CRIMINAL LAW

By

Steven L. Emanuel

Harvard Law School, J.D. 1976

**Fourth Edition prepared with
the assistance of**

Wendi Temkin-Nadel

**U. of Cal. Berkeley,
Boalt Hall School of Law,
J.D. 1991**

and

Helene Schonbrun

**New York University School of Law,
J.D. 1993**

Criminal Law, 4th Edition (2000-01)
Emanuel Publishing Corp. • 1328 Boston Post Road • Larchmont, NY 10538

Dedication

For Meredith Rachel

Preface

Thank you for buying this book.

We think three special features we've added to this edition will help you a lot. These are:

■ *Exam Tips* — We've compiled these by reviewing dozens of actual past essay questions, and 100s of multiple-choice questions, asked in past law-school and bar exams. We focus on the issues that are most likely to pop up on a real exam, and on the tricks and traps that professors have tried to spring on unsuspecting students throughout the years. The *Exam Tips* are at the end of each chapter.

■ *Quiz Yourself* questions — We've adapted these short-answer questions from the *Law in a Flash* flash-card deck on Criminal Law. (We've re-written most answers, to better mesh with the outline's approach). You'll find these distributed throughout the book, either at the end of a roman-numeraled section or at the end of a whole chapter. Each "pod" of Quiz Yourself questions can easily be located by using the Table of Contents.

■ *Casebook Correlation Chart* — This chart, located near the front of the book, works like this: if you have a topic that you're reading about in a particular place in your casebook, the Chart tells you where in the outline that topic is discussed.

I intend for you to use this book both throughout the semester and for exam preparation. Here are some suggestions about how to use it:[1]

1. During the semester, use the book in preparing each night for the next day's class. To do this, first read your casebook. Then, use the *Casebook Correlation Chart* at the front of the outline to get an idea of what part of the outline to read. Reading the outline will give you a sense of how the particular cases you've just read in your casebook fit into the overall structure of the subject. You may want to use a yellow highlighter to mark key portions of the *Emanuel*.

2. If you make your own outline for the course, use the *Emanuel* to give you a structure, and to supply black letter principles. You may want to rely especially on the *Capsule Summary* for this purpose. You are hereby authorized to copy small portions of the *Emanuel* into your own outline, provided that your outline will be used only by you or your study group, and provided that you are the owner of the *Emanuel*.

3. When you first start studying for exams, read the *Capsule Summary* to get an overview. This will probably take you all or part of two days.

4. Either during exam study or earlier in the semester, do some or all of the *Quiz Yourself* short-answer questions. When you do these questions: (1) record your short "answer" in the book after the question, but also: (2) try to write out a "mini essay" on a separate piece of paper. Remember that the only way to get good at writing essays is to write essays. At about the same time, do the Multistate-style multiple-choice questions at the back of the book.

5. A couple of days before the exam, review the *Exam Tips* that appear at the end of each chapter.

---

1. The suggestions below relate only to this book. I don't talk here about taking or reviewing class notes, using hornbooks or other study aids, joining a study group, or anything else. This doesn't mean I don't think these other steps are important — it's just that in this Preface, I've chosen to focus on how I think you can use this outline.

You may want to combine this step with step (4), so that you use the *Tips* to help you spot the issues in the short-answer questions. You'll also probably want to follow up from many of the *Tips* to the main outline's discussion of the topic.

6. Some time during the week or so before the exam, do some or all of the full-scale essay exams at the back of the book. Write out a full essay answer under exam-like conditions (e.g., closed-book if your exam will be closed book.) If you can, exchange papers with a classmate and critique each other's answer.

7. The night before the exam: (1) do some *Quiz Yourself* questions, just to get your writing juices flowing; and (2) re-read the various *Exam Tips* sections (you should be able to do this in 1-2 hours).

As part of continuing cooperation between LEXIS®-NEXIS® and Emanuel Publishing Corp., this edition of *Criminal Law* includes a special feature — sample LEXIS® searches, which you'll find at the end of many sections of the book. If you'd like to know more about a particular topic, just go on-line with LEXIS Research on the Web at **www.lexis.com/lawschool**. At "Search Sources," select from the "Explore Sources" option the following source: *Combined Federal & State Case Law - U.S.* Then run the appropriate sample search(es) from this book.

Alternatively, you can use LEXIS' "Search Advisor," a more structured way to do your searching. After you log in to **www.lexis.com/lawschool**, select the "Search Advisor" tab. Then select *Criminal Law & Procedure*, followed by *Criminal Offenses*. Select progressively-narrower topics as appropriate. When you've finished narrowing your category, select a jurisdiction from among the choices; a good general choice for jurisdiction is *Federal & State Cases -- Selected Criminal Materials*. Then, you can run the sample search(es) from this book against this pre-selected group of cases. (If you use Search Advisor, you can skip the phrase *"crime or criminal"* that is part of most of the sample searches.)

By the way, as part of that same LEXIS-Emanuel relationship, the ***full texts*** of the Capsule Summaries from this and other Emanuel Law Outlines are available for free download at the LEXIS website, **www.lexis.com/lawschool.**

We'd love your comments on this outline; be sure to fill out the survey at the back of the book. Each month we award a free outline or flashcard set to five people who have submitted surveys, so send yours in today!

Good luck. Write to me with any comments, corrections or suggestions. Or, better still, you can reach me via E-mail at: **semanuel@pobox.com**.

Also, check out our World Wide Web site: **http://www.emanuel.com**.

Steve Emanuel

Abbreviations Used in Text

B&P — Boyce and Perkins, *Cases and Materials on Criminal Law and Procedure*
  (Foundation Press, 8th Ed., 1999)

Fletcher — George Fletcher, *Rethinking Criminal Law* (Little Brown, 1978)

Johnson — Phillip Johnson, *Criminal Law, Cases, Materials and Text*
  (West Pubishing, 5th Ed., 1995)

K&S — Kadish and Schulhofer, *Criminal Law and its Processes*
  (Little Brown, 6th Ed., 1995)

LaFave — Wayne LaFave, *Modern Criminal Law, Cases, Comments and Questions*
  (West Publishing, 2nd Ed., 1988)

L — Wayne LaFave, *Criminal Law* (West Publishing, Hornbook Series, 3d Ed., 2000)

M.P.C. — *Model Penal Code*, Proposed Official Draft (1962) and Tentative Drafts 1-13
  (1953-1962) (American Law Institute) [Note: The Model Penal Code has not
  changed since 1962. However, the Official Commentaries to Parts I and II
  were revised in 1985 and 1980 respectively. All references in this outline to
  the Commentaries are to the revised Commentaries where applicable.]

CASEBOOK CORRELATION CHART

(**Note:** general sections of the outline are omitted from this chart. **NC** = not directly covered by this casebook.)
Any updates to this chart can be found at our web site — **http://www.emanuel.com**

Emanuel's Criminal Law Outline *(by chapter and section heading)*	Kadish & Schulhoffer **Criminal Law and Its Processes** (6th Ed. 1995)	Boyce & Perkins **Criminal Law and Procedure: Cases and Materials** (8th Ed. 1999)	Johnson **Criminal Law** (5th Ed. 1995)	Dressler **Cases and Materials on Criminal Law** (2nd Ed. 1999)	Kaplan, & Weisberg **Criminal Law: Cases and Materials** (3rd Ed. 1996)	LaFave **Modern Criminal Law** (2nd Ed. 1988)
CHAPTER 1 **ACTUS REUS AND MENS REA**		416-40, 371-9 805-47				
I. *Actus Reus*	171-79, 181-203		49-62	111-30, 662-80	121-47, 372-81	187-225
II. *Mens Rea*	204-82, 683-719	475-6, 480-6, 564-693	1-49, 62-81, 637-38	131-93, 923-43	195-302, 997-1032	96-186, 762-93
III. Concurrence	179-81	693-699	62	NC	NC	96
CHAPTER 2 **CAUSATION**						
II. Cause In Fact	NC	511-512	NC	196-200, 209-11	320-33	315-19
III. Proximate Cause Generally	547-60	512	NC	200-01	333-41	315-16
IV. Proximate Cause — Unintended Victims	560-61	673-683	NC	138-40, 207	NC	108
V. Proximate Cause — Unintended Manner of Harm	561-81	510-563	243-73	201-09	341-72	319-34
CHAPTER 3 **RESPONSIBILITY**						
I. The Insanity Defense	929-94	736-774	274-352	589-641	713-62	354-408
II. Diminished Responsibility	999-1010	740	339-52	641-55	303-07, 772-74	408-18
III. Automatism	173-79, 994-99	770-771	52-54	114-17	138-47, 765-72	187-203
IV. Intoxication	913-29, 1011-29	774-801	9-14, 66, 74-76, 322-33, 347-52	574-89, 662-80	147-52, 307-15, 762-65	419-54
V. Infancy	NC	703-736	NC	655-62	NC	455-59
CHAPTER 4 **JUSTIFICATION AND EXCUSE**						
II. Duress	896-913	801-4, 847-52, 859, 903	353-70	553-74	693-712	514-26
III. Necessity	860-80	847-60	356-60, 364, 370-79	526-48	661-93	527-33
IV. Self-Defense	801-46	930-75	379-406, 417-25	453-506	604-43	462-81
V. Defense of Others	836-37	975-87	407-17, 423-25	506-10	NC	481-84

CASEBOOK CORRELATION CHART (continued)

Emanuel's Criminal Law Outline *(by chapter and section heading)*	Kadish & Schulhoffer **Criminal Law and Its Processes** (6th Ed. 1995)	Boyce & Perkins **Criminal Law and Procedure: Cases and Materials** (8th Ed. 1999)	Johnson **Criminal Law** (5th Ed. 1995)	Dressler **Cases and Materials on Criminal Law** (2nd Ed. 1999)	Kaplan, & Weisberg **Criminal Law: Cases and Materials** (3rd Ed. 1996)	LaFave **Modern Criminal Law** (2nd Ed. 1988)
CHAPTER 4 **JUSTIFICAT. AND EXCUSE (Cont.)**						
VI. **Defense of Property**	846-51	987-1004	426-30	510-17	655-61	484-91
VII. **Law Enforcement (Arrest; Prevention of Escape and Crime)**	851-60	898-902, 917-30	430-37	517-26	643-55	491-509
VIII. **Maintaining Authority**	NC	906-16	NC	NC	NC	509-14
IX. **Consent**	329-32	860-79	437-40	NC	1033-35	533-39
X. **Entrapment**	673-4, 1046-7	1004-24	440-59	875	NC	NC
CHAPTER 5 **ATTEMPT**						
II. **Mental State**	585-93	405-06	581-86	704-13	786-94	540-49
III. **The Act — Attempt vs. "Mere Preparation"**	593-617	380-92	555-81	713-39	794-810	549-63
IV. **Impossibility**	623-40	392-405	586-97	739-52	822-48	563-75
V. **Renunciation**	599-600	412-14	560-64, 573-74	752-5	810-15	575-81
VI. **Attempt-Like Crimes**	308-14, 601-10	363-4, 407-9	83-91, 555-59	96-101, 697, 758-9	178-89, 799-802	583-95
VII. **Mechanics of Trial; Punishment**	581-85	416	576	698, 703-4	784-86	581-83
CHAPTER 6 **CONSPIRACY**						
II. **The Agreement**	743-51	442-4	564-72, 577-81, 607-11	794-801	931-37	598-610
III. **Mens Rea**	753-64	451-9	597-603, 643-49	778-94	939-49	610-32
IV. **The Conspiratorial Objective**	294-98, 729-31, 733-43, 751-53	441-2, 459-64	577, 655-59	765-71	949-61	632-46
V. **Scope: Multiple Parties**	764-74, 781-99	467-73	616-21, 659-78	807-12, 824-43	971-95	650-60, 683-96
VI. **Duration of Conspiracy**	720-5, 727-29	460-1, 474	611-15	822-24	937-39	661-70
VII. **Plurality**	774-80	444-51, 464-7	603-07	815-21	961-68	670-82
VIII. **Punishment**	731-33	474-5	574-76	767	920-31	676-77

CASEBOOK CORRELATION CHART (continued)

Emanuel's Criminal Law Outline *(by chapter and section heading)*	Kadish & Schulhoffer **Criminal Law and Its Processes** (6th Ed. 1995)	Boyce & Perkins **Criminal Law and Procedure: Cases and Materials** (8th Ed. 1999)	Johnson **Criminal Law** (5th Ed. 1995)	Dressler **Cases and Materials on Criminal Law** (2nd Ed. 1999)	Kaplan, & Weisberg **Criminal Law: Cases and Materials** (3rd Ed. 1996)	LaFave **Modern Criminal Law** (2nd Ed. 1988)
CHAPTER 7 **ACCOMPLICE LIABILITY AND SOLICITATION**						
I. **Parties to Crime**	641-44	487-90	638-39	844-6	860-62	704-06
II. **Accomplices — The Act Requirement**	666-71	495-6	621-26	847-51, 864-75	851-78	706-17, 732-37
III. **Accomplices — Mental State**	644-65	491-4	626-31, 639-42, 650-51	847-63	879-900	717-32
IV. **Accomplices — Additional Crimes By Principal**	647-49, 655-59	497-505	652-59	859-63	NC	737-45
V. **Guilt of the Principal**	671-83	476-9	631-37	875-86	906-17	745-56
VI. **Withdrawal By the Accomplice**	683	509-10	NC	888-90	878	757-60
VII. **Victims and Other Exceptions to Accomplice Liability**	681-83	509	NC	886-8	NC	760-62
VIII. **Post-Crime Assistance**	181-84, 186-87, 641	366, 490, 505-8	638	844-46	862	704, 793-807
IX. **Solicitation**	617-23	410-11	575-76	759-65	815-22	696-703
CHAPTER 8 **HOMICIDE AND OTHER CRIMES AGAINST THE PERSON**						
II. **Murder**	298-304, 385-93, 456-68	39-60, 68-71, 74-8, 152-4, 175-82	160-70, 183-95, 233-43	81-90, 212-29, 266-73	168-78, 383-98	47-60
III. **Felony Murder**	468-509	79-98, 538-54	206-32	284-312	498-542	296-313
IV. **Degrees of Murder**	393-405, 509-45	17-24, 99-107	123-46, 170-83	229-38, 314-52	399-416, 484-98, 543-90	264-96, 334-53
V. **Manslaughter — Voluntary**	405-37	61-8, 113-131, 144-7	147-60	238-66, 441-52	416-61	238-62
VI. **Manslaughter — Involuntary**	437-56, 476-78	71-4, 107-13, 131-44, 147-52	195-206	273-84, 312-14	463-84	313-15
VII. **Assault, Battery and Mayhem**	603-04	155-74, 192-3	584-86, 576-77	755-9	NC	101, 590-93
VIII. **Rape**	315-84	182-90	NC	353-434	1099-1155	165-75, 534
IX. **Kidnapping**	NC	174-5, 191-2	NC	NC	NC	NC

CASEBOOK CORRELATION CHART (continued)

Emanuel's Criminal Law Outline *(by chapter and section heading)*	Kadish & Schulhoffer **Criminal Law and Its Processes** (6th Ed. 1995)	Boyce & Perkins **Criminal Law and Procedure: Cases and Materials** (8th Ed. 1999)	Johnson **Criminal Law** (5th Ed. 1995)	Dressler **Cases and Materials on Criminal Law** (2nd Ed. 1999)	Kaplan, & Weisberg **Criminal Law: Cases and Materials** (3rd Ed. 1996)	LaFave **Modern Criminal Law** (2nd Ed. 1988)
CHAPTER 9 THEFT CRIMES						
II. Larceny	1041-49, 1090-1118, 1123-25	233-303	679-98	945-68, 981-2	1037-53	NC
III. Embezzlement	1049-64, 1118-22	309-14	698-702, 710-18	968-72	1045-47	NC
IV. False Pretenses	1064-79	314-32, 350-2	728-32, 738-57	972-84	1057-75	NC
V. Consolidation of Theft Crimes	1088-90	332-48	700	944	1054-57	NC
VI. Receiving Stolen Property	623-25	348-9	702-09	NC	822-35	NC
VII. Burglary	213, 602-03	195-228	13	NC	1095-98	109-12, 593-95
VIII. Robbery	1048-49	304-9	718-21	950	1093-95	NC
IX. Blackmail and Extortion	1048-49, 1079-88	352-7	721-38	NC	1075-93	NC

TABLE OF CONTENTS

Chapter 1

ACTUS REUS AND MENS REA

Chapter 2

CAUSATION

Chapter 3

RESPONSIBILITY

Chapter 4

JUSTIFICATION AND EXCUSE

Chapter 5

ATTEMPT

Chapter 6

CONSPIRACY

Chapter 7

ACCOMPLICE LIABILITY
AND SOLICITATION

Chapter 8

HOMICIDE, AND OTHER CRIMES AGAINST THE PERSON

xiv.

CRIMINAL LAW

F. **Felony is includible in homicide** 243
    1. Manslaughter 243
    2. Batteries and assaults 243
    3. Burglary with intent to assault 244
    4. Armed robbery 244
G. **Future of the felony-murder rule** 244

IV. **DEGREES OF MURDER** 246
  A. **Degrees of murder** 246
  B. **Death Penalty** 246
  C. **First-degree murder** 248
    1. Time required for premeditation 248
    2. Elements which must be shown 249
    3. Intoxication as negating deliberation 249
    4. Criticism of distinction 249
    5. Lying in wait, torture and poison 250
    6. Felony-murder 250
  D. **Second-degree murder** 250

V. **MANSLAUGHTER — VOLUNTARY** 250
  A. **Manslaughter generally** 250
  B. **Voluntary manslaughter based on "heat of passion"** 250
  C. **Requirements for voluntary manslaughter** 250
  D. **Reasonable provocation** 251
    1. Characteristics of the reasonable person 251
  E. **Actual provocation** 254
  F. **Reasonable "cooling off period"** 254
  G. **Actual cooling off** 254
  H. **Killing of one other than provoker** 255
  I. **Other kinds of voluntary manslaughter** 255
    1. "Imperfect" self-defense 255
    2. "Imperfect" defense of others 255
    3. "Imperfect" crime-prevention 255
    4. "Imperfect" coercion or necessity 256
    5. Other killings 256

VI. **MANSLAUGHTER — INVOLUNTARY** 257
  A. **Involuntary manslaughter based on criminal negligence** 257
    1. Vehicular homicide 259
  B. **Unlawful-act manslaughter ("misdemeanor-manslaughter")** .. 259
    1. What constitutes "unlawful act" 259
    2. Proximate cause 260
    3. Criticism of doctrine 261

Quiz Yourself on
HOMICIDE (ALL FORMS).. 261

VII. **ASSAULT, BATTERY AND MAYHEM** 266

Chapter 9

THEFT CRIMES

CAPSULE SUMMARY

This Capsule Summary is intended for review at the end of the semester. Reading it is not a substitute for mastering the material in the main outline. Numbers in brackets refer to the pages in the main outline where the topic is discussed. The order of topics is occasionally somewhat different from that in the main outline.

CHAPTER 1

ACTUS REUS AND *MENS REA*

I. GENERAL

A. Four elements: All crimes have several basic common elements: (1) a **voluntary act** ("*actus reus*"); (2) a **culpable intent** ("*mens rea*"); (3) **"concurrence"** between the *mens rea* and the *actus reus*; and (4) **causation** of harm. [1]

II. *ACTUS REUS*

A. Significance of concept: The defendant must have committed a **voluntary act**, or *"actus reus."* Look for an *actus reus* problem anytime you have one of the following situations: (1) D has not committed physical acts, but has "guilty" **thoughts**, **words**, states of **possession** or **status**; (2) D does an **involuntary act**; and (3) D has an **omission**, or failure to act. [1]

B. Thoughts, words, possession and status: *Mere thoughts* are never punishable as crimes. (*Example:* D writes in his diary, "I intend to kill V." This statement alone is not enough to constitute any crime, even attempted murder.) [1]

   1. Possession as criminal act: However, mere **possession** of an object may sometimes constitute the necessary criminal act. (*Example:* Possession of narcotics frequently constitutes a crime in itself.) [1-2]

      a. Knowledge: When mere possession is made a crime, the act of "possession" is almost always construed so as to include only **conscious** possession. (*Example:* If the prosecution fails to prove that D knew he had narcotics on his person, there can be no conviction.) [1]

C. Act must be voluntary: An act cannot satisfy the *actus reus* requirement unless it is **voluntary**. [3-5]

   1. Reflex or convulsion: An act consisting of a **reflex** or **convulsion** does not give rise to criminal liability. [3]

Example: D, while walking down the street, is striken by epileptic convulsions. His arm jerks back, and he strikes X in the face. The striking of X is not a voluntary act, so D cannot be held criminally liable. But if D had known beforehand that he was subject to such seizures, and unreasonably put himself in a position where he was likely to harm others — for instance, by driving a car — this initial act might subject him to criminal liability.

2. **Unconsciousness:** An act performed during a state of *"unconsiousness"* does not meet the *actus reus* requirement. But D will be found to have acted "unconsciously" only in rare situations. [3-4]

   Example: If D can show that at the time of the crime he was on "automatic pilot," and was completely unconscious of what he was doing, his act will be involuntary. (But the mere fact that D has *amnesia* concerning the period of the crime will *not* be a defense.)

3. **Hypnosis:** Courts are split about whether acts performed under *hypnosis* are sufficiently "involuntary" that they do not give rise to liability. The Model Penal Code (MPC) treats conduct under hypnosis as being involuntary. [4]

4. **Self-induced state:** In all cases involving allegedly involuntary acts, D's *earlier voluntary act* may deprive D of the "involuntary" defense. [4]

   Example: D, a member of a cult run by Leader, lets himself be hypnotized. Before undergoing hypnosis, D knows that Leader often gives his members orders under hypnosis to commit crimes. D can probably be held criminally liable for any crimes committed while under hypnosis, because he knowingly put himself in a position where this might result.

D. **Omissions:** The *actus reus* requirement means that in most situations, there is no criminal liability for an *omission* to act (as distinguished from an affirmative act). [5-9]

   Example: D sees V, a stranger, drowning in front of him. D could easily rescue V. D will normally not be criminally liable for failing to attempt to rescue V, because there is no general liability for omissions as distinguished from affirmative acts.

1. **Existence of legal duty:** But there are some "special situations" where courts deem D to have a *special legal duty to act*. Where this occurs, D's omission may be punished under a statute that speaks in terms of positive acts. [6-8]

   a. **Special relationship:** Where D and V have a *special relationship* — most notably a *close blood relationship* — D will be criminally liable for a failure to act. (*Example:* Parent fails to give food or water to Child, and Child dies. Even if there is no general statute dealing with child abuse, Parent can be held liable for murder or manslaughter, because the close relationship is construed to impose on Parent an affirmative duty to furnish necessities and thereby prevent death.) [6]

      i. **Permitting child abuse:** Some courts have applied this theory to hold one parent liable for child abuse for *failing to intervene* to stop affirmative abuse by the other parent.

   b. **Contract:** Similarly, a legal duty may arise out of a *contract*. (*Example:* Lifeguard is hired by City to guard a beach. Lifeguard intentionally fails to save Victim from drowning, even though he could easily do so. Lifeguard will probably be criminally liable despite the fact that his conduct was an omission rather than an act; his contract with City imposed a duty to take affirmative action.) [7]

   c. **D caused danger:** If the *danger was caused* (even innocently) by *D himself*, D generally has an affirmative duty to then save V. [7]

      Example: D digs a hole in the sidewalk in front of his house, acting legally under a building permit. D sees V about to step into the hole, but says nothing. V falls in and dies. D can be held criminally liable for manslaughter, because he created the condition — even though he did so innocently — and thus had an affirmative duty to protect those he knew to be in danger.

d. Undertaking: Finally, D may come under a duty to render assistance if he *undertakes* to give assistance. This is especially true where D leaves V *worse off* than he was before, or effectively dissuades other rescuers who believe that D is taking care of the problem. [8]

> **Example:** V is drowning, while D and three others are on shore. D says, "I'll swim out to save V." The others agree, and leave, thinking that D is taking care of the situation. Now, D will be criminally liable if he does not make reasonable efforts to save V.

III. *MENS REA*

A. Meaning: The term *"mens rea"* symbolizes the requirement that there be a *"culpable state of mind."* [11]

    1. Not necessarily state of mind: Most crimes require a true *"mens rea,"* that is, a state of mind that is truly guilty. But other crimes are defined to require merely "negligence" or "recklessness," which is not really a state of mind at all. Nonetheless, the term *"mens rea"* is sometimes used for these crimes as well: thus one can say that "for manslaughter, the *mens rea* is recklessness." There are also a few crimes defined so as to require no *mens rea* at all, the so called "strict liability" crimes. [11]

B. General vs. specific intent: Court traditionally classify the *mens rea* requirements of various crimes into three groups: (1) crimes requiring merely *"general intent"*; (2) crimes requiring *"specific intent"*; and (3) crimes requiring merely *recklessness* or *negligence*. (Strict liability crimes form a fourth category, as to which there is no culpable mental state required at all.) [12-13]

    1. "General intent": A crime requiring merely *"general intent"* is a crime for which it must merely be shown that D *desired to commit the act which served as the actus reus*. [12]

    2. "Specific intent": Where a crime requires *"specific intent"* or "special intent," this means that D, in addition to desiring to bring about the *actus reus*, must have desired to do *something further*. [13-13]

> **Example of general intent crime:** Battery is usually a "general intent" crime. The *actus reus* is a physical injury to or offensive touching of another. So long as D intends to touch another in an offensive way, he has the "general intent" that is all that is needed for battery. (Thus if D touches V with a knife, intending merely to graze his skin and frighten him, this will be all the (general) intent needed for battery, since D intended the touching, and no other intent (such as the intent to cause injury) is required.

> **Example of specific intent crime:** For common-law burglary, on the other hand, it must be shown that D not only intended to break and enter the dwelling of another, but that he also intended to commit a felony once inside the dwelling. This latter intent is a "specific intent" — it is an intent other than the one associated with the *actus reus* (the breaking and entering).

    3. Significance: The general/specific intent distinction usually matters in two situations: (1) where D is *intoxicated*; and (2) where D makes a *mistake* of law or fact. [13]

      a. Intoxication: *Intoxication* rarely negates a crime of general intent, but may sometimes negate the specific intent for a particular crime. (*Example:* D breaks and enters, but is too drunk to have any intent to commit larceny or any other felony inside; D probably is not guilty of burglary.) [13]

C
A
P
S
U
L
E

S
U
M
M
A
R
Y

   b. **Mistake:** Similarly, a *mistake* of fact is more likely to be enough to negate the required specific intent. [13]

       Example: D breaks and enters, in an attempt to carry away something which he mistakenly thinks belongs to him; D will probably be aquitted of burglary, where mistake will generally not negate a general intent (e.g., the intent to commit the breaking and entering by itself).

  4. **Abandonment of distinction:** However, many modern codes, and the Model Penal Code, have **abandoned** the general/specific distinction, and instead set forth the precise mental state required for each element of each crime. [13]

C. **"Purposely" as mental state:** Many crimes are defined to be committed only where a person acts *"purposely"* with respect to a particular element of a crime. Other crimes are defined to require the similar, but not identical, mental state of *"intentionally."* [14-16]

  1. **Definition of "purposely":** A person acts "purposely" with respect to a particular element if it his *"conscious object"* to engage in the particular conduct in question, or to cause the particular result in question. [14-15]

  2. **Not the same as "knowingly":** In modern statutes, "purposely" is not the same as "knowingly." If D does not desire a particular result, but is *aware* that the conduct or result is *certain to follow*, this is *not* "purposely." [16]

  Example: D consciously desires to kill A, and does so by putting a bomb on board a plane that contains both A and B. Although D knew B's death was certain, a modern court would probably not hold that D "purposely" killed B, (although D might nonetheless be guilty of murder on the grounds that he acted with a "depraved heart").

  3. **Motive:** D's *motive* will usually be *irrelevant* in determining whether he acted "purposely" or "intentionally." [16-16]

  Example: D, in an act of euthanasia, kills V, his wife, who has terminal cancer. D will be held to have "purposely" or "intentionally" killed V, even though he did it for ostensibly "good" motives.

    a. **Relevant to defenses:** Special motives may, however, be relevant to the existence of a *defense* (e.g., the defense of self-defense or necessity).

D. **"Knowingly":** Modern statutes, and the Model Penal Code, define some crimes to require that D *"knowingly"* take an act or produce a result. The biggest distinction between "purposely" and "knowingly" relates to D's awareness of the *consequences* of his act: if the crime is defined with respect to a certain result of D's conduct, D has acted knowingly (but not "purposely") if he was "aware that it is *practically certain* that his conduct will cause that result." [16-19]

  Example: On the facts of our earlier "bomb on the airplane" example, D will have "knowingly" killed B, but not "purposely" killed B, because he was aware that it was practically certain that his conduct would cause B's death.

  1. **Presumption of knowledge:** A statutory or judge-made *presumption* may be used to help prove that D acted "knowingly." (*Example:* In many statutes governing receipt of stolen property, D's unexplained possession of property which is in fact stolen gives rise to a presumption that D knew the property was stolen.) [18]

2. **Knowledge of attendant circumstances:** Where a statute specifies that D must act "knowingly," and the statute then specifies various ***attendant circumstances*** which the definition of the crime makes important, usually the requirement of knowledge is held applicable to ***all these attendant circumstances***. [18]

Example: A statute provides that any dealer in used merchandise must file a report with the police if the dealer "knowingly purchases a used item from one who is not in the business of selling such items, at a price less than half of the fair market value of the item." The statute's purpose is to cut down on the "fencing" of stolen goods. D, a used merchandise dealer, buys a vase for $500 that is really worth $2,000. Most courts would require the prosecution to show that D knew not only that he was purchasing the vase, but that he knew he was paying less than half of the vase's fair market value. In other words, D must be shown to have acted knowingly with respect to all of the attendant circumstances, including the circumstance that the purchase price was much less than the value.

E. **"Recklessly":** A person acts ***"recklessly"*** if he ***"consciously disregards a substantial and unjustifiable risk…."*** MPC §2.02(2). The idea is that D has behaved in a way that represents a ***gross deviation*** from the conduct of a law-abiding person. [19-20]

1. **Must be aware of risk:** Most courts, and the Model Penal Code, hold that D is reckless only if he was ***aware*** of the high risk of harm stemming from his conduct. This is a "subjective" standard for recklessness. But a substantial minority of courts and statutes hold that D can be reckless if he behaves extremely unreasonably even though he was unaware of the risk. [19]

Example: D runs a nightclub with inadequate fire exits. A fire breaks out, killing hundreds. Under the majority "subjective" standard for recklessness, D was reckless only if he actually knew of the high risk of harm posed by inadequate fire exits. Under the minority "objective" standard, it would be enough that D was extremely careless and that a reasonable person would have known of the great danger, even though D did not.

F. **"Negligently":** Some statutes make it a crime to behave ***"negligently"*** if certain results follow. For instance, the crime of "vehicular homicide" is sometimes defined to require a *mens rea* of "criminal negligence." [20-21]

1. **Awareness not required:** Most modern statutes, and the Model Penal Code, allow a finding of criminal negligence even if D was ***not aware*** of the risk imposed by his conduct (as in the above night-club fire example). [20]

2. **"Gross" negligence required:** Usually, criminal negligence is ***"gross"*** negligence. That is, the deviation from ordinary care must be greater than that which would be required for civil negligence. [21]

G. **Strict liability:** Some offenses are ***"strict liability."*** That is, no culpable mental state at all must be shown — it is enough that D performed the act in question, regardless of his mental state. [21-24]

Examples of strict liability crimes: The following are often defined as strict liability offenses: Statutory rape (D is generally guilty if he has intercourse with a girl below the prescribed age, regardless of whether he knew or should have known her true age); mislabelling of drugs; polluting of water or air; concealment of a dangerous weapon while boarding an aircraft.

1. **Constitutionality:** Generally there is no constitutional problem with punishing a defendant without regard to his mental state. [21]

2. **Interpretation:** The mere fact that the statute does not specify a mental state does not mean that the crime is a strict liability one — judges must determine whether a particular mental state was intended by the legislature. In general, the older the statute (especially if it is a codification of a common-law crime), the less likely it is to be a strict-liability offense. Most strict liability offenses are modern, and are of relatively low heinousness. [22-23]

   a. **Complex statute that is easy to violate innocently:** If the statute is *complex*, or *easy to violate innocently,* or *imposes serious penalties,* the court is likely to read in a *mens rea* requirement, and thus to refuse to treat the statute as imposing strict liability. [*Staples v. U.S.*] [22]

   b. **MPC:** Under the MPC, the only offenses that are strict liability are ones called *"violations."* These are minor offenses that do not constitute a "crime" and that may be punished only by fine or forfeiture. [23]

H. **Vicarious liability:** Statutes sometimes impose upon one person liability for the *act of another*; this is commonly called *"vicarious liability."* In essence, the requirement of an act (*actus reus*) has been dispensed with, not the requirement of the wrongful intent. [24-26]

   Example: Statutes frequently make an *automobile owner* liable for certain acts committed by those to whom he lends his car, even without a showing of culpable mental state on the part of the owner.

1. **Constitutionality:** Generally, the imposition of vicarious liability does *not* violate D's due process rights. However, there are exceptions: [24-25]

   a. **D has no control over offender:** If D did not have any *ability to control* the person who performed the actual *actus reus*, his conviction is probably unconstitutional. [24]

      Example: X steals D's car, and exceeds the speed limit. It is probably unconstitutional for the state to impose criminal sanctions upon D, since he had no ability to control X's conduct.

   b. **Imprisonment:** If D has been sentenced to *imprisonment* (or even if he is convicted of a crime for which imprisonment is authorized), some courts hold that his due process rights are violated unless he is shown to have at least *known* of the violation. [25]

      Example: D is a tavern owner whose employee served a minor. If D did not know of this act, or in any way acquiesce in its commission, some courts would hold that D may not constitutionally be imprisoned for it.

I. **Mistake:** Defendants raise the defense of *mistake* when they have been mistaken either about the facts or the law. Do not think of "mistake" as being a separate "doctrine." Instead, look at the effect of the particular mistake on D's *mental state*, and examine whether he was thereby prevented from having the mental state required for the crime. [26-32]

   Example: Assume that the requisite mental intent for larceny is the intent to take property which one knows or believes to belong to another. D takes V's umbrella from a restaurant, thinking that it is his own. D's factual mistake — his belief about who owns the umbrella — is a defense to the theft charge, because it negates the requisite mental state (intent to take the property which one knows or believes belongs to another).

1. **Crimes of "general intent":**   D's mistake is *least likely* to assist him where the crime is a *"general intent"* crime (i.e., one for which the most general kind of culpable intent will suffice). [26]

    Example: Murder is often thought of as a "general intent" crime in the sense that it will be enough that D either intends to kill, intends to commit grievous bodily injury, is recklessly indifferent to the value of human life or intends to commit any of certain non-homicide felonies. Suppose D shoots a gun at V, intending to hit V in the arm and thus create a painful but not serious flesh wound. D mistakenly believes that V is in ordinary health, when in fact he is a hemopheliac. D's mistake will not help him, because even had the facts been as D supposed them to be, D would have had a requisite mental state, the intent to commit grievous bodily injury.

2. **"Lesser crime" theory:**   D's mistake will almost never help him if, had the facts been as D mistakenly supposed them to be, his acts would still have been a crime, though a lesser one. This is the *"lesser crime"* theory. [29]

    Example: D steals a necklace from a costume jewelry store. The necklace is made of diamonds, and is worth $10,000, but D mistakenly believes it to be costume jewelry worth less than $500. In the jurisdiction, theft of something worth less than $500 is a misdemeanor, and theft of something worth more than that is a felony. D is guilty of a crime — a felony in most states — because even had the facts been as he supposed them to be, he still would have been guilty of some crime. (But some states, and the Model Penal Code, would scale his crime back to the crime that he would have committed had the facts been as he supposed, in this case, a misdemeanor.)

    a. **Moral wrong:**   Older decisions extend this principle to deny D of the defense of mistake if, under the facts as D believed them to be, his conduct and intent would have been *"immoral."* But modern statutes reject this view. [26]

3. **Mistake must be "reasonable":**   Older cases often impose the rule that a mistake cannot be a defense unless it was *"reasonable."* But the modern view, and the view of the MPC, is that *even an unreasonable mistake* will block conviction if the mistake prevented D from having the requisite intent or knowledge. [27]

    Example: D attempts (unsuccessfully) to have sex with a girl he meets on the street. He is charged with assault with intent to rape. D shows that he actually, but unreasonably, believed that V was a prostitute, because prostitutes frequented that area. A traditional court would probably hold that the mistake was no defense, since D's mistake was "unreasonable." But a modern court might allow the defense, since had the facts been as D supposed them to be, he would not have intended to commit a crime (unconsented-to sex).

    a. **Rejection by finder of fact:**   Remember that even in a "modern" jurisdiction, the finder of fact is always free to *disbelieve* that the mistake really occurred. Thus on the facts of the above example, the more "unreasonable" D's story that he thought V was a prostitute, the quicker the jury (or the judge in a bench trial) can be to conclude simply that D was not in fact mistaken. [27]

4. **Mistake of law:**   It is especially hard for D to prevail with a defense based on *"mistake of law."* [27]

a. **Generally no defense:** As a general rule, *"mistake of law is no defense."* More precisely, this means that **the fact that D mistakenly believes that no statute makes his conduct a crime does not furnish a defense**. [27]

Example: D, who is retarded, does not realize that unconsented-to intercourse is a crime. D has unconsented-to intercourse with V. D's ignorance that unconsented-to intercourse is a crime will not be a defense; so long as D intended the act of intercourse while knowing that V did not consent, he is guilty.

   i. **Reasonable mistake:** In this core "D mistakenly believes that no statute makes his conduct a crime" situation, even a **reasonable mistake** about the meaning of the statute will usually **not** protect D. In other words, so long as the crime is not itself defined in a way that makes D's guilty knowledge a prerequisite, there is usually no "reasonable mistake" exception to the core "mistake of law is no defense" rule.

b. **Mistake of law as to collateral fact:** It is important to remember that the oft-stated "rule," "ignorance of the law is no excuse," really only means *"ignorance that a statute makes one's conduct a crime is no excuse."* A mistake of law as to some **collateral fact** may negative the required mental state, just as a mistake of fact may do so. [29]

Example 1: D's car has been repossessed by Finance Co. D finds the car, breaks in, and takes it back. D's belief that the car is still legally his *will* absolve him, because it prevents him from having the requisite mental state for theft (intent to take property which one knows or believes to belong to another). (But if D had taken his neighbor's car, his ignorance that there is a statute making it a crime to take one's neighbor's property would not be a defense.)

Example 2: D reasonably believes that he has been divorced from W, his first wife, but in fact the "divorce" is an invalid foreign decree, which is not recognized under local law. D then marries V. D's "mistake of law" about the enforceability of the prior divorce *will* negative the intent needed for bigamy (intent to have two spouses at once).

c. **Mistake of law defense built in:** Of course, it's always possible for the legislature to write a statute in such a way that a mistake of law *will* constitute a defense (or so that awareness of the criminality of the conduct is an element of the offense). For instance, the legislature might do this by defining the crime to consist of a *"willful* violation" — the use of the word "willful" would probably be interpreted to require knowledge by the defendant that his act was prohibited by law. [32-33]

Example: A federal statute prohibits "structuring" bank transactions to evade the requirement that all transactions over $10,000 be reported to the government. Another statute makes it a crime to "willfully" violate the first statute. *Held*, D cannot be convicted of a willful violation of the statute unless the prosecution shows that he was aware of the ban on structuring. [*Ratzlaf v. U.S.*]

IV. CONCURRENCE

A. **Two types of concurrence required:** There are two ways in which there must be *"concurrence"* involving the *mens rea*: (1) there must be concurrence between D's **mental state** and the **act**; and (2) there must be concurrence between D's **mental state** and the **harmful result**, if the crime is one defined in terms of bad results. [35]

B. Concurrence between mind and act: There must be concurrence between the *mental state* and the *act*. [35-37]

  1. Same time: This requirement is not met if, *at the time of the act*, the required mental state does not exist. [35-37]

    Example: Common-law larceny is defined as the taking of another's property with intent to deprive him of it. D takes V's umbrella from a restaurant, thinking that it is his own. Five minutes later, he realizes that it belongs to V, and decides to keep it. D has not committed larceny, because at the time he committed the act (the taking), he did not have the requisite mental intent (the intent to deprive another of his property). The fact that D later acquired the requisite intent is irrelevant.

  2. Mental state must cause act: In fact, the mental state must *cause* the act. [36]

    Example: D intends to kill V. While driving to the store to buy a gun to carry out his intent, D accidentally runs over V and kills him. D is not guilty of murder, even though the intent to kill V existed at the time the act (driving the car over V) took place. This is because D's intent to kill did not "cause" the act (driving the car over V).

    a. Any action that is legal cause of harm: Most crimes are defined in terms of harmful results (e.g., homicide is the wrongful taking of a life). Where D takes *several acts* which together lead to the harmful result, the concurrence requirement is met if the mental state concurs with *any act that suffices as a legal cause* of the harm. [36-37]

      i. Destruction or concealment of a "body": Because of this rule, D will be guilty if he attempts to kill his victim, believes the victim to be dead, and then destroys or conceals the "body," killing the victim for real. (*Example:* D strikes V over the head, and thinking V is dead, pushes him over a cliff to destroy the body. The autopsy shows that the blows did not kill V and probably would not have killed him. V really died from the fall off the cliff. Most courts would find D guilty, probably on the theory that the blows to the head were a cause of harm, and the guilty intent (to kill V) caused the blows. [*Thabo Meli v. Regina*, 1 All E.R. 373 (Eng. 1954)])

C. Concurrence between mind and result: There must also be concurrence between the mental state and the *harmful result*, if the crime is one defined in terms of bad results (such as homicide, rape, larceny, etc.) Basically this aspect of concurrence means that if what actually occurred is *too far removed* from what was intended, there will be no concurrence and thus no liability. [37-40]

  1. Different crime: Thus if the harm which actually occurs is of a completely different *type* from what D intended, D will generally not be guilty of the other crime. In other words, the intent for one crime may not usually be linked with a result associated with a different crime. [37]

    Example: D attempts to shoot V to death while V is leaving his house. The shot misses and ruptures V's stove, causing V's house to burn down. Assuming that arson is defined so as to require an intent to burn, D will not be guilty of arson, because the intent for one crime (murder) cannot be matched with the result for another crime (burning) to produce guilt for the latter crime.

  2. Recklessly- or negligently-caused result: The same rule applies where D has *negligently* or *recklessly* acted with respect to the risk of a particular result, and a very different result occurs. [38]

Example: D recklessly takes target practice with his rifle in a crowded area; what makes his conduct reckless is the high risk that D will injure or kill a person. One of D's shots hits a gas tank, and causes a large fire. Assuming that the danger of causing a fire was not large, D will not be convicted of arson (even if arson is defined to include reckless burning), since his conduct was reckless only with respect to the risk of bodily harm, not the risk of burning.

3. **Felony-murder and misdemeanor-manslaughter rules:** But this general principle that there is no liability for a resulting harm which is substantially different from that intended or risked by D is subject to two very important *exceptions*, both relating to *homicide*: [38]

   a. **Felony-murder:** First, if D is engaged in the commission of certain *dangerous felonies*, he will be liable for certain deaths which occur, even if he did not intend the deaths. This is the *"felony-murder" rule*. [38]

   b. **Misdemeanor-manslaughter:** Second, if D was engaged in a *malum in se* misdemeanor (a misdemeanor that is immoral, not just regulatory), and a death occurs, D may be liable for involuntary manslaughter, even though his conduct imposed very little risk of that death and the death was a freak accident. This is the *"misdemeanor-manslaughter" rule*. [38]

4. **Same harm but different degree:** If the harm which results is of the *same general type* as D intended, but of a *more or less serious degree*, D gets the benefit of the rules on concurrence. [39-39]

   a. **Actual result more serious than intended:** Thus if the actual harm is *greater*, and related to, the intended result, D is generally *not liable* for the greater harm. [39]

   Example: Assume simple battery is defined as the intentional causing of minor bodily harm, and aggravated battery is defined as the intentional causing of grievous bodily harm. D gets into a minor scuffle with V, intending merely to hit him lightly on the chin. But V turns out to have a "glass jaw," which is fractured by the blow. D will not be held guilty of aggravated battery, just simple battery, since his intent was only to produce that lesser degree of injury required for simple battery.

      i. **Exceptions in homicide cases:** But again, we have two exceptions to this rule when death results. First, under the misdemeanor-manslaughter rule, if D's minor attack on V unexpectedly causes V to die, D is guilty of manslaughter (as he would be on the facts of the above example if V unexpectedly bled to death). Second, if D intended to *seriously injure* V but not kill him, in most states he will be guilty of murder if V dies from the attack, because most states have a form of murder as to which the mental state is intent-to-grievously-injure.

      Example: D intends to beat V to a pulp, but not to kill him; V dies unexpectedly. In a state defining murder to include a mental state of intent-to-grievously-injure, D is liable for murder.

CHAPTER 2

CAUSATION

I. INTRODUCTION

A. Two aspects of causation: "Causation" in criminal law relates to the link between the *act* and the *harmful result*. The prosecution must show that the defendant's *actus reus* "caused" the harmful result, in *two different senses*: (1) that the act was the *"cause in fact"* of the harm; and (2) that the act was the *"proximate"* cause (or the "legal" cause) of the harm. [44]

II. CAUSE IN FACT

A. Two ways: There are two ways in which an act can be the "cause in fact" of harm: (1) by being the *"but for"* cause of the harm; and (2) by being a *"substantial factor"* in creating the harm. These categories overlap, but not completely. [44]

B. The "but for" rule: Most often, the act will be the "cause in fact" of the harm by being the *"but for"* cause of that harm. To put the idea negatively, if the result *would have happened anyway*, even had the act not occurred, the act is *not a cause in fact* of that result. [44]

> **Example:** D shoots at V, but only grazes him, leaving V with a slightly bleeding flesh wound. X, who has always wanted to kill V, finds V (in the same place V would have been in had D not shot at V), and shoots V through the heart, killing him instantly. D's act is not a "cause in fact" of V's death, under the "but for" test — since V would have died, in just the manner and at the same time he did, even if D had not shot him, D's act was not the "but for" cause of V's death. Unless D's act is found to have been a "substantial factor" in V's death (the other test for causation in fact), which it probably would not, D's act is not the "cause in fact" of V's death, and D therefore cannot be punished for that death.

C. "Substantial factor" test: D's act will be found to be the cause in fact of harm, even if the act is not the "but for" cause, if the act was a *"substantial factor"* in bringing about the result. [44]

Example: At a time of widespread riots, D sets fire to a house at 99 Main Street, and X simultaneously sets fire to one at 103 Main Street. A house at 101 Main Street is consumed by the blaze from the two fires. D is charged with arson. He shows that even had he not torched 99, the flames from 103 would have been enough to burn down 101 at the same time it actually did burn. (Thus D's act was not the "but for" cause of the burning of 101.) However, since D's conduct was a (though not the sole) "substantial factor" in burning down 101, he was a "cause in fact" of the fire and will therefore be liable for arson.

1. D's act shortened V's life: In a homicide case, if D's act *shortened the victim's life*, this will strongly suggest that D's conduct was a "substantial factor" in producing the victim's death. [45]

> **Example:** X poisons D, in such a way that despite all medical efforts, V will definitely die within one day. One hour after V drinks the poison, D shoots V, killing him instantly. Since V would have died shortly anyway, it can be argued that D's shooting was not the "but for" cause of V's death. But since D shortened V's life, a court would certainly find that D was a "substantial factor" in causing V's death, and would find him guilty of murder.

> **a. Intervening act shortens V's life:** Where the *first* person to do harm is charged, and defends on the grounds that the second person's intervening act should relieve him of liability, it's a closer question, but many courts will find the first person to be guilty here as well. [45]
>
> **Example:** Same facts as above example, except now X, rather than D, is charged with murder. Assuming that V would inevitably have died from the poison had D not come along to shoot him, courts are split about whether D is relieved from liability by the intervening shooting.

2. Conspiracy: The above discussion of the "substantial factor" rule assumes that the two concurring acts occurred *independently* of each other. If the two occured as part of a *joint enterprise*, such as a *conspiracy*, the act of each person will be attributed to the other, and there will be no need to determine whether each act was a substantial factor in leading to the harm. [46]

Example: X and D each shoot V, as part of a successful conspiracy to kill V. Even if D's shot only caused a small flesh wound and did not really contribute to V's death, D is guilty of murder, because his co-conspirator's fatal shot will be attributable to D under the law of conspiracy.

III. PROXIMATE CAUSE GENERALLY

A. Definition of "proximate cause": It is not enough that D's act was a "cause in fact" of the harm. The prosecution must also show that the act and harm are sufficiently closely related that the act is a *"proximate"* or "legal" cause of that harm. This is a *policy* question: *Is the connection between the act and the harm so stretched that it is unfair to hold D liable for that harm?* [46]

1. No precise definition: There is no precise or mechanical definition of proximate cause — each case gets decided on its own facts. [46]

2. Model Penal Code formulation: Under the MPC, in most cases D's act will be the proximate cause of the harmful result if the result is "not too remote or accidental in its occurrence to have a [just] bearing on the actor's liability or on the gravity of his offense." MPC 2.03(2)(b). [46]

B. Year-and-a-day rule in homicide: One common-law rule that expresses the proximate-cause idea is the *"year and a day"* rule in homicide cases: D cannot be convicted if the victim did not die until a year and a day following D's act. Many states continue to impose this rule. [47]

C. Types of problems raised: Look for two main types of proximate cause problems: (1) situations where the type of harm intended occurred, and occurred in roughly the manner intended, but the *victim was not the intended one*; and (2) cases where the general type of harm intended did occur and occurred to the intended victim, but occurred in an *unintended manner*. [47]

1. Reckless and negligent crimes: Proximate cause issues are most common in cases where the *mens rea* for the crime is intent. But similar problems also arise where the mental state is recklessness or negligence. [47]

IV. PROXIMATE CAUSE — UNINTENDED VICTIMS

A. Transferred intent: It will not generally be a defense that the actual victim of D's act was *not the intended victim*. Instead, courts apply the doctrine of *"transferred intent,"* under which D's intent is "transferred" from the actual to the intended victim. [47-48]

Example: D, intending to kill X, shoots at X. Because of D's bad aim, D hits and kills V instead. D is guilty of the murder of V, because his intent is said to be "transferred" from X to V.

1. **Danger to actual V unforeseeable:** In most courts, the "unintended victim" rule probably applies even where the danger to the actual victim was *completely unforeseeable*. (*Example:* While D and X are out on the desert, D shoots at X, thinking the two are completely alone. V, sleeping behind some sagebrush, is hit by the errant bullet. Probably D may be convicted of murdering V.) [49]

B. **Same defense:** In general, D in an "unintended victim" case may raise the *same defenses* that he would have been able to raise had the intended victim been the one harmed. (*Example:* D shoots at X in legitimate self-defense. The bullet strikes V, a bystander. D may claim self-defense, just as he could if the bullet had struck the intended victim.) [49]

C. **Mistaken ID:** The fact that D is mistaken about the victim's *identity* will not be a defense. [49]

> **Example:** D shoots at V, mistakenly thinking that V is really X, D's enemy. D will be guilty of the murder of V, just as if he had been shooting at the person who was actually X, and had mistakenly hit V. The crime of murder requires an intent to kill, but does not require a correct belief as to the victim's identity.

D. **Crimes of recklessness or negligence:** The "unforeseen victim" problem also arises in crimes where the mental state is *recklessness* or *negligence*, rather than intent. But in these situations, a *tighter link* between D's act and V's injury is probably required than where the crime is intentional. [50]

V. PROXIMATE CAUSE — UNINTENDED MANNER OF HARM

A. **Generally:** If D's intended victim is harmed, but the harm occurs in an *unexpected manner* (though it is the same general type of harm intended), the unexpected manner of harm may or may not be enough to absolve D. In general, D will not be liable where the harm occurs through a *completely bizarre, unforeseeable chain of events*. [51]

> **Example:** D gets into a street fight with V, and tries to seriously injure him. As the result of the fight, V is knocked unconscious, recovers a few minutes later, drives away, and is hit by the 8:02 train at a crossing. D's act is certainly a "but for" cause of the harm to V, since had V not been knocked out, he would have continued on his way and crossed earlier than 8:02. And the general type of harm to V — severe bodily injury — is the same as that intended by D. Yet all courts would agree that the chain of events here was so unforeseeable from D's perspective that he should not be held liable for V's death.

1. **"Direct" causation vs. "intervening" events:** Courts often distinguish cases in which D's act was a *"direct"* cause of the harm from those in which there was an *"intervening"* cause between D's act and the harm. But the direct/intervening distinction is only one factor — D has a somewhat better chance, on average, of escaping liability where there was intervening cause than where there was not. [51]

B. **Direct causation:** We say that D's act was a *"direct"* of V's harm if the harm followed D's act without the presence of any clearly-defined act or event by an outside person or thing. In direct causation situations, D is rarely able to convince the court that the chain of events was so bizarre that D should be absolved. [51-53]

1. **Small differences in type of injury:**   If the same general *type of injury* (e.g., serious bodily harm, death, burning) occurs as was intended by D, the fact that the harm deviates in some small manner from that intended is irrelevant. [51]

2. **Slightly different mechanism:**   Similarly, if the general type of harm intended actually occurs, D will not be absolved because the harm occurred in a slightly different *way* than intended. [52]

   Example: D attempts to poison her husband, V, by putting strychnine in a glass of milk she serves him for breakfast. V drinks it, and becomes so dizzy from its effect that he falls while getting up from his chair, hitting his head on the table. He dies from the blow to the head, and the autopsy shows that the poison would not have been enough to kill him directly. Nearly all courts would hold that D is guilty of murder, because her act directly caused V's death, and there was nothing terribly bizarre about the chain of events leading to that death.

3. **Pre-existing weakness:**   If V has a *pre-existing condition*, unknown to D, that makes him much more *susceptible to injury or death* than a normal person would be, D *"takes his victim as he finds him."* Thus D may not argue that his own act was not the proximate cause of the unusually severe result. [52]

   Example: D beats V up, with intent to kill him. V runs away before many blows have fallen, and a person in ordinary health would not have been severely hurt by the blows that did fall. Unknown to D, however, V is a hemopheliac, who bleeds to death from one slight wound. D is guilty of murder, even though from D's viewpoint V's death from the slight wounds was unforeseeable.

   Note: When you are looking at a proximate cause problem, don't forget to also apply the rules of concurrence and to insist on the *correct mental state*. For instance, suppose D in the above example had only been trying to commit a minor battery on V, instead of trying to kill him. If V died as a result of his hemophelia, D would not be liable for common-law intent-to-kill murder, because he did not have the requisite mental state, the intent to kill. (But he would probably be liable for *manslaughter* under the misdemeanor- manslaughter rule.)

4. **Fright or stress:**   Where V's death results even *without physical impact*, as the result of a *fright* or *stress* caused by D, D's conduct can nonetheless be a proximate cause of the death. [52]

   Example: During a holdup by D, V, a storekeeper, has a fatal heart attack from the stress. In most courts, V's death will be held to be the proximate result of D's act of robbery; coupled with the felony-murder doctrine, this will be enough for D to be guilty of murder, even if there was no way he could have known of V's heart condition. [*People v. Stamp*]

C. **Intervening acts:**   D's odds of escaping liability are better where an *"intervening act"* or intervening *event* contributes to the result than where D has "directly" caused the harmful result. [53-60]

   1. **Dependent vs. independent intervening acts:**   Courts divide intervening acts into two categories: (1) *"dependent"* acts, which are ones which would not have occurred except for D's act (e.g., medical treatment for a wound caused by D); and (2) *"independent"* acts, which would have occurred even if D had not acted, but which combined with D's act produced the harmful result. [54]

Example of dependent act: D wounds V in a fight. X, a doctor, negligently treats V's wound, and V dies.

Example of independent act or event: D poisons V, weakening his immune system. D is then in a car accident which he would have been in even had the poisoning not taken place. V dies from the combined result of the accident and his pre-accident weakened condition.

    a. Significance: D's odds of escaping responsibility are somewhat better where the intervening act is *"independent."* An independent intervention will break the chain of events if it was *"unforeseeable"* for one in D's position. A dependent intervening cause will break the chain only if it was both unforeseeable and *"abnormal."* An act is less likely to be considered "abnormal" than it is to be considered merely "unforeseeable," so D typically does better in the independent case. [54]

  2. Intervening acts by third persons: [54-57]

    a. Medical treatment: The most common intervening act is *medical treatment* performed by a doctor or nurse upon V, where this treatment is necessitated by injuries inflicted by D. Here, the treatment is obviously in response to D's act, and therefore is a "dependent" intervening act, so it will only supersede if the treatment is *"abnormal."* [54-56]

      i. Negligent treatment: The fact that the treatment is *negligently performed* will *not*, by itself, usually be enough to make it so "abnormal" that it is a superceding event. But if the treatment is performed in a *reckless* or *grossly negligent* manner, the treatment *will* usually be found to be "abnormal" and thus superseding.

    b. Failure to act never supersedes: A third party's *failure to act* will almost *never* be a superseding cause. [57]

    Example: D shoots V. There is a doctor, X, standing by who could, with 100% certainty, prevent V from dying. X refuses to render assistance because he hates V and wants V to die. D will still be the proximate cause of death — a third party's failure to act will never supersede.

  3. Act by V: Sometimes the *victim herself* will take an action that is possibly a superseding intervening cause. Acts by victims are generally taken in direct response to D's act, so they will not be superseding unless they are "abnormal" (not merely "unforeseeable"). [57-59]

    a. Victim refuses medical aid: If the victim refuses to receive *medical assistance* which might prevent the severe harm imposed by D, the victim's refusal usually will *not* be superseding. [58]

    Example: D stabs V repeatedly. V refuses a blood transfusion because she is a Jehovah's Witness. *Held*, V's refusal to allow the transfusion is not a superseding cause. [*Regina v. Blaue*]

    b. Victim tries to avoid danger: If the victim attempts to *avoid the danger* posed by D, and this attempted escape results in additional injury, the attempt will be a superseding cause only if it is an "abnormal" reaction. [58]

    Example: D kidnaps V by locking her in a room. V tries to escape by knotting bed sheets together, and falls to her death while climbing down. V's escape would probably be found not to be "abnormal" even if it is was "unforeseeable," so it will not be a superseding cause, and D will be the proximate cause of death. The felony-murder rule will then make

D guilty of V's death, even though D did not have any of the mental states for ordinary murder.

    c. **V subjects self to danger:** Suppose D urges or encourages V to *expose himself to danger*. V's voluntary participation will *not* generally supersede, and D will be held to be a proximate cause of the result. [58-59]

    Examples: D persuades V to play Russian Roulette, or to engage in a drag race — many courts will hold D to be the proximate cause of the injury when V shoots himself or crashes.

CHAPTER 3

RESPONSIBILITY

I. THE INSANITY DEFENSE

  A. General purpose: If D can show he was *insane* at the time he committed a criminal act, he may be entitled to the verdict "not guilty by reason of insanity." [67]

    1. Mandatory commitment: If D succeeds with the insanity defense, he does not walk out of the courtroom free. In virtually every state, any D who succeeds with the insanity defense will be involuntarily *committed* to a mental institution. [67]

    2. Not constitutionally required: Virtually every state recognizes some form of the insanity defense. However, the federal constitution probably does *not require* the states to recognize insanity as a complete defense. [67]

    3. Limits use of mental disease: In many states, the insanity defense is coupled with a rule that *no evidence relating to mental disease or defect* may be introduced *except* as part of an insanity defense. (*Example:* D is charged with knifing his wife to death. In many states, D will not be permitted to show that his mental disease prevented him from forming an intent to kill her. In these states, D's sole method for showing the relevance of his mental disease is via the insanity defense.) [67]

  B. Tests for insanity: The principal tests for whether D was insane — each used in some jurisdictions — are as follows: [68-73]

    1. *M'Naghten* "right from wrong" rule: At least half the states apply the so-called *M'Naghten* rule: D must show: [68-69]

      a. Mental disease or defect: That he suffered a *mental disease* causing a *defect* in his reasoning powers [68]; and

      b. Result: That as a result, either: (1) he did not understand the *"nature and quality"* of his act; or (2) he did not know that his act was *wrong*. [69]

      Example 1: D strangles V, his wife, believing that he is squeezing a lemon. Even under the relatively strict *M'Naghten* test, D would probably be ruled insane, on the grounds that he did not understand the "nature and quality" of his act.

      Example 2: D is attracted to bright objects, and therefore shoplifts jewelry constantly, though intellectually he knows that this is morally wrong and also illegal. D is not insane under the *M'Naghten* test, because he understood the nature and quality of his act, and knew that his act was wrong. The fact that he may have acted under an "irresistible impulse" is irrelevant under the *M'Naghten* rule.

2. **"Irresistible impulse" test:**   Many states, including about half of those states that follow *M'Naghten*, have added a *second standard* by which D can establish his insanity: that D was *unable to control his conduct*. This is sometimes loosely called the *"irresistible impulse"* defense. (*Example:* On the facts of Example 2 above, D would be acquitted, because although he understood that it was wrong to shoplift shiny things, he was unable to control his conduct.) [70]

3. **Model Penal Code standard:**   The Model Penal Code (§4.01(1)) allows D to be acquitted if "as a result of mental disease or defect he lacks substantial capacity either to *appreciate the criminality* of his conduct or *to conform his conduct* to the requirements of the law." Thus D wins if he can show *either* that he didn't know his conduct was wrong, or that he couldn't control his conduct. Essentially, D wins if he satisfies either the *M'Naghten* test or the irresistible impulse test, under the MPC approach. [70-72]

4. **The federal standard:**   The modern *federal* standard (in force since 1984) sets a very stringent standard for federal prosecutions. D wins only if "as a result of a severe mental disease or defect, [he] was unable to appreciate the *nature and quality* or the *wrongfulness* of his acts…." This is essentially the *M'Naghten* standard. The fact that D was unable to conform his conduct to the requirements of the law is *irrelevant* — in other words, in federal suits, there is no "irresistible impulse" defense. [72]

C. **Raising and establishing the defense:**   [73-76]

1. **Who raises defense:**   In nearly all states, the insanity defense is an *affirmative defense*. That is, D is required to *come forward with evidence* showing that he is insane — only then does D's sanity enter the case. [73]

2. **Burden of persuasion:**   After D bears his burden of production by showing some evidence of insanity, courts are *split* about who bears the "burden of persuasion," i.e., the burden of convincing the fact-finder on the insanity issue. In half the states, the prosecution must prove beyond a reasonable doubt that D is not insane. In the remaining states, D bears the burden of proving his insanity, but only by a "preponderance of the evidence." In the federal system, the rule is even tougher on D: D must prove insanity by "clear and convincing evidence." [73]

3. **Psychiatric examination:**   A defendant who demonstrates that sanity will be a significant factor at his trial has a *constitutional right* to have the *assistance of a psychiatrist* at state expense. [*Ake v. Oklahoma*] [74-75]

    a. **Court-appointed expert:**   Whether or not a psychiatrist is appointed for D's benefit, in most states the court has the power to appoint a theoretically impartial psychiatrist to conduct an *independent examination* of D, the results of which will be admissible at the trial. Often, this appointment is done at the request of the prosecution. [74]

4. **Judge/jury allocation:**   If the case is tried before a jury, it is the jury that will have the task of deciding the merits of D's insanity defense, based on instructions from the judge. [75-76]

    a. **Decision left to jury:**   Courts try hard to ensure that the ultimate decision is in fact made by the jury, *not by the psychiatric expert witnesses*. The jury is always free to disregard or disbelieve the expert witness' evaluation of D's condition. In fact, in federal trials, the federal insanity statute *prevents* either side's expert from even *testifying* as to the ultimate issue of D's sanity. See FRE 704(b). [75]

D. **XYY chromosome defense:**   Some states allow D to buttress his insanity defense by showing that he has a certain chromosomal abnormality, the so-called "XYY chromosome defense," since XYY men are much more likely to commit certain kinds of crimes than men with normal chromosomes. [77-77]

E. **Commitment following insanity acquittal:**   In nearly every state, if D is acquitted by reason of insanity, he will end up being *committed* to a mental institution. In some states (and in the federal system) the judge is *required by law* to commit D to a mental institution, without even a hearing as to present sanity. [77] (Such a mandatory commitment procedure does not violate the constitution. [*Jones v. U.S.*, 463 U.S. 354 (1983)]) In other states, the judge or the jury conducts a *hearing* to decide whether D is still insane and in need of commitment. [77-78]

1. **Release:**   Once D has been committed to an institution and petitions for release, the release decision typically depends on: (1) whether D continues to be *insane*; and (2) whether D continues to be *dangerous*. [77-78]

    a. **Constitutional requirements:**   The Due Process Clause of the federal Constitution places limits on the conditions under which an insantiy acquitee may be kept in an institution. The state may automatically commit an insanity acquitee without a hearing, as noted above. But the state must then periodically offer D the opportunity to be released. The state must release D if he bears the burden of proving that he is *either no longer insane* or *no longer dangerous*. (Probably the state may not impose on D any burden more difficult than the "preponderance of the evidence" standard for establishing either that he is no longer insane or that he is no longer dangerous.) [*Foucha v. Louisiana*, 112 S.Ct. 1780 (1992)] [78]

F. **Fitness to stand trial:**   The insanity defense can also be asserted as a grounds for *not trying D* on the grounds that he is *incompetent to stand trial*. In general, D will be held to be incompetent to stand trial if he is unable to do *both* of the following: (1) *understand* the proceedings against him; and (2) *assist counsel* in his defense. [78-79]

1. **Burden of proof:**   Many jurisdictions place the *burden of proof* as toincompetence upon the *defendant*. The U.S. Supreme Court has held that it is *not unconstitutional* for the state to place upon D the burden of proving by a preponderance of the evidence that he is incompetent to stand trial. [*Medina v. California*, 505 U.S. 437 (1992)] [78]

G. **Insanity at time set for execution:**   If the defendant is insane *at the time set for his execution*, he may *not* be executed. Execution of a prisoner who is currently insane violates the Eighth Amendment's ban on cruel and unusual punishment. [*Ford v. Wainwright*, 477 U.S. 399 (1986)] [79]

II. DIMINISHED RESPONSIBILITY

A. **Where and how used:**   Under the defense of *"diminished responsibility,"* a non-insane D argues that he suffers such a mental impairment that he is *unable to formulate the requisite intent*. [80-83]

1. **Homicide cases:**   The defense is allowed most often in *homicide* cases, usually ones where D is charged with first-degree murder and attempts to reduce it to second-degree by showing that he was incapable of the requisite premeditation. [82]

B. Insanity supersedes: More than half of the states *reject* the doctrine of diminished responsibility. Usually, they do so by holding that *no evidence* that D suffers from a mental disease or defect may be introduced, except pursuant to a formal insanity defense. [81]

III. AUTOMATISM

A. Defense generally: Under the *"automatism"* defense, D tries to show that a mental or physical condition prevented his act from being *voluntary*. [83-84]

> **Example:** While D is in bed with his wife, V, he strangles her. D shows that the strangling occurred while he was in the throes of an epileptic seizure, and that he was not conscious of what he was doing. If the fact-finder believes this story, D will be acquitted, because the strangling was not a voluntary act.

B. Generally allowed: Most courts allow the automatism defense as a distinct defense from the insanity defense. [83]

   1. Model Penal Code allows: Thus the Model Penal Code effectively recognizes the defense: D is not liable if he does not commit a "voluntary act," and a "voluntary act" is defined so as to exclude a "reflex or convulsion" or movement during "unconsiousness." MPC §2.01(1) and (2). [83]

   2. Other variants: Apart from the common instance of epileptic seizures, the automatism defense might be used where: (1) D lapsed into unconsciousness because of low blood sugar; (2) D was unable to control her actions because of Premenstrual Syndrome; or (3) D was unable to control his conduct because of Post Traumatic Stress Disorder (PTSD) suffered as the result of wartime experiences. [83]

IV. INTOXICATION

A. Voluntary intoxication: *Voluntary self-induced intoxication* does *not "excuse"* criminal conduct, in general. [84-89]

> **Example:** D decides to rob a bank. Normally, he would be too timid to do so. However, he takes several drinks to increase his courage, and goes out and does the robbery. The fact that D was legally intoxicated when he committed the robbery will be completely irrelevant.

   1. Effect on mental state: Although voluntary intoxication is not an "excuse," it may *prevent D from having the required mental state*. If so, D will not be guilty. [85]

      a. General/specific intent distinction: Traditionally, courts have distinguished between crimes of "general intent" and "specific intent." In a crime of "general intent," intoxication would never be a defense. In a crime requiring "specific intent" (i.e., intent to do an act other than the *actus reus*, such as the intent to commit a felony as required for burglary), D would be allowed to show that intoxication prevented him from having the requisite specific intent. (*Example:* If D was charged with assault with intent to kill, he could show that he was too drunk to have an intent to kill.) [85]

   2. Modern trend: But modern courts usually don't distinguish between general and specific intent. Instead, modern courts generally allow D to show that his intoxication, even involuntary, *prevented him from having the requisite mental state*. See MPC §2.08(1) (self-induced intoxication "is not a defense unless it negatives an element of the offense"). [85]

3. **Negatives intent:**   Thus even self-induced intoxication may prevent D from having the requisite *intent*, if the crime is defined so as to require intent. [86]

    Example: Suppose that in a particular jurisdiction, first degree murder is defined so that D must be shown to have had the intent to kill, and it is not enough for him to recklessly disregard the risk of death. At a time when D has no intent to do anyone harm, he gets drunk in a bar. He then shoots his pistol towards V, intending only to frighten V as a joke. Had D been sober, he would have realized that V would be hit and possibly killed. D should be acquitted, because his drunken state prevented him from having the required intent, namely an intent to kill.

    a. **Pre-intoxication intent:**   Remember that it is not necessary for D to have the required intent *at the time of the actus reus*. Therefore, the fact that D's drunkenness prevented him from having the requisite intent at the time of the *actus reus* will not necessarily get him off the hook if he had the intent earlier. [87]

        Example: D, sober, decides to place a bomb under V's car, in the hopes that V will be blown up. D prepares the bomb. D then gets drunk. In his drunken stupor, he places the bomb under X's car; he is so drunk that he forgets why he is doing this, and at the moment the bomb is placed (and the moment a little while later when it goes off), D has no intent to harm anyone. D's drunkenness will not get him off the hook, because he had the requisite intent to kill at the moment he first prepared the bomb.

    b. **State may opt out of allowing this type of evidence:**   Also, states are free (constitutionally speaking) to legislate that D's intoxication shall not be admitted as evidence negating the required mental state. [*Montana v. Egelhoff*] [85]

4. **Doesn't negate recklessness:**   The most important single fact to remember about intoxication is that in most courts, intoxication *will not negate the element of recklessness*. In other words, if a particular element of a crime can be satisfied by a mental state of recklessness, D's intoxication will be irrelevant. [86]

    a. **Rape:**   For instance, in many *"date rape"* cases, D argues that V consented, or at least that D believed that V was consenting. But in most states (and under the MPC), D's *reckless* mistake about whether V consented will satisfy the *mens rea* requirements for that aspect of the crime. Consequently, if D's drunkenness prevents him from realizing that V is not consenting, D's defense of "I thought she was consenting" will *fail*, if a sober defendant would have realized V's lack of consent. [88]

    b. **Voluntary manslaughter:**   Similarly, D will generally not be allowed to introduce evidence of his intoxication in an attempt to get a murder charge reduced to *voluntary manslaughter*. This reduction is available only where D, acting in the heat of passion, acts under provocation that would have been enough to cause an ordinary person to lose control. But the assumption is that the ordinary man is sober, so D's drunkenness does not help him. [87]

        Example: D, after getting drunk in a bar, believes that V is attacking him with a deadly weapon. An ordinary sober man would have realized that V was merely holding his car keys. D shoots V in an honest attempt to save his own life, and now seeks a reduction from murder to voluntary manslaughter. Because the defense of self-defense is not available when D's belief in the need for that defense is reckless, D's drunkenness will not help him — the act of voluntarily getting drunk itself constitutes recklessness.

B. Involuntary intoxication: In the rare case where D can show that his intoxication was *"involuntary,"* D is much more likely to have a valid defense. [89-91]

    1. Mistake as to nature of substance: For instance, if D intentionally ingests a substance, but *mistakenly believes that it is not intoxicating*, he may have two related defenses: (1) a sort of "temporary insanity" defense, due to his temporary lack of mental capacity; and (2) a defense that the intoxication negated an element of the offense, even if the element was one for which recklessness will suffice. [90]

    Example: Assume the facts of the above example, except that D's intoxication is involuntary because his friend gave him LSD-laced punch. Now, D will probably win with his self-defense claims, since he did not act recklessly in getting drunk, and a reasonable person in his "unintentionally impaired" situation might have made the same mistake.

C. Alcoholism and narcotics addiction: Defendants who are *chronic alcoholics* or *narcotics addicts* sometimes try to use their condition as a defense. [91-92]

    1. Rejected: But courts almost always *reject* any defense based upon these diseases. For instance, D might argue that because he was an alcoholic, his intoxication was "involuntary," and he should therefore be subject to the more liberal standards for "involuntary" as opposed to "voluntary" self-intoxication described above. But almost all courts would reject the "involuntary" defense for alcoholics and addicts. [91]

    2. Crimes to gain funds: Similarly, many Ds commit crimes to *gain funds* to support their addictions. Arguments by such Ds that they lack free will or self-control, and should thus be acquitted, are even more certain to be rejected by the courts. [91]

CHAPTER 4

JUSTIFICATION AND EXCUSE

I. GENERAL PRINCIPLES

A. Justification and excuse generally: The twin doctrines of *"justification"* and *"excuse"* allow D to escape conviction even if the prosecution proves all elements of the case. There is no important distinction between those defenses referred to as "justification" and those referred to as "excuses." Here is a list of the main justifications/excuses: [98]

    1. *Duress*;

    2. *Necessity*;

    3. *Self-defense*;

    4. *Defense of others*;

    5. *Defense of property*;

    6. *Law enforcement* (arrest, prevention of crime and of escape);

    7. *Consent*;

    8. *Maintenance of domestic authority*;

    9. *Entrapment*.

B. Effect of mistake: The effect of a *mistake of fact* by D on these defenses has changed over time: [98-99]

   1. Traditional view: The traditional rule has generally been that D's *reasonable* mistake will not negate the privilege, but that an *unreasonable* mistake by D will negate the defense. [98]

   2. Modern view: But the modern trend, as exemplified by the MPC, is to hold that so long as D genuinely believes (even if *unreasonably*) that the facts are such that the defense is merited, the defense will stand. (There is an exception if D is charged with an act that may be committed "recklessly" or "negligently" — here, he loses the defense if the mistake was "reckless" or "negligent.") [99]

II. DURESS

A. General nature: D is said to have committed a crime under *"duress"* if he performed the crime because of a *threat of*, or *use of, force* by a third person sufficiently strong that D's will was *overborne*. The term applies to force placed upon D's *mind*, not his body. [100]

   Example: X forces D to rob Y, by threatening D with immediate death if he does not. D will be able to raise the defense of duress.

B. Elements: D must establish the following elements for duress: [100]

   1. Threat: A *threat* by a third person, [100]

   2. Fear: Which produces a *reasonable fear* in D, [100]

   3. Imminent danger: That he will suffer *immediate* or *imminent*, [100]

   4. Bodily harm: *Death* or *serious bodily injury*. [100]

C. Model Penal Code test: Under the MPC, the defense is available where the threat to D was sufficiently great that "a person of *reasonable firmness* in [D's] situation would have been *unable to resist*." MPC §2.09(1). [100]

D. Not available for homicide: Traditionally, the defense of duress is not available if D is charged with *homicide*, i.e., the intentional killing of another. [100-101]

   Example: D is a member of a gang run by X. X and the other gang members tell D that if D does not kill V, an innocent witness to one of the group's crimes, they will kill D immediately. D reasonably and honestly believes this threat. D kills V. Few if any courts will allow D to assert the defense of duress on these facts, because he is charged with the intentional killing of another. (The result probably would not change even if D had originally been coerced into joining the gang.)

   1. Reduction of crime: A few states allow duress to *reduce the severity* of an intentional homicide (e.g., from first-degree premeditated murder to second-degree spur-of-the-moment murder).

   2. Felony-murder: Also, duress is accepted as a defense to a charge of *felony-murder*. (*Example:* D is coerced into driving X to a robbery site. During the robbery, X intentionally kills V, a witness, to stop V from calling the police. Although in most states D would ordinarily be liable for felony-murder, most states would allow him to raise the defense of duress here.) [101]

E. Imminence of threatened harm: D must be threatened with *imminent* or *immediate* harm, in most courts. Thus the threat of *future harm* is not sufficient. But modern courts are more willing to relax this requirement. [101]

> **Example:** D witnesses X kill V. X phones D to say that if D testifies against X at X's murder trial, X will kill D after the trial. D lies on the stand to avoid implicating X. D is then charged with perjury. Traditionally, most courts would not allow D to raise the defense of duress, since the threatened harm was not imminent. But a modern court, and the Model Penal Code, might not impose this requirement of immediacy.

F. Threat directed at person other than defendant: Traditionally, most courts have required that the threatened harm be directed *at the defendant*. [101]

> **1. Modern view:**   But modern courts, and the MPC, are more liberal. Many courts now recognize the defense where the threat is made against a member of D's *family*. The MPC imposes no requirement at all about who must be threatened (but remember that under the MPC the test is whether a person of "reasonable firmness" would be coerced, and this may be hard to prove if D is coerced by the threat of harm to a complete stranger). [102]

G. Defendant subjects self to danger: Nearly all courts deny the defense to a D who has *voluntarily placed himself in a situation* where there is a substantial probability that he will be subjected to duress.

> **Example:** D voluntarily joins an organized crime group known to have the policy of *omerta*, or death to anyone who informs on the gang. D is called to the witness stand, and lies to protect other gang members. D will not be able to raise the defense of duress, since he voluntarily or at least recklessly placed himself in a position where he was likely to be subjected to duress. [102]

H. Guilt of coercer: Even though the person subjected to duress may have a valid defense on that ground, this will not absolve the person who did the coercing. [102]

> **Example:** A forces B to rob V, by threatening to kill B if he does not. Even though B probably has a duress defense to a robbery charge, A will be guilty of robbery, on an accomplice theory.

III. NECESSITY

A. Generally: The defense of *"necessity"* may be raised when D has been compelled to commit a criminal act, not by coercion from another human being, but by *non-human events*. The essence of the defense is that D has chosen the *lesser of two evils*. [103-106]

> **Example:** D needs to get his seriously ill wife to the hospital. He therefore violates the speed limit. Assuming that there is no available alternative, such as an ambulance, D may claim the defense of necessity, since the traffic violations were a lesser evil than letting his wife get sicker or die.

B. Requirements for defense: The principal requirements which D must meet for the necessity defense are: [104]

> **1. Greater harm:**   The harm sought to be avoided is *greater* than the harm committed; [104]
>
> **2. No alternative:**   There is no third *alternative* that would also avoid the harm, yet would be non-criminal or a less serious crime; [104]
>
> **3. Imminence:**   The harm is *imminent*, not merely future; and [104]

    4. Situation not caused by D: The situation was not brought about by D's carelessly or recklessly *putting himself in a position* where the emergency would arise. [104]

    Note: In contrast to the case of duress, the harm D is seeking to avoid need not be serious bodily harm, but may be non-serious bodily harm or even *property damage*.

C. Homicide: Courts have traditionally been very reluctant to permit the necessity defense where D is charged with an *intentional killing*. [105-106]

    1. Model Penal Code view: The MPC does not rule out the necessity defense even in intentional homicide cases. But under the MPC, one may not sacrifice one life to save another, since the Code requires the choice of the lesser of two evils, not merely the equal of two evils, and all lives are presumed to be of equal value. But if a life can be sacrificed to save two or more lives, the Code would allow the defense. (*Example:* D, a mountain climber, is roped to V, who has fallen over a cliff. If the only alternative is that both climbers will die, D may cut the rope even if this will inevitably cause V's death.) [106]

D. Economic necessity not sufficient: The harm that confronts D may be of a non-bodily nature, such as damage to his property. But courts do not accept the defense of *"economic necessity."* (*Example:* D, an unemployed worker, may not steal food and then claim the defense of necessity. But if he is actually about to starve to death, then the defense may be allowed.) [106]

E. Civil disobedience: The necessity defense is almost always rejected in cases of *"civil disobedience."* [106]

    Example: To protest U.S. military assistance to El Salvador, the Ds trespass in their local IRS office, splash blood on the walls, and do other criminal acts to draw attention to why U.S. policy is bad. *Held*, the Ds' necessity defense is invalid, because there were lawful ways of attempting to bring about changed government policies. [*U.S. v. Schoon*]

IV. SELF-DEFENSE

A. Self-defense generally: There is a general right to *defend oneself* against the use of *unlawful force*. When successfully asserted, the defense is a complete one, leading to acquittal. [107]

B. Requirements: The following requirements must generally be met: [107]

    1. Resist unlawful force: D must have been resisting the *present or imminent use* of *unlawful force*; [107]

    2. Force must not be excessive: The degree of force used by D must not have been *more than was reasonably necessary* to defend against the threatened harm; [107]

    3. Deadly force: The force used by D may not have been *deadly* (i.e., intended or likely to cause death or serious bodily injury) unless the danger being resisted was also deadly force; [107]

    4. Aggressor: D must not have been the *aggressor*, unless: (1) he was a *non-deadly aggressor* confronted with the unexpected use of deadly force; or (2) he *withdrew* after his initial aggression, and the other party continued to attack; and [107]

    5. Retreat: (In some states) D must not have been in a position from which he could *retreat* with complete safety, unless: (1) the attack took place in D's dwelling; or (2) D used only non-deadly force. [107]

C. Requirement of "unlawful force": Self-defense applies only where D is resisting force that is *unlawful*. [107-108]

   1. Other party commits tort or crime: Generally, this means that the other party must be committing a *crime or tort*. [107]

   a. Other party has privilege: Thus if the other party, even though he is using force, is *entitled* to do so, the force is not unlawful, and D may not use force to defend against it. For instance, a property owner who is using non-deadly force to defend his property against attempted theft is not using "unlawful" force. [107]

   Example: D tries to pick V's pocket. V, not a trained or dangerous fistfighter, hits D lightly with his fist. V has a privilege to use reasonable non-deadly force to defend his property, so V is not using "unlawful" force, and D therefore has no right to use any force in self-defense.

   b. Other party uses excessive force: However, if the other party is entitled to use some degree of force, but uses *more than is lawfully allowed*, the excess will probably be treated as unlawful, and D may resist it by using force himself. [107]

   Example: On the facts of the above example, suppose that V pulls out a gun and aims it at D and starts to pull the trigger, even though V realizes that D is unarmed and not dangerous. D may probably tackle V and knock away the gun, because V has gone beyond the scope of the privilege to use reasonable force to defend property.

   c. Reasonable mistake by D: If D makes a *reasonable mistake* about the unlawful status of the force being used against her, she will nonetheless be protected. (In general, the defense of self-defense is not voided by a reasonable mistake.) But in most states, D will lose the defense if her mistaken belief that the opposing force was unlawful was unreasonble. See the further discussion of mistake in self-defense below. [108-109]

D. Degree of force: D may not use more force than is *reasonably necessary* to protect himself. [108]

   1. Use of non-deadly force: D may use *non-deadly force* to resist virtually any kind of unlawful force (assuming that the level of non-deadly force D uses is not more than is necessary to meet the threat). [108]

   a. No need to retreat: D may use non-deadly force without *retreating* even if retreat could be safely done. [108]

   b. Prevention of theft: D may use non-deadly force to resist the other person's attempted theft of *property*. [108]

   2. Deadly force: D may defend himself with *deadly force* only if the attack threatens D with *serious bodily harm*. [108-109]

   a. Definition of "deadly force": Remember that "deadly force" is usually defined as force that is *intended or likely* to cause *death or serious bodily harm*. [109]

   i. Firing firearm: Generally, if D purposely *fires a gun* in the direction of another person, this will be considered use of deadly force. See MPC §3.11(2).

   ii. Result irrelevant: The *actual result* of the deadly force is *irrelevant*, either way.

Example 1: D shoots at V with a gun, and misses him entirely. D has used deadly force, and will be liable for assault and/or battery if deadly force was not permissible.

Example 2: D, not a particularly capable fistfighter, swings his fist at V's stomach, intending to immobilize V. V unexpectedly suffers a ruptured spleen, and dies. D will not be deemed to have used deadly force, since the force was neither intended nor likely to cause death or serious bodily harm.

   iii. Threats: D's verbal *threat* to use deadly force does *not* itself constitute use of deadly force, provided that D *does not intend to carry out the threat*. (MPC §3.11(2))

   b. Nature of attack: D may use deadly force to defend against the threat of *serious bodily harm*. Most courts also allow it to protect against *kidnapping* and forcible *rape*. [109]

   c. Effect of mistake: As with other sorts of mistakes, if D is reasonably mistaken in the belief that he is threatened with serious bodily harm, he will not lose the right to reply with deadly force. [109]

E. Imminence of harm: The harm being defended against must be reasonably *imminent*. [109]

   1. MPC liberal view: The MPC construes this requirement somewhat liberally — D may use force to protect himself against unlawful force that will be used *"on the present occasion."* [110]

   Example 1: V tells D on the telephone, "I will kill you tomorrow." D goes to V's house and shoots V. D may not claim self-defense, because V's threat was not for imminent force.

   Example 2: D is stranded in his broken-down car in the middle of a neighborhood he does not know well. V sees D defenseless, and says, "I'm gonna go get my friends and we're gonna come back and strip the tires off your car." Under the MPC, D may use non-violent force to prevent V from getting his friends, because the threat is that unlawful force will be used "on the present occasion," even though the force is not completely imminent.

   2. Withdrawal by aggressor: One consequence of the requirement that the danger be imminent is that if the *aggressor withdraws* from the conflict, the victim *loses his right to use force,* at least where the withdrawal should reasonably be interpreted as indicating that the danger is over. (But if the assailant seems to be getting *reinforcements*, that's not a "withdrawal," and the victim can keep using force.)

   Example: V and D are friends. They get into a verbal dispute, and V takes a swing at D. D starts to swing back. V stops swinging and says, "Wait a minute, we've always been friends, let's stop fighting." D (who has no reason to believe that V's offer to stop the fight is phony) continues to beat V up. D will not be able to use the defense of self-defense if he is charged with battery occurring after V's offer to stop — once V withdrew from the conflict, the occasion requiring self-defense was over.

F. Aggressor may not claim self-defense: If D is the *initial aggressor* — that is, one who strikes the first blow or otherwise precipitates the conflict — he may ordinarily *not claim self-defense*. [110-111]

   Example: D starts a fight in a bar with V, by brandishing a knife at V. V, using his own knife, tries to cut D's knife-wielding hand. D hits V in the face with his other hand, injuring him. D cannot claim self-defense, because he precipitated the conflict by brandishing the knife.

1. **Aggression without actual force:**   D can be treated as an aggressor, and thus lose the right of self-defense, even if D did not actually strike the first blow. It is enough if D did an *unlawful* (i.e., tortious or criminal) act which *"provoked"* the physical conflict. [110]

    Example: The above example illustrates this principle — D has merely brandished the knife, not used it, yet he is deemed the aggressor.

2. **Exceptions:**   There are two *exceptions* to the rule that the one who is the aggressor may not claim self-defense: [111]

    a. **Non-deadly force met with deadly force:**   First, if D provokes the exchange but uses no actual force or only *non-deadly force*, and the other party *responds with deadly force*, D may then defend himself (even with deadly force, if necessary). [111]

        Example: D attacks V with his fists. V defends by knocking D down, then starting to smash D's head against the wall, so that D is in danger of being killed or badly hurt. D manages to pull a knife, and kills X. Probably D is entitled to a claim of self-defense. V, by meeting non-deadly force with deadly force, was acting unlawfully, and D will be permitted to save his life. (All of this assumes that D did not have the duty and opportunity to retreat, a duty which he might have in some states under some circumstances.)

    b. **Withdrawal:**   Second, if D *withdraws from the conflict*, and the other party (V) initiates a *second conflict*, D may use non-deadly force (and even deadly force if he is threatened with death or serious bodily harm). This is true even if D started the initial conflict with the use of deadly force. All of this is so because once D (the initial aggressor) withdraws, the conflict is over, so V's use of force becomes unlawful force that D can defend against. [111]

        Example: In a bar, D attacks V with his fists, hits him several times, and knocks him down. D leaves the bar and gets into his car, intending to drive away. V, after getting up, follows D outside, and attacks D with his fists, just as D is getting to the car. D swings back, hitting and injuring V. D will be entitled to claim self-defense, because he withdrew from the conflict, and V was in effect starting a new conflict in which V was really the aggressor.

G. **Retreat:**   Some states (but not yet a majority) require that if D could *safely retreat*, he must do so *rather than use deadly force*. [112-113]

    1. **No retreat before non-deadly force:**   No states require retreat before the use of *non-deadly force*. [112]

        Example: V attacks D with non-deadly force. D could withdraw from the encounter with complete safety, by getting into his car and driving away. D instead stands his ground and fights back with his fists, with which he is not especially proficient. In all states, even those with a general "duty to retreat," D is privileged, because no reatreat is ever required before the use of non-deadly force.

    2. **Retreat only required where it can be safely done:**   The retreat rule, in states requiring it, only applies where D could retreat with *complete safety* to himself and others. Also, if D reasonably but mistakenly believes that retreat cannot be safely done, he will be protected. [112]

    3. **Retreat in D's dwelling:**   Those states requiring retreat do not generally require it where the attack takes place in *D's dwelling*. [112-113]

Example: D invites V to D's house, and the two parties get into a dispute. V attacks D with a knife. D could easily go into a bedroom which can be locked from the inside; while there, he could readily call the police. Instead, D grabs a knife — the only reasonably available means of combatting V, given D's inferior martial arts skills — and seriously wounds V. Even in states imposing a general duty of retreat, D is exempt from the duty here, since the attack is taking place in his own dwelling.

 a. Not applicable if D was aggressor: But this exception for a dwelling does not apply if D was the *aggressor*. [112]

 b. Assailant also resident: Also, some courts hold that the dwelling exception to the retreat requirement does not apply where the *assailant is also a resident* of the dwelling. But other courts, probably representing the more modern view, do not remove the exception in this situation. [113]

  Example: H and W are married. H attacks W at home. W could easily retreat to a lockable bedroom, but instead uses deadly force (though no more than reasonably necessary) to rebut the attack. Of the states requiring a duty to retreat, most would give W an exemption because she is in her dwelling, but a few would impose the duty of retreat even here because H is also a resident of the dwelling.

H. Effect of mistake: The effect of a *mistake* by D concerning the need for self-defense will depend largely on whether the mistake is *"reasonable."* Observe that there are various kinds of mistakes that D might make concerning the need for self-defense: (1) a mistaken belief that he is about to be attacked; (2) a mistake in belief that the force used against him is unlawful; (3) a mistaken belief that only deadly force will suffice to repel the threat; or (4) a mistaken belief that retreat could not be accomplished safely. [113-115]

 1. Reasonable: As long as D's mistaken belief as to any of these points is *reasonable*, all courts will allow him to claim self-defense. [113]

  Example: While D is walking down the street one evening, V says, "Your money or your life," and points what appears to be a gun at D. In fact, the "gun" is merely V's finger poking through V's jacket. A reasonable person in D's position would be likely to believe that there was a real gun. D also reasonably believes that V may shoot D even if D gives up the property, because this has happened in the neighborhood on several recent occasions. D pulls his own gun and shoots V to death. Later evidence shows that V, a career mugger, would never have dreamt of actually doing physical harm to a victim. Because D's mistakes (about the existence of a gun, and about whether it would be used against him) were "reasonable," D is entitled to claim self-defense despite the mistakes.

 2. Unreasonable mistake: But if D's mistake is *unreasonable*, most states hold that he *loses* the right to claim self-defense. [113-115]

  Example: D travels on a New York City subway while carrying an unlicensed loaded pistol. Four youths approach him, and one states, "Give me $5." D pulls out the gun and shoots at each of the four, one of whom is sitting on a bench and apparently posing no imminent threat to D at the time. D later admits that he did not think the youths had a gun, but that he had a fear, based on prior times when he was mugged, that he might be maimed as a result of this encounter.

  Held, D's claim of self-defense is valid only if he "reasonably believed" that one of the victims was about to use deadly physical force or about to commit one of certain violent crimes upon him. This imposes an objective standard, by which D's conduct must be that of a reasonable person in D's situation. [*People v. Goetz*, 497 N.E.2d 41 (N.Y. 1986)]

   a.   MPC/minority view: A minority of courts, and the Model Penal Code, hold that even an *unreasonable* (but genuine) mistake as to the need for self-defense will protect D. This is, in a sense, the more "modern" view. (But if the crime is one that can be committed by a "reckless" or "negligent" state of mind, even under the MPC D's reckless or negligent mistake as to the need for self-defense will not absolve him.) [115]

   b.   Not totally subjective: Even in courts following the majority "objective" standard for reasonableness of mistake, the standard is not completely objective.

   i.   D's physical disadvantages: Courts generally take D's *physical disadvantages* into account in determining the reasonableness of his mistake. [114]

   Example: If D is a small woman, and V is a large man, obviously it is reasonable for D to fear harm more readily than if the roles were reversed.

   ii.   D's past experiences and knowledge: Similarly, courts generally hold that D's *past experiences* and knowledge are to be taken into account in determining whether D's mistake was a "reasonable" one. [114]

   Example: In *People v. Goetz, supra,* D was allowed to put on evidence that he was previously mugged, thus contributing to his belief that danger to him was likely in the present encounter.

   c.   Intoxication: If the cause of D's unreasonable mistake as to the need for self-defense is his *intoxication*, all courts agree that the intoxication does not excuse the mistake, and D will not be entitled to a claim of self-defense. [115]

   Example: D gets drunk in a bar. He mistakenly believes that V is about to shoot him. He instead draws first, and shoots V to death. Had D been sober, he would have realized that V was not about to attack him. All courts agree that because D's mistake was caused by his intoxication, he loses the claim of self-defense.

I.   Battered women and self-defense: Where a woman *kills her spouse* because she believes this is the only way she can protect herself against ongoing *battering* by him, courts normally do not change the generally-applicable rules of self-defense. [115-118]

   1.   Standard for "reasonableness":   In a battered-woman case, the courts try not to allow too much subjectivity into the determination of whether the woman has acted reasonably. Most courts make the test, What would a reasonable woman do in the defendant's situation, taking into account the prior history of abuse, but not taking into account the particular psychology of the woman herself (e.g., that she is unusually depressed, or aggressive, or otherwise different)? [117]

   2.   Imminence of danger: Nearly all courts continue to require in battered-woman cases, as in other cases, that self-defense be used only where the danger is *imminent*. For instance, courts have not modified the traditional requirement of imminent danger to cover situations where the woman's counter-strike *does not come during a physical confrontation*. Thus D would probably be convicted of murder for killing her abusing husband, V, in any of the following situations:

   ❑   V, after abusing D, has *gone to sleep*, and D shoots him in the head while he sleeps;

❏ D *waits* for V to return home, and kills him immediately, before any kind of argument has arisen; and

❏ D *arranges with someone else* (at the most extreme, a hired killer) to kill V.

(But if the absense of confrontation is merely a *momentary lull* in the attack — e.g., V's back is temporarily turned, but D reasonably believes that the attack will resume any moment — then the requirement of imminence is typically found to be satisfied.) [117-118]

3. **Battered child:** Essentially the same rules apply where a *battered child* kills the abusive parent or step-parent, typically the father. Thus many courts allow psychologists to testify about a "battered child's syndrome." But courts apply the imminence requirement in the case of killings by children, just as in the case of killings by the wife. [118]

J. **Resisting arrest:** A person's right to use force to *resist an unlawful arrest* is much more limited than his right to use force to resist other kinds of unlawful attack. [118]

1. **Deadly force:** Virtually no state allows a suspect to use *deadly force* to resist an unlawful arrest. [118]

2. **Non-deadly force:** A substantial minority of states now bar even the use of *non-deadly force* against an unlawful arrest. The MPC, for instance, refuses to allow the use of force to resist an unlawful arrest, if D knows that the person doing the arresting is a police officer. MPC §3.04(2)(a)(i). [119]

Example: Officer comes to D's house to arrest D for a felony committed a long time ago, as to which the police have long suspected D. Officer does not have a warrant. D knows that Officer is a police officer, but D also knows that constitutionally, a warrant is required for entering a suspect's house to arrest him unless there are exigent circumstances. Although D thus knows that the arrest is unlawful, D may not use even non-deadly force — such as punching or kicking the officer — to resist arrest, under minority/MPC view.

a. **Traditional view:** But the traditional view, probably still followed by a bare majority of states, is that a suspect *may* use *non-deadly* force to resist an unlawful arrest. [119]

3. **Excessive force:** Nearly all states allow the use of non-deadly force to resist an arrest made with *excessive force*, or in any situation where D reasonably believes that he will be *injured*. (But even here, deadly force may not be used.) [119]

Example: In a Rodney King-like scenario, D is arrested properly, then kicked and beaten with truncheons for several minutes, while he does not resist. Nearly all states would allow D to punch or kick the arresting officer and to run away, in order to escape the blows. But D could not pull out a knife and stab the arresting officer, even in this extreme situation.

K. **Injury to third persons:** If while D is using force to protect himself, he *injures a bystander*, his criminal liability with respect to this injury will be measured by the same standards as if it was the assailant who was injured. [119]

1. **D not reckless or negligent:** Thus if D's conduct was not reckless or negligent with respect to the bystander, he will not be liable, assuming that self-defense as to the assailant was proper. [119]

2. **Recklessness or negligence:** Conversely, if D *is* reckless or negligent with respect to the risk of injuring a bystander, D may not claim self-defense if the charge is one that requires only recklessness or negligence (as the case may be). [120]

Example: X, wielding a knife, attacks D in a crowded bar. D pulls out what he knows to be a very powerful gun, and shoots at X. The bullet misses X and kills Y, a bystander. Even if, as seems likely, D had a general right to use deadly force in his own defense in this situation, a jury could find that D was reckless as to the risk of killing a bystander. If the jury so concluded, D would then be guilty of voluntary manslaughter, because his mental state with respect to Y — recklessness — suffices for manslaughter.

L. "Imperfect" self-defense: D may be entitled to a claim of *"imperfect"* self-defense, sufficient to reduce his crime from murder to *voluntary manslaughter*, if D killed in self-defense but failed to satisfy one of the requirements for acquittal by reason of self-defense. [120]

   1. Unreasonable mistake: Thus if D makes an *unreasonable mistake* as to the need for force, or as to the unlawfulness of the other party's force, most states give him the claim of imperfect self-defense. [120]

   2. Initial aggressor: Similarly, if D was the *initial aggressor*, and thus lost the right to claim true self-defense, he can still use imperfect self-defense to get his crime reduced to manslaughter. [120]

   Example: X insults D. D pulls a knife and advances towards X. X pulls a gun and is about to shoot D. With his spare hand, D pulls a gun and shoots X to death. Because D was the aggressor — and he was the first to use physical violence rather than mere words — he does not have a "full" claim of self-defense. However, he met all the requirements for use of deadly force except that he not have been the aggressor, so he'll probably be entitled to have the charge reduced from murder to voluntary manslaughter.

   3. Model Penal Code view: The MPC similarly says that an unreasonable belief in the need for deadly force will give rise to manslaughter if D was reckless in his mistake. (If D's unreasonable belief was merely negligent, under the MPC he cannot be charged with anything higher than criminally negligent homicide.) [120]

M. Burden of proof: Nearly all states make a claim of self-defense an *affirmative defense*, i.e., one which must be raised, in the first instance, by D. Many states also place the *burden of persuasion* on D, requiring him to prove by a *preponderance of the evidence* that all the requirements for the defense are met. It is constitutional for a state to put this burden of persuasion upon the defendant. [*Martin v. Ohio*, 480 U.S. 228 (1987)] [120]

V. DEFENSE OF OTHERS

A. Right to defend others in general: A person may use force to *defend another* in roughly the same circumstances in which he would be justified in using force in his own defense. [121]

B. Relation between defendant and aided person: At common law, a person was permitted to defend only his *relatives*. [121]

   1. Modern rule: Today, however, most courts and statutes permit one to use force to defend anyone, even a *total stranger*, from threat of harm from another. [121]

C. Requirements: D must generally meet the following requirements in order to have a claim of defense of others: [121]

   1. Danger to other: He reasonably believes that the other person is in *imminent danger* of *unlawful bodily harm*; [121]

2. **Degree of force:** The *degree of force* used by D is no greater than that which seems reasonably *necessary* to prevent the harm; and [121]

3. **Belief in the other person's right to use force:** D reasonably believes that the party being assisted would have the right to use in his *own defense* the force that D proposes to use in assistance. [121]

D. **Retreat:** Most courts hold that D may not use deadly force if he has reason to believe that the person being aided could *retreat with safety*. Thus the MPC requires that D at least "try to cause" the person being aided to retreat if retreat with safety is possible (although D may then use deadly force if his attempt at causing retreat fails). [121]

1. **Home of either party:** Probably retreat is not necessary if the place where the encounter takes place is the *dwelling* or *place of business* of either the defendant or the party assisted. [121]

E. **Mistake as to who is aggressor:** Courts are split about the effect of D's mistake concerning *who was really the aggressor*. [122-122]

1. **Traditional view:** The traditional view, called the *"alter ego"* rule, is that D "stands in the shoes" of the person he aids. Under this view, if the person aided would not have had the right to use that degree of force in his own defense, D's claim fails. [122]

   Example: D observes two middle-aged men beating and struggling with an 18-year-old youth; D reasonably concludes that these two are unlawfully attacking the youth. D hits X, one of the older men, in an attempt to get him off the youth; he breaks X's jaw. It turns out that X and the other older man were plainclothes police officers trying to make a lawful arrest of the youth for an attempted mugging. Under the traditional "alter ego" view, since the youth did not have the privilege to hit back to prevent a lawful arrest, D did not have that privilege to do so for the youth's benefit.

2. **Modern view:** But the modern view is that so long as D's belief that unlawful force is being used against the aidee is *reasonable*, D may assert a claim of defense of others even if his evaluation turns out to have been wrong. Thus the MPC gives the right based on "the circumstances as the actor believes them to be...." (*Example:* On the facts of the above example, the modern/MPC view would permit D to use the claim of defense of others.) [122]

VI. DEFENSE OF PROPERTY

A. **Generally:** A person has a limited right to use force to *defend his or her property* against a wrongful taking. [123]

1. **Non-deadly force:** *Non-deadly force* may be used to prevent a *wrongful entry on one's real property*, and the *wrongful taking of one's personal property*. [123]

2. **Reasonable degree:** The degree of force used must not be *more than appears reasonably necessary* to prevent the taking. For instance, if one in D's position should believe that a *request to desist* would be sufficient, force may not be used. [123]

   Example of proper use of non-deadly force: D sees X attempting to break into D's car, parked on the street. At least if D has no reason to believe that words alone will dissuade X, D may punch X, spray mace at him, or otherwise use non-deadly force to stop the break-in.

3. **Subsequent use of deadly force:** If D begins by using a reasonable degree of non-deadly force, and the wrongdoer responds with a personal attack, then the rules governing self-defense come into play. It may then become permissible for D to use deadly force to protect himself. [123]

B. **Deadly force:** In general, one may ***not use deadly force*** to defend personal property or real estate. [123-124]

   1. **Dwelling:** However, in limited circumstances, one may be able to use deadly force to defend ***one's dwelling***. [123-124]

      a. **Modern view requires violent felony:** Under the modern view, deadly force may be used ***only where the intrusion appears to pose a danger of a violent felony***. Under this view, a homeowner may ***not*** shoot a ***suspected burglar***, unless the the owner believes the burglar to be ***armed*** or ***dangerous to the safety of the inhabitants***. [123]

C. **Mechanical devices:** A property owner may ordinarily use ***mechanical devices*** to protect his property. [124-125]

   1. **Non-deadly devices:** A device that is ***non-deadly*** (i.e., one that is not likely or intended to cause death or serious bodily harm) may be used whenever it is ***reasonable*** to do so. Thus a property owner may put ***barbed wire*** or a ***spiked fence*** (but not an electrical fence) around his property. (Under the MPC, the owner must give a ***warning*** to intruders about the device unless it is one that is "customarily used for such a purpose.") [124]

   2. **Deadly force:** Courts are much less likely to allow a mechanical device that constitutes ***deadly force***. [124]

      a. **Traditional view:** Traditionally, D could use a mechanical deadly device if the situation were one in which D himself could use deadly force. [124]

      Example: D, a homeowner, sets up a spring gun attached to the door. The gun shoots X, who turns out to be an armed and dangerous burglar. Under the traditional view, D would not be guilty of anything, since he would have had the right to use deadly force against the burglar personally.

      b. **Modern view prohibits:** But the ***modern*** view ***prohibits*** the use of such devices altogether, even if they happen to go off in a situation where the owner himself would have been justified in using deadly force. [124]

      Example: Under the modern/MPC view, on the facts of the above example, D would be guilty of murder if the gun went off and shot to death even an armed and dangerous burglar.

D. **Recapture of chattel and re-entry on land:** A person has a privilege to use reasonable force to ***re-take*** his personal or real property. [125]

   1. **Personal property:** Where personal property has been taken, all courts agree that D may use reasonable non-deadly force to ***recapture*** it, provided that he does so ***immediately*** following the taking. [125]

      a. **Interval:** But if a substantial period of time has *elapsed* since the taking, courts are split. The modern/MPC view is that D may use force to retake his property at any time, provided that the owner believes that the other has no "claim of right" to possess the object. (*Example:* D's bicycle is stolen, and he sees X riding down the street on it several days later. If D reasonably believes he recognizes X as being the thief, he can use reasonable force to take back the bicycle. But if he sees that X is not the thief, and believes that X may have bought it from the thief, D cannot use reasonable force because X would be acting under a "claim of right to possession" of the bike, even though X does not have title.) [125]

2. **Re-entry on real estate:** Similarly, under the modern view, D may use force to *re-enter* his real estate, even if there has been a lapse of time, if the non-owner has no claim of right to possession and it would be a hardship for the owner to wait to get a court order. [125]

VII. LAW ENFORCEMENT (ARREST; PREVENTION OF ESCAPE AND CRIME)

A. **General privilege:** A person engaged in *law enforcement* has a general privilege to violate the law when it is reasonable to do so. [125]

   Example: D, a police officer, is chasing a fleeing convict. D may drive his car through a stop light, or 20 m.p.h. above the speed limit, provided that a reasonable officer in D's position would believe that this was necessary to recapture the escapee.

1. **Use of force:** The main question that arises is whether an officer's *use of force* was lawful. See below. [126]

B. **Arrest:** A law enforcement officer is privileged to use reasonable force in *effecting an arrest*. However, this privilege exists only where the arrest being made is a *lawful one*. [126-129]

1. **Summary of arrest rules:** The rules for determining whether an arrest is lawful depend in part on whether the arrest is for a felony or a misdemeanor: [126]

   a. **Felony:** At common law, a police officer may make an arrest for a *felony* if: (1) it was commited in the officer's presence; or (2) it was committed outside the officer's presence, but the officer has reasonable cause to believe that it was committed, and by the person to be arrested. [126]

      i. **Warrant not required:** In these situations, the arresting officer is *not required* to have a *warrant*.

   b. **Misdemeanor:** An officer may also arrest for a *misdemeanor*. [126]

      i. **Warrant:** If the misdemeanor occurred in the officer's presence, no warrant is required. But at common law, if the misdemeanor occurred outside of the officer's presence, then a warrant *is* required (though this rule has often been changed by statute).

2. **Arrest resisted:** If an officer who is attempting to make a lawful arrest meets resistance, he may use reasonable force to protect himself. In general, the rules applicable to self-defense apply here. [126]

   a. **No retreat:** There is one important difference: even in those states requiring one to retreat before using deadly force where it is safe to do so, an officer is *not required to retreat* rather than make the arrest. [126]

3. **Fleeing suspect:** An officer may use *non-deadly force* wherever it is reasonably necessary to arrest a *fleeing* suspect. But there are important limits on the use of *deadly* force where the suspect is fleeing: [127-128]

   a. **Misdemeanor:** If the suspect is fleeing from an arrest for a *misdemeanor*, deadly force may *not* be used against him. [127]

Example: If the police are chasing a garden-variety speeder, they may not shoot at him or at his car. If they shoot at the tires and cause a fatal crash, they will be liable for manslaughter, since shooting a gun in the direction of a person, even without intent to hit him, is generally considered to be the use of deadly force.

  b. Non-dangerous felony: Where the suspect is fleeing an arrest for a ***non-dangerous*** felony, the modern, and Supreme Court, view is that the police may ***not*** use deadly force to catch the suspect. [127-128]

  Example: Where an officer is chasing an escaping burglar whom the officer has no reason to believe is armed, the officer may not shoot the burglar in the back. This is true even if the burglar ignores a command to stop and raise his hands. [*Tennessee v. Garner*, 471 U.S. 1 (1985)]

  c. Dangerous felony: If the felony or the felon is a ***"dangerous"*** one, the arresting officer may use deadly force if that is the only way that the arrest can be made. The issue is whether the suspect poses a threat of ***serious physical harm***, either to the officer or to others. [128]

  Example: The typical car thief or burglar is not "dangerous," and thus cannot be stopped with deadly force. But the typical armed bank robbery suspect, and perhaps the typical rapist, is probably "dangerous" and thus may be stopped with deadly force.

 4. Arrest by private citizen: A ***private citizen*** who is attempting to make a "citizen's arrest" may use reasonable non-deadly force. The private citizen may also use deadly force, but only in extremely limited circumstances: the citizen takes the ***full risk of a mistake***. [129]

  Example: If it turns out that no dangerous felony was actually committed, or that the suspect was not the one who committed it, the citizen will be criminally liable for death or injury to the suspect.

  a. More extreme view: Some states, and the MPC, go further: they do not allow private citizens to use deadly force *at all* to make a citizen's arrest, even if the suspect really *has* committed a dangerous felony.

  b. Escape of non-deadly felon: Virtually all courts agree that a private citizen, like a police officer, may not use deadly force to stop a fleeing felon if the felon poses ***no immediate threat*** to the citizen or to others. That is, the rationale of *Tennessee v. Garner* (see *supra*) presumably applies to attempted arrests by private citizens just as to attempted arrests by police officers. (Of course, this rule would be invoked only where the court rejects — as most courts do — the MPC's blanket rule that the arresting citizen may *never* use deadly force, even to arrest a felon who *is* dangerous.) [129]

C. Prevention of escape: An officer may use reasonable force to ***prevent the escape*** of a suspect who has already been arrested. The above rules apply in this situation as well. [129]

D. Crime prevention: Similarly, officers may use force to ***prevent a crime*** from taking place, or from being completed. [129]

 1. Reasonable non-deadly force: Both law enforcement officers and private citizens may use reasonable ***non-deadly force*** to prevent the commission of a felony, or of a misdemeanor amounting to a breach of the peace. [129]

 2. Deadly force: Deadly force may be used to prevent only ***dangerous felonies***. [130]

VIII. MAINTAINING AUTHORITY

A. Right to maintain authority generally: *Parents* of minor children, *school teachers*, and other persons who have a duty of supervision, have a limited right to use force to discharge their duties. [130]

B. Parents of minor: Parents of a minor child may use a *reasonable degree of force* to guard the child's welfare. [130]

> **Example:** A parent who hits or spanks his child will not be guilty of battery, provided that the purpose is to promote the welfare of the child, including preventing or punishing misconduct. However, the parent loses the privilege if the degree of force is unreasonable under the circumstances.

IX. CONSENT

A. Effect of consent by victim: Generally, the fact that the victim of a crime has *consented* does not bar criminal liability. [131-131]

> **Example:** Suppose V, who is terminally ill, consents to have D perform a mercy killing on V. This consent does not protect D from murder charges.

However, there are two major exceptions to this rule that consent does not bar criminal liability:

1. Consent as element of crime: First, some crimes are defined in such a way that lack of consent is an *element of the crime*. [131]

> **Example:** Common-law rape is defined to include the element of lack of consent. Therefore, if V consents, there is automatically no crime, no matter how culpable D's mental state.

2. Consent as negating of harm: Second, for some crimes, in some courts, the fact that V has consented prevents D's conduct from constituting the *harm* from arising that the law is trying to prevent. [131]

    a. Athletic contest: Thus if the crime involves threatened or actual *bodily harm*, consent is a defense if the bodily harm is *not serious* or is part of a lawful *athletic contest* or *competitive sport*. [131]

> **Example:** D and V agree to a lawfully-sanctioned boxing match. D strikes V repeatedly, trying to injure V, knowing that V is already hurt. D will not be liable for battery, attempted murder, murder, or any other crime. See MPC §2.11(1).

B. Incapacity to consent: Even where the crime is one as to which consent can be a defense, consent will not be found where V is too *young*, mentally defective, intoxicated, or for other reasons unable to give a meaningful assent. [132]

1. Fraud: Similarly, if the consent was obtained by *fraud*, it will generally not be valid. However, the fraud will negate the consent only where it goes to the *essence* of the harmful activity. [132]

C. Contributory negligence of V: The fact that V may have been *contributorily negligent* will not, by itself, be a defense to any crime. [132]

> **Example:** D and V agree to drag race. D's car slams into V's, killing him. If D is prosecuted for criminally negligent homicide or voluntary manslaughter, V's consent will not be a

defense, though it might give D a chance to show that V's negligence, not his own, was the sole proximate cause of the accident.

D. Guilt of V: The fact that V is himself engaged in the same or a different illegal activity will not generally prevent the person who takes advantage of him from being criminally liable. (*Example:* D and V agree to an illegal boxing match, during which V is killed. V's equal culpability will not be a defense for D.) [132]

E. Forgiveness or settlement: The fact that V forgives the injury, is unwilling to prosecute, or *settles a civil suit* against D, will *not* absolve D from liability. The crime is considered to be against the people, not against V as an individual. [132]

X. ENTRAPMENT

A. Entrapment generally: The defense of *entrapment* exists where a *law enforcement official*, or someone cooperating with him, has *induced* D to commit the crime. [133-134]

B. Two tests for entrapment: There are two distinct tests used by courts for whether there has been entrapment: [133-134]

    1. "Predisposition" test: The majority test, and the one used in the federal system, is that entrapment exists where: (1) the government *originates* the crime and *induces* its commission; and (2) D is an *innocent person*, i.e., one who is *not predisposed* to committing this sort of crime. This is the so-called *"predisposition"* test. [133-134]

    Example: X, an undercover narcotics operative, offers to sell V heroin for V's own use. If the offer originated entirely with X, and V had never used or sought heroin, V would have a good chance at an entrapment defense, on the theory that he was an "innocent" person who was not predisposed to committing this sort of crime. But if the evidence showed that V had frequently purchased heroin from other sources, then V would not be entrapped under the "predisposition" test, even if the transaction between X and V was entirely at X's instigation.

    2. "Police conduct" rule: A minority of courts apply the *"police conduct"* rule. Under this rule, entrapment exists where the government agents originate the crime, and their participation is such as is likely to induce *unpredisposed* persons to commit the crime, regardless of whether D himself is predisposed. This test is usually easier for the defendant to meet. [134]

C. Other aspects of entrapment: [134]

    1. False representations regarding legality: A separate kind of entrapment exists where the government agent knowingly makes a *false representation* that the act in question is *legal*. [134]

    2. Violent crimes: Some courts refuse to allow the entrapment defense where the crime is one involving *violence*. [134]

    3. Distinguished from "missing element" cases: Distinguish entrapment situations from cases where, because of the participation of government agents, an *element* of the crime is *missing*. [134]

    Example: X, a government agent, suspects that D is a confidence man who swindles people out of their property. X pretends to go along with D's scheme, and gives D money which D appropriates. D is not guilty of obtaining money by false pretenses, because one of the elements of that crime is reliance on the part of the victim, and X was not really fooled.

CHAPTER 5

ATTEMPT

I. INTRODUCTION

A. Attempt generally: All states, in general, punish certain unsuccessful *attempts* to commit crimes. [146-147]

    1. General attempt statutes: Nearly all prosecutions for attempt occur under *general attempt statutes*. That is, the typical criminal code does not specifically make it a crime to attempt murder, to attempt robbery, etc. Instead, a separate statutory section makes it a crime to attempt to commit any of the substantive crimes enumerated elsewhere in the code. [147]

B. Two requirements: For most attempt statutes, there are two principal requirements, corresponding to the *mens rea* and the *actus reus*: [148]

    1. Mental state: First, D must have had a *mental state* which would have been enough to satisfy the *mens rea* requirement of the substantive crime itself. Typically, D will *intend* to commit the crime. But if a mental state less than intent (e.g., recklessness) suffices for the substantive crime, there may be instances where this same less-than-intent mental state will suffice for attempted commission of that crime. This is discussed further below (p. C39). [147]

    2. Act requirement: Second, D must be shown to have committed some *overt act* in furtherance of his plan of criminality. A leading modern view, that of the MPC, is that the act must constitute "a *substantial step*" in a course of conduct planned to culminate in the commission of the crime, but only if the substantial step is *"strongly corroborative"* of D's criminal purpose. MPC §5.01(1)(c). [147]

C. Broader liability: Modern courts impose attempt liability more *broadly* than older cases did. Two major illustrations of this broader trend are: [147-147]

    1. Looser act requirement: The overt act that D needs to commit can be further away from actual completion of the crime than used to be the case. [147]

    2. Impossibility: The defense of "legal impossibility" has been dramatically restricted. [147]

II. MENTAL STATE

A. Intent usually required: Generally, D will be liable for an attempt only if he *intended* to do acts which, if they had been carried out, would have resulted in the commission of that crime. [148-149]

    Example: D hits V in the jaw, intending only to slightly injure V. Instead, V suffers serious injuries due to hemophilia, but recovers. D will not be liable for attempted murder, even though he came close to killing V; this is because D is liable for attempted murder only if he had the mental state needed for actual murder (in this case, either an intent to kill or an intent to do serious bodily injury).

    1. Specific crime: Furthermore, D must have had an attempt to commit an act which would constitute the *same crime* as he is charged with attempting. [148]

Example: On the facts of the above example, it is not enough that D attempted a crime, namely battery against V. What must be shown by the prosecution is that D had the mental state needed for the very crime D is charged with attempting — murder.

2. **Knowledge of likely consequences:** Nor is it enough that D knew that certain consequences were *highly likely* to result from his act. [148]

   a. **"Substantially certain" results:** But if it is shown that D knew that a certain result was *"substantially certain"* to occur, then this may be enough to meet the intent requirement, even though D did not desire that result to occur. [148]

3. **Crimes defined by recklessness, negligence or strict liability:** Ordinarily, there can be no attempt to commit a crime defined in terms of *recklessness* or *negligence* or *strict liability*. [149]

   a. **Bringing about certain result:** This is clearly true as to crimes defined in terms of recklessly or negligently bringing about a *certain result* — there can be no attempt liability for these crimes. [149]

   Example: D gets into his car knowing that it has bad brakes, but recklessly decides to take a chance. D almost runs into V because he can't stop in time, but V dives out of the way. D will not be guilty of attempted involuntary manslaughter, because crimes defined in terms of recklessly or negligently bringing about a certain result cannot give rise to attempt liability.

   b. **Strict-liability crimes:** Generally, courts will not convict D of attempting a *strict-liability crime* unless D had a culpable state of mind. [149]

4. **Intent as to surrounding circumstances:** It is probably *not* necessary that D's intent encompass all of the *surrounding circumstances* that are elements of the crime. [149]

   Example: A federal statute makes it a federal crime to kill an FBI agent. Case law demonstrates that for the completed crime, it is enough that the defendant was reckless or even negligent with respect to the victim's identity. D tries to shoot V (an FBI agent) to death, but his shot misses; D recklessly disregarded the chance that V might be an FBI agent. Probably D may be found guilty of attempted killing of an FBI agent.

III. THE ACT — ATTEMPT VS. "MERE PREPARATION"

A. **The problem:** All courts agree that D cannot be convicted of attempt merely for thinking evil thoughts, or plotting in his mind to commit a crime. Thus all courts agree that D must have committed some *"overt act"* in furtherance of his plan of ciminality. But courts disagree about what sort of act will suffice. In general, modern courts hold that D must come much *less close to success* than older courts required. [150]

B. **Various approaches:** There are two main approaches which courts use to decide whether D's act was sufficient, the "proximity" approach and the "equivocality" approach. [150-156]

1. **The "proximity" approach:** Most courts have based their decision on *how close D came to completing the offense*. This is the *"proximity"* approach. In general, older decisions required D to come very close to success — thus older decisions frequently require D to achieve a *"dangerous proximity to success."* But modern courts tend to require merely that D take a *"substantial step"* towards carrying out his criminal plan. [150-153]

2. **The "equivocality" approach:** Other courts follow a completely different approach, concentrating not on how close D came to success, but on whether D's conduct **unequivocally manifested his criminal intent**. Under this **"equivocality"** approach, if D's conduct could indicate either a non-criminal intent or a criminal one, it is not sufficient — but if it does unequivocally manifest criminal intent, it suffices even though completion of the plan is many steps away. [153]

   a. **Confession excluded:** Under the "equivocality" test, any **confession** by D, made either to police or to other persons, is usually **not to be considered** in determining whether D's acts were unequivocally criminal in intent. [153]

3. **MPC's "substantial step" test:** The MPC incorporates aspects of both the "proximity" test and the "equivocality" test. But the incorporated aspects of each test are relatively unstringent in the MPC approach, so that almost any conduct meeting any of the variations of **either** of these tests would be sufficient under the Code. Under the MPC, conduct meets the act requirement if, under the circumstances as D believes them to be: (1) there occurs "an act or omission constituting a **substantial step** in a course of conduct planned to culminate in [D's] commission of the crime"; and (2) the act is **"strongly corroborative"** of the actor's criminal purpose. [154-156]

   a. **Illustrations:** Here are some illustrations of conduct that would suffice as overt acts under the MPC's "substantial step" approach: [155-156]

      i. **Lying in wait, searching** for or **following** the contemplated victim of the crime. [155]

      ii. **Enticing** or seeking to entice the contemplated victim to **go to the** place contemplated for its commission. [155]

      iii. **Reconnoitering** the place contemplated for commission of the crime. (**Example:** D is caught while hiding in the bushes observing V's residence, while V is away from home. This "casing the joint" will probably suffice.) [156]

      iv. Unlawful **entry** of a structure, vehicle or enclosure where the crime is to be committed. [156]

      v. **Possession of materials** to be employed in the commission of the crime, if the materials are **specially designed** for such unlawful use or can serve no lawful purpose of D under the circumstances. (**Example:** D is stopped on the street at night and is found to be in possession of lock-picking tools. Probably he can be convicted of attempted burglary.) [156]

   b. **Followed in many states:** The MPC's "substantial step" test is a popular one. About half the states, and two-thirds of the federal circuits, now use something like this test. [156]

IV. IMPOSSIBILITY

A. **Nature of "impossibility" defense:** The **"impossibility"** defense is raised where D has done everything in his power to accomplish the result he desires, but, due to external circumstances, no substantive crime has been committed. Most variants of the defense are **unsuccessful** today, but it is still important to be able to recognize situations where the defense might plausibly be raised. Here are some examples: [157]

   Example 1: D, a would-be pickpocket, reaches into V's pocket, but discovers that it is empty.

Example 2: D, a would-be rapist, achieves penetration of V, but discovers that V is a corpse, not a living woman.

Example 3: D buys a substance from V, thinking that it is heroin. In fact, the substance is sugar, because V is an undercover narcotics operative.

Note: In these three examples, a modern court would almost certainly hold that D is *liable* for attempt (to commit the substantive crime of larceny, rape and narcotics possession, respectively).

B. Factual impossibility: A claim of *factual* impossibility arises out of D's mistake concerning an issue of fact. D in effect says, "I made a mistake of fact. Had the facts been as I believed them to be, there would have been a crime. But under the true facts, my attempt to commit a crime could not possibly have succeeded." [157-158]

   1. Not accepted: The defense of factual impossibility is *rejected* by all modern courts. Impossibility is *no defense* in those cases where, *had the facts been as D believed them to be, there would have been a crime*. Thus D is guilty of an attempt (and his "factual impossibility" defense will fail) in all of the following examples: [157]

   Example 1: D points his gun at A, and pulls the trigger. The gun does not fire because, unbeknownst to D, it is not loaded.

   Example 2: D intends to rape X, but is unable to do so because he is impotent.

   Example 3: D is a "con man" who tries to get X to entrust money to him, which D intends to steal. Unbeknownst to D, X is a plainclothes police officer who is not fooled.

   Example 4: D attempts to poison X with a substance D believes is arsenic, but which is in fact harmless.

C. "True legal" impossibility: A different sort of defense arises where D is mistaken about *how an offense is defined*. That is, D engages in conduct which he believes is forbidden by a statute, but D has misunderstood the meaning of the statute. Here, D will be *acquitted* — the defense of "true legal" impossibility is a successful one. You can recognize the situation giving rise to the "true legal" impossibility defense by looking for situations where, *even had the facts been as D supposed them to be*, no crime would have been committed. [158]

   Example 1: D obtains a check for $2.50. He alters the numerals in the upper right hand corner, changing them to "12.50." But D does not change the written-out portion of the check, which remains "two and 50/100 dollars." Because the crime of forgery is defined as the material alteration of an instrument, and the numerals are considered an immaterial part of a check (the amount written out in words controls), D will be acquitted of attempted forgery. [*Wilson v. State*]

   Example 2: D is questioned by X, a police officer, during a criminal investigation. D lies, while believing that lying to the police constitutes perjury. D cannot be convicted of attempted perjury, because the act he was performing (and in fact the act he thought he was performing) is simply not a violation of the perjury statute.

   Note: The defense of "true legal impossibility" is the flip side of the rule that "mistake of law is no excuse." Just as D cannot defend on the grounds that he did not know that his acts were prohibited, so D will be acquitted where he commits an act that he thinks is forbidden but that is not forbidden.

D. Mistake of fact governing legal relationship: There is a third category, involving a *mistake of fact* that *bears upon legal relationships*. In this situation, D understands what the statute prohibits, but mistakenly believes that the facts bring his situation within the statute. Here, D will be *convicted* of attempt. This is because *had the facts been as D supposed them to be, his conduct would have been a crime.* [158-161]

> **Example:** D buys goods which he believes are stolen. In fact, the goods are police "bait," and D has been tricked by the seller, an undercover police officer, into thinking that they are stolen. D is guilty of attempted possession of stolen property.

> **Example:** D has intercourse with X, who he believes is in an unconscious drunken stupor. In fact, X is already dead at the time of intercourse. D is guilty of attempted rape, since had the facts been as he supposed them to be, his conduct would have been a crime. [*U.S. v. Thomas*, 13 U.S.C.M.A. 278 (1962)]

Note: All three categories — "factual" impossibility, "true legal impossibility" and "factual mistake bearing on legal relationship" — can be explained with one principle. Ask, "Would D's conduct have been criminal had the facts been as D supposed them to be?" For the "true legal impossibility" situation, the answer is "no." For the other two situations, the answer is "yes," so D is guilty of attempt in just the latter two situations.

E. "Inherent" impossibility (ineptness and superstition): If D's act is, to a reasonable observer, so *farfetched* that it had *no probability of success*, D may be able to successfully assert the defense of *"inherent impossibility."* [161]

1. Courts split: Courts are *split* about whether to recognize a defense of "inherent impossibility." The MPC authorizes a *conviction* in such cases, but also allows conviction of a lesser grade or degree, or in extreme circumstances even a dismissal, if the conduct charged "is so inherently unlikely to result or culminate in a commission of a crime that neither such conduct nor the actor presents a public danger...." [162]

> **Example:** D, a Haitian witch doctor, immigrates to the U.S. and continues practicing voodoo. A police officer sees D sticking pins in a doll representing V, in an attempt to kill V. D is charged with attempted murder of V. A court might conclude that D's conduct was so inherently unlikely to kill V (and that D himself was so unlikely to commit the substantive crime of murder or to make a more "serious" attempt to kill V) that D should be acquitted, or convicted of a lesser crime such as attempted battery.

V. RENUNCIATION

A. Defense generally accepted: Where D is charged with an attempted crime, most courts accept the defense of *renunciation*. To establish this defense, D must show that he *voluntarily abandoned* his attempt before completion of the substantive crime. [162-163]

> **Example:** D decides to shoot V when V comes out of V's house. D carries a loaded gun, and waits in the bushes outside V's house. Five minutes before he expects V to come out, D decides that he doesn't really want to kill V at all. D returns home, and is arrested and charged with attempted murder. All courts would acquit D in this circumstance, because he voluntarily abandoned his plan before completing it (even though the abandonment came after D took sufficient overt acts that he could have been arrested for an attempt right before the renunciation).

B. Voluntariness: All courts accepting the defense of abandonment require that the abandonment be *"voluntary."* [164-165]

   1. Threat of imminent apprehension: Thus if D, at the last moment, learns facts causing him to believe that he will be *caught* if he goes through with his plan, the abandonment will generally not be deemed voluntary. [164]

   Example: On the facts of the above example, just before V is scheduled to come out of his house, D spots a police officer on the sidewalk near D. D's abandonment has been motivated by the fear of imminent apprehension, so his abandonment will not be deemed voluntary, and D can be convicted of attempted murder.

   2. Generalized fear: On the other hand, if D abandons because of a *generalized* fear of apprehension, not linked to any *particular* threat or event, his abandonment will probably be deemed voluntary. [164]

   Example: On the facts of the above two examples, suppose that D's decision to abandon is motivated not by the appearance of a police officer, but by D's sudden thought, "If I get caught, I'll go to prison for life." D's abandonment will probably be treated as voluntary, and will be a bar to his prosecution for attempt.

   3. Other special circumstances: [164-165]

      a. Postponement: If D merely *postpones* his plan, because the scheduled time proves less advantageous than he thought it would be, this does *not* constitute a voluntary abandonment. [164]

      b. Dissuasion by victim: Similarly, if D's renunciation is the result of *dissuasion by the victim*, it will probably be deemed involuntary. [165]

      Example: D decides to rob V, a pedestrian, on a secluded street at night. D says, "Your money or your life," and brandishes a knife at V. V pulls out his own switchblade and says, "If you come any closer, I'll carve you up." D turns around and walks away. D's abandonment will almost certainly be found to be involuntary, because it was motivated by the victim's conduct. Therefore, D can be convicted of attempted robbery.

VI. ATTEMPT-LIKE CRIMES

A. Problem generally: Some *substantive* crimes punish incompleted or "inchoate" behavior. If D intends to commit acts which, if completed, would constitute one of these inchoate crimes, D may raise the defense that he cannot be convicted of "an attempt to commit a crime which is itself an attempt." [165-166]

   1. Occasionally successful: Very occasionally, defendants have succeeded with this defense. [165]

   Example: D, who is very weak, throws a rock at V, a police officer, but his arm is not strong enough to get the rock even close to V. One type of "assault" defined by statute in the jurisdiction is "an attempt to commit battery by one having present ability to do so." D is charged with "attempted assault." A court might hold that D should not be convicted, because the crime of assault (of the attempted-battery type) is intended to cover near-battery, and the crime here is effectively near-near-battery. But most courts would probably reject this defense and would convict D on these facts.

VII. MECHANICS OF TRIAL; PUNISHMENT

A. Relation between charge and conviction: Complications arise where D is: (1) charged with a completed substantive crime, but shown at trial to be guilty of at most an attempt; or (2) charged with attempt, but shown at trial to have committed the underlying substantive crime. [166]

    1. Substantive crime charged, attempt proved: If D is charged with a completed crime but shown to have committed only an attempt, the courts agree that D *may be convicted of attempt*. The attempt is said to be a "lesser included offense." [167]

    2. Attempt charged, completed crime proved: Conversely, if D is charged with an attempt and is shown at trial to have committed the underlying complete crime, D may normally be *convicted of attempt*. (But the attempt statute may be drafted so as to make failure an element of attempt; if so, D will escape liability.) [167]

CHAPTER 6

CONSPIRACY

I. INTRODUCTION

A. Definition of "conspiracy": The common-law crime of *conspiracy* is defined as *an agreement between two or more persons to do either an unlawful act or a lawful act by unlawful means*. At common law, the prosecution must show the following: [174]

    1. Agreement: An *agreement* between two or more persons; [174]

    2. Objective: To carry out an act which is either *unlawful* or which is lawful but to be accomplished by *unlawful means*; and [174]

    3. *Mens rea:* A *culpable intent* on the part of the defendant. [174]

B. Procedural advantages: The prosecution gets a number of *procedural* advantages in a conspiracy case. [175] The two most important are:

    1. Joint trial: Joinder laws generally let the prosecution try in a *single proceeding* all persons indicted on a single conspiracy charge. [175]

    2. Admission of hearsay: Statements made by any member of the conspiracy can generally be admitted against all, without constraint from the *hearsay* rule. *Any previous incriminating statement by any member of the conspiracy, if made in furtherance of the conspiracy, may be introduced into evidence against all of the conspirators*. See FRE 801(d)(2)(E). [175]

    Example: D1, D2 and D3 are charged with conspiracy to rob a bank. D1, the mastermind, tries to recruit X, an arms supplier, into the conspiracy, by telling X that D3 is also part of the conspiracy. X refuses to join the conspiracy. At the Ds' trial for conspiracy, X testifies as to D1's statements about D3's participation. This testimony will be admitted against D3 for the substantive purpose of showing that D3 was part of the conspiracy. This will be true even though the statement by D1 is hearsay as to D3.

    a. Hearsay considered in determining admissibility: In the federal system, and in many states, the judge may determine the admissibility of hearsay *without respect to the rules of evidence*. This means that the incriminating statement by a member of the alleged conspiracy *may itself be considered* in determining whether the conspiracy has been sufficiently documented that the hearsay should be admissible against the defendant. [175]

II. THE AGREEMENT

A. **"Meeting of the minds" not required:**   The essence of a conspiracy is an *agreement* for the joint pursuit of unlawful ends. However, no true "meeting of the minds" is necessary — all that is needed is that the parties communicate to each other in some way their intention to pursue a joint objective. [175-176]

   1. **Implied agreement:**   Thus words are not necessary — each party may, by his *actions alone*, make it clear to the other that they will pursue a common objective. [176]

      Example: A is in the process of mugging V on the street, when B comes along. B pins V to the ground, while A takes his wallet. A conspiracy to commit robbery could be found on these facts, even though there was no spoken communication between A and B.

   2. **Proof by circumstantial evidence:**   The prosecution may prove agreement by mere *circumstantial evidence*. That is, the prosecution can show that the parties committed acts in circumstances strongly suggesting that there *must* have been a *common plan*. [176]

      Example: V, a politician, is riding in a motorcade down a crowded city street. A and B both simultaneously shoot at V. The fact that both people shot simultaneously would be strong, and admissible, evidence that A and B had agreed to jointly attempt to kill V, and would thus support prosecution of the two for conspiracy to commit murder.

B. **Aiding and abetting:**   Suppose that A and B conspire to commit a crime (let's call the crime "X"). C then "aids and abets" A and B in the commission of crime X, but never reaches explicit agreement with A and B that he is helping them. It is clear that C will be liable for X if A and B actually commit X. But if A and B never commit X, courts are *split* about whether C, as a mere aider and abetter, is also liable for conspiracy to commit X. The MPC holds that a person does *not* become a co-conspirator merely by aiding and abetting the conspirators, if he himself does not reach agreement with them. [176]

      Example: D knows that A and B plan to kill X. D, without making any agreement with A and B, prevents a telegram of warning from reaching X. If X is thus unable to flee, and A and B kill X, it is clear that D is liable for the substantive crime of murder, since he aided and abetted A and B in carrying out the murder. But if X escapes, so there is no substantive crime of murder to be charged, can D be convicted of conspiracy to commit murder? Courts are split. The MPC would acquit D on these facts, since under the MPC an aider and abetter is not liable for the conspiracy if he did not reach any agreement with the conspirators.

C. **Parties don't agree to commit object crime:**   Although there must be an agreement, it is not necessary that each conspirator agree to commit the *substantive object crime(s)*. A particular D can be a conspirator even though he agreed to help only in the *planning stages*. (*Example:* D1, D2 and D3 work together to commit a bank robbery. D3's only participation is to agree to obtain the getaway car, not to participate in the bank robbery itself. D3 is still guilty of conspiracy to commit bank robbery.) [177]

D. **Feigned agreement:**   Courts disagree about the proper result where one of the parties to a "conspiracy" is merely *feigning* his agreement. The problem typically arises where one of the parties is secretly an *undercover agent*. [177]

Example: A and B agree that they will rob a bank. B is secretly an undercover agent, and never has any intention of committing the robbery. In fact, B makes sure that the FBI is present at the bank, and A is arrested when he and B show up. Courts disagree about whether the requisite "agreement" between A and B took place, and thus about whether A can be prosecuted for conspiracy to commit bank robbery.

1. **Traditional view that there is no conspiracy:** The traditional, common-law view is that there is *no agreement*, and therefore *no conspiracy*. Thus on the facts of the above example, A could not be charged with conspiracy to commit bank robbery. This traditional view is sometimes called the *"bilateral"* view, in the sense that the agreement must be a bilateral one if either party is to be bound. [177]

2. **Modern view allows conspiracy finding:** But the modern view is that regardless of one party's lack of subjective intent to carry out the object crime, *the other party may nonetheless be convicted of conspiracy*. [177]

   a. **Model Penal Code agrees:** The Model Penal Code agrees with the modern view. The Code follows a *"unilateral"* approach to conspiracy — a given individual is liable for conspiracy if he "agrees with another person or persons," whether or not the other person is really part of the plan. Thus under the MPC, A in the above example has clearly agreed to rob the bank (even though B has not truly agreed), and A can therefore be prosecuted for conspiracy. [178]

III. *MENS REA*

A. **Intent to commit object crime:** Normally, the conspirators must be shown to have agreed to commit a crime. It is then universally held that each of the conspirators must be shown to have had *at least the mental state required for the object crime*. [178-182]

   Example: A and B are caught trying to break into a dwelling at night. The prosecution shows only that A and B agreed to attempt to break and enter the dwelling, and does not show anything about what A and B intended to do once they were inside. A and B cannot be convicted of conspiracy to commit burglary, because there has been no showing that they had the intent necessary for the substantive crime of burglary, i.e., it has not been shown that they had the intent to commit any felony once they got inside.

   1. **Must have intent to achieve objective:** Also, where the substantive crime is defined in terms of causing a *harmful result*, for conspiracy to commit that crime the conspirators must be shown to have *intended to bring about that result*. This is true even though the intent is not necessary for conviction of the substantive crime. [179]

   Example: A and B plan to blow up a building by exploding a bomb. They know there are people in the building who are highly likely to be killed. If the bomb goes off and kills X, A and B are guilty of murder even though they did not intend to kill X (because one form of murder is the "depraved heart" or "reckless indifference to the value of human life" kind). But A and B are *not* guilty of conspiracy to murder X, because they did not have an affirmative intent to bring about X's death.

   2. **Crime of recklessness or negligence:** It's probably also the case that there can be no conspiracy to commit a crime that is defined in terms of recklessly or negligently causing a particular result. [179]

3. **Attendant circumstances:** But where the substantive crime contains some elements relating to the ***attendant circumstances*** surrounding the crime, and strict liability applies to those attendant circumstances, then two people ***can*** be convicted of conspiracy even though they had no knowledge or intent regarding the surrounding circumstances. [179-180]

   a. **Federal jurisdiction:** Elements relating to ***federal jurisdiction*** illustrate this problem. Even if the Ds are shown not to have been aware that the elements of federal jurisdiction were present, they can still be held liable for conspiracy to commit the underlying federal crime. [179]

      Example: It is a federal crime to assault a federal officer engaged in the performance of his duties. Cases on this crime hold that the defendant need not be shown to have been aware that his victim was a federal officer. D1 and D2 orally agree to attack V, thinking he is a rival drug dealer. In fact, V is a federal officer. D1 and D2 can be convicted of conspiracy to assault a federal officer, because V's status as such was merely an attendant circumstance, as to which intent need not be shown. [*U.S. v. Feola*, 420 U.S. 671 (1975)]

B. **Supplying of goods and services:** The Ds must be shown to have ***intended*** to further a criminal objective. It is not generally enough that a particular D merely ***knew*** that his acts might tend to enable others to pursue criminal ends. The issue arises most often where D is charged with conspiracy because he ***supplied goods or services*** to others who committed or planned to commit a substantive crime. [180-181]

   1. **Mere knowledge not sufficient:** It is ***not*** enough for the prosecution to show that D supplied goods or services with ***knowledge*** that his supplies might enable others to pursue a criminal objective. Instead, the supplier must be shown to have ***desired*** to further the criminal objective. On the other hand, this desire or intent can be shown by ***circumstantial*** evidence. [180-181]

      a. **"Stake in venture":** For instance, the requisite desire to further the criminal objective can be shown circumstantially by the fact that the supplier in some sense acquired a ***"stake in the venture."*** [180]

         Example: D and S agree that if S supplies D with equipment to make an illegal still, D will pay S 10% of the profits S makes from his illegal liquor operations. S will be held to have had such a stake in the venture that the jury may infer that he desired to bring about the illegal act of operating his still.

      b. **Controlled commodities:** The supplier is more likely to be found to be a participant in a conspiracy if the substance he sold was a ***governmentally controlled*** one that could only have been used for illegal purposes. (*Example:* S supplies the Ds with horse-racing information of benefit only to bookmakers, in a state where bookmaking is illegal.) [181]

      c. **Inflated charges:** The fact that the supplier is charging his criminal purchasers an ***inflated price*** compared with the cost of the items if sold for legal purposes, is evidence of intent. [181]

      d. **Large proportion of sales:** If sales to criminal purchasers represent a ***large portion*** of the supplier's overall sales of the item, the supplier is more likely to be held to have had the requisite intent. [181]

      e. **Serious crime:** The more ***serious*** the crime, the more likely it is that the supplier's participation will be found to be part of the conspiracy. [181]

IV. THE CONSPIRATORIAL OBJECTIVE

A. **Non-criminal objective:** Traditionally, and in England, the Ds could be convicted of conspiracy upon proof that they intended to commit acts that were *"immoral"* or "contrary to the public interest." In other words, the fact that the act or ultimate object was not explicitly criminal was not an automatic defense. [182-183]

    1. **Modern American view rejects:** But the modern American tendency is to allow a conspiracy conviction *only* if the Ds intended to perform an act that is *explicitly criminal*. Thus the MPC allows a conspiracy only where the defendants intend to commit a crime. [183]

    Example: D1 collaborates with various prostitutes, with the intention of publishing a directory of prostitutes. Under the traditional/English view, D1 and the prostitutes can be convicted of conspiracy to "corrupt public morals," even though actual publication of the directory would not itself have been a crime. But under the modern American view, there could be no conspiracy here, since no act was intended which would have been criminal. [*Shaw v. Dir. Pub. Prosec.*, 2 W.L.R. 897 (Eng. 1961)]

B. **The "overt act" requirement:** At common law, the crime of conspiracy is *complete as soon as the agreement has been made*. But about half the states have statutes requiring, in addition, that some *overt act* in furtherance of the conspiracy must also be committed. [183]

    1. **MPC limits requirement:** The MPC limits the overt act requirement to *non-serious crimes*. Under the MPC, a conspiracy to commit a felony of the first or second degree may be proved even without an overt act. [183]

    2. **Kind of act required:** The overt act, where required, may be *any act* which is taken in furtherance of the conspiracy. It does *not* have to be an act that is *criminal in itself*. Thus acts of *mere preparation* will be sufficient. (*Example:* If the conspiracy is to make moonshine liquor, purchase of sugar from a grocery store would meet the overt act requirement.) [183]

    3. **Act of one attributable to all:** Even in states requiring an overt act, it is not necessary that each D charged with the conspiracy be shown to have committed an overt act. Instead, if the overt act requirement applies, the overt act of a *single person* will be *attributable to all*. [183]

C. **Impossibility:** The same rules concerning *"impossibility"* apply in conspiracy as in attempt. [184-184] For instance, the defense of *"factual impossibility"* is always rejected. (*Example:* D1 and D2 agree to pick the pocket of a certain victim. The pocket turns out to be empty. The Ds are liable for conspiracy to commit larceny.) [184]

D. **Substantive liability for crimes of other conspirators:** The most frequently-tested aspect of conspiracy law relates to a member's liability for the *substantive crimes* committed by other members of the conspiracy. This subject is complicated, and requires close analysis. [184-185]

    1. **Aiding and abetting:** Normally, each conspirator *"aids and abets"* the others in furtherance of the aims of the conspiracy. Where this is the case, a D who has aided and abetted one of the others in accomplishing a particular substantive crime will be liable for that substantive crime — this is not a result having anything to do with conspiracy law, but is instead merely a product of the general rules about accomplice liability (discussed *infra*, pp. C53-C59). [184-185]

    Example: A and B agree to a scheme whereby A will steal a car, pick B up in it, and wait outside the First National Bank while B goes in and robs the teller. A steals the car, picks up B, and delivers B to the bank. Before B can even rob the teller, A is arrested out on the street. B robs the teller anyway. A is clearly liable for the substantive crime of bank robbery, because he has "aided and abetted" B in carrying out this crime. It is also true that A and B are guilty of conspiracy to commit bank robbery, but this fact is not necessary to a finding that A is liable for B's substantive crime — aiding and abetting is all that is required for A to be liable for bank robbery.

2. **Substantive liability without "aiding and abetting":** The more difficult question arises where A and B conspire to commit crime X, and B commits *additional crimes* "in furtherance" of the conspiracy, but without the direct assistance of A. Does A, by his *mere membership* in the conspiracy, become liable for these additional crimes by B in furtherance of the conspiracy? [184-185]

    a. **Traditional view:** The traditional "common law" view is that each member of a conspiracy, by virtue of his *membership alone*, is likely for reasonably foreseeable crimes committed by the others in *"furtherance"* of the conspiracy. [184]

    Example: Same basic fact pattern as prior example. Now, however, assume that A knows that B is carrying a gun into the bank, and A also knows that B would rather shoot anyone attempting to stop him than go to prison. However, A has done nothing to help B get the gun, and has not encouraged B to use the gun. B goes into the bank, and shoots V, a guard, while V is trying to capture B. V is seriously wounded. Under the traditional view, if B is liable for assault with a deadly weapon, A will be liable also, merely because he was a member of a conspiracy, and the crime was committed by another member in furtherance of the aims of the conspiracy (robbery with successful escape).

    b. **Modern/MPC view:** But modern courts, and the MPC, are *less likely to hold that mere membership in the conspiracy*, without anything more, automatically makes each member liable for substantive crimes committed by any other member in furtherance of the conspiracy. [185]

    Example: Same facts as above example. Assuming that A in no way encouraged or helped B to use his gun, a modern court might not hold A substantively liable for the assault on V, despite the fact that it was done in furtherance of the conspiracy.

V. SCOPE: MULTIPLE PARTIES

A. Not all parties know each other: When not all parties *know* each other, you may have to decide whether there was one large conspiracy or a series of smaller ones. [185]

B. "Wheel" conspiracies: In a *"wheel"* or *"circle"* conspiracy, a "ring leader" participates with each of the conspirators, but these conspirators deal only with the ring leader, not with each other. [186-186]

    1. **"Community of interest" test:** In the "wheel" situation, there can either be a single large conspiracy covering the entire wheel, or a series of smaller conspiracies, each involving the "hub" (the ring leader) and a single spoke (an individual who works with the ring leader). There will be a single conspiracy only if two requirements are met: (1) each spoke *knows that the other spokes exist* (though not necessarily the identity of each other spoke); and (2) the various spokes have, and realize that they have, a *"community of interest."* [186-186]

C. "Chain" conspiracies: In a *"chain"* conspiracy, there is a distribution chain of a commodity (usually *drugs*). As with "wheel" conspiracies, the main determinant of whether there is a single or multiple conspiracies is whether all the participants have a "community of interest." [187]

Example: A group of smugglers import illegal drugs; they sell the drugs to middlemen, who distribute them to retailers, who sell them to addicts. If all members of the conspiracy knew of each other's existence, and regarded themselves as being engaged in a single distribution venture, then a court might hold that there was a single conspiracy. Otherwise, there might be merely individual conspiracies, one involving smugglers and middlemen, another involving middlemen and retailers, etc.

D. Party who comes late or leaves early: Special problems arise as to a conspirator who *enters* the conspiracy *after* it has begun, or *leaves it before* it is finished. [188]

 1. Party comes late: One who enters a conspiracy that has *already committed substantive acts* will be a conspirator as to those acts only if he is not only told about them, but *accepts them* as part of the general scheme in which he is participating. [188]

   Example: D is a fence who buys from A and B, two jewelry thieves. D is clearly conspiring to receive stolen property. But he will normally *not* be a conspirator to the original crime of theft, unless he somehow involved himself in that venture, as by making the request for particular items in advance.

 2. Party who leaves early: One who *leaves* a conspiracy before it is finished is liable for acts that occur later only if those acts are *fairly within the confines of the conspiracy as it existed* at the time D was still present. [188]

   Example: D agrees to help A and B rob a bank; D is to procure the transportation, and to deliver it to A. D steals a car and delivers it to A, then leaves the conspiracy. D is guilty of conspiring to rob the bank even though he does nothing further, since the bank robbery is part of the original agreement. But if A and B, totally unbeknownst to D, decided after D left the conspiracy that they wished to use the car to rob a grocery store, D would not be guilty of conspiracy to rob the grocery store.

VI. DURATION OF THE CONSPIRACY

 A. Why it matters: You may have to determine the *ending point* of a conspiracy. Here are some issues on which the ending point may make a difference: [188]

 1. Who has joined: A person can be held to have *joined* the conspiracy only if it still existed at the time he got involved in it; [188]

 2. Statute of limitations: The *statute of limitations* on conspiracy does not start to run until the conspiracy has ended; and [188]

 3. Statements by co-defendants: Declarations of co-conspirators may be admissible against each other, despite the hearsay rule, but only if those declarations were made in furtherance of the conspiracy while it was still in progress. [188]

 B. Abandonment: A conspiracy will come to an end if it is *abandoned* by the participants. [189-191]

 1. Abandoned by all: If *all* the parties abandon the plan, this will be enough to end the conspiracy (and thus, for instance, to start the statute of limitations running). [189]

   a. No defense to conspiracy charge: But abandonment does *not* serve as a defense to the *conspiracy charge itself*. Under the common-law approach, the conspiracy is *complete as soon as the agreement is made*. Therefore, abandonment is irrelevant. [189]

C
A
P
S
U
L
E

S
U
M
M
A
R
Y

Example: A and B, while in their prison cell, decide to rob the first national bank the Tuesday after they are released. Before they are even released, they decide not to go through with the plan. However, X, to whom they previously confided their plans, turns them into the authorities. A and B are liable for conspiracy to commit bank robbery, even though they abandoned the plan — their crime of conspiracy was complete as soon as they made their agreement, and their subsequent abandonment did not, at common law, change the result.

2. **Withdrawal by individual conspirator:** A similar rule applies to the *withdrawal* by an *individual conspirator*. [189-190]

   a. **Procedural issues:** Thus for *procedural* purposes, D's withdrawal ends the conspiracy as to him. So long as D has made an *affirmative act* bringing home the fact of his withdrawal to his confederates, the conspiracy is over as to him, for purposes of: (1) running of the statute of limitations; (2) inadmissibility of declarations by other conspirators after he left; or (3) non-liability for the substantive crimes committed by the others after his departure. (Instead of notifying each of the other conspirators, the person withdrawing can instead notify the police.) [189]

   b. **As defense to conspiracy charge:** But if D tries to show withdrawal as a *substantive defense* against the conspiracy charge itself, he will fail: the common-law rule is that *no act of withdrawal*, even thwarting the conspiracy by turning others into the police, will be a defense. This comes from the principle that the crime is *complete* once the agreement has been made. [189]

      i. **More liberal Model Penal Code view:** But the MPC relaxes the common-law rule a bit. The MPC allows a limited defense of *"renunciation of criminal purpose."* D can avoid liability for the conspiracy itself if: (1) his renunciation was *voluntary*; and (2) he *thwarted* the conspiracy, typically by *informing the police*. (Good faith efforts by D to thwart the conspiracy, which fail for reasons beyond D's control, such as police inefficiency, are *not* enough, even under the liberal MPC view.) [190]

VII. PLURALITY

A. **Significance of the plurality requirement:** A conspiracy necessarily involves *two or more* persons. This is called the *"plurality"* requirement. [191]

B. **Wharton's Rule:** Under the common-law *Wharton's Rule*, where a substantive offense is defined so as to necessarily require more than one person, a prosecution for the substantive offense must be brought, rather than a conspiracy prosecution. The classic examples are *adultery*, *incest*, *bigamy* and *dueling* crimes. [191-193]

   Example: Howard and Wanda are husband and wife. Marsha is a single woman. Howard and Marsha agree to meet later one night at a specified motel, to have sex. They are arrested before the rendezvous can take place. Since the crime of adultery is defined so as to require at least two people, Howard and Marsha cannot be convicted of conspiracy to commit adultery, under the common law Wharton's Rule.

   1. **More persons than necessary:** A key *exception* to Wharton's Rule is that there is no bar to a conspiracy conviction where there were *more participants* than were logically necessary to complete the crime. [191]

Example: Same facts as above example. Now, however, assume that Steve, Howard's friend, has urged him to have sex with Marsha, and has reserved the hotel room for them. Despite Wharton's Rule, Howard, Marsha and Steve can all be prosecuted for conspiracy, because there were more persons involved than merely the two necessary direct parties to the substantive crime of adultery.

2. **Sometimes only a presumption:** Modern courts, including the federal system, frequently hold that Wharton's Rule is not an inflexible rule but merely a ***presumption*** about what the legislature intended. Under courts following this approach, if the legislative history behind the substantive crime is silent about whether the legislature intended to bar conspiracy convictions, a conspiracy charge is allowed. [192]

Example: A federal act makes it a federal crime for five or more persons to conduct a gambling business prohibited by state law. The five Ds are charged with conspiracy to violate this federal act. *Held*, the legislative history behind the federal act shows no congressional intent to merge conspiracy charges into the substantive crime, so a conspiracy charge is valid here. [*Iannelli v. U.S.*, 420 U.S. 770 (1975)]

3. **Model Penal Code rejects Rule:** The Model Penal Code almost completely ***rejects*** Wharton's Rule. [193]

   a. **No conviction for conspiracy and substantive offense:** However, the Code does provide that one may not be convicted of ***both*** a substantive crime and a conspiracy to commit that crime. (By contrast, most states ***allow*** this sort of ***"cumulative"*** punishment scheme, as long as the situation is not the classic Wharton's Rule scenario where only the parties logically necessary for the completed crime have been charged.) [193]

C. **Statutory purpose not to punish one party:** The court will not convict a party of conspiracy where it finds that the legislature intended not to punish such a party for the ***substantive*** crime. Typically, this situation arises where the legislature that defined the substantive crime recognized that two parties were necessarily involved, but chose to punish only one of those parties as being the "more guilty" one. [193-193]

Example: Stewart and Barbara, who are not married to each other, agree that Stewart will transport Barbara across state lines, so that they can have sex. The federal Mann Act prohibits the transportation of a woman across state lines for purposes of sexual intercourse. Cases interpreting the Mann Act itself hold that the woman is an innocent "victim" and thus does not violate the act merely by allowing herself to be transported interstate. Stewart and Barbara are arrested before they cross the state line, and are prosecuted for conspiracy to violate the Mann Act.

Held, Barbara may not be convicted of conspiracy, because the legislature did not intend to punish her for the substantive crime that she is accused of conspiring to commit. (A modern court would probably allow *Stewart* to be convicted, however.) [*Gebardi v. U.S.*, 287 U.S. 112 (1932)]

D. **Spouses and corporations:** [194]

1. **Spouses:** At common law, a ***husband and wife*** cannot by themselves make up a ***conspiracy***. But virtually all modern courts have ***rejected*** this common law rule, so a conspiracy composed solely of husband and wife is punishable. [194]

2. **Corporations:** There must at least be two ***human*** members of any conspiracy. Thus although a corporation can be punished as a conspirator, there can be no conspiracy when only

one corporation and one human being (e.g., an officer or stockholder of the corporation) are implicated. [194]

E. Inconsistent disposition: Look out for situations where one or more members of the alleged conspiracy are not convicted — does this prevent the conviction of the others? For now, let's assume that there are only two purported members, A and B. [194-195]

    1. Acquittal: Where A and B are tried in the *same proceeding*, and A is acquitted, all courts agree that B must also be acquitted. But if the two are tried in *separate* proceedings, courts are split. Most courts today hold that A's acquittal does *not* require B's release. [194]

        a. Model Penal Code rejects consistency requirement: The MPC, as the result of its "unilateral" approach, follows the majority rule of not requiring consistency where separate trials occur. [195]

        Example: A and B are the only two alleged conspirators. A is acquitted in his trial. B is then tried. B may be convicted, because under the "unilateral" approach, we look only at whether B conspired with anyone else, not whether "A and B conspired together."

    2. One conspirator not tried: If A is *not brought to justice* at all, this will *not* prevent conviction of B (assuming that the prosecution shows, in B's trial, that both A and B participated in the agreement). [195]

VIII. PUNISHMENT

A. Cumulative sentencing: May a member of the conspiracy be convicted of *both* conspiracy to commit the crime and the substantive crime itself? [195]

    1. Cumulative sentencing usually allowed: Most states allow a *cumulative sentence*, i.e., conviction for both conspiracy and the underlying crime. [195]

    2. MPC limits: But the Model Penal Code does not follow this majority approach — D may not be convicted simultaneously of crime X, and conspiracy to commit crime X. [195]

        a. Some objectives not realized: If, however, the conspiracy has a number of objectives, and less than all are carried out, even under the MPC there can be a conviction of both conspiracy and the carried-out crimes. [195]

CHAPTER 7

ACCOMPLICE LIABILITY AND SOLICITATION

I. PARTIES TO CRIME

A. Modern nomenclature: Modern courts and statutes dispense with common-law designations like "principal in the first degree," "accessory before the fact," "accessory after the fact," etc. Instead, modern courts and statutes usually refer only to two different types of criminal actors: "accomplices" and "principals." [205-206]

    1. Accomplice: An *"accomplice"* is one who *assists* or *encourages* the carrying out of a crime, but does not commit the *actus reus*. [206]

2. **Principal:** A *"principal,"* by contrast, is one who **commits** the *actus reus* (with or without the assistance of an accomplice). [206]

   Example: As part of a bank robbery plan, A steals a car, and drives B to the First National Bank. A remains in the car acting as lookout. B goes inside and demands money, which he receives and leaves the bank with. A drives the getaway car. Since B carried out the physical act of robbery, he is a "principal" to bank robbery. Since A merely assisted B, but did not carry out the physical act of bank robbery, he is an "accomplice" to bank robbery.

3. **Significance of distinction:** Relatively little turns today on the distinction between "accomplice" and "principal." The main significance of the distinction is that generally, the accomplice may not be convicted unless the prosecution also proves that the principal is guilty of the substantive crime in question. The most important rule to remember in dealing with accomplices is that generally, the accomplice is **guilty of the substantive crimes** he assisted or encouraged. [206]

II. ACCOMPLICES — THE ACT REQUIREMENT

A. **Liability for aiding and abetting:** The key principle of accomplice liability is that one who **aids**, **abets**, **encourages** or **assists** another to perform a crime, will himself be **liable for that crime**. [206-207]

   Example 1: Same facts as the above bank-robbery example. A is guilty of bank robbery, even though he did not himself use any violence, or even set foot inside the bank or touch the money.

   Example 2: A and B have a common enemy, V. A and B, in conversation, realize that they would both like V dead. A encourages B to kill V, and supplies B with a rifle with which to do the deed. B kills V with the rifle. A is guilty of murder — he assisted and encouraged another to commit murder, so he is himself guilty of murder.

1. **Words alone may be enough:** *Words*, by themselves, may be enough to constitute the requisite link between accomplice and principal — if the words constituted *encouragement* and *approval* of the crime, and thereby assisted commission of the crime, then the speaker is liable even if he did not take any physical acts. [206]

2. **Presence at crime scene not required:** One can be an accomplice even without ever being *present* at the *crime scene*. That is, the requisite encouragement, assistance, etc., may all take place before the actual occasion on which the crime takes place. [206]

   Example: On the facts of Example 2 above, A is not shielded from guilt of murder merely because he was a 1,000 miles away when B fired the rifle at V.

3. **Presence not sufficient:** Conversely, *mere presence* at the scene of the crime is *not*, by itself, sufficient to render one an accomplice. The prosecution must also show that D was at the crime scene for the *purpose of approving and encouraging* commission of the offense. [206]

   a. **Presence as evidence:** But D's presence at the crime scene can, of course, be convincing circumstantial *evidence* that D encouraged or assisted the crime. [207]

      Example: If the prosecution shows that A's presence at the crime was so that he could serve as a "look out" while B carried out the physical acts, A is obviously an accomplice and is thus guilty of the substantive crime.

4. **Failure to intervene:** Normally, the mere fact that D *failed to intervene* to prevent the crime will *not* make him an accomplice, even if the intervention could have been accomplished easily. [207]

   Example: A and B, who are good friends, walk down a city street together. B decides to shoplift a ring from a sidewalk vendor. A remains silent, when he could easily have dissuaded B. A is not an accomplice to theft of the ring.

   a. **Duty to intervene:** There are a few situations, however, where D has an *affirmative legal duty* to intervene. If he fails to exercise this duty, he may be an accomplice. [207]

      Example: Under general legal principles, both parents have an affirmative duty to safeguard the welfare of their child. Mother severely beats Child while Father remains silently by. Father is probably an accomplice to battery or child abuse, because he had an affirmative duty to protect Child and failed to carry out that duty.

B. **Aid not crucial:** Suppose that D gives assistance in furtherance of a crime, but the assistance turns out *not to have been necessary.* In this situation, D is generally *guilty* — as long as D intended to aid the crime, and took acts or spoke words in furtherance of this goal, the fact that the crime would probably have been carried out anyway will be irrelevant. [207-208]

   1. **Attempts to aid where no crime occurs:** If D attempts to give aid, but the substantive crime never takes place because the principal is *unsuccessful*, D may be liable for an *attempt*. [208]

      Example: A gives B a gun with which to kill V, and encourages B to do so. B shoots at V, but misses. A is guilty of attempted murder, just as B is.

      a. **Crime not attempted by the principal:** If, on the other hand, the principal does not even *attempt* the crime, most courts will *not* hold D guilty of even the crime of attempt on an accomplice theory. However, D is probably guilty of the crime of "solicitation," and a minority of courts might hold him guilty of attempt. [208]

         Example: A tries to persuade B to murder V, and gives B a rifle with which to do so. B turns A into the police, rather than trying to kill V. In most states, A is not liable for attempted murder on an accomplice theory, but may be liable for criminal solicitation. A few states, and the MPC, would hold D liable for attempted murder on these facts.

C. **Conspiracy as meeting the act requirement:** Some cases, especially older ones, hold that if D is found to have been in a *conspiracy* with another, he is automatically liable for any crimes committed by the other in furtherance of the conspiracy. (See *supra*, p. C-54.) [208]

   1. **Insufficient under modern view:** However, the modern view, and the view of the MPC, is that the act of joining a conspiracy is *not, by itself, enough* to make one an accomplice to all crimes carried out by any conspirator in furtherance of the conspiracy. But even in courts following this modern view, membership in the conspiracy will be strong *evidence* that D gave the other conspirators the required assistance or encouragement in the commission of the crimes that were the object of the conspiracy. [209]

III. ACCOMPLICES — MENTAL STATE

A. **General rule:** For D to have accomplice liability for a crime, the prosecution must generally show the following about D's mental state: (1) that D *intentionally aided or encouraged* the other to commit the criminal act; and (2) that D had the mental state *necessary for the crime* actually committed by the other. [209-212]

1. **Must have purpose to further crime:** The first requirement listed above means that it is not enough that D intends acts which have the *effect* of inducing another person to commit a crime — D must have the *purpose* of helping bring that crime about. [209]

   Example: D writes to X, "Your wife is sleeping with V." X, enraged, shoots V to death. D does not have the requisite mental state for accomplice liability for murder or manslaughter merely by virtue of intending to write the letter — the prosecution must also show that D intended to encourage X to kill V.

2. **Must have *mens rea* for crime actually committed:** D must be shown to have the *mens rea* for the *underlying crime*. Thus if the person assisted commits a *different crime* from that intended by D, D may escape liability. [209-210]

   Example: D believes that X will commit a burglary, and wants to help X do so. D procures a weapon for X, and drives X to the crime scene. Unbeknownst to D, X really intends all along to use the weapon to frighten V so that X can rape V; X carries out this scheme. D is not an accomplice to rape, because he did not have the *mens rea* — that is, he did not intend to cause unconsented-to sexual intercourse. The fact that D may have had the *mens rea* for burglary or robbery is irrelevant to the rape charge, though D might be held liable for attempted burglary or attempted robbery on these facts.

3. **Police undercover agents:** Where a *police undercover agent* helps bring about a crime by a suspect, the agent will usually have a valid defense based on his lack of the appropriate mental state.

B. **Knowledge, but not intent, as to criminal result:** The most important thing to watch out for regarding the mental state for accomplice is the situation where D *knows* that his conduct will encourage or assist another person in committing a crime, but D does not *intend* or *desire* to bring about that criminal result. [210-211]

   1. **Not usually sufficient:** Most courts hold that D is *not* an accomplice in this "knowledge but not intent" situation. [210]

      Example: X asks his friend D for a ride to a particular address. X is dressed all in black, and D knows that X has previously committed burglary. D does not desire that X commit a burglary, but figures, "If I don't give X a ride, someone else will, so I might as well stay on his good side." D drives X to the site, and X burgles the site. D is not guilty of burglary on an accomplice theory, because mere knowledge of X's purpose is not enough — D must be shown to have intended or desired to help X commit the crime.)

C. **Assistance with crime of recklessness or negligence:** If the underlying crime is not one that requires intent, but merely *recklessness or negligence*, *some* courts hold D liable as an accomplice upon a mere showing that D was reckless or negligent concerning the risk that the principal would commit the crime. [211-212]

   1. **Lending car to drunk driver:** Thus if D *lends his car to one that he knows to be drunk*, and the driver kills or wounds a pedestrian or other driver, some courts find D liable as an accomplice to manslaughter or battery. On these facts, D has had the mental state of recklessness (sufficient for involuntary manslaughter or battery), so a court may — but will not necessarily — hold that D's lack of intent to bring about the death or injury to another is irrelevant. [211]

    a. Negligence-manslaughter: Observe that in the above "lend car to drunk driver" scenario, D may be liable for manslaughter even if accomplice theory is not used — the crime of manslaughter is generally committed when one recklessly brings about the death of another, so D may, by entrusting his car to a known drunk, be guilty of manslaughter as a principal. [212]

IV. ACCOMPLICES — ADDITIONAL CRIMES BY PRINCIPAL

A. "Natural and probable" results that are not intended: A frequently-tested scenario involves a principal who commits not only the offense that the accomplice has assisted or encouraged, but *other offenses* as well. The accomplice will be liable for these additional crimes if: (1) the additional offenses are the *"natural and probable" consequences* of the conduct that D did intend to assist (even though D did not intend these additional offenses); *and* (2) the principal committed the additional crimes *in furtherance of the original criminal objective* that D was trying to assist. [212-215]

> **Example:** D1 and D2 agree to commit an armed robbery of a convenience store owned by V. D1 personally abhors violence. However, he knows that D2 is armed, and that D2 has been known to shoot in the course of prior robberies. D1 urges D2 not to shoot no matter what, but D2 refuses to make this promise. During the robbery, V attempts to trip an alarm, and D2 shoots her to death. A court would probably hold that D1 is liable for murder on an accomplice theory, since the shooting was a "natural and probable" consequence of armed robbery, and the shooting was carried out to further the original criminal objective of getting away with robbery.
>
> On the other hand, if D2 forcibly raped V instead of shooting her, and D1 had no reason to expect D2 to do this, D1 would not be liable for rape on an accomplice theory. This is because the rape was not the "natural and probable" consequence of the conduct encouraged by D1, nor was it committed in furtherance of the original objective of robbery.

    1. Unforeseeable: Thus if D can show that the additional offenses were *unlikely* or *unforeseeable*, D will not be liable for them. (*Example:* This is why D1 would not be liable for rape on the above hypothetical.)

    2. MPC rejects extended liability: The Model Penal Code rejects even the basic principle allowing an accomplice to be held liable for "natural and probable" crimes beyond those which he intended to aid or encourage. Under the MPC, only those crimes that D *intended* to aid or encourage will be laid at his door. [214]

    3. Felony-murder and misdemeanor-manslaughter rules: Wherever the additional offense is a *death*, the accomplice may end up being guilty not because of the "natural and probable consequences" rule, but because of the specialized *felony-murder* or *misdemeanor-manslaughter* rules. For instance, under the felony-murder rule (discussed *infra*, pp. C64-C67), if in the course of certain dangerous felonies the felon kills another, even *accidentally*, he is liable for murder. This can be combined with the general principles of accomplice liability to make the accessory liable for an unintended death. [214-215]

> **Example:** D1 and D2 agree to commit an armed robbery together, with D2 carrying the only gun. D1 does not desire that anybody be shot. D2 points his gun at V and asks for money; the gun accidentally goes off, killing V. D1 is probably guilty of murder on these facts. However, this is not because V's death was a "natural and probable consequence" of armed robbery.

Instead, it is because under the felony-murder doctrine, even an accidental death that directly stems from the commission of a dangerous felony such as armed robbery will constitute murder. By felony-murder alone, D2 is thus guilty of murder even though he did not intend to shoot, let alone kill, V. Then, since D1 was D2's accomplice in the armed robbery, D1 is liable for armed robbery. Since the killing occurred in the furtherance of the robbery *by D1* (even though he was not the shooter), and since D1 had the mental state required for felony-murder (intent to commit a dangerous felony), D1 is liable for murder without any use of the "natural and probable consequences" rule.

V. GUILT OF THE PRINCIPAL

A. **Principal must be guilty:** Generally, the accomplice cannot be convicted unless the prosecution shows that the person being aided or encouraged — the principal — is ***in fact guilty*** of the underlying crime. [216-217]

1. **Principal's conviction not necessary:** But it is not necessary that the principal be ***convicted***. (*Example:* A is charged with assisting B to commit a robbery. B is never arrested or brought to trial. Instead, B gets immunity and turns state's evidence against A. A can be convicted of being an accomplice to the robbery upon proof that B committed the robbery, and that A helped B carry it out — the fact that B is never charged or convicted is irrelevant.) [216]

2. **Inconsistent verdicts:** But if the principal is actually ***acquitted***, the accomplice must normally be acquitted as well. This is clearly true if the principal is acquitted in the ***same trial***, and probably true even if the principal is acquitted in an ***earlier*** trial. [*People v. Taylor*, 527 P.2d 622 (Cal. 1974)] [216]

VI. WITHDRAWAL BY THE ACCOMPLICE

A. **Withdrawal as defense:** One who has given aid or encouragement prior to a crime may ***withdraw*** and thus avoid accomplice liability. In other words, withdrawal is generally a ***defense*** to accomplice liability (in contrast to the conspiracy situation, where it is usually not a defense to the conspiracy charge itself, merely to substantive crimes later commited in furtherance of the conspiracy). The withdrawal will only be effective if D has ***undone*** the effects of his assistance or encouragement. [218]

> **Example:** X tells D that X wants to rob a gas station at gun point, and that he needs a gun to do so. D supplies X with a gun for this purpose. D then has second thoughts, and takes the gun back from X, while also telling X, "I don't think this robbery is a good idea." X gets a different gun from someone else, and carries out the same robbery of the same store. D is not guilty of being an accomplice to the robbery, because he withdrew, in a way that undid the effect of his earlier assistance and encouragement.

1. **Effect of aid must be undone:** It is not enough that D has a subjective change of heart, and gives no further assistance prior to the crime. He must, at the very least, make it ***clear to the other party*** that he is repudiating his past aid or encouragement. [219]

2. **Verbal withdrawal not always enough:** If D's aid has been only ***verbal***, he may be able to withdraw merely by stating to the "principal" that he now withdraws and disapproves of the project. But if D's assistance has been more ***tangible***, he probably has to take ***affirmative action*** to undo his affects. [219]

Example: On the facts of the prior example, where D supplies a gun to X, it probably would not be enough for D to say, "I think the robbery is a bad idea," while letting X keep the gun — D probably has to get the gun back.

    a. Warning to authorities: Alternatively, D can almost always make an effective withdrawal by *warning the authorities* prior to commission of the crime. [219]

3. Not required that crime be thwarted: Regardless of the means used to withdraw, it is *not necessary* that D actually *thwart* the crime. [219]

Example: D encourages X to commit a particular burglary at a specified time and place. X thinks better of it, and leaves a message at the local police station alerting the police to the place and time for the crime. He does not make any effort to talk X out of the crime, however. Due to police inefficiency, the message gets lost, and X carries out the crime. D's notice to the authorities will probably be held to be enough to constitute an effective withdrawal, even though D was not successful in actually thwarting the crime.

VII. VICTIMS AND OTHER EXCEPTIONS TO ACCOMPLICE LIABILITY

    A. Exceptions for certain classes: There are certain *classes* of persons as to whom no accomplice liablilty will be imposed: [220]

        1. Victims: Most obviously, where the legislature regards a certain type of person as being the *victim* of the crime, that victim will not be subject to accomplice liability. [220]

            a. Statutory rape: Thus a *female below the age of consent* will not be liable as an accessory to *statutory rape* of herself, even if she gives assistance and encouragement to the male. [220]

            b. Kidnapping and extortion: Similarly, a person who meets the demands of an *extortionist*, or a person who pays a ransom to *kidnappers* to secure the release of a loved one, will not be an accomplice to the extortion or kidnapping. [220]

        2. Crime logically requiring second person: Where a crime is defined so as to logically require participation by a second person, as to whom *no direct punishment* has been authorized by the legislature, that second person will not be liable as an accomplice. [220]

Examples: Since an abortion cannot be performed without a pregnant woman, the pregnant woman will not be liable as an accomplice to her own abortion, assuming that the legislature has not specifically authorized punishment for the woman in this situation. The same would be true of a customer who patronizes a prostitute, or one who purchases illegal drugs — if the legislature has not specifically punished customers of prostitutes or purchasers of drugs, these will not be liable as accomplices to prostitution/drug sales.

VIII. POST-CRIME ASSISTANCE

    A. Accessory after the fact: One who knowingly gives assistance to felon, for the purpose of helping him *avoid apprehension* following his crime, is an *accessory after the fact*. Under modern law, the accessory after the fact is *not liable* for the *felony itself*, as an accomplice would be. Instead, he has committed a distinct crime based upon obstruction of justice, and his punishment does not depend on the punishment for the underlying felony. [221]

B. Elements: Here are the elements for accessory after the fact: [221]

1. **Commission of a felony:** A *completed felony* must have been committed. (It is not enough that D *mistakenly believed* that the person he was assisting committed a felony — but the person aided need not have been formally charged, or even caught.) [221]

2. **Knowledge of felony:** D must be shown to have *known*, not merely *suspected*, that the felony was committed. [221]

3. **Assistance to felon personally:** The assistance must have been given to the *felon personally*. (Thus it is not enough that D knows that a crime has been committed by some unknown person, and D destroys evidence or otherwise obstructs prosecution.) [221]

4. **Affirmative acts:** D must be shown to have taken *affirmative acts* to hinder the felon's arrest. It is not enough that D *fails to report the felon*, or fails to turn in *evidence* that he possesses. [221]

C. Misprision of felony: At common law, one who simply fails to report a crime or known felon — without committing any affirmative acts to hinder the felon's arrest — is guilty of the separate crime of *"misprision of felony."* However, almost no states recognize this crime today. [221]

IX. SOLICITATION

A. Solicitation defined: The common-law crime of *solicitation* occurs when one *requests or encourages another* to perform a criminal act, regardless of whether the latter agrees. [222]

1. **Utility:** The main utility of the crime is that it allows punishment of the solicitor if the person who is requested to commit the crime *refuses*. [222]

    Example: Wendy is unhappily married to Herbert, and has been having an affair with Bart. Wendy says to Bart, "Won't you please kill Herbert? If you do, we can live happily ever after." Bart does not respond either way, but tells the police what has happened. The police arrest Wendy before Bart takes any action regarding Herbert. On these facts, Wendy is guilty of solicitation — she has requested or encouraged another to perform a criminal act, and it does not matter that the other has refused.

B. No overt act required: The crime of solicitation is never construed so as to require an *overt act* — as soon as D makes his request or proposal, the crime is complete (as in the above example). [222]

C. Communication not received: Courts disagree about whether D can be convicted of solicitation where he attempts to communicate his criminal proposal, but the proposal is never *received*. [223]

1. **Model Penal Code:** The Model Penal Code imposes liability in this "failed communication" situation. [223]

    Example: On the facts of the above example, Wendy sends a letter to Bart asking Bart to kill Herbert. The letter is intercepted by police before Bart can get it. Courts are split as to whether Wendy can be convicted of solicitation; the MPC would impose liability here. (Even courts not following the MPC approach would probably allow a conviction for "attempted solicitation" on these facts.) [223]

D. Renunciation: Some courts allow the defense that the solicitor *voluntarily renounced* his crime. Thus the MPC allows the defense of renunciation if D *prevents* the commission of the crime, and does so voluntarily. [223]

E. Solicitation as an attempted crime: If all D has done is to request or encourage another to commit a crime ("bare" solicitation), this is *not* enough to make D guilty of an *attempt* to commit the object crime. However, if D has gone further, by making extensive preparations with or on behalf of the solicitee, or otherwise making overt acts, this may be enough to cause him to be guilty of not only solicitation but an attempt [223] at the crime (even if the solicitee himself refuses to participate).

CHAPTER 8

HOMICIDE AND OTHER CRIMES AGAINST THE PERSON

I. HOMICIDE — INTRODUCTION

A. Different grades of homicide: Any unlawful taking of the life of another falls within the generic class *"homicide."* The two principal kinds of homicide are *murder* and *manslaughter*. [230]

1. **Degrees of murder:** In many jurisdictions, murder is divided into first-degree and second-degree murder. Generally, first-degree murder consists of murders committed "with premeditation and deliberation," and killings committed during the course of certain felonies. [230]

2. **Two kinds of manslaughter:** Similarly, manslaughter is usually divided into: (1) *voluntary* manslaughter (in most cases, a killing occurring the "heat of passion"); and (2) *involuntary* manslaughter (an unintentional killing committed recklessly, grossly negligently, or during commission of an unlawful act.) [230]

3. **Other statutory forms of homicide:** Additional forms of homicide exist by statute in some states. Many states have created the crime of *vehicular homicide* (an unintentional death caused by the driver of a moter vehicle). Similarly, some states, and the MPC, have created the crime of "negligent homicide." [230]

II. MURDER — GENERALLY

A. Definition of "murder": There is no simple definition of "murder" that is sufficient to distinguish killings that are murder from killings that are not. At the most general level, murder is defined as the *unlawful killing* of *another person*. [230]

1. **Four types:** In most states, there are four types of murder, distinguished principally by the defendant's mental state:

   [1] *intent-to-kill* murder;

   [2] *intent-to-commit-grievous-bodily-injury* murder;

   [3] *"depraved heart"* (a/k/a "reckless indifference to the value of human life") murder; and

   [4] *felony-murder*, i.e., a killing occurring during the course of a dangerous felony.

   Each of these types is discussed in detail below.

B. Taking of life: Murder exists only where a life has been taken. Therefore, be ready to spot situations where there is no murder because either: (1) the victim had not yet been born alive when D acted, and was never born alive; or (2) the victim's life had ended before D's act. [230-232]

1. **Fetus:** A *fetus* is not a human being for homicide purposes, in most states. Thus if D commits an act which kills the fetus, this does not fall within the general murder statute in most states. [231-231]

   Example: D shoots X, a pregnant woman. The bullet goes into X's uterus and instantly kills V, a fetus which has not yet started the birth process. In most states, D has not committed garden-variety murder of V, though he may have committed the separate statutory crime of feticide, defined in many states.

   a. **Fetus born alive:** But if the infant is *born alive* and then dies, D is guilty of murdering it even though his acts took place before the birth. (*Example:* Same facts as in the above example. Now, however, assume that the shooting causes X to go into premature labor, V is born alive, and immediately thereafter V dies of the bullet wound. D has murdered V.) [231]

2. **End of life:** Traditionally, *death* has been deemed to occur only when the victim's heart has stopped beating. The modern tendancy, however, is to recognize *"brain death"* as also being a type of death. [232]

   Example: D, a physician, concludes that V is "brain dead," and thus removes V's heart to use it in an organ transplant. Most courts today would probably hold that D has not murdered V, because V was already dead even though her heart was still beating.

C. **Elements of murder:** Here are the elements which the prosecution must prove to obtain a murder conviction: [232-233]

   1. *Actus reus:* There must be *conduct by the defendant* (an *"actus reus"*) either an affirmative act by D an omission by D where he had a duty to act. [232]

   2. *Corpus delecti:* There must be shown to have been a *death* of the victim. Death is the *"corpus delecti"* ("body of the crime") of murder. But the prosecution does *not* have to produce a *corpse*. Like any element of any crime, existence of death may be proved by *circumstantial evidence*. [232]

      Example: D and V are known to be getting along badly, and D has a motive — financial gain — for wanting V dead. V is last seen alive while about to visit D's remote mountain cabin. V is never seen again, and no body is ever found. V's wallet is found in the cabin. Seven years have gone by without a trace of V. A jury could probably reasonably conclude that V is now dead, and that D caused the death by methods unknown.

   3. *Mens rea:* D must be shown to have had an appropriate *mental state* for murder. The required mental state is sometimes called *"malice aforethought,"* but this is merely a term of art, which can be satisfied by any of several mental states. In most jurisdictions, any of the four following intents will suffice: [233]

      a. An intent to *kill*; [233-234]

      b. An intent to *commit grievous bodily injury*; [234-235]

      c. *Reckless indifference* to the *value of human life* (or a *"depraved heart,"* as the concept is sometimes put); [235-236] and

      d. An intent to commit any of certain non-homicide *dangerous felonies*. [237-246]

   4. **Proximate cause:** There must be a *causal relationship* between D's act and V's death. D's conduct must be both the "cause in fact" of the death and also its "proximate cause." [233]

a. **Year-and-a-day rule:** Most states continue a common-law proximate cause rule that applies only in murder cases: V must die within a *year and a day* of D's conduct. [233]

Note on four types of murder: Anytime D can be said to have killed V, you should go through all four types of murder before concluding that no murder has occurred. In other words, examine the possibility that D: (1) intended to kill V; (2) intended to inflict serious bodily harm upon V; (3) knew V or someone else had a substantial chance of dying, but with "reckless indifference" or "depraved heart" ignored this risk; or (4) intended to commit some dangerous felony, not itself a form of homicide (e.g., robbery, rape, kidnapping, etc.) Only if D's intent did not fall within any of these cases can you be confident that V's death does not constitute murder.

D. **Intent-to-kill murder:** The most common state of mind that suffices for murder is the *intent to kill*. [233-234]

1. **Desire to kill:** This intent exists, of course, when D has the *desire* to bring about the death of another. [233]

2. **Substantial certainty of death:** The requisite intent also exists where D knows that death is *substantially certain* to occur, but does not actively desire to bring about V's death. (*Example:* D, a terrorist, puts a bomb onto an airliner. He does not desire the death of any passengers, but knows that at least one death is almost certain to occur. D has the state of mind needed for "intent to kill" murder.) [233]

3. **Ill-will unnecessary:** The requisite intent to kill may exist even where D does not bear any *ill will* towards the victim. (*Example:* D's wife, V, is suffering from terminal cancer, but still has at least several weeks to live. D feeds her poison without telling her what this is, in order to spare her suffering. As a strictly legal matter, D has the mental state required for "intent to kill" murder, though a jury might well decide to convict only of manslaughter.) [234]

4. **Circumstantial evidence:** Intent to kill may be proved by *circumstantial evidence*. (*Example:* If death occurs as the result of a deadly weapon used by D, the jury is usually permitted to infer that D intended to bring about the death.) [234]

5. **Compare with voluntary manslaughter:** It does not automatically follow that because D intended to kill and did kill, that D is guilty of murder. (For instance, most cases of *voluntary manslaughter* — generally, a killing occurring in a "heat of passion" — are ones where D intended to kill.) In a prosecution for intent-to-kill murder, the mental state is an intent to kill *not accompanied by other redeeming or mitigating factors*. [234]

E. **Intent-to-do-serious-bodily-injury murder:** In most states, the *mens rea* requirement for murder is satisfied if D intended not to kill, but to do *serious bodily injury* to V. [234-235]

Example: D is angry at V for welching on a debt. D beats V with brass knuckles, intending only to break V's nose and jaw, and to knock out most of his teeth. In most states, D has the mental state required for murder of the "intent to do serious bodily injury" sort. Therefore, if V unexpectedly dies, D is guilty of murder in these states.

1. **Subjective standard:** Most states apply a *subjective* standard as to the risk of serious bodily harm — D has the requisite mental state only if he *actually realized* that there was a high probability of serious harm (not necessarily death) to V, and the fact that a "reasonable person" would have realized the danger is not sufficient. [235]

2. **"Serious bodily injury" defined:**   Some courts hold that only conduct which is likely to be *"life threatening"* suffices for "intent to commit serious bodily injury." Other courts take a broader view of what constitutes serious bodily harm. However, all courts recognizing this form of murder hold that a mere intent to commit some sort of bodily injury does not suffice. [235]

    Example: D punches V in the face, intending merely to knock V down. V strikes his head while falling, and dies. Probably no court would hold that D is liable for "intent to do serious bodily harm" murder on these facts, though he would be liable for manslaughter under the misdemeanor-manslaughter rule.

3. **Model Penal Code rejects:**   The Model Penal Code does *not* recognize "intent to do serious bodily harm" murder. The MPC regards the "reckless indifference to value of human life" or "depraved heart" standard, discussed below, as being enough to take care of cases where D wilfully endangers the life or safety of others and death results. [235]

F. **"Reckless indifference to value of human life" or "depraved heart" murder:**   Nearly all states hold D liable if he causes a death, while acting with such great *recklessness* that he can be said to have a *"depraved heart"* or an *"extreme indifference to the value of human life."* [235-236]

    1. **Illustrations:**   Here are some illustrations of "depraved heart" or "extreme indifference" murder: [236]

        Example 1: D sets fire to a building where he knows people are sleeping; he does not desire their death, but knows that there is a high risk of death. One inhabitant dies in the fire.

        Example 2: D fires a bullet into a passing passenger train, without any intent to kill any particular person. The bullet happens to strike and kill V, a passenger.

        Example 3: D, trying to escape from pursuing police, drives his car at 75 mph the wrong way down a one-way residential street that has a 30 mph speed limit. D hits V, a pedestrian.

    2. **Awareness of risk:**   Courts are split as to whether D shows the requisite "depravity" where he is *not aware* of the risk involved in his conduct. [236]

        a. **MPC view:**   The Model Penal Code follows the "subjective" approach to this problem: D shows the required extreme recklessness only if he *"consciously disregards"* a substantial and unjustifiable risk." [236]

        b. **Intoxication:**   If D fails to appreciate the risk of his conduct because he is *intoxicated*, even courts (and the MPC) that would ordinarily follow a "subjective" standard *allow a conviction*. [236]

III. FELONY-MURDER

A. **Generally:**   Under the *felony-murder rule*, *if D, while he is in the process of committing certain felonies, kills another (even accidentally), the killing is murder*. In other words, the intent to commit any of certain felonies (unrelated to homicide) is sufficient to meet the *mens rea* requirement for murder. [237]

    1. **Common law and today:**   The felony-murder rule was applied at common law, and continues to be applied by most states today. [237]

Example: D, while carrying a loaded gun, decides to rob V, a pedestrian. While D is pointing his gun at V and demanding money, the gun accidentally goes off, and kills V. Even though D never intended to kill V or even shoot at him, D is guilty of murder, because the killing occurred while D was in the course of carrying out a dangerous felony.

B. Dangerous felonies: Nearly all courts and legislatures today restrict application of the felony-murder doctrine to *certain felonies*. [237-238]

 1. "Inherently dangerous" felonies: Most courts today use the *"inherently dangerous"* test — only those felonies which are inherently dangerous to life and health count, for purposes of the felony-murder rule. [238]

   a. Two standards: Courts are *split* about how to determine whether a felony is "inherently dangerous." Some courts judge dangerousness in the *abstract* (e.g., by asking whether larceny is in general a dangerous crime), whereas others evaluate the felony based on the *facts of that particular case* (so that if, say, the particular larceny in question is committed in a very dangerous manner, the felony is "inherently dangerous" even though most other larcenies are not physically dangerous). [238]

   b. Listing: In courts that judge "inherent dangerousness" in the abstract, here are felonies that are typically considered inherently dangerous: *robbery*, *burglary*, *rape*, *arson*, *assault* and *kidnapping*. By contrast, the various theft-related felonies are generally not considered inherently dangerous: larceny, embezzlement and false pretenses. [238]

C. Causal relationship: There must be a *causal relationship* between the felony and the killing. First, the felony must in some sense be the "but for" cause of the killing. Second, the felony must be the *proximate cause* of the killing. [238-241]

 1. "Natural and probable" consequences: The requirement of proximate cause here is usually expressed by saying that D is only liable where the death is the *"natural and probable consequence"* of D's conduct. [239]

 2. Robberies and gunfights: Most commonly, proximate cause questions arise in the case of *robberies*. [239-241]

   a. Robber fires shot: If the fatal shot is fired by the *robber* (even if accidentally), virtually all courts agree that D is the proximate cause of death, and that the felony-murder doctrine should apply. This is true whether the shot kills the robbery victim, or a *bystander*. [239]

   Example 1: On a city street, D points a gun at V, and says, "Your money or your life." While V is reaching into his pocket for his wallet, D drops his gun. The gun strikes the pavement and goes off accidentally, killing V. D's acts of robbery are clearly the proximate cause of V's death, and D is guilty of murder under the felony-murder rule.

   Example 2: Same facts as above example. Now, assume that when the gun strikes the pavement and goes off, it kills B, a bystander 20 feet away. D's acts are the proximate cause of B's death, so D is guilty of murdering B under the felony-murder doctrine.

   b. Victim or police officer kills bystander: Where the fatal shot is fired by the *robbery victim* or by a *police officer*, and a *bystander* is accidentally killed, courts are split as to whether the robber is the proximate cause of the death. California, for instance, does not apply the felony-murder doctrine in any situation where the fatal shot comes from the gun of a person other than the robber. In other states, the result might depend on whether the robber fired the first shot, so that if the first shot was fired by the victim and struck a bystander, the robber would not be guilty. [239]

c. **Robber dies, shot by victim, police officer or other felon:** Where the person who dies is *one of the robbers*, and the fatal shot is fired by another robber, the robbery victim or by police officers, courts are even more reluctant to apply the felony-murder doctrine. Some courts hold that the felony-murder doctrine is intended to protect only innocent persons, so it should not apply where a robber is killed. Where a robber is killed not by one of his cohorts but by the robbery victim or the police, the case for applying the felony murder rule is the weakest of all. [240]

Example: D and X are co-robbers. X is killed by a police officer who is trying to apprehend the pair. *Held*, D is not guilty of felony murder. [*Comm. v. Redline*, 137 A.2d 472 (Pa. 1958)]

Note on "depraved heart" as alternative: In any robbery situation, in addition to the possibility of "felony murder" as a theory, examine the possibility of using "depraved heart" as an alternate theory. For instance, if D, while committing a robbery, initiates a gun fight, and a police officer shoots back, killing a bystander, it may be easier to argue that D behaved with reckless indifference to the value of human life (thus making him guilty of "depraved heart" murder) than to find that the felony murder doctrine should apply (since many courts hold that the felony-murder doctrine applies only where the killing is by the defendant's own hand or the hand of his accomplice). [241]

D. **Accomplice liability of co-felons:** Frequently, the doctrine of felony-murder combines with the rules on *accomplice* liability. The net result is that if two or more people work together to commit a felony, and one of them commits a killing during the felony, the others may also be guilty of felony-murder. [241-242]

1. **"In furtherance" test:** In most courts, all of the co-felons are liable for a killing committed by one of them, if the killing was: (1) committed *in furtherance of the felony*; and (2) a *"natural and probable" result* of the felony. [242-242]

a. **Accidental killing:** Thus one felon will commonly be guilty of murder based on another felon's *accidental* killing. [241]

Example: A and B decide to rob a convenience store together. A carries no gun. A knows that B is carrying a loaded gun, but also knows that B has never used a gun in similar robberies in the past, and that B does not believe in doing so. During the robbery, B accidentally drops the gun, and the gun goes off when it hits the floor, killing V, the convenience store operator. Because B was holding the gun "in furtherance" of the robbery when he dropped it, and because an accident involving a loaded gun is a somewhat "natural and probable" consequence of carrying the loaded gun during the felony, there is a good chance that the court will hold not only that B is guilty of felony-murder, but that A is also guilty of felony murder as an accomplice to B's act of felony murder.

b. **Intentional killing:** Similarly, if the killing by one co-felon is *intentional* rather than accidental, the other co-felons will probably still be liable under accomplice principles as long as the killing was committed "in furtherance" of the felony. This will normally be true even though the other co-felons can show that they did not desire or foresee the killing. But if the other co-felons can show that the killing was *not committed for the purpose of furthering the felony*, they may be able to escape accomplice liability. [242]

Example: A and B rob a convenience store together; as A knows, B is carrying a loaded gun, but B has never used the gun on any previous robberies and is generally opposed to violence. Unknown to either, the new owner of the store is V, an old enemy of B's. B decides to shoot V to death during the course of the robbery, even though V is not threatening to call the police or resisting the robbery in any way. A will have a good chance of persuading the court that the killing was not "in furtherance of" the robbery, and thus of escaping accomplice liability for felony-murder.

E. **"In commission of" a felony:**   The felony-murder doctrine applies only to killings which occur *"in the commission of"* a felony. [242-243]

   1. **Causal:**   There must be a *causal relationship* between felony and killing. [242]

   2. **Escape as part of felony:**   If the killing occurs while the felons are attempting to *escape*, it will probably be held to have occurred "in the commission of" the felony, at least if it occurred reasonably close, both in *time and place*, to the felony itself. [242]

   3. **Killing before felony:**   Even if the killing occurs *before* the accompanying felony, the felony-murder doctrine will apply if the killing was in some way in furtherance of the felony. [243]

   Example: D intends to rape V. In order to quiet her, he puts his hand over her mouth, thereby asphyxiating her. D is almost certainly liable for felony-murder, even though he killed V before he tried to rape her, and even though the final felony was only an attempted rape (since one cannot rape a corpse).

F. **Felony must be independent of the killing:** For applicaton of the felony-murder doctrine, the felony must be *independent* of the killing. This prevents the felony-murder rule from turning virtually any attack that culminates in death into automatic murder. [243-244]

   Example 1: D kills V in a heat of passion, under circumstances that would justify a conviction of voluntary manslaughter but not murder. Even though manslaughter is obviously a "dangerous felony," the felony-murder rule will not apply to upgrade the manslaughter to felony-murder. The reason is that the underlying felony must be independent of the killing, a requirement not satisfied here.

   Example 2: D intends to punch V in the jaw, but not to seriously injure him or kill him. V, while falling from the blow, hits his head on the curb and dies. Even though D was committing the dangerous felony of assault or battery, this will not be upgraded to felony-murder, because the felony was not independent of the killing.

G. **Model Penal Code approach:**   The Model Penal Code does *not* adopt the felony-murder rule *per se*. Instead, the MPC establishes a *rebuttable presumption* of "recklessness...manifesting extreme indifference to the value of life" where D is engaged in or an accomplice to robbery, rape, arson, burglary, kidnapping or felonious escape. Thus if an unintentional killing occurs during one of these crimes, the prosecution gets to the jury on the issue of "depraved heart" murder. But D is free to *rebut* the presumption that he acted with reckless indifference to the value of human life. The MPC provision is thus quite different from the usual felony-murder provision, by which D is *automatically* guilty of murder even if he can show that he was not reckless with respect to the risk of death. [245]

IV. DEGREES OF MURDER

A. Death penalty: At least 35 states now authorize the ***death penalty*** for some kinds of murder. [246-248]

1. **Not necessarily "cruel and unusual":** The death penalty is not necessarily a "cruel and unusual" punishment, and thus does not necessarily violate the Eighth Amendment. [*Gregg v. Georgia*, 428 U.S. 153 (1976)] [246]

2. **Must not be "arbitrary or capricious":** However, a state's death-penalty scheme must not be ***"arbitrary or capricious."*** That is, the state may not give too much discretion to juries in deciding whether or not to recommend the death penalty in a particular case. Typically, the state avoids undue discretion by listing in the death penalty statute certain **aggravating circumstances** (e.g., the presence of torture) — then, if the jury finds one or more of the aggravating circumstances to exist beyond a reasonable doubt, the jury may recommend the death penalty. In general, this "aggravating circumstance" approach has been upheld by the Supreme Court as constitutional. [246]

3. **Mandatory sentences not constitutional:** By contrast, it is usually ***unconstitutional*** for a state to try to avoid undue jury discretion by making a death sentence ***mandatory*** for certain crimes (e.g., killing of a police officer, or killing by one already under life sentence). The Supreme Court has held that the states must basically allow the jury to consider the ***individual circumstances*** of a particular case (e.g., the presence of extenuating circumstances), and a mandatory-sentence scheme by definition does not allow this. [*Woodson v. North Carolina*, 428 U.S. 280 (1976)] [247]

4. **Racial prejudice:** A defendant can avoid a death sentence by showing that the jury was motivated by ***racial*** considerations, in violation of his Eighth Amendment or equal protection rights. However, the Supreme Court has held that any proof of impermissible racial bias must be directed to the ***facts of the particular case***, and may not be proved by large-scale ***statistical studies***. [*McCleskey v. Kemp*, 481 U.S. 279 (1987).] [247]

5. **Non-intentional killings:** The Eighth Amendment appears to prevent use of the death penalty against a defendant who does not himself kill, attempt to kill or intend that a killing take place, or that lethal force be employed. [*Enmund v. Florida*, 458 U.S. 782 (1982).] [247]

   Example: D drives a getaway car while his two accomplices go into a farm house and murder the inhabitants. *Held*, since D did not commit the killing or desire it, he may not be executed, even though he is guilty of murder by virtue of the felony-murder doctrine and the rules on accomplice liability. [*Enmund, supra*]

6. **Non-murder cases:** The Supreme Court probably will not allow the death penalty for crimes ***other than murder***. Thus capital punishment may not constitutionally be imposed on one who commits ***rape***. [*Coker v. Georgia*, 433 U.S. 584 (1977)] [248]

B. First-degree murder: Most states recognize at least two degrees of murder. ***First-degree murder*** in most states is a killing that is ***"premeditated and deliberate."*** [248-250]

1. **Only short time required for premeditation:** Courts do not require a long period of premeditation. Traditionally, no substantial amount of time has needed to elapse between formation of the intent to kill and execution of the killing. Most modern courts require a reasonable period of time during which deliberation exists, but even this is not a very stringent requirement — five minutes, for example, would suffice in most courts even today. [248]

---

a. **Planning, motive or careful manner of killing:** Like any other form of intent, premeditation and deliberation can be shown by circumstantial evidence. Typical ways of showing that D premeditated are: (1) *planning activity* occurring prior to the killing (e.g., purchase of a weapon just before the crime); (2) evidence of a *"motive"* in contrast to a sudden impulse; and (3) a *manner* of killing so precise that it suggests D must have a preconceived design. [249]

2. **Intoxication as negating deliberation:** If D is so *intoxicated* that he lost the ability to deliberate or premeditate, this may be a defense to first-degree murder (though not a defense to murder generally, such as second-degree murder). [249]

3. **Certain felony murders:** Statutes in some states make some or all *felony-murders* (typically, those involving rape, robbery, arson and burglary) first-degree. [250]

4. **Model Penal Code:** The Model Penal Code does *not* divide murder into first- and second-degree, and attaches no significance to the fact that D did or did not premeditate/deliberate. [249]

C. **Second-degree murder:** Murders that are not first-degree are second-degree. These typically include the following classes: [250]

1. **No premeditation:** Cases in which there is *no premeditation*. [250]

2. **Intent to seriously injure:** Cases where D may have premeditated, but his intent was not to kill, but to do *serious bodily injury* (a *mens rea* sufficient for murder). [250]

3. **Reckless indifference:** Cases in which D did not intend to kill, but was *recklessly indifferent* to the value of human life. [250]

4. **Felony-murders:** Killings committed during the course of felonies other than those specified in the first-degree murder statute (i.e., typically felonies other than rape, robbery, arson and burglary). [250]

V. MANSLAUGHTER — VOLUNTARY

A. **Two types of manslaughter:** In most states, there are two types of manslaughter: (1) *voluntary manslaughter*, in which there is generally an *intent to kill*; and (2) *involuntary manslaughter*, in which the death is *accidental*. [250]

B. **"Heat of passion" manslaughter:** The most common kind of voluntary manslaughter is that in which D kills while in a *"heat of passion,"* i.e., an extremely *angry* or disturbed state. [250]

1. **Four elements:** Assuming that the facts would otherwise constitute murder, D is entitled to a conviction on the lesser charge of voluntary manslaughter if he meets four requirements: [250]

a. **Reasonable provocation:** He acted in response to a *provocation* that would have been sufficient to cause a *reasonable person* to *lose his self-control*. [250]

b. **Actually act in "heat of passion":** D was *in fact* in a "heat of passion" at the time he acted; [250]

c. **No time for reasonable person to cool off:** The lapse of time between the provocation and the killing was not great enough that a *reasonable person* would have *"cooled off,"* i.e., regained his self-control; [250] and

d. **D not in fact cooled off:** D did not *in fact* "cool off" by the time he killed. [250]

2. **Consequence of missing hurdle:** If D fails to clear hurdles (a) or (c) above (i.e., he is actually provoked, and has not cooled off, but a reasonable person would have either not lost his self-control or would have cooled off), D will normally be liable only for **second-degree** murder, not first-degree, since he will probably be found to have lacked the necessary premeditation. But if D trips up on hurdles (b) or (d) (i.e., he is not in fact driven into a heat of passion, or has in fact already cooled off), he is likely to be convicted of **first-degree** murder, since his act of killing is in "cold blood." [251]

C. **Provocation:** As noted, D's act must be in response to a **provocation** that is: (1) sufficiently strong that a **"reasonable person"** would have been **caused to lose his self control**; and (2) strong enough that **D himself** lost his self-control. [251-254]

   1. **Lost temper:** The provocation need not be enough to cause a reasonable person to kill. The provocation merely needs to be enough that it would make a reasonable person **lose his temper**. [251]

   2. **Objective standard for emotional characteristics:** Courts generally do **not** recognize the peculiar **emotional** characteristics of D in determining how a reasonable person would act. (*Example:* All courts agree that the fact that D is unusually bad-tempered, or unusually quick to anger, is not to be taken into account.) [251]

   3. **Particular categories:** Courts have established certain rules, as a matter of law, about what kind of provocation will suffice: [252]

      a. **Battery:** More-than-trivial **battery** committed on D is usually considered to be sufficient provocation. [252]

         Example: V, a man, slaps D, a man, because D has failed to pay back a debt. This will probably constitute adequate provocation, so if D then flies into a rage and kills V, this will be manslaughter rather than murder.

         i. **D initiates:** However, if D brought on the battery by his own initial aggressive conduct, he will **not** be entitled to a manslaughter verdict.

         ii. **Assault:** If V **attempts** to commit a battery on D, but fails (thereby committing a criminal assault), most courts regard this as sufficient provocation.

      b. **Mutual combat:** If D and V get into a **mutual combat**, in which neither one can be said to have been the aggressor, most courts will treat this as sufficient provocation to D. [252]

      c. **Adultery:** The classic voluntary manslaughter situation is that in which Husband surprises Wife in the act of **adultery** with her paramour, and kills either Wife or Lover. This will almost always be sufficient provocation. (But courts do not necessarily recognize provocation where the couple is **unmarried**.) [252]

      d. **Words alone:** Traditionally, **words alone** cannot constitute the requisite provocation — no matter how abusive, insulting or harassing, D will be guilty of murder, not manslaughter, if he kills in retaliation. [253]

         i. **Words carrying information:** But if the words **convey information**, most courts today hold that the words will suffice if a reasonable person would have lost his self-control upon hearing them.

            Example: V says to D, formerly his best friend, "You know, I've been having an affair with your wife for the last six months. She's a heck of a girl, and we'd like you to give her a divorce so that we can get married." This is probably sufficient provocation, so that if D kills V, he is probably entitled to a manslaughter verdict.

4. Effect of mistake: If D *reasonably* but *mistakenly* reaches a conclusion which, if accurate, would constitute sufficient provocation, courts will generally allow manslaughter. (*Example:* Based on circumstantial evidence, D reasonably but erroneously suspects that his wife has been sleeping with his best-friend. Probably this will suffice as provocation.) [254]

5. Actual provocation: Remember that the provocation must be not only sufficient to cause a reasonable person to lose his self-control, but also sufficient to have *in fact* enraged D. [254]

Example: D finds his wife together with V, his best friend. D has in fact suspected the affair for some time, and thus cooly says to himself, "Now's my chance to kill V and get off with just voluntary manslaughter." He cold-bloodedly shoots V in the heart. Even though the provocation would have been sufficient to cause a reasonable person to lose control, D does not qualify for manslaughter here because he was not in fact enraged at the moment of the shooting.

D. "Cooling off" period: The *time* between D's discovery of the upsetting facts and his act of killing must be sufficiently short that: (1) a *reasonable person* would not have had time to "cool off"; and (2) D himself did not *in fact* cool off. [254]

1. Rekindling: But even if there is a substantial cooling-off period between the initial provocation and the killing, if a *new provocation* occurs which would *rekindle* the passion of a reasonable person, the cooling-off rule is not violated. This is true even if the new provocation would not *by itself* be sufficient to inflame a reasonable person. [254]

E. Other kinds of voluntary manslaughter: In addition to manslaughter based upon a "heat of passion" killing, there are a number of other situations in which voluntary manslaughter may be found. [255-256]

1. "Imperfect" defenses: Mostly, these other kinds of voluntary manslaughter are situations in which what would otherwise be a *complete defense or justification* does not exist due to D's unreasonable mistake or for some other reason: [255]

a. Imperfect self-defense: Thus some states give D a manslaughter verdict for *"imperfect self-defense,"* where D killed to defend himself but is not entitled to an acquittal because: (1) he was unreasonably mistaken about the existence of danger; or (2) he was unreasonably mistaken about the need for deadly force; or (3) he was the aggressor. [255]

b. Imperfect defense of others: Similarly, if D uses deadly force in *defense of another*, but does not meet all of the requirements for exculpation, some courts give him the lesser charge of voluntary manslaughter. (*Example:* If D witnesses a fight between V and X, and honestly but unreasonably concludes that X was the aggressor, D may be entitled to manslaughter for killing V.) [255]

c. Other situations: If D comes close to qualifying for the defense of *prevention of crime*, or *necessity* or *coercion*, he may be similarly entitled to reduction to manslaughter. [255]

2. Mercy killings: Some courts — and many juries — frequently give D a lesser verdict of voluntary manslaughter when he commits a *mercy killing*, i.e., a killing to terminate the life of one suffering from a painful or incurable disease. [256]

3. Intoxication rarely suffices: Most states do *not* permit D's voluntary *intoxication* to reduce murder to manslaughter. [256]

VI. MANSLAUGHTER — INVOLUNTARY

A. **Involuntary manslaughter based on criminal negligence:** A person whose behavior is *grossly negligent* may be liable for *involuntary manslaughter* if his conduct results in the accidental death of another person. [257-259]

1. **Gross negligence required:** Nearly all states hold that *something more than ordinary tort negligence* must be shown before D is liable for involuntary manslaughter. Most states require *"gross negligence"*. Usually, D must be shown to have disregarded a very substantial danger not just of bodily harm, but of *serious* bodily harm or death. [257]

   a. **Model Penal Code:** The MPC requires that D act *"recklessly."* (The MPC also requires that D be aware of the risk, as discussed below.) [257]

2. **All circumstances considered:** The existence of gross negligence is to be measured in light of *all the "circumstances."* The *social utility* of any objective D is trying to fulfill is part of the equation. [257]

   Example: D kills V, a pedestrian, by driving at 50 mph in a 30 mph residential zone. D's conduct may be grossly negligent if D was out for a pleasure spin, but not if D was rushing his critically ill wife to the hospital.

3. **"Inherently dangerous" objects:** Where D uses an object that is *"inherently dangerous,"* the courts are quicker to find him guilty of involuntary manslaughter. This is especially true where the accident involves a *firearm*. [258]

4. **Defendant's awareness of risk:** Courts are split as to whether D may be liable for manslaughter if he was *unaware* of the risk posed by his conduct. [258]

   a. **Awareness usually required:** As noted, most states require D to have acted with "gross negligence" or "recklessness." In these states, courts usually require that D have been *actually aware* of the danger. [258]

      i. **Model Penal Code agrees:** The MPC, which requires "recklessness" for involuntary manslaughter, similarly requires actual awareness. Under the MPC, a person acts recklessly only when he *consciously disregards* a substantial and unjustifiable risk. [258]

5. **Victim's contributory negligence:** The fact that the *victim* was *contributorily negligent* is *not* a defense to manslaughter. (However, the victim's negligence may tend to show that the accident was proximately caused by this action on the victim's part, rather than by any gross negligence on D's part.) [259]

6. **Vehicular homicide:** Many states have defined the lesser crime of *vehicular homicide*, for cases in which death has occurred as the result of the defendant's poor driving, but where the driving was not reckless or grossly negligent. (Most successful involuntary manslaughter cases also involve death by automobile.) [259]

   a. **Intoxication statutes:** Also, some states have special statutes which make it a crime to cause death by *driving while intoxicated*. [259]

   b. **Criminally negligent homicide:** Additionally, some states define the crime of *"criminally negligent homicide,"* whose penalties are typically less than the penalties for involuntary manslaughter. These statutes are not limited to vehicular deaths. (*Example:* The MPC defines the crime of "negligent homicide," which covers cases where D behaves with gross negligence, but is *not aware* of the risk posed by his conduct.) [259]

B. **The misdemeanor-manslaughter rule:** Just as the felony-murder rule permits a *murder* conviction when a death occurs during the course of certain felonies, so the *"misdemeanor-manslaughter"* rule permits a conviction for *involuntary manslaughter* when a death occurs accidentally during the commission of a misdemeanor or other *unlawful act*. [259-261]

1. **Most states apply:** Most states continue to apply the misdemeanor-manslaughter rule. [259]

2. **Substitute for criminal negligence:** The theory behind the rule is that the unlawful act is treated as a *substitute for criminal negligence* (by analogy to the "negligence *per se*" doctrine in tort law). [259]

3. **"Unlawful act" defined:** *Any misdemeanor* may serve as the basis for application of the misdemeanor-manslaughter doctrine. Also, some states permit the prosecution to show that D violated a *local ordinance* or *administrative regulation*. And if a particular *felony* does not suffice for the felony-murder rule (e.g., because it is not "inherently dangerous to life"), it may be used. [259]

   a. **Battery:** The most common misdemeanor in misdemeanor-manslaughter cases is *battery*. [260]

      Example: D gets into an argument with V, and gives him a light tap on the chin with his fist. D intends only to stun V. Unbeknownst to D, V is a hemopheliac and bleeds to death. Since D has committed the misdemeanor of simple battery, and a death has resulted, he is guilty of manslaughter under the misdemeanor-manslaughter rule. The same result would occur if as the result of the light tap, V fell and fatally hit his head on the sidewalk.

   b. **Traffic violations:** The violation of *traffic laws* is another frequent source of misdemeanor-manslaughter liability. [260]

      Example: D fails to stop at a stop sign, and hits V, a pedestrian crossing at a crosswalk. V dies. Even if D does not have the "gross negligence" typically required for ordinary voluntary manslaughter, D's violation of the traffic rule requiring that one stop at stop signs will be enough to make him guilty of manslaughter under the misdemeanor-manslaughter rule.

4. **Causation:** There must be a *causal relation* between the violation and the death. [260]

   a. *Malum in se:* In the case of a violation that is *"malum in se"* (dangerous in itself, such as driving at an excessive speed), the requisite causal relationship is often found so long as the violation is the "cause in fact" of the death, even though it was not "natural and probable" or even "foreseeable" that the death would occur. That is, in *malum in se* cases, the usual requirement of "proximate cause" is often suspended. [260]

   b. *Malum prohibitum:* But if D's offense is *"malum prohibitum,"* (i.e., not dangerous in itself, but simply in violation of a *public-welfare* regulation), most states do require a showing that the violation was the proximate cause of the death. [260-261]

      i. **"Natural" or "foreseeable" result:** Some courts impose a requirement of proximate cause by holding that the death must be the *"natural"* or *"foreseeable"* consequence of the unlawful conduct. (*Example:* D fails to renew his driver's license, and then runs over V, a pedestrian. A court might well hold that since failure to renew a driver's license is *malum prohibitum*, and since V's death was not a "natural" or "probable" consequence of D's failure, D is not guilty under the misdemeanor-manslaughter rule.)

    ii. Violation irrelevant: Other courts simply do not apply the misdemeanor-manslaughter rule at all to conduct that is *malum prohibitum* — D's conduct must be shown to amount to actual criminal negligence, just as if there had been no violation.

  5. Model Penal Code abolishes: The Model Penal Code *rejects* the misdemeanor-manslaughter rule in its entirety. However, under the MPC, the fact that an act is unlawful may be *evidence* that the act was reckless (the Code's *mens rea* for manslaughter). [261]

VII. ASSAULT, BATTERY AND MAYHEM

A. Battery: The crime of *battery* exists where D causes either: (1) *bodily injury*; or (2) *offensive touching*. [266-267]

  1. Injury or offensive touching: Any kind of physical injury, even a bruise from a blow, will meet the physical harm requirement. Also, in most states an *offensive touching* will suffice. (*Example:* D, without V's consent, kisses V. Since this is an offensive touching, it will constitute battery in most states even though V was not physically injured.) [266]

  2. Mental state: D's *intent* to inflict the offensive touching or the injury will suffice, of course. But also, in most states, if the contact is committed *recklessly*, or with gross negligence, this will also suffice. [266]

    Example: D throws a baseball with a friend, in a crowded city street. The ball strikes V, a passerby. If a court finds that D behaved recklessly, he will probably be guilty of battery, even though he did not intend to touch or injure V.

  3. Degrees of battery: Simple battery is generally a misdemeanor. However, most states have one or more additional, aggravated, forms of battery, some of which are felonies. (*Examples:* Some states make it aggravated battery if D uses a deadly weapon, or acts with "intent to kill" or with "intent to rape.") [266]

B. Assault: The crime of *assault* exists where either: (1) D *attempts to commit a battery*, and fails; or (2) D places another in *fear of imminent injury*. [267-268]

  1. Attempted-battery assault: D is guilty of assault if he *unsuccessfully attempts* to commit a battery. (*Example:* D shoots at V, attempting to hit him in the leg. The bullet misses. D is guilty of the attempted-battery form of assault.) [267]

  2. Intentional-frightening assault: Some states also recognize a second form of assault, that in which D intentionally *frightens his victim* into fearing *immediate bodily harm*. [267]

    Example: During an attempted bank robbery, D points his gun at V, a customer at the bank, and says, "One false step and I'll fill you full of lead." This is assault of the intentional-frightening variety; the fact that D's threat is conditional does not prevent the crime from existing.

    a. Words alone: *Words alone* will *not* suffice for assault. The words must be accompanied by some overt gesture (e.g., the pointing of a gun) or other physical act. [267]

  3. Aggravated assault: Simple assault is a misdemeanor. However, most states recognize various kinds of felonious *aggravated assault* (e.g., "assault with intent to kill" or "assault with intent to rape"). [268]

C. Mayhem: The common-law crime of *mayhem* is committed whenever D intentionally *maims* or permanently *disables* his victim. Thus mayhem is a battery causing *great bodily harm*. [268]

   1. **Injury must be permanent:** The injury must not only be serious, but *permanent*. (*Example:* It is not mayhem to break V's jaw, or to cut him with a knife in a way that causes a small scar. On the other hand, it is mayhem to cut out V's eye, or to make him a cripple by shooting off his kneecap.) [268]

VIII. RAPE

   A. **Rape defined:** Rape is generally defined as *unlawful sexual intercourse with a female without her consent*. [268-271]

   1. **Intercourse:** It is not necessary that D achieve an emission. All that is required is that there be a sexual *penetration*, however slight. [268]

   2. **The spousal exception:** Common-law rape requires that the victim be one *other than the defendant's wife*. However, this complete spousal exemption at common law has been weakened by statutory reform. [269]

      a. **Forcible rape even while living together:** A substantial minority of states now permit prosecution for *forcible rape* even if H and W are living together. In other words, in these states, the spousal exemption is virtually eliminated. [269]

      b. **Separated or living apart:** An additional substantial minority eliminate the spousal exemption based on the parties' current living arrangements or marital status. Some of these eliminate the exemption where the parties are *not living together*. Others eliminate it only if the parties are separated by court order, or one has filed for divorce or separation. [269]

   3. **Without consent:** The intercourse must occur without the woman's *consent*. [269]

      a. **Victim drunk or drugged:** If D causes V to become *drunk*, *drugged* or *unconscious*, the requisite lack of consent is present. In some but not all states, consent is lacking if the woman is drunk, drugged or unconscious even if this condition was not induced by D. [269]

      b. **Fraud:** If consent is obtained by *fraud*, the status depends on the nature of the fraud. Where D tells a lie in order to induce V to agree to have what V knows is intercourse with him, the fraud is "in the inducement" and does *not* vitiate the consent. (*Example:* D says to V, "Have sex with me, and I promise we'll get married tomorrow." Even if D is knowingly misleading V about the probability of marriage, D has not committed rape.) [269]

         i. **Fraud in the essence:** But if the fraud is such that V does not even realize that she is having intercourse at all ("fraud in the essence"), this will suffice for rape. (*Example:* D, a doctor, has sex with V by telling her that he is treating her with a surgical instrument. This is rape.) [269]

      c. **Mistake as to consent:** If D makes a *reasonable mistake* as to whether V consented, he does *not* have the *mens rea* for rape. If D's mistake, however, is a negligent or reckless one, courts are split about whether it furnishes a defense. [269]

   4. **Force:** The vast majority of rape statutes apply only where the intercourse is committed by *"force"* or "forcible compulsion." In other words, it is not enough that the woman fails to consent; she must also be "forced" to have the intercourse. (If the woman is unconscious or drugged, or is under-age, force is not an element of the crime; but in other instances of rape, force is required.) [269-271]

    a. **Threat of force:** D's *threat* to commit *imminent serious bodily harm* on the woman will be a substitute for the use of actual physical force, in virtually all states. Some states also recognize the threat to do other kinds of acts not involving serious bodily harm (e.g., a threat of "extreme pain or kidnapping" may suffice under the Model Penal Code). [270]

        i. **Implied threats or threats of non-imminent harm:** On the other hand, *implied threats*, or threats to commit harm on some *future occasion*, or *duress* stemming from the victim's circumstances, are all things that will *not suffice*, because they are not threats to use force on the particular occasion. [270]

    b. **Resistance:** Traditionally, rape did not exist unless the woman *physically resisted*. This requirement is gradually being weakened. [270]

        i. **Reasonable resistance:** No state requires that the woman resist "to the utmost" anymore, as some states used to. Typically, the woman must now make merely *"reasonable"* resistance, as measured by the circumstances. (*Example:* Where D is threatening V with a gun or knife, presumably it is "reasonable" for V not to resist at all.) [270]

  5. **Homosexual rape:** Because common-law rape is defined so as to require both penetration and a female victim, there can be no common-law *homosexual rape*. (However, a majority of states have amended their rape statutes to be gender-neutral, so that homosexual rape is now the same crime as heterosexual rape in most states.) [271-271]

B. **Statutory rape:** All states establish an *age of consent*, below which the law regards a female's consent as *impossible*. One who has intercourse with a female below this age is punished for what is usually called "statutory rape." [271]

  1. **Reasonable mistake:** In most states, even a *reasonable belief* by D that the girl was over the age of consent is not a defense. [271]

    a. **MPC allows:** But the Model Penal Code allows the "reasonable mistake as to age" defense, at least where the offense is garden-variety statutory rape (intercourse with a girl under the age of 16). [272]

  2. **Encouragement by girl:** The fact that the under-age girl has *encouraged* the sex is irrelevant. Also, the fact that the girl has lied about her age is no defense (unless it contributes to D's reasonable mistake as to age, in a state recognizing reasonable mistake as a defense). [271]

IX. KIDNAPPING

A. **Definition of kidnapping:** Kidnapping is the *unlawful confinement* of another, accompanied by either a *moving* of the victim or a *secreting* of him. [272]

  1. **Asportation:** Assuming that the crime does not involve secret imprisonment, the prosecution must show that the victim was *moved* ("asportation"). [272]

    a. **Large distance not required:** The asportation need not be over a large distance. (*Example:* D accosts V on the street, and makes her walk a few feet to his car, where he detains her. The requisite asportation will probably be found.) [272]

    b. **Must not be incidental to some other offense:** However, the asportation must not be merely *incidental to some other offense*. [272]

Example: D, in order to rob V, forces him to stand up and put his hands against the wall, while D empties V's pockets. There is probably no asportation since there was no independent purpose to the confinement and movement; therefore, there is probably no kidnapping. But if B had been bound and gagged and left in a strange place to allow D to escape, this probably *would* be kidnapping.

CHAPTER 9

THEFT CRIMES

I. INTRODUCTION

A. List of theft crimes: There are seven crimes that can loosely be called "theft" crimes: [283]

1. *Larceny*

2. *Embezzlement*

3. *False pretenses*

4. *Receipt of stolen property*

5. *Burglary*

6. *Robbery*

7. *Extortion* (blackmail) [283]

B. Distinguishing the basic three: The three "basic" theft crimes are *larceny*, *embezzlement* and *false pretenses*. Most exam questions relating to theft focus on the distinctions among these three categories. Therefore, you must focus on two particular dividing lines: [283]

1. **Larceny vs. embezzlement:** First, focus on the dividing line between *larceny* and *embezzlement*. This comes down to the question, "Was possession originally obtained unlawfully [larceny] or lawfully [embezzlement]?" [283-284]

2. **Larceny vs. false pretenses:** Second, focus on the dividing line between *larceny* and *false pretenses*. This comes down to the question, "What was obtained unlawfully, mere possession [larceny] or title [false pretenses]?" [284]

Note on consolidation: Some American states have now consolidated the three main theft crimes into one basic crime of "theft." But for the most part, you will generally be called upon to make these distinctions among the three common-law crimes. [284]

II. LARCENY

A. Definition: Common-law larceny is defined as follows: [284]

1. The *trespassory*

2. *taking* and

3. *carrying away* of

4. *personal property*

5. of *another* with

6. *intent to steal*.

Example: D, a pickpocket, removes V's wallet from V's pocket, and runs away with it, without V discovering for some time what has happened. D has committed common-law larceny. That is, he has taken property that belonged to another and that was in the other's possession, and has carried it away, with an intent to steal it.

B. Trespassory taking: The requirement of a "trespassory taking" means that if D is *already in rightful possession* of the property at the time he appropriates it to his own use, he cannot be guilty of larceny. [284-288]

> **Example:** D rents a car from V, a car-rental agency. At the time D consummates the rental transaction, he intends to use the car for one week (and so notifies V), then return it. After the week has passed, D decides to keep the car permanently, without paying any further rental fee. At common law, D is not guilty of larceny. This is because at the time he made the decision to appropriate the car, he was already in rightful possession, under the rental contract. But if at the moment D rented the car he intended to steal it, this would be a "trespassory taking" and thus larceny.

1. Taking by employee: Where an *employee* steals property belonging to the employer, and the employee had at least some physical control over the property at the time he made the decision to steal it, the existence of the requisite "trespassory taking" can be unclear. [286-286]

a. Minor employee: If the employee is a relatively low-level one, the court is likely to hold that she had only *custody*, so that the employer retained possession. In this event, the employee would commit the necessary trespass, and would be guilty of common-law larceny. [286]

> **Example:** D is an entry-level bank clerk at V, a bank. D takes a stack of $100 bills out of her cash drawer, and walks out of the bank with them. A court would probably hold that D had only temporary "custody" of the bills in her cash register, not true "possession." Therefore, when D left the bank with the bills, she trespassorily took the bills from V's possession, and is guilty of common-law larceny.

i. Property received from third person: But if the low-level employee receives property for the employer's benefit from a *third person*, the employee will generally be deemed to have possession, not mere custody — if he then later appropriates it, he is not guilty of larceny.

> **Example:** D, a messenger, works for V, a business. D goes to the bank and picks up money from the bank, which is V's property needed for payroll. Here, D has possession, not mere custody, so if he then absconds with the money he is not guilty of larceny. Instead, he would be guilty of embezzlement.

b. High employee: If the employee is one who has a *high position*, with broad authority, he will usually be deemed to have possession, not just custody, of property that he holds for the employer's benefit. Therefore, if he subsequently appropriates the property for his own purposes, he is not guilty of larceny, but rather, embezzlement. [286]

> **Example:** D, the president of V, a publicly-held corporation, has the right to sign checks on V's bank accounts. He writes a check for $1,000, which he uses for his own purposes, and in a way that is not authorized by his employment contract with V. D has possession of the contents of the bank account, not mere custody, so his use of the money for his own purposes is embezzlement rather than larceny.

2. **Transactions in owner's presence:**   If the owner of property delivers it to D as part of an exchange transaction which the owner *intends to be completed in his presence*, D receives only custody, and the owner retains "constructive possession." Therefore, if D appropriates the property, the requisite trespass exists, and the crime is larceny. [286]

   Example: D drives into V's gas station. He asks for his tank to be filled up, and drives off without paying. Since the transaction was to be completed in V's presence, V retained "constructive possession" of the gas, and D's driving away was a trespassory taking and thus larceny. Some courts might call this "larceny by trick," but this is merely a particular way in which larceny can be committed, not a separate crime.

3. **Lost or mislaid property:**   Where D finds *lost or mislaid property*, he may or may not commit the requisite trespass, depending on his state of mind at the time of the finding. [287-288]

   a. **Initial intent to keep it:**   If D *intends to keep the property* at the time he finds it, he has committed the requisite trespass, and can be liable for larceny. (But he will not be guilty of larceny unless he also either knows who the owner is, or has reason to believe that he may be *able to find out* who and where the owner is. If D does not have such knowledge or reasonable belief at the time of finding, he does not become guilty of common-law larceny even if, subsequently, he discovers the owner's identity.) [287]

   b. **No initial intent to keep:**   Conversely, if D does *not* intend to keep the property at the time he finds it (that is, he intends to try to return it to the owner), his possession is rightful and there is no trespass. Then, if D later changes his mind and does keep the property, he is *not guilty of larceny* at common law, since he is already in lawful possession. [287]

   c. **Property delivered by mistake:**   The same rules apply where the owner of the property delivers it to D *by mistake* — D is not guilty of larceny, unless *at the time he receives the property*, he both realizes the mistake and intends to keep the property. [287]

   d. **MPC changes rule:**   The Model Penal Code changes the common-law trespass rules in cases of lost, mislaid or misdelivered property. Under the MPC, D's intent at the time he obtains the property is *irrelevant* — instead, D becomes liable for theft if "with purpose to deprive the owner thereof, he *fails to take reasonable measures* to *restore the property* to a person entitled to have it." [288]

   Example: D finds a wallet on the street, with money in it. At the time he picks it up, he intends to return it to V, its owner, who is identified on a driver's license inside the wallet. After D keeps the wallet on his dresser for two days, he decides, "I think I'll just keep it — no one will ever know." At common law, D is not guilty of larceny, because at the time he found the wallet, he intended to return it V. But under the MPC, D becomes guilty of larceny at the moment he decides to keep the property and fails to take reasonable steps to get it back to V.

4. **Larceny by trick:**   If D gains possession of property by *fraud or deceit*, the requisite trespassory taking takes place. The larceny in this situation is said to be *"by trick"* — larceny by trick is simply one way in which larceny may be committed, not a separate crime. [288]

   Example: D rents a car from V, a car rental agency. At the moment of the rental transaction, D has already decided that he will not return the car, and will not pay for it. D has committed larceny of the "by trick" variety, because his initial taking of possession was obtained by fraud or deceit.

a. **Distinguished from false pretenses:** Distinguish the taking of possession by fraud or deceit (leading to larceny by trick) from the taking of *title* by fraud or deceit (which is not larceny at all). If title passes, the crime is theft by false pretenses. [288]

C. **Carrying away ("asportation"):** D, to commit larceny, must not only commit a trespassory taking, but must also *carry the property away*. This is called *"asportation."* [289-289]

1. **Slight distance sufficient:** However, as long as every portion of the property is moved, even a *slight distance* will suffice. [289]

   Example: D enters V's car, turns on the lights and starts the engine. At that point he is arrested. At common law, this would probably not be enough movement to satisfy the asportation requirement. But many courts today would hold that since D brought the car under his dominion and control, he did enough to satisfy the requirement. If D drove the car even a few feet, *all* courts would agree that he had met the asportation requirement.

D. **Personal property of another:** Common-law larceny exists only where the property that is taken is *tangible personal property*. [289]

1. **Intangibles:** Thus at common law, one could not commit larceny of *intangible* personal property, such as stocks, bonds, checks, notes, etc. But today, all states have expanded larceny to cover many intangible items such as stocks and bonds; some states also cover such items as gas and electricity and services. [289]

2. **Trade secrets:** Some courts have held that the taking of *trade secrets* can constitute larceny. [289]

E. **Property of another:** The property taken, to constitute larceny, must be property *belonging to another*. Where D and another person are *co-owners*, the common-law view is that there can be no larceny. [290]

1. **Recapture of chattel:** If D is attempting to *retake* a *specific chattel* that belongs to him, D will not be guilty of larceny, because he is not taking property "of another." In most states, this is also true if D is genuinely *mistaken* (even if unreasonably) in thinking that the thing he is taking belongs to himself rather than the other person. But this rule does not apply where D is taking *cash* or some other property in satisfaction of a *debt* (though the "claim of right" defense may exist here; see *infra*, p. C-86). [290]

   Example 1: D's bicycle is stolen. Two days later he sees what is apparently the same bike, chained to a lamp post. D genuinely believes that this is his own stolen bike. He cuts the chain and removes the bike. If the bike was in fact his own, D is clearly not guilty of larceny, because he has not taken the property "of another." If D genuinely believes that the bike was his — even if this belief is unreasonable — most courts will similarly hold that he has not committed larceny.

   Example 2: D is owed $100 by V. D sees V's bicycle (worth $75) parked on the street. If D takes the bike as a substitute form of payment, he probably cannot defend on the grounds that the bike is not "property of another." On the other hand, most states would allow him to raise the "claim of right" defense, discussed in Par. F(2) below.

F. **Intent to steal:** Larceny is a crime that can only be committed *intentionally*, not negligently or recklessly. [291-293]

1. **Intent to permanently deprive owner:**   D must thus generally be shown to have an intent to *permanently deprive* the owner of his property. An intent to take property *temporarily* is not sufficient. [291]

    Example: D enters V's car, intending to take it on a three-mile "joy ride." After one mile, D crashes the car, destroying it totally. At common law, D is not guilty of larceny, because he did not intend to permanently deprive V of his property.

    a. **Substantial deprivation:**   But if D intends to use the property for such a long time, or in such a way, that the owner will be deprived of a *significant portion of the property's economic value*, the requisite intent to steal exists. [291]

        Example: D takes a lawnmower belonging to V, with an intent to keep it all summer and fall. This probably constitutes larceny, because D intends to deprive V of a substantial part of the useful life of the mower.

    b. **Issue is intent, not result:**   The issue regarding permanent-or-substantial-deprivation is D's *intent*, not what actually happens. [291]

        Example: In the above example concerning the joy ride, D did not meet the intent-to steal requirement because he did not intend to permanently deprive V of the car, even though this was the result of D's acts. Conversely, if D takes a car with intent to resell it or strip it for parts, D will not avoid a larceny conviction because the police stop him one block away with the car in perfect condition.

2. **Claim of right:**   If D takes another's property under a *claim of right*, D will not be found to have had the requisite guilty intent. [292-293]

    a. **Money taken to satisfy claim:**   Thus if D takes V's property with an intent to *collect a debt* which V owes D, or to satisfy some other kind of *claim* which D has against V, D will not be guilty of larceny. D is especially likely to have a good defense where D's claim against V is a "liquidated" one, that is, one is with a fixed monetary value. [292]

        Example: D works for V. V fires D, and illegally refuses to pay D D's last week of wages, equaling $100. D reaches into V's cash register and removes $100 and walks out with it. D is not guilty of larceny, because his intent was to collect a debt which V owed him.

        i. **Mistake:**   Most significantly, D lacks the requisite intent for larceny even if he is *mistaken* about the validity of his claim against V. And this is true even if D's mistake is *unreasonable*, so long as it is sincere. [292]

            Example: D works for V. V fires D, and refuses to pay him for three weeks of vacation pay, which D genuinely believes is owed to him. Assume that under applicable legal principles, and as any reasonably knowledgeable employee would understand, D was not entitled to any vacation pay, because D had taken all the vacation to which he was entitled up to the moment he was fired. D nonetheless reaches into V's cash register and removes three weeks' pay. D is not guilty of larceny, because he took pursuant to an honest, though unreasonable and mistaken, belief that he had a legally-enforceable claim against V for the money.

    b. **Usually not a defense to robbery:**   Most states hold that the "claim of right" defense is *not available* where D is charged with a crime of *violence*, including *robbery*. [292]

        Example: V owes D $25. D and V meet on the street, and V refuses to pay any of the money back, even though it is overdue. D sees that V has the entire sum owed, $25, on V's person. D takes the $25 back by force. Most courts would hold that this is robbery, because the "claim of right" defense is not available for crimes of violence such as robbery. [*People v. Reid*, 508 N.E.2d 661 (N.Y.1987)]

III. EMBEZZLEMENT

A. Definition: Embezzlement usually is defined as follows: [294-298]

1. A *fraudulent*

2. *conversion* of

3. the *property*

4. of *another*

5. by one who is *already in lawful possession* of it. [294]

B. No overlap with larceny: Embezzlement statutes are generally construed so as *not to overlap* with larceny — a given fact pattern must be either larceny or embezzlement, and cannot be both. [295]

C. Conversion: For most larceny, D needs only to take and carry away the property. But for embezzlement, D must *convert it*, i.e., deprive the owner of a significant part of its usefulness. If D merely uses the property for a short time, or moves it slightly, he is not guilty of embezzlement (regardless of whether he *intended* to convert it.) [295]

> **Example:** D's boss lends D the company car to do a company errand, and D decides to abscond with it or sell it. The police stop D after he has driven the car for one mile. D is not technically guilty of embezzlement, since he has not yet deprived the company of a significant part of the car's usefulness, and thus has not converted it.

D. Property of another: The property must be *"property of another."* [295-297]

1. **Meaning of "property":** Embezzlement statutes typically are somewhat broader than larceny statutes, in terms of the *property* covered. Anything that can be taken by larceny may be embezzled (i.e., not just tangible personal property but, for instance, stocks and bonds). Also, some embezzlement statutes cover real property (e.g., D uses a power of attorney received from O to deed O's property to D.) [295]

2. **Property "of another":** The property must be property belonging to *another* rather than to D. [295-297]

   a. **D to pay from own funds:** Thus if D has an obligation to *make payment from his own funds*, he *cannot embezzle* even if he fraudulently fails to make the payment. [295-296]

   Example: D, a coal mine operator, has his employees sign orders directing D to deduct from their wages the amount that each owes to a grocery store. D deducts the amount, but then fails to pay the store owner. D is not guilty of common-law embezzlement, because he did not misappropriate the employees' money, but rather, failed to make payment from his own funds. He is civilly liable but not criminally liable. [*Commonwealth v. Mitchneck*, 198 A. 463 (Pa. 1938)]

   i. **Model Penal Code changes:** The Model Penal Code changes the common law rule described above, by creating a new crime of "theft by failure to make the required disposition of funds received." The provision applies wherever D not only agrees to make a payment but ***reserves funds*** for this obligation. D in *Mitchneck, supra,* would be liable under the MPC rule.

b. Co-owners: One who is ***co-owner*** of the property together with another cannot, at common law, embezzle the joint property, because it is deemed to be his "own." Thus one ***partner*** in a business cannot commit common-law embezzlement against the other. (But some modern embezzlement statutes explicitly apply to co-owned property.)

c. Security interest: Suppose D ***buys goods on credit***, and gives the seller a *"security interest,"* entitling the seller to ***repossess*** the goods if D does not pay the price. If D then fails to repay the money and sells the goods in violation of the security agreement, this will usually ***not*** be treated as embezzlement. [296]

E. "By one in lawful possession": The main distinction between larceny and embezzlement is that embezzlement is committed by one who is ***already in lawful possession*** of the property before he appropriates it to his own use. [297-298]

Example: D, a lawyer, is appointed trustee of a trust for the benefit of V. The trust principal consists of $10,000, held by D in a bank account named "D in trust for V." D takes the money and buys a new car for himself. D is guilty of embezzlement, because he took property of which he was already in lawful possession.

1. Employees: Most commonly, embezzlers are ***employees*** who misappropriate property with which there employer has entrusted them. [297-298]

a. Minor employee: But remember that a ***low-level employee*** may be held to have received only ***custody*** of the item, not true "possession." If such a minor employee takes the property for his own purposes, he would be committing larceny rather than embezzlement. (Many states have changed this rule by statute, however — they make it embezzlement rather than larceny for any employee to take property in his possession or "under his care," thus covering even low-level employees who have only custody.) [298]

2. Finders: Recall that one who finds ***lost or mislaid property***, or to whom property is ***mistakenly delivered***, is not guilty of common law larceny if he gains possession without intent to steal (see *supra*, pp. C79-C79). But most embezzlement statutes don't cover this situation either. However, some states have special *"larceny by bailee"* statutes covering this situation, and other states have embezzlement statutes that explicitly cover finders and other bailees. [298]

F. Fraudulent taking: The taking must be *"fraudulent."* [298-299]

1. Claim of right: Thus if D honestly believes that he has a ***right*** to take the property, this will usually negate the existence of fraud. Thus if D mistakenly believes that the property is ***his***, or that he is authorized to use it in a certain way, this will be a defense (probably even if the mistake is unreasonable). [298]

2. Debt collection: Similarly, if D takes the property in order to ***collect a debt*** owed to him by the owner (or even a debt which D believes the owner owes him), D is not an embezzler. [298]

Example: D, president of V Corp., is dismissed by the board of directors. The board refuses to pay D a $20,000 bonus, which D genuinely believes the company was contractually committed to pay D for D's work in the prior year. D writes himself out a check for $20,000. D's taking here is probably not "fraudulent" and D is not an embezzler, even if D's claim of right was a mistaken one.

3. **Intent to repay:** If D takes *money*, it is *no defense* to an embezzlement charge that D *intended to repay* the money. This is true even if D has a complete *ability* to repay the money. [299]

Example: D, president of V Corp., "borrows" $10,000 from the corporate treasury with which to play the stock market. At the time of this borrowing, D has a net worth of several million dollars, and honestly intends to repay the money within one week. D is arrested before he can repay the money. It is clear that D is guilty of embezzlement, despite his intent and ability to repay.

Note: But if the property is something other than money, and D shows that he has an intent to return the *very property taken* (and has a substantial ability to do so at the time of taking), this *will* be a defense to embezzlement. (*Example:* D uses the company car for a two-hour personal trip, intending to return it. He is not an embezzler even if he accidentally destroys the car.)

IV. FALSE PRETENSES

A. **Definition:** The crime of obtaining property by false pretenses — usually called simply *"false pretenses"* — has these elements: [299]

1. A *false representation* of a

2. *material present or past fact*

3. which *causes* the person to whom it is made

4. to *pass title to*

5. his *property* to the misrepresenter, who

6. *knows* that his representation is false, and *intends to defraud*. [299]

B. **Nature of crime:** Thus false pretenses occurs where D uses fraud or deceit to obtain not only possession but also *ownership* (title). The crime differs from larceny with respect to what is obtained: in larceny, D obtains possession only, not title. [300]

C. **False representation of present or past fact:** There must be a *false representation* of a *material present or past fact*. [300-301]

1. **Non-disclosure and concealment:** The false representation is usually an explicit verbal one. But there are other types of misrepresentation that will qualify: [300]

   a. **Reinforcing false impressions:** It is a misrepresentation to knowingly *reinforce a false impression* held by another. [300]

   Example: Buyer wants to buy Seller's ring, which as Seller knows Buyer thinks is diamond. Seller knows that the ring is really glass. Seller quotes a price that would be a low price for diamonds, but hundreds of times too high for glass. Seller has probably committed a false representation as to the nature of the ring by reinforcing what he knows to be Buyer's misconception.

   b. **Concealment:** Similarly, the requisite misrepresentation can exist if D takes affirmative acts to *conceal* a material fact. [300]

   Example: D, owner of a car whose engine block is broken, paints the engine block in such a way as to conceal the defect, then sells the car to V at a price that would be a fair price for a car with a good engine. D would probably be held to have made a misrepresentation by his act of concealment and would therefore be guilty of false pretenses.

c. **Fiduciary relationship:** If D is in a *fiduciary relationship* with the other party, he will generally have an affirmative duty to speak the truth, and is thus not free to remain silent. [300]

Example: D has long been the family jeweler for V and his family. D knows that V trusts D in matters relating to jewelry. V sees a ring in D's window and says, "Oh, what a lovely diamond ring; I'll pay you $1,000." D knows that the ring is cubic zirconium, but remains silent and accepts the $1,000. Because D probably had a fiduciary relationship with V based on their past dealing and V's extra trust in D, D has probably made a misrepresentation and can be guilty of false pretenses.

d. **Silence normally not enough:** But these are all *exceptions* to the *general rule*: a party to a bargaining situation may generally *remain silent* even though he knows that the other party is under a false impression (provided that D did not cause that false impression in the first place). [300]

2. **False promises not sufficient:** Most courts hold that the representation must relate to a *past or present fact*. *False promises*, even when made with an intent not to keep them, are *not* sufficient in most courts. (But an increasing *minority* of courts do treat knowingly false promises as sufficient.) [301-301]

Example: D borrows money from V Bank, promising to repay it on a particular date. D in reality has no intention of ever repaying the money, and plans to abscond with it to South America. In most courts, this is not taking money by false pretenses, but in an increasing minority of courts it is.

D. **Reliance:** The victim must *rely* upon the representation. [301]

1. **Belief required:** Thus if the victim does *not believe* the representation, there is no crime of false pretenses. [301]

2. **Materiality:** Also, the false representation must be a *"material"* one. That is, it must be a representation which would play an important role in a *reasonable person's decision* whether to enter into the transaction. [301]

E. **Passing of title:** Remember that *title*, not merely possession, must pass for false pretenses. Generally, this turns on what the *victim intends* to do. [302-302]

1. **Sale as opposed to loan or lease:** If the victim parts with property in return for other property or money, there is a transfer of title if a *sale* occurs, of course. But if the victim merely *lends* or *leases* his property, only possession has been transferred, so that the offense is larceny by trick rather than false pretenses. [302]

2. **Handing over money:** Where V *hands over money* to D, this will usually be a passing of title, and the crime will thus be false pretenses. (*Example:* D borrows money from V, a bank, by lying on the credit application. The bank is deemed to have passed over title to the money in return for D's promise to repay with interest, so D has committed false pretenses.) [302]

a. **Money for specific purposes:** But if V gives D money with the understanding that D will apply it towards a *particular purpose*, this is likely to be a passage of possession rather than title, and thus larceny rather than false pretenses. This is especially the case where it can be argued that D has taken the money in "constructive trust" for V.

Example: V, a client, gives $1,000 to D, a lawyer who is assisting V in the sale of some property. V tells D that D should use the money to pay off a tax lien against the property. Instead, D gambles away the money. Assuming that from the very moment of the transfer of funds D intended to misuse the money — thus preventing the case from being embezzlement — D would be guilty of larceny rather than false pretenses, because the property was given to him earmarked for a specific purpose.

F. **Property "of another":** The property received by D must have belonged to *"another."* [303]

1. **Joint ownership:** Thus as in embezzlement and larceny, most courts still hold that property D *co-owns* with V is not property of another. [303]

a. **Modern view finds liability:** But modern courts are increasingly likely to hold that where D takes property belonging to himself and a co-owner, this *is* property of "another" and thus false pretenses. [303]

G. **D's mental state:** False pretenses is essentially a crime requiring intent. However, the intent requirement is deemed met if either: (1) D *knows* that the representation is untrue; (2) D *believes*, but does not know, that the representation is untrue; or (3) D *knows that he does not know* whether the representation is true or false. [303]

Example: D has a painting found in his attic, signed "van Gogh." D knows nothing about art or the circumstances in which the painting came to be in his attic. D nonetheless tells V, a prospective amateur buyer who also knows nothing about art, "This painting is a genuine van Gogh." Because D knows that he does not in fact know the provenance of the painting, D has committed the requisite false representation. He is therefore guilty of false pretenses when he makes the sale to V at a price that would be appropriate for a genuine van Gogh.

1. **Unreasonable belief in truth:** But if D *believes* the representation to be true, he is not liable for false pretenses even if his belief is *unreasonable*. [303]

2. **Claim of right:** If D goes through the transaction under a *claim of right*, this will be a defense to false pretenses just as to embezzlement or larceny. This is true, for instance, where D uses subterfuge to collect a debt. [304]

Example: V owes D $1,000, which V has refused to repay in a timely way. D then offers to sell V a ring which D says is a true diamond worth $2,000. The ring is in fact cubic zirconium worth $20. V agrees to buy the ring for $1,000. Assuming that D's purpose in entering into the "fraudulent" transaction was merely to recoup the $1,000 that V owed him, D's misrepresentation is not truly fraudulent, and D is not guilty of false pretenses.

a. **Mistake:** The same is probably true even if D is *mistaken* as to the validity of his claim of right.

H. **Defenses:** [304]

1. **Gullibility of victim:** D may *not* defend a false pretenses case by showing that the misrepresentation was one which would not have deceived an ordinarily intelligent person. In other words, the *victim's gullibility* is no defense. [304]

2. **No pecuniary loss:** Similarly, the fact that V has suffered no actual *pecuniary loss* is usually not a defense. So long as D has knowingly made the requisite material false representation of fact that causes V to transfer property, the fact that the trade may be approximately "even" is irrelevant. [304]

Example: D sells office supplies to V, a large company, by bribing V's purchasing agent. The prices charged by D are "ordinary" prices in the trade, neither as low as some charge nor as high as others charge. D cannot defend a false pretenses prosecution on the grounds that V has suffered no financial loss. This is because D has acquired property (V's money) by fraud, and V would not have paid the money had it known that the sales were procured by bribery of an employee.

I. **Related crimes:** Here are some statutory crimes, found in many jurisdictions, that are related to false pretenses but deal with slightly different situations: [304]

   1. **Bad checks:** Most jurisdictions make it a crime to obtain property by writing a *bad check*. This crime is committed even if the check never clears and the title never transfers (which would not be the case for false pretenses). [304]

   2. **Federal mail fraud:** The *federal mail fraud* statute makes it a crime to use the mails as part of a scheme to defraud a victim of his property. Here, too, the scheme *does not have to be successful* for liability to exist. [304]

   3. **Forgery:** The crime of *forgery* exists where a document (usually a check or other negotiable instrument) is *falsified*. The falsification must relate to the *genuineness* of the instrument itself. Again, it is not necessary that the forged document actually be used to obtain property from another. (*Example:* D steals checks from V, then signs V's name to them. If D is found with the checks in his possession, he is already liable for forgery even if he has not used the checks to gain property.) [305]

V. CONSOLIDATION OF THEFT CRIMES

A. **Consolidation generally:** Some states, though still a minority, have joined two or more of the group of larceny, embezzlement and false pretenses into a *unified* crime called "theft." [305-306]

   1. **MPC consolidation:** The MPC achieves a similar, though not identical, consolidation. Larceny and embezzlement are consolidated as "theft by unlawful taking or disposition." "Larceny by trick" (classically a form of larceny) and false pretenses are combined into "theft by deception." Also, several new crimes are created, including "theft of property lost, mislaid, or delivered by mistake" (which previously could have been either larceny or embezzlement, depending on the facts). [305]

VI. RECEIVING STOLEN PROPERTY

A. **Targetted at fences:** The crime of *"receipt of stolen property"* is directed primarily at *"fences,"* middlemen who buy goods at a very low price from thieves and resell them to end-users. [306]

B. **Elements of offense:** Most stolen property statutes make it a crime to: [306-307]

   1. *receive*

   2. *stolen property*

   3. with *knowledge* that it has been stolen and

   4. with *intent to deprive* the owner. [306]

C. **Discussion:**

1. **"Stolen":** Most statutes cover not only property taken by larceny, but also property that was taken by *embezzlement* or *false pretenses*. [306]

2. **Trap laid by police:** If property is sold by a thief who is cooperating with the police, or by the police themselves, the fence who buys it is *not guilty* of receiving stolen property, even if he believes the property is stolen. This is because the property is no longer in fact stolen. However, the fence will typically be guilty of *attempted* receipt of stolen goods. [306]

3. **Knowledge that property is stolen:** Statutes typically say that D must have *"known"* that the property was stolen. However, knowledge in the sense of certainty is typically *not* required. [306]

   a. **Belief:** Thus in all states, it is enough that D *believes that the goods are stolen*.

   b. **Suspicion:** On the other hand, if D merely *suspected* that the goods might be stolen (in the sense that he recognized a possibility that they were stolen), this will not meet the knowledge requirement. And needless to say, the mere fact that a *reasonable person* in D's position would have suspected that the goods were stolen, or would have believed them to be stolen, is not enough (though this will of course be circumstantial evidence as to what D actually believed). [307]

   c. **Model Penal Code applies presumption:** The MPC institutes a *presumption* that a dealer possesses the required knowledge or belief in some circumstances (e.g., he is found in possession of property stolen from two or more persons on separate occasions, or buys for far below the goods' reasonable value). But under the MPC, the dealer can rebut this presumption. [307]

VII. BURGLARY

A. **Common-law definition:** The common-law crime of burglary is defined as follows: [307]

   1. The *breaking* and

   2. *entering* of

   3. the *dwelling of another*

   4. at *night*

   5. with *intent to commit a felony* therein. [307]

   a. **Modern statutes:** Modern statutes eliminate most of these requirements (as discussed below) for at least the lowest degree of the crime. [307]

B. **Breaking:** At common law, there must be a *"breaking."* This means that an *opening* must be *created* by the burglar. [307-307]

   Example: If Owner simply leaves his door or window *open*, the requisite breaking does not exist. However, no force or violence is needed; the mere opening of a closed but unlocked door, followed by entry, suffices.

   1. **No consent:** Also, breaking does not exist at common law if D is *invited* into the house (assuming that he does not stray into a portion of the house where he was not invited).

   2. **Statutes modify:** Most states no longer require breaking for all degrees of burglary. [307]

C. **Entry:** There must also be, at common law, an *entry* following a breaking. However, it is sufficient that *any part* of D's anatomy enters the structure, even for a moment. [307]

Example: D reaches his hand through a window to grab an item just on the inside of the window; this suffices for breaking and entering, so if D carries the property away, he has committed common-law burglary.

1. **Maintained:** Nearly all states continue to impose the requirement of an entry. [308]

D. **Dwelling of another:** The common law required that the structure be the *dwelling of another*. Thus a place of business did not suffice. [308]

1. **Modified by statute:** All states now have at least one form of statutory burglary that does not require that the structure be a dwelling (though nearly all require that there be either a building or a vehicle). [308]

E. **Nighttime:** At common law, the breaking and entering had to occur *at night*. [308]

1. **Not now required:** No state now requires, for all degrees of burglary, that entry be at night. [308]

F. **Intent to commit felony therein:** At common law, the burglar must, at the time he entered, have *intended to commit a felony* once he got inside. [308]

1. **Crime intended:** Today, an intent to commit a *felony* is not required. However, all states require that D have an intent to commit *some crime* (at least a misdemeanor) within the structure. [308]

VIII. ROBBERY

A. **Definition:** Robbery is defined as *larceny* committed with two additional elements: [308]

1. The property is taken from the *person or presence* of the owner [309]; and

2. The taking is accomplished by using *force* or putting the owner in *fear*. [309]

Example: D accosts V on the street at night, and says to V, "Give me your wallet or I'll punch you in the face." V complies, and D carries the property away. D has committed robbery, because D has committed larceny (the taking and carrying away of the property of another with intent to permanently deprive him of it), and has done so by taking the property from V's person, and putting V in fear of what would happen if he did not comply with D's demand.

B. **Presence or person of V:** The property must be taken from the *presence or person* of its owner. [309]

1. **"Presence" of victim:** Most robberies take place directly from the victim's "person." But it is enough that the taking is from V's *"presence."* The test for "presence" is whether V, if he had not been intimidated or forcibly restrained, could have prevented the taking. [309]

Example: D enters V's house and bedroom. While pointing a gun at V, who is on the bed, D takes V's purse from her dresser, and carries it away. Since the property was taken from V's "presence" — V could have prevented the taking if not intimidated — robbery has taken place even though the taking was not from V's "person."

C. **Use of violence or intimidation:** The taking must be by use of *violence* or *intimidation*. [309]

Example 1: V is walking down the street, and is momentarily distracted by a near collision. D stealthily plucks V's wallet out of V's half-open purse. V does not realize what has happened until some time later. D has committed larceny but not robbery, because D did not use violence or intimidation.

Example 2: Same basic fact pattern as prior example, except that D simply snatches V's purse from her grasp. V has no chance to resist, though she is aware for a fleeting second of what is happening. This is not robbery, because there has been no violence or intimidation. (But if V had been able to put up even a brief struggle, the requisite violence would exist for robbery.)

1. **Intimidation:** A *threat of harm* may suffice in lieu of violence. V must be placed in *apprehension* of harm. (*Example:* D pulls a gun on V, and says, "Your money or your life." This is robbery even though no actual force is used.) [309]

   a. **"Reasonable person" standard not applied:** It is irrelevant that a *"reasonable person"* would not have been apprehensive of bodily harm. Thus if V is frightened of bodily harm due to his unusual timidity, robbery will exist even though most people would not have been afraid. [309]

D. **No simultaneous larceny and robbery:** The same transaction *cannot* give rise to *simultaneous convictions* for larceny and robbery. This is because robbery is a form of larceny, with the additional element of force present. [309]

E. **"Armed" robbery:** One aggravated form of robbery, defined in most states, is *"armed"* robbery. This exists where D uses a *deadly weapon*. [309]

1. **Gun need not be loaded:** Armed robbery is usually found even though D's gun is *unloaded*. Some cases hold that even a *toy pistol* suffices, though probably this would happen only if V is shown to have believed that the pistol was real. [309]

IX. BLACKMAIL AND EXTORTION

A. **Definition:** If D obtains property by a threat of *future harm*, he is guilty of *extortion*. The crime is called "blackmail" in some states (but there is no significant difference between what some states call blackmail and other call extortion). [310]

1. **Distinction:** Distinguish extortion from robbery: robbery exists where the property is taken by use of violence or threat of *immediate* harm, whereas extortion exists where the threat is of future harm. [310]

B. **Nature of threat:** The threat can be of various types: to cause physical harm to V or his family or relatives; to *cause economic injury*; or (most commonly) to *accuse V* of a crime, or to divulge disgracing information about V. [310]

   Example: D secretly photographs V, a married man, in the arms of V's lover. D shows V copies of the photos, and threatens to send the photos to V's wife if V does not pay D $2,000. This is extortion, because D has threatened to cause V future harm (exposure) if V does not give D property.

C. **Attempt by D to recover property:** Suppose D uses threats of future harm to *recover property* that V has taken from D. Courts are split as to whether D may defend against an extortion charge by showing that he was operating under a *"claim of right."* Most courts today would probably allow this defense, provided that D is merely recovering the same property or value that V previously, and wrongfully, took from him. [310]

   Example: D, a storekeeper, watches V shoplift $50 worth of merchandise. D is unable to stop V as V leaves the store. The next day, V comes back to the store. D, after writing down V's license plate number, tells V, "If you don't sign a confession to shoplifting and pay me $50, I will turn you in to the police." Most courts today would probably hold that this is not extortion by D, because D is merely making an effort to reclaim property which V has taken from him.

1. **Reasonable mistake:** Some of the courts allowing D a defense on facts like those in the above example would probably also grant a defense where D has made a ***reasonable mistake*** about whether V owed the property or money to D. (*Example:* On the facts of the above example, some courts would grant D a defense to extortion if he showed that he mistakenly, but reasonably, believed that V had stolen $50 of merchandise.) [310]

    a. **MPC allows:** The Model Penal Code seems to take this approach, by granting a defense if D "honestly claimed [the property] as restitution…or as compensation for property or lawful services." [310]

CHAPTER 1

ACTUS REUS AND *MENS REA*

Introductory note: All crimes have several basic common elements. This chapter treats all but one of the major ones: (1) a *voluntary act* ("*actus reus*"); (2) a *culpable intent* ("*mens rea*"); and (3) *"concurrence"* between the *mens rea* and the *actus reus* (i.e., a showing that the act was the result of the culpable intention). The fourth major element, *causation* of harm, is discussed in the following chapter, *infra*, p. 44.

I. *ACTUS REUS*

A. Significance of *"actus reus"* concept: The requirement that the defendant have committed a voluntary act ("*actus reus*") can best be understood by analyzing three basic kinds of situations in which the requirement may be held not to have been met. The required voluntary act is distinguished from: (1) *thoughts*, *words*, states of *possession* and *status*; (2) *involuntary acts* (e.g. sleep-walking); and (3) *omissions* (i.e., failure to act).

B. Distinguished from thoughts, words, possession and status: *Mere thoughts* are never punishable as crimes. Even the crime of conspiracy, and the various crimes of attempt, exist only where the defendant has gone beyond thoughts, however evil and detailed, and committed an *overt act*. The refusal to punish mere thoughts stems both from fears of "thought control" as well as from practical problems of enforcement and proof.

1. Statement of intent made to third party: Even if the defendant has confessed his evil intent to some third person, this will usually not be enough to constitute the *actus reus*. For instance, a statement "I intend to kill X" would not constitute the requisite criminal act. See K&S, p. 179-181.

  a. Words as acts: But there a few situations in which, by the nature of the crime in question, words may constitute the requisite act. For instance, in some jurisdictions, an agreement between two persons to commit a crime is a sufficient act to constitute conspiracy; similarly, words spoken to encourage another to commit a crime might well be enough to give rise to a prosecution for aiding and abetting criminal activity. See K&S, p. 179-181.

2. Possession as criminal act: Mere *possession* of an object may sometimes constitute the necessary criminal act. For instance, possession of narcotics frequently constitutes a crime in itself.

  a. Knowledge of possession: However, the act of "possession" is almost always construed so as to include only *conscious* possession. Thus if the prosecution fails to prove that the defendant knew that he had narcotics on his person, there can be no conviction.

b. Knowledge of guilty character of object: But for possession to be a criminal act, it is not necessarily required that the defendant have been aware of the object's *illegal or contraband nature*.

Example: D is prosecuted for possession of marijuana, and is convicted.

Held, on appeal, D was entitled to have the jury instructed that it could not find him guilty unless it was convinced that he knew that he had the marijuana in his possession. But he was not entitled to have an instruction that he could be convicted only if he knew that the drug was illegal contraband. *People v. Gory*, 170 P.2d 433 (Cal. 1946).

c. Model Penal Code: The Model Penal Code provides that possession can be a criminal act only if the defendant knew he had possession of the object, *and* "was aware of his control thereof for a sufficient period to have been able to terminate his possession." M.P.C. § 2.01(4).

d. Presumptions: The prosecutor's burden of proving knowing possession is frequently made easier by *statutory presumptions*. For instance, New York Penal Law § 265.15(3) provides that if an illegal weapon is found in an automobile, all persons in the car shall be presumed to be in possession of the weapon, unless it is on the person of one of them.

i. Overcoming presumption: However, a defendant can always overcome such a presumption of possession by producing evidence that he did not know of the object's presence, or that he had no control over it.

ii. Possible unconstitutionality: Such presumptions, even though rebuttable, have occasionally been held unconstitutional.

iii. Weapons presumption upheld: Most presumptions, however, have been found *constitutional*. For instance, the New York weapon-in-automobile presumption referred to above was found to be *constitutional* by the Supreme Court, at least as it was applied on the facts of that case; *County Court of Ulster County v. Allen*, 442 U.S. 140 (1979). The Court held that the test of the validity of a "permissive" presumption, such as this one, is *whether the presumed fact is "more likely than not" to follow from the basic fact*. The Court also held that in making this determination, all evidence presented to the jury may be considered. Since the defendants were adult males, and the weapons were large handguns found in the open pocketbook of their 16-year-old female co-passenger, it was "more likely than not" that the defendants' presence in the car indicated that they had possession (defined as "dominion or control") of the weapons.

3. Status: A defendant may not be convicted for merely having a certain *status or condition*, rather than committing an act. Thus the Supreme Court has held that a statute making it a crime to be a *narcotics addict* imposed an unconstitutional cruel and unusual punishment. *Robinson v. State of California*, 370 U.S. 660 (1962).

a. Act stemming from condition: But the Supreme Court and other courts have refused to extend very far the *Robinson* court's prohibition on status crimes. For instance, the Court held that a defendant could constitutionally be punished for the crime of public drunkenness, even though some evidence suggested that he was a chronic alcoholic who once he became intoxicated had no control over his actions (and could thus not prevent himself from being found drunk in public). *Powell v. State of Texas*, 392 U.S. 514 (1968).

C. Act must be voluntary: An act cannot satisfy the *actus reus* requirement unless it is *voluntary*.

1. **Model Penal Code examples:** The Model Penal Code, § 2.01(2), lists three particular kinds of acts which it holds to be *involuntary*:

   a. **Reflex or convulsion:** "A *reflex* or *convulsion*";

   b. **Unconsciousness or sleep:** "A bodily movement during *unconsciousness* or *sleep*";

   c. **Hypnosis:** "Conduct during *hypnosis* or resulting from hypnotic suggestion."

   d. **Other acts:** The Code also provides that an act is involuntary if it is "a bodily movement that otherwise is not a product of the effort or determination of the actor, either conscious or habitual." § 2.01(2)(d).

2. **Reflex or convulsion:** An act consisting of a *reflex or convulsion* presents the clearest case for being involuntary, and thus not giving rise to criminal liability.

   Example: D is walking down the street, when he is stricken by epileptic convulsions. While in the midst of these convulsions, his arm jerks back, and he strikes X in the face. The striking of X was not a voluntary act, and cannot give rise to criminal liability.

   Note: But if D knew beforehand that he was subject to such seizures, and unreasonably put himself in a position where he was likely to harm others (e.g., by driving a car), this initial act might subject him to criminal liability. See the discussion of *People v. Decina*, *infra*, p. 5.

   a. **Quick but conscious decision:** But an act is voluntary, not reflexive, as long as the defendant has *time to make some decision* as to whether to take that action. For instance, if D is about to fall, and reaches out to grab someone or something to stop himself, he has not acted reflexively, since his mind has "quickly grasped the situation and dictated some action." L, p. 210.

3. **Unconsciousness:** It is universally agreed that an act performed during a state of "*unconsciousness*" does not meet the *actus reus* requirement. But there is a great deal of dispute about exactly what constitutes "unconsciousness."

   a. **Defendant who "blacks out":** The most difficult issue, which arises frequently, occurs when the defendant testifies that prior to the crime, he "blacked out," and has no recollection of committing the crime. Virtually all courts agree that his *amnesia* by itself does not constitute a defense. But if the defendant can demonstrate that *at the time of the crime*, he was on "*automatic pilot*," so to speak, and was not conscious of what he was doing, there is a good chance that his act will be held to be involuntary.

   Example: D (the black radical, Huey Newton) is tried for the murder of a police officer. D testifies that he and the officer were involved in a skirmish, that the officer shot him in the stomach, that D felt a "sensation like…boiling hot soup had been spilled on my stomach," and that he does not remember anything that happened next until he was found at the entrance of a hospital. A doctor also testifies on D's behalf that such a gunshot wound in the stomach is very likely to produce shock and unconsciousness.

Held (on appeal), the California Penal Code prevents anyone from being convicted for an act he committed "without being conscious thereof." D produced enough evidence of unconsciousness that he was entitled to have the jury instructed that if it found him to have been unconscious, it could not convict him. The conviction is therefore reversed. *People v. Newton*, 87 Cal. Rptr. 394 (Cal. Ct. App. 1970).

  i. **Relation to insanity defense:** At first glance, this unconsciousness defense, often called the defense of *automatism*, appears almost indistinguishable from the insanity defense. But there are some important practical differences between the two defenses. First, in most states, there is a statutory requirement that any defendant acquitted by reason of insanity be *committed* to a mental institution automatically; there is seldom such a requirement as to a defendant successfully using the automatism defense.

  ii. **Burden of proof:** Another difference is that the insanity defendant often has the burden of establishing, by a preponderance of the evidence, that he was insane at the time of the crime. Many courts, however, require the defendant merely to present *some evidence* supporting his automatism defense, and then shift to the prosecution the burden of proving (beyond a reasonable doubt) that the defendant was not acting unconsciously.

  iii. **Contrary view:** But see *State v. Caddell*, 215 S.E.2d 348 (N. C. 1975), as an example of a case making the defendant establish the automatism defense by a preponderance of the evidence. Where this rule applies, the defendant will presumably never be entitled to have the jury instructed on the automatism issue merely by his testimony that he "blacked out" at the time of the crime and does not remember anything.

4. **Hypnotism:** There is dispute about whether acts performed under *hypnosis* are always (or indeed ever) sufficiently "involuntary" that they cannot give rise to liability. The Model Penal Code, as noted, provides in § 2.01(2)(c) that such acts are always involuntary.

  a. **Contrasting view:** But the opposite view, that liability should attach even to acts performed under hypnosis, relies on the often-stated view that no one will perform acts under hypnosis that are deeply repugnant to him (and that therefore the hypnotized subject must be exercising his will to some extent).

5. **Self-induced state:** Although the defendant's acts while unconscious, while in the midst of an epileptic seizure, etc., will not meet the *actus reus* requirement, his acts *prior to* such a state may be enough to meet the requirement. For instance, if the defendant had himself hypnotized for the purpose of emboldening him to commit a crime, the act requirement would be met; this would probably be the case, for instance, if a *cult member* allowed himself to be hypnotized by a leader known to induce his subjects to commit crimes while hypnotized. See Nutshell, p. 139.

a. Risk knowingly imposed on others: Similarly, the act requirement may be met where a person *knowingly puts himself* in the position of *imposing risk* on others. For instance, a driver who drinks heavily, and then falls asleep at the wheel, could undoubtedly be held guilty of manslaughter or vehicular homicide; his act consists of drinking and getting in the driver's seat, not of losing consciousness while driving. This principle was carried even further in one case, in which a driver who knew that he was subject to *epileptic seizures* nonetheless drove, and caused a fatal accident; he was convicted of negligent homicide. *People v. Decina*, 138 N.E.2d 799 (N. Y. 1956). (A dissent pointed out, however, that the defendant was being punished for merely driving at all, something which his driver's license explicitly allowed him to do.)

D. Omissions: A completely distinct effect of the *actus reus* requirement is to prevent criminal liability from arising from most *omissions* to act (as distinguished from affirmative actions). For instance, if the defendant sees a stranger drowning in front of him, the defendant will normally *not be criminally liable* for failing to attempt to rescue, even though this could have been done with perfect ease and safety. (This principle also bars tort liability; see Emanuel on *Torts*.)

1. Distinguished from affirmative acts: In most situations, it is not difficult to distinguish between an affirmative action and an omission to act. If A pushes B into a lake, where he drowns, we would all agree that A has acted affirmatively; if A merely comes upon B already in the water, and walks away, we would agree that A has simply failed to act to save B. But there are situations in which the line between acting and failing to act is fuzzier.

a. Respirator cases: One such situation arises when a physician is faced with the care of a *comatose patient*, whose life can only be maintained by the use of artificial means, such as a *respirator*. If the physician fails to use the respirator, or uses it and then turns it off, has he acted affirmatively, or has he simply omitted to act?

i. Omission to act: Most commentators agree that the physician's decision not to use the respirator, or to turn it off, constitutes an omission to act; that is, it is "not a positive act of killing the patient, but a decision not to strive any longer to save him." (Glanville Williams, quoted in K,S&P, pp. 214-15.) As Williams points out, if a respirator is so constructed that it turns itself off every 24 hours, we would all probably agree that the doctor's decision not to turn it back on again was an omission; there should be no moral difference between failing to reset such a machine and switching off a machine that has been constructed so as to run continuously. (*Ibid.*)

Note: The switched-off respirator problem is considered further *infra*, p. 9.

2. Limited liability for omissions: Anglo-American law has always been much less willing to impose liability for omissions than for affirmative acts. Various reasons for this have been advanced, including: (1) the fact that rules governing failure to act would necessarily be much vaguer than rules prohibiting affirmative conduct and would be likely to violate the principle that forbidden conduct must be carefully specified; (2) the difficulties of deciding which of the various people who could have acted and did not should be prosecuted (e.g., which of the 38 people who watched Kitty Genovese get stabbed to death, if any, should be charged?); and (3) the general feeling that there is an important causal difference between precipitating an event and merely failing to intervene to prevent it. (E.g., if an old woman dies of pneumonia in New Jersey, does it make sense to say that the failure of a particular physician in Florida to attend to her "caused" her death, just as did the failure of every other physician in the world to do so?). As to this last point, see Fletcher, p. 596.

a. **Bases for liability:** Liability for omissions has been limited by restricting it to a few kinds of situations. These may be summarized by saying that there is liability only where there is either: (1) a statute which explicitly makes it a crime to omit the act in question; or (2) there are other factors giving rise to a distinct *legal duty* to act.

Example: D is charged with abusing two young children of a friend of hers, and involuntarily causing the death of one of them. The prosecution claims that the children lived with D under an agreement whereby their mother paid for their care. The evidence shows that the children were malnourished and did not get proper medical attention. The judge's instructions to the jury do not suggest that the jury must, in order to convict, find that D had a legal duty of care that she breached.

Held, D's conviction reversed. "[T]he duty neglected must be a legal duty, and not a mere moral obligation." In the absence of a statute imposing a duty, the legal duty can arise because of one's status relation to another (e.g., mother to child); because one has assumed a contractual duty to care for another; or because one has "voluntarily assumed the care of another and so secluded the helpless person as to prevent others from rendering aid." Here, it may well have been the case that, as the prosecution charged, the "contractual duty" or "voluntary assumption of care" grounds was applicable. But because the jury was not instructed that they must find a legal duty to exist before they may convict, D's conviction cannot stand. *Jones v. U.S.*, 308 F.2d 307 (D.C. Cir. 1962).

3. **Statutory requirement:** There are a number of *statutes* which impose a *duty to take affirmative action* in particular situations. For instance, the Internal Revenue laws make it a crime to fail to file an income tax return. Similarly, many states have statutes making it a crime to fail to report a crime in a certain situation. Where omission is explicitly made a crime, most of the practical conceptual difficulties mentioned above are not present.

4. **Existence of "legal duty":** A different situation is presented when the defendant has omitted to act, and the state attempts to prosecute him under a statute that speaks in terms of *positive acts*. For instance, the statute may proscribe "unlawful killing," and the defendant is prosecuted for simply failing to prevent a death. The courts have worked out four principal categories in which the defendant will be held to have been under a *special legal duty to act*, so that his failure to do so may make him criminally liable.

a. **Special relationship:** A *special relationship* between the defendant and the victim may give rise to such a duty to act. A close *blood relationship* is the clearest example. Thus a parent who fails to give food or medical attention to his child could be held liable for murder or manslaughter, based upon the parent-child relationship and the corresponding duty to furnish necessities.

Example: D knows that her husband has repeatedly abused her two children physically and sexually. D takes no action to stop the abuse, and in fact leaves the children in the husband's physical care for hours at a time, during which he abuses them. D is charged with the crime of child abuse, defined to cover one who "subjects a child to cruel maltreatment." D defends on the grounds that she did not commit any overt act, and her omission to act is not covered by the statute.

Held, D may be convicted under the statute. D's conduct was a "substantial factor" which contributed to the abuse. One can be liable for a crime not just by committing an overt act, but by omitting to act when there is a legal duty to act. The relationship between a parent and a child exemplifies a special relationship where the duty to protect is imposed. (A dissent argues that it is up to the legislature to prescribe a legal duty to act, and that the court should not, in effect, legislate by expanding the coverage of the statute to cover a parent's omission to act.) *State v. Williquette*, 385 N.W.2d 145 (Wisc. 1986).

    i. Interdependence: Other relationships, not involving ties of blood or marriage, may be characterized by such ***mutual dependence*** that a failure to aid may give rise to liability. For instance, it has been suggested that if two mountain climbers are alone together, and one falls into a crevasse, the other has a duty to attempt a rescue (if it could be done with reasonable safety). Similarly, two roommates living together might have a duty to render assistance to each other. L, p. 216.

    ii. *Beardsley* case: But if the relationship is more casual, there will probably be no duty to assist. Thus in the well-known case of *People v. Beardsley*, 113 N.W. 1128 (Mich. 1907), the defendant and his mistress went on a drunken and adulterous weekend fling; she took an overdose of morphine towards the end of it, and he did nothing to save her (other than to ensconce her in the apartment of a friend of his, lest she be found by the defendant's wife in their own apartment). The court held that the defendant had had no legal duty to render aid to her; the decision stressed that the mistress knew the risk involved, and that she had had "ample experience in such affairs."

  b. Duty based on contract: A legal duty may arise out of a ***contract***. The contract need not be between the defendant and the victim; thus if a lifeguard is hired to guard a city beach, he may be criminally liable if he stands by and does not attempt to save a drowning swimmer (perhaps even if the swimmer had no apparent right to be on this particular beach). L, p. 217. Similarly, if the defendant is hired by a baby's mother to feed and care for the baby, the defendant will be liable for the infant's death by malnutrition. *Jones v. U.S.*, *supra*, p. 6.

    i. Extent of duty: But it does not follow, of course, that every breach of a contractual duty can give rise to liability-by-omission. The prosecution almost certainly needs to show ***willfulness*** and ***knowledge of the danger***, and the defendant has a chance to show excuse or justification. See *infra*, p. 98.

  c. Danger caused by defendant: A duty to assist may arise from the fact that the ***danger was caused*** (innocently or otherwise) by the ***defendant***. The courts are obviously quicker to impose such a duty where the danger was caused by a negligent or intentional act on the part of the defendant, but will also sometimes impose such a duty where the danger was caused completely innocently.

Example: D starts a fire in a building in which he has an indirect ownership. Evidence indicates that he started the fire accidentally, but that once the fire was underway, he refrained from calling the fire department or trying to extinguish it (allegedly to collect insurance proceeds).

Held, D may be convicted of arson. *Commonwealth v. Cali*, 141 N.E. 510 (Mass. 1923).

d. **Undertaking:** Even if the defendant starts out by being under no duty to render assistance to a person in distress, he may come under such a duty if he *undertakes to give assistance*. This will be particularly true if he leaves the victim worse off than he was before (e.g., by moving an accident victim so that his bleeding and bone injuries are worsened). But it may also be true even if all that has happened is that other potential rescuers are dissuaded from helping, in reliance on the fact that the defendant is already doing so. However, there would probably be no liability if the defendant has not even worsened the victim's position to this latter extent; see L, p. 218.

e. **Statutory duty:** It was noted previously that a statute may explicitly provide for liability based upon an omission. But a statute may also *indirectly* give rise to liability, by imposing a duty of care that the defendant has not met. For instance, many states have statutes requiring a motorist who has played even an innocent role in an accident to render and/or call for first aid for his victim. If the motorist fails to do so (e.g., a hit-and-run driver), and the victim dies, the violation of the statute (which by itself might only be a misdemeanor) might serve as the basis for a manslaughter conviction.

f. **Knowledge required for conviction:** A defendant may attempt to raise the defense of ignorance, either of the facts or of the law giving rise to the duty to act.

i. **Ignorance of facts:** The prosecution must normally show that the defendant was *aware of the facts* that gave rise to the duty, and that constituted the emergency. Thus if the defendant in *Commonwealth v. Cali, supra*, did not realize that he had set the building on fire, he would presumably have been under no duty to call the fire department.

ii. **Strict liability:** But in a few situations, a person may be *strictly liable* for failing to know the facts giving rise to a duty. For example, an adult can be found guilty of statutory rape for having sex with a 15 year-old, even though the adult did not know (and had no reason to know) that his lover was under-aged.

iii. **Ignorance of law:** Generally speaking, the fact that the defendant did not know that the *law imputes a legal duty* in a certain situation will not constitute a defense. The defendant in *Cali, supra*, for instance, could not defend on the ground that he didn't know that one who causes a danger must take steps to alleviate it. See L, p. 220. Thus the maxim, *"Ignorance of the law is no excuse,"* is generally a correct statement.

(1) **Exception where duty unusual:** But there is an exception to this rule in situations where the duty is *so unusual* that the average person *could not be*

expected to know that it existed. See, e.g., *Lambert v. California*, 355 U.S. 225 (1957), in which D's conviction for failing to register as a convicted felon was reversed; the court held that since there was a complete lack of circumstances that would have made her aware of her duty to register, she should be entitled to assert the defense of ignorance of the registration requirement.

5. **Degree of risk and effort required:** One of the reasons courts have been reluctant to impose broad-sweeping liability for omissions is that it is frequently very hard to tell exactly how far the duty to act should extend. There is no general rule, and the degree of risk and inconvenience to which the defendant must subject himself probably varies with the circumstances. For instance, a parent whose child is drowning is certainly required to expose himself to greater risks than is a stranger in the same situation, whose duty arises only because he has started to attempt to rescue, thus dissuading other potential rescuers (*supra*, p. 8).

   a. **Duty arising out of contract:** Where the duty arises out of a ***contract***, the contract itself may govern the extent of the duty, or at least have an evidentiary bearing on it. For instance, suppose that a babysitter is hired to watch a child until midnight, at which time the parents have promised to be home. If the sitter leaves at midnight, and a fatal fire occurs shortly thereafter, she might be able to escape liability on the grounds that she did all that the contract required. However, the court might hold that her duty went beyond the contractual requirement, at least unless she had some other important conflicting obligation (e.g., another appointment; see Fletcher, pp. 622-23.)

   b. **Respirators:** The difficulty of determining the bounds of the duty to act is illustrated by cases in which a patient is on a ***respirator*** or other life-sustaining apparatus, and the doctor wishes to terminate the apparatus' use. As noted previously (*supra*, p. 5), his failure to continue the treatment would probably be treated as an omission; does this mean that the physician who disconnects the apparatus cannot have criminal liability?

      i. ***Barber* case:** At least one court has held that a physician who, at the request of the patient's family, disconnects life-sustaining equipment is ***not criminally liable*** if the victim had virtually no chance of benefitting from the life-sustaining measures. See *Barber v. Superior Court*, 195 Cal. Rptr. 484 (Cal. App. 1983).

      ii. **Interference by third person:** The fact that a physician might be allowed to terminate respirator or other extraordinary treatment without liability does not mean that a ***third person*** could turn off the respirator with equal impunity. Certainly, if a stranger had walked into the hospital room of the patient in *Barber* and pulled the plug, he would have been prosecuted and probably convicted. In this situation, the court would be likely to say that there was not an omission (i.e., a decision not to continue with further treatment) but rather an affirmative action on the part of one who had no prior connection with the treatment.

Quiz Yourself on
ACTUS REUS

1. Cain hates Abel and wants to kill him. Cain, Abel and their third brother, Seth, visit the Grand Canyon. Abel is peering over the edge.

(A) Cain pushes Seth into Abel, causing Abel to fall to his death. Has *Seth* committed an act that could result in criminal liability?

(B) Instead of the facts in Part A, assume that Cain tells Seth: "If you don't kill Abel, I'll tell Mom you've been eating forbidden fruit." If Seth pushes Abel off a cliff under this threat, has he committed an act that could result in criminal liability?

2. King George III, an epileptic, has a seizure in a crowded bus. During his seizure, he hits another passenger, breaking his jaw. In hitting the passenger, has George committed the actus reus required for a crime (in this case, battery)?

3. Sigmund Freud is addicted to cocaine.

(A) First, assume Freud is arrested under a state statute making it a crime to be addicted to a controlled substance. (The arrest comes about because Freud's doctor realizes that Freud is addicted, and informs the police of this fact.) Is the statute constitutionally valid, as applied to Freud?

(B) Now, assume that Freud is arrested for possession of cocaine when a police officer spots a baggy of the stuff on the passenger seat of Freud's car during a routine traffic stop. The statute makes it a crime to possess cocaine, even if the possession is exclusively for the defendant's own use on account of the defendant's drug addiction. Is the possession statute constitutionally valid, as applied to Freud?

4. India Hauser, champion swimmer, is lounging on a riverbank reading John Stuart Mill's autobiography. Ima Gonner, India's sworn enemy, strolls up in her bathing suit and goes for a dip in the river. In fact the water is deeper than Ima expected, and she begins to drown. India looks up from her book and watches, laughing, as Ima drowns. When Ima goes down for the last time, India sighs and says: "Oh well. Back to the Mill."

(A) Is India criminally liable for Ima's death?

(B) Assume the same facts as above, except that Ima went into the river because India told her, "Go on in and swim. The water's only three feet deep." (India actually believed this, because a friend whom India had reason to trust told her that the water was only three feet deep.) Is India criminally liable for Ima's death?

Answers

1. **(A) No.** All crimes require an "*actus reus*" (an act). The act must be a voluntary one. Here, the actus reus requirement is not satisfied, because Seth's act was not voluntary; he was, in effect, Cain's weapon. Since there was no voluntary act on Seth's part, he cannot be criminally liable.

   (B) Yes. Here, Seth's actual act was voluntary, even if he wouldn't have done it "but for" Cain's threat. (Note that Seth may be able to defend against criminal charges due to duress, discussed in Chap. 4 (II), although it's doubtful he'd win because duress is generally not available for homicide offenses.)

2. **No.** In order to be criminal, an act must be voluntary – that is, the act must have been committed under the actor's will and control. Where the act is the result of an epileptic seizure, it is not voluntary and thus no criminal liability will attach. (However, an epileptic might become criminally liable for *putting himself in a position* where his potential loss of muscle control is likely to cause serious damage, e.g., by driving a car. Here, the actus reus would be the reckless act of driving while knowingly subject to seizures.)

3. **(A) No.** Crimes that punish status (instead of acts or omissions) are considered unconstitutional, in violation of due process and the prohibition against cruel and unusual punishment under the Eighth Amend-

ment. *Robinson v. Cal.* These include conditions like mental illness and addiction. Note, however, that a state can outlaw, say, public drunkenness – here, it's not one's status as an alcoholic that's being proscribed, but the act of being sloshed in public.

(B) Yes. Statutes outlawing possession of narcotics are valid, provided they require that the person charged knew that he possessed the substance in question. (Note that he does not have to know it is illegal to possess the substance; he just has to know that he has it.) The fact that the possession was the direct result of an addiction, and/or the fact that the possession was for the defendant's own use, makes no difference.

4. **(A) No, because she was under no duty to act.** Normally speaking, in Anglo-American law a bystander will not be subjected to criminal liability merely for failing to assist another in distress, even though that assistance could have been given easily and without risk. Only where the bystander has some special *legal duty* to assist can there be liability for failure to assist. Here, nothing caused such a duty to come into existence. India's intense dislike for Ima is irrelevant, since bad thoughts alone are not punishable, and India's bad thoughts did not cause India to have a duty to assist.

(B) Yes. Although normally a bystander has no duty to render assistance, there are some special situations that *will* cause a duty to assist to come into existence. One of those situations is that the defendant *caused the dangerous situation to arise* (whether the defendant acted negligently, intentionally, or even completely innocently). Since India's statement caused the danger to exist — even though India may have behaved non-negligently in making the statement — India then had a duty to render reasonable assistance when Ima started to drown.

LEXIS®-NEXIS® Searches on **ACTUS REUS**

Sub-Topic	Suggested Searches
Requirement of voluntariness — Unconsciousness	`(crime or criminal) and ((voluntary w/10 act!) w/25 unconscious!)`

II. *MENS REA*

A. **Introduction:** Just as the term *"actus reus"* symbolizes the requirement that there be a voluntary act, so the term *"mens rea"* symbolizes the requirement that there be what might be called a *"culpable state of mind."*

1. **Not necessarily state of mind:** In most situations, the requirement of *mens rea* refers to what we would all agree is a mental state, either "intent" or "knowledge." But some crimes are defined in such a way that the *"mens rea"* is merely "negligence" or "recklessness"; in these cases, it is often stretching things to say that there is a particular state of mind involved at all.

    a. **Negligence and recklessness:** When one acts negligently (even with "criminal negligence," a term that usually refers to a greater deviation from the ordinary standard of care than the deviation that would be enough to give rise to civil liability), it is hard to say that he has had any special mental state; the essence of his act is that he acted *without consciousness* of the risk that he was imposing. Even "recklessness" is defined in some courts as acting without consciousness of an extremely great risk (although, as is discussed further, *infra*, p. 19, other statutes, and the Model Penal Code, require that there be a ***conscious*** disregard of a known risk for an act to be reckless.) Nonetheless, negligence and recklessness are said to fulfill the *mens rea* requirements of certain crimes.

    b. Strict liability: Finally, some crimes are defined so as to require no *mens rea* at all. These are generally referred to as ***"strict liability"*** crimes, and are discussed *infra*, p. 21. Generally, they tend to be what might be called "public welfare" violations (e.g., parking without putting money in the meter). They are usually punishable only by fine and not by imprisonment, and carry no great social opprobrium.

2. Ambiguity in statute: Most crimes have a number of ***material elements,*** each of which the prosecution is required to prove (and prove, generally speaking, "beyond a reasonable doubt"). In many cases, the mental state required as to each of these material elements may not all be the same.

Example: The crime of rape requires that the defendant have intended sexual relations; it is also generally required that the defendant not be married to the victim, and that the victim not have consented. The prosecution must certainly show that the defendant ***intended*** to have sexual relations. But if the defendant argues that he mistakenly thought that the victim was his wife (e.g., he thought she was his wife, when she was in fact his wife's twin sister), or if he mistakenly thought that the victim had consented, it is not at all clear that the defendant will win. That is, it may suffice that the defendant behaved negligently, rather than intentionally, with respect to marriage or consent. See M.P.C., Comment 1 to § 2.02 (Tent. Dr. No. 4).

    a. Unclear statutes: Notwithstanding this possibility that there may be different mental states required for the various elements of the crime, most statutes are not drawn so as to make it clear which state is required for each element. For instance, suppose that a statute provides that "Whoever shall knowingly receive stolen property" is guilty of the crime of receiving stolen goods. Must the defendant be shown to have known that the property which he was receiving was stolen, or must he merely be shown to have known that he was receiving property, and simply negligent in failing to realize that the property was in fact stolen? The Model Penal Code attempts to avoid such ambiguity in its definitions of crimes, and a Comment states that "The problem of the kind of culpability that is required for conviction must be faced separately with respect to each material element of the offense, although the answer may in many cases be the same with respect to each element." (M.P.C., § 2.02, Comment 1, Tent. Dr. No. 4.)

B. General versus specific intent: Courts have traditionally classified the *mens rea* requirements of the various crimes into three groups: (1) crimes requiring merely ***"general intent"***; (2) crimes requiring ***"specific intent"***; and (3) crimes requiring merely ***negligence.*** (Obviously this classification does not encompass crimes as to which no culpable mental state is required at all, i.e., strict liability crimes.)

1. "General intent": When courts hold that a crime requires merely ***"general intent,"*** they usually mean that all that must be shown is that the defendant ***desired to commit the act which served as the actus reus.***

2. **Specific intent:** Where a crime is said to require *"specific intent"* or "special intent," on the other hand, the courts usually mean that the defendant, in addition to desiring to bring about the *actus reus*, must have desired to do *something further.* L, pp. 238-39.

   a. **Distinction illustrated:** The distinction between "general" and "specific" intent can best be illustrated by considering a crime for which general intent is usually held to be sufficient (simple assault) and a crime for which specific intent is usually held necessary (common law burglary).

      i. **Assault:** It is enough for *assault* if the defendant had an "intent to willfully commit an act the direct, natural and probable consequences of which if successfully completed would be…injury to another." *People v. Rocha,* 479 P.2d 372 (Cal. 1971). The prosecution is not required to show that the defendant thought that his conduct was wrong or unlawful, or even that he intended to cause bodily harm; thus if the defendant touches the victim with a knife, intending merely to graze his skin and frighten him, this will be sufficient intent, even though no actual injury is intended.

      ii. **Burglary:** For common law *burglary*, on the other hand, it must be shown that the defendant not only intended to break and enter the dwelling of another, but also that he intended to commit a felony once he was inside the dwelling. This latter intent is a "specific intent," in the sense that it is an intent other than the one associated with the *actus reus* (the breaking and entering).

   b. **Significance of distinction:** Those courts that adhere to the distinction between "general" and "specific" intent rely on it principally to dispose of two issues: (1) the effect of the defendant's *intoxication*; and (2) the effect of a *mistake* of law or fact. Intoxication is usually held insufficient to negate a crime of general intent, but possibly sufficient to negate the specific intent for a particular crime (e.g., a defendant who breaks and enters, but is too drunk to have any intent to commit larceny or any other felony.) See *infra*, p. 84. Similarly, a mistake of fact may be enough to negate the required specific intent (e.g., a defendant who breaks and enters, in an attempt to carry away something which he mistakenly thinks belongs to him) where the mistake might not negate the general intent (e.g., the intent to commit the breaking and entering by itself).

      i. **Abandonment of distinction:** However, the terms "general" and "specific" intent are sufficiently ambiguous that many jurisdictions are now turning away from them, as does the Model Penal Code. The latter, for instance, specifies as to most crimes the precise mental state (e.g., "recklessly") required as to each material element. Where the crime is not defined with this precision, the Code, rather than providing that a "general intent" is sufficient, states that "where the culpability sufficient to establish a material element of an offense is not prescribed by law, such element is established if a person acts *purposely, knowingly* or *recklessly* with respect thereto." M.P.C. § 2.02(3).

C. **Common law vs. statutory crimes:** When the criminal law developed in England, it did so principally as *common law* (i.e., "judge-made" law or "case law"). In most American jurisdictions, the original English common-law crimes have been *codified* in *statutory form*. Thus in many jurisdictions, there are no common-law crimes at all any more, and in others there are only a few. By and large, American criminal law is statutory law. That is, conduct is criminal only if it is prohibited by statute.

1. **Statutory offenses not existing at common law:** In addition to statutory codifications of the common-law crimes, American legislatures have also enacted a huge body of modern statutory crimes that have no common-law counterpart. Many of these are defined so as to have elaborate *mens rea* requirements, similar to those of most common-law crimes. But many others are essentially strict liability crimes; these are often referred to as "public welfare" offenses or "violations," and are discussed *infra*, p. 21.

D. **Presumption of intent:** It will often be quite difficult for the prosecution to prove, beyond a reasonable doubt, that the defendant did something with a particular state of mind (especially "purposely" or "intentionally"). This burden is made easier by statutory and judge-made ***presumptions*** under which, from the existence of what might be called the "basic" fact, the jury is permitted to ***infer***, beyond a reasonable doubt, the presumed fact (e.g., the fact that the defendant acted purposely or intentionally).

> **Example:** A receipt-of-stolen-property statute might say that where *A* is a dealer in a particular type of object who is found in possession of stolen property of that type, *A* will be presumed to have known the stolen character of the object. *A* would of course be permitted to rebut the presumption, but the point is that if he didn't, the jury could infer that, beyond a reasonable doubt, *A* knew that the goods were stolen even if there was no direct evidence that he had such knowledge.

1. **Constitutional test:** It is now required, as a matter of constitutional due process, that the defendant not be convicted of a crime unless he has been proved guilty "beyond a reasonable doubt." *In Re Winship*, 397 U.S. 358 (1970). A judge-made or statutory presumption, insofar as it allows the jury to find that a material element of the crime exists merely because some other fact (the basic fact) exists, may run afoul of this due process standard. But this won't happen very often. That's because the U.S. Supreme Court's decision in *County Court of Ulster County v. Allen, supra*, p. 2, probably means that it is only necessary that the presumed fact be ***"more likely than not"*** to follow from the basic fact. (Furthermore, all the evidence in the case, not just the presumption, may be used to determine whether the presumed fact exists beyond a reasonable doubt.)

> **Example:** On the facts of the above stolen-property example, if it is "more likely than not" that a dealer who is in possession of stolen goods of a type the dealer customarily sells knows their stolen character, then the presumption in the example would not violate constitutional due process.

E. **Different states of mind:** The Model Penal Code sets forth four distinct states of mind that may give rise to culpability, depending on how the crime in question is defined: (1) "purposely"; (2) "knowingly"; (3) "recklessly"; and (4) "negligently." Because this Model Penal Code scheme has had a substantial impact upon the drafting of criminal statutes in the seventeen years since its publication, we will focus on that scheme here. Then, we will discuss crimes and offenses not requiring any culpable mental state, i.e., strict liability.

F. **"Purposely":** Under the Model Penal Code, § 2.02(2)(a), a person acts ***purposely*** with respect to a particular element of a crime if it is his ***"conscious object"*** to engage in the particular conduct in question, or to cause the particular result in question. If the element in question relates not to conduct or result, but to "attendant circumstances," then the defendant has acted purposely with respect to those circumstances if he is "aware of the existence of such circumstances or he believes or hopes that they exist."

1. **Distinguished from "intentionally":** Most pre-Model Penal Code statutes do not use the word "purposely," but rather, the word "intentionally." Within the term "intentionally" is often included not only a conscious desire to bring about the results, or to engage in the conduct in question, but also the *awareness* that the conduct or result is *certain to follow*. That is, most older decisions do not distinguish between "purposely" and "knowingly." For instance, if the defendant has a conscious desire to kill A, and he does so by putting a bomb on board a plane that contains both A and B, he would be held by these courts to have "intended" to kill B as well as A since, although he did not desire to kill B, he knew that B's death was substantially certain to result from his actions.

2. **"Maliciously":** Pre-Model Penal Code statutes often use the word *"malice"* to denote a particular *mens rea*. The term always includes intentional conduct by the defendant, but is also usually interpreted to include *reckless conduct*, i.e., conduct taken in disregard of a known high probability of risk. But most decisions hold that neither negligence, nor the fact that the defendant was intentionally engaging in some other, unrelated, crime, is enough to establish that he acted "maliciously" with respect to the harm that in fact occurred.

   Example: D steals a gas meter from the home of his prospective mother-in-law. However, D fails to turn off the stop tap to the meter, located only two feet away, and coal gas seeps through the walls, partially asphyxiating V, a woman sleeping next door. The applicable statute requires a finding that D acted "maliciously." The trial court judge defines "malicious" as a generally "wicked" state of mind during the commission of an act.

   Held (on appeal), for D. In order to establish that D acted maliciously, the prosecution must prove that D either (1) *intended* to harm V or (2) acted recklessly in that he foresaw a risk of harm to V but imposed the risk on her anyway. It was not sufficient that D was "wicked," which he clearly was by stealing the meter at all. *Regina v. Cunningham*, 41 Crim. App. 155 (1957).

   Note: Despite the decision in *Cunningham*, there are many situations in which a defendant who intends or desires to produce one result will be treated as if he intended or desired a different, even unexpected, one. For instance, if the defendant shoots at A, desiring to kill him, and instead the bullet hits B and kills him, the defendant will be held to have purposely killed B, under the doctrine of transferred intent. Most of the problems of unintended results of wrongful conduct are treated in the material on concurrence, *infra*, p. 35 and causation, *infra*, p. 44.

3. **Conditional intent:** The defendant may intend to commit a particular act only *upon a certain condition*. If so, shall he be deemed to have "intended" that act? The Model Penal Code, in § 2.02(6), provides that the existence of such a condition is irrelevant, "unless the condition negatives the harm or evil sought to be prevented by the law defining the offense."

Example: Suppose D breaks into a house, intending to steal something only if no one is at home. He will be found to have had the necessary intent for burglary (i.e., intent to break and enter and also intent to commit a felony; see *infra*, p. 307), since the evils sought to be prevented by laws against burglary (breaking and entering, and subsequent commissions of felonies) are present despite the condition. But if D had broken in for the purpose of having sex with the dwelling's owner, but only on condition that she consent, he will be held not to have had the necessary intent for burglary (since there is no statutory purpose to discourage consented-to sexual intercourse). See M.P.C., § 2.02(6), Comment 8 (Tent. Dr. No. 4).

4. **Motive:**   It is often said that the defendant's *"motive"* in committing a certain act, as distinguished from his "intent" or "purpose," is irrelevant. The dividing line between "motive" and "intent" is often blurry, but the idea of motive usually refers to an "ulterior" or "ultimate" intent. As one well-known illustration puts it, if A murders B in order to obtain B's money, A's "intent" is to kill, and his "motive" is to get the money. L, p. 241-42.

   a. **Good motives no defense:**   Good motives will not normally negate a state of mind that otherwise furnishes the required intent. This is most frequently demonstrated in *mercy-killing* cases, in which the defendant has killed a close relative to spare the latter the suffering of a terminal illness; the defendant can certainly be convicted of murder or voluntary manslaughter, even though his ultimate objective, his motive, may have been the lofty humanitarian one of sparing needless pain.

   b. **Defenses of necessity, self-defense, etc.:**   But there are a number of special, well-recognized, defenses as to which motive may be relevant. For instance, a defendant who commits what would otherwise be a criminal act may be entitled to the defense of *necessity*, if he can show that he was preventing a greater harm; his desire to prevent that greater harm might be said to be his "motive." Similarly, a person who has killed another in self-defense might be said to have had the "motive" of self-defense. But unless the defendant's conduct and mental state fit within one of these fairly well-defined defenses (discussed *infra*, p. 98), his motive will be irrelevant to his liability (although it may have a bearing on the sentence imposed by the court).

G. **"Knowingly":**   The Model Penal Code marks a new tendency to distinguish between acting "purposely" and merely *"knowingly."* A person acts "knowingly" under the Code, with respect to the nature of his conduct or the surrounding circumstances, if he is *"aware"* that his conduct is of a certain kind or that certain circumstances exist. More significantly, if the crime is defined with respect to a certain *result* of the defendant's conduct, the defendant has acted knowingly if he was "aware that it is *practically certain* that his conduct will cause" that result. M.P.C., § 2.02(2)(b).

1. **"Willfully":**   Statutes often use the ambiguous term *"willfully."* The Model Penal Code takes the position that for a person to have acted willfully, it is not necessary that he acted "purposely"; it is sufficient if he acted "knowingly," unless the statute indicates otherwise. M.P.C. § 2.02(8). For instance, if murder is defined in a particular statute as the "willful taking of the life of another," the defendant can be convicted if it is shown that he knew that the victim's life was substantially certain to be taken, even if he did not desire that result (e.g., he put a bomb on board a plane carrying the victim, for the purpose of killing one of the other passengers).

2. **Subjective test:** The Model Penal Code, and most recent decisions, impose a *subjective test* for determining the defendant's knowledge. That is, the test is whether the defendant *actually* knew or believed something, not merely whether a reasonable person in the position of the defendant would have had that knowledge or belief. The effect of this is that if the defendant can show that he was unusually stupid or gullible, he may escape having knowledge imputed to him.

Example: D runs an antique store. One of his customers notices that some of the antiques that D is selling were stolen from her house. After she tells her suspicions to the police, D hides or sells the objects in question, and is arrested for knowingly concealing stolen property. That crime is defined by local statute so as to apply only where the defendant acted "knowing [the goods] to be stolen."

Held, the prosecution must prove that D *actually* knew or believed that the goods had been stolen, and it is not enough to prove that a "reasonable person" with the information available to D, would have known that the goods were stolen. (However, it does not have to be proven that D was *certain* that the goods were stolen; "it is enough if he was made aware of circumstances which caused him to believe that they were stolen." A stricter requirement would make the various "possession of stolen property" crimes virtually unprovable, since a thief almost never admits to his fence that the goods are stolen.) *State v. Beale*, 299 A.2d 921 (Me. 1973).

a. **"Willful blindness":** There is one situation in which the defendant is not required to have had actual knowledge or belief of a fact for him to be held to have acted "knowingly." This is the situation that has often been called *"willful blindness."* It occurs where the defendant has a suspicion that something is the case, but in order to be able to deny knowledge, has purposely refrained from making inquiries which would have led to the knowledge in question. As the Model Penal Code, § 2.02(7), puts the idea, such knowledge is established if the defendant is "aware of a high probability of its existence," unless he actually believes that the fact in question does not exist.

Example: D is arrested when driving into the U.S. from Mexico, for having 110 pounds of marijuana concealed in a secret compartment in his trunk. He testifies at his trial that he was paid $100 by the owner of the car to drive it across the border, and that he, D, knew that there was some kind of void in the trunk, but did not know what was in it. The trial judge instructs the jury that it may convict if the government has proved that D's lack of knowledge of the contents of the trunk "was solely and entirely a result of his having made a conscious decision to disregard the nature of that which was in the vehicle, with a conscious purpose to avoid learning the truth." The jury convicts.

Held, conviction affirmed. The jury instruction as to D's willful refusal to ascertain for certain that which he suspected (the presence of the marijuana) was a correct statement of the "willful blindness" doctrine. (A dissent argued that this instruction did not meet the Model Penal Code requirements, principally because it may have confused the jury into thinking that D could be convicted if he actually believed that there was no marijuana, if his belief was unreasonable.) *U.S. v. Jewell*, 532 F.2d 697 (9th Cir. 1976).

3. **Presumption of knowledge:**   A statutory or judge-made ***presumption*** may be used to help prove that the defendant acted "knowingly," just as it may be used to show that the defendant had a particular "intent." One frequent illustration of this kind of presumption is in statutes governing stolen property, which typically provide that the defendant's unexplained possession of property which is in fact stolen gives rise to a presumption that he knew that it was stolen.

    Example: D is charged with, *inter alia*, possession of treasury checks stolen from the mails; the statute requires the prosecution to prove that D knew the checks were stolen. The jury is instructed that "possession of recently stolen property, if not satisfactorily explained, is ordinarily a circumstance from which you may reasonably draw the inference …that the person in possession knew the property had been stolen." D is convicted and appeals.

    Held, the presumption is not unconstitutional since, at least in this case, the evidence (that D possessed recently stolen treasury checks payable to persons he did not know, and provided no plausible explanation) would allow a reasonable juror to find beyond a reasonable doubt that D knew the checks were stolen. *Barnes v. U.S.*, 412 U.S. 837 (1973).

    Note: A dissent argued that it could not be said that all or virtually all U.S. treasury checks, even ones already endorsed, have been stolen, since people often use them to make direct payments for goods or services. Therefore, the presumption that D knew the checks were stolen was not supported empirically.

4. **Knowledge of attendant circumstances:**   Statutes requiring that the defendant act "knowingly" are often very ambiguous grammatically, because it will often be unclear exactly ***what*** the defendant must know. In particular, it will often be unclear whether the defendant must not only know the basic nature of his action but the ***attendant circumstances*** which the definition of the crime makes important.

    Example: Suppose that a statute provides that any dealer in used merchandise must file a report with the police anytime the dealer "knowingly purchases a used item from one who is not in the business of selling such items, at a price less than half of the fair market value of the item." The statute's purpose is to cut down on the "fencing" of stolen goods. D, a used merchandise dealer, buys a vase for $500 that is really worth $2000. Clearly D cannot be convicted unless he is shown to have known that he was purchasing the vase. But must D also be shown to have known that the price he was paying was less than half of the vase's fair market value? In general, the modern tendency is to interpret the term "knowingly" broadly, as applicable to ***all of the material elements*** of the crime, including the attendant circumstances. See MPC, § 2.02(4) and Comment 5 thereto. Thus most courts today, and the Model Penal Code, would probably acquit D if there were no proof that he knew that the item he was buying for $500 was really worth $2,000.

    a. **Knowledge of illegality:**   A special case of the "knowledge of *what?*" problem is presented by statutes that refer to exemptions or prohibitions that are not part of the core statutory provision. Again, the modern tendency is to interpret "knowingly" broadly, so that D cannot be convicted unless he is shown to have known of the illegality. For instance, the combination of a "knowingly" requirement and a requirement that D's conduct be ***"unauthorized"*** (or an exception for conduct that is "authorized") will usually be taken together to create, in effect, a defense of ***mistake of law***.

Example: A federal statute that attempts to combat food stamp fraud provides that "whoever knowingly uses, transfers, acquires, alters, or possesses [food stamp] coupons or authorization cards in any manner not authorized by [the statute] or the regulations" is subject to fine and imprisonment. D, a restaurant owner, is charged with violating the statute by buying food stamps at a wholesale discount. He argues that he can be convicted only if he is shown to have known that his conduct was "not authorized by" the statute.

Held (by the U.S. Supreme Court), for D. Since there is no indication, in the statutory language or legislative history, that Congress intended otherwise, the quoted language "requires a showing that the defendant knew his conduct to be unauthorized by statute or regulations." If the requirement of knowledge were not read to cover the unauthorizedness of D's conduct, the result would be to "criminalize a broad range of apparently innocent conduct" (e.g., a nonrecipient of food stamps who "possessed" stamps because officials mistakenly sent them to him through the mail due to administrative error would be committing a crime).

(A two-Justice dissent argues that the word "knowingly" in the statute merely requires that D be aware of the relevant aspects of his conduct, not aware that his conduct violates the law. To these dissenters, the majority's view creates a defense of mistake of law, which Congress did not intend.) *Liparota v. U.S.*, 471 U.S. 419 (1985).

H. "Recklessly": A person is said to act *"recklessly,"* under the Model Penal Code, when he *"consciously disregards a substantial and unjustifiable risk...."* The Code gives a further explanation of what constitutes a "substantial and unjustifiable" risk, by saying that the risk "must be of such a nature and degree that, considering the nature and purpose of the actor's conduct and the circumstances known to him, its disregard involves a *gross deviation* from the standard of conduct that a law-abiding person would observe in the actor's situation." M.P.C. § 2.02(2)(c).

1. Must be aware of risk: The Code thus takes the position that for the defendant to be reckless, he must have been *aware* of the high risk of harm stemming from his conduct. To put it another way, the Code applies a *subjective standard* for recklessness.

   a. View of some courts: The M.P.C.'s subjective standard is in sharp contrast to the "objective" standard applied by a number of courts and statutes, under which the defendant can be reckless if he behaves extremely unreasonably (i.e., disregards an extremely high risk of harm) even where he was *unaware* of this risk.

   Example: D owns and runs the "New Coconut Grove," a Boston nightclub. One night, a sixteen-year old employee, while trying to replace a lightbulb in the club's basement, accidentally sets fire to some flammable decorations with a match he is using for a light. The fire spreads to the main floor of the crowded club, a panic results, and many customers die from burns and smoke inhalation. Several emergency exits are later shown to have been locked at the time. Although D himself is in the hospital at the time of the fire, he is charged with manslaughter.

   Held, D's manslaughter conviction is affirmed because he acted recklessly, not just negligently. It is irrelevant whether D knew that he was creating a large danger by the inadequate fire exits. "[E]ven if a particular defendant is so stupid [or] so heedless

...that in fact he did not realize the grave danger, he cannot escape the imputation of wanton or reckless conduct in his dangerous act or omission, if an ordinary normal man under the same circumstances would have realized the gravity of the danger. A man may be reckless within the meaning of the law although he himself thought he was careful." (Nor does it matter that D did not directly cause the fire, since his reckless omission to perform his duty to protect the safety of his patrons was the equivalent of an affirmative act.) *Commonwealth v. Welansky*, 55 N.E.2d 902 (Mass. 1944).

2. **All circumstances considered:** In determining whether the risk was "substantial and unjustifiable," *all the circumstances* known to the defendant must be considered. These would include the end that he is seeking (which might be called his "motive"; see *supra*, p. 16). Thus if the defendant drives very fast through a residential area, his conduct might be reckless if he was simply trying to avoid being late for a movie, but would not be reckless if he were trying to get an injured person to the hospital. This would be true even though the risk imposed on the outside world would be the same in both situations; the gravity of the potential harm must be weighed against the "social benefit" that the defendant is attempting to obtain.

3. **Necessity for objective danger:** Under the M.P.C. formulation, "recklessness" would seem to require that there be an actual, not merely apparent, risk of harm. But not all courts have agreed. Thus where a statute provided for punishment of the crime of "recklessly endangering another person," and the statute provided for a presumption that "recklessness and danger" existed "where a person knowingly points a firearm at or in the direction of another, whether or not the actor believed the firearm to be loaded," the court held that even the pointing of a gun that was *actually* unloaded was reckless endangerment. "The most dangerous weapon is the 'unloaded gun' and the legislature's intent was to proscribe the pointing of all firearms at others." *State v. Cushman*, 329 A.2d 648 (Vt. 1974).

   a. **Criticism:** The result in *Cushman* seems clearly wrong. There was no actual danger at all, so either the court misinterpreted the legislature's intent, or the presumption is unconstitutional, since it is not even "more likely than not" that there is danger and recklessness in each case in which an unloaded gun is pointed at someone.

I. **"Negligently":** A number of statutes make it a crime to behave *"negligently"* if certain results follow. The most common such crime is probably that of "vehicular homicide," which is in some states a variety of "criminal negligence." The Model Penal Code defines the term "negligently" so as to apply an objective, not subjective standard: a person is negligent "when he should be aware of a substantial and unjustifiable risk.... The risk must be of such a nature and degree that the actor's failure to perceive it, considering the nature and purpose of his conduct and the circumstances known to him, involves a gross deviation from the standard of care that a reasonable person would observe in the actor's situation."

1. **Distinguished from civil negligence:** Most courts and statutes require a greater degree of culpability for conviction of a crime involving negligence than for the imposition of *civil liability* for negligence. Sometimes this is done by holding that there is no negligence unless the defendant is shown to have been *aware* of the risk imposed by his conduct; the Model Penal Code rejects this approach, at least as far as it is merely the defendant's *mental attributes* (e.g., the "heredity, intelligence or temperament of the actor") which are con-

cerned; otherwise, the negligence standard would be "deprive[d]...of all its objectivity." M.P.C. § 2.02, Comment 4.

    a. Physical attributes: But the defendant's *physical characteristics* are relevant, if they prevent him from perceiving or avoiding a risk. "If the actor were blind or if he had just suffered a blow or experienced a heart attack, these would certainly be facts to be considered, as they would be under present law." M.P.C., *ibid.*

2. Gross negligence: The other respect in which many courts and statutes have imposed a different standard for criminal negligence than for civil negligence is by requiring a *greater deviation* from the standard of care which would be shown by a reasonable person. This is sometimes expressed by saying that criminal negligence is *"gross"* negligence. The Model Penal Code agrees with this view, insofar as it imposes liability for negligence only where there is a *"gross deviation* from the standard of care that a reasonable person would observe...." M.P.C., § 2.02(2)(d).

Example: D is tried under a statute providing for the punishment of anyone who, "while on a hunting trip...negligently or carelessly shoots and wounds, or kills any human being...."

Held, on appeal, the statute, since it is a penal one, must be strictly construed. Therefore, it will be interpreted to punish only gross, not ordinary, negligence. *State v. Jones*, 126 A.2d 273 (Me. 1956).

3. Unforeseeable results: Suppose the defendant should have known that there was a substantial risk that a particular harm would come from his act, and instead a *different harm occurs*, or the same harm occurs in a *different manner* from that which was foreseeable, or a *different victim* is harmed. For instance, suppose that on the facts of *Jones, supra*, the defendant was negligent in disregarding the risk that he might hit his hunting companion with a shot, and the shot in fact hit some third person whose presence was completely unforeseeable; has D committed the crime of negligent shooting while hunting? These questions of unforeseeable results (which may also arise in cases where an intentional act, or a knowing or reckless one, is involved) are discussed elsewhere, partly in the treatment of concurrence, *infra*, p. 35, and partly in the material on causation, *infra*, p. 44.

J. Strict liability: The traditional common-law crimes are all defined in such a way that they are committed only if the defendant acted intentionally, knowingly, recklessly, or at least negligently. As legislatures have become more and more active in defining crimes, however, so-called *"strict liability"* crimes have come into existence. These are crimes for which no culpable mental state at all must be shown; it is enough that the defendant has performed the act in question, regardless of his mental state. Among the more serious strict liability crimes are those of *statutory rape* (in which the defendant is guilty if he has intercourse with a girl below the prescribed age, regardless of whether he knew or should have known her true age) and *bigamy* (under which the defendant is guilty even if he reasonably thought that a purported divorce decree was valid, or that the prior spouse had died).

1. Constitutionality: The constitutionality of such strict-liability statutes, particularly ones which impose substantial criminal penalties such as imprisonment, has often been attacked by defendants, usually on the grounds that conviction without a showing of culpable intent violates the *due process clause* of the Fifth and Fourteenth Amendments. But such an argument has practically never succeeded. Thus in *U.S. v. Balint*, 258 U.S. 250 (1922), the Supreme Court upheld a federal statute making it a crime to sell certain drugs including opium, without a written order on a form printed by the Commissioner of Internal Revenue. "The state may in the maintenance of public policy provide, as to certain acts, 'that he who shall do them shall do them at his peril and will not be heard to plead in defense good faith or ignorance.' "

2. **Interpretation:**   The legislature seldom makes it clear that strict liability is to be imposed. Instead, statutes typically simply omit any particular mental requirement. Since many statutes (particularly old ones) fail to specify a mental state even where some *mens rea* requirement *is* intended, the courts are often faced with a difficult problem of statutory interpretation: did the legislature intend to impose strict liability, or did it simply omit an intended mental requirement?

    a. **Rules for interpretation:**   In deciding what the legislature intended, courts often rely upon factors listed by the Supreme Court in *Morisette v. U.S.*, 342 U.S. 246 (1952); there, the Court stated that "public welfare offenses" (as the less serious strict-liability offenses are often labeled) are generally characterized by the following factors, among others: (1) the violation is in the nature of *neglect* or *inaction*, rather than positive aggression; (2) there is no direct injury to person or property, but simply a *danger* of such, and it is this danger that the statute seeks to curtail; (3) the *penalty* prescribed is small; and (4) conviction does no grave damage to the defendant's *reputation*.

    b. **Not applicable where statute codifies common law:**   Another important factor is that where the statute is more or less a *codification* of a *common law crime*, it is much less likely to be held to be a strict-liability offense than where the statute has brought into being a whole new kind of offense not known to the common law. This factor was, in fact, the deciding one in *Morissette*, *supra*, the facts of which are set forth in the following example.

        Example: D enters an Air Force practice bombing range, and takes used bomb casings that have been lying around for years rusting away. He sells them as junk for an $84 profit. He is tried and convicted of "knowingly converting" government property. He defends on the grounds that he honestly believed that the casings had been abandoned, and that he was not violating the government's rights by taking them.

        Held, the statute in question was not a strict-liability one, and required the prosecution to show an intent to steal (which apparently, according to the Court, was negated by D's belief that the property had been abandoned.) The statute was merely a codification of the common-law crime of larceny; therefore, the fact that Congress did not specify a requirement of intent to steal does not warrant the assumption that strict liability was intended, since intent to steal has always been an element of common-law larceny. *Morissette v. U.S.*, 342 U.S. 246 (1952).

    c. **Complex statute that is easy to violate innocently:**   If the statute is *complex*, *easy to violate innocently*, and/or *imposes a stiff penalty* for its violation, the court is likely to read in a *mens rea* requirement, and thus to refuse to treat the statute as imposing strict liability. The 1994 Supreme Court decision set forth in the following example illustrates this tendency.

Example: A federal statute, the National Firearms Act, makes it a crime (punishable by up to 10 years in prison) to possess a "machinegun" without proper registration. The Act defines "machinegun" to include "any weapon which shoots, ... or can be readily restored to shoot, automatically more than one shot, without manual reloading, by a single function of the trigger." D is found to be in possession of an AR-15 rifle, which is a semi-automatic weapon that can be modified to fire as an automatic one. (When officers test D's weapon, the weapon fires more than one shot with a single pull of the trigger.) D is charged with unlawful possession of an unregistered machinegun. At trial, D argues that he did not know of the gun's automatic firing capability, and that his ignorance should shield him from any criminal liability under the statute.

Held (by the Supreme Court), for D. Although Congress was silent as to any *mens rea* requirement in this statute, one must be inferred, since the penalty for failure to comply with the statute is so severe. "In a system that generally requires a 'vicious will' to establish a crime, imposing severe punishments for offenses that require no *mens rea* would seem incongruous. ... In such a case, the usual presumption that a defendant must know the facts that make his conduct illegal should apply." *Staples v. U.S.*, 511 U.S. 600 (1994).

Note: A dissent in *Staples* noted that the weapon in question here was a particularly dangerous one, making it reasonable to hold D accountable for failure to register it. According to the dissent, the absence of an express knowledge requirement in the statute "suggests that Congress did not intend to require proof that the defendant knew all of the facts that made his conduct illegal."

d. **Can only be "violation" under Model Penal Code:** The Model Penal Code provides that if strict (or, as the Code calls it, "absolute") liability is imposed as to any material element of an offense, the offense can only be a *"violation."* A violation, under the Code, is a minor offense that does not constitute a crime, and that may be punished only by fine or forfeiture. (M.P.C. § 1.04(5)). The commentary to the Code (Comment 1 to § 2.05, Tent. Dr. No. 4) explains this position by stating: "[t]he liabilities involved [in conviction] are indefensible in principle, unless reduced to terms that insulate conviction from the type of moral condemnation that is and ought to be implicit when a sentence of probation or imprisonment may be imposed. In the absence of minimal culpability, the law has neither a deterrent nor corrective nor an incapacitative function to perform."

i. **Applicability to other statutes:** The Model Penal Code also would impose the rule reducing all strict-liability offenses to violations even where the relevant statute or regulation is outside of the Code (e.g., a special statute preventing adulteration of food, enforced under administrative regulations). As to such non-Code statutes, the Code provides that these will be deemed to impose strict liability only "insofar as a legislative purpose to impose absolute liability...*plainly appears*."

3. **Typical strict-liability provisions:** Following are a few examples of statutes which have been interpreted to impose strict liability, and to be constitutional:

a. Mislabeling of drugs: The putting into interstate commerce of any drug that is *"adulterated* or *misbranded"*; 21 U.S.C. § 331(a). *U.S. v. Dotterweich*, 320 U.S. 277 (1943).

b. Pollution: The causing or permitting of certain *pollutants* to enter the atmosphere; Ariz. R. S. § 36-779.

c. Anti-hijacking statute: The concealment of a *dangerous weapon* while boarding an *aircraft*; 9 U.S.C. § 1472(1).

K. Vicarious liability: In the strict-liability situations discussed above, a person who committed acts proscribed by a statute was made liable, notwithstanding the absence of wrongful intent. A distinct kind of absolute liability may be imposed upon one person for the *act of another*; this is commonly called *"vicarious liability."* Where vicarious liability exists, it is probably more accurate to say that it is the requirement of an *act* (*actus reus*) that has been dispensed with, not the requirement of a wrongful intent.

1. Employer liability: The most common form of vicarious liability is that which makes an *employer* or *principal* liable for the acts of his employee or agent.

Example: D is the general manager of a drug corporation. The corporation receives an order from an out-of-state physician, and one of the employees fills it by shipping him a bottle of "Cascera Compound" pills. Unbeknownst to anyone at the corporation, the pills are mislabeled (due to a change in the official composition of such pills), in violation of a Federal statute prohibiting the interstate shipment of "adulterated or misbranded" drugs. D himself has nothing to do with this particular shipment. Nonetheless, he is convicted of violating the statute, on a vicarious liability theory.

Held, by the U.S. Supreme Court, conviction affirmed. Anyone who has a "responsible share" in the distribution of misbranded drugs in interstate commerce can be convicted under the statute, even if that person did not physically handle the shipment. *U.S. v. Dotterweich*, 320 U.S. 277 (1943).

2. Automobile owner: Another area in which vicarious liability is frequently imposed is that of *automobile ownership*. Statutes frequently make a car owner liable for certain acts committed by those to whom he lends his car (e.g., parking violations), even without a showing of culpable mental state on the part of the owner.

3. Constitutionality: Convictions based on a vicarious liability theory, like those based on strict liability, are often subjected to *constitutional attack* by the defendant. The defendant typically argues that his conviction on a vicarious liability theory violates his federal *due process* rights. In general, defendants have not fared well with this theory, though there are exceptions.

a. Defendant must have had control over offender: If the defendant did not have any *ability to control* the person who performed the actual *actus reus*, his conviction is probably *unconstitutional*. See L, p. 270.

b. Fine: Where the defendant has merely been *fined* rather than imprisoned, the use of vicarious liability is virtually never a due process violation. This is true even if the defendant did not *know* that the violation was taking place, and behaved with reasonable care.

c. **Imprisonment:**   But if the defendant has been sentenced to *imprisonment* (or even if he is convicted of a crime for which imprisonment is *authorized*) he has a better chance — courts are *split* about whether imprisonment based on a vicarious liability theory violates the defendant's due process rights.

    i. **Tavern cases:**   The issue often arises in connection with *tavern owners*: May the owner be sentenced to prison where his employee serves minors, if the owner was *not aware* that the service to a minor was taking place, and did not behave negligently? Most states have *upheld* the constitutionality of imprisonment in this situation; see K&S, p. 313. But some courts find a due process violation. See, e.g., *State v. Guminga*, 395 N.W.2d 344 (Minn. 1986), holding that it is a violation of due process for D to be "convicted of a crime punishable by imprisonment for an act he did not commit, did not have knowledge of, or give express or implied consent to the commission thereof."

4. **Interpretation:**   It is not always clear whether the legislature *intended* a particular statute to give rise to vicarious liability.

    a. **Statutory reference:**   Sometimes, the statute may contain words indicating that the employer or principal will be liable; e.g., "any sale of liquor [to a minor] is the act of the employer as well of that of the person actually making the sale...."

    b. **Statute requires culpability:**   If the statute is silent on the issue of vicarious liability, but requires a culpable mental state on the part of the person actually committing the act (e.g., "intentionally," "recklessly"), then normally the employer/principal cannot be convicted without a showing that he, too, had the same culpable mental state. L, p. 267.

    c. **No-fault statute:**   If the statute is silent on the issue of vicarious liability, and it is interpreted so as to place strict liability on the employee, the odds are that it will also be interpreted to provide for vicarious liability without a showing of the employer's fault. Thus in *U.S. v. Dotterweich, supra*, p. 24, the Supreme Court jumped from a finding that the statute was intended to impose strict liability on one who actually makes a mislabeled shipment, to the conclusion that vicarious liability for a higher-up was also intended. This conclusion is criticized in L, pp. 268-69.

    d. **Severity of punishment:**   The severity of the punishment for violation of the statute is perhaps the most important factor in interpreting the legislative intent. If the punishment is relatively light (e.g., a fine), the court is likely to find both that strict liability for the actor was intended and that vicarious liability was intended. If a prison sentence is authorized by statute, on the other hand, both of these conclusions are less likely to be reached.

        i. ***U.S. v. Park* authorizes potential imprisonment:**   However, the fact that a substantial prison sentence is authorized won't *automatically* prove that the legislature did not intend to create vicarious liability. Thus in *U.S. v. Park*, 421 U.S. 658 (1975), the U.S. Supreme Court upheld a corporate executive's strict-liability conviction under a statute theoretically authorizing imprisonment for up to a year on a first conviction, and up to three years upon a second.

(1) Facts: D, president of Acme Markets, was convicted of violating an FDA-enforced statute prohibiting shipment of adulterated food. The government showed that D had been informed of unsanitary conditions at one of the company's sixteen warehouses, and that these conditions were not rectified. D attempted to defend on the grounds that he had delegated responsibility for remedying the situation to responsible subordinates, and that he himself was not guilty even of negligence.

(2) Holding: But the Court disagreed, holding that to further the statute's public welfare purposes, D could be convicted merely upon a showing that he was theoretically "responsible" for maintenance of sanitary conditions (just as he apparently was responsible for everything else that happened in the company).

L. Mistakes of fact or law: Courts have often tended to treat *mistakes* of fact or law by the defendant as involving a whole separate body of law, distinct from the general principles of *mens rea*. In reality, however, many questions of mistake, particularly mistakes relating to factual issues, simply pose *mens rea* issues under a different guise. Frequently, the defendant's mistake will simply *prevent the requisite mental state* from existing at all, and the case should be disposed of on this ground.

Example: Suppose that rape is defined as intentionally having intercourse with one whom the defendant knows does not consent. If the defendant mistakenly believes that his victim was consenting, he should be acquitted, not because of any special doctrine of "mistake," but simply because the special intent required for the crime of rape (the intent to have intercourse where there is no consent) is lacking.

1. Grounds for confusion: Courts have traditionally limited the mileage a defendant can get out of his mistake in three ways: (1) by holding that the mental state required for the crime is a very general, rather than specific, one (e.g., by holding that rape requires only intent to have intercourse, not intent to have intercourse with a non-consenting woman); (2) by holding that a mistake is never a defense unless it is "reasonable"; and (3) by holding that a "mistake of law" can never be a defense.

2. General mental state: Since many statutes, particularly older ones, do not make clear precisely what mental state is required, there has been much scope for courts to hold that the most general kind of culpable intent suffices, and that the defendant's mistake did not negate that broad culpable intent.

a. Moral wrong: One way that this has often been done is by application of the doctrine that the requisite general mental state exists if, under the facts as the defendant believed them to be, his conduct and intent would have been either criminal or *"immoral."*

Example: D is tried for the offense of taking an unmarried girl under the age of sixteen out of her father's possession against his will. D defends on the grounds that he reasonably believed that the girl was eighteen, as she told him she was.

Held, conviction affirmed. Even had the facts been as D thought they were, he would still have been guilty of the moral wrong of taking a girl out of her parent's possession (despite the fact that this would not have been a crime, since she was over sixteen.) Accordingly, D will be held to have had a culpable mental state. But if D's mistake had been that he erroneously thought that her father had consented, this would be a defense since, had his understanding been correct, he would have committed no moral wrong. (A dissent argued that the "look at the facts as the defendant assumed them to be" rationale should only be applied where, on the facts as supposed by D, his conduct would have been a lesser crime, not merely a moral wrong.) *Regina v. Prince,* L.R. 2 Cr. Cas. Res. 154 (Eng. 1875).

3. **Mistake must be "reasonable":** Older cases have frequently made the blanket statement that a mistake can never be a defense unless it was *"reasonable."* This statement is generally made without consideration of the fact that the mistake, reasonable or otherwise, may negate the required specific mental state.

    Example: D, a soldier, attempts to have intercourse with a young Japanese girl he meets on the street in Tokyo. He is tried for assault with intent to commit rape, and defends on the grounds that the area was one in which prostitution was common, and that he mistakenly believed that the girl was a prostitute. D contends that he is entitled to the defense of mistake, even if his belief that the victim was a prostitute (and therefore was consenting) was unreasonable.

    Held, an unreasonable mistake is no defense. "When consent is in issue, whether or not it was given is a question of fact for the court. It, not the accused, must determine whether the woman's conduct was such as to lead the accused to believe she had consented to his acts." *U.S. v. Short,* 4 U.S.C.M.A. 437 (Ct. Mil. App. 1954).

4. **Mistake of law:** Finally, the traditional view has been that a *"mistake of law,"* even if completely reasonable, can never be a defense. Many cases have blindly applied this rule not only where the defendant is ignorant of the fact that there was a statute proscribing his conduct (in which the "mistake of law is no excuse" doctrine is still agreed to be generally sound; see *infra,* p. 30) but also where the mistake of law is as to a *collateral fact,* and the mistake negates a required mental state.

    Example: Suppose D honestly but mistakenly believes that she has been validly divorced, because her husband, H, has so informed here. In fact, however, the Mexican divorce procured by H would not be recognized by an American court. Now, D purports to re-marry X. According to the traditional view, D would be guilty of bigamy, because she has made a "mistake of law" about the validity of a Mexican divorce, and a mistake of law cannot be a defense.

5. **Modern view:** But *modern* law gives a *much bigger role* for mistakes. The modern approach to mistake is exemplified by the Model Penal Code. M.P.C. § 2.04(1) provides that "ignorance or mistake as to a matter of fact or law is a defense if: (a) the ignorance or mistake negatives the purpose, knowledge, belief, recklessness or negligence required to establish a material element of the offense; or (b) the law provides that the state of mind established by such ignorance or mistake constitutes a defense."

    a. **Effect of this view:** This approach makes two principal changes in the traditional case-law discussed above, one with respect to the effect of an unreasonable mistake, the other with respect to the effect of a mistake of law on a collateral factual issue. Each of these changes is discussed below.

6. **Unreasonable mistake:**   If the crime is one as to which a showing of intent or knowledge is required, then an ***unreasonable mistake*** negating such intent or knowledge will ***block conviction*** under the Model Penal Code. Thus on the facts of *U.S. v. Short, supra,* assuming that the court recognized that the crime of assault with intent to rape required an intent to have unconsented-to intercourse, the defendant's belief that there was consent (***however unreasonable***) would be a defense (or, more precisely, would block a *prima facie* showing of liability).

   a. **Effect on rape convictions:**   Even where the court does subscribe to the Model Penal Code rule, however, the effect of that rule will obviously depend on how the court defines the required mental state. For instance, if the court holds that the crime of rape requires merely an intent to have intercourse, not an intent to have unconsented-to intercourse, then the Model Penal Code rule will not block liability where the defendant believes that there has been consent. However, where absence of a belief that there has been consent is found to be part of the *mens rea* of rape, the Model Penal Code can produce dramatic results, as occurred in the case set forth in the following example.

      Example: One of the Ds, Morgan, is convicted of aiding and abetting rape; the other three Ds are convicted of rape as well as aiding and abetting rape. The Ds defend by claiming that Morgan invited the other three Ds to have sex with his wife, telling them beforehand that his wife "might put up a show of struggling," but that this would be only a "charade stimulating her sexual excitement, as in reality she would welcome intercourse with them." The wife does indeed put up a struggle, and it is subsequently clear to the jury that she did not in fact consent.

      Held, by the House of Lords, if the three Ds did indeed believe Morgan's story, and thus believed that there was consent, they cannot be convicted of rape or aiding and abetting it, since those crimes require an intent to have non-consensual intercourse. This is true even if their belief was unreasonable. *Director of Public Prosecutions v. Morgan,* 61 C.A. 136 (Eng. 1975).

      Note: The House of Lords upheld the Ds' conviction in *Morgan,* however, on the grounds that even if the jury had been instructed that an unreasonable (but honest) mistake was a defense, a reasonable jury could not possibly have believed the story. (This finding was in turn probably due to the fact that the defendants had changed their story, having previously in the trial contended that the victim had willingly entered into an orgy. See L, p. 171, fn. c.) This result demonstrates that the finder of fact is of course always free to disbelieve the defendant's testimony that he was actually mistaken.

   b. **Statutory rape:**   A similar result has been reached in some jurisdictions with respect to the crime of ***statutory rape*** (i.e., intercourse with a woman below a certain age, regardless of actual "psychological" consent on her part). Thus in *People v. Hernandez,* 393 P.2d 673 (Cal. 1964), the California Supreme Court interpreted a statute making it rape to have sexual intercourse with a female under the age of eighteen years; the statute specified no particular mental state. The court held that the defendant's reasonable belief that the girl was over eighteen (she was in fact only three months less than eighteen) was a defense, since his reasonable belief negated any criminal intent.

(The Court implied that an ***unreasonable*** belief that the girl was over eighteen would not have been a defense.)

   i. **Model Penal Code position:** The Model Penal Code contains a special provision governing mistake as to the other party's age in a sex-offense crime. M.P.C. § 213.6(1) provides that a reasonable mistake as to a child's age is a defense if the criminality depends on the child's being below a critical age other than ten, but is not a defense if the crime is based upon the child's being below the age of ten. This rule is explained as follows: if the victim is in fact under ten, "no credible error of perception would be sufficient to recharacterize a child of such tender years as an appropriate subject of sexual gratification." On the other hand, where the girl is over ten, but under sixteen (making the man potentially liable for corruption of a minor but not rape), the man "evidences no abnormality.... At most, he has disregarded religious precept or social convention." M.P.C., Comment 2 to § 213.6.

7. **"Lesser crime" theory retained:** As noted above, the traditional view was that if, even on the facts as the defendant mistakenly supposed them to be, his acts would have been either a moral wrong or a lesser crime, his mistake cannot be a defense. The Model Penal Code follows this rule with respect to conduct that would be a lesser crime, but rejects it as to conduct that would merely be a moral wrong. M.P.C. § 2.04(2) provides that "although ignorance or mistake would otherwise afford a defense to the offense charged, the defense is not available if the defendant would be guilty of another offense had the situation been as he supposed."

    Example: Suppose D steals a necklace from a costume jewelry store. The necklace is made of diamonds, and is worth $10,000, but D shows that he believed it to be merely costume jewelry worth less than $500. Since D's act would have been a crime (a misdemeanor under the Model Penal Code) even had the facts been as he thought them to be, his mistake will be no defense to the felony (more than $500 stolen) charge. See M.P.C., § 223.1(2). (An earlier draft of the Model Penal Code would, however, have made the defendant's reasonable belief as to the value of the property relevant; see Tent. Dr. No. 2, § 206.15, Comment 3.)

    a. **Conviction treated as being of lesser offense:** But where the defendant makes such a showing that he mistakenly believed facts that would have made his conduct a lesser crime, the Model Penal Code does provide that upon conviction, the "grade and offense" of the crime (e.g., third-degree felony) shall be reduced to those of the crime which the defendant would have committed had the facts been as he supposed. Thus the defendant in the above example could be convicted only of a misdemeanor (non-violent theft of less than $500), not a third-degree felony (violent theft or theft of over $500). This amounts to virtually the same thing as treating the defendant as having been convicted of the lesser offense. M.P.C. § 2.04(2).

8. **Mistake of law as to collateral fact:** Modern cases have also been more willing to recognize that the general rule that "mistake of law is no defense" should not apply at all when the mistake relates to the application of law to fact, and the fact is a collateral one. These cases recognize the validity of the rule that the defendant's mistaken belief that no statute makes the particular conduct a crime is not a defense. (This rule, and the few

exceptions to it, are discussed *infra*, p. 30.) But other mistakes involving questions of law may very well constitute a defense, just as mistakes of fact can, if they **negative the required mental state**.

Example 1: D, whose car has been repossessed by Finance Company (as the Company has a right to do under its loan agreement), breaks into the car and takes it back. His mistaken belief that the car is still his **will** be a defense to a theft prosecution, under the modern view, since the requisite mental intent for theft is intent to take property which one knows or believes to belong to another. The fact that D's mistake has legal aspects (i.e., who has proper title to the car) is irrelevant. But if D had taken his neighbor's car, and attempted to raise the defense that he didn't know that there was a statute making it a crime to take one's neighbor's property, this would not be a defense.

Example 2: The Ds are tried for the crime of kidnapping, which is defined to require an intent to imprison the victim "without authority of law." The Ds testify that they believed that the person they confined was the murderer of the Lindbergh baby, and that they had been assured by a police officer that he was appointing them a "special deputy" to aid with the case.

Held, even if the Ds were unreasonable in their mistaken belief that they had authority of law, this belief negated the required intent to act "without authority of law," and they may not be convicted. *People v. Weiss*, 12 N.E.2d 514 (N.Y. 1938).

Note: But if the Ds in the *Weiss* case had testified that the police officer had assured them that no statute made it a crime to seize a crime suspect, this would probably not have been a defense. In this situation, their belief would not have been as to a collateral factual issue (whether they had "authority of law"), but whether there was a statute making their conduct a crime. Admittedly there may be a blurred line between believing that one has special authority, and believing that one's act is not a crime, but the distinction is an important one in principle.

    a. Bigamy and adultery statutes: The recognition that a mistake of law leading to a mistake of collateral fact may be a defense, has led some courts to hold that a defendant may not be convicted of **adultery** or **bigamy** where he reasonably believes that a prior divorce is valid. See, e.g., *People v. Vogel*, 299 P.2d 850 (Cal. 1956), holding that a good faith belief that the defendant's former wife had obtained a valid divorce was a defense to a charge of bigamy.

        i. Defense of reasonable attempt to learn law: The same result was reached on different grounds in *Long v. State*, 65 A.2d 489 (Del. 1949), in which the defendant's conviction of bigamy was reversed on the grounds that he had made full and diligent efforts to learn whether his wife's foreign divorce decree was valid. The reversal was based not on the ground that the defendant was mistaken as to a matter of fact negativing his intent, but on the theory that he had consulted a lawyer and had relied upon the latter's advice as to a matter of law. The vast majority of courts would probably not recognize this as a valid defense.

9. Mistaken belief that conduct is not a crime: As just stated, the rule that "mistake of law is no defense" is properly limited to situations in which the defendant **mistakenly believes that no statute makes his conduct a crime**.

Example: Suppose that D is retarded, and does not know that rape is a crime. He can nonetheless be convicted of rape, as long as it can be shown that he intended to have unconsented-to sexual intercourse.

a. **Reasonable mistake:** In this core "D mistakenly believes that no statute makes his conduct a crime" situation, even a *reasonable mistake* about the meaning of the statute will *not* protect D. In other words, so long as the crime is not itself defined in a way that makes D's guilty knowledge a prerequisite, there is no "reasonable mistake" exception to the core "mistake of law is no defense" rule.

Example: A New York statute makes it a crime to possess a loaded pistol without a license. A provision in that statute expressly exempts "peace officers," defined in a different statute to include "correction officers of any state correctional facility or of any penal correctional institution." D is a corrections officer at a federal prison, and is charged with carrying an unlicensed pistol. He first defends (successfully in the trial court) on the grounds that he *is* a corrections officer as defined in the statute, but an appeals court rules against him on this issue, holding that the statute applies only to corrections officers at state prisons. D is then tried, and asserts the defense that he reasonably believed that the statute did not apply to him.

Held, for the prosecution. A defendant's mistaken belief that the statute does not apply to his conduct, even if that mistake is reasonable, does not by itself establish a defense. True, New York statutory law gives a defense for a "mistaken belief … founded upon an official statement of the law contained in (a) a statute or other enactment…." However, this language was not meant by the legislature to apply to a misreading of a statute, but only to a correct reading of the statute that turns out to be invalid for some other reason. If D's "I reasonably misread the statute" defense were accepted, "the exception would swallow the rule. Mistakes about the law would be encouraged, rather than respect for and adherence to law." (But a dissent contends that D should be given the benefit of the statutory provision referring to "mistaken belief …founded upon an official statement of the law contained in…a statute or other enactment….") *People v. Marrero*, 507 N.E.2d 1068 (N.Y. 1987).

10. **Exceptions to general rule:** However, many states, and the Model Penal Code, recognize a few *exceptions* even to the generally-accepted rule that D may not defend on the grounds that he believed that no statute made his conduct a crime. M.P.C. § 2.04(3) recognizes two principal types of situations in which ignorance of the statute that makes the defendant's conduct a crime may constitute a defense.

a. **Law not promulgated:** First, the defendant will escape liability if he can show that the statute or regulation defining the offense was not known to him, and was not *"published or otherwise reasonably made available* prior to the conduct alleged." (M.P.C. § 2.04(3)(a).) This result is probably required by the U.S. Constitution's prohibition of *ex post facto* laws, i.e., laws which make an action a crime that was not a crime at the time it was committed. Thus the defendant will escape liability, for instance, if a statute makes it a crime to fail to follow certain administrative regulations, and the regulations are not published in any systematic codified way (which is unfortunately the case in most states). This defense is much more likely to be available where the wrong is one which could be called *"malum prohibitum"* (conduct whose criminality and wrongfulness is not obvious, such as failing to comply with an unusual state product-labeling requirement) than where the crime is *"malum in se"* (obviously immoral, such as murder).

    i.   Traditional expansion: Similarly, even a statute that was published at the time of the defendant's act may not be used as the basis for punishment if, after the act, there occurs an unforeseeable **judicial enlargement** of the application of the statute. For instance, in *Bouie v. City of Columbia*, 378 U.S. 347 (1964), two blacks took seats in a restaurant and refused to leave upon demand; a statute existing at the time of the sit-in made it criminal trespass for a person to enter another's property "after notice" forbidding such conduct. The South Carolina Supreme Court affirmed the defendants' convictions by expanding its interpretation of the statute to cover the wholly different act of **remaining** on property after receiving notice to leave. The U.S. Supreme Court reversed, on the grounds that the South Carolina court's ruling was "unforeseeable" and that where an "unforeseeable state-court construction of a criminal statute is applied retroactively to subject a person to criminal liability for past conduct, the effect is to deprive him of due process of law in the sense of fair warning that his contemplated conduct constitutes a crime."

  b.   Interpretation later found to be invalid: Second, the defendant may raise the defense that he reasonably relied upon one of the following **official statements** of the law, which later turned out to be **erroneous**: (1) A statute or other enactment (e.g., a statute purporting to repeal a different statute, where the later statute is ultimately held to be unconstitutional); (2) A judicial decision, opinion or judgment; (3) An "administrative order or grant of permission"; and (4) An "official interpretation" of the public officer or body "charged by law with responsibility for the interpretation, administration or enforcement of the law defining the offense." See M.P.C. § 2.04(3)(b).

  c.   Mistake of law defense built into statute: It is always possible for the legislature to write a statute in such a way that a mistake of law *will* constitute a defense (or so that awareness of the criminality of the conduct is an element of the offense). The statute might provide, for instance, that whoever does a certain action, with knowledge that that action is in violation of the statute, shall be convicted. Unfortunately, statutes are often ambiguously drafted when it comes to determining whether or not awareness that the conduct in question is illegal is an element of the offense.

    i.   "Knowingly" requirement: For instance, the legislature frequently requires that the defendant take some action "knowingly," and the statute then mentions other statutory provisions or regulations in a kind of shorthand manner. The defendant will typically claim that the presence of the word "knowingly" means that D must be shown to have known that the other statutory provisions or regulations were being violated; the prosecutor claims that "knowingly" merely means that D must have known the basic nature of his own acts, not known that they violated the statute. There is no strong majority approach to deciding such cases — the modern tendency is probably to benefit D by reading the word "knowingly" broadly. See, e.g., *Liparota v. U.S.* (*supra*, p. 19), where the Supreme Court held that a statute punishing "whoever knowingly uses, transfers, acquires...[food stamp] coupons in any manner not authorized by [the statute] or the regulations" required the prosecutor to show that D *knew* his conduct was in violation of the regulations.

ii. **"Willfully" requirement:** The same ambiguity arises when the legislature defines a crime in a way that requires the defendant to act ***"willfully."*** In the case set out in the following example, the U.S. Supreme Court said that D could be guilty of a "willful" violation of the statute only if he ***in fact knew that his actions amounted to a criminal offense at the time he undertook them.***

Example: D tries to discharge a large gambling debt owed to a Reno casino by paying it off with $100,000 in cash. He is informed by the casino that it has to report to the federal government any cash transaction of $10,000 or more. Rather than risk having his gambling activities reported, he goes to a bank to try to get a cashier's check. When the bank informs him it has the same legal constraints, he decides to purchase numerous cashiers checks, each for less than $10,000, and each from a different bank. A federal statute prohibits "structuring" a financial transaction, by dividing it up into several smaller ones merely to avoid the federal reporting requirements, and another statute makes it a federal crime to "willfully" violate the first statute. D is charged with the crime of violating the latter statute.

Held, for D: the requirement of a willful statutory violation means that D may only be convicted if the prosecution proves not only that he structured his transaction to avoid having the bank report it, but that he *knew* such structuring was illegal at the time he did it. *Ratzlaf v. United States*, 114 S. Ct. 665 (1994).

Quiz Yourself on
MENS REA

5. John Wilkes Booth decides to kill Lincoln, because he thinks Lincoln is a tyrant. Booth notes in his diary, "I have decided to kill Lincoln the day after tomorrow." Before anything further happens, Booth is arrested by the FBI. Is Booth subject to criminal liability?

6. Kramer and George are motorists in the State of Seinfeld. The two approach an empty parking spot at the same time. After each yells at the other about who is entitled to the spot, Kramer leaves his car and walks over to George's car. Kramer pulls a screwdriver from his pocket and touches it to George's throat, hoping that the touch will scare George away. In fact, however, George reacts by twisting his head, and in so doing, cuts himself severely against the blade of the screwdriver. Kramer did not intend to physically injure George, merely to frighten him. The State of Seinfeld defines the crime of assault as occurring where one "purposely causes bodily injury to another...." A decision of the Seinfeld Supreme Court states that assault is a crime which requires "general intent." May Kramer properly be found guilty of assault?

7. The State of Mane enacts a criminal statute stating that "Any person who sells misbranded hair care products shall be guilty of a misdemeanor, punishable by up to 7 days in jail." Delilah is charged with selling to Samson a can of hair spray labelled "Makes your hair grow longer," when in fact the can makes your hair all fall out.

(A) Assume for this part that the statute's legislative history makes it clear that the Mane legislature intended that the statute shall apply even though the seller does not know (and has no reason to know) of the mislabelling. Assume further that Delilah demonstrates that she neither knew nor had any particular reason to know that the can she sold Samson was mislabelled. May Delilah constitutionally be convicted of a statutory violation and sentenced to 6 days in jail?

(B) Assume for this part that everything specified in Part (A) remains true, except that: (1) There is no legislative history shedding any light on whether the Mane legislature intended to require any particular mental state for a violation of the statute; and (2) The statute mandates a jail sentence of between 30 days and one year upon any conviction. Should a court convict Delilah of the violation?

8. Abbott and Costello, who do not know each other, meet on the street one day and begin to talk. Abbott tells Costello that he is late for an appointment in the building they are standing near, and that he will pay Costello $250 to do him a favor. Abbott explains that he has borrowed his friend's red Porsche and parked it down the street, but has lost the keys. Having learned that Costello is an auto mechanic, Abbott asks Costello to break into the Porsche, hot-wire it, and deliver it to an address that Abbott scribbles on a piece of paper. Costello accepts the offer and carries it out. The story later turns out to be false — in fact, the Porsche belongs to a stranger, and Abbott is really a thief who has duped Costello into delivering the car to Abbott's fence. Costello is charged with auto theft, defined in the jurisdiction as "knowingly or purposefully taking a vehicle belonging to another." The case is tried before a judge, who finds that Costello actually believed Abbott's story, but that a "reasonable person" would not have believed the story. If the state follows the Model Penal Code approach to mistake, can Costello be convicted?

Answers

5. **No.** Intent is a state of mind and, with nothing more, is not criminal. Here, Booth has not yet committed any kind of action designed to bring about the desired result, so his intent cannot by itself give rise to criminal liability. (However, once Booth's intent was combined with some action designed to bring about the desired results, it could become culpable, even though the final act — killing — hadn't yet occurred. As we'll see in later chapters, this is the basis for the crimes of attempt and conspiracy.)

6. **Yes.** When courts hold that a crime requires merely "general intent," they usually mean that all that must be shown is that the defendant desired to commit the act which served as the actus reus. Here, the act that served as the actus reus was the placing of the screwdriver against George's throat. Once the prosecution shows that Kramer desired to unlawfully touch George's throat for the purpose of frightening him, the fact that Kramer did not intend to injure George will be viewed as irrelevant.

7. **(A) Yes.** State legislatures have the power to enact criminal statutes that do not require a mens rea, particularly where the statutes regulate food, drugs and misbranded articles. Such statutes are known as "strict liability" statutes. The fact that the statute may be violated innocently does not make a conviction (or even a short jail sentence) a violation of the defendant's constitutional due process rights.

(B) No. In a series of cases, the Supreme Court has held set out rules of thumb for determining when a statute was intended as a strict-liability (or as it is sometimes called, "public welfare offense") statute. See, e.g., *Staples v. U.S.* One of these rules of thumb is that if the penalties for violation are relatively severe, it is unlikely that the statute was intended to impose strict-liability. Here, this factor cut strongly in favor of non-strict-liability, since a minimum sentence of 30 days in jail (with a maximum of 1 year) is relatively severe. Therefore, the judge should infer that the legislature intended that at least, the defendant must have behaved negligently in selling the mislabelled product. Consequently, the court should acquit Delilah.

8. **No.** Some older cases contain broad statements to the effect that a mistake of fact cannot be a defense unless the mistake was "reasonable." But the Model Penal Code, and nearly all modern statutes, hold that

if intent or knowledge is required as an element of a crime, then even an ***unreasonable mistake*** will block conviction if it negated such intent or knowledge. See M.P.C. §2.04(1)(a). Here, Costello's belief in the truth of Abbott's story prevented Costello from having the requisite intent to take another's property or the requisite knowledge that it belonged to another — the fact that Costello was unreasonably credulous is irrelevant. Of course, the more unreasonable Costello's belief in the truth of Abbott's story is, the less likely the judge or jury is to find that Costello *in fact believed* that story. But the facts here tell us that Costello actually believed the story, so this by itself is enough to negate purpose or knowledge.

LEXIS®-NEXIS® Searches on **MENS REA**

Sub-Topic	Suggested Searches
Different states of mind	
Purposely	`(crime or criminal) and (purpose! w/25 ((mens rea) or (mental state)))`
Recklessly	`(crime or criminal) and ((reckless! or (conscious! disregard!)) w/25 (mens rea or mental state))`
Mistakes of fact or law	`(crime or criminal) and (specific intent w/10 mistake)`

III. CONCURRENCE

A. Concurrence generally: It is often said that there must be *"concurrence"* between the *mens rea* and the *actus reus*. This requirement exists principally to deal with two kinds of problems:

1. What happens when the defendant at some point has the *mens rea* necessary for a particular crime, and later commits an act meeting the physical requirements for that crime, but the mental state did not exist at the time the act occurred (e.g., D stabs his victim, intending to kill him, but just wounds him and, thinking the victim to be dead, throws the body into a river, so that drowning is the actual cause of death)?; and

2. What happens when the defendant has the *mens rea* necessary for one crime, and his act meets the requirements for a different crime (e.g., D intends to commit a simple battery on his victim, but the victim turns out to be a hemophiliac and unforeseeably bleeds to death)?

The first of these situations might be called the "temporal concurrence" problem, and the second might be called the problem of concurrence between "mind and result."

B. Concurrence between mind and act ("temporal concurrence"): The requirement that there be concurrence between the mental state and the act (the *actus reus*) is often called the requirement of *"temporal concurrence"* because, generally speaking, the requirement is not met if, at the time of the act, the required mental state does not exist. This may be so either because the defendant, before acting, had both formed the mental state and then abandoned it, or because he did not acquire the requisite mental state until *after* his act.

Example: The crime of common-law larceny is defined as the taking of another's property with intent to deprive him of it. D takes V's umbrella from a restaurant, thinking that it is his own. Five minutes later, he realizes that it belongs to V, and decides to keep it. D has not committed larceny, because at the time he committed the act (the taking), he did not have the requisite mental intent (the intent to deprive another of his property). ***The fact that he later acquired the requisite intent is irrelevant.***

1. **Mental state must cause act:** Close analysis shows, however, that concurrence requires more than merely that the right *mens rea* must exist at the time the *actus reus* occurs. It must be the case that the *mens rea caused*, or "actuated," the *actus reus*. L, p. 284.

    Example: D intends to kill V. While driving to a store to buy a gun to carry out his intent, D accidentally runs over V, killing him. D is not guilty of murder, even though the intent to kill V existed at the time the act (driving the car over V) took place. The act "must be done for the actual carrying out of the intent and not merely to prepare for its execution." L, p. 286.

2. **Voluntary intoxication:** There is at least one situation in which the *mens rea* does not even have to be in existence any more when the *actus reus* occurs, so long as a causal relation between the two can be found. That is the situation in which the defendant, in order to gather up his courage to commit a certain crime, **voluntarily intoxicates** himself. If he commits the crime in a drunken stupor, he will probably not successfully defend on the grounds that he no longer had the mental state necessary for the crime, since that mental state will indirectly have caused the act. See L, p. 286 and fn. 21 thereto.

3. **Concurrence must be with act, not results:** The concurrence principle requires merely that there be concurrence between the *mens rea* and the *actus reus*, not concurrence between *mens rea* and the bad results. For instance, if the defendant purposely shoots his victim, attempting to kill him, and the victim lingers in the hospital for six months, the necessary concurrence (of intent and the act of shooting) exists, even though by the time the victim dies, the defendant no longer desires his death. L, pp. 286-87.

4. **Concurrence may be with any act that is legal cause of harm:** Most crimes are defined in terms of harmful results (e.g., homicide is the wrongful taking of a life; rape is a non-consensual intercourse, etc.). Where the defendant takes **several acts** which together lead to the harmful result, it will not always be clear with which of those acts the *mens rea* must concur. In general, the concurrence requirement is met if the mental state concurs with **any act that suffices as a legal cause** of the harm. (What constitutes a legal cause is discussed *infra*, p. 46.)

    Example: D, knowing he is subject to frequent epileptic fits, conceals this fact from his state's Motor Vehicle Department, and obtains a driver's license. While driving he suddenly has a seizure, goes out of control, and kills V, a pedestrian. If D is prosecuted for involuntary manslaughter (which usually requires a mental state of recklessness), concurrence between his mental state and his act will probably be found, since his act will be the act of driving with knowledge of his susceptibility to seizures, not the losing of control and running over V.

    a. **Defendant mistaken as to victim's death:** The problem of determining which act must concur with the mental state arises in cases where the defendant has attempted to kill his victim, believes the victim to be dead, and ***destroys or conceals the body***. If it turns out that the original murder attempt was unsuccessful, and that the efforts to conceal the body are what really killed the victim, is there concurrence? The defendant can argue that when he made the original murder attempt, there was no concurrence since the act did not lead to death, and that when he hid the body, there was no concurrence since the requisite intent to kill was no longer present.

    i. Argument generally rejected: Most courts have ***rejected*** this type of argument. They have usually done so on the grounds that the killing-and-concealing was all part of one transaction, which should be treated as one act for purposes of the concurrence rule. Thus in *Thabo Meli v. Regina*, 1 All E. R. 373 (Eng. 1954), the defendant struck the victim over the head, and, thinking he was dead, pushed him over a cliff. Medical evidence showed that the victim was actually alive when he was rolled over the cliff, and died of exposure thereafter. The appellate court held that the defendant had set out to do both the murder and the concealment as part of one plan, and that there was therefore concurrence between *mens rea* and the acts causing death.

    ii. View first act as legal cause of death: LaFave & Scott (p. 271-273) suggest that a better way to sustain a conviction in such situations is to concentrate solely on the first act (in *Thabo Meli*, the blows on the head). There is clearly concurrence between *mens rea* and this first act; the only possible difficulty is that this first act might not be viewed as the legal cause of death. However, since disposal of a body is not an unforeseen or unusual thing, particularly when it is done by the person who did the killing, the concealment is not necessarily a superseding cause, and it is not unreasonable to hold that the original act is at least one of the legal causes of death. This aspect of legal cause is discussed further *infra*, p. 59.

C. Concurrence between mind and result: The second aspect of the concurrence requirement is that there must be concurrence between the *mens rea* and the ***harmful result***, at least in the case of those crimes defined in terms of bad results (e.g., homicide, rape, etc.) It is not necessary that the actual results correspond exactly to the mental state; thus if the crime charged is an intentional one, it is not necessary that the harm match precisely in degree, manner of occurrence and victim the defendant's intention. But if what actually occurs is too far removed from what was intended, there will be held to be no concurrence, and no liability.

1. Different crime occurs: Thus if the harm which actually occurs is of a completely different type from what the defendant intended, so that it is a result associated with a ***different, more heinous, crime,*** the defendant will ***not be guilty*** of the graver crime.

Example: Suppose D, a seaman, enters the hold of his ship for the purpose of stealing rum from the cargo. He lights a match to see what he's doing, and inadvertently causes the ship to catch fire. D will not be guilty of arson (defined so as to require an intent to burn), since his intent to steal cannot be substituted for the required intent to cause a fire.

    a. Different, but not more serious, result: The same principle also applies even where the actual result is ***not more serious*** than the intended result, but the intended result is nonetheless associated with a ***different crime*** than the intended one. In other words, the general principle is that ***the intent for one crime may not usually be linked with a***

result associated with a different crime. For instance, if D attempts to shoot V to death while the latter is coming out of his house, D will not be liable for arson if the shot misses and ruptures the stove, causing the house to burn down. (This assumes that arson is defined so as to require an intent to burn, rather than merely negligence or recklessness with respect to the risk of burning.)

    b. **Model Penal Code formulation:** The Model Penal Code follows this general rule; § 2.03(2) provides that where purposely or knowingly causing a particular result is a required element of a crime, the element is not established if the actual result is "not within the purpose or the contemplation of the actor." The Code contains several exceptions to this general principle, which are discussed at various places *infra*. (None of these exceptions would make the seaman in *Faulkner*, or D in the above example, guilty of arson.)

2. **Recklessly- or negligently-caused result:** Essentially the same rule applies where the defendant has *negligently* or *recklessly* acted with respect to the risk of a particular result, and a materially different result occurs. The necessary concurrence between the defendant's mental state and the actual harm will be found lacking. See Model Penal Code, § 2.03(3).

Example: D recklessly takes target practice with his rifle in a heavily populated area; his conduct is reckless because of the high risk that D will injure or kill a person. One of D's shots, instead of hitting a person, hits an automobile's gas tank, leading to a large fire. Assuming that the danger of causing such a fire was not large, D will not be convicted of even a lesser degree of arson (e.g., burning caused by recklessness), since his conduct was reckless only with respect to the risk of bodily harm, not burning.

3. **Felony-murder and misdemeanor-manslaughter rules:** The common-law rules on *homicide* contain two very important exceptions to the general principle that there will be no liability for a resulting harm that is substantially different from that intended or risked by the defendant.

    a. **Felony-murder:** First, if the defendant was engaged in the commission of certain *dangerous felonies*, he will be liable for certain deaths which occur, even if he did not intend the deaths. This is known as the *felony-murder* rule, and is discussed *infra*, p. 237.

    b. **Misdemeanor-manslaughter:** Second, if the defendant was engaged in a *malum in se* misdemeanor (i.e., a misdemeanor that is immoral, not merely contrary to some regulation), and a death occurs, the defendant may be liable for involuntary manslaughter, even though his conduct imposed very little risk of that death, and the death was a freak accident. This is known as the *misdemeanor-manslaughter* rule, and is discussed *infra*, p. 259.

    c. **Peculiar rules of homicide:** These two rules should probably be viewed not as exceptions to the general rules of concurrence, but rather, as special ways of defining murder and manslaughter. Thus the felony-murder rule can be viewed as a special crime the *mens rea* for which is intent to commit one of the dangerous felonies; similarly, the misdemeanor-manslaughter rule establishes a special kind of involuntary manslaughter, as to which the *mens rea* is the intentional commission of a misdemeanor.

4. **Same kind of harm but different degree:** Related to the different-kind-of-harm-than-intended problem just discussed, is the situation where the harm which results is of the *same general type* as that intended by the defendant, but of either *more or less serious degree*. Such a problem would arise if the defendant merely intends to make a simple battery on the victim, and the victim turns out to be a hemophiliac who bleeds to death, or, conversely, the defendant intends to kill his victim, but the victim suffers only a superficial wound.

   a. **Actual result more serious than intended one:** If the actual harm is *greater*, and related to, the intended result, the general principle is that there is *no liability for the greater harm.*

      Example: Assume that the jurisdiction in question has a statute defining the crimes of simple battery (applicable to minor bodily harm) and aggravated battery (applicable to assault which produces "grievous bodily harm"); assume also that each statutory provision requires an intent to produce the requisite bodily harm. D gets into a minor scuffle with V, intending merely to hit him lightly on the chin; however, V turns out to have a "glass jaw," which is fractured by the blow. D will not be held guilty of aggravated battery, since his intent was only to produce the lesser degree of bodily injury required for simple battery.

      i. **Apparent exceptions for resulting death:** But once again, the various degrees of *homicide* are defined in such a way that this principle's force is often negated. For instance, if D intends just to wound V slightly, and V bleeds to death because he is a hemophiliac, D will be guilty of involuntary manslaughter; see L, p. 291. This result occurs not because the rules of concurrence are suspended for involuntary manslaughter, but because one kind of involuntary manslaughter is "misdemeanor-manslaughter," and battery is one of the kinds of misdemeanors that will trigger the rule; see *infra*, pp. 259-261.

      ii. **Intent-to-grievously-injure murder:** Similarly, if D intends to *seriously injure* V (e.g., by trying to shoot at his eye), in most states he will be guilty of *murder* if V dies from the attack. This is because most states have a form of murder as to which the *mens rea* is not intent-to-kill, but intent-to-grievously-injure. See *infra*, p. 234.

   b. **Actual harm less serious:** If the harm which actually occurs is *less serious* than that intended, and is of the *same general type* as that intended, but associated with a different (and less serious) crime, the defendant *is* liable for the less severe crime. In this situation, courts have simply felt that it is not unjust to hold the defendant for the less serious crime.

      Example: D shoots at V, attempting to kill him. Instead, the bullet just grazes V. D can be convicted of battery (and also of attempted murder).

5. **Manner of harm:** Suppose that the harm which actually occurs is of the same type as that intended by the defendant, but it occurs in a radically *different manner* from that

anticipated or intended. In this situation, the rules of *causation*, discussed *infra*, p. 44, may shield the defendant from liability if the harm came about through an extraordinary intervening cause. But there is no *concurrence* problem in this situation.

6. **Different victim:**   Similarly, suppose the defendant intends to injure one victim, and ends up injuring a *different one* (e.g., D shoots at X, and hits V). Here again, there is no concurrence problem; the court will hold that there is sufficient relationship between the *mens rea* and the harmful result. (Nor will there generally be a causation problem; see the discussion of "transferred intent" *infra*, p. 47.)

Quiz Yourself on
CONCURRENCE

9. Guy Fawkes goes to the corner bar and says to himself, "I'm going to drink until I'm completely smashed, and then I'm going to stagger drunkenly around town until they lock me up." He drinks until, as he knows, he's completely smashed. He then leaves the bar and wanders around drunkenly. At one point, he he stops to light a cigarette, drops the match, and burns down his neighbor's garage. The jurisdiction's public intoxication statute applies to "a person who intentionally appears in public in a state of intoxication." The jurisdiction's arson statute applies to one who "intentionally sets fire to real property not his own." Can Guy be convicted of arson on the grounds that his general criminal intent to commit the crime of public intoxication is transferred to his commission of the crime of arson?

10. On July 4, Dr. Evil firmly decides to do away with Austin Powers by killing him with a super-sonic freeze gun. He plans to commit the crime on July 5.

(A) For this part only, assume that during the night of July 4-5, Dr. Evil has a dream in which he is damned to hell. On the morning of July 5, he wakes up with a change of heart, and no longer plans to kill Powers. Later that day, while he is walking down the street with his supersonic freeze gun, he happens to pass Powers. He is so startled that he reflexively and unintentionally squeezes the trigger of the gun, and it goes off, freezing Powers to death. Is Dr. Evil guilty of murder?

(B) Same facts as above, except that Dr. Evil does not have the dream or the change of heart. He plans to kill Powers at Powers' home at 8:00 pm using the freeze gun. At 5:30 p.m., while Dr. Evil is en route to his favorite restaurant with the gun in hand, Powers passes by. Dr. Evil is so startled that he reflexively squeezes the trigger and the gun goes off, freezing Powers to death. Is Dr. Evil guilty of murder?

Answers

9. **No, because there is no concurrence between Guy's mens rea and the result.** In the case of a crime defined in terms of a bad result, the requirement of concurrence normally means that the mental state must relate to that harmful result, not to some other, quite different, harmful result associated with some other crime. So here, the mental state for public intoxication (intentionally appearing drunk in public) cannot be "transferred" to satisfy the mental-state requirement for some other crime (here, intent to burn). There are some exceptions to this requirement of concurrence (e.g., the felony-murder rule and the misdemeanor-manslaughter rule), but none of those exceptions applies on these facts.

10. **(A) No.** Although Dr. Evil had the mens rea for murder at one point, he did not have it at the time of the act that led to Austin Power's death. The requirement of *"temporal concurrence"* means that the mens rea and the actus reus must exist at the same time, and, indeed, that the mens rea must *"cause"* the actus

reus. Here, by the time of the actus reus (the squeezing), the mental state (intent to shoot) was no longer present. Therefore, the requirement of temporal concurrence is not satisfied.

(B) Still no. Although Dr. Evil did intend (eventually) to kill Austin Powers under these facts, his act of shooting was not caused by his desire to kill. For the requirement of "temporal concurrence" to be satisfied, the mens rea must in some way "cause" the act in order. Since that was not the case here, Dr. Evil gets off. That's true despite the fact that Dr. Evil in a sense still possessed the desire to (eventually) kill at the time he squeezed the trigger. (Of course, Dr. Evil might have a hard time convincing the trier of fact that he didn't intend to shoot at the time of the shooting — but if he could do this, he's entitled to an acquittal on the murder charges.)

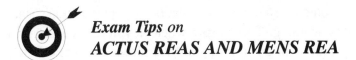

Exam Tips on
ACTUS REAS AND MENS REA

The most common issues that arise on exams regarding the requirements of an "actus reus" and a "mens rea" are the following:

Duty to act

☛ Duty-to-act is tested with some frequency on exams, because it calls for the close analysis of a fact pattern. Look for a party who *fails to help another party in distress.* Remember that a party is criminally liable for an omission *only if there exists a duty for her to act.*

   ☞ **Trap:** Profs will try to distract you by presenting a very callous witness to an accident — one who fails to render aid. Don't be swayed by unsympathetic feelings toward the bystander. Instead, concentrate on whether she had a duty to act. *The ordinary bystander, who has no previous involvement with the peril, has no duty to act.*

   Example: A lifeguard at a public swimming pool leaves work early with the permission of her employer. While the pool is unattended a child falls in, striking her head against the edge of the pool. A bystander, B, witnesses the child's fall, but fails to act, despite her knowledge that there is no lifeguard on duty and the fact that she is a strong swimmer. B had no duty to act and cannot be found guilty of any common-law crime.

      ☞ **Exceptions:** There are two kinds of situations to watch for, exceptions in which there will be a duty to assist:

      [1] A *contractual obligation* to act.

         Example: D, an apartment-house landlord, receives repeated complaints about a malfunctioning heating system, and fails to respond. The lease says that the landlord will maintain the furnace. The furnace explodes and causes a fire, which leads to the death of V, the complaining tenant. D had a contractual obligation to fix the furnace, and therefore his failure to fix it met the actus reus requirement.

[2] A party ***undertakes to give assistance*** and fails to follow through.

> *Example:* D, a prominent heart surgeon, is called by the U.S. Government and asked to perform an unusual heart operation for free on V, an public official. D agrees, but then without warning fails to show up at the appointed time. It's too late to find another surgeon, and V dies without the surgery. (Timely surgery would almost surely have saved him.) When D undertook to do the operation — in circumstances where he knew the search for a surgeon would stop — he incurred an obligation to do what he said he'd do, or at least to notify the government of a change of mind. His failure to perform that duty supplies the actus reus needed for criminal liability in V's death.

Statutory Language (as to both Actus Reus and Mens Rea)

☛ Whenever a question asks you to contemplate a party's violation of a jurisdiction's statute, pay close attention to the statute's wording. This is true whether you're focusing on the actus reus or the mens rea. *Trap:* Profs will try to fool you by drafting a statute differently than the rule prevalent in most jurisdictions or different than the common law. Remember to distinguish between *strict liability* statutes and those requiring *intent.*

These "statutory interpretation" question are pretty much freebies — you don't really need to know any substantive law to answer them, you just need to read and think carefully. So *don't waste these freebies by carelessness.*

☛ Tips on statutory interpretation:

☞ **Knowledge:** Look for the words "knowledge" or "knowing." This will often be a clue that a required element (knowledge as to some aspect) is missing.

> *Example:* A statute provides: "Any person who sells an intoxicating substance to a person with knowledge that the person is under the age of 18 years shall be guilty of a misdemeanor." Observe that although most statutes that forbid the sale of alcohol to minors impose strict liability, this one does not. And, under this statute, if a bartender believes (reasonably or unreasonably) that a patron is over 18, then that required element is lacking and there is no violation.

☞ **Ambiguous elements:** If it's unclear from the wording whether knowledge is a requirement, ***argue both ways.***

> *Example:* A statute provides: "Whoever assaults with a deadly weapon any federal officer engaged in the performance of his duties is guilty of a felony." It's plausible that this statute might be interpreted to require that the defendant have known or believed that the victim was a federal officer. So you should make arguments both ways on this point.

☞ Identify the specific conduct prohibited, and make sure that the conduct in question qualifies.

> *Example:* A statute provides that "Any person who knowingly sells an intoxicating substance to a person under the age of 18 years shall be guilty of a misdemeanor." This statute prohibits a *sale* of an intoxicating substance, without any further conduct by the customer. So the fact that the customer never *drank* the

liquor (or didn't get drunk) is irrelevant.

☛ **Ignorance of law:** Watch for an indication that a defendant was unaware of or did not understand a statute. Because all people are ***conclusively presumed to know the law***, this is not a general defense.

  ☞ **Exceptions:** However, there are some (modern) crimes that are expressly defined so as to require that the defendant know of the statutory prohibition. But if that's the case, your prof will have to signal this fact to you. So if you don't see any such signal, you can presume that the general rule of "ignorance of the law is no excuse" applies.

☛ **Arson:** Pay special attention to ***arson*** problems, because element-of-the-crime issues abound when arson is involved.

  Example: At common law, arson could be committed only on another's *dwelling*. But many modern statutes extend the definition to buildings other than dwellings, and profs often test this point. If your prof wants to test you on a modern statutory variation on the common-law arson requirements, he/she will *have* to specify the text of the statute, so when you see the statutory text be on the lookout for coverage of buildings other than dwellings.

☛ **Civil statutory violation as evidence of mens rea**: Fact patterns often involve violations of *civil* (as opposed to criminal) statutes. Note that, although violation of a civil statute may be *evidence* of negligence or recklessness, a civil statutory violation alone does not automatically *satisfy* the mens rea requirement for negligence or recklessness.

  Example: A state statute requires that any person engaging in the use of fireworks have a license which is issued upon the completion of a safety course. D, who does not have a license, believes he is competent to use fireworks and brings some to X's party. D sets off some of the fireworks in X's backyard. Although D acts "reasonably," one of the fireworks explodes prematurely, causing a fire which completely destroys X's home. The criminal arson statute requires recklessness or intent to start a fire. D cannot be found guilty of arson solely because of his violation of the statute requiring a license for the use of fireworks — the prosecutor will have to show that D's overall behavior constituted recklessness.

CHAPTER 2

CAUSATION

Introductory Note: This chapter examines the requirement that the defendant's actus reus must have "caused" the harmful result. The prosecutor must make two distinct showings of causation: (1) that the act was the *"cause in fact"* of the harm; and (2) that the act was the *"proximate"* or *"legal"* cause of the harm. Problems like that of the unintended victim, or the intervening act, fall within category (2).

I. INTRODUCTION

A. Causation generally: The problems of concurrence, discussed in the previous chapter, related to the links between mental state and act, and between mental state and harmful result. We turn now to the link between *act and harmful result.* Where the links between the defendant's act and the harmful result that ensues are unduly tenuous, we say that there is no *causal relationship* between the two, and therefore no liability.

B. Two aspects of causation: In the case of any crime which is defined in terms of harmful results (e.g., murder, rape, arson etc.), the prosecution must prove that the defendant's *actus reus* "caused" the harmful result. To do this the prosecution must in reality make two different showings: (1) that the act was the *"cause in fact"* of the harm; and (2) that the act was the *"proximate"* cause (or, as the Model Penal Code puts it, the "legal" cause) of the harm. We consider each of these aspects in turn.

II. CAUSE IN FACT

A. Cause in fact generally: For an act to be a *"cause in fact"* of a result, it is often said that it must be the *"but for"* antecedent of that result. By this is meant that if the result *would have happened anyway*, even had the act not occurred, the act is *not a cause in fact* of that result.

Example: D shoots at V, but only grazes him, leaving V with a slightly-bleeding flesh wound. X then comes along and shoots V through the heart, killing him instantly. D's act is clearly not a "cause in fact" of V's death, since V would have died, and in just the manner he did, even if D had not shot him.

1. **Expansive test:** This "but for" test is obviously a very expansive one, under which every result will have literally thousands of antecedent "but for" causes in fact. In the above example, for instance, X's act is obviously a cause in fact of V's death, since he would not have died when he did without that act. But the act of the weapons' manufacturer in making X's gun was also a "but for" cause, since if X had not had the gun, he couldn't have shot V. Similarly, the marriage between X's parents was a "but for" cause, since otherwise X wouldn't have been around at all to do the shooting.

2. **"Substantial factor" test:** But as expansive as the "but for" test is, it leaves out one category of acts which almost all courts would hold to be "causes in fact," even though they

are not "but for" causes. Such a cause occurs where an act other than that of the defendant would have been sufficient to bring about the result, but the defendant's act is a "*substantial factor*" in bringing about the result nonetheless. Sometimes the defendant's act in this situation would have been sufficient by *itself* to bring about the result, but this is not necessary for it to be held to be a "substantial factor," and therefore a cause in fact.

Example: D shoots V in the leg, causing him to bleed a serious amount. X then shoots V in the arm. V dies from loss of blood from the two wounds. Medical evidence shows that V would have died from the loss of blood from the X wound even without the D wound, but that he would not have died from the D wound without the X wound. Even though D's act is therefore not a "but for" cause of V's death, D will be held to have been a cause in fact of V's death, because his act was a "substantial factor" in producing that death.

3. **Shortening of life:** In determining whether the defendant's act is a "substantial factor" in bringing about death, one obviously relevant fact is whether the act *shortened the victim's life.* For instance, suppose that V is shot by X, and will definitely die within a day. If D comes along and shoots V, killing him instantly, D will undoubtedly have been a "cause in fact" of the death, since his act directly shortened V's life. See L, p. 296.

   a. **Intervening act shortens life:** The converse situation is more difficult. That is, in the above example, is *X* also a cause in fact of V's death? He can argue that D was the only precipitating cause of death, and the fact that V might have died later is irrelevant. This argument has sometimes succeeded; thus in a California case on almost exactly these facts, the court found that the earlier aggressor had been prevented from killing his victim as effectively "as he would have been if some obstacle had turned aside the bullet from its course and left [V] unwounded." *People v. Lewis*, 57 P. 470 (Cal. 1899). See B&P, p. 430.

      i. **Contrary view:** But other courts have held otherwise in this situation. In any event, if the court is inclined to convict, it may tend to find that the victim died of the effect of both wounds; for instance, in the above example, it might find that V might have survived the second shooting had he not already been lying in a mortally weakened state.

   b. **Lengthening of life:** Although the fact that the victim's life has been shortened is one indication that the defendant's act was a "substantial factor," and therefore a cause in fact, of death, it is possible to imagine a situation where an act could be a cause of death even though it *lengthened* the victim's life. Suppose, for instance, that V is scheduled to take a plane trip, but is poisoned by D, and dies a week later. If the plane crashed, killing all aboard, V will have lived almost an extra week, but D will nonetheless be a cause in fact of his death. See L, p. 297, fn. 25.

4. **Murder victim must have been alive at time of act:** One obvious application of the "cause in fact" requirement is that in a homicide case, the prosecution must prove that the victim was *alive* at the time of the defendant's act. This will not always be an easy evidentiary burden.

   Example: D, driving his car, hits V, a pedestrian. D flees the scene of the accident, dragging V with him under the car. D is charged with manslaughter, on the theory that he was criminally negligent in continuing to drive after the impact. The medical evidence is inconclusive as to whether V was killed upon impact, or only after he had been dragged.

Held, D cannot be convicted, because it has not been shown beyond a reasonable doubt that V was still alive at the time of D's negligent conduct (the driving after the accident). (There was no showing that D was negligent in the first instance in hitting V.) *State v. Rose*, 311 A.2d 281 (R. I. 1973).

5. **Two people working together:** The above discussion assumes that the two concurring acts occur independently of each other. If the two occurred as part of a joint enterprise (e.g., X and D each shoot V, as part of a conspiracy to kill him), the act of each will be attributed to the other, and there will be no need to determine whether each wound was a substantial factor in killing V.

III. PROXIMATE CAUSE GENERALLY

A. **Proximate cause, in general:** Once it has been established that the defendant's act was a cause in fact of the harm, it remains for the prosecution to demonstrate that the act and the harm are sufficiently closely related that the act is a ***"proximate"*** or "legal" cause of that harm. This is really a problem not of "cause" as the layman understands the term, but rather of ***policy***: is the connection between the act and the harm so attenuated that it is unfair to hold the defendant liable for that harm?

1. **Distinguished from tort concept of proximate cause:** Proximate cause in criminal law is related, but by no means identical to, the tort concept of proximate cause. Tort law, insofar as it is concerned with compensating an innocent victim, will be inclined to charge a defendant with far-reaching consequences of his act. Criminal law, on the other hand, being based upon the concept of moral fault and punishment, generally insists upon a substantially closer connection between the defendant's act and the ensuing harm. See *Commonwealth v. Root*, 170 A.2d 310 (Pa. 1961), discussed further *infra*, p. 59, which establishes a stricter rule for proximate cause in criminal than in tort cases.

2. **More than one proximate cause possible:** Just as every event has more than one "cause in fact," so an event may have ***more than one*** "proximate" or "legal" cause. For instance, if X and Y both shoot V so that either wound would have been fatal, and he in fact dies from the combined effect of both wounds, both X and Y will be held to be proximate causes of V's death.

B. **No mechanical principles:** Courts have struggled for centuries to set forth mechanical principles that would establish, for all cases, when an act or event is the proximate cause of a particular result. Ultimately, however, it has come to be realized that no such mechanical rules are possible, and that the existence of proximate cause is a policy issue that must be decided on a case-by-case basis.

1. **Model Penal Code approach:** Thus the Model Penal Code expressly puts the issue in terms of the finder of fact's sense of justice: at least where the actual result involves the same "kind of injury or harm" as that intended by the defendant, the act is the proximate cause of the harmful result if it is ***"not too remote or accidental in its occurrence to have a [just] bearing on the actor's liability or on the gravity of his offense."*** M.P.C.

§ 2.03(2)(b). (The word "just" is in brackets because it is an "alternative" formulation in the Code.)

2. **Year-and-a-day rule in homicide:**   One common-law attempt to establish mechanical rules concerning causation has survived to the present day: this is the rule that in homicide cases, the defendant cannot be convicted if the victim did not die until *"a year and a day"* following the defendant's act.

   a. **Rationale:**   The theory behind this rule was that, because of the inexactness of medical science, it was impossible to say that the defendant's act was a sufficiently direct factor in producing death if the victim survived that long. Many commentators have criticized this rule in light of present-day medical knowledge, but it still exists, either in the form of statute or case law, in the substantial majority of American states. However, "the modern trend is to abolish the rule." L, p. 318 and fn. 161 thereto.

3. **Types of problems raised:**   Cases raising serious proximate cause issues tend to fall into two general categories: (1) those in which the type of harm intended occurred, and occurred in roughly the manner intended, but the *victim was not the intended one*; and (2) cases in which the general type of harm intended did occur and occurred to the intended victim, but in an *unintended manner*. Our discussion below is thus divided into these "unintended victim" and "unintended manner of harm" categories.

   a. **Reckless and negligent crimes:**   Proximate cause issues can also arise where the *mens rea* for the crime is not intent, but *recklessness* or *negligence*. Here, the problems arise where either (1) the victim is one as to whom there was not a great (in the case of recklessness) or unreasonable (in the case of negligence) risk of harm; or (2) the harm occurred in a manner that was not extremely likely (in the case of recklessness) or unreasonably likely (in the case of negligence). Accordingly, we shall treat crimes defined in terms of recklessness or negligence during the course of the two-category breakdown referred to above.

IV. PROXIMATE CAUSE — UNINTENDED VICTIMS

A. **Unintended victims generally:**   Generally speaking, the fact that the actual victim of the defendant's act was *not the intended victim*, will not prevent the defendant's act from being the proximate cause of the actual harm. Instead, courts apply the doctrine of *"transferred intent,"* under which the defendant's intent is *"transferred" from the actual to the intended victim*. Of course, this "transfer" is just a legal fiction, but the result, that there is still proximate cause between act and result, is well-established.

Example: D, intending to kill X, shoots at him, but because of his bad aim, hits and kills V. D is guilty of the murder of V, because his intent is said to be transferred from X to V. See, e.g., *Regina v. Smith*, 169 Eng. Rep. 845 (1855).

1. **Model Penal Code supports this view:**   The Model Penal Code expresses this rule without using the notion of "transferred intent." The defendant's act is not prevented from being the proximate cause of a result if the result differs from that intended "only in the respect that a different person or different property is injured or affected…." M.P.C. § 2.03(2)(a).

2. **Applies only where particular result is element of crime:**   The "transferred intent" rule
    (or, as it might be better called, the "unintended victim" rule) applies only to those crimes
    of which causing a particular bad result is an element. Thus it has no application to crimes
    of ***attempt.***

    Example: D tries to shoot X to death, and merely wounds V, rather than killing him. D
    may be convicted of battery against V (by combining the "unintended victim" rule with
    the rule discussed *supra*, p. 39, that allows the *mens rea* for a more serious crime to suffice
    for conviction of a less serious, related, crime.) And D may also be convicted of the
    attempted murder of X. But he may ***not*** be convicted of the attempted murder of V. See
    B&P, p. 564-69.

B. **Resulting crime is more serious:**   Suppose that D hurts an unintended victim, but also hurts
    that victim in a very different, and much more ***serious manner***, than he intended vis-a-vis his
    actual target. In this situation, some courts (and the MPC) hold that the doctrine of transferred
    intent applies, but only enough to make the defendant guilty of the ***lesser*** (intended) crime.

    Example: D swings his fist at A, intending only to hurt A without causing him serious bodily
    harm. The punch misses A, and hits B in the jaw. B falls down, strikes his head on the curb,
    and dies. At least according to the Model Penal Code, D is liable only for manslaughter, not
    murder, because D's intent is "transferred" to the limited extent of making him guilty for hurt-
    ing B even though he intended to hurt A; however, he is not liable for the "excess" damage
    caused to B over what he intended to inflict on A. See MPC § 2.03(2)(a), Note.

    Note: The result in the above Example follows from the rules on ***concurrence***. Recall (see
    supra, p. 35) that the *mens rea* and *actus reus* must "match up," in the sense that the former
    must "motivate" the latter. Above, when D intended merely to commit an assault or battery,
    and death resulted, the necessary concurrence was not present. The use of the doctrine of
    transferred intent does not overcome this lack of concurrence.

    1. **Higher degree because of victim's special identity:**   Now suppose that the same type of
        harm results to the unintended victim as D intended to impose on the target, but that due to
        the victim's ***special identity***, a more serious ***punishment*** is imposed. Here, D typically
        does ***not*** get relief — he is treated as if he had intended that harm to the actual victim
        rather than to the target.

        Example: D shoots at A, a civilian, intending to kill him. The bullet accidentally hits B, a
        police officer. A statute imposes higher penalties on killing a police officer than killing a
        civilian. D may probably be convicted of killing a police officer, with the higher penalties.
        See 93 Yale L.J. 609, 649.

C. **Application where different property destroyed:**   The "unintended victim" rule can also
    apply where the crime is against ***property***, rather than against the person. For instance, sup-
    pose that D tries to burn down X's house, but instead the fire spreads or veers due to a change
    of wind, and burns down V's house. D is guilty of arson as to V's house. (But if the fire also
    kills Y, the "unintended victim" rule will not make D guilty of Y's murder. He might be guilty
    of murder under the felony-murder doctrine, or under a statute making "depraved indifference
    to life" one of the permissible mental states for murder or manslaughter, but this result would
    then be due to the definitional peculiarities of homicide, not the "transferred intent" rule.)

D. Actual victim not foreseeable: The "unintended victim" rule probably applies even where the danger to the actual victim was ***completely unforeseeable.*** For instance, Lafave suggests that if, when D shoots at X, the two are out in the desert, and think they are alone, but V is sleeping behind some sagebrush when he is hit by the errant bullet, D may nonetheless probably be convicted of murdering V. L, pp. 301-01.

   1. Model Penal Code might be exception: The Model Penal Code might allow D to escape in this situation. While, as noted, the Code does not let the defendant escape merely because a different person was injured than the defendant intended, the defendant may escape under the alternate theory that the actual result was "too remote or accidental in its occurrence to have a [just] bearing on the [defendant's] liability...." (M.P.C. § 2.03(2)(b)).

E. Must be linked to "manner of harm" problems: The fact that an unintended victim was injured does not prevent the defendant from showing that in ***some other respect***, his act was not the proximate cause of the result.

   1. Illustration: Suppose, for instance, that D shoots at X, and misses, and that X reacts by tracking D down and, two days later, shooting at him and hitting V by mistake. *X* might be guilty of murdering V under the "unintended victim" rule, but *D* will not; he will be able to show that although his shooting at X might be a "but for" cause of V's death (and therefore "a cause in fact" of that death; see *supra*, p. 44), X's own act was a superseding cause of V's death, which made the causal link between D's act and V's death too remote for D to be liable for it. (See the discussion of superseding causes, including acts by third persons, *infra*, pp. 54-57.)

   2. Must be linked with concurrence rules: Similarly, the defendant may escape by showing that the rules of concurrence, discussed *supra*, p. 35, have not been complied with.

   Example: D, trying to kill X, shoots at him. The bullet misses, and instead ruptures a gas line in V's house, causing the house to burn down. Had the bullet killed V, D would be guilty of murder, as we have noted. But he will not be guilty of arson of V's house, since he did not have the *mens rea* (intent to burn) required of arson.

F. Defense assertable against intended victim: By and large, the defendant in an "unintended victim" case is entitled to raise the ***same defenses*** that he would have been able to raise had the intended victim been the one harmed.

   1. Illustration: For instance, if D shoots at X out of legitimate self-defense, this will prevent him from being guilty of the murder of V if the bullet strikes the wrong target (assuming that D has acted reasonably, which might not be the case if the transaction took place in a crowded street.) Similarly, if D tries to shoot X to death in the heat of passion, after discovering X with D's wife, and the bullet actually strikes V, D would probably be able to get the charge reduced to voluntary manslaughter.

G. Mistake of identity: A related "unintended victim" problem is posed in "***mistaken identity***" cases. If D shoots at V, mistakenly thinking that V is really X (D's enemy), D will be guilty of the murder of V just as if he had been shooting at the person who was actually X and mistakenly hit V. As was noted previously (*supra*, p. 27), a "mistake of fact" will generally be a defense only if it negates the particular mental state required for the crime. The crime of murder may require an intent to kill, but it does not require a correct belief as to the victim's identity. See L, p. 303.

H. Crimes of recklessness or negligence: Where the crime is one for which the mental state is merely *recklessness* or *negligence*, the problem of the unforeseen victim may also arise. In the case of a crime requiring recklessness, the problem would arise if the defendant was aware that his conduct posed a high degree of risk to X (or to a class of which X is a member), and instead harm occurred to V, as to whom the defendant had not been aware of a high risk. In a negligence type of crime, the problem would arise where there was an unreasonable risk of danger to X (or to a class of which X was a member), and the harm occurred to V, as to whom there was not an unreasonable danger.

1. **Tighter link required:**   A *tighter link* between the defendant's act and the actual victim's injury is probably required where the crime is defined in terms of recklessness or negligence, than where it is intentional. See L, pp. 303-04. This would parallel the *tort rule*, where a defendant is liable for practically all the far-reaching consequences of his intentional torts, but only for a much narrower spectrum of unusual results from his negligent conduct; see, e.g., *Palsgraf v. L.I.R.R.*, 162 N.E. 99 (N.Y. 1928), holding that there is no liability to an "unforeseeable plaintiff" injured by the defendant's negligent act.

    a. **Recklessness:**   In *recklessness* crimes, this principle would probably mean that the defendant would *not be liable* for harm to a victim as to whom there was not a *high risk* of harm foreseeable from the defendant's position. (If one follows the Model Penal Code view that recklessness requires that the defendant be *aware* of the high risk of harm, there would be a further requirement that the defendant have been actually aware of such a high risk of harm to the actual victim.)

        Example: D decides to take target practice with his rifle in his backyard. He is aware that there is substantial risk that he will hit someone in his next-door neighbor's house, but he shoots anyway. Unbeknownst to him, the neighbor has been storing explosives in the house; the bullet hits the explosives, an explosion occurs which starts a fire, and the fire kills V, who lives a block away, and to whom D's shooting did not impose a foreseeably high risk of harm. D will not be liable for recklessness-manslaughter, i.e., manslaughter defined so as to have a *mens rea* of recklessness. (See *infra*, p. 257). (He might be liable for misdemeanor-manslaughter, arising out of the unlawful act of taking target practice in a residential area; however, even as to the misdemeanor-manslaughter rule, the unusual chain of causation might be enough to absolve D; see *infra*, pp. 259-261.)

    b. **Negligence:**   If the crime were one committable through *negligence*, the defendant would probably not be liable for an injury to a *victim who was not in the foreseeable zone of danger*. That is, there would be no "transferred negligence." Suppose, for instance, that in the above example, D was charged with merely being negligent (not reckless) as to the risk of harming his next-door neighbor. D would escape liability for the injury to V if there had been no foreseeable risk of such danger to V.

    c. **Model Penal Code view:**   The Model Penal Code apparently would not allow a defendant to escape from the consequences of his negligent or reckless conduct merely because the actual victim was not within the zone of foreseeable danger. See

M.P.C. § 2.03(3)(a). However, the defendant might be able to take advantage of § 2.03(3)(b), making him not liable where the result is "too remote or accidental in its occurrence to have a [just] bearing on the [defendant's] liability...."

V. PROXIMATE CAUSE — UNINTENDED MANNER OF HARM

A. Unintended manner of harm generally: Suppose the defendant's intended victim is harmed, and the harm is of the same general kind as that intended, but it occurs in an *unexpected manner.* Does the unexpectedness of the way the harm occurs absolve the defendant of liability, on the theory that his act was not the proximate cause of the result? No general answer can be given; the courts have developed a number of specialized rules for different kinds of situations. Cases are generally divided into those in which the defendant's act was a "direct" cause of the harm, and those in which there was an "intervening" cause between the defendant's act and the harm. The discussion below follows this division.

  1. No liability for bizarre results: The general principle common to all of the cases, however, is that the defendant should *not be liable* if the actual result occurs through a *completely bizarre, unforeseeable chain of events*. For instance, suppose D gets into a street fight with V, as a result of which V is knocked unconscious, recovers a few minutes later, drives away, and gets into an accident which would not have occurred had D not punched him (since he would have driven away earlier and not been at the place where the accident occurred when it occurred.) In this situation, all courts would agree that the harm to V from the accident was simply too fortuitous a result of the battery by D to make D liable for it.

  2. Classification not followed by Model Penal Code: The Model Penal Code does not follow the distinction between "direct" causation cases and "intervening" causation ones. The Code recognizes that the problem is essentially one of deciding whether the link between the defendant's act and the eventual result is so remote as to make it unfair to hold the defendant liable. Thus for an intentional crime, if the actual result is "not within the purpose or the contemplation" of the defendant, there is no liability if the actual result is "too remote or accidental in its occurrence to have a [just] bearing on the [defendant's] liability or on the gravity of his offense." M.P.C. § 2.03(2)(b).

B. Direct causation: In some cases the type of harm intended by the defendant may come about in an unintended manner, yet without the presence of any clearly-defined act by an outside person or thing. In this situation, the defendant's act is said to be the "direct cause" of the victim's injury, and it usually will be extremely difficult for the defendant to convince the court that the manner in which the harm occurred was so bizarre that the defendant was not the proximate cause of that harm.

  1. Small differences in type of injury: Thus if the same general *type of injury* (e.g., serious bodily harm, death, burning) occurs as was intended by the defendant, the fact that it deviates in some small manner from that intended is irrelevant. (This problem is also discussed in the treatment of concurrence, *supra*, p. 39).

  Example: D, a member of the Italian Red Brigade, shoots at V, trying to hit him in the knee-caps to cripple him. Instead, he hits V in the eye, blinding him. D will be guilty of mayhem (the intentional causing of grievous bodily injury; see *infra*, p. 268) even though the precise type of harm intended did not occur.

2. **Slightly different mechanism:**   Similarly, if the general type of harm intended actually occurs, the defendant will not be absolved because the harm occurred in a *slightly different way* than intended. (Again, we are assuming for the moment that there is no distinct "intervening cause.")

Example: D attempts to poison her husband, V, by putting five grains of strychnine in a glass of milk she serves him for breakfast. He drinks it, and becomes so dizzy from its effect that he falls while getting up from the chair, hitting his head on the table. He dies, and the evidence indicates that he may have died from the blow to his head, rather than the poison.

   Held, D is nonetheless guilty of murder. D created the condition which made the normal routine act of standing up dangerous, and the death is therefore the direct result of her act. *People v. Cobbler*, 37 P.2d 869 (Cal. App. 1934).

3. **Pre-existing weakness:**   The most common "direct causation" problem occurs when the victim has a *pre-existing condition*, unknown to the defendant, that makes him much more *susceptible to injury or death* than a normal person would be. The defendant in this situation is said to *"take his victim as he finds him"*, and may not argue that the defendant's own act was not the proximate cause of the unusually severe result.

Example: D beats V up, with intent to kill him. V runs away before very many blows fall, and a person in ordinary health would not have been severely hurt by the blows that did fall. Unknown to D, however, V is a hemophiliac, who bleeds to death from one slight wound. D is guilty of murder, notwithstanding the fact that, from his viewpoint, V's death from the slight wounds was unforeseeable.

Note on concurrence: In dealing with proximate cause problems, it is always necessary to remember the rules of concurrence, discussed *supra*, p. 35, relating to the link between intent and result. For instance, suppose that D had only been trying to commit a minor battery on V, rather than trying to kill him. If V died as a result of his hemophilia, D would not be liable for common-law intent-to-kill murder, because he did not have the requisite mental state, the intent to kill. (But he would probably be liable for manslaughter under the misdemeanor-manslaughter rule; see *infra*, pp. 259-261.)

4. **Death caused without physical impact:**   Courts today are generally willing to find that where death results *even without physical impact*, as the result of *fright* or *stress* caused by the defendant, the defendant's conduct can nonetheless be a proximate cause of the death. Although courts sometimes say that there can be no liability for effects on the "mind alone," there is almost always some physical effect in the victim's body (e.g., a heart attack) which is the direct cause of the death, and this physical result is enough to confer liability on the defendant even without physical impact.

Example: The Ds hold up V's business. They require V and his employees to lie down on the floor while the money is taken. V, who is an obese 60-year-old man with a history of heart disease, and who leads a generally stressful life because of his competitive business, is very frightened, and has a heart attack fifteen minutes after the robbery. The heart attack is fatal, and the Ds are prosecuted for his death under the felony-murder rule.

Held, the Ds may be convicted. Medical evidence indicated that the robbery was the "direct" cause of the heart attack, and it is irrelevant that the Ds had no reason to know of V's heart condition, and that V might have died soon anyway. *People v. Stamp*, 82 Cal. Rptr. 598 (Cal. App. 1969).

   a. Danger to third persons: One court has even gone so far as to find that the defendant caused the death-through-fright of his victim where the defendant's actions were *directed solely at a third person*. In *Ex Parte Heigho*, 110 P. 1029 (Id. 1910), D struck V's son-in-law in the face during an altercation; V was so frightened that she had a fatal heart attack. The appellate court held that D could be found guilty of misdemeanor-manslaughter.

5. "Come to rest in apparent safety": The defendant's liability for the results of which he is the "direct" cause is sometimes limited by an *exception* where the dangerous force unleashed by the defendant *"came to rest in a position of apparent safety"*. See P&B, p. 780-81.

   Example: D forces his wife, V, out of the house at night in freezing weather. She walks to the nearby house of her father without ill consequences, where she would have been taken in at any hour. Not wanting to disturb him in the middle of the night, however, she lies down outside, and freezes to death.

   Held, D is not guilty of manslaughter. V had reached a position of apparent safety, thus preventing D's act from being the proximate cause of her death. *State v. Preslar*, 48 N.C. 421 (1856).

   Note: This case might alternatively be viewed as one in which the victim's own acts (her gross contributory negligence) acted as an intervening, superseding, act. See *infra*, pp. 57-58.

6. Recklessness and negligence crimes: Where the crime requires a mental state merely of *negligence* or *recklessness*, and the type of harm that made the conduct negligent or reckless occurs, but in an unexpected manner, the defendant is likely to be liable, just as where the crime involves intent.

   a. Slightly more liberal standard: However, courts probably have some tendency to take the defendant's mental state into account in solving proximate cause problems, and a defendant who is only negligent or reckless may be somewhat less likely to be held for harm occurring in an unforeseen manner than if he had acted intentionally. Thus if D negligently shoots V in a hunting accident, giving V a small wound, and V unforeseeably bleeds to death because he is a hemophiliac, D will have a somewhat better chance of avoiding a conviction for involuntary manslaughter or criminally negligent homicide than he would of avoiding a murder conviction had he intended to kill V. (Nonetheless, in this particular situation he would probably be convicted, due to the strength of the general principle that one takes one's victim as one finds him.) See L, p. 310.

C. Intervening acts: The defendant's odds of escaping liability for harm occurring in an unanticipated manner are better where an *"intervening act"* or event contributes to the result than where the defendant has "directly" caused the harmful result.

1. **Dependent vs. independent intervening acts:** Courts have tended to divide intervening acts and events into two conceptually different categories: (1) those acts and events which would not have occurred except for the defendant's act; these are "dependent" acts (e.g., medical treatment for a wound caused by the defendant); and (2) acts and events which would have occurred even had the defendant not acted, but which combined with the defendant's act to produce the harmful result; these are called "independent" causes (e.g., V is in a car accident, which he would have been in even had D not previously beaten him up, but D dies from the combined result of the accident and his weakened condition stemming from the beating).

   a. **Significance of distinction:** The courts have used somewhat different tests to determine whether a *"dependent"* intervening cause is *superseding* (i.e., relieves the defendant of liability) than where the intervention is "independent." An independent intervention, which is by definition merely a coincidence, will usually break the chain of causation if it was *"unforeseeable"* from one in the defendant's position. A dependent intervening cause, on the other hand, since it is by definition a direct response to the defendant's conduct, will break the chain of causation only if it was not only unforeseeable, but also *abnormal*. See L, pp. 305-06. The significance of the distinction is that an act is less likely to be considered "abnormal" than it is to be considered merely "unforeseeable."

   Example: D beats up V, and leaves him by the side of the road. An ambulance picks him up, and while rushing him to the hospital, gets into a collision, killing V. D might be held responsible for this death, since the ambulance's picking up of V, and travelling at a high rate of speed, was a direct response to D's act (a "dependent cause") and is probably not "abnormal" (even though the accident itself was not particularly "foreseeable"). If, on the other hand, V had gotten up from the beating, and taken a later bus to visit his girlfriend than he would have taken had he not been beaten up, and the bus got into a fatal accident, D would probably not be liable. In this case, V's bus trip and accident would be merely an independent intervening act (a coincidence), and since the accident would probably be held to have been unforeseeable, it would be held to be a superseding cause.

   Note: LaFave, p. 308, suggests that even where the accident occurs during the ambulance ride, in the above example, D might not be held liable for V's death, on the grounds that the death is purely from new, medically-unrelated injuries.

2. **Four kinds of acts:** Our discussion below is organized according to the source of the intervening act: (1) intervening acts by *third persons*, (2) intervening acts by the *victim*; (3) intervening acts by the *defendant*; and (4) *non-human* intervening events.

3. **Intervening acts by third person:** If an intervening act is committed by someone who is neither the victim nor the defendant, that act will generally be superseding only if: (1) it was *independent* of the defendant's act (coincidental) and *unforeseeable*; or (2) it was *dependent* on the defendant's act (i.e., a response to it), and was *"abnormal"* (not merely unforeseeable).

   a. **Medical treatment:** The most common such intervening act is *medical treatment* performed by a doctor or nurse upon the victim, where this treatment is necessitated by the defendant's act. Such treatment is obviously a response to the defendant's act, and therefore will not be a superseding intervening cause unless the treatment is abnormal.

i. **Negligent treatment:** The fact that the treatment is *negligently performed* generally will *not*, by itself, be enough to make it so "abnormal" that it is a superseding event. Thus in *State v. Clark*, 248 A.2d 559 (N.J. 1968), the defendant argued that the victim, whom he had shot, would have survived an operation performed on her after the shooting had she not been given insufficient blood transfusions during it. The court held that as long as the treatment was part of the "usual course of practice" followed by the medical profession, neither any incidental negligence, nor the fact that a different treatment might have saved the victim, would make the treatment a superseding cause.

ii. **Reckless or grossly negligent treatment:** But if the medical treatment is "abnormal," which it would be if it was shown to have been performed *recklessly* or *in a grossly negligent manner*, this treatment *will* be a superseding intervening cause, and the defendant will not be responsible for harm (e.g., death) stemming directly from the treatment.

iii. **Departure from required surgery:** Similarly, if the treatment goes beyond what is necessary to care for the harm done by the defendant, and an attempt is made to *cure* other, *unrelated* problems, ill results occurring during the extended treatment will be superseding.

Example: D stabs V in the stomach. V is operated on for the stab wound, during the course of which operation the doctors discover a hernia. While they are attempting to correct the hernia, V has a heart attack and suffers fatal brain damage.

Held, for D. Since the hernia was unrelated to the stab wounds, and V would have survived had the hernia never been cured, the work on the hernia (which was going on when the heart attack occurred) is a superseding cause. (Also, there is some evidence that death may have been due solely to the anesthesiologist's failure to give adequate oxygen; this might constitute gross negligence, which would itself be a superseding cause.) *People v. Stewart*, 358 N.E.2d 487 (N.Y. 1976).

iv. **Disease or infection caught in hospital:** If the victim catches a *disease or infection* as a result of being in the hospital, the court will have to decide whether this disease or infection related directly to the wounds being treated, or was merely a coincidental by-product of the victim's presence in the hospital. If the former, this will be a superseding cause only if it was "abnormal." But if the latter, the disease or infection will supersede so long as it was not foreseeable. Thus in one well-known case, the victim of a gunshot wound died not from the wound, but from scarlet fever which she contracted from her attending physician; the scarlet fever was held to be a superseding cause, absolving the defendant of responsibility. *Bush v. Commonwealth*, 78 Ky. 268 (1880). (But L, at p. 309-10, fn. 06, 103, suggests that if the defendant had been aware that there was a scarlet fever epidemic, the victim's getting the disease would be a foreseeable intervention, and therefore not superseding.)

   v.   Non-fatal wound: The rule imposing liability on the defendant even where the direct cause of death is bad medical treatment probably applies even where the wounds caused by the defendant would definitely ***not have been fatal*** except for the medical treatment. (Of course, the defendant would be liable for murder in the case of the non-fatal wounds only if he inflicted them with intent to kill. See L, p. 307-08, fn.87.) However, if the wound was not just non-mortal, but actually ***superficial*** (e.g., a small cut), it is not so clear that the defendant will be liable for ensuing death from bad treatment.

b.   Nonmedical harm: The same distinction between dependent and independent causes is generally followed where the intervention is ***non-medical.***

Example: The Ds meet V in a bar, and decide to rob him. They encourage V to get drunk, and then take him for a car ride, during which they take his money, his boots and his eye glasses. They put him out on an unlit road in the middle of a cold and windy night. Half an hour later, as V is sitting in the middle of the road, he is run over by X, who is driving ten miles above the speed limit; V dies of the injuries he sustains. The Ds are tried for second degree murder, the statutory mental state for which is "depraved indifference to human life," accompanied by recklessness.

   Held (by a federal court acting on a *habeas corpus* petition after the Ds' conviction), the jury should have been instructed that the Ds "caused" V's death only if V's death was ***foreseeable*** to them. Lack of an instruction on causation deprived the Ds of due process, since it may have induced the jury to believe that causation could be inferred merely from the fact that V's death followed the Ds' conduct. *Kibbe v. Henderson,* 534 F.2d 493 (2d Cir. 1976).

Note: The prosecution appealed the *Kibbe* case to the U.S. Supreme Court, and got the decision cited above reversed. The Supreme Court held that while an instruction on "foreseeability" as it related to causation might have been desirable, its absence was not an unconstitutional deprivation of due process. The Court relied on the fact that the jury, in convicting, must necessarily have found that the Ds behaved "recklessly." One who behaves recklessly with respect to a particular risk (the risk of death, as the New York statute is written) must have foreseen that risk or, at least, that risk must have been ***foreseeable*** to him, said the Court. *Henderson v. Kibbe,* 431 U.S. 145 (1977).

c.   Intended result never superseded: If the intervening act leads to a result that is not only of the same general type (e.g., death, bodily harm) as that intended by the defendant, but is further ***almost identical*** to the desired result in its ***manner of occurrence,*** the intervening act will not be a superseding one. This is true even though the intervention may have been quite unforeseeable or abnormal.

Example: D, intending to have her nine-month-old son killed, gives a bottle of poison to the boy's nurse, saying that it is medicine that he is to be given. The nurse decides that the baby doesn't need the medicine, and puts it on top of the mantel piece. Several days later, the nurse's five-year-old son gives the poison to the baby, killing him.

Held, D is guilty of murder. *Regina v. Michael*, 169 Eng. Rep. 48 (1840).

d. **Negative act never supersedes:** A third party's *failure to act* will never be a superseding cause. For instance, suppose that D shoots V, and there is a doctor standing close by who could, with 100% certainty, prevent V from dying. Despite the fact that the doctor refuses to render assistance (even if he does so because he hates V and wants him to die), D will still be the proximate cause of death. And this will be true even if the third person has an affirmative duty to intervene (e.g., a parent with the duty to rescue his child who has been thrown into deep water by the defendant).

4. **Act by victim:** The *victim himself* may sometimes take actions which are potentially superseding intervening causes. Again, the test is generally the foreseeability and/or "normality" of the victim's act. Generally speaking, acts by victims tend to be taken in direct response to the defendant's act, so they will not be superseding unless they are "abnormal" (not merely "unforeseeable").

a. **Suicide:** Suppose D wounds or maims V, leading V to *commit suicide.* Is V's suicide a superseding event?

i. **Insanity:** If the evidence indicates that V was *driven insane*, or was otherwise not acting rationally, because of D's act, the suicide will not be superseding.

Example: D kidnaps V, a young woman, and commits various sexual perversions upon her, including putting mutilating bite marks all over her body. V becomes so distraught and ashamed that she takes poison. While V is in agony from the poison and screaming for a doctor, D fails to get her one. V eventually dies, of the combined effect of the poison, exhaustion, lack of medical treatment, and possibly an infection from one of the wounds.

Held, V's act of taking the poison was not a superseding act. The evidence showed that V was rendered "mentally irresponsible" by D's acts, and D's conduct was therefore a direct cause of her death. *Stephenson v. State*, 179 N.E. 633 (Ind. 1932).

ii. **Victim prefers death to life:** If the victim is not made "insane" or "mentally irresponsible" by the defendant's conduct, but is maimed in such a horrible way that he makes a decision that death is preferable to life, it is not clear whether his suicide will be an intervening cause. LaFave and Scott argue that suicide should not be a superseding act in this situation; L, p. 307.

b. **Encouraging suicide:** If the defendant *encourages* the victim to commit suicide, the former will normally be prosecuted for the crime of aiding and abetting suicide, not murder. But if a murder prosecution does take place, there is dispute about whether the defendant's act is either the cause in fact or the proximate cause of the death. See L, p. 307, fn. 86.

i. **Model Penal Code view:** The Model Penal Code, in § 210.5(1), makes it criminal homicide to cause another to commit suicide, if the defendant "purposely causes such suicide by force, duress or deception." The criminal homicide in this situation would normally be murder, though it might be voluntary manslaughter if the defendant was acting under certain types of mental or emotional disturbance.

(If the suicide is caused without "force, duress or deception," the defendant is guilty under the Code of the independent offense of "aiding or soliciting suicide," a second-degree felony if it is done purposely.)

c. **Victim refuses medical aid:** If the victim, rather than committing suicide, simply *refuses to avail himself of medical assistance* which would probably have prevented the injuries or death caused by the defendant, the victim's refusal will *not be superseding.*

Example: D stabs V four times. While she is in the hospital, V is told that if she does not have blood transfusions she will die. Because she is a Jehovah's Witness, she refuses the transfusions, and dies.

Held, V's refusal to allow the transfusions is not a superseding cause that relieves D of liability. "It has long been the policy of the law that those who use violence on other people must take their victims as they find them. This in our judgment means the whole man, not just the physical man." *Regina v. Blaue*, 3 Eng. Rep. 446 (Eng. 1975).

Note: If *Blaue* were a tort suit brought by the victim's parents for recovery against the defendant, the victim's refusal to "mitigate her damages" would probably have prevented the parents from receiving full compensation for their daughter's death. Thus the criminal law is more stringent than the civil law in this situation; this result has been criticized. See Glanville Williams, quoted in L., p. 327, note 1.

d. **Victim's attempt to avoid danger:** The victim may attempt to *avoid the danger* posed by the defendant. If this attempt at escape results in additional injury, the attempt will be a superseding cause only if it can be said to be an "abnormal" reaction. For example, suppose D locks the door of his bedroom and assaults his wife, V, with a knife, threatening to kill her. V is so frightened that she tries to escape from an upstairs window, and is killed in a fall. Since V's escape attempt would not be considered an "abnormal" reaction, D would be held to be the proximate cause of her death.

   i. **Lesser crimes:** The same principle would apply if the victim's escape attempt led to injury rather than death. For instance, if D in the above example had attacked V with intent merely to injure her, rather than to kill her, and she had broken her leg jumping out of the window, he would have been guilty of battery.

   ii. **Act not required to be prudent or foreseeable:** The defendant will be the cause of the victim's injury or death even if the victim's attempt to escape the danger was *unreasonable* and *imprudent*, as long as it was instinctual and not completely bizarre.

e. **Victim subjects self to danger:** With the defendant's urging or encouragement, the victim may sometimes *expose himself to danger*; if the danger materializes, the defendant will often be held to be a proximate cause of the result, despite the victim's own voluntary participation.

Example: The two Ds and V decide to play "Russian Roulette," in which each takes a turn spinning the chamber of a revolver containing one bullet, and pressing the trigger with the barrel held to the player's own head. The Ds each take a turn, and the gun does not fire. V tries it and the gun fires, causing V's death.

Held, the Ds may be convicted of manslaughter, and the fact that V voluntarily pressed the trigger is no bar to liability. Their conduct constituted reckless endangerment of V's life, insofar as they either encouraged him or at least cooperated with him in playing the dangerous game. (Cases involving drag racing, in which one competitor is sometimes held not responsible for the death of the other due to the latter's bad driving, were distinguished, on the grounds that they involved games left to the skill of the competitors. See *infra*, this page.) *Commonwealth v. Atencio*, 189 N.E.2d 223 (Mass. 1963).

i. **Drag racing:** A similar situation arises where the defendant and the victim participate in a ***drag race*** together, and the victim is killed or injured. Some cases have held that the victim's voluntary participation in the race, and/or his careless driving, are not superseding causes. Thus in *State v. Petersen*, 522 P.2d 912 (Ore. 1974), the defendant was held guilty of manslaughter for participating in a drag race in which a passenger in the other car was killed; the defendant "helped create the dangerous situation, and was a part of it. His conduct was a substantial factor in bringing about the decedent's death." The court refused to hold that there should be no liability because the decedent voluntarily assumed the risk of a crash (even though this would probably have been a defense to a civil action against D).

ii. **Different result:** Other cases, however, have held that, at least where the victim was a voluntary participant in the drag race, his own act *is* superseding. In one case, the court held that where the defendant drove one car, and the victim drove the other, the defendant was not the proximate cause of death where the victim "recklessly and suicidally" swerved his car into the path of an oncoming truck in an attempt to pass the defendant's car. The court stressed that proximate cause in criminal cases should be more narrowly defined than in civil cases. *Commonwealth v. Root*, 170 A.2d 310 (Pa. 1961).

5. **Act by defendant:** The defendant himself may commit not only the *actus reus*, but also an intervening act. In this situation, the courts are, not surprisingly, very reluctant to recognize the defendant's second act as something that supersedes the causal impact of his first act.

a. **Mistake as to death:** This happens most frequently in the ***mistake-as-to-death*** cases (*supra*, p. 36), in which the defendant intends to kill the victim, erroneously believes he has done so, and then ***destroys or conceals the "corpse"*** in a way that actually causes death.

i. **Not superseding:** The defendant cannot be charged with homicide based on the act that actually causes death (since, because there was no longer an intent to kill at the time of this latter act, there is no concurrence). But the court may well hold that the first act (which, by hypothesis, was accompanied by the requisite intent to kill) was the legal cause of death, and that the defendant's second act of concealment was ***not a superseding intervention***. LaFave believes that such a holding would be justified, on the grounds that "acts by the defendant himself to dispose of the body are not abnormal and thus do not break the causal chain...." L, p. 309.

6. **Non-human event:** An intervening cause may be in the form of a ***non-human event***. Such events will generally be coincidences, not responses to the defendant's act, and will therefore be superseding if they were not foreseeable.

   a. ***Bush* case:** *Bush v. Commonwealth, supra*, p. 55, in which the victim of wounds inflicted by the defendant caught scarlet fever from her physician, might be viewed as falling into this class. The scarlet fever was an unforeseeable coincidental event, and therefore superseding. (Alternatively, the fact that the doctor treated the patient could be viewed as a "response" to the defendant's acts, but even here, liability would probably be denied on the theory that the result was highly abnormal.)

7. **Recklessness or negligence crime:** If the crime is defined to require merely ***recklessness*** or ***negligence***, probably the same general rules regarding intervening causes apply as where the crime is one of intent. That is, if D has behaved recklessly with respect to the risk that V will suffer a certain kind of harm, and that general type of harm occurs, but only through an intervening act by X, the intervening act will be superseding if it was abnormal and unforeseeable, but not if it was foreseeable or usual. Similarly, if D was negligent concerning the risk of harm to V, and an intervening act helps bring about that type of harm, the intervention will be superseding if it was not foreseeable.

   Example: D lives with her lover and her 20-month-old baby. The lover gives frequent beatings to the baby, from which he eventually dies. D is charged with manslaughter.

   Held, D can be held to be a proximate cause of the baby's death. D had a duty (by virtue of her status as parent; see *supra*, p. 6) not to allow the baby to be exposed to unreasonable risk of harm. She breached that duty, and the lover's intervening acts (the beatings) were foreseeable, as was the death which resulted from them. *Palmer v. State*, 164 A.2d 467 (Md. 1960).

   a. **Less strict standard:** It is, however, possible that courts and/or juries will instinctively require a somewhat greater causal link between the defendant's act and the eventual result where the crime is merely one of negligence or recklessness. For instance, if the defendant recklessly or negligently injured the victim, and then thinking the victim was dead, threw him in the river to avoid detection, this latter act might be held to be "unforeseeable" and "abnormal," where it would not be had the defendant acted with an original intent to kill. See L, p. 312.

   b. **Model Penal Code standard:** The Model Penal Code appears to impose much the same standard for intervening acts in recklessness and negligence cases as in intentional crimes. Assuming that the problem is not one of "transferred intent" (i.e., a different victim) or concurrence (a completely different type of harm, such as burning where death from shooting was the principal risk of the defendant's conduct), the defendant will be relieved of liability unless both: (1) "the actual result involves the same kind of injury or harm as the probable result [of the defendant's conduct]"; and (2) the actual result "is not too remote or accidental in its occurrence to have a [just] bearing on the actor's liability or on the gravity of his offense." M.P.C. § 2.03(3)(b).

D. **Causation in felony-murder and misdemeanor-manslaughter cases:** The doctrines of ***felony-murder*** and ***misdemeanor-manslaughter*** allow the defendant to be convicted of homicide where he had no intent to kill. In some jurisdictions these crimes have apparently been so construed as to almost completely dispense with the requirement of proximate cause. For instance, some commentators have even suggested that if D kidnaps V, and during the kidnapping, gets into a car accident that is fatal to V, this will be felony-murder; see L, p. 314, fn. 131.

1. **Contrary view:** But in keeping with the recent tendency of courts to construe felony-murder and misdemeanor-manslaughter statutes more narrowly than previously, the same proximate causation rules might be applied to these two types of crimes as to any other crime. Thus in the above kidnapping example, since the intervening event (the car accident) was unforeseeable (assuming that it was not part of a high speed chase), that accident might be held to be a superseding cause relieving D of felony-murder liability. (See L, p. 314.) Another illustration of this narrowing of causal principles is set forth in the following Example.

> **Example:** D steals money from a church collection plate and flees. One of the congregants, V, follows him by car, and dies of a heart attack during the chase. *Held,* the petty theft was not the legal cause of V's death. The crime itself was a petty property offense, and "did not encompass the kind of direct, foreseeable risk of physical harm that would support a conviction of manslaughter." *Todd v. State,* 594 So. 2d 802 (Fla. Dist. App. 1992)

E. **Strict liability crimes:** Where the crime is one imposing ***strict liability*** (i.e., liability without any requisite mental state (see *supra,* p. 21)), a few courts have dispensed with the need for proximate causation, and have required merely that the defendant's act be the "but for" cause of the harm. But the Model Penal Code, in § 2.03(4), provides that there is no liability unless the actual result is a "***probable consequence***" of the defendant's conduct.

Example: A statute makes it a crime to cause to be shipped in interstate commerce any drug not properly labeled. D, a drug dealer, receives improperly labeled stock from a supplier, and puts it aside in his drawer, intending to relabel it. That night a thief breaks in, steals the drugs, and sells them through the mails. Under the Model Penal Code, D would not be liable, since theft-and-resale was not a "probable consequence" of his conduct.

Quiz Yourself on
CAUSATION (ENTIRE CHAPTER)

11. Jesse James is trapped at the I'm O.K. Corral. Doc Holiday fires a bullet at James, and hits him. 1/2 second later, Wyatt Earp fires a shot at James, and also hits him (while he's still standing). (Holliday and Earp are not acting in concern, they each independently have it in for James.) James dies immediately. Either bullet would have been enough to kill James. Who is the cause-in-fact of James' death, Holliday, Earp, both or neither?

12. Yosemite Sam has his heart set on rabbit stew for dinner. He sees Bugs Bunny off in the distance, aims his gun right at him, and fires. (Assume that if Sam had hit Bugs, this would have been murder, i.e., there's no defense of rabbit-hunting.) Unfortunately, Sam's aim is very bad and he instead hits and kills Daffy Duck, whom he never even saw.

(A) Is Yosemite Sam guilty of murdering Daffy Duck?

(B) Same facts as (A), except that instead of killing Daffy Duck, he merely wounds him. What crimes is

Sam guilty of now?

13. Cheshire Cat is tired of being chased by Tweedle Dee all day long and decides to "off" him. He buys an AK-47 at the local convenience store and hides in the bushes, waiting for his victim to pass by. Tweedle Dum, Tweedle Dee's twin brother, happens to walk by. Thinking that he's looking at Tweedle Dee, Cheshire Cat aims right at him and fires. Tweedle Dum is killed instantly. Since Cheshire Cat only had the intention to kill Tweedle Dee, is he guilty of the murder of Tweedle Dum?

14. Antony gives Cleopatra a glass of wine tainted with arsenic, intending to kill her. However, the poison does not instantly kill Cleo.

   (A) For this part only, assume that the arsenic was (unbeknownst to Antony) so weak that it would almost certainly not have killed Cleo, even if she had had no medical treatment. Cleo was rushed to the hospital. A nurse there gave her a potion that was intended to be an antidote. What the nurse didn't know was that the potion was in fact a rat poison intended to exterminate the hospital's growing rat population, which had been mislabelled due to another nurse's gross negligence. Cleo died principally from the effects of the rat poison, but had she not been weakened from the earlier arsenic poisoning, she probably would have survived. Will Antony's act be deemed a proximate cause of Cleo's death?

   (B) For this part, assume that Cleo refused to go to the hospital – even though she knew she would not otherwise likely recover from the poison. She died several hours later. Will Antony's act be deemed the proximate cause of Cleo's death?

15. Bob Ford intends to kill Jesse James. He shoots at James, but misses. In an attempt to escape Ford's shots, James turns his horse and gallops off in the opposite direction. Shortly after he starts the escape gallop, he is struck and killed by a boulder from an unexpected rockfall. Is Ford's conduct a proximate cause of James' death?

Answers

11. **Both Holiday and Earp are causes in fact.** Although something that is a "but for" cause will always be a cause-in-fact, the conversely is not true: something can be a cause-in-fact even though it was not a but-for cause. In particular, if two acts are each a *"substantial factor"* in bringing about a result, then each is a cause-in-fact even though the other act would have sufficed. That's what happened here: neither shot was a but-for cause of the death (since the death would have happened anyway without that shot), but each was undeniably a "substantial factor" in bringing about the death. (Each shot contributed significantly to the result — James' death — so that's enough to make it a "substantial factor".)

12. **(A) Yes.** Under the doctrine of *"transferred intent,"* if a defendant intends to bring about a certain sort of harm and then does bring about that general type of harm, the fact that the victim is different than the intended one will not make a difference. The doctrine applies here: since Yosemite Sam intended to kill someone, the fact that the one who ended up dead was Daffy instead of Bugs won't prevent Sam from meeting the requirements for murder.

   (B) Battery against Daffy, and attempted murder of Bugs. First, Yosemite Sam will be guilty of battery against Daffy Duck — Sam's intent to kill Bugs will be transferred to his act of battery against Daffy, even though the crimes are not the same. (Note that this works because battery is sort of a lesser version of murder. If the two crimes were totally unrelated, such as murder and arson, the intent could not be transferred.) Second, Yosemite Sam will also be guilty of attempted murder of Bugs, since he had the intent to kill him (the mens rea) and took an act in furtherance of that goal (shooting towards him). However, Yosemite Sam will *not* be guilty of the attempted murder of Daffy Duck — the doctrine of "transferred intent" does not apply to crimes of attempt.

13. **Yes.** A case of mistaken identity does not save the defendant. As long as Cheshire Cat had the intention to kill someone, and engaged in an act designed to carry that intention out, the fact that he was mistaken regarding the identity of his victim is irrelevant. A "mistake of fact" will generally only be a defense if it negates the particular mental state required for the crime. That is not the case here, because a correct belief about the victim's identity is not part of the mental state required for murder (or practically any other crime, for that matter.)

14. **(A) No.** When the defendant causes injury or illness, resulting medical treatment will be viewed as a "dependent" intervening cause. A dependent intervening cause will be viewed as ***"superseding"*** (i.e., as preventing the defendant's action from being a proximate cause) only if that dependent cause was ***"abnormal."*** Where medical treatment is performed in a grossly-negligent way, that will usually meet the hard-to-satisfy "abnormal" standard. The treatment here was certainly gross negligence — hospitals may commit garden-variety negligence with some frequency (and that ordinary negligence won't be superseding), but giving a patient rat poison because of a labelling error goes way beyond ordinary negligence. Therefore, the rat poison will be treated as a superseding cause. (But if the hospital had acted just a bit negligently, say by not having the most-effective antidote available, or by delaying treatment for 10 minutes because of emergency-room congestion, this would not have been enough to break the chain of causation if Cleo had died, and here Antony's act *would* have the proximate cause of her death.)

    (B) No. Where a crime victim refuses to avail herself of medical assistance, most courts hold that the refusal is not a superseding cause. That's true even if the victim's conduct is irrational.

15. **No.** Ford's conduct is certainly a cause-in-fact of the death. (The death wouldn't have occurred "but for" Ford's conduct, since James wouldn't have been at the spot where the boulder occurred.) But the shooting is not a *proximate* cause. The falling of the boulder was an "independent" intervening event. (That is, the boulder didn't fall because of the shooting.) An independent intervening event will be superseding if it was ***"unforeseeable"*** (even if it wasn't "abnormal," in the sense of deeply unusual or bizarre). There's no particular reason for anyone to have foreseen a rockfall at the time James passed by (and the facts say that the rockfall was "unexpected"), so the unforeseeable rockfall will be a superseding event.

LEXIS®-NEXIS® Searches on **PROXIMATE CAUSE**

Sub-Topic	Suggested Searches
Unintended manner of harm — transferred intent	`(crime or criminal) and (transferred intent w/5 (theory or doctrine or concept))`
Intervening acts	
Independent intervening acts	`(crime or criminal) and (intervening w/30 independent!)`
Dependent intervening acts	`(crime or criminal) and (intervening w/30 dependent!)`

Exam Tips on
CAUSATION

Be on the lookout for causation issues, especially in fact patterns that involve homicide — the fact that V (victim) ended up dead doesn't mean that D caused the death, as a legal matter.

Cause In Fact

☞ First determine whether the defendant's act was the cause-in-fact of the harm. Usually, this will be because D's act was the but-for cause of the harm.

    ☞ Analyze the situation to determine ***whether the result would have happened anyway (in exactly the same way) even had D's act not occurred.*** If it would have, then D's act won't be the but-for cause, or cause-in-fact, of the harm, and D can't be guilty.

    Example: D, A prominent heart surgeon, agrees at the request of the U.S. Government to perform a heart operation on V, an important official. Relying on his agreement, the government ceases its search for another physician. D then fails to show up to do the operation, and it's too late for the government to find another. V dies. D could plausibly contend that, even if he had performed the operation, it is uncertain that it would have been successful. If he can show this, then his wrongful act (his promising to do the operation and then not doing it) has not been proved beyond a reasonable doubt to have been the cause-in-fact of V's death.

    ☞ Remember that for D's act to be the cause in fact of a homicide, the victim must be ***alive at the time of the act.***

    Example: D shoots to kill V, whom he believes is asleep, but who actually died of a heart attack moments before. D's act of shooting is not the cause in fact of V's death. Therefore, regardless of D's culpable state of mind and wrongful act, D can't be guilty of homicide.

    ☞ Remember that a death may have ***several causes-in-fact.*** That is, there may be several acts or events each of which is a cause in fact, because the death wouldn't have happened without all of those acts/events. When this happens, the person who does a single one of the acts can be guilty (because he's *a* cause-in-fact even though not *the sole* cause in fact).

Proximate Cause

☞ **Generally:** Proximate cause is very frequently tested. Several things to watch out for:

    ☞ **Year-and-a-Day-Rule:** Remember that at common law (and still in most states), if a death occurs ***at least a year-and-a-day after D's act***, D can't be the proximate cause of the death.

    ☞ **Unintended victim:** Profs will try to sidetrack you by presenting a fact pattern where there is an inadvertent killing of a person who was not the original target. Remember that, as long as the defendant shows the requisite mental state, ***it is inconsequential*** *that the victim is different than the one D was focusing on* (assuming the victim suffers a harm similar to what was intended). Distinguish between the two similar situations of transferred intent and mistaken identity (D will be on the hook in both):

☞ **Transferred intent:** In a fact pattern involving *transferred intent*, the defendant aims at his targeted party (X) but because of bad aim, a ricocheting bullet, or something of that sort, another person (V) is hit. If D had the requisite mental state vis a vis X, D is guilty of the same crime against V as D would have been had the harm that befell V really befallen X.

Example: D returns home and catches B climbing out the window of his home. He pursues B down the street. D fires a shot at B with a hunting rifle, attempting to shoot him in the leg. The bullet misses B, but hits V, who is driving a car down the street. V later dies. D's intent to cause serious bodily harm to B (a mental state sufficient for murder) would be transferred to V. Therefore, D is the proximate cause of V's death, and can be found guilty of murder, assuming that no defense applies.

☞ **Mistaken identity:** In a fact pattern involving *mistaken identity*, the defendant injures or kills the party at which he aimed; but the victim is not who the defendant thought he was. Here, too, the mistake doesn't prevent D from being guilty.

Example: V, who has just robbed a casino, encounters D on the steps of the casino. D is not aware of V's criminal activity. In fact, D is waiting on the steps of the casino so that he can shoot its owner because D has just lost all his savings there. When D sees V, he mistakenly believes that V is the casino owner. He shouts, "Death to gamblers," and shoots at V, killing him. Knowledge of the victim's identity is not an essential element of the crime. Because D yelled, "Death to gamblers," and fired at V, he showed the necessary intent to kill or cause serious bodily harm. Therefore, D is guilty of murdering X notwithstanding his mistake about X's identity.

☞ **Intervening causes:** Determine whether the intervening act is *"independent"* or *"dependent."* Remember that an independent act will break the causation chain if it's *"unforeseeable"* but a dependent act will only break the chain if it's *"abnormal"* (*plus* unforeseeable). "Abnormal" is rarer, so an independent act is more likely to break the chain than a dependent one.

☞ **Medical aid:** Most common scenario for dependent intervening cause: the victim is given *medical aid*, and something goes wrong during the aid-giving process.

Example: D attacks V, a basketball player, with a baseball bat, inflicting serious injuries. V is admitted to the hospital and is injected with a pain reliever to which he has a fatal allergic reaction. Because the drug was given to relieve pain which resulted from the beating, the administration of the pain reliever and the reaction to it are dependent acts. Therefore, as long as these events are not abnormal (and mere negligence, as opposed to gross negligence, is probably not an "abnormal" response to a need for medical assistance), the chain of causation has not been broken.

☞ **Victim's intervening act:**   Look for a situation where. after the initial harm caused by D, the victim *exposes himself to additional danger.* If the exposure is brought about by D's act, the exposure is a dependent event, and won't be superseding unless abnormal.

Example: D sets fire to X's home. X flees the burning home, then reenters to rescue his baby trapped inside. He later dies of burns. Since it is not uncommon for someone to risk his life to save his child, the act would be foreseeable (and certainly not "abnormal"), so even if it was in some sense a bad move for X from a risk-reward perspective, it won't be deemed superseding.

☞ **Defendant's intervening act:** Look for a situation where D has the intent to kill, erroneously believes his victim is dead, and attempts to destroy or conceal the "corpse." Usually, this second act by D won't be superseding.

Example: D beats V to the point of unconsciousness. Then, thinking that V is dead, D takes the "corpse" to a secluded spot. V ultimately dies of exposure. D's intervening act of moving V's body (and not checking to see that V was dead) was a dependent act. The act was not unforeseeable or abnormal, and was therefore not superseding. Therefore, the death will be deemed to have been proximately caused by the original beating, so D can be prosecuted for some version of homicide. (*Which* type would depend on his mental state during the beating.)

CHAPTER 3

RESPONSIBILITY

Introductory Note: This chapter considers several defenses which the defendant may raise regarding his *lack of mental responsibility* for the alleged offense. These include: (1) the *insanity* defense (including the "XYY chromosome" defense); (2) the defense of *diminished responsibility* (which can negate the existence of the required *mens rea*); (3) *automatism* (the doing of acts while in an unconscious state); (4) the defense of *intoxication*; and (5) *infancy*.

I. THE INSANITY DEFENSE

A. General purpose: If the defendant can show that he was *insane* at the time he committed a criminal act, he may be entitled to the verdict "not guilty by reason of insanity." This defense has been recognized in Anglo-American law for several hundred years. Its principal justification is that where the defendant's mental disease has prevented him from distinguishing between "right" and "wrong," or from controlling his conduct (depending on the test employed in the particular jurisdiction) the *punishment* and *deterrence* objects of the criminal law would not be served by convicting. It is felt that it would be inappropriate and unfair to punish the defendant for something that he could not help, and futile to attempt to deter him from similar misconduct by convicting him.

   1. Incarceration as objective: But another significant reason for the defense has also been noted. Most serious crimes are defined in terms of intent; thus in most states, first-degree murder may be committed only by causing the death of another with intent to do so. If no insanity defense existed, an insane defendant might very well be able to show that his insanity prevented him from forming the intent to kill; this would be the case, for instance, in the frequently-cited hypothetical of the man who strangles his wife believing that he is squeezing a lemon. (See M.P.C., Comment 2 to § 4.01). The strangler might therefore go free.

      a. Limits use of mental disease: But in many (perhaps most) states, the insanity defense is coupled with a rule that *no evidence relating to mental disease or defect* may be introduced except as part of an insanity defense. This means that the strangler must either plead insanity, or not be allowed to show that his mental disease prevented him from forming an intent to kill. Coupled with the fact that in virtually every state, an insanity acquittal leads almost inevitably to the defendant's involuntary commitment to a mental institution (see *infra*, p. 77), this means that the insanity defense serves as a means of *avoiding the outright release* of certain defendants who would otherwise be acquitted for lack of the necessary *mens rea*. See L, p. 324-25.

   2. Not constitutionally required: Virtually every state recognizes some form of the insanity defense. Johnson, p. 280. However, probably the federal Constitution does *not require* the states to recognize insanity as a complete defense. *Id.* See also *Foucha v. Louisiana,*

112 S.Ct. 1780 (1992) (Justice O'Connor, concurring, notes that the states are not required to make the insanity defense available).

B. Tests for insanity: Several different formulations exist for determining whether a defendant was insane, in a way entitling him to acquittal. The principal ones are as follows:

C. *M'Naghten* "right-wrong" rule: At least half of the states apply, as their sole criterion for application of the insanity defense, a rule first set forth in *M'Naghten's case*, 8 Eng. Rep. 718 (1843). In that case, the defendant shot and killed Edward Drummond, private secretary to Sir Robert Peel, Prime Minister of England. The defendant believed that Peel had been conspiring to murder him, and shot Drummond thinking him to be Peel. A jury found him not guilty by reason of insanity.

1. **Ruling:** The House of Lords then asked the Justices of the Queen's Bench what the proper test for insanity should be. They responded, in what has come to be known as the ***"M'Naghten rule,"*** as follows: the defendant should be presumed to be sane unless he proves that, at the time he acted, he was "labouring under such a defect of reason, from disease of the mind, as ***not to know the nature and quality of the act he was doing***; or, if he did know it, that he ***did not know he was doing what was wrong***."

2. **Reformulation:** Thus for the defendant to establish his insanity under the *M'Naghten* rule, he must show:

    a. **Mental defect or disease:** That he suffered a mental disease causing a defect in his reasoning powers; and

    b. **Result:** That as a result, either (1) he did not understand the "nature and quality" of his act; or (2) he did not know that his act was wrong.

3. **What constitutes "mental disease":** Courts applying the *M'Naghten* test have generally not agreed on exactly what constitutes a "disease of the mind."

    a. **"Psychopathic" or "sociopathic" personality:** One thing that seems to be agreed upon is that the fact that the defendant is a ***"psychopath"*** or ***"sociopath"*** does not mean that he has the requisite mental disease. These terms refer solely to the fact that the defendant has a ***long history of criminal behavior***, and do not mean that he necessarily has different mental functions than a normal person. For obvious reasons, courts have refused to allow a mere history of repetitious criminal acts to be considered as a kind of mental disease; otherwise the insanity defense might swallow up most of the criminal justice system.

    b. **"Know":** When the *M'Naghten* court said that the defendant must not "know" the nature and quality of his act, or that it was wrong, it did not make clear whether "know" was used solely in the *cognitive* sense (i.e., rational understanding), or in the emotive sense as well. For instance, if the defendant knew that he was killing his victim, and knew that it was against the law to kill, but thought that killing was morally required in this situation (e.g., because "God told me to do it"), is he insane under the *M'Naghten* test?

        i. **Includes emotive test:** Most courts that have considered the issue have concluded that the defendant can be insane if he lacks such an emotional understanding of the wrongfulness of his conduct, even though he may have a rational awareness that society condemns it. In California, for instance, the defendant will meet the *M'Naghten* test if he did not "understand" what he was doing, or did not "understand that it was wrong *and a violation of the rights of another*." *People v. Wolff*, 394 P.2d 959 (Cal. 1964). Presumably under the California test, the murderer who could show that he believed that God had told him to kill would be insane.

c. **"Nature and quality of his act":**   Most courts have not similarly broadened their interpretation of the requirement that the defendant have known the "nature and quality of his act." In general, this refers merely to knowledge of the physical consequences; thus if the defendant has shot his victim to death, he will meet the "nature and quality" requirement if he knew that pressing a trigger would discharge a bullet which might cause death. One or two courts have gone further, and have required a knowledge of the moral consequences. L, p. 333-34.

d. **Knowledge that the act is "wrong":**   A similar question is raised by the requirement that the defendant know that his act was "*wrong*." Does "wrong" mean merely knowledge that the act is legally forbidden, or is there a further requirement of knowledge that the act is morally wrong? The previously-mentioned hypothetical murderer who believes that God has commanded the murder, for instance, might very well understand that murder is legally wrong, but believe that it is morally acceptable in this case. In most cases, if the defendant realizes that the conduct is legally prohibited, he will also realize that *society* would regard it as morally wrong, so the question is really whether the *defendant's own belief* that the conduct is morally acceptable meets the *M'Naghten* test.

   i. **Not resolved:**   Few courts have explicitly confronted this question. To the extent that some courts have held (*supra*) that the defendant "knows" his conduct to be wrong only where he has an emotional understanding that it violates another's rights, his belief that the act is morally acceptable would probably be enough to meet the *M'Naghten* test.

   ii. **"Right and wrong" apply to particular case:**   In any event, the defendant is not required to have a *general* inability to differentiate between right and wrong. The issue is whether, *as to the act charged*, he was able to distinguish right from wrong. If he couldn't do so, he will be insane even though in general he may be capable of making the distinction.

e. **Delusions:**   In many cases the defendant will try to show that he lacked the requisite knowledge or understanding by showing that he had *delusions* (e.g., that God spoke to him and demanded that he commit a murder). No special rule applies to such cases; the question is simply whether, because of the delusions or anything else, the defendant lacked the ability to appreciate the nature and quality of his act or its wrongfulness. See L, pp. 336-37.

4. **Criticism of *M'Naghten* test:**   The *M'Naghten* test has been criticized, principally in academic circles, for decades, and a number of American courts have abandoned it. The main criticism has been that the test is *too narrow*, and that the law should regard as insane not only those defendants who do not "know right from wrong," but also those who might

have such knowledge, but who are ***incapable of obeying the law*** anyway. This criticism has led nearly half of American jurisdictions to accept the insanity defense for the latter group of people, usually under the heading of "irresistible impulse" (discussed *infra*).

D. "Irresistible impulse":   As noted, a principal objection to the *M'Naghten* rule is that it does not allow a finding of insanity if the defendant understood the difference between right and wrong, but was ***unable to control his conduct***. To remedy this effect, almost half of those states that follow *M'Naghten* (which are in a majority) have added such an inability to control one's act as a separate ground for an insanity finding.

  1. "Irresistible impulse" is misnomer: This additional ground has sometimes colloquially been called the ***"irresistible impulse"*** defense, but this is a misnomer. It is not required that the defendant's inability to control himself be an "impulse," in the sense of a sudden desire to commit the act in question; even if the defendant broods upon and plans his act, he may still avail himself of the defense.

  2. Complete "irresistibility" not required: Nor have most courts required that a defendant's need to commit the act be ***totally*** "irresistible," in the sense that he would have committed the offense even if there had been a ***"policeman at his elbow."*** Rather, it has generally been sufficient that the defendant's ability to control himself was ***"substantially"*** impaired. (The Model Penal Code, in its reformulation of the lack-of-control test, explicitly uses the requirement of "substantial" impairment; see *infra*).

E. The *Durham* "product" test: In 1954, the U.S. Court of Appeals for the District of Columbia announced a new test, which would in theory encompass all cases meeting either the *M'Naghten* or "irresistible impulse" standards, and perhaps other situations as well. In *Durham v. U.S.,* 214 F.2d 862 (D.C. Cir. 1954), the court stated that the defendant would be entitled to an insanity acquittal "if his unlawful act was the ***product of mental disease or defect.***" One objective of this rule was to permit psychiatrists, testifying as expert witnesses, to give a broader range of information to the jury than they could under the *M'Naghten* test (under which they were forced to restrict their opinion to whether the defendant "knew right from wrong").

  1. Not accepted: No state courts, and only one state legislature (Maine) enacted the *Durham* test. Furthermore, the *Durham* court itself later more or less abandoned that test, in favor of the Model Penal Code formulation (discussed *infra*).

  2. Difficult to define "product":   One of the principal reasons for this lack of success has been the difficulty of formulating a standard for deciding whether the act was a "product" of the disease or defect. A "but for" test, under which the act is a product of the disease if it would not have occurred but for that disease, seems to be much too broad and would include virtually every mental disease, regardless of whether there was a close connection with the ensuing act. No other definition of the term "product" has proven any more acceptable, however.

F. Model Penal Code standard: The Model Penal Code, like *Durham*, attempts to broaden the *M'Naghten* and "irresistible impulse" tests. M.P.C. § 4.01(1) provides that "a person is not responsible for criminal conduct if at the time of such conduct as a result of mental disease or defect he lacks substantial capacity either to appreciate the criminality [wrongfulness] of his conduct or to conform his conduct to the requirements of the law."

1. **Similarity to older tests:**   The Model Penal Code test thus focuses on roughly the same two elements as the *M'Naghten* and "irresistible impulse" tests: (1) the defendant's lack of understanding of the wrongfulness of his conduct (the "cognitive" prong); and (2) his inability to control his conduct (the "volitional" prong). If the defendant can show either of these two things, he is entitled to an insanity verdict.

2. **Only "substantial capacity" might be lacking:**   While the "irresistible impulse" test is open to the interpretation that the defendant must be totally lacking in the ability to control himself (e.g., so that he would have committed the crime even with a "policeman at his elbow"), the Model Penal Code explicitly provides that merely *"substantial capacity,"* not total capacity, to exercise control must be lacking.

    a. **No "impulse" required:**   Nor does the Model Penal Code test require, where the defense is based upon the defendant's inability to control his acts, that the act be the product of a sudden *"impulse."* Under the Model Penal Code, even acts that are the product of *brooding and deliberation* may qualify.

3. **Emotional awareness of wrongful conduct:**   And it is sufficient for meeting the cognitive portion of the Model Penal Code test (i.e., that the defendant lacks substantial capacity to "appreciate the criminality" of his conduct) that the defendant is unable to have an emotional, "affective," understanding of the *wrongfulness* of his conduct. The word "appreciate," as opposed to "know," is used for this reason. See LS, p. 349.

    a. **Unclear standard:**   But observe that this formulation does not answer the question whether it is the defendant's own moral sense, or his perception of the community's moral sense, that is relevant. If the defendant "appreciates" that the community considers it wrong to kill, but he himself believes that it is not only right but required by God, has he met the Model Penal Code test? This is not clear.

4. **Psychopaths and sociopaths:** The Model Penal Code explicitly provides, in § 4.01(2), that for purposes of the Code's insanity defense, the terms "mental disease or defect" do not include "an abnormality manifested only by repeated criminal or otherwise anti-social conduct." A commentary explains that this provision is intended to exclude the case of so-called *"psychopathic* personality"; the psychopath "differs from a normal person only quantitatively or in degree, not qualitatively, and the diagnosis of psychopathic personality does not carry with it any explanation of the causes of the abnormality." (Comment 6 to § 4.01, Tent. Dr. No. 4.)

5. **Criticisms:** The Model Penal Code formulation has been subject to much criticism. Most has centered on the "volitional" prong, i.e., the requirement that the defendant lack "substantial capacity…to conform his conduct to the requirements of the law." See, e.g., *U.S. v. Lyons*, 731 F.2d 243 (5th Cir. 1984), rejecting the volitional prong and thus holding that "a person is not responsible for criminal conduct on the grounds of insanity only if at the time of that conduct, as a result of a mental disease or defect, he is unable to appreciate the wrongfulness of that conduct." Some of the criticisms of the volitional prong are:

    a. **Limits of psychiatry:**   That even most psychiatrists "now believe that they do not possess sufficient accurate scientific bases for *measuring* a person's capacity for self-control or for calibrating the impairment of that capacity." *Lyons, supra.* As one writer has put it, there is "no objective basis for distinguishing between offenders who are undeterrable and those who are merely undeterred, between the impulse that was irresistible and the impulse not resisted, or between substantial impairment of capacity and some lesser impairment." 69 A.B.A.J. 194, at 196 (1983).

b. **Fabrication:** That the volitional prong increases the *risks of fabrication*, since it is easier to feign an inability to "help oneself" than it is for one to feign an inability to tell right from wrong.

c. **Reasonable doubt:** That in those jurisdictions requiring proof of insanity beyond a reasonable doubt (originally including all federal courts, but since changed by statute; see *infra*), proof beyond a reasonable doubt that the defendant lacked substantial capacity to conform his conduct to the requirements of the law is virtually impossible.

6. **Limited adoption:** The Model Penal Code has been adopted in a significant minority of jurisdictions, including Massachusetts, Rhode Island, Tennessee, and West Virginia. (See L, p. 350, fn. 68.)

   a. **Federal:** Virtually all of the U.S. Courts of Appeals at one time adopted the M.P.C. standard. However, in 1984, Congress passed a statute (18 U.S.C.A. § 20(a)) to replace the M.P.C. rule with what is essentially the *M'Naghten* rule. The federal insanity standard is discussed extensively, *infra*.

   b. **California:** California has made a similar round-trip.

      i. **Judicial adoption:** In *People v. Drew*, 583 P.2d 1318 (Cal. 1978), the California Supreme Court adopted the M.P.C. standard.

      ii. **Statute overturns:** But in 1982, the voters of California approved a new statute that repudiates the M.P.C. formulation, and that is in fact even more restrictive than the *M'Naghten* rule. § 25 of the California Penal Code now limits the insanity defense to a defendant who "was incapable of knowing or understanding the nature and quality of his or her act *and* of distinguishing right from wrong at the time of the commission of the offense." (The "and" replaces the *M'Naghten* rule's "or.")

G. **The federal standard:** In *federal* trials, the insanity defense is now governed by a statute passed by Congress in 1984, in the wake of John Hinckley's insanity acquittal for the attempted assassination of President Reagan. Because the federal standard has undergone several major changes over the last forty years, a brief review of the development of federal insanity defense law is worthwhile.

1. **The Durham "product" test:** The *Durham* "product" test, discussed *supra*, p. 70, was never accepted anywhere in the federal system except in the District of Columbia Circuit that originated it. L, p. 345.

2. **Model Penal Code:** Virtually all of the United States Courts of Appeals eventually adopted the Model Penal Code Test. L, p. 350. Even the D.C. Court of Appeals, which created *Durham*, eventually rejected its own creation in favor of the M.P.C. approach. See *U.S. v. Brawner*, 471 F.2d 969 (D.C. Cir. 1972).

3. **Federal statute:** The federal jury in the Hinckley trial was instructed that it must acquit Hinckley if there was a reasonable doubt about whether he could either appreciate the

wrongfulness of his conduct or conform his conduct to the law (the Model Penal Code standard). To the surprise and chagrin of many observers, the jury took its instructions seriously and delivered a verdict of not guilty by reason of insanity. The resulting public outcry, when added to a number of scholarly and professional expressions of unhappiness with the Model Penal Code standard (e.g., the repudiation of the M.P.C. standard by the American Psychiatric Association, the American Bar Association, and the American Medical Association all in the same year, 1983) led Congress to respond with a new statute.

a. **Terms of federal statute:** The new federal insanity statute, 18 U.S.C. § 17 et seq. (the Insanity Defense Reform Act of 1984), *drastically narrows* the insanity defense in federal criminal cases to essentially *M'Naghten* proportions.

   i. **General standard:** The defense is allowed only if the defendant "as a result of a severe mental disease or defect, was unable to appreciate the nature and quality or the wrongfulness of his acts" at the time of the offense. This is essentially the *M'Naghten* standard. Most importantly, the fact that the defendant may have been unable to "conform his conduct to the requirements of the law" (the "volitional" branch of the Model Penal Code standard) is *not* a basis for assertion of the defense under the new federal statute.

   ii. **Burden:** Whereas the burden of proof on insanity was previously on the prosecution, the new statute places *upon the defendant* the burden of proving his insanity by *clear and convincing evidence*.

   iii. **Commitment and release:** After a federal insanity acquittal, the defendant is given a commitment hearing. If the crime charged was one of violence, the defendant has the burden of proving by clear and convincing evidence that his release would not be dangerous. If he cannot meet this burden, he is subjected to involuntary civil commitment, and can be released only upon findings by both the director of the mental institution then housing him and a judge that he is no longer dangerous. 18 U.S.C. § 4243.

   See generally Johnson, pp. 311-19.

H. **Raising and establishing the defense:** We examine now a number of procedural issues regarding the raising and establishing of the insanity defense.

   1. **Who raises defense:** Virtually all states have statutes making the insanity defense an *affirmative defense*; that is, the defendant is required to *come forward with evidence* showing that he is insane, before insanity will become part of the case. States vary as to how much evidence is necessary to meet this "burden of production"; in general, even the testimony of lay witnesses as to the defendant's bizarre conduct will be enough to place the defense into issue.

   2. **Burden of persuasion:** Once the defendant has come forward with some evidence of insanity, he has met his burden of production. The issue then becomes who has the *"burden of persuasion,"* i.e., the burden of convincing the fact-finder on the insanity issue. In about half the states, the prosecution must prove *beyond a reasonable doubt* that the defendant is not insane. In the remaining states, the defendant bears the burden of persuasion, but only has to prove by a *"preponderance of the evidence"* that he is insane. The

federal system requires the defendant to prove insanity by "clear and convincing evidence." See L, 375-76.

a. **Constitutionality:** The Supreme Court has held that *placing this burden upon the defendant is not unconstitutional*. It is true that the constitution requires that every "element of the offense" must be proved by the prosecution beyond a reasonable doubt. *In re Winship*, 397 U.S. 358 (1970). But the Court has taken the position that the sanity of the defendant is not an "element of the offense." See *Patterson v. New York*, 432 U.S. 197 (1977), stating that "once the facts constituting a crime are established beyond a reasonable doubt, based on all the evidence including the evidence of the defendant's mental state, the State may refuse to sustain the affirmative defense of insanity unless demonstrated by a preponderance of the evidence."

3. **When defense must be raised:** If the prosecution did not become aware of the defendant's intention to rely upon an insanity defense until the start of the trial itself, the prosecution's ability to rebut the defense effectively might be hurt. Therefore, nearly half the states have provisions which require the defense to *notify* the prosecution of its intention to rely upon the insanity defense prior to the trial; sometimes this is done by making a special plea of "not guilty by reason of insanity."

    a. **Model Penal Code:** The Model Penal Code, in § 4.03(2), requires that a written notice of intent to rely on the defense be filed at the time the "not guilty" plea is entered, or within ten days thereafter, unless the court gives a longer period "for good cause."

4. **Psychiatric examination:** A defendant who demonstrates to the trial court that sanity will be a significant factor at his trial has a *constitutional right* to have the *assistance of a psychiatrist* at state expense. The Supreme Court so held in *Ake v. Oklahoma*, 105 S. Ct. 1087 (1985).

    a. **Role of psychiatrist:** This court-appointed psychiatrist will examine the defendant and must then "assist in evaluation, preparation, and presentation of the [insanity] defense." *Ake*, *supra*.

    b. **Partisan expert:** The Supreme Court in *Ake* left it unclear whether the indigent defendant is entitled to a psychiatrist who will serve as the defendant's own, partisan, expert. The Court explained that its holding did not give the defendant "a constitutional right to choose a psychiatrist of his personal liking or to receive funds to hire his own." However, the Court's statement that the defendant is entitled to a psychiatrist who will "assist in evaluation, preparation, and presentation of the defense" is probably hard to satisfy by appointment of a psychiatrist who is not essentially acting as the defendant's partisan expert. For instance, if the court appoints a psychiatrist who is employed by the state and who declines to give testimony that is helpful to the defendant, the defendant may well have a due process claim under *Ake*. Therefore, most states will probably find it easier to let the defendant hire a partisan psychiatrist rather than risk a successful challenge by the defendant to the adequacy of a purportedly neutral one. 99 Harv. L. Rev. at 136-37.

    c. **Prosecution expert:** Regardless of whether a psychiatrist is appointed for the defendant's benefit, in most states the court has the power to appoint a theoretically impartial psychiatrist to conduct an ***independent examination*** of the defendant, the results of which will be admissible at the trial. Such an independent expert's testimony or report will often be taken more seriously by the trier of fact than will the opinion of a psychiatrist retained by the prosecution or the defense. L, p. 367-68.

d. Self-incrimination: Once the court-appointed "impartial" psychiatrist begins testifying, an issue of the defendant's right against ***self-incrimination*** arises. Courts have generally held that those statements made by the defendant during the court-ordered psychiatric examination that would tend to incriminate the defendant (e.g., "Yes, I shot him") are covered by the privilege against self-incrimination. L, p. 368-69.

  i. Consequence: However, the fact that the defendant's statements are covered by the privilege does not mean that the trier of fact can never learn about them. It merely means that the statements cannot be admitted as part of the prosecution's case in chief, to establish guilt. Most courts have allowed the psychiatrist to describe these statements if they form part of the basis for the expert's opinion on the defendant's sanity. The only protection the defendant usually gets is an instruction to the jury that they not consider the admission on the question of guilt. *Id.*

  ii. No right to refuse exam: Furthermore, courts have almost universally concluded that the defendant's privilege against self-incrimination does not permit him to ***refuse to undergo*** the court-ordered examination. The Supreme Court has not yet ruled on this issue, but when it does it is likely to agree with the prevailing view. An important rationale against allowing the defendant to refuse to undergo an examination is that without such an examination, the prosecution has no way to combat spurious claims.

5. Role of the jury: If the case is tried before a jury, the jury will have the task of deciding the merits of the defendant's insanity defense, just as it will decide the other factual issues in the case. In most jurisdictions, the judge will instruct the jury that it is not to consider the insanity defense unless it finds that all material elements of the offense have been proved beyond a reasonable doubt by the prosecution, so that the choice is between conviction or an insanity acquittal.

a. Decision left to jury: The courts have tried hard to ensure that the ultimate decision is in fact made by the jury, ***not by the psychiatric expert witnesses***. The jury is always free to disregard or disbelieve the witnesses' evaluation of the defendant's condition. Also, it is always free to conclude that even though the defendant may have the requisite mental disease or defect, this did not prevent him from knowing "right from wrong," from controlling his actions, or whatever the relevant test in that jurisdiction is.

  i. *Wolff* case: Thus in *People v. Wolff*, 394 P.2d 959 (Cal. 1964), the California Supreme Court refused to overturn the jury's finding of no insanity, where all the expert witnesses had agreed that the defendant suffered from schizophrenia. The court stated that "to hold otherwise would be in effect to substitute trial by 'experts' for a trial by jury, for it would require that the jurors accept the psychiatric testimony as conclusive on an issue — the legal sanity of the defendant —

which under our present law is exclusively within the province of the trier of fact to determine."

    ii. Federal law: The federal insanity statute (the Insanity Defense Reform Act of 1984, see *supra*, p. 73) in fact ***prevents*** either side's expert from even ***testifying*** as to the ultimate issue of the defendant's sanity. The Act amends Federal Rule of Evidence 704 so as to read, "No expert witness testifying with respect to the mental state or condition of a defendant in a criminal case may state an opinion or inference as to whether the defendant did or did not have the mental state or condition constituting an element of the crime charged or of a defense thereto. Such ultimate issues are matters for the trier of fact alone." FRE 704(b). (This provision was found constitutional, as applied to the insanity defense, in *U.S. v. Freeman*, 804 F.2d 1574 (11th Cir. 1986).)

  b. Telling jury about mandatory commitment: In nearly all jurisdictions, a defendant who successfully raises the insanity defense will be subject either to mandatory commitment or to procedures that are extremely likely to lead to commitment. The question has therefore arisen, should the jury be told that this is the likely result of an insanity verdict?

    i. Traditionally jury not told: The traditional view has been that no mention should be made of the likely consequences of an insanity acquittal, on the grounds that the jury should not be distracted from their function.

    ii. Jury told: But some modern cases have held otherwise. Thus in *Commonwealth v. Mutina*, 323 N.E.2d 294 (Mass. 1975), a case in which the jury was not told that commitment would almost certainly follow from an insanity acquittal, the appellate court held that the guilty verdict was in the face of overwhelming evidence of insanity, and that this verdict was probably "designed to ensure the confinement of the defendant for his own safety and that of the community."

6. Bifurcated trial: In a few jurisdictions, principally California, the issue of the defendant's guilt is tried in a ***different trial*** from that of his insanity. The first trial is on the guilt issue; if the verdict is "guilty," a second trial is held, with the same or a different jury, on the insanity issue. This approach supposedly has the merit of not distracting or misleading the jury with extensive testimony about the defendant's mental state, until guilt has already been decided. But this advantage has generally not materialized, since during the trial on the issue of guilt, often there will be extensive psychiatric testimony on the issue of whether the defendant had the requisite *mens rea* (e.g., the capacity to premeditate and deliberate). See L, p. 379.

7. Insanity defense as "all or nothing": Some states take the view that the defendant will be allowed to present evidence showing that he suffers from a mental disease or defect ***only if this is done pursuant to an insanity defense***. See L, p. 391. This means for instance, that the defendant is not free to show that his extreme irrationality prevented him from doing the requisite "deliberation" or "premeditation" required in most states for first-degree murder.

  a. Partial responsibility: But most courts now accept the defense of "diminished responsibility," discussed *infra*, p. 80, by which evidence of mental disease or other mental condition may be accepted as showing that the defendant may not have the requisite *mens rea*, or that he should be subjected to a less severe punishment.

I. XYY chromosome defense: Studies done in the last two decades have shown that men whose chromosomes contain a certain abnormality (three sex chromosomes, one X and two Y's, rather than the usual X and Y) are much more likely to commit certain kinds of crimes than men whose chromosomes are normal. In particular, they commit crimes against property in extremely high proportions, and share other characteristics, including some degree of retardation, extreme height, and acne. A number of defendants have sought to introduce their chromosomal abnormality at trial, in support of an insanity defense. This is the so-called *"XYY chromosome defense."* See L, pp. 401-05.

    1. Sometimes accepted: The XYY abnormality has been accepted in several countries other than the U.S. (including Australia and France) as evidence of insanity. In this country, however, only a very small number of cases have allowed such evidence to go to the jury. Most American cases that have considered the issue have held that the relation between XYY and criminal conduct are not sufficiently well-documented that the condition is probative evidence of the sort that a jury should hear.

    2. Relevance of insanity tests used: The likelihood that a court will accept evidence of the XYY condition will be influenced by which test for insanity is in use in that jurisdiction. A jurisdiction following the *M'Naghten* rule, without an "irresistible impulse" addition to it, for instance, is very unlikely to accept evidence of the defect, since there is little reason to believe that the defect prevents the defendant from "knowing right from wrong." But where the "irresistible impulse" or "lack of substantial capacity to conform conduct to the law" tests are in use, the XYY defense will have a greater possibility of success. See generally L, pp. 404-05.

J. Commitment following insanity acquittal: If the defendant is acquitted by reason of insanity- he almost never walks free out of the courtroom. In a minority of states and in the federal courts the judge is *required by law* to commit him to a mental institution (L, pp. 382-83), without even a hearing as to whether he is still insane. In other states, the trial judge or the jury must conduct a hearing to decide whether the defendant is still insane and in need of commitment. In a few states, the decision whether to seek commitment is left to the prosecutor.

    1. Constitutionality of mandatory commitment: It is *not unconstitutional* for the state to impose *mandatory commitment* on an insanity acquittee, without any hearing as to whether he is still insane and in need of commitment. An insanity acquittal establishes that the defendant committed an act constituting a criminal offense, and that he did so because of mental illness. From these two facts, it is not unconstitutional for the state to *infer* that at the time of the verdict, the defendant is still mentally ill and dangerous, and thus may be committed. *Jones v. U.S.*, 463 U.S. 354 (1983).

    2. Release: Since the substantial majority of insanity-acquitted defendants will be committed following their trial, either with or without a hearing, the main issue regarding commitment is the *standard for release*. The two factors usually considered are: (1) Does the defendant's insanity continue? and (2) Is the defendant dangerous to society? If the answer to both questions is "yes," the state will obviously keep the defendant committed; if the answer to both is "no," the state will obviously release the defendant. The interesting questions arise where the answer to one question is "yes" but the answer to the other is "no."

    a. **Sane but still dangerous:** Where the defendant is *now sane*, but *still dangerous*, a modern Supreme Court decision apparently means that the defendant must be *released*. In *Foucha v. Louisiana*, 112 S.Ct. 1780 (1992), the Court found unconstitutional (by a 5-4 vote) a Louisiana law that allowed an insanity acquittee to be kept in a mental hospital indefinitely, until he bore the burden of proving that he was no longer dangerous. The majority relied on several reasons for striking down the law, including the theory that since the insanity acquittee is not being punished (the insanity acquittal absolves him of criminal responsibility for his act), only reasons independent of punishment may justify commitment. Since D could not be *civilly* committed (the Court has held that this requires both a showing of dangerousness and of mental illness), and since no other rationale would justify depriving D of his liberty interest protected by the due process clause, he must be released despite his dangerousness.

        i. **Dissent:** The four dissenters in *Foucha* argued that where the defendant has been found to have committed the act in question, this fact justifies treating him differently from a person who has been civilly committed. In their judgment, this difference was great enough to justify holding the defendant while sane but dangerous, at least as long as the total period during which he was detained was not longer than the maximum sentence which he could have been given had he been convicted.

    b. **Insane but not dangerous:** Similarly, it appears to be the case that the state may not continue to incarcerate a defendant who continues to be *insane*, but is *not dangerous*. *Foucha v. Louisiana*, *supra* (dictum by the majority).

    c. **Summary:** In other words, it now seems to be the case that the state may automatically commit an insanity acquittee, but must then periodically offer him the opportunity to be released. The state must release D if he bears the burden of proving that he is *either* no longer insane or no longer dangerous. (Probably the state may not impose on the defendant any burden more difficult that the "preponderance of the evidence" standard.)

K. Fitness to stand trial: The insanity defense is actually asserted at trial much less frequently than it is asserted as a grounds for *not trying the defendant* on the grounds that he is *incompetent to stand trial*. In general, the defendant will be held to be incompetent to stand trial if he is unable to do both of the following: (1) understand the proceedings against him; and (2) assist counsel in his defense. L, p. 353.

    1. **Burden of proof:** Many jurisdictions place the *burden of proof* on incompetence upon the *defendant*, particularly where he is the one who raises the issue. The U.S. Supreme Court has held that it is *not unconstitutional* for the state to place upon the defendant the burden of proving by a preponderance of the evidence that he is incompetent to stand trial. See *Medina v. California*, 60 U.S.L.W. 4684 (June 22, 1992).

    2. **Waiver not permitted:** If there is substantial evidence that the defendant is incompetent, he will not be permitted to *waive* his incompetence and proceed to trial. Instead, the court must hold a full hearing to determine the competency issue. As the Supreme Court has noted, "it is contradictory to argue that a defendant may be incompetent, and yet knowingly or intelligently 'waive' his right to have the court determine his capacity to stand trial." *Pate v. Robinson*, 383 U.S. 375 (1966). (In *Pate*, the Court found that the defendant's counsel had not even attempted to waive the defense of competency, and that the trial judge had erred in going forward with the trial in face of substantial evidence of the accused's irrationality.)

   a. **May be raised by prosecution or court:** As a corollary of the courts' reluctance to allow waiver, the issue of incompetency may be raised by the ***prosecution or the court***, if the defendant does not raise it. See L, p. 355.

3. **Procedures following commitment:** If the defendant is found incompetent to stand trial, he is invariably committed, generally to a state mental institution. In the past, such commitment has tended to be ***indefinite*** in length, and frequently longer than the maximum sentence that could have been imposed had the defendant been convicted of the offense charged. However, in recent years, many courts, including the Supreme Court, have imposed various limits on the length and nature of the commitment, based on due process and equal protection grounds.

   a. **Must have some prospect of recovery:** The theoretical purpose of committing the incompetent defendant is to permit him to regain his ability to stand trial. Where there is no real prospect that the ability to stand trial will ever be regained, the Supreme Court has held that the defendant must either be ***released***, or ***recommitted*** under the same ***civil commitment procedures*** as a defendant not charged with a crime. *Jackson v. Indiana*, 406 U.S. 715 (1972).

L. **Insanity at time set for execution:** If the defendant is insane ***at the time set for his execution***, he may ***not*** be executed. (Obviously, this can only occur where the defendant has ***become*** insane since his trial; otherwise, he would have been entitled to an insanity acquittal.) The Supreme Court has held that execution of a prisoner who is currently insane violates the Eighth Amendment's ban on ***cruel and unusual punishment***. *Ford v. Wainwright*, 477 U.S. 399 (1986).

Quiz Yourself on
THE INSANITY DEFENSE

16. Jack T. Ripper knows that killing a person is legally wrong. Nevertheless, he slashes the throats of several prostitutes for the purpose of killing them. He does this because he believes that has been instructed by God to "kill all prostitutes — they are evil." Jack tries to resist God's instructions (because he really doesn't enjoy the killing), but is powerless to prevent himself from obeying what he believes are God's orders.

   (A) Is Jack insane under the *M'Naghten* Rule?

   (B) Is Jack insane under the federal insanity statute?

   (C) Is Jack insane under the Model Penal Code?

   (D) Under the federal insanity statute, which party (Jack or the prosecution) will bear the burden of (1) raising the issue of sanity; and (2) proving sanity/insanity?

Answer

16. **(A) Probably not.** Under the *M'Naghten* test, a defendant must show that on account of his mental disease, either: (1) he did not understand the "nature and quality" of his act; or (2) he did not know that his act was wrong. Ripper clearly does not qualify under (1), since he knows that he's killing humans when he slashes throats. The interesting question is whether Ripper qualifies under (2). A court might hold that even though Ripper knew that what he did was legally wrong, his belief that God was commanding him to do the act prevented him from "knowing" that the act was "wrong" in the moral sense. However, it's more likely — in view of the strongly law-and-order approach to insanity followed by most *M'Naghten* jurisdictions today — that a court would say that Ripper's knowledge that the act was legally forbidden prevents him from qualifying under (2).

   (B) Probably not. The federal insanity statute essentially follows the *M'Naghten* standard: D prevails only if he shows that "as a result of a several mental disease or defect, [he] was unable to appreciate the nature and quality or the wrongfulness of his acts." Since D would probably lose under M'Naghten, he'd probably lose under the federal rule.

   (C) Yes. M.P.C. § 4.01(1) provides that "a person is not responsible for criminal conduct if at the time of such conduct as a result of mental disease or defect he lacks substantial capacity either to appreciate the criminality [wrongfulness] of his conduct or to **conform his conduct to the requirements of the law**." Thus the M.P.C. incorporates both the *M'Naghten* test and a variant of the "irresistible impulse" test — D wins if he satisfies *either* test. Here, the facts make it clear that Ripper is powerless to avoid killing, and that he therefore "lacks substantial capacity … to conform his conduct to the requirements of the law."

   (D) Jack as to both. That is, Jack must first come forward with some evidence of his insanity even to make sanity part of the case. (This is true in nearly all states courts as well, by the way.) Then, Jack must prove, by **"clear and convincing evidence,"** that he is insane. (This is one of the ways in which the federal statute makes it much tougher for defendants to win on insanity than in state courts — nearly all states either put the burden of persuasion on the prosecution, or make the defendant prove insanity but only by a "preponderance of the evidence.")

LEXIS®-NEXIS® Searches on **THE INSANITY DEFENSE**

Sub-Topic	Suggested Searches
M'Naghten Rule	`insan! w/5 (M'Naghten)`
Irresistible impulse test	`insan! w/20 (irresistible impulse)`
Federal insanity test	`(18 w/3 17) w/25 (insanity w/3 defense)`

II. DIMINISHED RESPONSIBILITY

A. **Meaning of diminished responsibility:** Many crimes are loosely said to be "specific intent" crimes; see *supra* p. 13. This is, they are defined in such a way that the defendant does not have the appropriate *mens rea* unless he has something more than a general wrongful intent. In most states, for instance, first degree murder is defined so as to require the "willful, deliberate, and premeditated taking of another's life." If a defendant who is not insane nonetheless suffers from such a mental impairment that he is **unable to formulate the requisite intent**, in a substantial minority of states he may prove this, and thus avoid conviction of that particular offense. A defense made on these grounds is generally called the defense of "*diminished responsibility*" or "*partial responsibility.*" L, p. 391.

> **Example:** D is charged with first degree murder, which is defined in the particular jurisdiction as a "willful, deliberate and premeditated killing." He seeks to prove that he has had a surgical lobotomy, as a result of which he does not have the mental capacity to form the required intent.
>
> *Held*, D may be allowed to present psychiatric expert testimony to this effect. Psychiatric testimony is admissible on such questions as whether D was insane at the time of the crime. There is no good reason not to accept such testimony when it would tend to show that the accused lacked the ability to form the requisite intent. *Commonwealth v. Walzack*, 360 A.2d 914 (Pa. 1976).

1. **Effect is to reduce to lesser offense:** The vast majority of those cases allowing the defense of diminished responsibility have been in homicide cases, usually ones in which the defendant is charged with first-degree murder and attempts to reduce it to second-degree by showing that he was incapable of the requisite premeditation. Accordingly, when the defense has been successful, it has resulted merely in the diminution of the offense from first-degree murder to second-degree, or from murder to manslaughter. This is because the lesser offense is usually a "lesser included offense," the elements of which are the same as the graver one except for the *mens rea*.

   a. **Defendant seldom goes free:** It is quite rare that successful use of the diminished responsibility defense allows the defendant to walk away free; where this would be the result of successful use of the defense, courts have sometimes refused to allow it, for this very reason.

2. **Special statutory provisions:** The term "diminished responsibility" or "partial responsibility" usually is used to refer to the judge-made doctrine whereby the defendant can use his mental impairment to establish that he did not have the requisite specific intent. But the same effect is sometimes given by express ***statutory provisions*** which allow or require the judge to take into account the defendant's mental impairment in deciding upon the severity of his offense. For instance, in New York the defendant may get a murder charge reduced to manslaughter if he acts "under the influence of extreme emotional disturbance." N.Y. Penal L. § 125.20(2).

B. **Insanity defense sometimes held to be superseding:** At least half of all American jurisdictions reject the doctrine of diminished responsibility. Usually, they do so by holding that ***no evidence*** that the defendant suffers from a mental disease or defect may be introduced, except pursuant to a formal insanity defense. L, p. 391.

1. **Practical consequence:** That is, either the defendant attempts to show that he is entitled to an insanity acquittal, or he will be held to be capable of formulating whatever specific intent is required for the crime, at least insofar as mental disease or defects are concerned. In these states, the insanity defense "supersedes" the defense of diminished responsibility.

   a. **Rejected in Ohio:** For instance, Ohio has rejected the doctrine of diminished responsibility by holding that it is superseded by the insanity defense. *State v. Wilcox*, 436 N.E.2d 523 (Ohio 1982). The court in *Wilcox* pointed out that a defendant who successfully asserts the defense of a diminished responsibility will typically have his crime reduced to a lesser one, and will thus receive a short prison sentence — rather than being involuntarily committed to a mental institution, as would happen in the case of an insanity acquittal. The court was therefore concerned that the diminished responsibility defense "could swallow up the insanity defense and its attendant commitment provisions." It also worried that the defense would not lead to "principled and consistent decision-making in criminal cases."

   i.   Result: The net result of the *Wilcox* holding is that "a defendant may not offer expert psychiatric testimony, unrelated to the insanity defense, to show that the defendant lacked the mental capacity to form the specific mental state required for a particular crime or degree of crime."

   b.   Statutory narrowing in California: The state best known for its expansive use of the diminished responsibility defense, California, has *narrowed* the defense by statute. One statutory provision purports to "abolish" the defense of diminished capacity; a companion provision seems to mean that evidence of a defendant's mental condition (other than insanity) is not admissible to show his lack of *capacity* to form the mental state required for the crime charged, but *is* admissible to show that he did *not in fact* form a required specific intent. Cal. Penal Code §§ 25, 28. An expert testifying about the defendant's mental condition is prevented from testifying as to "whether the defendant had or did not have the required mental states," an issue which is to be "decided by the trier of fact." *Id.*, § 29. This statute is a symptom of the disfavor into which the diminished responsibility defense has fallen in recent years.

C. Specific applications: As noted, the principal use of the diminished responsibility defense has been to reduce first-degree murder to second-degree, by a showing that the defendant was not capable of premeditation. But the defense has also been used in some other situations:

1. Murder reduced to manslaughter: The defendant may be allowed to show that he did not have the mental capacity to entertain "malice aforethought," and thus cannot be convicted of even second-degree murder, so that his crime must be reduced to manslaughter.

   a.   Use to negate "implied malice":   The defense is particularly likely to succeed in California, where a defendant may be convicted of second degree murder based upon an act "involving a high degree of probability that it would result in death," but only where he is shown to have had "implied malice." The California courts hold that implied malice exists only where the accused both knew his duty to act within the law, and acted in a manner likely to cause death or serious injury despite that awareness. In *People v. Poddar*, 518 P.2d 342 (Cal. 1974), D was held to be entitled to show that by reason of mental impairment not amounting to insanity, he was unable to control his conduct and therefore did not have the requisite "implied malice."

   Note: The popularity of the "diminished responsibility" defense in California is probably due mostly to the fact that California does not accept the "irresistible impulse" insanity defense, so that a defendant cannot gain an insanity acquittal by showing that he was unable to control his conduct. The "diminished responsibility" defense is therefore the next best way of using this inability.

2. **"Heat of passion" manslaughter:** In nearly all states, the defendant may get a murder charge reduced to manslaughter on the grounds that he acted *"in the heat of passion"* under extreme provocation; the defendant may be allowed to present testimony of his impaired mental condition to show that he did indeed act in the heat of passion. Thus in *Commonwealth v. McCusker*, 292 A.2d 287 (Pa. 1972), the defendant was allowed to present psychiatric testimony that at the time of the murder, he was "incapable of cool reflection" because of an affair between his wife (the victim) and the defendant's step-brother, her threats to retain custody of the defendant's son, etc.

III. AUTOMATISM

A. Nature of automatism defense: We saw previously (*supra*, pp. 3-4) that the defendant has not committed a crime unless he has committed a *voluntary act*. There are certain mental or physical conditions which may, at least in the opinion of a doctor, if not a judge, be considered to prevent a defendant's act from being considered voluntary. An *epileptic seizure* is the most frequent example of such a condition. When the defendant argues that such a seizure or other condition has prevented his act from being voluntary, he is asserting what is frequently called the defense of *"automatism"* (discussed briefly *supra*, p. 3.)

B. Defense sometimes superseded by insanity: Just as some courts have refused to allow the defense of "diminished responsibility," on the grounds that this defense is superseded by the insanity defense (see *supra*, p. 81), so some jurisdictions have refused to allow the defense of automatism, on the grounds that any condition which affects the defendant's mind so as to render his conduct involuntary constitutes a mental disease or defect, which may be asserted only by use of the insanity defense.

C. Generally allowed in America: American courts have, in general, allowed the automatism defense as distinct from the insanity defense. This would seem to be the position of the Model Penal Code, which in § 2.01(1) and (2) prevents liability from existing where the defendant does not commit a "voluntary act," and defines "voluntary act" to exclude, *inter alia*, a "reflex or convulsion" and movement during "unconsciousness."

1. *People v. Grant:* A case from Illinois, which has enacted provisions substantially similar to those of the Model Penal Code with respect to both insanity and involuntary acts, upheld the automatism defense. In *People v. Grant*, 360 N.E.2d 809 (1977), the defendant claimed that prior to the aggravated assault with which he was charged, he suffered a "blackout," and that this was due to "psychomotor epilepsy." The appellate court held that he was entitled to have the jury instructed that he could not be convicted if his act was not "voluntary," and that his defense could be asserted apart from the insanity defense (which he also asserted).

2. **Low blood sugar:** The automatism defense has also been allowed in at least one case involving *low blood sugar*. In *Regina v. Quick*, 3 W.L.R. 26 (Eng. 1973), the defendant was a diabetic who took insulin every morning. On the day in question, the defendant had too much insulin for the amount of sugar in his blood, and developed hypoglycemia, commonly called "low blood sugar." He lapsed into semi-unconsciousness, and attacked another person, a violence characteristic of hypoglycemia.

a. **Rationale:**   The court noted that the attack could have been prevented if the patient had eaten a lump of sugar beforehand, and that the case was therefore distinguishable from *Bratty, supra,* in that hypoglycemia was not "the sort of disease for which a person should be detained in a hospital rather than be given an unqualified acquittal" (as the court in *Bratty* indicated that epilepsy was.) Insanity is only applicable where there is a "malfunctioning of the mind caused by disease." A mental malfunctioning "of transitory effect caused by the application to the body of some external factor such as violence, drugs, including anesthetics, alcohol and hypnotic influences cannot be said to be due to disease." Here, the illness was due to insulin, not to basic mental disorder.

3. **Premenstrual Syndrome defense:**   It has been argued that the automatism defense should be allowed to women defendants who can show that they were unable to control their actions at the time of the crime because of *Premenstrual Syndrome*, or PMS. L, p. 407. Apparently no American court has allowed the defense.

4. **Post-traumatic stress disorder:**   Similarly, a defendant suffering from *post-traumatic stress disorder*, or PTSD, might be able to use this disorder to support an automatism defense. L, p. 407. A Vietnam veteran suffering from PTSD as the result of combat trauma might, for instance, argue that the resulting nightmares, reduction in emotional response, memory loss, loss of sleep, etc., entitle him to an acquittal on grounds of automatism.

IV. INTOXICATION

A. **The problem generally:**   A defendant who at the time of a criminal act was *intoxicated,* either from alcohol or drugs, may make several different kinds of arguments as to why his intoxication should constitute a defense.

1. **Voluntarily induced:**   If the intoxication was *"self-induced,"* he may argue: (1) that he would not have committed the crime if he had not been intoxicated, and therefore that he should not be punished merely because he was drunk. (2) Alternatively, he may make the more forceful argument that his intoxication prevented him from having the requisite *mens rea* for the crime. (3) Lastly, he may argue that as a result of his intoxication, he did not "know right from wrong," and should therefore be treated like an insane person.

2. **Involuntary:**   If, on the other hand, the intoxication was *"involuntary"* (a term of art including not only cases of duress, but also cases in which the intoxication was not foreseeable even though the ingestion of alcohol or drugs was intended), he may argue that this fact alone prevents him from having committed a voluntary act, and that he is therefore not liable for any crime.

3. **Balancing of interests:**   All of these arguments have been frowned on, to a greater or lesser degree, by the courts; the defendant's chances are better in the case of involuntary intoxication. The courts have strived to reach a balancing between society's interest in not having intoxicated defendants commit antisocial acts, and the fundamental principle of the criminal law that a person should not be convicted for conduct unless he had the appropriate mental state (*mens rea*).

B. **Voluntary intoxication:**   *Voluntary self-induced intoxication* does *not "excuse"* criminal conduct, in the same way that, say, self-defense or duress might constitute excuses. To take the clearest example, if the defendant decides to rob a bank, and voluntarily takes several drinks to increase his courage, the fact that he may be legally intoxicated when he actually commits the robbery will have absolutely no mitigating effect.

1. **Effect upon mental state:** However, the defendant's intoxication may, rather than constituting an "excuse," *negative the required mental state*, and therefore prevent an element of the crime from existing at all.

Example: D shoots at X with a loaded pistol. He is charged with "assault with intent to murder." D shows at trial that he was severely intoxicated at the time of the event.

Held, if D's intoxication was so severe that it prevented him from forming an intent to murder, he cannot be convicted of "assault with intent to kill." (But for this to be the case, he must show that he was so drunk that he did not know what he was doing or did not realize that death might result; it is not enough that he was too drunk to appreciate the "moral qualities" of his act. Also, if he did entertain the requisite intent, it is irrelevant that he would not have done so but for his intoxication.) *Roberts v. People*, 19 Mich. 401 (1870).

a. **States free to "opt out" of allowing this type of evidence:** Although evidence of voluntary intoxication could prove that the defendant did not possess the required mental state, states are free to legislate that such evidence shall be excluded. The Supreme Court has held that this type of statute does not violate the 14th Amendment's Due Process Clause. *Montana v. Egelhoff*, 518 U.S. 37 (1996).

2. **"Specific intent" crimes:** The mental state required in many of the common-law crimes is somewhat ill-defined, so that it has often been hard to identify the precise mental state required, and therefore to evaluate the defendant's contention that intoxication prevented him from having that mental state. Accordingly, courts have tended to divide crimes into those requiring *"specific intent,"* usually defined to mean an intent to do an act other than the *actus reus* (e.g., in burglary, the intent to commit a felony) and those requiring only *"general intent."* See *supra*, p. 12. As to the former (but not the latter), courts have generally held that intoxication is *admissible to show that the defendant lacked the specific intent in question.* Thus a defendant charged with burglary might show that he was too drunk to formulate the intent to commit a felony once he had committed the breaking and entering into a dwelling. Similarly, a defendant might escape liability for "assault with intent to kill" by showing he was too drunk to form an intent to kill (as in *Roberts, supra*). In each case, the mental state that has been negated by intoxication is the "specific intent" to do an act other than the *actus reus* (the breaking and entering, the discharging of the pistol).

3. **Categories abandoned:** However, modern courts have come increasingly to feel that the labels "specific intent" and "general intent" are really conclusions, and that the decision whether to recognize intoxication as a defense is better made on a crime-by-crime basis. Usually this will be done by looking at the *precise mental state* required in the definition of the crime, and determining whether this has been negated by intoxication. As to those crimes where it is not clear what mental state should be required, the decision should be made on policy grounds, i.e., will the purposes of the criminal law be best served by convicting or exculpating a defendant who acted while intoxicated?

a. Model Penal Code approach: Thus the Model Penal Code, in § 2.08(1), provides that self-induced intoxication "is not a defense unless it **negatives an element of the offense**."

b. *People v. Hood:* Similarly, the Supreme Court of California has rejected the significance of the labels "specific intent" and "general intent," at least as these concern the crime of "assault with a deadly weapon." In *People v. Hood*, 462 P.2d 370 (Cal. 1969), the court held that intoxication should not be allowed as a defense to a charge of assault with a deadly weapon; this conclusion was reached not by characterizing such assaults as being crimes of "specific intent" or "general intent," but rather because it would be "anomalous to allow evidence of intoxication to relieve a man of responsibility for the crimes of assault with a deadly weapon or simple assault, which are so frequently committed in just such a manner." The court's decision thus turned on the fact that the harm that the prohibition on assault is designed to curb is particularly likely to be induced by intoxication, and that an intoxication defense would defeat the purpose of making assault a crime. (But the court in *Hood* maintained the principle that intoxication can be a defense to a charge of battery with intent to rape or kill.)

c. Difficult standard to meet: Those states that follow the modern view of asking whether the intoxication has negated the particular mental state needed for the crime, often impose a **difficult standard** for the defendant to meet in showing that he was "drunk enough." See, e.g., *State v. Cameron*, 514 A.2d 1302 (N.J. 1986), a case interpreting a "negatives an element of the offense" provision identical to MPC § 2.08(1). The court held that the intoxication must be of "an extremely high level" amounting to ***"prostration of faculties."*** The fact that the intoxication may have led D to behave bizarrely or violently was irrelevant; the intoxication would suffice only if it rendered D "[in]capable of forming that bizarre or violent purpose...."

4. Defense to traditional "general intent" crimes: As a corollary of the lessening significance of the general intent/specific intent distinction, some courts are now willing to recognize that intoxication may serve as a defense to certain kinds of homicide and to rape, **even though these have traditionally been defined as "general intent" crimes.**

a. Rape: Thus a defendant who is so intoxicated that, although he has intercourse with an unconsenting victim, he did not have an intent to have that intercourse, might obtain an acquittal under modern principles. L, p. 414. (Many older cases refuse to allow such a defense).

i. Lack of consent not realized: Suppose instead that the defendant argued that his intoxication prevented him from *realizing that the victim was not consenting.* This would be a defense only if knowledge of the lack of consent, rather than recklessness as to the lack of consent, was the required mental state. Generally, however, recklessness has been held to be sufficient to make out the "general intent" required for the general intent crimes, so the "I didn't know she wasn't consenting" defense *doesn't work* if the defendant's failure to realize there was no consent was due to intoxication (generally considered to be a manifestation of recklessness).

b. Premeditated murder: Similarly, where first degree *murder* is defined so as to require "premeditation" or "deliberateness," most courts allow the defendant to show that intoxication prevented him from entertaining the requisite premeditation or deliberation. See L, p. 415. But, as noted, if the defendant started out with the requisite premeditation or deliberation, he will not escape conviction by the fact that he subsequently got drunk before committing the crime; so long as the original mental state actuates the crime, the fact that that state did not exist at the time of the crime is irrelevant, under the principles of concurrence (see *supra*, p. 35).

    i. No reduction to involuntary manslaughter: Also, the defendant will *not* generally be able to reduce a second-degree murder charge to *involuntary manslaughter* by virtue of his intoxication. This is principally because, in most states, second-degree murder is defined so as to include killings that stem from "reckless disregard for the value of human life," a "depraved heart," or some such formulation; courts generally hold that the act of becoming voluntarily intoxicated manifests the requisite degree of reckless endangerment. L, p. 415.

    ii. Voluntary manslaughter: Similarly, the defendant will not generally be allowed to introduce evidence of his intoxication in an attempt to get a murder charge reduced to *voluntary manslaughter*. Voluntary manslaughter exists where the defendant has killed in the "heat of passion." The crime is defined so as to include an objective component: the provocation must have been such as would cause an ordinary man to lose control. This is interpreted to refer to an ordinary *sober* man, so that the fact that the defendant might not have been provoked had he been sober will be irrelevant. (But, conversely, if the provocation would have been sufficient to inflame a reasonable sober man, the defendant will not lose his eligibility for voluntary manslaughter merely because he happened to be drunk. On the contrary, the drunkenness may be taken into account in determining whether the defendant *in fact* acted in the heat of passion, also a requirement.) See L, pp. 417-18.

c. Other crimes: There has probably been an increasing tendency to allow intoxication as a defense to other crimes as well, again provided that these are defined so as to require "intent," and not merely "recklessness." Thus in *U.S. v. Nix*, 501 F.2d 516 (7th Cir. 1974), it was held that intoxication could serve as a defense to a charge of *escape from prison* (and *a fortiori*, attempted escape), if the defendant could show that he was too drunk to form an intent to depart the prison and an intent to avoid confinement. The court explicitly rejected the traditional distinction between "general" and "specific" intent as a basis for determining whether intoxication should be a defense.

5. Recklessness: With respect to those crimes that have traditionally been called crimes of "general intent," the defendant's *recklessness* has usually been enough to meet the *mens rea* requirement, and a purposeful or knowing act has not usually been required. For instance, the crime of battery has usually been defined so as to require merely the reckless disregard of the risk of inflicting bodily harm on another. In cases of intoxication, courts have further decided, generally, that *intoxication will never be considered to negate the existence of recklessness*. The consequence of this is that intoxication will not negate the *mens rea* of crimes that may be committed through recklessness.

a. **Model Penal Code agrees:** The Model Penal Code agrees that drunkenness may not negate recklessness. M.P.C. § 2.08(2). Since acting "recklessly" is defined in § 2.02(2)(c) of the Code as occurring when a person "consciously disregards" a high risk of harm, the rule on drunkenness is clearly a special exception to the definition of recklessness, because the drunk defendant will often simply not be aware of the high risk that his conduct poses.

  i. **Rationale:** The Code draftsmen decided that such a special rule was not only well-recognized, but justified: "awareness of the potential consequences of excessive drinking on the capacity of human beings to gauge the risks incident to their conduct is by now so dispersed in our culture that it is not unfair to postulate a general equivalence between the risks created by the conduct of the drunken actor and the risks created by his conduct in becoming drunk." Furthermore, a contrary rule would force the prosecution to show that the defendant consciously disregarded the high risk of danger at the time he became drunk, and this would frequently be extremely difficult to prove. Comment 1(d) to M.P.C. § 2.08.

  ii. **Relation to crimes of "general intent":** The Code provision concerning intoxication and recklessness is quite significant, because under Code § 2.02(3), if a crime defined in the Code or elsewhere contains no provision as to the requisite mental state, that mental state may be established by showing that the defendant acted "purposely, knowingly or recklessly" with respect to the element in question. For instance, the Code definition of "rape," in § 213.1(1), does not mention any requisite mental state with respect to either the act of intercourse, or the woman's lack of consent. Thus if a rape defendant drunkenly believes that the woman is consenting, when she is not, intoxication would not be a defense, at least in those situations where he would have realized the lack of consent had he been sober.

6. **Negligence:** Not surprisingly, intoxication is also not accepted to negate ***criminal negligence***. The usual definition of criminal negligence does not include a requirement that the actor be aware of the risk that he has created (so long as he ***should*** be aware of that risk), so no special rule or exception is required to prevent drunkenness from negating negligence.

Example: D is charged with criminal assault for having stabbed a police officer. D pleads intoxication as a defense. The voluntary intoxication statute provides that "no act committed by a person while in a state of voluntary intoxication shall be deemed less criminal by reason of his condition, but whenever the actual existence of any particular mental state is a necessary element to constitute a particular species or degree of crime, the fact of his intoxication may be taken into consideration in determining such mental state." The jurisdiction defines "criminal negligence" as being present where a person "[fails] to be aware of a substantial risk that a wrongful act may occur and his failure to be aware of such substantial risk constitutes a gross deviation from the standard of care that a reasonable man would exercise in the same situation."

Held, because criminal negligence is thus defined by reference to an objective standard (the "reasonable man"), D's drunkenness cannot prevent him from having the requisite mental state, and is therefore not a defense. *State v. Coates*, 735 P.2d 64 (Wash. 1987).

7. **Self-defense:** Similarly, the defendant may not establish the defense of *self-defense* (*infra* p. 107) by showing that, because of his drunkenness, he mistakenly believed that he was being attacked. The test is again whether a *reasonable sober* man would have believed that self-defense was necessary. L, p. 417.

8. **Insanity:** The defendant will generally not be allowed to try to prove that his intoxication prevented him from knowing "right from wrong," and thereby amounted to a type of "temporary *insanity.*"

    Example: D voluntarily takes amphetamines for several days. He then suffers from "toxic psychosis," and drives around recklessly, shoots at a policeman, and kidnaps someone. He raises the defense of insanity, caused by the drugs.

    Held, where a defendant suffers from a "temporary episode of mental incapacity caused by the voluntary use of liquor or drugs," he may not assert the defense of insanity. (But, the court said, had D been suffering from an "existing state of mental illness," he could have used the insanity defense, even if this more-or-less permanent state had originally been brought about by prolonged use of liquor or drugs.) *State v. Cooper*, 529 P.2d 231 (Ariz. 1974).

    a. **"Permanent" insanity:** As the court noted in *Cooper, supra*, if the defendant suffers from a mental disease or defect which is more-or-less "*permanent*" rather than transitory, the insanity defense may be used even though that disease or defect may have resulted from prolonged use of drugs or alcohol. A chronic alcoholic who suffers from *delirium tremens*, for instance, could assert an insanity defense. L, p. 420.

        i. **Prolonged illness from one episode:** If the defendant developed a permanent disease or defect as a result of one or just a few episodes of drug-use, however, it is not clear whether insanity could be asserted. A defendant who was thrown into a long-term hallucinating state by one bad LSD trip, for instance, might have some chance of establishing the insanity defense, although courts are not likely to be sympathetic to such an argument in view of the self-induced nature of the illness. (But such a case might come within the definition of "pathological intoxication," discussed *infra*.)

C. **Involuntary intoxication:** If the defendant is fortunate enough to be able to show that his intoxication was not "self-induced" and "voluntary" but rather, "*involuntary*," he is much more likely to be able to make good use of it in defending a criminal charge. The principal benefit to him is that not only may the intoxication negate a specific mental element of the crime, but it may also amount to an *insanity defense*, if it prevented him from "knowing right from wrong," "being substantially able to conform his conduct to the requirements of the law," or whatever formulation of the insanity defense is in use in the particular jurisdiction.

    1. **Several kinds of involuntary intoxication:** Courts have recognized several kinds of situations in which the defendant's intoxication will be held to have been "involuntary."

        a. **Duress:** The defendant's intoxication is involuntary if he ingested the drugs or alcohol only *under duress*. Courts have traditionally been quite strict about what constitutes duress. The Model Penal Code, for instance, would allow the defense only where the defendant was subjected to the actual or threatened use of force "which a person of *reasonable firmness* in his situation would have been unable to resist." (M.P.C.,

§ 2.09(1)). Thus if the defendant goes out with friends, who insist that he take a drink, and who threaten to ostracize him if he doesn't, his intoxication would almost certainly not be "involuntary."

i.　***Burrows* case:**　The leading case on what constitutes duress for purposes of involuntary intoxication is *Burrows v. State*, 297 P. 1029 (Ariz. 1931). There D, an 18-year-old who had never tasted alcohol, was picked up as a hitchhiker on a road running through the Arizona desert. The driver insisted that D drink first beer and then whiskey, threatening to throw him out in the middle of the desert, without any money, if he did not. D complied, and then apparently went into an alcoholic fit in which he killed the driver. The court held that the jury could properly consider whether the defendant had acted under duress (which the jury found not to have been the case).

ii.　**Model Penal Code:**　Observe that under the Model Penal Code, it would probably be held that as a matter of law, there was no duress in *Burrows*; the highway was a reasonably well-traveled one, and it certainly does not seem that a person of "reasonable firmness" in the defendant's situation would have been "unable" to resist the command to drink. (But the Model Penal Code also makes the "choice of evils," or "necessity," defense available in the involuntary intoxication situation. See § 3.02(1), and the Comments to the final version of § 2.08. Thus the defendant in *Burrows* might argue that getting drunk was a lesser evil than being put out on the desert with no money.)

b.　**Drugs taken under medical advice:**　Intoxication will also be involuntary if it occurs ***pursuant to medical advice***. See M.P.C. § 2.08(5)(b). Thus in *City of Minneapolis v. Altimus*, 238 N.W.2d 851 (Minn. 1976), the defendant, accused of careless driving and hit-and-run, was held entitled to a temporary insanity defense if he could show that the drug he had taken (Valium) was taken pursuant to medical advice, without knowledge of its intoxicating capacities, and served to prevent him from knowing either the nature of his act or that it was wrong.

c.　**Mistake as to nature of substance:**　If the defendant intentionally ingests a substance, but ***mistakenly believes that it is not intoxicating***, he may be able to have this considered "involuntary" intoxication. But his mistake must be a ***reasonable*** one. Thus in one case the defendant was given some tablets which he was told were "breath purifiers," but which were in fact cocaine tablets; he was held to have been involuntarily intoxicated and entitled to an insanity acquittal if the tablets had caused him to become temporarily insane. *People v. Penman,* 110 N.E. 894 (Ill. 1915). Similarly, if the defendant had never had an opportunity to learn, even vicariously, that a certain drug (e.g., LSD) caused intoxication, his intoxication might be involuntary even if he knew that what he was taking was the drug in question. See Comment 1 to M.P.C. § 2.08.

i.　**Strict definition of "mistake":**　But the defendant will not generally be entitled to use the "mistake" doctrine merely because he did not know the *precise* qualities of the substance he was taking, if he did know that the substance had *some* kind of intoxicating nature. Thus in *State v. Hall*, 214 N.W.2d 205 (Iowa 1974), the defendant was given LSD by a friend, who told him that it was a "little sunshine" and would make him feel "groovy." The defendant went into hallucinations, and killed another, whom he thought was a rabid dog. *Held* the defendant acted voluntarily in taking the drug. This was not a situation in which he was totally mistaken about the nature of the substance (e.g., he did not think it was candy), and he knew that it had some mind-affecting qualities.

    ii. Pathological-reaction possibilities: But under the Model Penal Code, the defendant in *Hall* might have been able to establish that his intoxication was "pathological," i.e., grossly excessive in degree due to his unusual susceptibility to the drug. (See *infra*, this page, sub-par. (d)). Such a rationale is hinted at by the dissent, which argued that in view of the defendant's lack of knowledge about hallucinations and other possible serious effects, his conduct should not be considered voluntary.

  d. Pathological response: A final kind of involuntary intoxication occurs when the defendant knowingly takes a relatively small amount of intoxicant, but because of an ***abnormal sensitivity*** that he was not aware of, his reaction is much ***more severe*** than it would be for a normal person. Such intoxication is often called "***pathological intoxication***." See M.P.C. § 2.08(5)(c). Thus if the defendant knows that one can get drunk on alcohol, but has never taken a drink, and upon taking his first drink is driven into a murderous frenzy due to his unknown and abnormal sensitivity to it, he will be treated as involuntarily intoxicated, and therefore eligible for the insanity defense.

D. Alcoholism and narcotics addiction: If the defendant is a ***chronic alcoholic***, or a ***narcotics addict***, he may make the argument that he had reached a point where even taking the first drink of the day, or the first "fix," is no longer a matter of choice but of physical compulsion stemming from disease. If he were able to succeed with this argument, he would then presumably be entitled to be treated as "involuntarily" intoxicated, and therefore eligible for the insanity defense.

  1. Defense not well-accepted: But courts have not been sympathetic to this approach. For one thing, it is very hard to convince a court that the defendant has literally no free choice whether to take that first fix or drink of the day. For another, the anti-social behavior engaged in by such defendants, particularly narcotics addicts, is so great that there is great judicial fear of opening the door to such claims. See L, p. 423.

  2. Crimes committed to gain funds: Some defendants have gone even farther, and have claimed not that their addiction or alcoholism rendered them insane, but that they committed crimes ***to gain funds to avoid withdrawal symptoms***. Such a defense has apparently never succeeded, and is not likely to. Courts are all too aware of the large number of crimes that are committed under precisely these circumstances.

    a. The *Moore* case: Thus in *U.S. V. Moore*, 486 F.2d 1139 (D.C. Cir. 1973), D, charged with possession of heroin, argued that he had "lost the power of self-control with regard to his addiction," and therefore should not be responsible for possession. The court rejected his contention, stating that if absence of free will would excuse possession of the addicting drugs, "the more desperate bank robber for drug money has an even more demonstrable lack of free will" derived from the same factors that, according to D, should absolve the mere possessor. Accordingly, the court decided, D's addiction, and loss of control, was a self-induced disease, and therefore not exculpating.

3. **Constitutional arguments:**   Addicts and alcoholics have also made ***constitutional*** arguments stemming from the alleged compulsory nature of their intoxications. These arguments have received some, but not much, sympathy from the Supreme Court. The two principal cases governing the constitutionality of punishing behavior related to alcoholism and addiction are *Robinson v. California* and *Powell v. Texas*.

   a. *Robinson:*   In *Robinson v. California*, 370 U.S. 660 (1962), the Supreme Court held that it was an unconstitutional cruel and unusual punishment to make it a crime for a person to "be addicted to the use of narcotics." The Court made a number of arguments in support of this holding, but, at least according to later decisions by the Court, the principal basis was that this statute punished "status" as opposed to "conduct." (See *supra*, p. 2.)

   b. *Powell:*   The Court subsequently refused to extend the rationale of *Robinson* to situations involving crimes requiring some affirmative conduct, not mere "status" as addict or alcoholic. In *Powell v. Texas*, 392 U.S. 514 (1968), the defendant was convicted of being found in a state of intoxication in a public place. The Supreme Court held (by a 5-4 vote) that the defendant had not been punished for "status," but for the act of appearing drunk in public, and that *Robinson* therefore did not control. The Court rejected the defendant's contention that his conduct consisted merely of the natural result of his "compulsion" to drink; the Court relied first on the absence of any evidence showing that the defendant was powerless to resist taking the first drink, and also on the principle that there should be no constitutional doctrine of *mens rea* or *actus reus* (i.e., that such matters are better left to the individual states).

Quiz Yourself on
INTOXICATION

17. Hansel goes to the local tavern one night and ties one on. He stumbles out, and drives away. Hansel then forcibly opens the door to Witch Hazel's house, believing it's his own (which is really one block over in their development of nearly-identical tract homes). When Witch Hazel walks into the room Hansel thinks she's a burglar and beats her up. Hansel is criminally charged with both burglary and battery. Burglary is defined in the jurisdiction as an intentional entry into the dwelling of another at night, with an intent to commit a felony therein. Battery is defined as intentionally or recklessly causing a harmful or offensive contact with the body of another. To which (if either) of these two charges — burglary and battery — will Hansel's intoxication be a defense?

18. Popeye spends the afternoon drinking in a bar and gets plastered. As he is leaving to go home, he encounters Brutus, who approaches him while waving his arms wildly to swat away a fly. Popeye, believing that Brutus is going to attack him, picks up a bar stool and hits Brutus over the head with it. (A sober man in Popeye's position would not have believed that Brutus was attacking him.) Can Popeye successfully plead self-defense?

19. Othello has for some time suspected that his beloved wife Desdemona may have been unfaithful to him. One evening he gets quite drunk at a neighboring tavern, and then comes home to discover that his wife's favorite handkerchief is missing. As the result of Othello's drunken logic (plus a little help from his evil

friend Iago, who has planted the idea of Desdemona's infidelity in Othello's head), Othello incorrectly believes that the missing handkerchief is proof that Desdemona has cheated on him. He kills Desdemona in a jealous rage. Assume that a sober man in Othello's position would not have believed that the missing handkerchief suggested anything about Dedemona's fidelity. Assume further that where a man reasonably believes that his spouse has been unfaithful, his killing of the spouse in a fit of jealous rage may be reduced from murder to manslaughter. May Othello successfully plead manslaughter on these facts?

Answers

17. **It will be a defense to burglary but not to battery.** First, let's consider burglary. Voluntary intoxication can be a defense to crimes requiring intent or knowledge (beyond the intent to do the actus reus itself), if the intoxication prevented defendant from forming the mental state necessary. Burglary requires an intent to enter another's dwelling plus an intent to "commit a felony therein." Hansel did not have the intent to enter another's dwelling, and he certainly didn't have any intent (at the time of entry) to commit a felony inside the dwelling. So his intoxication, although voluntary, prevented him from having the mental state needed for burglary.

    Battery, on the other hand, is defined quite differently with respect to the required mental state. As the question stipulates (and in this, the stipulation matches the law of most states), battery can be committed either by intending to commit a harmful/offensive contact, or by recklessly committing such a contact. Virtually all states (and the M.P.C.) agree that voluntary intoxication will never negate the existence of recklessness. In a sense, Hansel's recklessness in getting drunk will "carry over" and be deemed recklessness existing at the time of the attack on Witch. Therefore, Hansel meets the mental-state requirement for battery (reckless infliction of a harmful or offensive contact) even though his mistake about whether Witch was a burglar was caused by his intoxication.

18. **No.** The test for self-defense is an objective one: whether a reasonable, *sober* person would have believed that self-defense was necessary. It is irrelevant that Popeye's intoxication made him believe self-defense was necessary.

19. **No.** The lesser crime of manslaughter is defined so as to include an *objective* component: the provocation must have been such as would cause an ordinary "reasonable" person in the defendant's position to lose control. The ordinary reasonable person is presumed to be a *sober* one. Therefore, the fact that Othello's intoxication made him unable to rationally process the information won't help him.

LEXIS®-NEXIS® Searches on **INTOXICATION**

Sub-Topic	Suggested Searches
Voluntary intoxication	`crime or criminal) and (intoxicat! w/3 (intent or mens rea) and (atleast2(intox!) or atleast2(drunk!))`
Involuntary intoxication	`crime or criminal) and (intoxicat! w/3 voluntary w/10 (intent or mens rea))`

V. INFANCY

A. Common-law treatment: An extensive discussion of the law governing *minors* accused of crimes is beyond the scope of this outline. In general, it may be said that the common-law view of the criminal capacity of children is as follows:

    1. Under seven: Children under seven are conclusively presumed to have no criminal capacities;

    2. Between seven and fourteen: Children between seven and fourteen are presumed to have no criminal capacity, but this presumption may be rebutted by a showing of malice or awareness of the wrongfulness of the conduct (e.g., attempting to conceal a crime);

    3. Over fourteen: Children over the age of fourteen are treated the same as adults for purposes of criminal capacity.

B. Effect of legislation: But legislation in almost every state has made the importance of these common-law rules much less great. First, many states have raised the minimum age of responsibility, which in some states is now as high as sixteen. Even more significantly, almost all states have enacted *juvenile court legislation*, in which youths who have committed acts that would be crimes if committed by adults are handled in juvenile court, and may be sent to reformatories.

    1. Constitutional issues: The use of juvenile court proceedings has raised a number of constitutional questions on which the Supreme Court has spoken.

        a. Due process rights: The juvenile offender, if charged with an act that would be a crime if it were committed by an adult, has the right to *adequate written notice* of the charge, the right of representation by *counsel*, the privilege against *self-incrimination*, and the right to *confront witnesses*. *In Re Gault*, 387 U.S. 1 (1967). The state must meet the "beyond a reasonable doubt" standard of proof. *In Re Winship*, 397 U.S. 358 (1971). However, there is no right to a jury trial. *McKeiver v. Pennsylvania*, 403 U.S. 528 (1970).

        b. Waiver: Statutes setting up such juvenile courts often provide that the youthful offender may *waive* his right to be tried in the juvenile system, and may then be handled within the regular criminal court system. The Supreme Court, in construing the District of Columbia statute, has held that the juvenile court must hold a hearing on waiver, and must give adequate reasons for its decision to have the case transferred to the regular criminal system. *Kent v. U.S.*, 383 U.S. 541 (1966). It is not clear whether this holding was reached on constitutional, as opposed to statutory, grounds.

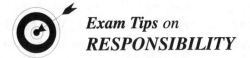 *Exam Tips on*
RESPONSIBILITY

Many exam questions involve issues of insanity or intoxication. So always be attuned to the possibility of a defendant raising these defenses.

Insanity

☛ Don't come to a quick conclusion that a defendant is legally insane just because the fact pattern depicts outlandish behavior by her. Always check the jurisdiction's definition of insanity and analyze carefully the behavior against the required elements.

☞ *M'Naghten* **test:** *M'Naghten* is the test most frequently used on exams. Remember, D meets the test if *either* he (1) didn't ***know the nature and quality of the act*** he was doing; or (2) he didn't know that what he was doing was ***wrong***.

Key things to look for:

☞ **When the insanity occurs:** Make sure the elements of the test were present ***at the time of the offense*** in question. *Trap:* Don't be fooled by a fact pattern that tells you that D has already been declared insane in another case or at another time — this doesn't matter. Nor is it enough that D has been diagnosed with "mental illness."

☞ **"Understood that act was wrong" prong:** Look in the fact pattern for information indicating that this prong was satisfied, such as that D knew his conduct to be "unlawful" or knew that he could be imprisoned for it.

Conversely, look for objective signs that D was ***unaware*** of the wrongfulness of the act.

Example: D, who has been previously diagnosed with schizophrenia, strangles his fiancee, Marie. Just before he does that, he says to his psychiatrist, "I'm being stalked by a robot who's hidden Marie and impersonated her. I've got to disable the robot by strangling it, and then I'll work on finding Marie." You should say that if D was telling the truth to his psychiatrist, this is a strong indication that he didn't understand that he was killing Marie, and that he thought instead that he was disabling a robot. In that case, he'd qualify under the "didn't know that what he was doing was wrong" prong (and also the "didn't know the nature and quality of the act" prong) of *M'Naghten*.

☞ **"Understood the nature and quality of the act" prong:** This prong is usually held to be satisfied if D merely understood the physical consequences of his act — the fact that D had some crazy motive for doing the act won't help him.

☞ **Delusions:** This principle is often shown by fact patterns involving ***delusions***. If the delusion just relates to D's motive for the act, and doesn't prevent D from understanding both that his act is illegal and that it will have certain physical consequences, then D can't take advantage of *M'Naghten*, in most states.

Example: D is mentally ill, and, as a result, believes that his wife W is building a bomb in the basement of their house and that she plans to blow up the world. Although he knows that he could be punished for murder, he pushes W down a flight of stairs in order to save the world by killing her. D's delusion probably won't help him under *M'Naghten*, because D understood that pushing W down the stairs was illegal and would probably kill her. The fact that D had what he thought was a good motive (save the world) won't make a difference.

☞ **"Irresistible impulse" test:** If the fact pattern doesn't specify what insanity test applies in the jurisdiction, consider whether *irresistible impulse* might produce a different result on your facts than *M'Naghten*. Generally, for irresistible-impulse to apply, the fact pattern will have to signal to you that D feels powerless to stop even though he realizes what he's doing is wrong. (*Example:* D, who's very religious, hears God telling him to kill his wife — if the trier believes this, irresistible-impulse probably applies.)

☞ **Diminished capacity:** If an insanity defense is likely to fail, consider the defense of *diminished capacity.* A defendant in a specific intent crime may negate the specific intent element by claiming that he had a mental defect that prevented him from forming the required mens rea. This defense is usually used to reduce a charge from murder to voluntary manslaughter.

Intoxication

☛ Often a fact pattern will indicate that a defendant has been drinking or taking drugs. In the usual case, the intoxication will be *"voluntary,"* and the basic discussion below assumes that this is so.

☞ **Specific mental state:** Most important, figure out whether the intoxication *blocked the defendant from forming the requisite mental state.* If it did, the intoxication will require a finding of not guilty. In deciding this issue, the classic general-intent/specific-intent distinction isn't dispositive, but it still has some value.

☞ **General intent:** Where the crime is a so-called *"general intent"* crime — i.e., the only intent needed is the intent is to do the actus reus — voluntary intoxication usually *won't* prevent the requisite intent from being formed. (But this is just a generalization, and isn't always accurate.)

Example 1 — Sexual assault: D rapes V — the only intent needed is the intent to have intercourse, and intoxication probably won't negate that intent. (Intoxication that prevents D from *noticing that V isn't consenting* won't negate the requisite intent).

Example 2 — Battery: D physically attacks V — the only intent needed for battery is intent to make harmful contact, and intoxication that makes D belligerent (or that causes him to be insulted where a sober person wouldn't be) isn't inconsistent with that intent.

☞ **Specific intent:** Where the crime is a so-called *"specific intent"* crime (i.e., the intent needed is something beyond the mere intent to do the actus reus), voluntary intoxication is *more likely to block* the requisite intent. So analyze D's state of mind closely against *all* mental elements.

Example 1 — Pre-meditated murder: If D is very drunk, his intoxication may have prevented him from doing the requisite pre-meditation. (But check to make sure he didn't do the pre-meditating before he got drunk, in which case he meets the requirement even if he was incapable of still pre-meditating just before the killing.)

Example 2 — Larceny: If D is so drunk that he didn't know the property he was taking belonged to another, the requisite intent (to wrongfully take property of another) will be missing.

☞ **Involuntary intoxication:** Look out for facts suggesting *"involuntary"* intoxication. This occurs most often where either: (1) D is mistaken about the nature of what he's taking (e.g., he doesn't realize there's LSD in the fruit punch); or (2) D knowingly takes a small quantity of a psychoactive substance, but has a grossly excessive, unpredictable reaction to it (e.g., D gets totally drunk and enraged the first time he has a single drink). Here, if D was not reckless in ingesting the substance, he may be able to avoid meeting the mental state for any crime requiring recklessness or intent.

☞ **Wanton or Reckless:** But in any involuntary-intoxication case, analyze the facts to determine whether the defendant's actions in ingesting the substance may be considered reckless or wanton. If they are, the wanton or reckless state of mind may be enough for the crime.

Example: D suffers from paranoid schizophrenia that becomes acute whenever he drinks an excessive quantity of alcohol. D drinks five glasses of beer while having lunch with his friend, F, at a bar/restaurant. F insults D and D shouts that he will kill him. D leaves the bar, comes back with a gun, and shoots F. D may well be deemed to have been intoxicated and unable to form the requisite mens rea for pre-meditation-style murder. But if he knows that his paranoia spikes whenever he drinks and often causes him to attack others, you could argue that by the mere act of drinking heavily, D acted with wanton indifference to the safety of others. Therefore, he might be guilty of wanton-indifference-to-the-value-of-human-life murder.

On the other hand, if D had no history of violent behavior as a consequence of his condition, his conduct would probably rise at most to the level of recklessness, in which case he couldn't be convicted of any crime more serious than involuntary manslaughter (for which recklessness meets the mental-state requirement).

CHAPTER 4

JUSTIFICATION AND EXCUSE

Introductory note: Grouped within this chapter are a number of affirmative defenses (that is, defenses as to which, generally, the defendant must bear the burden of proof) that will allow the defendant to escape conviction, even though the prosecution may be able to prove all the elements of the crime. These defenses are: (1) *duress*; (2) *necessity*; (3) *self-defense*; (4) *defense of others*; (5) defense of *property*; (6) *law enforcement* (arrest, prevention of crime and escape); (7) *consent*; (8) *maintenance of authority*; and (9) *entrapment*. While the underlying rationale varies somewhat from defense to defense, there are two recurring reasons for exculpating the defendant: (1) because his conduct was a choice of the lesser of two evils; and (2) because his conduct, even if not a choice of the lesser of two evils, was all that a person of ordinary firmness or courage would do in the situation.

I. GENERAL PRINCIPLES

A. Justification vs. excuse: Courts occasionally denominate some of the defenses discussed in this chapter as being "justifications," or, on the contrary, "excuses." Thus the defense of "necessity" (*infra*, p. 103) is usually thought to be a justification, whereas duress is generally thought of as an excuse. The theory behind the two labels is that "justification" applies where the defendant took the better, more socially useful, and morally defensible of two actions; "excuse" applies where he did not necessarily do so, but did all that he could have been expected to do. For instance, if the defendant is forced by terrorists to join in a bank robbery or else be killed, his doing so would be "excused," not "justified," under the doctrine of duress.

1. Significance of distinction: Generally, there is no great significance to the distinction. However, it has been suggested that a claim of justification is transferable to a third party, whereas a claim of excuse is not. Suppose that a starving woman steals bread to feed herself and her child; if her claim of necessity is a justification, then a third person ought to be able to take the bread on her behalf. But if her conduct is merely excused, then the defense would be personal to her, and a third person could not commit the act for her and claim the defense. See Fletcher, pp. 761-62. It is not clear that courts would recognize this distinction, however.

B. Effect of mistake of fact: One problem that arises with respect to almost all of the defenses in this chapter is the *effect of a mistake of fact* by the defendant. That is, if the defendant is mistaken about the need for, say, self-defense, does he lose his right to assert that defense? The courts have frequently divided the problem into two categories: (1) the effect of a reasonable mistake; and (2) the effect of an unreasonable one.

1. Common-law approach has no unified rule: In general (but not always), the common-law approach has been that a reasonable mistake will not negate the privilege. (But see the privilege of arrest, and that of prevention of crime by private citizens, both of which are voided by a reasonable mistake; *infra*, p. 129). An ***unreasonable*** mistake, however, will negate virtually all of these defenses, under the common law.

    a. Criticism of rule: Requiring the defendant not to make an unreasonable mistake has often been criticized, on the grounds that it may allow the defendant to be convicted of a crime requiring intent (e.g., first-degree murder) when his only relevant mental state was negligence. For instance, suppose the defendant is somewhat stupid and somewhat paranoid, and he reasonably believes that X, his acknowledged enemy, who has reached into his pocket, is about to shoot him. If in reality, X is merely reaching for a handkerchief, and D fatally shoots him in "self defense," under the common-law rule his negligent mistake is wiped out — the case is treated as if D behaved maliciously. This result has seemed to many to be unjust.

        i. Model Penal Code view: Accordingly, the Model Penal Code requires, as to all the defenses discussed here, merely that the defendant really believe ***(whether reasonably or not)*** that the facts are such that the defense is merited. The only exception to this rule is that, if the defendant is prosecuted for an act that may be committed "recklessly" or "negligently," he will lose the defense if his mistake was "reckless" or "negligent," as the case may be. M.P.C. § 3.09(2).

        Example: Consider the hypothetical given above, in which D fatally shoots X, in the unreasonable and mistaken belief that X was about to kill him. Under the Model Penal Code approach, D will be able to assert the defense of self-defense to a charge of first-degree murder, since the definition of that crime provides that the killing must be committed "purposely or knowingly," or with "extreme indifference to the value of human life." (See M.P.C. § 210.2(1)). But if the charge against D is manslaughter, he will not be able to assert self-defense if it is shown that his mistake was "reckless," since manslaughter, under the Code, may be committed recklessly. (See M.P.C. § 210.3(1)(a)). Similarly, self-defense would be no defense against a charge of negligent homicide (M.P.C. § 210.4) if the mistake were shown to have been a negligent one.

C. Overlapping of defenses: In some situations, more than one of the defenses in this chapter might be applicable. For instance, a homeowner who shoots a burglar might assert self-defense, defense of others (his family), prevention of crime (larceny), and arrest. Since, particularly under the common-law approach, there may be significant disparities in the requirements for these defenses (e.g., the consequences of a reasonable mistake), it can be important to pick the correct defense to assert.

    1. Model Penal Code attempts unified rules: For this reason, the Model Penal Code draftsmen have attempted to reduce the disparities in the rules governing the various defenses. For instance, as noted, an unreasonable but genuine belief in the need to assert any of these defenses will not negate the defense under the Code, unless the offense charged is one which may be committed recklessly or negligently.

II. DURESS

A. Nature of duress: A defendant can be said to have committed a crime under duress if he performed it because of a ***threat*** of, or ***use*** of, ***force*** by a ***third person*** sufficiently strong that the defendant's will was ***overborne***. The term applies to force placed upon the defendant's ***mind***, not his body.

Example: Suppose X forces D to rob Y, by threatening D with immediate death if he does not. This is duress, since the force from X operates on D's mind. But if X had given D an epilepsy-producing drug, so that D went into convulsions and attacked someone, D would not raise the defense of duress; instead, he would assert that he had not committed any voluntary act, and therefore had no liability (see *supra*, p. 3).

B. Elements of the defense: In most jurisdictions, the defendant must establish the following elements in order to claim the duress defense:

1. **Threat:**   A ***threat*** by a third person,

2. **Fear:**   which produces a ***reasonable fear*** in the defendant

3. **Imminent danger:**   that he will suffer ***immediate***, or ***imminent***

4. **Bodily harm:**   ***death*** or ***serious bodily injury.***

C. Rationale for defense: The rationale that is sometimes expressed for the defense is that, generally speaking, the harm that is likely to befall the defendant (death or serious bodily injury) is greater than the harm he will cause by doing crime. If the defendant is threatened with death unless he helps carry out a robbery, for instance, his acquiescence represents a choice of the lesser harm (the robbery) over the greater harm (death). Accordingly, some courts would probably refuse to allow the defense where the harm feared by the defendant is not as great as that which he commits. (This theory probably explains the generally-accepted rule that duress is no defense to intentional homicide; see *infra*.)

1. **Model Penal Code view:**   But the Model Penal Code does not contain such a requirement that the harm avoided be greater than the harm brought about. Instead, the Code's test is whether the threat was sufficiently great that "a person of ***reasonable firmness*** in [the defendant's] situation would have been unable to resist." M.P.C. § 2.09(1). Presumably, however, the enormity of the harm which the defendant will be committing is one of the factors which a reasonable person would evaluate in reaching a decision whether to resist. A reasonable person confronted with a choice between losing a finger and killing an innocent victim, for instance, might be "able" to resist, where he would not resist the choice between his own death and cutting off the victim's finger.

D. Homicide cases: Courts have traditionally held that the defense of duress is not available where the defendant is charged with the ***intentional killing of another*** (i.e., murder or voluntary manslaughter). This is true even though the defendant is threatened with his own death if he refuses and, in theory, true if the defendant is asked to sacrifice the life of one innocent person, in order to save those of several. Some states have changed this rule by statute — by not imposing an automatic ban on the duress defense in homicide cases — but most states appear still to follow it. L, pp. 468-69, 472.

1. **Justifications:**   Two principal justifications for this rule have been articulated:

   a. **Greater good required:** At least where the choice is between the defendant's life and that of an innocent victim, morality demands that the defendant sacrifice his own life. (Presumably, this would not apply where the threat is that more than one person, say, the defendant's entire family, will be killed if the defendant does not kill one victim.)

   b. **Immunization of terrorists:** More forcefully, allowing the duress defense to murder charges would permit the leader of a *terrorist gang*, or of a gang of kidnappers, to immunize his entire gang against all murder charges. Each member of the gang could say, perhaps truthfully, "I would have been killed had I not obeyed."

2. **Felony-murder:** Duress has always been accepted as a defense to a charge of *felony-murder*. For instance, suppose D is coerced into driving X to a robbery site, and during the robbery, X accidentally or intentionally kills a bystander. Under the felony-murder doctrine, D would ordinarily be liable for murder. But since D would be allowed to assert the duress defense to the underlying accomplice-to-robbery charge, he would not be liable of any underlying felony, and therefore could not be convicted of felony-murder. See L, p. 470.

E. **Imminence of threatened harm:** The harm with which the defendant is threatened must, according to most courts, be *immediate* or *imminent*. That is, threat of a *future harm* is generally not sufficient. The theory behind this requirement is probably that where harm is threatened for the future, the defendant almost always has some other, non-criminal, alternative available to him (e.g., calling the police and asking for protection).

   1. **Rule breaking down:** But there has been a mild tendency towards abandonment of this requirement of imminence. The Model Penal Code, in § 2.09, does not require that the threatened harm be imminent, but merely that the threat be such that a person of "reasonable firmness" would be "unable to resist" it.

      a. **Telephone threats:** Similarly, see *State v. Toscano*, 378 A.2d 755 (N.J. 1977), where the defendant asserted that a third person had *threatened him over the telephone* several times, to induce him to prepare a fraudulent insurance claim. The court held that no *per se* rule requiring imminence of harm should be applied, provided that the Model Penal Code's "person of reasonable firmness" test is met.

F. **Death or serious bodily injury:** Traditionally, the defendant must be threatened with *death or serious bodily injury*. L, pp. 470-71. But this rule, too, may be breaking down. The Model Penal Code in § 2.09(1), requires only a threat of "bodily harm," not serious bodily harm. Furthermore, there seems to be no reason why a threat of extreme *property damage* or *economic sanction* (e.g., that the defendant will be bankrupted) should not suffice to excuse at least a relatively minor crime against property (e.g., cooperation in filing a false insurance claim, as in *Toscano, supra*). Under the Model Penal Code, such a threat might give rise to the justification, or "lesser of two evils," defense of § 3.02.

G. **Threat directed at person other than defendant:** Some states require that the threatened harm be directed *at the defendant*. But the vast majority of states today are more liberal, recognizing the defense where the threat is made against a third party, including a member of the defendant's *family*. L, p. 472.

1. **Model Penal Code's liberal view:** The Model Penal Code, in § 2.09(1), follows the modern liberal trend of allowing harm to third persons to suffice: The threat may be against "[the defendant's] person or the person of another…." But the Code's "person of reasonable firmness" test must, of course, be met, so that the threat of, say, minor harm to an absolute stranger may not be enough where the defendant is induced to commit a serious crime.

H. **Effect of mistake:** The defendant normally has no way of knowing whether or not the threat will be carried out if he fails to comply. If it is subsequently shown that the threat definitely would not or could not have been carried out, does the defendant lose his duress defense? All courts apparently agree that, as long as the defendant's mistake was *reasonable*, he does not forfeit the defense. But if his belief that the harm will occur is *unreasonable*, in most states he will lose the defense.

1. **Model Penal Code view:** The Model Penal Code does not require that the defendant's belief that the threat will be made good be reasonable. But this requirement may be implied by the requirement that the threat be such that a "person of reasonable firmness" would be unable to resist it; if it would be clear to such a person that the threat will not be carried out, he would presumably be able to resist.

I. **Defendant who voluntarily subjects himself to danger:** Virtually all courts deny the defense to a defendant who has *voluntarily* placed himself in a situation where there is a substantial probability that he will be subjected to duress. Thus one who voluntarily joins a terrorist group that is rumored to kill any member who attempts to defect, might be held to have waived the duress defense as to any act which the group coerces him into taking.

1. **Model Penal Code view:** The Model Penal Code would similarly deny the defense if the defendant "recklessly placed himself in a situation in which it was probable that he would be subjected to duress." Furthermore, if he was merely negligent, not reckless, in doing so, he could be convicted of a crime as to which negligence meets the required *mens rea* (e.g., negligent homicide), but not of a crime requiring intent or recklessness. M.P.C. § 2.09(2).

J. **Wife coerced by husband:** At common law, a wife who could show that her husband commanded her to perform a criminal act had a good chance of successfully asserting the duress defense, just by that fact alone. But the more modern view, and that of the Model Penal Code, is that pressure by a husband against his wife is to be treated the same as any other kind of coercion, with no special presumption of duress. See M.P.C. § 2.09(3); see also L, pp. 475-76.

K. **Military orders:** Closely related to the defense of duress is the defense that one was *obeying military orders* issued by a superior. It is generally agreed that if the defendant *neither knows nor has reason to know* that the act ordered is unlawful, he cannot be convicted if the act is a crime. Conversely, it is agreed that if the defendant *does* know that the act ordered is unlawful, he may be convicted if he performs it. Thus the most common form of the Nuremberg Defense ("I was only following orders….") is unavailing.

L. **Guilt of coercer:** Even though the person subjected to duress may have a valid defense on that ground, this will not absolve the person who did the coercing. The latter is likely to be convicted based on general principles of principal-and-agent liability, just as one may be convicted of murder if one induces a child or mental incompetent to carry out the killing. See L, p. 475.

M. Relation to "choice of evils" or "necessity" defense: The defense of "necessity," discussed in the next section, is similar to that of duress, except that the source of pressure comes not from a human being, but from circumstances or events (e.g., a shipwreck). The basis of the necessity doctrine is that the defendant may, in some circumstances, choose the "lesser of two evils," even if that evil is a crime. If the defendant is pressured by a human being, but is unable to make out a traditional duress defense (e.g., the threat is to destroy the defendant's property, rather than harm her person), may the defendant employ a "choice of evils" defense?

   1. Model Penal Code allows: Most courts have been reluctant to allow the defense of necessity where the coercion comes from a human source. But the Model Penal Code explicitly provides, in § 2.09(4), that the defendant may employ the "choice of evils" defense of § 3.02 even where the motivating force is another human being, and the duress defense would not be available.

LEXIS®-NEXIS® Searches on **DURESS**

Sub-Topic	Suggested Searches
Duress, generally	`(crime or criminal) and atleast2(duress)`
Homicide cases	`(crime or criminal) and (duress w/10 (homicide or murder))`
Requirement that threatened harm be imminent	`(crime or criminal) and (duress w/20 imminen!) and atleast2(imminen!)`

III. NECESSITY

A. The necessity defense generally: The defense of *"necessity"* may be raised when the defendant has been compelled to commit a criminal act, not by coercion from another human being, but by *non-human events*. For instance, a husband who needs to get his seriously ill wife to the hospital could claim the necessity defense, if he violated the speed limit.

   1. Choice of evils: The essence of the defense is that the defendant has chosen the *lesser of two evils*. Thus in the case of the man with the sick wife, it is presumably a lesser evil to violate the speed limit (assuming that one is otherwise careful) than to leave a person in danger of sickness or death.

   a. Model Penal Code formulation: The Model Penal Code explicitly recognizes that the balancing of evils is the basis of the defense. The Code defense is called that of *"justification,"* and it is available where "the harm or evil sought to be avoided...is greater than that sought to be prevented by the law defining the offense charged...." M.P.C. § 3.02(1)(a). (Unlike the common-law defense of necessity, the Code defense is also available where the source of the emergency is coercion by another person rather than an event.)

   b. Harm must be greater, not merely equal: The harm sought to be avoided by the defendant must be *greater than*, not merely equal to, the harm caused by the defendant's conduct. The most tangible demonstration of this principle is the rule that one may not take another's life to save one's own (the presumption being that all lives are of equal value). See the discussion of the defense in homicide cases, *infra*, p. 105.

c. **Test is objective, not subjective:** It is up to the court, not the defendant, to make the final determination of whether the harm sought to be avoided was indeed greater than that committed by the defendant's criminal act. There is also a requirement that the defendant have ***believed*** that he was making a choice of the lesser of two evils, (i.e., if he did not have this belief, and merely discovered the necessity after the fact, he will not have the defense), but the ultimate balancing of interests is done by the court. See L, pp. 482-83.

   i. **Innocent mistake:** But if a reasonable ordinary person in the defendant's situation would have agreed that the harm sought to be avoided was greater than the harm caused, the defendant will not lose the benefit of his defense merely because it later turns out that the choice of evils was unnecessary. For instance, if D speeds to the hospital to bring his wife there, and it later turns out that there was nothing seriously wrong with her, he will not lose his defense so long as a reasonable man would have agreed with his belief that speeding seemed necessary.

B. **Requirements for defense:** The principal requirements which the defendant must meet to be entitled to the necessity defense are, according to most courts:

1. **Greater harm:** The harm sought to be avoided is greater than the harm committed (or, in any event, the harm which the defendant thinks he is committing);

2. **No alternative:** There is no ***alternative*** that would also avoid the harm, and would be non-criminal or a less serious crime;

3. **Imminence:** The harm is ***imminent***, not merely future;

4. **Situation not caused by defendant:** The situation has not been brought about by D's carelessly or recklessly putting himself in a position where the emergency would arise;

5. **Nature of harm:** The harm sought to be avoided is not usually required to be serious bodily harm (as it generally must be for duress; see *supra*, p. 101), but may be non-serious bodily harm, or even ***property damage***.

C. **Illustrative examples:** Following are some situations in which the necessity defense has been accepted or, under the Model Penal Code, would be accepted:

1. A druggist may dispense a drug without the required prescription to alleviate distress in an emergency;

2. An ambulance may pass a traffic light;

3. Property may be destroyed to stop the spread of fire;

4. A mountain climber, roped to a companion who has fallen over a cliff, may cut the rope, if the only alternative is that both will die. (But many courts, as discussed below, refuse to allow the necessity of defense in any intentional homicide case.)

5. A prisoner threatened with homosexual rape by other prisoners may escape (providing other alternatives, such as reporting the threat to the authorities, are unavailable or futile). *People v. Unger*, 362 N.E.2d 319 (Ill. 1977). See also *State v. Reese*, 272 N.W.2d 863

(Iowa 1978), allowing the necessity defense to an escaped prisoner, but only upon full compliance with five specific requirements: (1) The prisoner is faced with "a *specific threat* of death, forcible sexual attack, or substantial bodily injury in the *immediate future*"; (2) "There is *no time for a complaint* to the authorities or there exists a history of futile complaints…."; (3) "There is no time or opportunity to *resort to the courts*"; (4) There is no evidence that the defendant used *force or violence* towards prison personnel or other "innocent" persons during the escape; and (5) The prisoner "*immediately reports* to the proper authorities" once he has obtained safety from the immediate threat.

6. A professional "deprogrammer" may kidnap a twenty-year-old man to "save" him from "indoctrination and domination" by a religious group which he had joined. (A case involving Ted Patrick, not officially reported but reported in the *New York Times*, August 7, 1973, p. 24, col. 5.)

For situations 1 to 3 above, see Model Penal Code, Comment 2 to M.P.C. § 3.02.

D. Homicide: Courts have traditionally been extremely reluctant to permit the necessity defense where the defendant is charged with an ***intentional killing.***

1. ***Dudley & Stephens:*** The best known case on the subject is *Regina v. Dudley & Stephens*, 14 Q.B.D. 273 (Eng. 1884). The two Ds had been shipwrecked, along with a 17-year-old boy, and were compelled to spend more than three weeks on a lifeboat, without food or fresh water. After 18 days, the Ds killed the boy, and ate his flesh and drank his blood. They were picked up four days later. They argued that had they not killed the boy, they would have died within the four days, and that the boy would certainly have died first. Nonetheless, the court refused to accept their necessity defense. The following reasons were given:

   a. **Morality:** Morality demands that one die rather than take the life of an innocent person;

   b. **Rescue:** A rescue might have occurred before any of the three had died (or not until they had all died), so that it was not at all certain that a greater evil would be avoided by the killing;

   c. **Unfairness:** Any means for deciding who is to die is fraught with a danger of unfairness; here, for instance, the weakest and youngest was chosen;

   d. **Abuse:** If the defense is allowed, it may be abused, and "made the legal cloak for unbridled passion and atrocious crime."

2. ***Holmes* case:** An American case, *U.S. v. Holmes*, 26 F. Cas. 360 (C.C.E.D. Pa. 1842) also involved a lifeboat situation. There, the defendant was one of several seamen who, with 32 passengers, were adrift in a lifeboat following a shipwreck. The first mate decided that the boat was overcrowded, and that those male passengers not accompanied by their wives should be thrown overboard. The defendant helped in the jettisoning, and was charged with manslaughter. (The grand jury refused to indict for murder.) The court instructed the jury that necessity was not a defense, particularly since the seamen bore a duty to sacrifice themselves before the passengers. In any event, the court stated, the proper procedure was to ***draw lots*** to decide who should be thrown overboard.

3. Model Penal Code view: The Model Penal Code, however, does not rule out the necessity defense in intentional homicide cases. Even under the Code, one may not sacrifice one life to save another, since the Code requires the choice of the lesser of two evils, not merely the equal of two evils, and all lives are presumed to be of equal value. But if a life can be sacrificed to save two or more lives, the Code would allow the defense. See Comment 3 to M.P.C. § 3.02.

    a. Mountaineer: Thus the Code would grant the necessity defense to a mountaineer who, roped to a companion who has fallen over a precipice, cuts the rope so that instead of the inevitable death of both of them, one will survive. *(Ibid.)*

E. Economic necessity not sufficient: The harm that confronts the defendant, may, as noted, be of a non-bodily nature (e.g., damage to his property). But the courts have not accepted the defense of *"economic necessity."* Thus an unemployed worker will not be excused if he steals food. (But if he is actually starving to death, then the defense may be allowed.) See L, p. 480.

F. Civil disobedience: The necessity defense has frequently been asserted in cases of *civil disobedience*, in which the defendant has committed an act of protest to manifest his disapproval of government policies. The defense has seldom, if ever, been allowed in such a situation. The courts' refusal is often based in part on the theory that there is a non-criminal alternative way of expressing protest.

    Example: The Ds want to protest the U.S.'s involvement in El Salvador. They therefore enter their local IRS office, chant, "keep America's tax dollars out of El Salvador," splash simulated blood on the counters, walls and carpeting, and obstruct the office's operation. After several warnings by police to leave or face arrest, Ds are arrested. At trial, they assert the defense of necessity, contending that their acts of protest were necessary to prevent further bloodshed in El Salvador.

    Held, the defense of necessity can never apply to cases involving indirect civil disobedience. Cases of *direct* civil disobedience must be distinguished from those of *indirect* civil disobedience. In the former, protestors seek to challenge the very laws under which they are charged (e.g., an African American sit-in at a lunch counter at a time when African Americans were prevented from sitting at lunch counters); direct civil disobedience might satisfy the requirements for necessity. In contrast, *indirect* civil disobedience involves breaking one law (e.g., trespass) to call attention to another (e.g., our statutes authorizing U.S. involvement in El Salvador). Cases of indirect civil disobedience fail to meet several of the prerequisites for the necessity defense. For example, the disobedience cannot be considered the "lesser of two harms," since the policy being questioned (here, U.S. involvement in El Salvador) is by hypothesis one that was validly enacted by the legislature and therefore cannot constitute a cognizable harm at all. Similarly, the necessity defense requires the absence of any legal alternative that could abate the evil, and in the case of indirect civil disobedience there is always a legal alternative — working to change government policy. *United States v. Schoon*, 971 F.2d 193 (9th Cir. 1991).

G. Prevention of "possible future harm" not sufficient: If D's actions were undertaken with the object of preventing a non-imminent *future harm* that is *speculative* rather than nearly certain to occur, the necessity defense will fail.

Example: D operates a free needle-exchange program for drug addicts in an effort to stop the spread of AIDS in his neighborhood. He is charged with violating a state law that prohibits the distribution of hypodermic needles without a prescription. *Held*, D may not use the necessity defense, since the harm he sought to prevent was "debatable or speculative" rather than imminent. *Commonwealth v. Leno*, 616 N.E.2d 453 (Mass., 1993). (The court also held that the defense should fail because D had a legal alternative to abate the danger: to try to change the law through the initiative process.)

IV. SELF-DEFENSE

A. Self-defense generally: There is a general right to **defend oneself** against the use of unlawful force. In some circumstances, the defense may be by means of **deadly force**; at other times, it is limited to non-deadly force. When successfully asserted, the defense is a complete one, and can result in an acquittal not only on homicide charges, but on other charges, such as aggravated assault, attempted murder, assault and battery, etc.

B. Requirements: The following requirements must generally be met for use of the defense:

1. **Resist unlawful force:** The defendant must have been resisting the **present or imminent use** of **unlawful force;**

2. **Force must not be excessive:** The degree of force used by the defendant must not be **more than is reasonably necessary** to defend against the threatened harm;

3. **Deadly force:** The force used by the defendant may not be **deadly** (i.e., likely to cause death or serious bodily injury) unless the danger being resisted was also deadly force;

4. **Aggressor:** The defendant must not have been the **aggressor** (unless (1) he was a non-deadly aggressor confronted with the unexpected use of deadly force, or (2) he withdrew after his initial aggression, and the other party continued to attack);

5. **Retreat:** The defendant must not have been in a position from which he could **retreat** with complete safety, unless (1) the attack takes place in the defendant's dwelling, or, by the modern view, his place of work or (2) the defendant uses only non-deadly force.

C. What constitutes unlawful force: Self-defense applies only where the defendant is resisting force that is **unlawful**. In general, this means that the other party must be committing a **crime** or **tort**. If the other party, even though he is using force, is entitled to do so (e.g., a property owner using non-deadly force to defend his property against attempted theft by the defendant), the force is not unlawful and the defendant may not use force to defend against it.

1. **Excessive force:** However, if the other party is entitled to use some degree of force, but uses **more than is lawfully allowed**, the excess will probably be treated as unlawful, and the defendant may resist it by using force himself. Thus if the property owner uses deadly force to defend his property (which is more force than the law allows in most situations; see *infra*, pp. 123-124), the defendant may presumably use deadly force to protect himself. (In this situation, the defendant is the aggressor, but under the rules discussed *infra*, pp. 111, an aggressor who uses non-deadly force may resist when the other party answers with deadly force.)

2. **Force which would be excused:**   If the other party's use of force is not justifiable, but merely "excusable," it may be treated the same as if it were unlawful, for purposes of the defendant's right to defend himself against it.

   Example: D is a policeman who is trying to check whether a store belonging to S has been broken into. D tries the door, and S, reasonably believing that D is a thief who intends not only to rob him, but to harm him, starts shooting at D. S's use of force is not, strictly speaking, unlawful, since he may claim self-defense (because, even though he is mistaken, his belief is reasonable; see *infra*, p. 113). Nonetheless, it would probably be held that D is entitled to resist, even by using deadly force if non-deadly force would not suffice. See Fletcher, pp. 763-66.

3. **Effect of mistake:**   If the defendant makes a *reasonable mistake* about the unlawful status of the force being used against him, he will nonetheless be protected. This is in keeping with the general rule in self-defense cases that reasonable errors as to factual matters do not void the defense. See *infra*, pp. 113-115.

4. **Consent:**   If the defendant has *consented* to the other party's use of force, the defendant may not use force in self-defense. Thus if a woman has consented to sexual intercourse, she may not suddenly change her mind and stab her partner in the back. (But she would have the right to withdraw her consent at any time, and if the partner failed to stop, she would then be allowed to resist.)

D. **Degree of force:**   The defendant may not use more force than is *reasonably necessary* to protect himself.

   1. **Use of non-deadly force:**   One is entitled to use *non-deadly force* to resist virtually any kind of unlawful force (assuming that the level of non-deadly force is not more than is necessary to meet the threat.)

      a. **No need to retreat:**   One may use non-deadly force without *retreating* even if this could be safely done (whereas retreat may be necessary before the use of deadly force; see *infra*, pp. 112-113).

      b. **Prevention of theft:**   Also, if the other party is attempting to steal property, one has the right to resist by non-deadly force, and is not required to surrender the property sought to be stolen. See Comment 4(d) to M.P.C. § 3.04.

      c. **Threats:**   A *threat* to use deadly force is generally not considered to be the equivalent of the use of deadly force. Thus if one is attacked by a person using only his fists (which, generally, will not constitute use of deadly force), one may resist by threatening to shoot or stab the assailant. But this threat may be made *only if there is no intention to carry it out*, at least according to the Model Penal Code § 3.11(2). See the fuller discussion of the meaning of "deadly force" shortly below.

E. **Deadly force:**   One may defend oneself with *deadly force* only if the attack threatens him with *serious bodily harm*. This rule stems from the principle that the level of resistance should be roughly proportional to the level of the threat, and that a minor attack not dangerous to life or limb should not be met with an annihilating response.

   Example: D gets into a shouting match with X. X, who as D knows is not a particularly effective street fighter, starts swinging his fists at D. D has the right to use non-deadly force (e.g., his own fists) to protect himself. But he may not use deadly force, such as a gun or a knife. (If he does so, he himself will be behaving unlawfully, and X will have the right to counter with deadly force of his own: see *infra*, p. 111.)

1. **Definition of "deadly force":** "Deadly force" is usually defined as force that is *intended or likely* to cause *death or serious bodily harm*. The Model Penal Code, in § 3.11(2), defines the term to include "purposely firing a firearm in the direction of another person or at a vehicle in which another person is believed to be...."

    a. **Result irrelevant:** Whether or not death or serious bodily harm actually occurs is theoretically irrelevant to determining whether a particular force is deadly. Thus if D shoots at his assailant with a gun, and either misses him entirely, or just gives him a superficial flesh wound, D has used deadly force, and may be liable for assault and/or battery if deadly force was not permissible.

        i. **Death or serious bodily harm unexpectedly occurring:** Conversely, if a particular kind of force is not used for the purpose of causing death or serious bodily harm, and is not likely to cause it, the force will be treated as non-deadly even if death or serious bodily harm *unexpectedly results*.

    b. **Depends on situation:** A particular kind of resistance may constitute deadly force if used by one person, but not by another. A heavyweight boxing champion or karate expert who used his hands to attack an assailant might well be held to have used deadly force, where this would not be so of an ordinary person.

    c. **Threats:** As noted, a *threat* to use deadly force does not itself constitute use of deadly force, provided that the threatener does not intend to carry out the threat. See M.P.C. § 3.11(2).

2. **Nature of attack defended against:** The Model Penal Code allows deadly force to be used to protect against not only death and serious bodily harm, but "kidnapping or sexual intercourse compelled by force or threat...." The privilege of self-defense thus blends into the privilege to prevent violent felonies by use of deadly force (*infra*, p. 130).

3. **Effect of mistake:** If the defendant is mistaken in his belief that he is threatened with serious bodily harm, he will nonetheless not lose the right to reply with deadly force so long as his mistaken belief was reasonable. See the full discussion of mistake *infra*, pp. 113-115.

F. **Imminence of harm:** The harm being defended against must be reasonably *imminent*. The danger that one may be attacked tomorrow (even if the attack is virtually certain) will not suffice; this rule derives principally from the desire of courts to encourage non-violent dispute-resolution, particularly where there is time to take other measures (e.g., asking for police protection.)

    1. **Not unduly strict standard:** But the courts have not required that the defendant wait until the very last second before the attack prior to defending himself. Thus, in *People v. Williams*, 205 N.E.2d 749 (Ill. App. 1965), the defendant was a cab driver who stopped his cab to prevent some youths from continuing their beating of an old man. As he stopped, his cab was hit by a brick thrown by one of the muggers. The defendant got out of his cab and fired two shots towards the boys (to frighten them), one of which caused a fatal

wound. The court held that the muggers had a "present ability" to harm the defendant and were "a short distance" from him. Therefore, the requirement of imminence was met even though no attack on him was in progress.

   a. Model Penal Code requirement: The Model Penal Code is even more liberal with respect to the degree of immediacy of the threat. A person may use force in self-defense if he is protecting himself against unlawful force that will be used *"on the present occasion."* M.P.C. § 3.04(1). Commentary to the Code explains that this would permit the defendant to use defensive force to "prevent an assailant from going to summon reinforcements…." Comment 2(c) to M.P.C. § 3.04.

  2. Withdrawal by aggressor: One consequence of the requirement that the danger be imminent is that if the *aggressor withdraws* from the conflict, the victim *loses his right to use force,* at least where the withdrawal should reasonably be interpreted as indicating that the danger is over. (But as the M.P.C. notes in the quotation above, if the assailant seems to be getting reinforcements, that's not a "withdrawal," and the victim can keep using force.)

   Example: V and D are friends. They get into a verbal dispute, and V takes a swing at D. D starts to swing back. V stops swinging and says, "Wait a minute, we've always been friends, let's stop fighting." D (who has no reason to believe that V's offer to stop the fight is phony) continues to beat V up. D will not be able to use the defense of self-defense if he is charged with battery occurring after V's offer to stop — once V withdrew from the conflict, the occasion requiring self-defense was over.

G. Aggressor may not defend himself: One who is the *initial aggressor* (i.e., one who strikes the first blow or otherwise precipitates the conflict) may *not claim self-defense*. This principle follows from the general rule that one may use self-defense only against unlawful force; since the aggressor has, by hypothesis, used force, the other party is justified in resisting it, so that resistance is not unlawful.

  1. Aggression without use of actual force: One can be an aggressor, and thus lose the right of self-defense, even if one did not actually strike the first blow. It is enough if one does an unlawful (i.e., tortious or criminal) act which "provokes" the physical conflict.

   Example: X and two friends drive up to the rear of D's house, and attempt to take the windshield wipers from D's wrecked car. D comes out of the house and starts yelling at X. According to D's later testimony, X picks up a lug wrench, so D goes into the house to get his pistol. When he comes out, X is back in the car, ready to depart. D walks up to the car and says "If you move, I will shoot." X gets out of the car and walks towards D, exclaiming, "What the hell do you think you are going to do with that?" (Apparently, X has the lug wrench in a raised position.) D shoots X when they are ten feet apart, and kills him. A jury finds D guilty of manslaughter, thus implicitly rejecting D's claim of self-defense.
   Held, the jury could properly find that D was the aggressor, and thus forfeited his right of self-defense. It is true that X provoked the first quarrel, by trying to steal the wipers, but this was only a misdemeanor against D's property; in any event, the initial quarrel had ended when X went back to his car prepared to drive away. D was therefore the actual provoker of the second round of hostilities. "The fact that the deceased struck the first blow, fired the first shot or made the first menacing gesture does not legalize the self-defense claim if in fact the claimant was the actual provoker…. An affirmative unlawful act rea-

sonably calculated to produce an affray foreboding injurious or fatal consequences is an aggression which, unless renounced, nullified the right of homicidal self-defense." D's walking towards X with a loaded pistol, and threatening to shoot, was such an act. *U.S. v. Peterson*, 483 F.2d 1222 (D.C. Cir. 1973).

2. **Two exceptions:** There are two exceptions to the rule that one who is the aggressor may not claim self-defense.

    a. **Non-deadly force met with deadly force:** First, if the defendant provoked the exchange but used no actual force or only ***non-deadly force***, and the other party ***responds with deadly force***, the defendant may then defend himself (even with deadly force, if necessary). In this situation, the victim's use of force is unlawful, since it is excessive, so there is no strong reason to prevent the defendant from countering it.

    Example: D attacks X with his fists. X defends himself by knocking D down; he then starts to smash D's head against the wall, so that D is in danger of being killed or badly hurt. D manages to pull a knife, and kills X. Most present-day courts would hold that D is entitled to a claim of self-defense. X, insofar as he met non-deadly force with deadly force, was acting unlawfully, and D should be permitted to save his life. Comment 4(b) to M.P.C. § 3.04.

    Note: The above analysis assumes that D did not have the opportunity to ***retreat safely***, and that his choices were either to use the knife or be killed or maimed. If D had had the chance to retreat, and the jurisdiction was one which requires retreat before the use of deadly force (see *infra*), D would have lost the right to rely on the defense if he did not retreat. If the jurisdiction was one not requiring retreat, the court might have been inclined to hold that D lost his right of self-defense because he was the aggressor, even though the use of non-deadly force was met with deadly force; this would simply be a judicial means for encouraging retreat at least upon the part of aggressors. See M.P.C., *ibid*.

    b. **Withdrawal:** The second exception to the aggressor rule is that if the defendant-aggressor ***withdraws from the conflict***, and the other party initiates a second conflict, the defendant may use non-deadly force, and may use deadly force if he is threatened with death or serious bodily harm. This is true even if the defendant started the initial conflict with the use of deadly force, and an intent to kill or maim.

        Example: D starts a knife fight with V, finds himself getting the worst of the encounter, tries unsuccessfully to escape, and finally stabs V to death. *Held*, D was entitled to claim self-defense because he withdrew. *State v. Mayberry*, 226 S.W.2d 725 (Mo. 1950).

        i. **Rationale:** This result stems from the rule, discussed earlier, that if the aggressor withdraws, the victim may no longer use force. If the aggressor withdraws and the victim continues to use force, the aggressor is now the one in the right, and is himself entitled to use force in his own defense.

        ii. **Must be brought home to other party:** However, the defendant-aggressor's act of withdrawal must be such that the other party ***realizes***, or ***should realize***, that the defendant has tried to end the hostilities.

H. Retreat: Courts have been understandably reluctant to encourage the use of deadly force when there is an alternative means available for ending an encounter. Therefore, a number of states (still a minority, but probably close to half now) require that if one could *safely retreat*, he must do so rather than use deadly force. The majority that has rejected this requirement has generally done so on the ground that a person should not be required to do an act that is commonly regarded as a sign of cowardice.

1. **No retreat required before non-deadly force:** Even jurisdictions imposing the retreat requirement will hold that, assuming one had the right to use self-defense, it is never necessary to retreat before the use of *non-deadly force*. Thus if X attacks D in either a deadly or non-deadly manner, and D could withdraw from the encounter with complete safety (e.g., by getting into his car and driving away), D is nonetheless privileged everywhere to stand his ground and fight back with his fists.

2. **Only required where it can be safely done:** The retreat rule, in those states adopting it, only applies where the defendant could retreat with *complete safety* to himself and to others. Furthermore, a defendant who reasonably but mistakenly believes that retreat cannot be safely done will be protected; "…the issue is not whether in retrospect it can be found [that] the defendant could have retreated unharmed. Rather the question is whether he knew the opportunity was there, and of course in that inquiry the total circumstances including the attendant excitement can be considered." *State v. Abbott*, 174 A.2d 881 (N.J. 1961).

   a. **Safety depends on circumstances:** Obviously the nature of the weapon, if any, possessed by the other party will be relevant in determining whether the defendant believed or should have believed that retreat with safety was possible. If the other party had a high-powered rifle, the court is exceptionally unlikely to find a duty to retreat. On the other hand, if the weapon is a knife, and the assailant is obviously less quick on his feet than the defendant, a duty to retreat is likely to be found.

   b. **Unreasonable but genuine mistake:** If the defendant genuinely believes that retreat could not be done safely, but this mistake is *unreasonable*, the court would presumably treat the situation just as it would treat other unreasonable mistakes. The various treatments of such mistakes are discussed *infra*, pp. 113-115.

      i. **Model Penal Code:** The Model Penal Code, in § 3.04(b)(ii), requires retreat only where the defendant "*knows* that he can avoid the necessity of using such force with complete safety by retreating…." But if his mistaken belief that he cannot safely retreat amounts to recklessness or negligence, he may be convicted of a crime requiring only recklessness or negligence, as the case may be; see M.P.C. § 3.09(2).

3. **Retreat in defendant's dwelling:** Those states requiring retreat *do not require it* where the attack takes place in the *defendant's dwelling*. This stems from the deep-rooted historical belief that "a man's home is his castle." See M.P.C. § 3.04(2)(b)(ii)(1).

   a. **Not applicable if defendant was aggressor:** But the exception for a dwelling does not apply if the defendant was the *aggressor*; this stems from the overall position that the aggressor has, in general, no right of self-defense at all (see *supra*, p. 110). Thus in *U.S. v. Peterson*, 483 F.2d 1222 (D.C. Cir. 1973) (discussed more fully *supra*, p. 110), the court held that since the jury could properly have found that D was the aggressor, he had a duty to retreat if that was possible, even though the encounter took place on his property.

b. Assailant also resident of dwelling: A few courts have held that the dwelling exception to the retreat requirement does not apply where the *assailant is also a resident* of the dwelling (e.g., husband attacked by wife in their house). These courts apparently rely upon the theory that where the dwelling is also the "castle" of the assailant, the reasons for the exception (that the defendant's home is his castle) are nullified.

   i. Modern view: But the modern view does not remove the exception in this situation. See, e.g., *People v. Lenkevich*, 229 N.W.2d 298 (Mich. 1975) ("why…should one retreat from his own house when assailed by a partner or co-tenant, anymore than when assailed by a stranger who is lawfully upon the premises? Whither shall he flee, and how far, and when may he be permitted to return?") See also M.P.C. § 3.04(2)(b)(ii)(1).

c. Offices, hotels and clubs: Courts have been liberal in extending the dwelling exception to include not only the defendant's house, but his *place of work*, the *hotel* where he is staying, and such places as his social club.

I. Effect of mistake: It may happen that the defendant is mistaken about one of several aspects of the situation confronting him. He may be mistaken in his belief that he is about to be attacked, mistaken in his belief that the force used against him is unlawful, mistaken in his belief that only deadly force will suffice to repel the threat, or mistaken in his belief that retreat could not be accomplished with safety. But so long as his mistaken belief as to any of these points is *reasonable*, he will still be able to claim self-defense.

Example: X, D's sworn enemy, comes up to D and points a pistol at him, saying "Your time has come." D shoots X to death before X can pull the trigger. It later turns out that X's gun was not loaded, and his motive was simply to frighten D. Nonetheless, D will be able to successfully claim self-defense.

1. "Detached reflection" not required: The reason for this rule is that in a typical situation the defendant is confronted with the need for immediate action, and should not be penalized for an innocent mistake. As Justice Holmes said, "Detached reflection cannot be demanded in the presence of an uplifted knife." *Brown v. U.S.*, 256 U.S. 335 (1921).

2. Unreasonable belief: But if the defendant's mistake is *unreasonable*, most states hold that he loses the right to claim self-defense. "It is not enough that the party believed himself in danger, unless the facts and circumstances were such that the jury can say he had reasonable grounds for his belief…." *Shorter v. People,* 2 N.Y. 193 (1849).

Example: D boards a New York City subway, while carrying an unlicensed loaded pistol. Four youths approach D, and one states, "Give me $5." D pulls out the gun and shoots at each of the four, wounding them all (and permanently paralyzing one). After an initial round of shots, which is enough to wound or scare each of the four, D fires a final shot at one of them, who is sitting on a bench at the time (and apparently posing no imminent threat to D). D later tells the police that he was certain that none of the youths had a gun, but he had a fear, based on prior occasions on which he had been mugged, that he might be "maimed." The prosecutor charges the grand jury that D was entitled to act as he did only if a reasonable person in D's situation would have done so. The grand jury indicts D (for attempted murder, assault and weapons possession), but a lower court dismisses the indictment on the grounds that all that is required is that D's beliefs and reactions have been "reasonable to him."

Held (on appeal), for the prosecution. New York's statute on self-defense allows a person to use physical force against another "when and to the extent he *reasonably believes* such to be necessary to defend himself…from what he reasonably believes to be the use or imminent use of unlawful physical force…." The lower court's interpretation of this statute (that "reasonably believes" requires only that D's belief have been "reasonable to him") would make "reasonably believes" the equivalent of "genuinely believes," and thus strip the word "reasonably" of all of its meaning. Such an interpretation would also "allow citizens to set their own standards for the permissible use of force…." Instead, the correct interpretation of "reasonably believes" is that it imposes an *objective standard*, i.e., the defendant's conduct must be that of a reasonable person in the defendant's situation. *People v. Goetz*, 497 N.E.2d 41 (N.Y. 1986).

Note: *People v. Goetz* involved the celebrated case of Bernhard Goetz. When Goetz was eventually tried on the charges, the jury convicted him on the weapons charge, but acquitted him on all other counts. It appears that the jury simply disregarded the judge's instructions that Goetz, in deciding whether and how to use deadly force, must have behaved as a reasonable person would have behaved in the circumstances.

a. **Defendant's physical disadvantages:** Courts generally take the defendant's *physical disadvantages* into account in determining the reasonableness of his mistake. Thus in *State v. Wanrow*, 559 P.2d 548 (Wash. 1977), D was a 5'4" woman with a cast on her leg, and V was a 6'2" intoxicated man suspected (reasonably) of being a child molester. The court held that these facts should be considered by the jury in determining whether D's frightened, reflexive shooting of V was a reasonable mistake (in which case self-defense would still apply).

b. **Defendant's knowledge and past experiences:** Courts generally hold that the defendant's *past experiences* and *knowledge* are to be taken into consideration in deciding whether defendant's mistake was a "reasonable" one.

Example: In *People v. Goetz*, *supra*, the court said that D could present evidence as to "any prior experiences he had which could provide a reasonable basis for a belief that another person's intentions were to injure or rob him or that the use of deadly force was necessary under the circumstances." At the trial, D was allowed to put on evidence that he had previously been mugged. (By the way, the evidence in *Goetz* showed that although none of the four youths was carrying a conventional weapon, two of the four had screwdrivers inside their coats, which they admitted were to be used to break into the coin boxes of video machines. So Goetz's perception that these youths were prospective robbers was indeed a correct one.)

c. **Belief must be *bona fide*:** The defendant's belief must be an honest, *genuine* one. If the defendant's purpose in killing is not to defend himself, but to get rid of the other party, the claim of self-defense is not available even if it later turns out that the other party was indeed, unknown to the defendant, about to kill the latter.

    i. Surrounding circumstances: In determining what the defendant's motive was, the circumstances surrounding the death will of course be considered; thus where the defendant was a prostitute who killed a prospective customer, the jury was allowed to consider the fact that he had promised her two ten-dollar bills but had given her only two one-dollar bills. It was held that the jury could properly find that the defendant's anger over being short-changed, not her fear of violence from the customer, led her to shoot him. *State v. Goodseal*, 183 N.W.2d 258 (Neb. 1971).

    d. Model Penal Code view: A few courts have held that even an **unreasonable** (but genuine) belief as to the need for self-defense will protect the defendant. This view is more or less shared by the Model Penal Code, which requires merely that the defendant "believe" that force is necessary for self-defense, with no requirement of reasonableness. However, M.P.C. § 3.09(2) provides that if the defendant's mistaken belief as to the need for force is "reckless" or "negligent," the claim of self-defense is unavailable if the crime charged is one which may be committed recklessly or negligently, as the case may be. (The MPC's approach has attracted little support from state legislators, however. See K&S, p. 851.)

    e. Intoxication: Frequently, the cause of the defendant's unreasonable mistake as to the need for self-defense will be his **intoxication**. In this situation, virtually all courts agree that the intoxication does not excuse the mistake, and the defendant will not be entitled to a claim of self-defense. See L, p. 494.

    3. Imperfect defense: While an unreasonable mistake will, as noted, generally block a claim of self-defense, such a mistake may entitle the defendant to conviction of a **lesser offense**, particularly a reduction of a murder charge to manslaughter. See the discussion of "imperfect self-defense" *infra*, p. 120.

J. Battered women and self-defense: One context in which a claim of self-defense is often raised is that of a woman who **kills her spouse** because, she says, this is the only way she could protect herself against ongoing **battering** or other abuse. Courts have usually not changed the generally-applicable rules of self-defense to deal with this "battered woman" situation, but they have increasingly attempted to give women defendants a fair chance to assert the defense.

    1. The "battered woman's syndrome": Psychologists have identified a *"battered woman's syndrome,"* ("BWS") a series of common characteristics that appear in women who have been abused physically and psychologically over a long time by their mate or other dominant male in their lives. Experts who have studied BWS say that most domestic violence occurs in a series of three-phase cycles: phase 1 is the "tension-building stage," during which the male engages in minor battering incidents and verbal abuse, while the woman tries to placate him; phase 2 is the "acute battering incident," during which the more serious violence occurs; and in phase 3, the male becomes extremely contrite and loving. Proponents of the BWS say that women often stay in the abusive relationship because the male's loving behavior during phase 3 leads the woman to believe that the male will reform. The woman also frequently sinks into a state of psychological paralysis, believing that she cannot prevent or escape from the violence; this reaction is sometimes called "learned helplessness." Also, she may come to believe, with good reason, that if she attempts to escape, the male will find her and beat her even worse.

2. **Admissibility of expert testimony about BWS:** Women who kill their abusing spouse or lover frequently seek to introduce *expert testimony* about BWS. Such testimony is now *admitted* by the vast majority of American jurisdictions, provided that the defendant comes forward with some evidence that she was in fact repeatedly beaten by the victim. Under the law of evidence, expert testimony may generally be admitted only where it would help the jury understand a matter better than they would understand it without the testimony. Courts typically allow BWS testimony to be admitted in self-defense cases to shed light on two issues:

   a. **"Why didn't you leave?":** First, if the defendant puts on extensive evidence of her history of being abused by the victim (as nearly all courts let her do to show that she had reason to fear for her safety), the jury is likely to say to itself, *"If the abuse was really as bad as you say, why didn't you simply leave the victim?"* Expert testimony about BWS tends to answer this question, by showing that many women in the defendant's situation have the "learned helplessness" reaction, and do not believe that they can successfully escape (and, in fact, are often correct in assuming that if they leave, the male is likely to find them and to beat them even worse). So the BWS testimony provides a general buttressing of the woman's credibility on the self-defense claim.

   b. **Did D reasonably fear imminent danger?:** Second, the BWS testimony helps establish that D had a *genuine and reasonable fear* of *imminent danger* to herself. In particular, the expert will frequently testify that a battered woman, through her long experience with abuse at the hands of the male in question, will frequently know his behavioral patterns better than anyone else possibly could, and will realize that something the male has just done or said, which might seem innocuous to an outsider, strongly predicts that the violence will escalate imminently. On this point, the BWS testimony has both a *subjective* dimension (it tends to establish that because D reacted the way other women who really *were* in fear behaved, probably D *genuinely felt* the fear) and an *objective* component (because the woman knows her abuser best, probably D was *right* in predicting that the danger was especially great this time, so her fear and her consequent behavior were *"reasonable"*).

   See generally *State v. Kelly*, 478 A.2d 364 (N.J. 1984), the first major state supreme court case allowing BWS testimony to buttress the woman's claim of self-defense, and *People v. Humphrey*, 921 P.2d 1 (Cal. 1996), in which the court held that evidence of BWS was relevant to the reasonableness of D's belief that she needed to act in self-defense.

   Note: Most courts that have considered the issue have not limited the use of BWS testimony to *wives* — a woman who can show that her *lover* or other dominant male figure has repeatedly abused her will generally be allowed to present BWS testimony, even though the defendant and victim were not married.

3. Standard for "reasonableness": Most cases in which the woman kills her abusing mate turn on the "reasonableness" of the woman's conduct — assuming that her belief in the danger was genuine, was that belief reasonable? And was the level of force used also "reasonable"? Recall that in most courts, the reasonableness of the defendant's self-defense is to be determined by a basically ***objective*** "reasonable person" standard (see *supra*, p. 113), but that some of the personal characteristics of the defendant (e.g., physical characteristics like small stature) may be taken into account. How subjective should the determination of "reasonableness" be in the case of a battered woman?

    a. Not too subjective: In general, the courts have tried ***not*** to allow too much subjectivity into the analysis of reasonableness in the BWS situation. Commonly, the test is articulated as being, what would a reasonable woman do in the defendant's situation, taking into account the prior history of abuse, but not taking into account the particular psychology of the woman herself (e.g., that she is unusually depressed, or aggressive, or otherwise different)? See, e.g., *State v. Stewart*, 763 P.2d 572 (Kansas 1988), holding that "[I]n cases involving battered spouses 'the objective test is how a ***reasonably prudent battered wife*** would perceive [the aggressor's] demeanor.' "

4. Imminence of danger: Many battered-woman homicide cases turn on whether the danger to the woman was ***imminent***. Recall that as a general rule of self-defense, the danger must be imminent — D cannot, for example, kill today to avoid even an extremely great likelihood of serious bodily harm or death tomorrow. (See *supra*, p. 109) Courts have struggled with whether to change the requirement of imminence for battered-woman self-defense cases.

    a. Use of BWS testimony: As noted *supra*, courts have taken the limited step of allowing the use of BWS testimony to bear on the reasonableness of D's belief that the danger to her was imminent.

    b. Non-confrontational situation: The harder question is whether to modify the traditional requirement of imminent danger to cover situations where the defendant's counter-strike ***does not occur during a physical confrontation***. There are several non-confrontational fact patterns where the lack of imminent danger is a big problem for the defense: (1) Most commonly, the victim, after abusing the defendant, has ***gone to sleep***, and the defendant shoots him in the head while he sleeps; (2) the defendant ***waits*** for the victim to return home, and kills him immediately, before any kind of argument has arisen; and (3) the defendant ***arranges with someone else*** (at the most extreme, a hired killer) to kill the victim.

        i. Defendant usually loses: In these clearly non-confrontational situations, the defendant generally ***loses***. The trial judge typically does not even give the jury a self-defense instruction (or gives one that makes it clear that self-defense applies only if physical danger was imminent, with imminence defined to mean "immediate"). Also typically, the appellate court refuses to reverse for the trial court's refusal to give a self-defense instruction.

        Example: D shoots her husband to death while he is asleep. She shows at trial that he had tormented, physically abused and humiliated her for years.

Held, D was not entitled to a self-defense instruction. "The imminence requirement ensures that deadly force will be used only where it is necessary as a last resort in the exercise of the inherent right of self preservation.... The evidence in this case did not tend to show that the defendant reasonably believed she was confronted by a threat of imminent death or great bodily harm.... The uncontroverted evidence was that her husband had been asleep for some time when she walked to her mother's house, returned with the pistol, fixed the pistol after it jammed and then shot her husband three times in the back of the head. The defendant was not faced with an instantaneous choice between killing her husband or being killed or seriously injured. Instead, all of the evidence tended to show that the defendant had ample time and opportunity to resort to other means of preventing further abuse by her husband." *North Carolina v. Norman*, 378 S.E.2d 8 (N.C. 1989).

    ii. Rationale: It is not hard to see why courts have resisted relaxing the imminence requirement, even in cases involving horrible abuse. As the Kansas Supreme Court put it in *State v. Stewart* (*supra* p. 117), to abandon the imminence requirement "would in effect allow the ***execution of the abuser*** for past or future acts and conduct." As another court said, "It is difficult enough to justify capital punishment as an appropriate response of society to criminal acts even after the circumstances have been carefully evaluated by a number of people. To permit capital punishment to be imposed upon the subjective conclusion of the individual that prior acts and conduct of the deceased justify the killing would amount to a leap into the abyss of anarchy." *Jahnke v. State* (discussed *infra*).

    iii. Momentary lull: But if the absence of confrontation is merely a ***momentary lull*** in the attack — e.g., the victim's back is temporarily turned, but D reasonably believes that the attack will resume any moment — then the requirement of imminence is typically found to be satisfied.

  5. Battered child: There are also an increasing number of cases in which a ***battered child*** kills the abusive parent or step-parent, typically the father. Some psychologists have reported a "battered child's syndrome" ("BCS") analogous to BWS. Courts have occasionally allowed BCS expert testimony. However, in general, courts have been slower to allow such testimony than in the battered-woman situation, probably because there has been less scientific study of the battered-child situation. And, of course, courts have applied the imminence requirement in the case of killings by children, just as in the case of killings by the wife. See, e.g., *Jahnke v. State*, 682 P.2d 991 (Wyo. 1984) (16-year-old boy waits with shotgun for an hour and a half for his parents to return from dinner, and then shoots his father to death; *held*, it was not error to refuse to allow testimony about the "battered child's syndrome," because such evidence is only relevant where there was a "confrontation or conflict with the deceased not at the defendant's instigation," and none occurred here).

K. Resisting arrest: Related to garden-variety self-defense is the use of force to ***resist an unlawful arrest***. Here, the courts have been much less willing to encourage the use of force, since society has a strong interest in discouraging resistance to police officers. Accordingly, virtually no jurisdictions permit a suspect to use deadly force to resist an unlawful arrest.

1. **Non-deadly force:** Furthermore, a substantial number of states (though probably still a minority) now bar even the use of *non-deadly force* against an unlawful arrest (e.g., one made without probable cause, or without a warrant in a situation where a warrant is required).

    a. *Curtis* **case:** Thus the Supreme Court of California has held that there is no constitutional right to resist an unlawful arrest, even though the arrest itself might be an "unreasonable seizure" violative of the Fourth Amendment. In *People v. Curtis*, 450 P.2d 33 (Cal. 1969), the police had received a description of a prowler as being "male Negro, about six feet tall, wearing a white shirt and tan trousers." An officer stopped D, who matched that description, and arrested him for burglary. D resisted the officer's attempt to take hold of his arm, and a violent struggle took place, injuring both men. D was eventually acquitted of the burglary charge, but was convicted of resisting arrest.

        i. **No constitutional right to resist:** The California Supreme Court held that even assuming that D's arrest was unlawful (because made without probable cause), he did not have a constitutional right to resist the arrest. A defendant's rights are admittedly violated by such an arrest, but the use of self-help is less likely to vindicate him, and more likely to injure him, than the use of available judicial remedies. (But the court also held that D could not be convicted of the felony of resisting an officer "engaged in the performance of his duties," because such "duties" do not include the making of unlawful arrests; only the misdemeanor of resisting arrest could be charged.)

    b. **Model Penal Code view:** The Model Penal Code similarly refuses to allow the use of force to resist an unlawful arrest, assuming that the defendant knows that the person doing the arresting is a policeman. M.P.C. § 3.04(2)(a)(i).

2. **May resist excessive force:** But even those states denying the right to resist an unlawful arrest generally allow the use of force to resist an arrest made with *excessive force*, or in any situation in which the defendant reasonably believes that he will be injured (probably even where he fears that he will be injured in jail). Comment 3(a) to M.P.C. § 3.04. Similarly, the court in *People v. Curtis, supra*, held that D would have been justified in using reasonable force to defend himself if it was found that the arresting officer used excessive force.

3. **Courts allowing resistance:** In those courts which do allow resistance, deadly force may not be used, as noted. If the defendant does use deadly force, and the arresting officer dies, some of these states permit an almost automatic reduction of the charge from murder to manslaughter.

L. **Injury to third person:** It may happen that while the defendant is using force to protect himself against his assailant, he *injures a bystander*. Assuming that the defendant's conduct was not reckless or negligent with respect to this bystander, he will not be liable, assuming that self-defense as to the assailant was proper.

   Example: D is being repeatedly fired upon by X, who is in a slow-moving car with Y and several others. D shoots back, attempting to hit X. However, the bullet misses X and strikes Y, killing her. Assuming that D's use of deadly force was not reckless or negligent (taking into account what D knew about the proximity of others), and would have been justified vis a vis X, D will not be guilty of homicide in the death of Y.

1. **Recklessness or negligence:**   Conversely, if the defendant *is* reckless or negligent with respect to the risk of injuring a bystander, the common approach, and the one followed by M.P.C. § 3.09(3), is that the defendant may not claim self-defense if the charge is one that requires only recklessness or negligence (as the case may be). Thus if the bystander is killed, the charge will typically be one of manslaughter (death arising from recklessness), and the defendant will not be able to claim self-defense if he was reckless as to the risk of injuring the bystander. For instance, in the above example, if it was reckless of D not to realize that there was a large risk he'd hit a non-participant, he'd be guilty of manslaughter in Y's death.

M. **"Imperfect" self-defense:**   Suppose that the defendant kills in self-defense, but has made an *unreasonable mistake* as to the need for force, the unlawfulness of the other party's force, etc. Or, suppose that the defendant was the initial aggressor, and has therefore lost the right to claim self-defense. In any of these situations, the defendant would normally be guilty of murder, since the justification of self-defense is not available to him, and the death itself is purposely caused. But a number of states grant the defendant what might be called a claim of *"imperfect"* self-defense, sufficient to reduce his crime from murder to *manslaughter*.

1. **Model Penal Code view:**   The Model Penal Code agrees, taking the position that an unreasonable belief in the need for deadly force will give rise to manslaughter if the defendant was reckless in his mistake. See § 3.09(2), and Comment 12 to § 2.02 (Tent. Dr. No. 4). The Code is unusually liberal, in the sense that if the defendant's unreasonable belief was merely negligent, he cannot be charged with anything higher than criminally negligent homicide. M.P.C. § 3.09(2).

N. **Burden of proof:**   Virtually all states make a claim of self-defense an *affirmative defense*, i.e., one which must be raised, at least in the first instance, by the defendant. Many states also place the *burden of persuasion* upon him, requiring him to *prove by a preponderance of the evidence* that all the requirements for the defense are met.

1. **Constitutionally permissible:**   It is *constitutional* for the state to put the burden of persuasion upon the defendant as to self-defense. In *Martin v. Ohio*, 480 U.S. 228 (1987), the Supreme Court upheld a state law requiring the defendant to prove self-defense by a preponderance of the evidence. The Court reasoned that D was not being forced to prove any of the elements of the crime (murder, in this case), but was merely allowed to establish the "justification" of self-defense, a justification whose elements did not overlap with the elements of the crime charged. (But the Court noted that defendants must be allowed to introduce self-defense *evidence* that does not rise to the level of preponderance-of-the-evidence, because such evidence still may help the defendant establish reasonable doubt about whether he is guilty of the substantive crime.)

LEXIS®-NEXIS® Searches on **SELF-DEFENSE**

Sub-Topic	Suggested Searches
Self-defense, generally	`(crime or criminal) and (self-defense or self w/2 defense or selfdefense)`

Permissible degree of force	`(crime or criminal) and (self-defense w/20 ((excessive force) or (degree w/3 force)))`
Aggressor, self-defense by	`(crime or criminal) and (self-defense w/30 aggressor)`
Retreat, duty of	`(crime or criminal) and (self-defense w/30 (duty w/10 retreat))`

V. DEFENSE OF OTHERS

A. Right to defend others in general: A person may use force to ***defend another*** in roughly the same circumstances in which he would be justified in using force in his own defense.

B. Relation between defendant and aided person: The common-law traditionally limited the right to come to the assistance of others; many courts refused to permit a person to assist anyone except his relatives.

1. **Modern rule:** Today, however, most courts and statutes permit one to use force to defend a friend, or even a total stranger, from threat of harm from another. For instance, the court in *Commonwealth v. Martin*, 341 N.E.2d 885 (Mass. 1976), went so far as to permit one prisoner to raise the claim of defense of another when he attacked a prison guard who was apparently beating up the other prisoner. (The consequences of the fact that the defendant was mistaken as to who was the aggressor are discussed *infra*, p. 122). See also M.P.C. § 3.05(1), allowing defense of others without regard to the relation between the defendant and the person aided.

C. Requirements for defense: The defendant must generally meet the following requirements, in order to assert a claim of defense of others:

1. **Danger to other:** He reasonably believes that the other person is in ***imminent danger*** of ***unlawful bodily harm***;

2. **Degree of force:** The ***degree of force*** used by the defendant is no greater than that which seems reasonably ***necessary*** to prevent the harm; and

3. **Belief in another person's right to use force:** The defendant reasonably believes that the party being assisted would have the right to use in his own defense the force that the defendant proposes to use in his assistance.

D. Retreat: Most courts would probably hold that the defendant may not use deadly force if he has reason to believe that the person being aided could ***retreat with safety***. Thus Model Penal Code § 3.05(2)(b) requires that the defendant at least "try to cause" the person aided to retreat if retreat with safety is possible (although the defendant may use deadly force if his attempt at encouraging retreat fails).

1. **Home of either party:** The Model Penal Code does not require that either the defendant or the party assisted retreat if the place where the encounter takes place is the dwelling or place of business of either of them. Thus if the attack occurred in the defendant's home, he would not be required to encourage the party aided to retreat even if that party did not live there. M.P.C. § 3.05(2)(c).

E. Mistake as to who is aggressor: Courts have been sharply in dispute about the effect of one particular kind of mistake. This mistake arises when the defendant happens upon a struggle, and reasonably but erroneously believes that the force being used against one party is unlawful. The belief might be mistaken because *that party was really the aggressor* (and thus lost the right to use force in his own self-defense; see *supra*, p. 110), or because he is being arrested by, say, plainclothes policemen. Does the defendant lose his claim of defense of others by going to such a person's defense?

1. **Traditional view:** The traditional view, sometimes called the *"alter ego"* rule, is that the defendant *"stands in the shoes"* of the person he aids. Under this view, if the person aided would not have had the right to use that degree of force in his own defense, the defendant's claim fails.

   Example: D, a forty-year-old man with a virtually clean police record, observes two middle-aged men beating and struggling with an 18-year-old youth in the middle of Manhattan. The youth is crying and trying to pull away, and one of the older men has almost pulled his pants off. D attempts to go to the youth's rescue, and during the struggle with one of the older men, the latter falls and breaks his leg. It turns out that the two older men were plainclothes policemen who were arresting the youth, and that D had no way of knowing this. D is convicted of criminal assault.

   Held, "…one who goes to the aid of a third person does so at his own peril…. The right of a person to defend another ordinarily should not be greater than such person's right to defend himself." A contrary policy "would not be conducive to an orderly society." Because the youth would not have been entitled to use force in his own defense (since the arrest was lawful), D could not use force on his behalf. *People v. Young*, 183 N.E.2d 319 (N.Y. 1962).

   Note: Several years after the decision in *Young*, the New York legislature changed the law. N.Y. Penal Law § 35.15(1) now provides that one may use physical force to defend another from what one "reasonably believes" to be the use or imminent use of unlawful force against that person.

   a. **Modern view allows defense:** The more modern view is that so long as the defendant's belief that unlawful force is being used against the person to be aided is *reasonable*, the defendant may assert a claim of defense of others even if his evaluation turns out in retrospect to have been *wrong*. This is the rule imposed by Model Penal Code § 3.05(1)(b), which refers to "the circumstances as the actor believes them to be…."

      i. **Determination of reasonableness:** In determining whether the defendant's mistake was reasonable, the courts are likely to examine all the circumstances as known to the defendant. Thus in *Commonwealth v. Martin*, 341 N.E.2d 885 (Mass. 1976), the court held that one prison inmate might have the right to use force in defense of another in an altercation with a guard, but also noted that prison guards have the right to use reasonable force to control inmates, and that knowledge of this fact must be imputed to the defendant. Thus if the guard had merely taken the other inmate into custody, and had not been beating him, the defendant's belief in the necessity for force would not be reasonable.

VI. DEFENSE OF PROPERTY

A. **Right to defend property generally:** One has a limited right to use force to *defend one's property* against a wrongful taking.

1. **Non-deadly force:** *Non-deadly force* may be used to prevent a *wrongful entry on one's real property*, and the *wrongful taking of one's personal property.*

2. **Limited to reasonable degree:** The degree of force used must not be *more than appears reasonably necessary* to prevent the taking. For instance, if there is reason to believe that a *request to desist* would be sufficient, force may not be used. See M.P.C. § 3.06(3)(a).

3. **Subsequent use of deadly force:** If one begins by using a reasonable degree of non-deadly force, and the wrongdoer responds with a personal attack, then the rules governing self-defense (*supra*, p. 107) come into play. Thus it may be permissible to use deadly force to protect oneself.

B. **Deadly force not generally allowed:** Generally speaking, one may *not use deadly force* to defend personal property or real estate. The law regards human life as more valuable than property rights, and therefore refuses to allow the former to be endangered to protect the latter.

1. **Defense of dwelling:** However, one may sometimes be entitled to use deadly force to defend *one's dwelling.*

   a. **Broad right:** A few courts hold that one may use deadly force whenever any forcible entry of one's dwelling is occurring, provided that a warning does not suffice. L, p. 505.

   b. **Must be felony or pose serious danger:** Other courts follow a somewhat stricter view, that deadly force may be used only where the intrusion appears to be for purposes of committing a *felony* or of doing harm to someone inside the dwelling. L, *id.* By this standard, one would have the right to *shoot a burglar* (since, by the definition of burglary, the intruder intends to commit a felony), even if there were no reason to believe that the burglar was armed or dangerous.

   c. **Must be dangerous felony:** But the modern view, exemplified by the Model Penal Code, is even more limited. Under this view, deadly force may be used *only where the intrusion appears to pose a danger of a violent felony*. Under this view, there is not an automatic right to shoot a suspected burglar, unless he is believed to be *armed* or *dangerous to the safety of the inhabitants.*

   Example: D, a black who has recently moved into a white neighborhood, has his house burglarized. A week later, a well-meaning neighbor thinks that another burglary is in progress in D's house, and calls the police. The police find what they think are signs of entry, and try to enter the house themselves. D, meanwhile, thinks that the sounds of the police represent a new burglary, so he shoots through the door, killing one of the policemen. D is charged with and convicted of murder.

   Held, conviction affirmed. One who is defending his dwelling may use deadly force to prevent a felony only if it is "committed by forcible means, violence, and surprise such as murder, robbery, burglary, rape or arson." Furthermore, it is required that the deadly force be *necessary*; if other means would prevent the felony, these must be used. The jury could properly find that D should have used such other means. *Law v. State*, 318 A. 2d 859 (Md. 1974).

   d. Model Penal Code view: The Model Penal Code is even more specific: deadly force may be used only where the user believes that the intruder is trying to commit a felony, and also believes either that the intruder has employed or threatened the use of ***deadly force***, or that the dwelling's inhabitants will be exposed to "substantial danger of serious bodily harm." M.P.C. § 3.06(3)(d)(ii). Thus where a homeowner has no reason to believe that a burglar is armed, or threatens bodily harm to the inhabitants, he is not allowed to shoot.

   e. Definition of "dwelling":   What is a *"dwelling"* for purposes of the deadly force rule? Some cases have defined the term broadly. See, e.g., *State v. Mitcheson*, 560 P.2d 1120 (Utah 1977), concluding that the term should be interpreted "in the broad sense," so as to include "not only a person's actual residence, but also whatever place he may be occupying peacefully as a substitute home or habitation, such as a hotel, motel, or even where he is a guest in the home of another; and so would apply to the defendant in his sister's home...."

C. Use of mechanical devices: Property owners are sometimes tempted to use various ***mechanical devices*** to protect their property. These devices may be of either the deadly or non-deadly variety, and have given rise to some special rules.

   1. Non-deadly devices: A device that is ***non-deadly*** (i.e., one that is not likely or intended to cause death or serious bodily harm) may be used, generally speaking, whenever it is reasonable to do so. Barbed wire or spiked fence (but not an electrical fence) would fall within this category.

   a. Model Penal Code: The Model Penal Code further requires either that the non-deadly device be one that is "customarily used for such a purpose" or that reasonable care be taken to ***warn*** intruders that the device is being used. M.P.C. § 3.06(5)(c).

   2. Deadly force: Where the device constitutes ***deadly force***, on the other hand, courts are much less willing to allow its use.

   a. Traditional view: The traditional view has been that such devices may at least be used in situations where the owner, if he were present, would be entitled to use deadly force himself. Suppose, for instance, that a homeowner sets up a ***spring gun*** (a gun whose trigger is attached to a door or window, so that it fires when entry is made). If the gun shoots an armed burglar, the owner will probably escape liability, since he would in most jurisdictions have had the right to use deadly force against the burglar personally.

   b. Modern view prohibits: But the modern view prohibits the use of such devices altogether, even if they happen to go off in a situation where the owner himself would have been justified in using deadly force.

   Example: D attaches a loaded pistol to the door of his house, after he has been burglarized. Two unarmed teenagers, X and Y, then try to break into the house; while X is forcing open the door, the gun goes off and hits him in the face. D is convicted of assault with a deadly weapon.

Held, conviction affirmed. California will not allow the use of deadly mechanical devices under any circumstances. "Allowing persons, at their own risk, to employ deadly mechanical devices imperils the lives of children, firemen and policemen acting within the scope of their employment, and others." Where the homeowner is present, there is always a chance he will realize that what he thinks is a burglar is really not; a mechanical device cannot make such judgments. Furthermore, deadly force is allowable, if used in person, only where the intruder creates a danger of great bodily harm; since the house was empty when X and Y entered, there was no danger to inhabitants, so even under the traditional common-law rule the use of the spring gun was unlawful. Nor can the use of the gun be justified on the grounds that D was attempting to apprehend a felon, since there is no evidence that D intended to apprehend rather than to maim. *People v. Ceballos*, 526 P.2d 241 (Cal. 1974).

    i. Model Penal Code follows modern view: The Model Penal Code similarly holds that a deadly mechanical device may never be used. M.P.C. § 3.06(5)(a).

D. Recapture of chattel and of re-entry on land: A similar privilege to use reasonable force exists where the taking of personal or real property has been *consummated.*

    1. Personal property: Where personal property has been taken, all courts agree that the defendant may use reasonable non-deadly force to *recapture* it, provided that he does so immediately following the taking. L, p. 506.

        a. Interval: But if a substantial period of time has elapsed since the taking, the traditional view is that reasonable force may not be used to reclaim the property, and that resort to the courts must be had instead.

            i. Model Penal Code: However, the Model Penal Code, in § 3.06(1)(b), allows the use of such force to retake property at any time, provided that the owner believes that the other person has no "claim of right" to possess the object. Thus if D's bicycle is stolen, and he sees X riding down the street on it several days later, he cannot use force to take it from X if he has reason to believe that X may have bought it from the thief; in this situation, X would be acting under a "claim of right to possession" even though he does not have title. If, on the other hand, D thought that he recognized X as being the thief, he could then use reasonable force to take back the bicycle.

    2. Re-entry on real estate: Similar rules exist with respect to a person who is ousted from real property which he owns. That is, the common-law rule is that reentry by force may not be made unless it is done immediately. Again, however, the Model Penal Code would allow forcible re-entry after a lapse of time, at least where the non-owner has no claim of right to possession, and it would be an "exceptional hardship" for the owner to wait to get a court order. M.P.C. § 3.06(1)(b)(ii).

VII. LAW ENFORCEMENT (ARREST; PREVENTION OF ESCAPE AND CRIME)

    A. Law Enforcement privilege generally: A person engaged in *law enforcement* has a general privilege to violate the law when it is reasonable to do so.

Example: D, who has been charged with possession and sale of heroin, claims that he was acting at the request of the police, who wanted to find and arrest dope dealers. *Held*, if D can demonstrate this, he will be entitled to an acquittal, on the grounds that he did not possess a "felonious" intent. *Kohler v. Commonwealth*, 492 S.W.2d 198 (Ky. App. 1973)

1. **Use of force:** The question of privilege to engage in law enforcement usually arises in the context of the *use of force* by the defendant. Accordingly, our discussion of the three principal areas of law enforcement (arrest, prevention of escape, and prevention of crime) focuses on when force may be used.

B. **Arrest:** Law enforcement officers are sometimes privileged to use reasonable force in effecting an arrest. However, this privilege exists only where the arrest being made is a *lawful one*. Therefore, it is necessary to have a general idea of what constitutes a lawful arrest.

1. **Summary of arrest rules:** The rules governing when arrests may be made can be summarized as follows (see L, pp. 508-09):

    a. **Felonies:** At common law, a policeman may make an arrest for a *felony* if it was committed in his presence, or if it was committed outside of his presence but he has reasonable cause to believe that it was committed, and committed by the person to be arrested.

       i. **Warrant not required:** In these situations, the arresting officer is *not required* to have a *warrant*.

       ii. **Private person:** A *private citizen*, on the other hand, may generally arrest for a felony only if the felony has *in fact* been committed, and some states may require that it in fact have been committed by the person arrested. In other words, a private citizen will not receive the benefit of a reasonable mistake, where a law enforcement officer will.

    b. **Misdemeanors:** A law enforcement officer may also arrest for a *misdemeanor*, without a warrant, if it occurred in his presence. But the common-law rule is that if the misdemeanor occurred outside of the officer's presence, then a warrant is required. (This rule has frequently been changed by a statute).

       i. **Private citizen:** In most states, a *private citizen* may arrest for misdemeanors actually committed in his presence, but generally not for ones committed outside his presence, or in situations where the citizen has made a reasonable mistake about whether the offense really occurred.

2. **Arrest resisted:** If an officer who is attempting to make a lawful arrest meets resistance, which makes him reasonably believe that he will be hurt, he may use reasonable force to protect himself. If he reasonably believes that he is in danger of serious bodily harm or death, he may even use *deadly force* to protect himself. In general, the rules applicable to self-defense (*supra*, p. 107) apply in this situation.

    a. **No need to retreat:** However, there is one important difference: even in those jurisdictions which require one to retreat before using deadly force if it is safe to do so (*supra*, p. 112), an officer is *not required to retreat rather than make the arrest*. L, p. 509-10.

3. **Suspect fleeing:** The most frequent kind of controversy involves the use of force against a suspect who, rather than resisting, merely *flees*. Since the arresting officer is not in any danger of harm, the reasons for allowing him to use force are less compelling. Accordingly, while an officer may use *non-deadly force* wherever it is reasonably necessary to make the arrest, limits have been placed on the use of deadly force.

   a. **Misdemeanors:** If the suspect is fleeing from an arrest for a *misdemeanor*, it is universally agreed that *deadly force may not be used against him.*

      Example: D, a game warden, attempts to arrest X for illegal fishing (a misdemeanor). X tries to escape in his boat, and D chases him. X hits D on the head with an oar, and D shoots him in the arm. D is tried for assault and battery.

      Held, since the arrest was for a misdemeanor, D had no right to use deadly force (a gun) merely to prevent X from escaping. But if the shooting was in response to dangerous resistance by X, then it may have been justified. *Durham v. State*, 159 N.E. 145 (Ind. 1927).

      i. **Speeders:** This rule normally will mean that when the police are chasing a *speeder* (generally a misdemeanant), they may not shoot at him or his car. If they shoot at the tires and cause a fatal crash, they will be liable for manslaughter. See L, p. 510. (Shooting a gun in the direction of a person, even without an intent to hit that person, is generally considered to be the use of "deadly force"; see M.P.C. § 3.11(2)).

   b. **Non-dangerous felony:** Where the suspect is fleeing from an arrest for a *non-dangerous felony*, may the arresting officer use deadly force to apprehend him?

      i. **Common-law view:** The common-law view was that the officer could use deadly force to prevent the escape of a person fleeing from an arrest for any felony, even if the felony was not one involving violence or physical danger to others. L, p. 510. Thus if an officer spotted a burglar leaving a house, the officer could (at least after shouting a warning) shoot the fleeing suspect, even if there was no reason to believe that the suspect was armed or dangerous.

      ii. **Supreme Court disallows:** But the arresting officer's right to use deadly force to stop one fleeing arrest for a non-dangerous felony is now drastically restricted, as the result of a Supreme Court constitutional law decision, *Tennessee v. Garner*, 471 U.S. 1 (1985). In *Garner*, the Court held that "where the suspect poses *no immediate threat* to the officer and *no threat to others*, the harm resulting from failure to apprehend him does *not justify the use of deadly force* to do so." In constitutional terms, the Court decided that use of deadly force to apprehend a non-dangerous fleeing suspect amounts to an *unreasonable seizure* under the Fourth Amendment.

      iii. **Significance for prosecution of officer:** *Garner* was not a criminal prosecution at all. Rather, it was a private suit brought by the suspect's estate against the police department, for damages stemming from the asserted violation of the suspect's constitutional (Fourth Amendment) rights. But *Garner* probably has great significance in the event the arresting officer were tried for murder or manslaughter —

the fact that the officer had violated the suspect's Fourth Amendment rights would probably by itself be sufficient to deprive the officer of the defense of force-used-pursuant-to-lawful-arrest. See, e.g., *People v. Couch*, 439 N.W.2d 354 (Mich. App. 1989), holding that the rationale of *Garner* applies to criminal cases, and that a criminal defendant may not defend on the grounds that deadly force was needed to stop the flight of an escaping non-dangerous felon.

iv. **Application to facts:** The facts of *Garner* illustrate the kind of situation in which the use of deadly force will not be constitutionally permissible. A police officer received a report that a burglary was in progress at a private residence. He arrived on the scene, and saw in the darkness a young man, who refused to stop when ordered to do so. As the suspect started to climb over a fence in order to escape, the officer shot him dead in the back. Since the officer had no reason to believe that the suspect was either armed or dangerous to anyone, the use of the gun to "seize" (and, unfortunately, kill) him was "unreasonable" under the Fourth Amendment.

v. **When deadly force can be used:** *Garner* does not mean that deadly force may *never* be used where a suspect escapes following a non-dangerous felony. As the Court explained in *Garner*, "where the officer has probable cause to believe that the suspect poses a threat of *serious physical harm*, either to the officer or to others, it is not constitutionally unreasonable to prevent escape by using deadly force." Even where the felony was non-dangerous, the officer may use deadly force if the suspect *threatens the officer with a weapon*; he must, however, give some warning if it is feasible to do so.

vi. **Model Penal Code view:** The Model Penal Code's rules on when deadly force may be used to apprehend a felon are constitutional under *Garner*. By M.P.C. § 3.07(2)(b), deadly force may be used only if the officer believes that the force to be used "creates no substantial risk of injury to innocent persons," and also believes either (1) that the suspect used or threatened the use of deadly force; or (2) that there is a substantial risk that the suspect will "cause death or serious bodily harm" if he is not immediately apprehended. That is, under the M.P.C., deadly force may not be used unless the felon is dangerous, so the *Garner* situation (deadly force used against non-dangerous fleeing felon) would not be sanctioned by the M.P.C.

c. **Dangerous felony:** If the felony is a *"dangerous"* one, the arresting officer may use deadly force if that is the only way that the arrest can be made. Under the Model Penal Code formulation mentioned *supra*, the suspect may be considered "dangerous" only if he is believed to have used or threatened deadly force while committing the crime, or is believed to pose a threat of death or serious harm to others if he is not immediately captured. The *Garner* decision seems to set out similar requirements for "dangerousness" — it allows deadly force "[w]here the officer has probable cause to believe that the suspect poses a threat of serious physical harm, either to the officer or to others." Under this formulation, the typical car thief or burglar would not fall within the "dangerous" category.

4. **Arrest by private citizen:** The foregoing discussion assumes that the person attempting to make the arrest by use of deadly force is a law officer. If, however, the arrest is to be made by a ***private citizen***, the situations where deadly force may be used are even rarer.

   a. **Assistance rendered to policemen:** If the private citizen is responding to a ***policeman's call for assistance***, he will have roughly the same right to use deadly force as the officer would. (In fact, if he reasonably believed that the officer was trying to make a lawful arrest, he will be protected even if it turns out that the officer lacked probable cause or that the arrest was unlawful in some other way.) L, p. 512. This approach is followed by the Model Penal Code, in § 3.07(2)(b)(ii) and § 3.07(4)(a).

   b. **Arrest on one's own:** But if the private citizen is ***acting on his own***, attempting to make a "citizen's arrest," he acts at his peril if he uses deadly force. If it turns out that no dangerous felony was committed, or that the suspect was not the one who committed it, the citizen will be criminally liable for death or injury to the suspect. L, p. 512.

   c. **Model Penal Code bars use:** The Model Penal Code goes even further; a private citizen who is not responding to what he believes to be an officer's call for assistance ***may not use deadly force at all***, even if he correctly believes that the suspect has committed a dangerous felony. M.P.C. § 3.07(2)(b)(ii). The Code drafters justified this rule on the grounds that private citizens should be discouraged from shooting at fleeing felons, because citizens have normally not been trained to use firearms properly, and may therefore injure innocent bystanders.

   d. **Right to use deadly force to prevent escape of non-deadly felon:** A private citizen, like a police officer, may not use deadly force to ***stop a fleeing felon***, if the felon poses ***no immediate threat*** to the citizen or to others. In other words, the rationale of *Tennessee v. Garner* (see *supra*, p. 127) presumably applies to attempted arrests by private citizens just as to attempted arrests by police officers. (Of course, this rule would be invoked only where the court rejects — as most courts do — the MPC's blanket rule that the arresting citizen may *never* use deadly force, even to arrest a felon who *is* dangerous.)

C. **Prevention of escape:** The same rules apply to the use of force to ***prevent the escape*** of a suspect who has already been arrested. Thus an officer who has arrested a misdemeanant may not use deadly force to prevent him from escaping, since he would not be permitted to use deadly force to make the arrest in the first place. See L, p. 513.

D. **Crime prevention:** It may also be permissible to use force to ***prevent a crime*** from taking place, or from being consummated once it is begun. This privilege overlaps several others: (1) the right to arrest (since one might arrest for a burglary, and want to prevent the completion of the underlying felony, e.g., larceny); (2) self-defense or defense of others; and (3) defense of property (e.g., by preventing arson or burglary).

1. **Reasonable non-deadly force:** In general, both law enforcement officers and private citizens may use a reasonable degree of ***non-deadly force*** to prevent the commission of a felony, or of a misdemeanor amounting to a breach of the peace (e.g., fighting, but not a parking violation). L, pp. 513-14.

2. **Deadly force:** But the right to use *deadly force* is much more limited. The modern rule is that deadly force may be used to prevent only *dangerous felonies*. Thus just as the right to defend one's property does not furnish an automatic right to use deadly force against a burglar not believed to be armed (*supra*, p. 123), so deadly force may not be used against such a burglar under the guise of prevention of crime. Only if the burglar is believed to be armed, and likely to do serious bodily harm to the inhabitants, may he be shot at. And, of course, deadly force may never be used unless it appears that lesser force will not suffice. See M.P.C. § 3.07(5)(a)(ii)(1).

LEXIS®-NEXIS® Searches on **LAW ENFORCEMENT**

Sub-Topic	Suggested Searches
Arrest of fleeing suspect, generally	`(crime or criminal) and (arrest w/30 ((flee! or flight) w/30 force))`
Arrest of fleeing suspect, *Tenn. v. Garner* case	`arrest w/30 (flee! or flight! or run!) w/30 (Tenn! w/4 garner)`

VIII. MAINTAINING AUTHORITY

A. **Right to maintain authority generally:** *Parents* of minor children, *school teachers,* and other persons who have a duty of supervision, have a limited right to use force to discharge their duties.

B. **Parents of minor:** *Parents* of a minor child may use a *reasonable degree of force* to guard the child's welfare. Thus a parent who hits or spanks his child will not be guilty of battery, provided that the degree of force is not unreasonable under the circumstances. The "circumstances" include the child's age, sex, severity of his misbehavior, etc.

1. **Objective vs. subjective standard:** Courts are in dispute about whether the standard for determining the reasonableness of the force is an objective or a subjective one. The "objectivists" look to whether a "reasonable parent" would have used that degree of force in the circumstances. The "subjectivists" would look to whether the parent was motivated by a genuine desire to guard his child's welfare, as opposed to a malicious desire to punish and inflict pain.

2. **Model Penal Code:** The Model Penal Code imposes a test which has aspects of both the objective and subjective approach. First, the parent must be acting "for the purpose of safeguarding or promoting the welfare of the minor, including the prevention or punishment of his misconduct...." (subjective standard). Additionally, the force must be "not designed to cause or known to create a substantial risk of causing death, serious bodily harm, disfigurement, extreme pain or mental distress or gross degradation...." (a somewhat objective standard, since a purpose of promoting the child's welfare will not exculpate a parent who knew that there was a substantial risk of causing, e.g., "extreme mental distress" by the punishment.) M.P.C. § 3.08(1).

a. **Negligence or recklessness:** If the parent negligently or recklessly fails to realize that he is creating such a risk, he loses the defense of maintaining authority only with respect to crimes as to which the *mens rea* is negligence or recklessness, as the case may be. M.P.C. § 3.09(2). Thus if death resulted, the parent who negligently failed to realize that the beating administered might cause death could not be convicted, under the Code, of murder or manslaughter (both of which require at least recklessness), but could be convicted of criminally negligent homicide.

C. **School teacher:** A *school teacher* may similarly use reasonable force to maintain order or to promote a student's welfare, assuming that there is no statute barring corporal punishment. As with parental authority, the courts are split on whether the test should be an objective test (force that a reasonable man would use) or a subjective one (whether there was "malice"). See, e.g., *People v. Ball,* 303 N.E.2d 516 (Ill. App. 1973), in which the majority held that corporal punishment may be used, as long as it is not "wantonly or maliciously" inflicted, and that it is irrelevant whether the punishment is "just and reasonable." (But a dissent argued that the modern trend, of imposing a reasonableness requirement, should be followed.)

IX. CONSENT

A. **Effect of consent by victim:** Generally, the fact that the victim of a crime has **consented** does not bar criminal liability. For example, if a terminally ill patient asks a physician to help him commit suicide, the doctor can be found guilty of the crime of assisting in a suicide, even though his actions were done with the victim's consent.[1] However, there are two major types of situations in which the victim's consent may bar liability:

1. **Consent as element of the offense:** Some crimes are defined in such a way that lack of consent is an *element of the crime.* The most obvious example of this is *rape*: if the woman consents, there has been no rape.

2. **Consent as relevant factor:** There are other crimes as to which lack of consent is not an element, but where consent may induce the offense to occur where it would otherwise not have. In this situation, courts are in dispute about whether the victim's consent negates the existence of a crime.

   a. **Model Penal Code view:** The Model Penal Code view is that consent of the victim negates the crime if the consent "precludes the infliction of the harm or evil sought to be prevented by the law defining the offense." M.P.C. § 2.11(1). More particularly, the Code provides that where a crime involves threatened or actual bodily harm, consent is a defense if the bodily harm is *not serious* or is part of a lawful *athletic contest* or *competitive sport.* Thus if one participant in a boxing match injured the other, the former could not be prosecuted for battery, assuming that the boxing match was not in violation of law.

      i. **Masochist:** A rationale similar to that of the Model Penal Code was used to hold a *sadist* guilty of assault and sodomy for beating up a masochist. In *People v. Samuels,* 58 Cal. Rptr. 439 (Cal. App. 1967), the court held that in this situation, consent was no defense, principally because (according to the court) the victim could

---

1. Thus the Supreme Court has held that a state ban on assisted suicide does not violate the substantive due process clause of the Fourteenth Amendment. *Washington v. Glucksberg,* 521 U.S. 702 (1997).

not have been a "normal person in full possession of his mental faculties" if he consented to the beating, and secondly because consent is no defense where there is severe or mortal injury.

B. Incapacity to consent: Even where the crime is one as to which consent can be a defense, consent will not be found where the victim is too *young, mentally defective, intoxicated*, or for other reasons unable to give a meaningful assent.

   1. Deception: Similarly, if the consent was obtained by *fraud*, it will generally not be valid. However, the fraud will negate the consent, generally speaking, only where it goes to the *essence* of the harmful activity, rather than to a *collateral matter.*

      a. Illustration: For instance, if M.D., a gynecologist, induced Patient to have sexual intercourse with him by blindfolding her and telling her he was performing an examination procedure, this would be fraud in the essence, and M.D. would be guilty of rape. But if M.D. merely told Patient that sex would be a beneficial treatment for her, this would be fraud in the inducement, and the consent would not be vitiated. M.D. would thus not be guilty of rape. See L, p. 518.

C. Contributory negligence of victim: The fact that the victim may have been *contributorily negligent* will not, by itself, be a defense to any crime. Contributory negligence is a tort doctrine based on the theory that even an injured plaintiff should not be entitled to recover where he is partially at fault. Insofar as the function of the criminal law is to protect the state's interest in proper behavior by all citizens, the plaintiff's contributory negligence does not negate the need to punish the defendant.

   1. Relevant as evidence: However, the plaintiff's contributory negligence may have an *evidentiary bearing* on the defendant's guilt. Thus a defendant charged with manslaughter arising out of an auto accident might try to show that it was the deceased's negligence, not his own, that caused the accident. See *infra,* p. 259. See L, p. 520.

D. Guilt of victim: The fact that the victim is himself engaged in the same or a different illegal activity will not necessarily prevent the person who takes advantage of him from being criminally liable. For instance, in a situation like that of the movie *The Sting* (A swindles B, who is involved in the running of an illegal betting parlor), A will nonetheless be guilty of larceny by trick.

E. Condonation and compromise: Generally speaking, the fact that the victim *forgives* the injury, is unwilling to prosecute, or *settles a civil suit* against the party who injured him, will *not* absolve the latter from liability. The crime is considered to be against the people, not against the individual victim, and only the people's representative (the prosecutor) has authority to drop the charges. Of course, as a practical matter, if the victim is unwilling to cooperate, there will usually not be a prosecution if the offense is a minor one (and sometimes even a major one, such as rape).

   1. Compromise statutes: However, a number of states have *"compromise"* statutes, by which if the wrongdoer and the victim reach a civil settlement, there is no criminal liability. Frequently, these statutes apply only to misdemeanors, not felonies.

      a. *Garouette* case: Such a compromise statute was at issue in *State v. Garouette*, 388 P.2d 809 (Ariz. 1964). The defendant, while driving, collided with his victim and killed him. The Arizona compromise statute provided that civil settlement would absolve liability in all misdemeanor cases. Since under Arizona law manslaughter in the driving of a motor vehicle is a misdemeanor, the court had no choice but to apply the compromise statute. However, it urged the legislature to change the wording of the compromise statute to bar such a result in the future, stating that "it was never thought that the taking of a human life could be paid for and forgotten." As the court noted, if a drunk or reckless driver does not hit anyone, he can go to jail. But if he hits someone, and is lucky enough to have the money to settle a civil suit, he can escape punishment entirely under the Arizona scheme.

X. ENTRAPMENT

A. **Entrapment generally:** The defense of *entrapment* exists where a *law enforcement official*, or some one cooperating with him, has induced the defendant to commit the crime.

1. **Two rationales for defense:** Two rationales for the entrapment defense have been commonly stated. The first, accepted by a majority of state courts and the U.S. Supreme Court, is that the legislature, in enacting the substantive criminal statute, did not intend it to cover one who was led into the crime by a government agent. The other, minority, rationale is that courts as a matter of public policy should not encourage police officials to "manufacture" cases or commit other improper acts.

2. **Two rules for entrapment:** Each of these two rationales has given rise to a test for determining whether entrapment exists:

   a. **"Predisposition" test:** The majority, and U.S. Supreme Court, rule is that entrapment exists "when the criminal design originates with the officials of the Government, and they implant *in the mind of an innocent person* the disposition to commit the alleged offense and induce its commission in order that they may prosecute." See *Sorrells v. U.S.*, 287 U.S. 435 (1932). Thus entrapment exists where: (1) the government originates the crime and induces its commission; and (2) the defendant is an innocent person, i.e., one who is *not predisposed* to committing this sort of crime.

   Example: The Ds run a small laboratory to manufacture illegal amphetamines. X, a federal narcotics undercover agent, tells the Ds that he wants to participate in the manufacture and distribution of such drugs, and that he is willing to supply propanone, a necessary and hard-to-get substance, as his part of the bargain. The Ds show X that they are already producing the drug, with their own source of propanone, but agree to his proposal. X supplies some propanone, the Ds produce amphetamines from it, and X arrests them. The Ds raise the defense of entrapment.

   Held, the Ds' conviction affirmed. It is clear that the Ds were predisposed to commit the crime in question, since they had been previously manufacturing the drug on their own. Therefore, the defense of entrapment cannot be asserted; the court declines to broaden the doctrine to allow its use by one predisposed to commit the crime. Nor does X's supplying of a hard-to-get (though legal) component violate any constitutional right of the Ds. Prosecution of this type of offense would be impossible unless government agents were permitted to gain a suspect's confidence by supplying something of value to the enterprise. *U.S. v. Russell*, 411 U.S. 423 (1973).

    b. **Police conduct rule:** The minority test for entrapment is that entrapment exists where the government agents originate the crime, and their participation is such as is likely to induce unpredisposed persons to commit the crime, ***regardless of whether the defendant himself is predisposed***. Thus on the facts of *Russell*, under the minority view entrapment would probably not be found, since the supplying of a necessary and hard-to-obtain component is sufficient to cause persons not previously engaged in narcotics manufacture to commence such operations. See, e.g., *People v. Barraza*, 591 P.2d 947 (Cal. 1979).

        i. **Model Penal Code follows minority rule:** The Model Penal Code follows the minority position. M.P.C. § 2.13(1)(b) permits the entrapment defense where the government agent induces the crime by "employing methods of persuasion or inducement which create a substantial risk that such offense will be committed by persons *other than those who are ready to commit it.*"

    3. **False representations regarding legality:** A separate kind of entrapment is recognized to exist where the government agent ***knowingly makes a false representation that the act in question is legal***. Thus if X, in *Russell*, had told the Ds that amphetamines could be legally manufactured, the defense of entrapment would be recognized (presumably even by courts following the Supreme Court-majority rule). See M.P.C. § 2.13(1)(a).

    4. **Exception for violent crimes:** Some courts have refused to allow the entrapment defense where the crime is one involving ***violence***. See, e.g., M.P.C. § 2.13(3), making the defense unavailable where "causing or threatening bodily injury is an element of the offense charged," and the violence alleged was committed by one other than the government agent.

B. **Evidence:** When the majority test for entrapment is followed, the prosecution is permitted to show the defendant's "predisposition" by evidence of his ***past criminal activities of a similar nature***. The theory behind allowing such evidence is that if the defendant was willing to commit such crimes in the past, he was probably predisposed to do so on this occasion. Thus the prosecution in *Russell* was permitted to show that the Ds had previously been engaged in the manufacture of amphetamines.

    1. **Danger of prejudice:** Allowing such evidence runs counter to the usual principle that evidence of past criminality by the defendant is not admissible. Where the entrapment issue is decided as a matter of fact by the jury (as is usually the case), there is a substantial risk that the jury will consider this evidence not just on the entrapment issue, but also on the merits. For this reason, the majority "predisposition" rule is often criticized (as in a dissent to *Russell, supra*, p. 134).

C. **Distinguish from "missing element" cases:** Situations involving entrapment should be distinguished from similar ones where, because of the participation of government agents, ***an element of the crime is missing***.

    1. **Illustration:** For instance, if X, a government agent, suspects that D is a confidence man who swindles people out of their property by a "bunco scheme" (as in *People v. Orndorff*, *infra*, p. 152), and he feigns participation in the scheme by giving money to D, D cannot be convicted of obtaining money by false pretenses. This is not due to any entrapment defense, but because the crime of false pretenses requires actual reliance by the victim (*infra*, p. 301), and X was not really fooled. See L&S(1st), p. 370.

LEXIS®-NEXIS® Searches on **ENTRAPMENT**

Sub-Topic	Suggested Searches
Entrapment, generally	`(crime or criminal) and atleast2(entrap!)`
Predisposition test	`(crime or criminal) and (entrap! w/20 predisposition) and atleast2(entrap!)`
Police conduct rule	`(crime or criminal) and (entrap! w/30 (conduct w/10 police))`

Quiz Yourself on

JUSTIFICATION AND EXCUSE (ENTIRE CHAPTER)

20. Lewis threatens to kill Clark if Clark does not steal certain valuable camping equipment from their employer, Sacagewea, before they leave for the next leg of their trip the following week. Clark reasonably believes that Lewis will do what he says, given Lewis' past violent behavior. Clark steals the equipment and is charged with larceny.

(A) What defense offers Clark his best chance at an acquittal?

(B) In most states, will the defense you listed in (A) be accepted on these facts?

(C) Will the defense you listed in (A) be accepted on these facts under the Model Penal Code?

21. Norton holds a knife to the throat of Alice, Ralph's wife, and threatens to kill her unless Ralph robs the local convenience store.

(A) If Ralph robs the store, is he guilty of larceny?

(B) Same facts as above, except that Norton's threat is that he will kill Alice unless Ralph kills Trixie, Norton's wife. Ralph does so, and Norton releases Alice, thanking Ralph for making him a free man. Is Ralph guilty of criminal homicide?

22. Etta is kidnapped by Sundance and forced at gunpoint to participate in a bank robbery. (Before she participates in the robbery, Etta realizes that Sundance may well use deadly force to complete the robbery.) During the robbery, Sundance shoots and kills a bank teller, who is trying to summon the police. Etta is charged with felony-murder. Guilty or not guilty?

23. Phineas Phogg is piloting a hot air balloon around the world, accompanied by five paying passengers. The balloon starts to lose altitude, and Phineas must take immediate action.

(A) For this part only, assume that Phineas throws all the passengers' belongings overboard, hoping to lighten the basket's load and regain altitude. If Phineas is charged with larceny, what defense should he assert, and will that defense prevail?

(B) Say instead that after Phineas throws overboard all the belongings (including his own), and anything else that's not human, the balloon is still plunging at an alarming rate. Phineas makes the reasonable determination that unless he throws one passenger overboard, the balloon will crash land at a speed that is likely to kill anyone aboard. He therefore throws overboard the heaviest passenger. If Phineas is charged with murder, will the defense you asserted in part (A) prevail?

24. Dorothy sees a tornado heading toward her while she is walking home from school with her dog Toto. In order to escape the danger, she breaks a window to get into the only nearby structure, a house, and runs into the basement. Is Dorothy guilty of trespass?

25. Rocky and Rambo meet on a sidewalk one day. Without any apparent provocation, Rocky begins to physically attack Rambo. Rambo reasonably fears that Rocky is about to kill him or do him serious bodily harm.

    (A) For this part only, assume the following additional facts: Rambo knows that Rocky is a skilled and brutal fighter, and reasonably believes that if he, Rambo, fights back with non-deadly force (such as his own fists), Rocky is likely to overpower him and hurt him badly. Rambo also realizes that he could simply run away, because he's a faster runner than Rocky. But Rambo does not want to do anything so cowardly as that. Therefore, without any warning, Rambo whips out a hidden gun and shoots Rocky to death. Under the approach of most states, is Rambo guilty of homicide in Rocky's death?

    (B) Assume the same facts as in part (A), except that: shortly after the Rocky's attack starts — before Rambo has made any real decision about how to defend himself — Rocky calms down, and starts to walk away. As Rocky is walking away, Rambo whips out his gun and shoots Rocky in the back. Rambo does this not because he fears that Rocky will change his mind and re-attack, but because he's enraged that Rocky had the gall to assault him in the first place. Can Rambo successfully plead self-defense against a charge of murder?

26. Alfalfa insults Butch's mother. Butch responds by slapping Alfalfa once on the cheek. Alfalfa (who thinks that the slap is just a prelude to a bigger attack) fights back by swinging with a closed fist. Butch, who reasonably fears that Alfalfa may slightly hurt him with his swings, swings back, breaking Alfalfa's jaw.

    (A) If Butch is charged with battery for the swing that broke Alfalfa's jaw, will he be found guilty?

    (B) Assume the same facts, except as follows: Alfalfa, instead of merely swinging at Butch after Butch's slap, wraps his hands around Butch's throat, and starts to squeeze hard. Butch responds by punching Alfalfa in the face (in order to break the choke-hold), and as in part (A) breaks Alfalfa's jaw. If Butch is charged with battery for the jaw-breaking, will he be found guilty?

27. Juliet is in her fifth month of pregnancy. Romeo walks up to her with a knife, and tells her, "Once you have the baby, I'm going to kill you." Juliet pulls out a gun and shoots him. Can Juliet defend on self-defense grounds?

28. Fletcher Christian shoots and kills Captain Bligh because he thinks Bligh is about to shoot and kill him. Actually, Bligh pulled out his gun to shoot deckhand Dick Hand, who was standing behind Christian and looking like he was about to strangle Christian with a clothesline. Can Christian successfully assert the defense of self-defense?

29. Papa Bear and his family are asleep in their home when he is awakened by mysterious noises coming from downstairs. He gets up and picks up a baseball bat from his son's room, and goes downstairs. There he confronts an apparently-unarmed Goldilocks, who is stealing silverware.

    (A) For this part only, assume that Goldilocks is startled, but makes no move to leave. Nor does she put down the silverware. Papa Bear tells her to leave, and she starts walking out, taking the silverware with her. Papa Bear (who knows he's very strong) swings a baseball bat at Goldilocks' head, intending to knock her unconscious so he can retrieve the silverware. Goldilocks dies from the blow. Papa Bear is charged with manslaughter. Under the Model Penal Code, should he be convicted?

(B) For this part, assume the same facts, except that after Papa Bear tells Goldilocks to leave, she runs towards the carving knives at the side of the kitchen. Before she can pick up a knife, Papa Bear swings at her with the baseball bat, fearing that if he doesn't, Goldilocks may attack him with the knife. (In fact, Goldilocks just wants to grab a few knives so she can steal them for their silver value.) Goldilocks dies from the blow. Again, Papa Bear is charged with manslaughter. Under the Model Penal Code, should he be convicted?

30. Paul Bunyon owns a hunting cabin in Northwoods that has been broken into several times during his absences. He devises a trap door just inside the entryway which, when triggered, drops an intruder into a rattlesnake pit. Several weeks later, Daniel Goon, unarmed, breaks into the cabin, intending to take away with him whatever he can carry. However, he falls through the trap door and into the pit, where he is bitten to death by the snakes. Can Paul Bunyon defend a murder charge on the grounds of privilege to defend his property?

31. Police officer Dudley Do-Righteous, walking the beat in the financial district, gets a call on his police radio that there has been an embezzlement at the Awesome Bank, and that the suspect is about to leave the scene with a large satchel in which to carry cash. (The report does not indicate that the suspect is armed.) Dudley happens to be right in front of the bank. He sees Snively Whiplash run out of the building carrying a large satchel, jump in a car, and start to drive away. Dudley yells "Stop, Embezzler!" Snively keeps going. The only way Dudley will be able to detain and arrest Snively is by shooting at him. Can Dudley do so?

32. John Gotti is a law-abiding citizen. One afternoon, while walking down a street in Little Italy, John observes a teenager running out of a store, holding a box. An old man chases the teenager, screaming in Italian (a language that John recognizes but doesn't understand). Some of the other people in the street around him begin speaking Italian and pointing towards the teenager. John reasonably believes that the boy has just committed shoplifting (a felony in the jurisdiction) from the man. Therefore, John gives chase. As he gets close to the boy, John makes a flying tackle, hoping just to bring the teenager down. Instead, the teenager, while falling, cracks his head and suffers serious injuries. It later turns out that the teenager was the grandson of the old man, and that there had not been any crime, merely a family argument. Assume that John acted reasonably (at least given his lack of ability to understand Italian) in concluding that the teenager was a fleeing thief. If John is charged with the crime of assault, will he be able to raise the defense of private arrest?

33. Bunko, a police officer, convinces Ratso that Bunko is a junkie and that he'll pay anything to get a fix. Ratso refuses to sell him anything, saying he has nothing to do with drugs. Bunko pleads, "Come on, Pal. Have a heart. I'll give you $100 for yourself, plus whatever the stuff itself costs, if you'll help me out." Ratso finally agrees. When Ratso hands over the drugs, Bunko arrests him on narcotics charges.

(A) Assume for this part only that at the time of the transaction Ratso had in fact never dealt in narcotics. Will Ratso have a valid entrapment defense under the majority approach to entrapment?

(B) For this part, assume that Ratso had, in the previous two years, been arrested twice on drug-selling charges, and convicted once. Will Ratso have a valid entrapment defense under the majority approach to entrapment?

34. Annie Oakley, age 17, repeatedly asks Jessie James, a rifle dealer, to sell her a firearm. She finally succeeds, by telling James (who has long been attracted to Annie) that she'll have sex with him if he makes the sale. It's not a crime in the jurisdiction for an adult to have sex with a 17-year-old minor. It is, however, a crime to sell a firearm to a person under 18. James has never sold a firearm to a minor before. As soon as the sale is complete, Annie (who is secretly motivated by a desire to get unregistered firearms off the streets) turns Jessie in to the police. Can Jessie defend on grounds of entrapment, according to the majority definition of entrapment?

Answers

20. **(A) Duress.** The defense of duress is available where D commits a crime on account of a threat by a third person, which threat produces a reasonable fear in the defendant that he will suffer imminent death or serious bodily harm if he does not comply with the third person's demands.

    (B) No, because the harm wasn't imminent. Traditionally, courts have required that the harm with which the defendant is threatened must be immediate or at least imminent. Here, the threat is that Clark will be killed if he doesn't take an action during the course of the next week. Although the requirement of imminence is not as iron-clad as it once was, it's still followed by most courts.

    (C) Yes. M.P.C. § 2.09 does not impose any requirement that the threatened harm be imminent. All that is required is that the threat be such that a person of "reasonable firmness" would be "unable to resist" it. It seems likely that a person of reasonable firmness would choose to steal rather than die (and would believe Lewis' threat, given his past conduct), so Clark should be entitled to the defense under the M.P.C.

21. **(A) No.** In the vast majority of states today, the defense of duress is available whether the harm threatened is to the defendant himself, or to another. Since Ralph reasonably believed that the threat to Alice was real and immediate (and since the social harm from robbery is less than from murder), his crime will be excused under the doctrine of duress.

    (B) Yes, probably. In most states duress cannot be an excuse to commit homicide, even where the defendant reasonably believes that he or his close relative will be killed if he doesn't carry out the homicide. (However, most courts *do* allow duress to be a mitigating factor that reduces a murder charge to manslaughter.)

22. **Not guilty.** Although duress is normally not allowed as a defense to homicide charges (see part (B) to previous question), this is not true where the homicide is felony-murder. In other words, if duress would otherwise be usable as a defense to the underlying felony, duress may be used to prevent the felony from giving rise to felony-murder. Here, if no killing had occurred, Etta would have been entitled to use duress as a defense to her participation in the bank robbery, since the threat that she'd be shot would have been enough to induce a reasonable person in her position to participate in such a robbery. The duress defense thus means that Etta is not guilty of robbery. Therefore, there is no underlying felony on which the felony-murder doctrine can operate.

23. **(A) He should assert the defense of "necessity," which will be successful.** Where a person is forced to choose between a violation of law or a greater (and imminent) harm, and he chooses to violate the law in order to avoid the greater harm, he is free of criminal responsibility under the doctrine of necessity. The destruction-of-property situation is, in fact, the classic kind of situation in which the defense is often successful.

    (B) Unclear. Courts have generally been extremely reluctant — and in most cases unwilling — to allow the necessity defense when the crime involved is an intentional killing. However, the Model Penal Code allows the defense even in homicide cases, if the killing is necessary to save two or more other lives. Here, since sacrifice of one life was apparently the only way to avoid the likely loss of five other lives, the M.P.C. (and perhaps some courts) would allow the defense.

24. **No.** Dorothy can defend against the charge of trespass by asserting the defense of "necessity." The situation here meets all the requirements for the defense: (1) the harm of possibly being killed by the tornado was *greater* than the harm of breaking a window and trespassing; (2) there seems to have been *no lawful alternative method* of avoiding the harm; (3) the harm was *imminent*; and (4) Dorothy didn't *cause the danger* by recklessly or negligently putting herself in a position where the emergency was likely to arise.

25. **(A) No.** To begin with, the facts meet the basic requirements for self-defense: (1) Rambo was resisting the present or imminent use of unlawful force (since the act was completely unprovoked); (2) the degree of force was not more than was reasonably necessary to defend against threatened harm (since the facts say that Rambo realized he probably couldn't repel the act using non-deadly means); (3) deadly force was justified since the threat itself consisted of deadly force (i.e., force that in these circumstances — given Rocky's skills — was likely to kill or seriously injure Rambo); and (4) Rambo was not the aggressor. The question, of course, is whether Rocky was required to *retreat*.

The majority answer to this question is no — perhaps surprisingly, most courts continue to hold that there is no duty to retreat before using deadly force, even where retreat can be accomplished with complete safety. Note, however, that a growing *minority* of courts has held that there *is* a duty to retreat before using deadly force, but even those courts hold there is no duty to retreat where, among other factors: (1) The victim cannot retreat in complete safety, or (2) the attack occurs in the victim's home or place of business, or (3) the attack occurs where the victim is making a lawful arrest. (None of these factors applies here, so in the minority of states sometimes requiring retreat, Rambo is guilty of homicide.)

(B) No. Once the danger of the attack is over, the defense of self-defense is no longer available to the defendant. As soon as Rocky turned and began to leave the scene, Rambo lost his ability to use any sort of force against him. (It would have been different if, say, Rambo reasonably believed that Rocky was leaving just in order to recruit his friends to come back and group-attack Rambo — then, Rocky's leaving wouldn't have been a true withdrawal, and Rocky would have been justified in shooting if there was no other apparent way to prevent a life-threatening group attack.)

26. **(A) Yes.** In general, the "aggressor" — the one who first committed a battery or other legal infraction against the other party — thereby loses the right to use force in his own defense. Since Butch began the encounter by committing a battery, he thereby lost the right to defend himself, even by the use of what would otherwise have been an appropriate level of force. (The fact that Alfalfa began the hostilities by insulting Butch's mother is irrelevant — insults not accompanied by force or threat of force aren't unlawful, and may not be responded to by force.)

(B) No. These facts illustrate an important exception to the general rule that the aggressor has no right to use force in his own defense: when the victim *escalates* the fight, the aggressor may respond with a level of force appropriate to the escalation. Here, Butch was the aggressor but he started only a minor altercation. Alfalfa, the "victim," is the one who escalated the fight into one involving deadly force. Once that happened, Butch lost his status as aggressor, and was entitled to use self-defense as if he had never been an aggressor. Since a blow to Alfalfa's head was the only way he could reasonably defeat the potentially-deadly chokehold, he was entitled to use that level of force. (Indeed, he would have even been entitled to use deadly force, such as a gun or knife, if non-deadly force would not have sufficed.)

27. **No.** The defense of self-defense is available only where the threatened force is ***imminent***. Where the threat refers to the future (i.e., a time beyond the "present occasion," in the words of the M.P.C.), physical violence is not necessary, because other means, such as police help, are presumably available. Here, Romeo's words revealed that Juliet was not under an immediate threat of physical violence, so she was not entitled to use physical force, let alone deadly force.

28. **Yes, if Fletcher's mistake was reasonable.** Even though the defendant is mistaken about the actual need for self-defense, his use of the defense is not nullified so long as his mistake was a reasonable one. Here, the facts strongly suggest that Fletcher's belief was a reasonable, though tragically mistaken, one. If so, Fletcher will prevail with the defense.

29. **(A) Yes.** A person has the right to defend his property. However, under the M.P.C. (and in many states today), a homeowner may not use deadly force to defend his home or other property from an intruder, unless either: (1) the intruder has used or threatened the use of deadly force; or (2) the owner or his family are exposed to a substantial danger of serious bodily harm. Here, Goldilocks was unarmed and not posing any apparent physical threat to Papa or any of the other Bears. Therefore, Papa was entitled to use only non-deadly force. The baseball bat — especially given Papa's strength — was likely to produce serious bodily harm if swung at Goldilocks' head, so its use constituted deadly force. Consequently, Papa exceeded the bounds of permissible force in defense of his property, and he will have no defense. (He would probably be able to defeat a *murder* charge, because his "imperfect self defense" would entitle him to have the charge reduced to voluntary manslaughter.)

    (B) No. As noted in part (A), there is no privilege under the M.P.C. to use force likely to cause death or serious bodily injury if property alone is threatened. But where the threat to property is coupled with a serious bodily threat to the defender, then deadly force can be used in defense, even under the M.P.C. That's what happened here. (The fact that Papa was wrong about what Goldilocks intended is irrelevant — he reasonably believed that she was about to attack him with a knife, and that was enough.)

30. **No.** Although a property owner is sometimes privileged to protect his property against intruders by the use of mechanical devices, he may use only non-deadly ones. Under the modern view and the M.P.C., the use of a deadly mechanical device is *never* privileged – even if the homeowner would have been able to use deadly force himself had he been there at the time of the break-in. But even in a jurisdiction following the traditional view on mechanical devices, the device here would not have been privileged: under that view, the mechanical device may only be used under circumstances that would have entitled the homeowner to use deadly force in person. Here, where Goon did not pose a threat of serious bodily harm to anyone, Bunyon would not have been privileged to use deadly force in person, and was therefore not privileged to do so by proxy.

31. **No.** Although the common-law view was that an officer could use deadly force to prevent a person escaping the arrest of any felony, the Supreme Court, in *Tennessee v. Garner*, restricted that right. According to *Garner*, use of deadly force to stop a suspect fleeing from a non-dangerous felony is only constitutionally permissible if the suspect poses an immediate threat of serious physical harm, either to the officer or others. Here, Dudley would be violating the Fourth Amendment's ban on unreasonable seizures if he were to shoot Snively, since embezzlement is not a dangerous felony and there's no reason to believe that Snively poses a physical threat to anyone. Given that the shooting would be unreasonable, Dudley would lose his common-law privilege to use force in making an arrest, since that privilege is limited to the *reasonable* use of force. (But Dudley could have used *non*-deadly force, such as parking his car in the middle of the road to block Snively's escape.)

32. No. A *police officer* gets a privilege to use force (at least non-deadly force) to make an arrest for any felony, and he does not waive this privilege by making a reasonable mistake. But when a ***private citizen*** uses force (even non-deadly force) to make an arrest, he does not get the benefit of a reasonable mistake, and acts ***at his own peril***. Since here, no felony was in fact committed, John cannot escape liability based on his reasonable error. Nor does John get any protection from the fact that he used non-deadly force — a private citizen may not use even non-deadly force based on a reasonable mistake (though John would be protected if the teenager had in fact committed a felony for which John was trying to arrest him).

33. (A) Yes. Under the majority approach to entrapment, entrapment exists where: (1) the government originates the crime and induces its commission; and (2) the defendant is one who was not predisposed to committing this sort of crime. Here, both elements are satisfied: (1) Bunko came up with the idea of a drug transaction, and by pleading induced Ratso to go along; and (2) Ratso's lack of any prior involvement in narcotics sales indicates that he was not predisposed to commit this sort of crime.

(B) No. Here, Ratso does not satisfy element (2) of the majority rule: his record indicates that he was in fact predisposed to sell narcotics. (But note that under the minority "police conduct" rule for determining entrapment, Ratso might win — under that test, if the government originates the crime and the behavior of the government agents is such that a non-predisposed person would be likely to be induced, the fact that the particular defendant himself may have been predisposed is viewed as irrelevant.)

34. No, because Annie is not a government agent, nor is she working with the police. Entrapment arises as a defense where government agents (or those working under their direction) instigate private persons to commit a crime that they were not "predisposed" to commit. The fact that Annie turned Jessie over to the police immediately after the crime (or even the fact that she always planned to do so) is irrelevant — a private citizen will be deemed to be working with the police, and thus a potential agent for entrapment, only if the police are directing or encouraging the operation while it progresses. (If the police had put a wire on Annie before the sale, that probably *would* be enough to make Annie a government agent for entrapment purposes, in which case Jessie might win.)

Exam Tips on
JUSTIFICATION AND EXCUSE

Consider all possible justifications and excuses discussed in this chapter when analyzing a fact pattern, because it is possible to assert several of them at the same time. Be aware that the defenses of self-defense, defense of property, and the "fleeing felon" defense present themselves most frequently.

Self-defense

☛ Key issues to consider when a party uses deadly force to defend herself from an attack or threat of an attack from another person:

   ☞ **Serious bodily harm:** When D has been attacked, concentrate on analyzing whether the attack threatened him with what D reasonably believed was ***serious bodily harm.*** This matters because you can only use ***deadly force*** (force likely to kill or do serious bodily harm) to repel an attack that you reasonably believe threatens serious bodily harm.

☞ **Mistaken perception of threat:** When deadly force has not yet been used, you must analyze the *reasonableness* of D's belief that there was an imminent threat of deadly force. Even if D is wrong in this belief, he can plead self-defense so long as his belief was reasonable.

> *Example (reasonable belief):* D is selling cocaine outside a high school. T sticks his hand in his pocket, thrusts a finger forward, jabs D with it, and says, "I've got a gun. Give me the dope or I'll blow you away." D shoots T. It doesn't matter that T didn't really have a gun — so long as D's belief that there was a gun (and that T might use that gun) was reasonable, D was entitled to use deadly force in return.

> *Example (unreasonable belief):* D brings her watch in to be repaired and the jewelry store owner sells it to V. At a bowling alley, D notices her watch on V's wrist. D angrily demands the watch. Concerned because of a previous argument with D, V fumbles in her pockets for the receipt to show she had purchased the watch. Thinking that V is reaching for a weapon, D strikes V on the head with a heavy metal ashtray, seriously injuring her. D would probably not be able to assert the privilege of self-defense, because her belief that V was reaching for a gun when she put her hands in her pockets was probably unreasonable in the circumstances.

☞ *Trap:* Don't be fooled by a fact pattern in which D shoots a *police officer* — if D had a reasonable belief that the police officer was a dangerous intruder, this may still be self-defense.

> *Example:* D, the owner of a tavern, has been burglarized several times. As a result, he sleeps at the tavern with a pistol. V, a police officer, sees the tavern window open at night and climbs in to investigate. D cocks his pistol at V. V doesn't say he's a police officer, but shouts, "Drop that gun or I'll shoot." D, believing that V is an armed burglar, shoots V. D's belief that V was an armed burglar may well have been reasonable; if so (and if he reasonably feared that V would use deadly force), this was valid self-defense.

☞ **Belief must be bona fide:** Remember that even if a reasonable person might have believed that a threat exists, if the defendant did not *actually* believe that there was one, then the defense may not be asserted.

☛ **Retreat or otherwise incapable of inflicting harm:** Remember that if the *initial threat no longer exists*, the defense of self-defense no longer applies.

> *Example:* Following a rape, the rapist falls asleep. The victim ties his hands and feet to the posts of the bed, and beats him severely. The victim may not assert the privilege of self-defense as to the serious injury because once the rapist was tied up, the threat was over.

☞ **Aggressor may not assert privilege:** Also, look for a fact pattern where the initial aggressor's actual threat of or use of deadly force is responded to with force (perhaps deadly force) and the initial aggressor then defends himself. Remember that *a wrongful aggressor has no right of self-defense against a reasonable response to her ini-*

tial aggression.

☞ *Example:* After an exchange of insults, D pulls a gun and points it at V. V pulls out a knife and moves towards D. D shoots V. Since D was the wrongful aggressor and used deadly force, V's response was permissible (deadly force proportional to the threat). Therefore, D was not permitted to use deadly force to counter it.

☞ **Exception for withdrawal:** But remember that even this rule has an exception: if the initial (wrongful) aggressor retreats, attempting to end the encounter, the aggressor is entitled to use force — even, where necessary, deadly force — to protect himself if the target persists in his defense. (And, the target's use of deadly force following the retreat is itself not reasonable). So be on the lookout for the retreat of the initial aggressor.

Example: D attends weekly sessions with a psychotherapist. While in the waiting room of the psychotherapist's office, D draws a knife, waving it at N, the nurse, and screaming, "Vader must die. The Empire will be restored." N takes a heavy, replica of a medieval sword and holds it in front of him. D hands the knife to N, kneels before him and says, "Forgive me, Lord of the Galaxy." N, who should (but doesn't) realize that he is no longer in danger of being injured by D, swings at D with the sword, narrowly missing him. D then grabs back his knife and stabs N. Despite the fact that D was the initial aggressor, his initial aggression had ended by the time N swung the sword. Therefore, N's response was not reasonable. This unreasonableness entitled D to use self-defense just as if N had never been a wrongful aggressor in the first place. So if D's use of the knife was proportional to the threat he reasonably perceived from N, D can successfully plead self-defense.

Defense of property

☛ **Deadly force not privileged:** When a party uses *deadly force* to protect his property, you should write in your answer that, generally, the use of deadly force is not privileged. However, note that in some jurisdictions, a party may use deadly force to prevent another from invading that party's *home*. In that case you must analyze the following:

   ☞ **Definition of dwelling:** The privilege applies only to intrusion of a *dwelling*, i.e., an occupied residence. So, for instance, a tool shed on the property would probably not be covered. But any room within the residence would be covered even if the room is used only for business (e.g., a doctor's office inside the doctor's house).

☛ **Degree of force:** Under the modern view, deadly force may be used only when the home occupier reasonably believes that an intruder is about to *commit a violent felony* within the premises and poses a danger to the inhabitants. So there's *no automatic right to shoot at a burglar.*

Fleeing Felons and Law Enforcement

☛ **Private citizens:** The most common fact pattern in this area concerns a *private citizen* using force to *stop a fleeing felon.* If a party has just committed a dangerous felony and is fleeing, a private citizen is justified in using deadly force only if the felon poses an *immediate threat* to the citizen or others. Check for the following:

☞ Make sure the party asserting the defense *actually believes* that the victim has just committed a felony.

> *Example:* X, Y and Z commit a robbery in a casino. As they are leaving, on the steps of a gambling casino, D approaches them, believing them to be the operators of the casino. He shouts, "Death to gamblers," and shoots at them. D was unaware of the robbery — his motive for shooting was to close down the casino because he had lost all his savings there and his life had been ruined. Therefore, although X, Y and Z were in fact fleeing felons, D may not assert apprehension-of-felons as a defense.

☞ Make sure the party asserting the defense was *correct* in his belief that the victim had just committed a felony. If he is mistaken, he bears the risk of his mistake, even if the mistake is "reasonable".

> *Example:* U, an undercover police agent, participates in the robbery of a drugstore with members of a group of thieves that U has infiltrated. U approaches the store owner, O, draws her gun, and hands to O a note that reads: "I am a police undercover agent. Pretend to be frightened. Give me the money in the cash register." O is illiterate, and therefore doesn't read the note. When U turns to leave, O shoots at her. Since U was not in fact a fleeing felon, O is not entitled to the fleeing-felon defense.

☛ **Police arrest:** Remember that a *police officer* who has probable cause to believe that a person has committed a *felony* (and is *dangerous* to others) may use *deadly force* to make an arrest. But where the officer believes that the person has merely committed a *misdemeanor*, or has committed a felony but poses *no threat* to others, the officer may *not* use deadly force to make the arrest.

☞ Don't be fooled by a fact pattern in which the arrestee has committed a dangerous felony, but the officer is making the arrest for a different crime, which is a mere misdemeanor or non-dangerous felony. What matters is what the officer reasonably believes, not the underlying facts.

> *Example:* After fatally stabbing somebody in a bar brawl, X drives away in her car. A few blocks away, a police officer, D, observes X going through a stop sign and begins to chase her. X speeds away because she thinks she is being chased regarding the stabbing. D fires at X's tires, but the shot accidentally kills a pedestrian, V. If D is charged with homicide in the death of V, he probably won't succeed, because he was trying to arrest X for a misdemeanor (running a stop sign), and D wasn't privileged to use deadly force in doing so. The fact that X may have been guilty of a dangerous felony and could have been arrested with use of deadly force for that won't bail D out, since he didn't know these facts and his state of mind is the issue.

Entrapment

☛ **Requirements:** Remember that D usually must prove that (1) the government agent *originated* the crime and *induced* D to commit it; *and* (2) D was *not predisposed* to committing the crime.

☛ **Induce commission:** You will usually find that the police officer (or agent) did not *induce or instigate* the commission of the crime.

☞ **Absence of inducement:** Watch for a police officer who involves himself heavily in the planning or commission of the crime, but is not the actual one to suggest that it be committed. This won't be entrapment, because of the lack of inducement.

> *Example:* X and Y are suspected of having committed a series of recent robberies. P, an undercover police agent, invites X and Y to her home for drinks and mentions to them that she is impressed with the perpetrators of the recent robberies in the neighborhood. X then suggests that a neighborhood drugstore would be an easy target for a robbery. P agrees to join in the robbery, in order to obtain evidence of X's and Y's past crimes. X and Y are arrested as they enter the drugstore accompanied by P. Since P never suggested the commission of the crime, or otherwise induced X and Y to commit it, there's no entrapment despite her participation in the planning.

☞ **Predisposition:** You will also usually find that the party asserting the defense was predisposed to commit the crime, again blocking a finding of entrapment.

Example: P agrees to assist the police in return for reduced charges on a drug-related crime. The police set him up in a used-car business and spread the rumor that he deals in stolen vehicles. With police permission, P purchases a stolen vehicle from X. Then D comes to P's place of business requesting to purchase a stolen vehicle. With police permission, P sells the stolen vehicle to D. This is not entrapment, because by seeking out the dealership and asking for a stolen vehicle, D showed a predisposition to commit the crime.

Duress

☛ **Duress generally:** When considering the defense of duress, the most important things to remember are:

☞ The defense *may not be used* in a *murder* charge.

☞ D's fear of harm must have been both *reasonable* and *actual*.

CHAPTER 5

ATTEMPT

Introductory Note: Even if a person does not complete the commission of a substantive crime, she can in some instances be convicted of the separate crime of "attempting" to commit that substantive crime. The most important elements of liability for attempt are: (1) To be liable for attempting crime X, D must have had the *intent* to do acts which, if they had been carried out, would have resulted in the commission of crime X; (2) Thoughts alone won't suffice — D must have committed some *act* in furtherance of the crime (though exactly what types of act will suffice varies among jurisdictions); and (3) The claim that D couldn't possibly have succeeded — that is, the defense of *"impossibility"* — usually fails.

I. INTRODUCTION

A. **Concept of attempt generally:** It has long been recognized that there are sound reasons for punishing a person who tries to commit a substantive crime and who, for reasons beyond his control, comes close to succeeding but in the end fails. For instance, if A shoots at B with an intent to kill him, and he fails only because his aim is faulty, A is obviously a dangerous person whom it is desirable to punish. Otherwise, he may try again, either against B or against someone else.

   1. **Need to have police intervene:** Furthermore, if attempts were not punishable, the police would be severely impeded in their ability to stop the commission of substantive crimes. Suppose, for instance, that the police knew that A would try to kill B. If they were forced to wait to see whether A were successful, and allowed to arrest him only if he were, their prevention powers would obviously be destroyed. Furthermore, their prevention powers would even be severely diminished under a rule of law that allowed them to arrest A for attempted murder after he shot at B and missed, but not to arrest him before he pulled the trigger for the first time.

      a. **Social interest:** Therefore, there is a strong social interest not only in making unsuccessful efforts to commit a substantive crime criminal in themselves, but also in moving forward in time the point at which the planning and preparation of a crime becomes a punishable attempt.

   2. **Countervailing issues:** On the other hand, if unsuccessful efforts become criminal too soon in the continuum between conception and execution, undesirable effects may also occur:

      a. **Punishment of innocent:** First, since the external evidence that someone is planning a crime is often ambiguous, there is a risk that this evidence may be wrongly interpreted, and will lead to the conviction of persons who had no intention at all of ever executing a substantive crime.

b. No chance for abandonment: Secondly, even assuming that the person in question did have an intention to commit a crime, by making his conduct punishable too early, we may be punishing someone who ultimately would have abandoned his efforts, perhaps before he even came reasonably close to committing the crime. We would thus run the danger of punishing him for little more than *evil thoughts*; as noted *supra* (p. 1), punishment for thoughts alone is not a desirable feature of a criminal justice system.

3. Modern trend toward broader attempt liability: Prior to this century, the tendency in Anglo-American law was to give great weight to the arguments urging strict limitation on liability for attempts. But the tendency in this century, particularly within the last twenty years, has been almost universally towards an extreme *broadening of attempt liability*. This broadening can be seen by considering briefly each of the three major aspects of attempt liability:

a. The mental state requirement: It has traditionally been required that for a defendant to be convicted of attempting a particular substantive crime, he must have had an *intent to commit that crime*. There has been a greater willingness to convict for an attempt if the defendant had a mental state short of intent, but one which would have been enough to satisfy the *mens rea* requirement of the substantive crime itself. For instance, if A shoots at B with an intent to do him serious bodily harm, but not to kill him, this will be enough for murder in most jurisdictions (see *infra*, p. 234). However, the traditional, but probably not the modern, view is that if A misses, he is not guilty of attempted murder. This area is discussed *infra*.

b. The act requirement: Similarly, the traditional view has been that the defendant cannot be convicted of an attempt to commit a substantive crime unless he performed acts which came very close to commission of the substantive crime itself. But the modern view is that almost any sort of overt act that represents a substantial step towards the offense, and that is strongly corroborative of the defendant's intent to commit the substantive crime, will suffice. See *infra*, p. 154.

c. Impossibility: Lastly, the traditional attitude has been to give reasonably broad scope to a defense called the defense of "legal impossibility." In contrast, the modern view has been to limit this defense sharply. See *infra*, p. 158.

4. General attempt statutes: The vast majority of prosecutions for attempt today occur under *general attempt statutes*. That is, the typical criminal code does not specifically make it a crime to attempt murder, to attempt robbery, etc. Instead, a separate statutory section makes it a crime to attempt to commit any of the substantive crimes enumerated elsewhere in the code. Unfortunately, these statutes are not usually very specific as to what constitutes an attempt; a statute may say, for instance, simply that "it shall be an offense to attempt to commit any of the crimes enumerated in...," without specifying the requisite mental state, the kind of act which will suffice, or the scope of the impossibility defense.

a. Completed offense: However, the statutes do usually say that they apply only where the defendant does not succeed in committing the substantive crime; thus it is sometimes held that the defendant cannot be convicted of an attempt if the completed crime is proved. See *infra*, p. 167.

II. MENTAL STATE

A. **Intent usually required:** As a general rule, for a defendant to be convicted of attempting a particular substantive crime, he must have had an *intent* to do acts which, if they had been carried out, would have resulted in the commission of that crime. This view is in accord with the common understanding of what it means to "attempt" something. For instance, under this approach one can attempt to kill another person only if one *intends to kill that person*, and not if a danger of death to that other person arises from some other mental state (e.g., recklessness). This is true even though mental states other than intent might suffice for a conviction of committing the substantive crime.

> **Example:** D, hoping to scare V (but not physically injure him), fires a gun in V's direction. The shot narrowly misses V, and lands harmlessly. If the shot had hit and killed V, D would probably have been guilty of reckless-indifference murder. But reckless-indifference does not suffice as a mental state for attempt. Therefore, D will not be guilty of attempted murder.

1. **Specific crime in question:** Furthermore, the defendant must not only have an intent to commit a criminal act, but an intent to commit an act which would constitute *the same crime as he is charged with attempting*. It is not enough that the defendant is shown to have intended some other sort of criminality.

> **Example:** D accosts X, a woman, on the sidewalk, grabs her arm, and waves a screwdriver. He orders her to unlock the door of her car, and tells her that "we're going in your car." X is too frightened to find the keys, so she gives the purse to D, who looks for them. Another car pulls up, D is frightened, and X escapes. D is charged with attempted kidnapping, and convicted.
>
> *Held*, D's statement that "we're going in your car" did not necessarily demonstrate an intent to kidnap, but may have signified merely an intent to rape X inside her car, or to steal from her. An intent to commit some crime other than kidnapping would not support a conviction of attempted kidnapping. Therefore, D's appellate counsel was incompetent in not raising this defense, and D is entitled to a new appeal. *In Re Smith*, 474 P.2d 969 (Cal. 1970).

2. **Knowledge of likely consequences:** It has also been generally held that the mere fact that the defendant knew that certain consequences were *highly likely* to result from his act is *not equivalent* to intending those consequences.

> **Example:** D fires a gun in V's direction, knowing that it's highly likely that the bullet will hit V. (But D doesn't intend to hit V, just to frighten him.) The bullet misses. D is probably not guilty of attempted murder — his knowledge that death was highly likely was not equivalent to an intent to bring about that death.

   a. **"Substantially certain" results:** But if it can be shown that the defendant knew that a certain result was *"substantially certain"* to occur, then this may be enough to meet the intent requirement, even though the defendant may not have desired that result to occur. For instance, the commentary to the Model Penal Code puts the case of a defendant who desires to demolish a building, and accordingly detonates a bomb, knowing that people inside will almost certainly be killed; according to the Code draftsmen, the defendant could be convicted of attempted murder. See Comment 2 to M.P.C. § 5.01.

3. **Crimes defined by recklessness, negligence or strict liability:** Since an intent to bring about a certain result is generally required for crimes of attempt, it would seem at first glance that there can be no attempt to commit a crime defined in terms of recklessness or negligence.

     a. **Bringing about certain result:** This is clearly true as to those crimes defined in terms of recklessly or negligently bringing about a *certain result*. For instance, involuntary manslaughter is generally defined (see *infra*, p. 257) as grossly negligent causing of death. There can be no such thing as attempted involuntary manslaughter; either the defendant intended to bring about death, in which case he can be liable for attempted murder, or he did not intend it, in which case he is not guilty of any sort of attempted homicide. Thus suppose that D gets into his car knowing that it has bad brakes, but negligently (or recklessly) deciding to take a chance. If he almost runs into X because he can't stop in time, he will not be guilty of attempted involuntary manslaughter.

     b. **Crime not defined by result:** But if a crime defined in terms of recklessness or negligence does not require a particular physical consequence to occur, it may be possible to attempt to commit it. Suppose, once again, that D knows his car has bad brakes. If he gets into the car intending to drive it notwithstanding the risk, but is unsuccessful in starting the engine, he might theoretically be convicted of attempted negligent driving. See L, pp. 542.

     c. **Strict-liability crimes:** It is not clear whether one can be convicted of attempting a *strict-liability crime* without a culpable state of mind. LaFave (pp. 543-44) suggests that the justification for strict-liability crimes in general is "shaky," and that therefore conviction of an attempt to commit such a crime should not be premised on anything less than intent. Thus if it is a crime to sell adulterated milk even though one does not know that the milk is adulterated, one should nonetheless not be convicted of an attempt to sell adulterated milk unless one knows that it is.

4. **Proving intent by circumstantial evidence:** It is important to remember that the defendant's intent may be proved by *circumstantial evidence*. And one of the kinds of circumstantial evidence that would tend to demonstrate intent might be that the defendant has acted in circumstances where he must have had at least an awareness of the likely consequences of his conduct.

     Example: Suppose D shoots twice at X, each shot missing by only eighteen inches from a distance of one hundred feet. D claims that he did not intend to kill X, but merely to frighten him. A jury could infer from D's acts that, beyond a reasonable doubt, D intended to kill X. Therefore, the jury could properly find D guilty of attempted murder, based on circumstantial evidence of D's intent.

5. **Intent as to surrounding circumstances:** It is probably not necessary that the defendant's intent encompass all of the *surrounding circumstances* that are elements of the crime. The draftsmen of the Model Penal Code, for instance, put the case of a statute making it a federal crime to kill an F. B. I. agent. Supposing that recklessness or even negligence with respect to the victim's identity suffices for the completed crime, according to the Code an attempt to violate the statute can be found if the defendant intended to kill X,

but was merely reckless or negligent with respect to whether X was an F.B.I. agent. See Comment 2 to M.P.C. § 5.01.

III. THE ACT — ATTEMPT VS. "MERE PREPARATION"

A. **Attempt distinguished from mere preparation:**   Everyone agrees that attempt liability should be premised on something more than mere thoughts or verbal expressions of thoughts. Thus it is uniformly required that, before the defendant can be convicted of an attempt, he must have committed *some act* in furtherance of his plan of criminality. But there has been great dispute about what kind of act suffices. In the nineteenth century, it was usually held that only an act that came quite close to successful commission of the substantive crime could suffice. In this century, there has been a tendency to find that acts much earlier in the sequence of conception-to-commission are enough.

1. **Different views:**   Nor have courts been in agreement even on what factors should be looked to in determining whether or not an act is sufficiently demonstrative of criminal intent to meet the *actus reus* requirement for an attempt. In general, courts have gone in one of two directions: (1) focusing on **how close** the defendant came to committing the substantive crime (the "proximity" approach); and (2) focusing on how clear it is from the act that the defendant indeed intended to commit the substantive crime (the "equivocality" approach). Each of these approaches, and the variations upon it, are discussed below. Finally, we discuss the view of the Model Penal Code, which is more or less a combination of these two approaches.

B. **The proximity approach:**   Most courts have based their decision about whether a particular act is sufficient on *how close the defendant came to completing the offense*. But whereas it was once required that the defendant have committed *every act which was in his power* towards completion of the offense (the "last act" test), in recent decades acts significantly further removed from completion have sufficed.

1. **The "last act" test:**   The *"last act"* test dates from a well-known English case, *Regina v. Eagleton*, 6 Cox C. C. 559 (Eng. 1855). In that case, D was a baker who was hired by a welfare office to provide bread for the poor. Each poor person was to present D with a ticket, in return for which D would give him a loaf of bread; D would then turn the tickets in to the welfare office, and receive a credit on their books, against which he would be paid at a later time. D delivered underweight loaves, and turned in his tickets. He was charged with attempting to obtain money by false pretenses from the welfare office; he defended on the grounds that by turning in the tickets, he received only a credit, not money, and that he had therefore not come close enough to successful completion of the crime to be liable for attempt.

   a. **Holding:**   The court held, however, that D was liable for attempted obtaining of money by false pretenses. The holding was based on the fact that "no other act on the part of D would have been required." Turning in the tickets was the "last act depending on himself" toward obtaining the money, and this was therefore sufficient for attempt liability.

2. **"Dangerous proximity to success" test:**   It quickly became apparent that the "last act" test was too restrictive, and that it prevented liability from attaching in situations where common sense dictated that it ought to. For instance, suppose that D decided to embark on a course of systematically poisoning X by the administration of small doses of arsenic. If he administered the first one or two doses, common sense would dictate that he had gone far enough to be liable for attempted murder; yet, he clearly had not committed the "last act," and would not do so until he set out the final dose of poison, by which time the only prosecution likely to occur would be for murder, not attempted murder. Accordingly, courts articulated the rule that so long as the defendant achieved a ***"dangerous proximity to success,"*** he would be liable.

   a. **Preparation may be enough:**   It followed from this rule that what might be called ***"mere preparation"*** on the part of the defendant could nonetheless be a sufficiently overt act to confer liability. For instance, in *Commonwealth v. Peaslee*, 59 N.E. 55 (Mass. 1901), the defendant was charged with attempted arson; he had arranged combustible materials inside the building in question, but his plan required the additional step of taking a candle from a shelf, lighting it, and moving it across the room. The court suggested (but did not decide) that even without the lighting of the candle, the defendant had done enough to meet the act requirement; "Some preparations may amount to an attempt. It is a question of degree. If the preparation comes very near to the accomplishment of the act, the intent to complete it renders the crime so probable that the act will be a [crime]...."

   b. **Some preparations not enough:**   But the "dangerous proximity" requirement nonetheless means that some acts, although they very clearly indicate the defendant's intent to commit a substantive crime, are not sufficient to meet the act requirement. This is generally because there are circumstances ***outside the defendant's control*** which either may, or do, turn up to block successful completion of the crime. The following two examples illustrate this result.

   Example 1: D, with three others, plans to rob Rao while he is carrying from the bank a payroll for his company. On the day when Rao is expected to carry the payroll, the four set out by car looking for him. They go first to the bank, then to sites where Rao's company is working, but do not find Rao or any other payroll messenger. As they are searching, they are arrested by the police, who have become suspicious. D is charged with attempted robbery.

   Held, D is not guilty of the crime. For him to have been guilty, he would have had to commit an act which was "so near to [the crime's] accomplishment that in all reasonable probability the crime itself would have been committed, but for timely interference." Here, however, D did not come "dangerously" close to robbing Rao. At the very least, it was necessary that D locate the robbery victim; just as one cannot be convicted of an attempt to burglarize a building if one has merely searched for the building without finding it, so one cannot attempt a robbery before locating the victim. *People v. Rizzo*, 158 N.E. 888 (N. Y. 1927).

   Example 2: D1 requests a $20 withdrawal from an ATM at Bank. She then fails to remove the bill. This "bill trap" causes the machine to be shut down and a service technician to be dispatched. (D1 knows that this is how things work, because she previously worked for Bank.) Shortly thereafter — apparently before the arrival of the technician — police find D1 and two other Ds sitting in a rental car near Bank. A search reveals several weapons and ammunition, as well as a stun gun and two pair of latex surgical gloves. One of the Ds also has someone else's ATM card. The Ds are charged with attempted bank robbery. The prosecution reasons that the Ds caused the bill trap in the expectation that once the technician arrived and opened the ATM, the Ds could rob the machine.

Held, there is insufficient evidence to convict on the attempt charge. The Ds never made a move toward the technician or Bank to accomplish the criminal portion of their intended mission. Therefore, they had not yet taken a step of "'such substantiality that, unless frustrated, the crime would have occurred'. … Making an appointment with a potential victim is not of itself such a commitment to an intended crime as to constitute an attempt, even though it may make a later attempt possible." *United States v. Harper,* 33 F.3d 1143 (9th. Cir. 1994).

3. **The "probable desistance" approach:**   A third variation of the proximity test is that the defendant's conduct meets the act requirement if it has gone beyond the point where the defendant is likely to *voluntarily* (i.e., without interference from an outside source) stop short of completing the events. That is, if it is no longer probable that the defendant would, on his own, *"desist"*, he has met the act requirement.

    Example: D, a prisoner, arranges to have two hacksaw blades sent to him from outside the prison. During a search of the prison, officials discover the two blades, and D is charged with attempted escape.

    Held, for D. D's procuring of the blades amounted to a preparation only, since at the time of their discovery he had plenty of time to change his mind and abandon his escape plan. *Commonwealth v. Skipper,* 294 A.2d 780 (Pa. 1972).

    a. **Same as "proximity" test:**   The "probable desistance test" is generally criticized on the grounds that there is no way to tell whether it is likely that the defendant reached a point where he would go through with the crime, unless one looks at how close to completing the crime he was. If this is what one does, then the test is really exactly the same as the "dangerous proximity" test.

4. **"Reasonable man" standard:**   A slightly different standard is that the defendant's conduct satisfies the act requirement if it goes beyond the point of where a *"reasonable, law-abiding citizen,"* if he had originally formulated the criminal intent, would abandon it. However, it is doubtful that a reasonable, law-abiding citizen would go more than a very short way towards committing a crime. And it does not seem desirable to punish all conduct that goes beyond this.

5. **"Indispensable element" test:**   Still other cases look at whether the defendant's plan, to succeed, required cooperation or action by *third persons,* which had not yet taken place. If so, the defendant's conduct, by this test, does not yet amount to an attempt.

    Example: D, a professional con man, intends to bilk X of her money by a "bunco" scheme. The scheme requires D and henchman to convince X that D is afraid he will lose his money if he puts it in the bank, and to persuade X to withdraw her own money so that D will be convinced of the bank's safety; after X withdraws her money, the plan is to take it by a sleight-of-hand switch for counterfeit money. However, while X is in the bank, D decides to drive away; he is later arrested by the police, and charged with attempted grand theft.

Held, D did not go far enough to be liable for an attempt. The scheme could not have succeeded until, *inter alia*, X withdrew her money and gave it to D. "Too many potential slips remained before the cup of success would reach the defendant's lips for us to say that there was here anything more than preparation." *People v. Orndorff*, 67 Cal. Rptr. 824 (Cal. App. 1968).

a. **"Mere solicitation" not enough:** A related principle is that if all the defendant has done was to try to convince another person to commit a crime, he has not met the act requirement. That is, one who has merely committed the offense of *"solicitation"* (discussed *infra*, p. 222) has not committed an attempt. Thus in *State v. Davis*, 6 S.W.2d 609 (Mo. 1928), D wished to procure the murder of his mistress' husband. He tried to persuade X to find him a paid assassin, but X tipped off Y, a police officer, who then posed as an ex-convict willing to do the job. When D paid Y $600 to carry out the plan, the police were waiting to arrest D. The court held that D was not guilty of attempted murder, since he had merely solicited Y. (The court relied in part on the fact that Y never had any intention of carrying out the crime. But it is not clear whether the result would or should be different if Y had had such an intent; why should Y's intent be imputed, one way or the other, to D?)

b. **Rejection of "indispensable element":** It seems clear that most modern courts are not willing to accept the principle that there cannot be an attempt where the action of a third party is necessary for completion of a crime. For instance, in *D.P.P. v. Stonehouse*, 2 All E.R. 909 (Eng. 1977), D, who was in financial difficulties, faked his death by drowning, in order that his wife might obtain his life insurance proceeds. However, D was discovered before the wife (who was ignorant of the scheme) could make her claim. D's conviction of attempted fraud was affirmed, the court not being troubled by either the fact that the wife had not yet made her claim, or the fact that the insurance company (which might have denied the claim on suspicion of fraud) had not yet made payment. The fact that the defendant had done all that he could do in furtherance of the scheme was deemed sufficient.

C. **The "equivocality" test:** All of the tests described above are similar, in that they look to how close the defendant came to succeeding. An entirely different test, usually called the *"equivocality"* test, requires instead merely that the defendant's conduct *unequivocally manifest his criminal intent*. If the conduct could be indicative either of a non-criminal intent or of a criminal one, it is not sufficient. But if it does unequivocally manifest criminality of intent, it suffices even though completion of the plan is many steps away.

1. **Confessions excluded:** Perhaps the most significant aspect of this test is that any *confession* by the defendant, made either to police or to other persons, is *not to be considered* in determining whether the defendant's acts were unequivocally criminal in intent. As one court put it, "That a man's unfulfilled criminal purposes should be punishable they must be manifested not by his words merely, or by acts which are in themselves of innocent or ambiguous significance, but by overt acts which are sufficient in themselves to declare or

proclaim the guilty purpose with which they are done." *The King v. Barker*, 1924 N.Z.L.R. 865 (N.Z. 1924).

Example: The Ds, two men, are admitted with two female companions to the house of X, an 80-year-old woman. A neighbor gets suspicious, and calls the police. When the police arrive, they find jewelry and other belongings of X strewn around the house, but find none of her property on either of the Ds. The Ds are tried for attempted larceny, and the trial judge instructs the jury that it may convict if it finds that the Ds entered X's house with the intention of stealing from her.

Held, the trial judge erred. The Ds' mere entry into X's house does not meet the act requirement, because it was not an unambiguous, unequivocal manifestation of intent to rob. There was evidence that the Ds had previously done housework for X, and from their entry into the building it is not possible to say that this was not their reason this time. "…It is as though a cinematographic film, which has so far depicted merely the accused person's acts without stating what was his intention, had been suddenly stopped, and the audience were asked to say to what end those acts were directed. If there is only one reasonable answer to this question then the accused has done what amounts to an 'attempt' to attain that end. If there is more than one reasonably possible answer, then the accused has not yet done enough." *People v. Bowen*, 158 N.W.2d 794 (Mich. App. 1968).

2. **Criticism:** The equivocality test is often criticized principally on the grounds that there is *no act that is completely unequivocal*. For instance, suppose the defendant is arrested after lighting a match next to a haystack, and is charged with attempted arson. If he happens to be carrying a pipe, he can argue that he was merely going to light the pipe; since any confession to the contrary would be disregarded in measuring the equivocality of his conduct, the defendant would have to be acquitted. To carry the point to an even further extreme, suppose the defendant were stopped just before he fired a bullet into a car's windshield, with a driver sitting behind. Under the "cinematographic" test referred to in *Bowen*, the defendant could point out that this conduct was consistent with an innocent desire to test whether the windshield in the car was bullet proof!

3. **Uselessness of confession:** Even assuming that the equivocality test is interpreted so as to require only a "reasonable" degree of unambiguity, the test is open to the serious objection that it drastically undermines the utility of *confessions*. Suppose, for instance, that the Ds in *Bowen* had confessed to the police, after proper *Miranda* warnings, that they had intended to steal X's jewelry. By the terms of the test, these confessions could not be consulted in determining whether their act of entering the house was unambiguous. Although it is true that this approach prevents an innocent person who has confessed under police pressure from being convicted of an attempt, it would seem possible to guard against convicting the innocent without letting manifestly dangerous persons escape liability for their unconsummated criminal plans.

D. **Model Penal Code's "substantial step" test:** The Model Penal Code incorporates aspects of both the "proximity" test and the "unequivocality" test. Yet the aspects of each that it incorporates are relatively unstringent, so that almost any conduct meeting any of the variations of either of these tests would be sufficient under the Code, and many acts that would fail some or all of these tests would also be sufficient under the Code.

1. **"Substantial step" test:** Conduct meets the act requirement under the Code if, under circumstances as the defendant believes them to be, there occurs "...an act or omission constituting a *substantial step* in a course of conduct planned to culminate in [the defendant's] commission of the crime." M.P.C. § 5.01(1)(c).

   a. **"Strongly corroborative" requirement:** However, the Code adds that conduct meeting this "substantial step" test will not suffice unless, in addition, "...it is *strongly corroborative* of the actor's criminal purpose."

2. **Combination of proximity and equivocality test:** Thus a very watered-down version of the proximity test is contained in the requirement that the act be a "substantial step" towards completion of the crime, and a watered-down version of the equivocality test is contained in the requirement that the act be "strongly corroborative" of the defendant's criminal purpose.

3. **Close proximity not required:** The Model Penal Code test will frequently confer attempt liability even where the defendant does not get very far along the path to consummation of his crime, as can be seen from the following example.

   Example: X is a government undercover narcotics agent. He tells D, a reputed drug dealer, that he is looking for some heroin. D first makes four telephone calls to locate a source, and when that doesn't work, offers to visit his contact if X will give him $650. D leaves to look for his contact, and an hour later comes back without having found him. He returns the money to X. D is arrested and charged with attempted distribution of heroin.

   Held, D's conviction affirmed. The jury could properly find that, under the Model Penal Code test, D's requesting and accepting the money was a "substantial step" towards distribution of heroin, and that it was "strongly corroborative" of D's intent to complete the crime. This was true even though the jury did not find beyond a reasonable doubt that D made any telephone calls to obtain heroin. *U.S. v. Mandujano*, 499 F.2d 370 (5th Cir. 1974).

   a. **Examples given by Code:** The tendency of the Code to require relatively little to meet the act requirement is further enhanced by a number of examples given in M.P.C. § 5.01(2)(a) through (g). These subsections give illustrations of conduct which, according to the Code, shall not be held to be, as a matter of law, insufficiently substantial steps, provided that they are "strongly corroborative" of the defendant's criminal purpose. These illustrations include the following:

      i. **"Lying in wait, searching for** or following the contemplated victim, of the crime." This subsection thus overrules *People v. Rizzo, supra*, where the defendant's act of searching for his robbery victim was held insufficient.

      ii. **"Enticing** or seeking to entice the contemplated victim of the crime to **go to the place** contemplated for its commission." (Note that this subsection is inconsistent with the holding in *U.S. v. Harper, supra*, p. 152, in which the court held that setting a "bill trap" in an ATM to entice a technician to appear so the ATM could be robbed was not a sufficient act to constitute an attempt.)

iii. ***"Reconnoitering*** the place contemplated for the commission of the crime." Thus a would-be burglar who is caught while "casing the joint" might be charged with attempted burglary.

iv. "Unlawful ***entry*** of a structure, vehicle or enclosure in which it is contemplated that the crime will be committed."

v. ***"Possession of materials*** to be employed in the commission of the crime, which are specially designed for such unlawful use or which can serve no lawful purpose of the actor under the circumstances." A would-be burglar who is stopped on the street, and found to be in possession of lock-picking tools, might be convicted of attempted burglary under this subsection.

vi. ***"Possession***, collection or fabrication of ***materials*** to be ***employed in the commission of the crime***, at or near the place contemplated for its commission, where such possession, collection or fabrication serves no lawful purpose of the actor under the circumstances." This provision, according to Comment 6(b)(vi) to M.P.C. § 5.01, is intended to be used principally in prosecutions for attempted arson. Recall, for instance, the defendant in *Commonwealth v. Peaslee*, *supra*, p. 151, who arranged combustibles in a building, but intended that they not be ignited until a later time. Under the Code, this arranging of flammable substances would itself be sufficient for an attempt (whereas the *Peaslee* court indicated that the defendant's solicitation of a third party to light the candle was also required before there could be an attempt.)

vii. ***"Soliciting*** an innocent agent to engage in conduct constituting an element of the crime." This provision is not designed to apply where the crime of solicitation has occurred. (That crime only occurs where the solicited party would be guilty of a completed crime if he did as he was asked.) Thus if the solicitee is an innocent party because the solicitor has withheld facts from him (e.g., A asks B to pick up a suit from the cleaners, and unbeknownst to B the cleaning ticket stub was stolen by A), this is not the crime of solicitation, but it can be an attempted crime (here, attempted larceny by A).

b. **Misrepresentation:**   Although the Code itself does not furnish any examples dealing with attempts to commit crimes of ***misrepresentation*** (e.g., attempted obtaining money by false pretenses), the Comment 6(b)(viii) to M.P.C. § 5.01 indicate that ***actual communication*** with the party to be defrauded is ***not necessary***, as long as the defendant has done what he believes to be necessary to make the communication.

Example: D fakes the theft of his jewelry, reports the theft to the police, and mails a claim form to Insurance Co. Even if the claim letter is never received, D has, under the Code, committed an attempt to obtain money by false pretenses, since he has taken all action which he believed necessary to communicate the misrepresentation.

4. Followed in many states: The M.P.C.'s "substantial step" test has been popular. About half the states, and two-thirds of the federal circuits, now use something like this test. K&S, p. 651.

LEXIS®-NEXIS® Searches on **THE ACT — ATTEMPT VS. MERE PREPARATION**

Sub-Topic	Suggested Searches
The proximity-to-success test	`(crime or criminal) and atleast2(attempt) and (attempt w/10 proximity w/10 success)`
The "substantial step" test	`(crime or criminal) and atleast2(attempt) and (attempt w/10 (substantial step))`

IV. IMPOSSIBILITY

A. Nature of "impossibility" defense: It frequently happens that the defendant has done everything in his power to accomplish the result he desires, but that due to external circumstances, no substantive crime is committed. He may, for instance, be a would-be pickpocket who reaches into his victim's pocket, but discovers that it is empty. Or, he may be a would-be rapist who achieves penetration, but discovers, for instance, either (a) that the victim is his wife; or (b) that the victim is dead. In such situations, the defendant will often make the argument that not only did the completed offense not occur, it *could not have occurred*. That is, there was no way, theoretically, to pick the empty pocket, or to rape either one's wife or a corpse. This sort of defense has come to be called the *"impossibility"* defense.

   1. Several kinds of "impossibility": However, the broad category of "impossibility" masks the fact that there are at least three analytically distinct kinds of situations where a claim that "the crime could not have possibly been committed" may be raised. For our purposes these will be called the defenses of "actual impossibility," "true legal impossibility" and "impossibility as to a fact governing a legal relationship." As we shall see, claims of *"factual"* impossibility almost *never succeed*, claims of *"true legal"* impossibility *always succeed*, and claims of *"factual impossibility related to legal relationships"* formerly succeeded frequently, but are much *less likely* to do so today.

B. Factual impossibility: A claim of *"factual"* impossibility arises out of the defendant's mistake concerning an issue of fact, such that had the defendant not been mistaken, he would have known that his attempt had no possibility of success. A classic example of this is the would-be pickpocket who reaches into an empty pocket; had the criminal known that the pocket was empty, he would have realized that there was no possibility of succeeding in his criminal enterprise.

   1. Not accepted as defense: Except for a few nineteenth century cases, the defense of factual impossibility has almost *never been successful*. Thus the would-be pickpocket just discussed would almost definitely be convicted of attempted larceny. As the idea is often put, impossibility is no defense in those cases where, *had the facts been as the defendant believed them to be, there would have been a crime*. Thus had the victim's pocket been filled with money, our would-be pickpocket would have been a successful one, so his claim of impossibility must fail.

   2. Other examples of factual impossibility: Thus claims of impossibility would fail in the following typical sorts of situations:

a. D points his gun at X, and pulls the trigger, but the gun does not fire because, unbeknownst to D, it is not loaded;

b. D intends to rape X, but he is unable to do so because he is impotent;

c. D is a confidence man who attempts to pull a "bunco" scheme on X (see *People v. Orndorff, supra,* p. 152), but X is a plainclothes police officer who is not fooled for a second;

d. D attempts to poison X with what his pharmacist has labeled as arsenic, but which in fact turns out to be a harmless substance.

3. Rationale for convictions: It is not hard to see why courts have generally refused to acquit in situations of "factual" impossibility like those listed above. The defendant in these situations is a *manifestly dangerous person*, whose intent is every bit as culpable as it would have been had he been right about the facts. The principal theory behind the entire law of attempts, that unsuccessful efforts should sometimes be punished, would be nullified if a mistake about external facts was exculpatory.

C. "True legal" impossibility: A different sort of impossibility defense arises where it is not only the case that what the defendant has done could not possibly be a crime, but also that *even had the facts been as the defendant supposed them to be,* no crime would have been committed. This situation occurs when the defendant is mistaken about *how an offense is defined.* That is, the defendant engages in conduct which he believes is proscribed by a statute, but he has misconstrued the meaning of the statute. In this situation, which we shall call the case of "true legal impossibility," courts will *always acquit.*

Example: D obtains a check for $2.50. He alters the numerals in the upper righthand corner, making them read "$12.50." But he does not change the written-out portion of the check, which continues to read "Two and 50/100 dollars." D is charged with attempted forgery.

Held, conviction reversed. The crime of forgery is defined as the *material* alteration of an instrument. Because the numerals are considered to be an immaterial part of the check (the amount written out in words controls), D cannot be convicted of an attempt, because what he tried to do did not violate any statute. *Wilson v. State,* 38 So. 46 (Miss. 1905).

1. Statement to policeman not perjury: Similarly, suppose that D, when questioned by a policeman during a criminal investigation, lies, and believes that lying to a policeman constitutes perjury. D will certainly not be convicted of attempted perjury, because the act he was performing (and more importantly, the act he thought he was performing) is simply not a violation of the perjury statute.

2. Relation to rule of "ignorance of law no excuse": The defense of "true legal impossibility" is a corollary of the rule that a "mistake of law" cannot be an *excuse* (see *supra,* p. 30). That is, just as a defendant who commits an act proscribed by statute cannot defend on the grounds that he did not know that such acts were prohibited, so a defendant who commits an act that he believes to be proscribed will not be guilty of an attempt.

D. Mistake of fact governing legal relationship: If the label of "legal impossibility" were applied only to cases of what we have called "true legal impossibility," there would be relatively little dispute about the validity of the legal impossibility defense. Unfortunately, however, another, analytically quite different, situation is also termed "legal impossibility" by many courts. This is the situation where the defendant has made a ***mistake of fact*** that ***bears upon legal relationships***. The classic illustration of this category is the case set forth in the following example.

Example: D is offered goods belonging to X. The goods have previously been stolen from X, but by the time the offer is made to D, they have been recovered by the police and returned to X, thereby losing their character as stolen goods. The offer to D is made as part of an undercover scheme; D makes the purchase. He is tried for an attempted violation of the statute prohibiting the knowing receipt of stolen property.

Held, conviction reversed. What D intended to do was to buy the goods in question; his act when carried out would not be a crime, since the goods were not in fact stolen. Therefore, D cannot be liable for an attempt, in part because the statute prohibiting receipt of stolen goods requires that the receipt be "knowing," and D cannot "know" goods to be stolen if they are not. (But most courts would decide the issue differently today, as is discussed below.) *People v. Jaffe*, 78 N.E. 169 (N.Y. 1906).

1. **Other illustrations:** Similarly, it has been held that where game wardens set up a stuffed deer as a decoy, and the defendant shoots it thinking that he is shooting a live deer, and knowing that it is not the hunting season, the defendant is not liable for an attempt to hunt out of season. And one who tries to bribe a person thinking that that person is a juror has been held not guilty of attempted bribery when the recipient turned out not to be a juror. See L, p. 557.

2. **Distinguished from "true legal" impossibility cases:** It is obvious that these cases are different in principle from those which we called cases of "true legal impossibility." In the true legal impossibility case, the defendant is mistaken as to ***what kind of conduct the statute prohibits***. In the "mistake of fact relating to legal relationship" case, on the other hand, the defendant understands what the statute prohibits, but mistakenly believes that the facts bring his situation within that statute. Thus the defendant in *Jaffe*, *supra*, presumably understood that it was a crime knowingly to receive stolen goods; his mistake was in believing that the goods in question were stolen.

3. **Defense now seldom accepted:** The "mistake of fact relating to legal relationships" defense has fallen on hard times in recent years. It is probably the case that the substantial majority of American jurisdictions would ***convict*** the defendant in the *Jaffe* "receipt of goods that are not really stolen" situation. Similarly, it is now standard practice for undercover narcotics agents to sell suspects a substance that purports to be heroin, but which is really sugar; the suspects are routinely convicted of attempted possession of narcotics.

   a. **Rationale:** The rationale for the modern view is that the purpose of punishing attempts is principally to ***deter dangerous conduct***. The defendant who not only believes that he is violating a statute, but who would be violating a statute if he had not made a mistake of fact, is probably at least as dangerous as the defendant who fails to commit a crime for other reasons (e.g., because he aims his gun badly.) Nor is there a compelling reason for treating mistakes as to legal relationships differently from mistakes as to other factual matters. Why should one who mistakenly believes that goods are stolen be handled more leniently than one who mistakenly believes that the substance he is administering is poison when it is really sugar?

4. **Model Penal Code view:** This modern rejection of the "mistake of fact relating to legal relationships" defense is typified by the Model Penal Code. M.P.C. § 5.01(1)(a) makes it an attempt to "purposely engage in conduct which would constitute the crime if the attendant circumstances were as [the defendant] believes them to be...." Comment 3 to M.P.C. § 5.01 states that the Code approach "...is to *eliminate the defense of impossibility in all situations*." (However, Comment 4 makes it clear that what we have called the defense of "true legal impossibility" remains: "If, according to his belief as to facts and legal relationships, the result desired or intended is not a crime, the actor will not be guilty of an attempt even though he firmly believes that his goal is criminal.")

   a. **Illustration of Model Penal Code view:** The Model Penal Code view, abolishing the defense of impossibility as to factual mistakes relating to legal issues, is illustrated by *U.S. v. Thomas*, 13 U.S.C.M.A. 278 (1962). The Ds were two Navy enlisted men who picked up a girl, X, in a bar. While one of the Ds was dancing with her, she appeared to faint from drunkenness, and the two put her in their car and had intercourse with her. It turned out that X had not fainted at the bar, but had died of a heart attack. The Ds were tried and convicted of attempted rape, and argued on appeal that since it was legally impossible to rape a corpse, they could not be guilty of attempt.

      i. **Holding:** The appellate court, however, *affirmed the convictions*, on the grounds that modern authorities such as the Model Penal Code are in favor of abolishing the defense of "legal" impossibility. (But the court noted that "...if what an accused believed to be a substantive crime was actually no crime at all, he cannot be guilty of an attempt to commit such a crime." This refers to what we have called the "true legal impossibility" defense.)

      ii. **Dissent:** A dissent in *Thomas* reviewed the classic cases allowing the legal impossibility defense, including *People v. Jaffe (supra*, p. 159), and concluded that these cases all stand for the proposition that there cannot be a conviction for attempt where "there is simply no 'victim' or thing which the particular law intended to be broken is designed to protect." Since at the moment of intercourse there was no longer a victim (but merely a corpse), there could be no attempt, according to the dissent. The dissent also stressed that the majority's view "unnecessarily emphasizes the accused's mental frame of reference at the expense of what they actually did. The common-law concept that danger to society lay chiefly in action rather than in thought has much to commend it...."

5. **Modern view criticized:** The Model Penal Code rejection of the defense of "factual impossibility related to legal relations," although it may now represent a majority position, has not been without some sound criticisms. The three principal criticisms are: (1) that the *risk of an erroneous conviction* is measurably raised; (2) that it is unwise to punish for *evil thoughts* not accompanied by evil deeds; and (3) that there is little reason to distinguish this defense from the defense of "true legal impossibility."

   a. **Risk of erroneous conviction:** When one convicts a defendant who has made a mistake of fact regarding a legal relationship, one is by hypothesis punishing him for conduct which is, to an external observer, innocent. As the proponents of the "equivocality" test for distinguishing between preparations and attempts (*supra*, p.

153) point out, punishing innocent physical acts increases the risks of convicting a completely innocent (and non-evil-intending) defendant.

   i.   Illustration from *Jaffe*:   For instance, consider the situation in *People v. Jaffe* (*supra*, p. 159), where D buys goods which, according to the prosecution, D believes to have been stolen. If the goods are not really stolen, then we have relatively little objective evidence from which to conclude that D believed them to have been stolen. If, on the other hand, the goods are *in fact* stolen, we have at least that fact to corroborate the accusation that the defendant knew them to be stolen. Since the defendant's intent can only be proved by circumstantial evidence anyway (frequently by unreliable confessions), there is a greater risk of convicting a man for intentions which were not evil if no evil conduct is required. See L, p. 559, fn. 77.

b.   Punishment for thoughts alone undesirable: Related to this argument, but analytically somewhat different, is that even putting aside the danger of convicting a man whose intentions were not evil, it is not desirable to punish *thoughts alone*, however evil they may be. This argument, too, appears in the debate about when preparations should be treated as attempts (*supra*, p. 147).

c.   Distinction unimportant: Acceptance of the Model Penal Code's view requires, as we have noted, that one distinguish between situations where the defendant's mistake is as to the scope of the relevant law (the "true legal impossibility" defense, which requires acquittal) and situations in which the defendant is mistaken as to a factual issue bearing on a legal relationship (where, as we have seen, the Code requires conviction.) A number of commentators have noted that while this distinction is real, *there is no reason to attach so much importance to it*.

   i.   Illustration: Consider, for instance, a hypothetical posed by Kadish & Schulhofer (pp. 638-40): Two friends, Mr. Fact and Mr. Law, go hunting on October 15, in a state whose law makes it a misdemeanor to hunt any time other than from October 1 to November 30. Both kill deer. Mr. Fact is under the erroneous belief that the date is September 15; Mr. Law is under the erroneous belief that the hunting season is confined to the month of November, as it was the previous year. Mr. Fact can be convicted, under the Model Penal Code view, of an attempted violation, since his mistake was one of fact regarding a legal relation (and, on the facts as he believed them to be, he would have committed a crime). Mr. Law, however, since he is mistaken about the scope of the statute on hunting, would have to be acquitted. There does not seem to be any good policy reason why different results should be reached in the two cases; certainly the two men are equally "dangerous," since they have both indicated their willingness to commit what they believe to be a violation of the same law.

E.   "Inherent" impossibility (inaptness and superstition):   So far we have considered actions by defendants which, although unsuccessful, bore a reasonable chance of culminating in a completed substantive crime. The defendant in *Jaffe*, for instance, might very well have bought goods that had in fact remained stolen; similarly, the defendants in *U.S. v. Thomas* might very well have committed rape on a living victim, except for the bizarre fortuity of her death. But suppose that the defendant's act is, to a reasonable observer, so farfetched that it had *no probability of success*. Should this fact induce us to acquit, based on a doctrine that might be called *"inherent impossibility"*?

1. **Voodoo practitioner:** The problem is most commonly posed by the hypothetical of a Haitian witch-doctor who comes to the U.S. and continues practicing voodoo. If the prosecution can show that the witch-doctor intends to kill X and believes that he can do so by sticking pins in a doll resembling X, is this attempted murder?

2. **No clear consensus:** Such situations obviously do not arise very often, and it is therefore hard to say what most courts would do in this kind of case. On the one hand, it may be argued that such a defendant should not be convicted because he is not dangerous; there was, by hypothesis, virtually no chance that he would have succeeded. On the other hand, although it is true that there was little chance that he would succeed on this particular attempt, he may try other, more reasonable means next time. The witch-doctor, for instance, may try a gun when the voodoo doesn't work.

3. **Model Penal Code allows conviction:** The Model Penal Code authorizes a *conviction* even in such cases of "inherent impossibility." See Comment 3 to M.P.C. § 5.01. However, a separate Code section, § 5.05(2), provides that "If the particular conduct charged to constitute a criminal attempt…is so inherently unlikely to result or culminate in a commission of a crime that neither such conduct nor the actor presents a public danger…the court shall exercise its power…to enter judgment and impose sentence for a crime of lower grade or degree or, in extreme cases, may dismiss the prosecution."

   a. **Witch-doctor might be convicted:** Observe that by this formulation, a prosecution against, say, the witch-doctor would be dismissed only if it were shown not only that the black magic could not possibly have succeeded, but also that the defendant himself is not dangerous to the public. This in turn requires that the court be satisfied that the defendant will not turn to other, more reasonable, means.

LEXIS®-NEXIS® Searches on **IMPOSSIBLITY**

Sub-Topic	Suggested Searches
Factual impossibility	`(crime or criminal) and attempt and (factual impossibility w/20 defense)`
Legal impossibility	`(crime or criminal) and attempt and (legal impossibility)`

V. RENUNCIATION

A. **Renunciation of criminal purpose:** Suppose that D proceeds far enough with his plan that he has committed an overt act that satisfies the *actus reus* requirement. Assuming that he has the appropriate mental state, he is now guilty of an attempt. Suppose further, however, that he then *changes his mind*, and abandons the plan. Should this for some reason "purge" him of criminality?

1. **Distinguished from substantive crimes:** If the offense were a substantive one, it is clear that no such purging would result from a change of heart; thus one who takes another's

property with intention to deprive him of it will not escape a larceny conviction by returning the goods the next day. But in the case of attempts, there are several reasons why it might be sensible to recognize the defense of *"abandonment"* or *"renunciation of purpose"*:

    a. Encourage desistance: Such a defense would encourage people to *stop short* of the completed substantive crime. Since the defense would only be relevant where the line between mere preparation and attempt had been crossed, we would be encouraging desistance by the very people we are most interested in motivating: those who are relatively close to the final crime.

    b. Lack of dangerousness: Also, if the person has abandoned his scheme, then a strong argument can be made that he has shown his *lack of dangerousness*. Since one of the purposes of punishing attempts is to incarcerate dangerous persons, this goal would not be served by denying the defense of abandonment.

    c. Lack of intent to carry through: Finally, the abandonment is relevant to the question of *mens rea* in two respects. First of all, the fact that the defendant has abandoned may show that he never had the requisite *mens rea* in the first place. Secondly, even if he did once have it, by hypothesis he no longer does, and it can be argued that it is this continuing "intent to carry through," which the defendant does not possess, that should be the required *mens rea*. See Fletcher, pp. 187-8.

  2. Arguments against defense: Reasonable arguments can be made against each of these rationales, however.

    a. Little deterrent effect: With respect to the deterrence argument ((a) above), it will be quite rare that anyone who has committed the requisite overt act, and who is willing to run the risk of being prosecuted for the completed substantive crime, will be deterred by the thought that he will not be punished for an attempt if he stops now.

    b. Dangerousness: With respect to the defendant's dangerousness (argument (b) above), while the defendant may have shown himself not to be dangerous with respect to this particular episode, it is not at all clear that he will not prove dangerous in the future, with respect to a different offense — he has already shown his theoretical willingness to violate the law.

    c. Mental state: With respect to the defendant's mental state (argument (c) above), there is no reason to treat the required *mens rea* as an ongoing "intent to carry through." Certainly if the defendant is caught by the police before he can consummate his plan, we would not require proof that he ultimately would have gone through with it (due to the universally-accepted requirement that the abandonment be voluntary, discussed *infra*); why should we make lack of an ongoing intent relevant where the abandonment is not due to external factors?

B. Modern view accepts defense: Many modern courts and statutes *recognize the defense* of abandonment in at least some situations. See Fletcher, p. 185; L, pp. 563-64.

  1. Model Penal Code allows defense: Similarly, the Model Penal Code recognizes the defense, which it calls "renunciation of criminal purpose." § 5.01(4) provides that where there has been what would otherwise be an attempt, "it is an affirmative defense that [the defendant] abandoned his effort to commit the crime or otherwise prevented its commission...." However, the Code, like virtually all case-law and statutes accepting the defense, requires that the abandonment be a ***voluntary*** one.

C. Voluntariness requirement: Suppose that D intends to shoot X to death at a particular place and time. D arrives at the projected shooting ground, but realizes that there is a police car cruising nearby, and decides to postpone his plan indefinitely so that he will not get caught. It seems apparent that we should not recognize a defense of abandonment in this situation; D has not been deterred in the long run, and he is as dangerous and self-willed as ever.

1. **Universal requirement:**   Thus it is not surprising that virtually all courts and statutes accepting the defense of abandonment require that the abandonment be *"voluntary"*. Precisely what constitutes a "voluntary" abandonment, however, is a subtle issue on which there are differences of opinion.

    a. **Threat of immediate apprehension:**   Where the defendant learns that if he goes through with his plans, he is likely to be ***immediately apprehended*** (e.g., D, the would-be murderer who sees the police car), it is clear that his abandonment should be treated as *"involuntary."*

    b. **General timidity or fear of apprehension:**   On the other hand, if the defendant abandons because of a ***generalized*** timidity or general fear of apprehension, not linked to any particular threat or occurrence, most jurisdictions will treat this as voluntary. Thus if D in the above example had simply decided that murderers are likely to get caught, and had made his decision to renounce on that basis rather than because he saw a police car, he would probably be successful with his renunciation defense. However, it will often be difficult to tell whether the defendant's abandonment was in response to a specific threat or a generalized fear; for this reason, the defense of abandonment is usually held to be an ***affirmative defense*** (one which the defendant must establish).

    c. **Postponement for better time:**   If the defendant merely ***postpones his plan***, because the scheduled time proves to be less advantageous than he thought it would be, this does ***not*** constitute a voluntary abandonment. Thus the Model Penal Code, in § 5.01(4), rules out renunciation that is "motivated by a decision to postpone the criminal conduct until a more advantageous time...."

    d. **Different victim:**   Similarly, if the defendant decides to transfer his efforts to a different, but similar, ***victim***, this will not be treated as a voluntary abandonment. See M.P.C. § 5.01(4).

    e. **Disappointment of small fruits:**   If the cause of the defendant's change of heart is that the ***anticipated fruits of the crime*** are ***smaller*** than expected, it is not clear whether most courts would regard this as voluntary. Suppose, for instance, that D is a would-be mugger who walks up to his victim, says "Your money or your life," and when he finds out that the victim has only $10, walks away in disgust. While D's motive for abandoning is certainly not morally commendable, at least one commentator (Fletcher, p. 191) states that "[o]ne finds it hard to think of [D's] activity as attempted robbery."

    f. **Dissuasion by victim:** A difficult situation is also presented where the defendant's renunciation is the result of ***dissuasion by the victim***. In general, courts are probably not too likely to find such a renunciation voluntary. For instance, if D throws X on the ground, saying that he intends to rape her, and X says "Don't do it here on the ground; if you come back to my apartment this evening I'll be glad to accommodate you," D's acceptance of the proposal will probably not be held to be voluntary.

        i. **Product of defendant's will:** But Fletcher (pp. 192-94) suggests that this case should be decided not on whether the defendant's motives were commendable, but on whether he abandoned his attempt as an exercise of will, rather than as a response to the threat of apprehension or other undesirable occurrence. Here, although X's proposal is an external factor, D has made his own decision, just as he would if he responded to X's appeals to his moral sensibilities. Thus according to Fletcher, D should be acquitted of attempted rape.

  2. **Time to abandon:** If one accepts the merits of allowing an abandonment defense, then it would seem sensible to allow the defense even once the defendant has done his ***"last act."*** Thus if D plans to burn down a building, and lights the fuse, the abandonment defense should be allowed if he comes back and stamps the fuse out. This is the approach of the Model Penal Code; See Comment 8 to M.P.C. § 5.01(4).

    a. **Forces which no longer can be stopped:** But if the defendant has not only committed his "last act," but has put in motion forces which he ***cannot stop***, then he can no longer claim abandonment. Thus if D tries to shoot X, and misses, it is too late to abandon. See M.P.C., *ibid*.

VI. ATTEMPT-LIKE CRIMES

  A. **Inchoate crimes generally:** In addition to the generalized law of attempt, there are a number of ***substantive*** crimes which also punish incompleted (***"inchoate"***) behavior.

    1. **Burglary and assault:** For instance, common-law burglary is defined as the breaking and entering of a dwelling at night with an intent to commit a felony therein (*infra*, p. 307). And one kind of assault is defined as an attempted battery. While these crimes have an aspect of completeness about them, they are in an important sense crimes which have not been brought to complete fruition; the burglar has not necessarily committed the intended felony inside the dwelling, and the assailant has not caused bodily injury to his target.

    2. **Possession crimes:** Similarly, many statutes proscribing ***possession*** of certain items represent attempts to prevent more dangerous conduct from occurring. Where possession of ***burglar's tools*** without a lawful purpose is made a statutory crime, for instance, the purpose is obviously to prevent the more serious crimes of breaking and entering, burglary, etc.

  B. **Attempt to commit attempt-like crimes:** Where defendants have been charged with attempting to commit these attempt-like crimes, they have, not surprisingly, raised the argument that it is logically impossible to ***"attempt to attempt"***, and that they therefore may not be convicted. This argument has generally ***not*** fared well.

1. **Assault:** Where the charge is for ***attempted assault***, and the assault is of the attempted-battery type, defendants have occasionally been able to get the charge dismissed on the grounds that it is logically impossible to attempt to attempt a battery. But other courts have sustained such charges, on the grounds that they do not violate common sense.

   Example: D comes looking for V, his wife, at her place of business. D is carrying a shotgun, intending to shoot V. V's co-workers hide her, so that D is unable to find her. *Held*, D's conviction of attempted assault is affirmed. It is reasonable to distinguish between assault and attempted assault, since in the former case the defendant has a *present ability* to commit harm and in the latter case he does not. *State v. Wilson*, 346 P.2d 115 (Ore. 1959).

2. **Burglary:** Defendants charged with ***attempted burglary*** have had even less success arguing that the charge is a logical absurdity than in the case of attempted assault. For instance, if D is apprehended near a jewelry store, and the police find signs of tampering on the door but no evidence that there has been actual entry, D is quite likely to be convicted of attempted burglary. See K&S, pp. 642-43.

C. **Constitutional objections to attempt-like crimes:** Where the legislature goes to unusual lengths to punish conduct on the grounds that it poses the threat of subsequent substantive criminal violation, the statute in question may be ***unconstitutional***. This has sometimes been the case with respect to *vagrancy* and *loitering* statutes.

1. ***Papachristou* case:** Thus in *Papachristou v. City of Jacksonville*, 405 U.S. 156 (1972), the Ds were charged with violating a vagrancy ordinance allowing for punishment of numerous classes of persons, including "persons wandering or strolling around from place to place without any lawful purpose or object," "habitual loafers," and "persons able to work but habitually living on the earnings of their wives or minor children...." The Supreme Court reversed, holding that the statute was ***void for vagueness*** under the 14th Amendment, because it "fails to give a person of ordinary intelligence fair notice that his contemplated conduct is forbidden by the statute," and also because it "encourages arbitrary and erratic arrests and convictions."

LEXIS®-NEXIS® Searches on **PROXIMATE CAUSE**

Sub-Topic	Suggested Searches
Renunciation of purpose, generally	crime or criminal) and attempt and ((renunciat! or renounc! or abandon! or withdraw! or withdrew) w/20 (crime))
Voluntariness requirement	crime or criminal) and attempt and ((renuncia! or renounc! or abandon! or withdraw!) w/20 voluntar!))

VII. MECHANICS OF TRIAL; PUNISHMENT

A. **Relation between charge and conviction:** It may happen that D is charged with a completed substantive crime, but the evidence at trial shows that he is guilty at most of an attempt. Conversely, he may be charged with attempt, but proof at trial may show that, if he did anything, he committed the underlying substantive crime. Such situations raise two kinds of issues:

1. **Substantive crime charged, attempt proved:** If the defendant is charged with a completed crime, and the proof shows that he committed only an attempt, American courts virtually all agree that the defendant *may be convicted of attempt*. The attempt is said to be a "lesser included offense" (that is, a lesser offense included within the indictment on the substantive crime).

2. **Attempt charged, completed crime proved:** Where the defendant is charged with an attempt, he obviously cannot be convicted of a completed crime; this would violate the principle that one is entitled to fair notice of the charges against him.

   a. **Conviction of attempt:** But the defendant in this situation may sometimes be convicted of an attempt, *even though the proof shows that the complete crime occurred*. For instance, if D is charged with attempted burglary, and it develops at trial that he actually entered the dwelling in question, he may be convicted of attempted burglary notwithstanding proof of completed burglary. Such a result is justified on the theory that the defendant should not be allowed to complain "where the determination of his case was more favorable to him than the evidence warranted." See L, pp. 566-67. (But the attempt statute may be drafted so as to make failure an element of attempt; if so, D would escape liability.)

B. **Penalties:** The penalties for attempts vary a great deal from state to state; in general, they are significantly less severe than for the completed substantive crime. Many states, for instance, authorize a sentence of up to one-half the authorized sentence for the substantive crime.

   1. **Model Penal Code takes stricter position:** The Model Penal Code is somewhat stricter. For all misdemeanors, and all felonies except those of the "first-degree," the same sentence may be given for an attempt as for the completed substantive crime. As to the first-degree felonies (e.g., murder, some kinds of rape, and kidnapping where the victim is not voluntarily released alive and in a safe place), the sentence for an attempt is limited to that which may be imposed for completed second-degree felonies (ten years maximum).

Quiz Yourself on
ATTEMPT (ENTIRE CHAPTER)

35. Boris Badanov wants to make a political statement by blowing up the United Nations Building. He does not particularly want to kill any people – he just wants to destroy the building. He sets a very powerful charge, one that if detonated will almost certainly cause the entire multi-story building to collapse. Just as he is about to press the detonator on a Friday afternoon at 3 p.m., he is arrested by the police, and the explosion does not occur. Obviously Boris can be convicted of attempted bombing; but may he be convicted of attempted *murder*?

36. Hatshepsut likes to drive fast. She gets behind the wheel one day and races through a school zone at 90 m.p.h., not caring about the possibility she may hit a child. She hits Tut King, who is crossing at a crosswalk, and serious injures him.

   (A) Suppose Hatshepsut is brought up on attempted murder charges. Can she be convicted?

(B) Suppose instead that Hatshepsut is charged with attempted involuntary manslaughter. Can she be convicted?

37. Nero, who makes a habit of torching buildings belonging to his employers, gathers a bunch of rags, papers and other combustibles in the basement of a warehouse with the intention of returning later to ignite them. He also buys 2 gallons of lighter fluid, which he stores on site. The combustibles are discovered, and Nero is tracked down and arrested. Under the Model Penal Code, can Nero be convicted of attempted arson?

38. In mid-October, Don Juan and Sancho Panza plan to burglarize Zorro's home (which they have never seen) sometime during the following week. Their plans are overheard by Zorro, who calls the police. The police arrest Don Juan and Sancho Panza on their way out of a costume shop where they have rented black masks, which they consider essential to a successful burglary. The two have not yet taken any other acts in furtherance of their burglary plan. Can Juan and Panza be convicted of attempted burglary?

39. Lucrezia Borgia slips a small amount of poison into her husband's morning coffee, intending to slowly poison him. Lucrezia knows her poisons, and knows it will take at least seven doses to kill him. After the first cup of coffee, hubby suspects something's wrong, and has the coffee analyzed in a lab. Lucrezia is immediately arrested and charged with attempted murder. Can she properly be convicted?

40. Mickey Spillane intends to kill Mike Hammer. He pulls out his gun (which he believes to be a .357 Magnum) and aims it at Hammer, saying, "Prepare to die." Unbeknownst to him, his gun has been switched with a toy, and a paper banner reading "bang" pops out when he pulls the trigger. Is Mickey guilty of attempted murder?

41. Irving Brilliant fancies himself as a legal scholar. While lacking formal training, he watches "People's Court" faithfully, and buys every alcoholic beverage endorsed by famous trial lawyers. Irving's back yard is a popular watering hole for crows. One day, Irv takes out his shotgun and shoots at one of the crows, even though he believes this violates the Migratory Birds Act of 1918. Unbeknownst to Irving, the Migratory Birds Act does not apply to crows, because they don't migrate in the way the act covers. Can Irving be convicted for attempted violation of the Migratory Birds Act?

42. Phil Goode is a small-time drug dealer. After his previous supplier is arrested, Phil changes to a new supplier, Yuwanna Bye. In their first transaction, Yuwanna sells Phil 10 packets that he says are cocaine. Phil goes out on the street, and begins "advertising" the bags as cocaine, and selling them. He sells one bag to Narco, who unbeknownst to Phil is an undercover narcotics officer. Narco immediately arrests Phil. Upon testing, the packet proves to contain only talcum powder, a substance that is not banned. Phil is charged with attempting to distribute cocaine, and evidence at his trial shows that Phil in fact believed that the substance was cocaine. May Phil properly be convicted?

————————————————————

Answers

35. Yes, probably. In general, crimes of attempt require that the defendant have the specific intention of bringing about the criminal result required for the underlying crime he is charged with attempting. Thus normally, one could not be convicted of attempted murder by recklessly bringing about a near-killing, since the result embodied in the definition of murder is a killing, and for attempted murder one must therefore intend (not merely recklessly disregard the possibility of) a killing. But where the defendant *knows with substantial certainty* that a particular result will follow from his contemplated action, most courts (and the M.P.C.) take the position that this is tantamount to an intent to bring about that result. So here, since Boris knows with substantial certainty that if he carries out his plan people will die (after all, the building is full on a Friday afternoon and Boris knows the building will collapse if there's an explosion), Boris will be deemed to have intended to bring about killings. Consequently, he may be convicted of attempted murder.

36. **(A) No.** Where a crime is defined in terms of bringing about a certain result, the mental state required for an attempt to commit that crime is normally an *intent* to bring about that result. The mere fact that the defendant had a mental state that would have sufficed for the underlying crime does not suffice. Murder is defined to require, inter alia, a killing of another. Therefore, a person can be convicted of attempted murder only if she intends to kill another. The fact that Hatshepsut may have behaved with a mental state adequate for reckless-indifference murder (a wanton indifference to the value of human life) will not suffice for the crime of attempted murder.

(B) No, for the same reason as in (A). That is, where a crime is defined as recklessly bringing about a certain result (here, a death), there can be no attempt to commit that crime. So the fact that Hatshepsut had the mental state that would suffice for involuntary manslaughter (recklessly causing the death of another) is irrelevant on the attempted manslaughter charge.

37. **Yes, because he took a "substantial step" towards committing the crime.** As in all jurisdictions, under the M.P.C. a defendant cannot be convicted of an attempt unless he takes some sort of act in furtherance of his criminal plan. Under the M.P.C., that act (or multiple acts) must satisfy two requirements: (1) it constitutes a "substantial step" in a course of conduct planned to culminate in the commission of a crime; and (2) it is "strongly corroborative" of the defendant's criminal purpose. Here, Nero's conduct satisfies both requirements: (1) gathering all the materials needed for a crime will generally constitute a "substantial step" towards commission of that crime, and certainly does so here; and (2) there is no innocent explanation for Nero's gathering activities, so they're "strongly corroborative" of the proposition that he planned to burn down the building. Indeed, M.P.C. § 5.01(2)(f) contains a special provision covering these facts quite precisely: activities shall be considered sufficiently corroborative if they consist of "possession [or] collection … of materials to be employed in the commission of the crime, at or near the place contemplated for its commission, where such possession [or] collection … serves no lawful purpose of the actor under the circumstances."

38. **Probably not, because their preparations have not come close enough to success.** Courts vary as to how far along the defendants' preparations must have advanced before they give rise to attempt liability. But under virtually any test, it's unlikely that the Ds here advanced sufficiently. Under the popular "dangerous proximity to success" test, for instance, the purchase of the masks did not make the Ds dangerously close to success — there's no evidence that they picked a particular time for the burglary, for instance, and they haven't reconnoitered the scene to determine a point of entry. Even under the relatively easy-to-satisfy 2-part M.P.C. test (summarized in the answer to the previous question), the preparations here probably would not succeed: the purchase of the masks might be a "substantial step" towards commission of the crime (though this is debatable), but it's unlikely that a court would find that the rental of the masks "strongly corroborated" the burglary — the masks might have been rented just for upcoming Halloween, for instance.

39. **Yes, probably.** The precise analysis will depend on exactly what test is used by the court. Under the "dangerous proximity to success" test, the prosecution's case is probably the weakest, but even here, a court would probably conclude that if hubby had drunk the first cup without complaint, it wouldn't have taken too long for him to consume another six cups on, say, six consecutive mornings. The "probable desistance" approach is almost certain to lead to a conviction, since one who administers one dose of a poison is unlikely to voluntarily abandon the plan. The "equivocality" test is also easily satisfied, since Lucre-

zia's actions are not the slightest bit equivocal — it's perfectly obvious that one who puts poison in a person's cup wants to kill or at least seriously injure the drinker. Finally, the M.P.C.'s "substantial step" approach is clearly satisfied: administering the first dose of fatal poison is obviously a substantial step towards carrying out the completed poisoning, and it's certainly a step that's "strongly corroborative" of the defendant's ultimate criminal plan (there's no alternative explanation for the poison).

40. **Yes, because "factual impossibility" is not a defense.** Mickey certainly satisfies the mental state for attempted murder (intent to commit a killing), and has done everything reasonably in his power to bring that result about. The question, of course, is whether Mickey can use the defense of impossibility. Here, the defense would have to be "factual impossibility" — that is, Mickey is claiming that he made a mistake on an issue of fact, such that had he not made the mistake, he would have known that his plan had no possibility of success. The defense of factual impossibility is not accepted by any court. Indeed, the present setting — defendant uses a weapon that malfunctions — is almost the archetypal illustration of the universally-rejected factual-impossibility defense.

41. **No.** This is a case of *"true legal impossibility."* That is, the mistake is a pure mistake of law — Irving's only mistake is about *how a particular offense is defined.* Even if all the surrounding facts (except for legal definitions) had been as Irving believed them to be, his actions would still not have been a crime, because it is simply not a crime to shoot crows. Therefore, the defense of true legal impossibility — which is accepted in all courts — protects Irving from attempt liability.

42. **Yes.** Phil could assert a variant of the impossibility defense, namely, what might be called *"factual impossibility related to legal relationships."* But in general, courts reject this defense almost universally now, just as they reject garden-variety claims of factual impossibility. The issue for most courts is whether, had the facts been as the defendant supposed, the defendant would have committed a crime. Here, had the packet really contained cocaine rather than talcum powder, Phil would have committed the crime of drug sale; therefore, he can be convicted of attempting to commit that crime. (In an analogous situation, defendants are convicted every day of "attempted purchase" of drugs, where they buy from an undercover officer what they think is an illegal drug but what is in fact a harmless substance such as sugar.)

Be sure to distinguish the unsuccessful defense of "factual impossibility related to legal relationships," which is what's at issue here, from the successful defense of "true legal impossibility," as in the previous question. Where the defendant's mistake consists of a mistake about how an offense is defined, that's true legal impossibility, and is successful. (For instance, had Phil mistakenly believed that it was a crime to sell talcum powder without a license and then sold what he knew was talcum powder without a license, he'd have a valid defense to, say, a charge of attempted illegal sales of merchandise.) But where the defendant's mistake consists of a mistaken belief about the nature of a particular object, the fact that the mistake relates to the object's legal status doesn't help the defendant. So here, Phil's mistake was a factual mistake about the nature of the bags he was selling (not a "purely legal" mistake about how a particular crime is defined), so he's no different than a person who makes a mistake of fact about some non-legal subject, like whether a gun is loaded — his essentially factual mistake doesn't lead to a valid defense.

 *Exam Tips on*
ATTEMPT

When a defendant is unsuccessful in committing a substantive crime, consider a charge of criminal attempt.

☛ **Definition of "attempt":** You should have a general definition of "attempt" in mind. A good definition (but not necessarily precisely the law in any particular jurisdiction) would be: A person is guilty of a criminal attempt when: (1) with an *intent to commit acts* that are the *actus reus* for a particular *substantive crime*, she (2) takes a *substantial step* towards the commission of that crime.

Mental State

☛ **Specific intent required:** Remember that *specific intent* is required, regardless of the level of intent necessary to be convicted of the completed offense. That is, D must *intend to take an act* (or bring about a result) that, if committed, would constitute the underlying crime.

   ☞ **Strict liability, negligence or recklessness:** Thus if an underlying crime is defined to require only negligence, recklessness or even no mental state at all (i.e., a strict liability crime), that state of mind won't be enough for an attempt to commit that underlying crime.

   Example: The state Liquor Sales Act prohibits the sale of liquor between the hours of midnight and 8 A.M., regardless of the mental state of the seller. V, an undercover police officer pretending to be a customer, enters a liquor store and asks to buy a bottle of vodka. D, an employee, looks at the clock and it reads five minutes after eleven in the evening. D does not realize that there was a change to daylight savings time the night before and that the store's clock has not been changed. Just as D is about to hand over the bottle and receive V's money, V arrests him, and charges him with an attempt to violate the Liquor Sales Act. D can't be convicted, under the majority view, because he didn't intend to commit an act (*after-hours* sale of liquor) that was prohibited by the underlying statute. This is so even though D would have been guilty of violating the underlying statute had he finished the transaction.

   ☞ **Attempted murder:** If the crime is defined in terms of a particular result, the required mental state is the desire to bring about that result. Thus, since murder is defined in terms of a result (death of another), in order to successfully prosecute for *attempted murder* the defendant must have had the specific intent to cause that result (*death of another*).

   Example: D, while trying to study for an exam, hears a loud argument coming from V's house across the street. She fires a rifle out her own window and into the front window of the living room of V's house, which D thinks is vacant. D's motive is merely to frighten V and the other arguer into silence. Unbeknownst to D, V is in fact in the living room, and is hit in the leg. V survives. D can't be convicted of attempted murder, because she didn't intend to bring about V's death. That's true even though, had V died from the shot, D would probably have been guilty of actual murder (of the depraved-indifference variety).

Requirement of Act

☛ **"Substantial step" test):** Remember that under the modern/Model-Penal-Code approach, the requirement of an act is met by any act that is a *"substantial step"* towards completion of the underlying crime.

> *Example:* X wants to test the faithfulness of his girlfriend, G, and if she proves to be unfaithful, to kill her. X plans with Y to give Y a box of chocolates laced with poison. Y is to pretend to like G, and to offer her the chocolates. If she accepts the chocolates, then X will believe her to be unfaithful and deserving to die (from the poison). X brings the box of poisoned chocolates to the pool hall he and Y frequent and places the chocolates near his coat on the bench. Somebody else takes the chocolates (and throws them away without eating them), so X can't give them to Y. X's act of poisoning the chocolates and bringing them to the pool hall would probably be found to constitute a substantial step toward completion of the crime of murdering G, despite the fact that the chocolates were never given to G.

Impossibility

☞ **Factual impossibility:** Look for a fact pattern where: (1) *had the facts been as D believed them to be, his act would have constituted a crime*; but (2) under the facts as they really were, his act did not constitute a completed crime. This is *"factual impossibility,"* and it is *not a valid defense*.

Examples:

[1] D shoots to kill V, whom he believes is asleep, but V actually died of a heart attack moments before. (This is still attempted murder.)

[2] D shoots to kill V with an unloaded gun, although D thinks it's loaded. (This is still attempted murder.)

[3] D puts LSD into chocolate intending to kill the person consuming it, but does not know that the amount of LSD put into the food cannot cause death. (This is still attempted murder).

☞ **Factual mistake bearing on legal relations:** Where D's mistake is a factual mistake about the *legal status* of some person or thing, the mistake is still not a defense, any more than any other kind of factual mistake is a defense. So if D is mistaken about whether V is still alive (Example 1 above) or mistaken about whether a car is stolen (see example below), this won't be a defense to an attempt charge.

Example: X and Y, undercover police officers, pretend to be criminals in order to catch D, a criminal known to buy and sell stolen cars. X meets D and tells him that Y is looking for a buyer for stolen cars. After D says that he might be interested in buying one for resale, X offers to buy it with him as a partner. X sets up a meeting between D and Y. Y offers to sell D what he says is a stolen car. (The car has actually been requisitioned from the police department.) D pays Y for the car.

Although the car was not actually "stolen property" (so D cannot be convicted of receiving stolen property), he's guilty of attempt to receive stolen property. That's because D's factual mistake about legal status (whether the car was stolen) is irrelevant, since had the facts been as D thought they were, he would have completed the crime of receiving stolen property.

☞ **True legal impossibility (mistake about how a crime is defined):** On the other hand, if D's mistake is about *how a particular crime is defined* — that is, D thinks his act matches the definition but it really doesn't — then this *is* a defense. This is the defense of *"true legal impossibility."* (But be sure to distinguish between this true legal-impossibility situation, and the "factual mistake bearing on legal relations" situation, described above, that *isn't* a defense).

Example 1: Due to the advice of an attorney, D believes that the crime of arson in her jurisdiction covers the intentional burning of any dwelling, although it actually applies only to the dwelling of "another." With a belief that she is committing arson, D burns down her house in order to collect insurance proceeds. D thought she was committing arson, but she may not be charged with attempted arson. The defense of "legal impossibility" applies: D's mistake was a mistake about how the crime of arson is defined.

Example 2: Until recently, the hunting season for the flivver, a rare migratory bird, was restricted to March and April. The law fixing the hunting season was recently amended to permit hunting during May and June. D, unaware of the change in the law, decides to go flivver hunting in May, because he does not like to compete with other hunters. D shoots and kills a flivver. Despite the fact that D thought he was in violation of the hunting law, he may not be charged with an attempt to violate it. Again, the defense of legal impossibility applies: D's mistake was a mistake about how the crime of flivver-hunting is defined.

Merger, and Convictions of Both Attempt and the Underlying Crime

☛ **Merger:** Remember that a lesser included offense, such as attempt, *merges* with the more serious one if the crime was completed — merger means that D can't be convicted of both.

☞ **No merger of attempt and conspiracy:** However, remember that the crime of attempt *does not merge with conspiracy*, so a person can be convicted of both, arising out of a single fact pattern and a single underlying crime.

Example: X and Y agree to kill V. Y loads the gun, and X pulls the trigger. The bullet misses. X and Y can each be convicted of *both* attempted murder *and* conspiracy to commit murder.

☛ **Standalone prosecution for attempt:** Also, remember that the prosecutor can choose to charge the defendant *only* with attempt, even if a conviction for the substantive crime could have been attained.

Example: D shoots at V, intending to kill him. V is wounded, and dies in the hospital. D can't be convicted of both murder and attempted murder. But the prosecutor may choose to bring just an attempted-murder charge; D may be convicted of that charge, even though the facts might also support a murder conviction.

CHAPTER 6

CONSPIRACY

Introductory Note: When two or more people agree to commit an act that is a crime, they can be convicted of "conspiracy" to do that act. This is true even if they don't ever carry out the crime itself. (In fact, in most states, they can be convicted even if they don't do anything more than make the agreement, and never carry out *any acts* in furtherance of the conspiracy). Conspiracy is an increasingly important prosecutorial tool whenever groups of people plan to commit crimes together.

I. INTRODUCTION

A. **Definition of "conspiracy":** The common-law crime of *conspiracy* is defined as *an agreement between two or more persons to do either an unlawful act or a lawful act by unlawful means.* At common law, the prosecution is required to show the following elements:

1. **Agreement:** An *agreement* between two or more persons;

2. **Objective:** To carry out an act which is either *unlawful* or which is lawful but to be accomplished by unlawful means;

3. *Mens rea:* A *culpable intent* on the part of the defendant. In the usual case of a conspiracy to commit an act that would be a crime, the intent must consist of at least the mental state *required for the object crime.* (For instance, for conspiracy to commit murder, each conspirator must have an intent that would suffice for the crime of murder.)

B. **Purposes of conspiracy law:** There are two principal purposes that are served by defining and proscribing the crime of conspiracy:

1. **Inchoate crime:** First, since a conspiracy may be (and frequently is) found where no substantive crime is ever committed, society is able to stop conduct before the harmful effects of substantive criminality occur. Thus conspiracy is an "inchoate" crime, and serves the same functions as the law of attempts (*supra*, p. 146).

2. **Group activity:** Secondly, it is often felt that *group activity* of a criminal nature is *more dangerous* than criminal conduct engaged in by an individual working alone. Under conventional theory, persons working in combination will give each other courage, dissuade each other from abandoning the criminal plan, and render each other mutual assistance that makes the ultimate success of the crime more likely. Thus the law of conspiracy serves a function of policing group activity.

   a. **Contrary view:** Others have pointed out, however, that there is no empirical evidence that group criminality is more likely to succeed than solo activity, and that there are theoretical reasons why this may not be so. For instance, the risk of a *leak* to law enforcement authorities, and the risk that one of the participants may be an undercover agent, are obviously potent anti-success factors that are not present when an individual works alone. See Commentary to M.P.C. § 5.03, fn. 17.

C. **Procedural advantages:** Conspiracy law furnishes the prosecutor with a potent weapon. Substantively, he is given extraordinary latitude in some states, which define conspiracy as an agreement to do not only criminal acts, but acts that are "immoral," "contrary to the public interest," or some other vague phrase. (See the fuller discussion of this aspect *infra*, p. 182). Even more significantly, a number of *procedural* advantages come to the prosecutor in a conspiracy case. We discuss two of these advantages here.

1. **Joint trial:** Joinder laws in virtually all states permit the prosecution to try in a ***single proceeding*** all persons indicted on a single conspiracy charge. Such a joint trial saves the prosecution a great deal of work, since the case only has to be presented once; furthermore, witnesses are likely to be much more willing to testify a single time than in multiple proceedings.

2. **Admission of hearsay:** Perhaps the most devastating procedural advantage available to the prosecution in a conspiracy trial is the ***exclusion*** from normal ***hearsay*** evidence rules given for statements made by a defendant's ***co-conspirator*** in furtherance of the conspiracy. Normally, the rule against hearsay evidence prevents the in-court repetition of a previous statement by one person to be used against a different person (i.e., the defendant). But in a conspiracy case, the rule is that ***any previous incriminating statement by any member of the conspiracy, if made in furtherance of the conspiracy, may be introduced into evidence against all of the conspirators***. See, e.g., Federal Rule of Evidence 801(d)(2)(E), codifying the common-law rule that a statement is admissible, and not excludable hearsay, if it is offered against a party and is "a statement by a co-conspirator of [the] party during the course and in furtherance of the conspiracy."

   a. **Rationale:** This rule is generally defended on the grounds that, by agreeing to pursue criminal ends together, all of the conspirators have authorized each of them to act as "agent" for all of them, and an agent's statements are binding against his "principal." The use of this exception to the hearsay rule can be demonstrated by the following example.

   Example: D1, D2 and D3 are charged with conspiracy to rob a bank. Before the robbery occurs, D1, the organizer of the plan, tells his mistress, X, that D3's part in the plan is to steal a getaway car. (D3 makes this statement in an unsuccessful attempt to recruit X to the conspiracy.) At trial, the prosecution has X repeat this statement in its case against D3, who is convicted with D1 and D2. Assuming that there is enough *non*-hearsay evidence to show, by a preponderance of the evidence, that D3 and D1 were a part of a conspiracy, the statements to X were properly admitted against D3, on the theory that the statement were acts in furtherance of the conspiracy, and were implicitly authorized by D3.

II. THE AGREEMENT

A. **"Meeting of the minds" not required:** As noted, the essence of a conspiracy is an ***agreement*** for the joint pursuit of unlawful ends. However, the sort of "agreement" that is required is not a true "meeting of the minds" of the kind necessary for a legally enforceable contract.

All that is necessary is that the parties communicate to each other in some way their intention to pursue a joint objective.

1. **Implied agreement:** The agreement does not have to be reached in words; each of two parties might, *by his actions alone*, make it clear to the other that they will pursue a common objective. For instance, if A is in the process of mugging X on the street, and V comes along and helps pin X to the ground while A takes his wallet, a conspiracy to commit larceny or robbery might well be found, despite the absence of any spoken communication.

2. **Proof by circumstantial evidence:** Furthermore, courts are very liberal as to the *proof* that must be given of the agreement's existence. Unless one of the co-conspirators turns state's evidence, the prosecution is unlikely to be able to prove through direct testimony that an agreement was reached. Therefore, the prosecution is normally permitted to prove the agreement merely by *circumstantial evidence*, that is, evidence of the acts committed by the party, in circumstances strongly suggesting that *there must have been a common plan*.

   Example: The Ds claim to be "citizens" of the "Republic of New Africa" (RNA) in Jackson, Mississippi; RNA is composed of black Americans who are descended from African slaves. In the midst of a stake-out by FBI agents, several RNA members shoot and wound some of the agents and kill a local policeman. The gunmen, and several other RNA members, are charged with, *inter alia*, conspiracy to assault a Federal officer. The evidence shows that the gunmen acted almost simultaneously, in what appears to have been a coordinated attack on the agents.

   Held, convictions affirmed. The conduct of the shoot-out was "strong evidence of a common plan and certainly showed concerted action." The existence of an agreement, rather than haphazard self-defense, is buttressed by testimony that the RNA members organized highly regimented "combat-win" drills to train for an anticipated attack by law enforcement personnel. (Also, even those defendants who were not present at the shoot-out, but who participated in the drills, may be convicted of the conspiracy.) *U.S. v. James*, 528 F.2d 999 (5th Cir. 1976).

   a. **But must be some agreement:** But the rule permitting proof of agreement by circumstantial evidence does not dispense with the need for showing that there was indeed an agreement. Suppose, for instance, that the jury in *James, supra*, believed that the RNA members spontaneously and individually decided to shoot at the FBI agents; the mere fact that they were pursuing a common objective would not have been enough to sustain a conspiracy conviction. "[C]oncurrence of acts is only evidence of conspiracy, not equivalent to conspiracy." (Glanville Williams, quoted in K&S, p. 801.)

B. **Aiding and abetting:** As is discussed *infra*, p. 205, under the rules of accomplice liability a person may become liable for the substantive crimes of another merely by *furnishing assistance* to that other person. Does accomplice liability extend to the substantive crime of conspiracy, so that one who "aids and abets" a conspiracy is guilty of conspiracy, despite the fact that he has not reached even a tacit agreement with the conspirators to help them?

1. **Illustration:** The question is illustrated by a well-known murder case, *State ex rel. Attorney General v. Tally*, 15 So. 722 (Ala. 1894). D, a judge, knew that A and B planned to kill X. D, without making any agreement with A and B, prevented a telegram of warning from reaching X; X therefore did not flee, and A and B killed him. D was convicted of aiding and abetting the murder of X, and was therefore held liable of the substantive crime of murder under accomplice liability principles. Our present question becomes: is D also guilty of *conspiracy* to murder X, even though there was no agreement between him and A and B? Courts are split on this question.

    a. **View favoring liability:** In favor of finding a conspiracy in this situation, it can be argued that D knew he was serving an existing conspiracy, and he therefore had as great an evil intent, and as much willingness to act affirmatively in furtherance of that intent, as if he had made an agreement with A and B.

    b. **View against liability:** On the other hand, since conspiracy is defined as an "agreement," it can be argued that one aids and abets conspiracy only by *aiding the act of agreement* (e.g., by bringing A and B together and helping them agree on a plan), not by aiding and abetting the substantive object crime. (See L, p. 578.)

        i. **Unfairness:** Furthermore, as the draftsmen of the Model Penal Code point out, there are so many severe implications to being treated as a member of a conspiracy (e.g., admissibility of declarations by one conspirator against another, despite hearsay rule) that it may be unfair to treat the aider and abettor as a full-fledged conspirator when he has not become part of the agreement. See Comment 2(c)(iv) to M.P.C. § 5.03. Accordingly, under the Code, the aider and abettor is liable for the substantive object crime if the conspirators commit it. But he does *not* become a co-conspirator merely by aiding and abetting the conspirators.

C. **Parties do not agree to commit object crime:**   Although there must be an agreement, it is not necessary that each conspirator agree to commit the *substantive object crime(s)* (or "immoral act," etc.; see *infra*, p. 182). A particular defendant can be a conspirator even though he agreed to help only in the *planning stages*. Thus in the example on p. 175), D3 would be guilty of conspiracy to commit bank robbery even though he has only agreed to obtain the getaway car, not to participate in the bank robbery itself.

D. **Feigned agreement:** Suppose A and B verbally agree with each other that they will rob a bank, but B is secretly an *undercover agent*, and never has any intention of committing the robbery (and in fact plans to have A arrested before he can go much further). In this situation, has the requirement of an "agreement" been met?

    1. **Traditional view that there is no conspiracy:** The traditional view is that there is *no agreement*, and therefore *no conspiracy*.

    2. **Modern view allows conspiracy finding:** Modern courts, however, generally hold that despite the lack of subjective intent on the part of one conspirator to carry out the object crime, *the other party may nonetheless be convicted of conspiracy*.

        Example: D agrees with his cousin that the two of them will murder D's mother. The cousin turns D into the police, and testifies at D's conspiracy trial that he, the cousin, never had any intention of carrying out the plan. *Held*, D was properly convicted. "[A] man who believes he is conspiring to commit a crime and wishes to conspire to commit a crime has a guilty mind and has done all in his power to plot the commission of an unlawful purpose," even if the other party has no intention of cooperating. *State v. St. Christopher*, 232 N.W.2d 798 (Minn. 1975).

    a. Model Penal Code agrees: The Model Penal Code agrees with this result, although it reaches it in a slightly different way. The Code follows a *"unilateral"* approach to conspiracy, rather than the traditional "bilateral" one. That is, it does not define conspiracy as an agreement "between two or more persons," but rather, makes an individual liable for conspiracy if he "agrees with [an] other person or persons." M.P.C. § 5.03(1)(a). Under this formulation, since the individual defendant has intended to reach an agreement, he meets the statutory requirement even though the other person is in reality not part of the plan. Comment 2(c)(iv) to M.P.C. § 5.03 concedes that "the project's chances of success have not been increased by the agreement; indeed, its doom may have been sealed by this turn of events." But in view of the evidence that the defendant has had a firm purpose to carry out the plan, the Code draftsmen believe a conspiracy conviction to be justified.

E. Knowledge of the identity of other conspirator: Because the necessary "agreement" does not have to be an explicit one (*supra*, p. 176), it may be the case that a defendant is held to have conspired with a person whom he had never met, and whose precise *identity he was not aware of.* For instance, if A agrees with B to rob a bank, and B then agrees with C with respect to a different aspect of the same bank robbery plan, A and C may be held to have been part of the same conspiracy, even though they may never have met each other, or even known of each other's precise identity. (However, it is probably necessary that each of them at least knew that there was some person other than B in the conspiracy.) This topic is discussed further in the treatment of "wheel" and "chain" conspiracies *infra*, p. 186.

III. *MENS REA*

A. The intent requirement generally: Since, as noted, the essence of a conspiracy is an "agreement," there must be, on the part of each conspirator, an *intent to agree*. (An "agreement" is, by definition, a product of intent.) But beyond the intent to reach an agreement, the conspirator must be shown to have had a *further, unlawful, intent*. It is this further intent that we now examine.

B. Intent to commit object crime: In many jurisdictions, the conspirators must be shown to have agreed to commit a *crime* (although some jurisdictions permit conviction based upon an agreement to accomplish an "immoral act"; see *infra*, p. 182). Assuming that the prosecution is for conspiracy to commit a criminal act, it is universally held that each of the conspirators must be shown to have had *at least the mental state required for the object crime.*

Example: Suppose that A and B are caught trying to break into a dwelling at night. They can be convicted of conspiracy to commit burglary only if it is shown that they had the intent necessary for the crime of burglary, i.e., not only an intent to break and enter, but also an intent to commit a felony once they got inside.

1. **Must have intent to achieve objective:** Furthermore, a conspiracy to commit certain crimes defined in terms of causing a *harmful result* may require a mental state that is *more culpable* than needed for the object crime itself. The conspirators must be shown to have *intended to bring about that result*, even though such an intent may not be necessary for conviction of the substantive crime.

    a. **Illustration:** Consider an example put by the draftsmen of the Model Penal Code: assume that A and B plan to blow up a building by exploding a bomb. If they know that there are persons in the building who are highly likely to be killed, and they go through with the plan, they will be liable for the completed crime of murder if death results (because murder may be committed with "reckless disregard" of the danger of death, rather than intent to kill; see *infra*, p. 235). But they will *not* be guilty of conspiracy to murder the inhabitants, because they did not have an *affirmative intent to bring about death*. See Comment 2(c)(i) to M.P.C. § 5.03.

2. **Crime of recklessness or negligence:** It follows from the intent requirement that there can be no conspiracy to commit a crime that is defined in terms of *recklessly or negligently* causing a particular result. For instance, where the crime of involuntary manslaughter is defined as the causing of death due to criminal negligence (*infra*, p. 257), there can be no conspiracy to commit such manslaughter; either one plans to bring about a death, in which case it is conspiracy to murder, or one behaves negligently (even in conjunction with the negligence of others) in which case there is no conspiracy to commit any homicide crime.

3. **Strict-liability crimes:** Where the defendants are charged with conspiring to commit a crime that has no *mens rea* requirement (i.e., a *strict-liability* crime; see *supra*, p. 21), it is usually agreed that they must be shown to have *intended* to bring about the result in question. As Learned Hand put it, "While one may, for instance, be guilty of running past a traffic light of whose existence one is ignorant, one cannot be guilty of conspiring to run past such a light, for one cannot agree to run past a light unless one supposes that there is a light to run past." *U.S. v. Crimmins*, 123 F.2d 271 (2d Cir. 1941).

    a. **Ignorance of law:** But it is not usually required that, to be liable for conspiracy, the defendants have understood that the act they intended to commit was a crime. If A and B agree to race their cars through a red light, they can be convicted of a conspiracy to do so even if they are able to prove that they did not know it was a crime to go through a red light.

4. **Attendant circumstances:** An offense defined completely in strict-liability terms must be distinguished from a crime with *several elements*, as to which only *some* require intent or knowledge. As a result of a Supreme Court ruling, one *can be convicted* of conspiring to commit such a crime even though one may have been unaware of the facts fulfilling the strict-liability elements of the crime. These strict-liability elements typically have to do with *"attendant circumstances"* surrounding commission of the crime.

    a. **Federal jurisdiction:** The issue arises most frequently with respect to crimes some elements of which relate principally or solely to the existence of *federal jurisdiction*. For instance, the federal mail fraud statute applies only where fraud is committed through use of the mails. One who actually uses the mails may be convicted of the substantive crime of mail fraud, even though it is not shown that he knew that the mails had been used. But until the Supreme Court's decision in *U.S. v. Feola*, 420 U.S. 671 (1975), it was not clear whether a defendant could be convicted of **conspiracy** to commit mail fraud if it were not shown that he intended to use the mails. *Feola* shows that the answer is yes.

    b. ***Feola* case:**   In *Feola*, the Ds were involved in a classic narcotics "scam," in which they attempted to have their victim pay them for heroin, but give him merely powdered sugar. When the victim got suspicious, the Ds attempted to beat him up. Unbeknownst to them, the victim was a federal narcotics agent. The Ds were charged with conspiring to commit an assault on a federal officer engaged in performance of his duties. The Ds argued that, since they did not know that the victim was a federal officer, they could not be convicted of conspiracy to assault a federal official.

        i. **Conviction affirmed:**   The Supreme Court *rejected* this contention. The Court noted first that the "federal officer" requirement is ***purely jurisdictional***. Furthermore, the Court found that Congress, in enacting the substantive statute, had intended in part to protect federal law enforcement personnel, and that a strict *mens rea* requirement in conspiracy cases would tend to defeat this congressional purpose.

    c. **Model Penal Code view:**   In state prosecutions, where a crime is similarly defined so as to include attendant circumstances as to which knowledge or intent does not have to be proved, it is not clear whether the states will follow the lead of *Feola* and allow conspiracy conviction where such intent or knowledge is absent. The Model Penal Code does not explicitly resolve this problem, but the draftsmen state that they believe it to be "strongly arguable" that the *mens rea* requirement should be found to be met in such a conspiracy prosecution, even though intent or knowledge with respect to the attendant circumstances is lacking. See Comment 2(c)(ii) to M.P.C. § 5.03.

C. Supplying of goods and services: The defendants must, as noted, be shown to have *intended* to further a criminal objective. It is generally not enough that a particular defendant merely *knew* that his acts might tend to enable others to pursue criminal ends. One situation in which courts are often required to distinguish between intent and mere knowledge occurs when a person *supplies goods or services* to others with knowledge that what he supplies will be used to further criminal ends. Can the supplier be said to have joined a conspiracy?

    1. Mere knowledge usually insufficient: Generally, *something more than mere knowledge* is necessary to show an intent to further the criminal objective. Courts have found the following elements to be enough "extra" (beyond knowledge) to make the supplier a member of the conspiracy:

        a. "Stake in venture":   The supplier will be held to have joined the conspiracy if the nature of his sales shows that he in some sense acquired a *"stake in the venture."* (But this is not shown merely by the fact that he made profits from selling items which the conspirators would not have bought had they not been engaged in the criminal activity in question.) For instance, if he agrees to postpone payment until he can be paid out of proceeds of the crime — or if he agrees to be paid a fixed percentage of the proceeds from the crime — he'll have a stake in the venture and therefore be deemed to be part of the conspiracy.

b. Controlled commodities: The supplier is more likely to be held to have been a participant in the conspiracy if the substance sold was a ***governmentally-controlled*** one that, in the quantities in question, could, to the supplier's knowledge, only have been used for illegal purposes.

c. Inflated charges: If the supplier is charging his criminal purchasers an ***inflated price*** compared with what the items would cost when sold for legal purposes, this is evidence of his intent to further the criminal purposes. See *People v. Lauria*, discussed *infra*, citing this factor.

d. Large proportion of sales: If sales to criminal purchasers represent a ***large proportion*** of the supplier's overall sales of the item, he is more likely to be held to have had the requisite intent.

e. Serious crime: The supplier's participation in illegal activity is more likely to be found where the illegal activity is known to the supplier to constitute a ***serious crime***, than where the end use is a misdemeanor.

Example: D1 runs a telephone answering service. The service numbers among its clients several prostitutes, for whom the service processes messages from potential clients. D1 and the prostitutes are charged with conspiracy to commit prostitution; prostitution is a misdemeanor. The evidence shows that D1 knew that the clients in question were prostitutes, but no acts by him in furtherance of their trade are proven except for the taking of messages.

Held, D1's conviction reversed. If one supplies goods or services that one knows will be used for a serious crime, his intent to facilitate that crime may be inferred from this alone. "For instance, we think the operator of a telephone answering service with positive knowledge that his service was being used to facilitate the extortion of ransom, the distribution of heroin, or the passing of counterfeit money who continued to furnish the service with knowledge of its use, might be chargeable on knowledge alone with participation in a scheme to extort money, to distribute narcotics, or to pass counterfeit money. The same result would follow the seller of gasoline who knew the buyer was using his product to make Molotov cocktails for terroristic use." But where, as here, the end use constitutes only a misdemeanor, mere knowledge of it is not enough. Since there are no other indications of D1's intent to participate in the venture (e.g., he did not charge inflated prices to the prostitutes, and they did not account for a large share of his business), the necessary intent has not been shown. *People v. Lauria*, 59 Cal. Rptr. 628 (Cal. App. 1967).

D. Differing mental states: It will often be the case that the alleged conspirators have different mental states. Each defendant's mental state must, of course, be judged on its own. Thus if A, B and C all agree to break into X's house at night, but only A and B intend to steal something when they get inside (and C is just going along as a lark), C cannot be convicted of conspiracy to commit burglary. See L, p. 585-86.

1. **Plurality requirement:**   Furthermore, since under the traditional definition conspiracy requires an agreement between two or more persons, if only one defendant has the requisite mental state, he must normally be acquitted of conspiracy. Thus if, in the housebreaking hypothetical above, neither B or C intended to commit a felony inside the house, A would be entitled to acquittal, since there is no "agreement" between him and the others to commit the substantive offense of burglary. See L, p. 586.

    a. **Model Penal Code rejects this result:**   But the Model Penal Code, with its "unilateral" approach to conspiracy (see *supra*, p. 178)), would reject this result. A would be held to have had the necessary intent to agree, regardless of whether B and C had the appropriate subjective intent.

    b. **Inconsistent results:**   Furthermore, even in a jurisdiction not accepting the Model Penal Code's unilateral approach, it would not be necessary that B and C actually be *convicted* in order for A's conviction to stand. For instance, if B turned state's evidence, and C was simply not prosecuted, A would not be able to defend on the grounds that this showed that B and C did not have the requisite intent. (But A could still argue that the evidence at his own trial showed that B and C did not have the needed intent.) See the discussion of inconsistent results, *infra*, p. 194.

LEXIS®-NEXIS® Searches on **MENS REA**

Sub-Topic	Suggested Searches
Intent to commit target crime	`(crime or criminal) and atleast2(conspiracy)` `and (conspir! w/5 (mens rea))`
Supplying of goods and services	`(crime or criminal) and atleast2(conspiracy)` `and (conspir! w/50 (suppl! w/20 stake))`

IV. THE CONSPIRATORIAL OBJECTIVE

A. **Non-criminal objectives:**   The definition of common-law conspiracy is usually construed to require an agreement to pursue an *"unlawful objective"* or a lawful objective by *"unlawful means"*. However, courts have traditionally interpreted the term "unlawful" to include not only acts that have explicitly been made *criminal* if pursued by a single person, but also acts that are *"immoral"*, "contrary to the public interest," "fraudulent," etc.

   Example: Suppose that a state makes any loan above 15% unenforceable as usury, but does not make making the loan a crime. If D1 and D2 agree to write such loans, under the common-law approach they could be convicted of conspiracy, for jointly pursuing an immoral (but non-criminal) objective.

1. **English view:**   The punishment of conspiracies to perform acts that are not by themselves criminal is still very much a part of *British* law. For instance, in *Shaw v. Director of Public Prosecutions*, 2 W.L.R. 897 (Eng. 1961), the defendant was convicted of conspiracy to "corrupt public morals," by collaborating with prostitutes for the publication of a "Ladies Directory," containing the "names, addresses and telephone numbers of prostitutes with photographs of nude female figures, and in some cases details which conveyed to the ini-

tiates willingness to indulge not only in ordinary sexual intercourse but also in various perverse practices." The court held that the conviction could stand, regardless of whether a substantive, non-conspiratorial, crime would have been committed by similar conduct. (The court left open the question of whether such conduct, if pursued by an individual acting alone, could or should be made criminal as a "common law" crime.)

2. **Modern American view rejects this approach:** But the modern American tendency is to allow a conspiracy conviction *only* if the defendants intended to perform an act that was *explicitly criminal*. Thus Model Penal Code, § 5.03(1), speaks only of conspiracy "to commit a crime." The Code draftsmen state that statutes imposing conspiratorial liability for acts which would not be criminal in themselves generally "fail to provide a sufficiently definite standard of conduct to have any place in a penal code." See Comment 2(a) to M.P.C. § 5.03.

   a. **Conspiracy to defraud government:** But one area in which a broad definition of conspiratorial objective still exists occurs in statutes making it a crime to conspire to *"defraud" the government*. The best known such statute is the federal one, making it a crime to "conspire to defraud the United States." This statute has been broadly construed, so as to make it a crime not only to conspire to obtain pecuniary gain at the expense of the government, but also to conspire to commit many other kinds of interference with the functions of government.

B. **Overt act requirement:** The common-law doctrine of conspiracy provides that the crime is complete once the agreement has been made. But about half the states have statutes requiring, in addition, that in some circumstances an *overt act* in furtherance of the conspiracy must also be committed.

   1. **Rationale:** The usual explanation for this requirement is that it is needed to verify that there has been a reasonably *firm intent* on the part of the conspirators to go through with the crime; the requirement is therefore similar to the requirement in the law of attempts (*supra*, p. 151) that the defendant have come reasonably close to success.

   2. **Model Penal Code limits requirement:** The Model Penal Code limits the overt act requirement to *non-serious crimes*. A conspiracy to commit a felony of the first or second degree may be proved without an overt act, because of the greater importance of "preventive intervention" in such cases than in less serious conspiracies. See Comment 5 to M.P.C. § 5.03(5).

   3. **Kind of act required:** The overt act may be *any act* which is taken in furtherance of the conspiracy. It does *not* have to be an act that is *criminal in itself*, or even one which represents the beginning of the commission of the substantive offense. Thus acts of *mere preparation* will be sufficient; for instance, if the conspiracy is to make moonshine liquor, purchase of sugar from a grocery store would meet the overt act requirement.

   4. **Act of one attributable to all:** It is not necessary that every defendant charged with the conspiracy be shown to have committed an overt act. Instead, the overt act of one will be *attributable to all* (since, by hypothesis, the act is in furtherance of the conspiracy that all have joined). See *Pinkerton v. U.S.*, 328 U.S. 640 (1946) (dictum).

C. Impossibility: Recall that in the law of attempts, the defense of so-called "legal impossibility" is often asserted, though rarely accepted. For instance, one who buys goods thinking they are stolen property, when in fact they are not, might try to escape conviction for attempted receiving of stolen goods. (See *supra*, p. 159). Can such a defense of legal impossibility succeed in conspiracy cases?

1. **Generally rejected:** Where the impossibility is of the sort we have termed (*supra*, p. 158) "factual impossibility relating to legal relations," which corresponds to the common label "legal impossibility," most courts have ***not accepted*** the impossibility defense for conspiracy, any more than they have accepted it in attempt cases. For instance, if two Ds conspire to purchase property which they believed to be stolen, it is unlikely that they would succeed with their impossibility defense.

2. **Mistake as to coverage of statute:** If the defendants' mistake, rather than being a factual one that relates to legal matters, is instead one relating to ***interpretation of the criminal statute itself***, presumably this will be a defense against conspiracy just as against attempt. (See *supra*, p. 158). For instance, suppose that the defendants believe that it constitutes the crime of perjury to lie to a police officer investigating a crime; if the defendants agree to tell such a lie, they would presumably not be guilty of conspiracy to commit perjury, any more than of attempt to commit perjury.

3. **Factual impossibility:** Where the impossibility is so-called "factual impossibility," it will virtually never be a defense to conspiracy (or to attempt; see *supra*, p. 157). Thus if the Ds agree to pick the pocket of a certain victim, and the pocket turns out to be empty, they will be liable for conspiracy to commit larceny.

D. Substantive liability for crimes of other conspirators: Suppose that the members of a conspiracy proceed to commit actual crimes. Assuming that the crimes are in "furtherance" of the conspiracy, is each member of the conspiracy, by virtue of his *membership alone*, ***liable for the substantive crimes committed by his colleagues***?

1. ***Pinkerton* case imposes liability:** The U.S. Supreme Court has answered "yes" to this question, in *Pinkerton v. U.S.*, 328 U.S. 640 (1946). (However, *Pinkerton* is not only an older case, it's a case that is not binding on the states when they decides matters of state criminal law.)

   a. **Facts of *Pinkerton*:** In *Pinkerton*, two brothers, Daniel and Walter, were charged with violating the Internal Revenue laws by conducting a moonshining business, as well as with conspiracy to violate those laws. There was no evidence that Daniel had participated directly in the commission of the substantive offenses (and in fact he was in prison when some of them were committed by Walter).

   b. **Held liable:** Nonetheless, the Court upheld Daniel's conviction of the substantive crimes as well as the conspiracy, on the grounds that Walter had committed them in furtherance of the conspiracy between the two brothers. Since the requirement of an overt act can be met as to all defendants by showing an overt act by one (see *supra*, p. 183), the Court saw no reason why liability for substantive crimes committed in furtherance of a conspiracy should not also be imputed to all defendants. (The Court conceded that Daniel would not have been liable if the crimes were not done in furtherance of the conspiracy, or were not "reasonably foreseeable" as "necessary or natural consequence" of the agreement when it was entered into.)

   c. Dissent: A dissent stressed that there was no evidence that Daniel even counseled, advised or knew of the particular substantive crimes committed by Walter, and argued that such vicarious criminal liability was even broader than the vicarious civil liability of a partner for acts done by a co-partner in furtherance of the partnership's business.

2. Modern view limits *Pinkerton:* It is well accepted that one conspirator may, by actively "aiding and abetting" another to commit a substantive crime in furtherance of the conspiracy, become liable for that substantive crime. This is a product of the rules on accomplice liability (discussed *infra*, p. 205). The difficult issue, however, is whether, ***even without proof of "aiding and abetting,"*** a conspirator is necessarily liable for the substantive crimes committed by his colleagues in furtherance of the conspiracy. Despite the decision in *Pinkerton*, most modern courts have tended to ***reject*** such substantive liability founded upon mere membership. See L, p. 634-35.

   a. Model Penal Code view: Similarly, the Model Penal Code does not make "conspiracy," without more, a basis for imposing liability for the substantive crimes of others. The Code draftsmen pose the case of a large prostitution ring, in which the ringleaders place many girls in houses of prostitution and receive money for doing so. It is justified to hold the ringleaders liable for each individual act of prostitution; this can be done on an "aiding and abetting" theory. But would it be justified to hold ***each girl*** liable for the acts of prostitution committed by each of the ***others***, on the sole grounds that they were all part of the same conspiracy? The draftsmen suggest that the answer is clearly "no": "Law would lose all sense of just proportion if in virtue of that one crime [of conspiracy], each were held accountable for thousands of offenses that [s]he did not influence at all." See Comment 6(a) to M.P.C. § 2.06(3).

LEXIS®-NEXIS® Searches on **THE CONSPIRATORIAL OBJECTIVE**

Sub-Topic	Suggested Searches
Overt act requirement	```(crime or criminal) and atleast2(conspiracy) and (conspir! w/5 (overt act))```
Impossibility	```(crime or criminal) and atleast2(conspiracy) and (conspir! w/20 impossib! w/20 defen!)```
Substantive liability for other conspirators' crimes	```(crime or criminal) and atleast2(conspiracy) and (conspir! w/20 (substantive or pinkerton))```

V. SCOPE: MULTIPLE PARTIES

   A. Parties not in contact with each other: It may happen that some of the parties involved in a substantial criminal undertaking do not know each other personally, and are not even aware of each others' identities. This is particularly likely to be the case with respect to the activities of organized crime. When this happens, it will be important to have a way of deciding whether there is ***one large conspiracy***, some members of which will not even know the others, or a *series of smaller ones*, composed of sets of participants who know each other and work together. The question is often discussed in terms of two sorts of organizations: (1) *"wheel"* or *"circle"* conspiracies; and (2) *"chain"* conspiracies.

B.   "Wheel" conspiracies: The term *"wheel"* or *"circle"* conspiracy is applied to an arrangement in which a "ringleader" participates with each of the conspirators, but these conspirators deal only with the ringleader, and not with each other. The ringleader may be thought of as the "hub," to which the other members are connected like "spokes." These peripheral "spokes" do not have any contact with each other.

1.   **"Community of interest" test:**   In many cases, there will be found to be a series of separate conspiracies, each one composed of a single spoke and the hub. For a "wheel" arrangement to be considered a *single conspiracy* rather than a series of smaller ones, it will usually be necessary that: (1) each spoke knows that the other spokes exist (although he does not necessarily have to know their precise identity) and; (2) the various spokes have, and realize that they have, a *"community of interest."* This second requirement means that it must be the case that each spoke realizes that the success of the venture depends on the performance of the other spokes.

> **Example:** Several bookmakers each independently agree to subscribe to an illegal horse-racing wire service. *Held*, each bookmaker may be convicted of participating in an overall wire-service conspiracy involving all of the bookmakers, because the evidence showed that each subscriber realized that subscriptions from others were necessary to make the service feasible. That is, all the bookmakers recognized that they had a community of interest. *State v. McLaughlin*, 44 A.2d 116 (Conn. 1945).

a.   **Multiple conspiracies found:**   Conversely, if there is no "community of interest" among the various spokes, or each individual spoke does not know of the existence of the others, there will be multiple small conspiracies. The best-known such case is *Kotteakos v. U.S.*, 328 U.S. 750 (1946). The hub, one Brown, helped a number of individuals obtain FHA loans based on fraudulent applications. In many cases, the loan recipients did not know each other. The Court held that there was a series of conspiracies (each one between one loan recipient and Brown), not a single large conspiracy. While the Court appeared to base its decision principally on the grounds that the loan recipients had no direct connection with each other, a subsequent Supreme Court case (*Blumenthal v. U.S.*, discussed *infra*) explained the result in *Kotteakos* by saying that "each loan was an end in itself, separate from all the others, although all were alike in having similar illegal objects. Except for Brown, the common figure, no conspirator was interested in whether any loan except his own went through."

i.   **Consequence of *Kotteakos*:**   The consequence of the ruling in *Kotteakos* was that the defendants' convictions were reversed. The faulty premise that there was only one conspiracy had led the trial judge to allow declarations made by various loan recipients to be admissible in evidence against all, and to hold that an overt act committed by one recipient could be attributed to all for purposes of meeting the overt act requirement.

C. "Chain" conspiracies: In a "chain" conspiracy, on the other hand, there is a sequence of distribution of a commodity (usually **drugs**) from, say, importer to wholesaler to retailer to consumer. Here, as in the "wheel" conspiracies, it will often be the case that not all participants know each other; thus the importer may not know the retailers, and one retailer may not know the others (though they will all know the wholesaler).

1. "Community of interest" test: The principal test for determining whether there is one conspiracy or several is, as with "wheel" conspiracies, the existence of a *"community of interest"* among the participants.

a. Knowledge of others' identity not necessary: It is not necessary that each member of the chain know the others' precise identity for there to be a single conspiracy, so long as the members are aware that there are others involved in the scheme, fulfilling certain general functions.

Example: X, the owner of two carloads of whiskey, arranges for its resale by Francisco Distributing Co., a wholesale liquor agency run by D1 and D2. D1 and D2 arrange for D3 and D4, who have no connection with Francisco Distributing, each to sell and deliver a portion of the whiskey to local taverns at an illegally high price. All the Ds are charged with having conspired with X (whose identity was never divulged in court) to violate the price laws.

Held, by the U.S. Supreme Court, there was a single conspiracy among the Ds and X, notwithstanding the fact that D3 and D4 never knew who X was. "The salesmen knew or must have known that others unknown to them were sharing in so large a project; and it hardly can be sufficient to relieve them that they did not know, when they joined the scheme, who those people were or exactly the parts they were playing in carrying out the common design and object of all. By their separate agreements, if such they were, they became parties to the larger common plan, joined together by their knowledge of its essential features and broad scope, though not of its exact limits, and by their common single goal." The *Kotteakos* case (*supra*, p. 186) is distinguishable, because there, each loan was an end in itself; here, each salesman knew that he was helping to further a larger common objective (disposition of the entire lot of whiskey). *Blumenthal v. U.S.*, 332 U.S. 539 (1947).

D. Organized crime: Whether the conspiracy at issue is a "wheel" or a "chain," it will, as noted, be necessary to show that each member being prosecuted was joined with the others in pursuit of a common objective. In the case of *organized crime*, this can be a very difficult showing to make, since organized crime "cells" or "families" often engage in a variety of different crimes, committed by many persons, each of whom may be unaware of what the others are doing.

1. RICO statute: To facilitate prosecution of such organized crime groups, Congress in 1970 passed the Racketeer Influenced and Corrupt Organizations Act (*RICO*), which makes it a substantive crime to engage in a "pattern of racketeering activity" in connection with the affairs of an interstate "enterprise." "Racketeering" is defined to include a large number of crimes (e.g., murder, narcotics violations, arson, bribery, extortion, etc.); anyone who commits two such crimes in association with an enterprise has engaged in the necessary "pattern" of racketeering, and has violated the Act.

2. **Conspiracy:** The Act also has its own *conspiracy provisions*. The net result is that anyone who commits or even agrees to commit two of the enumerated crimes can be lumped together with all others who do so in connection with the same "enterprise," and all can be convicted of conspiracy. This is so even though the individual defendants did not know each other, and *did not even have any idea of the sorts of activities the others were engaging in.*

   a. *Elliott* **case:** Thus in *U.S. v. Elliott*, 571 F.2d 880 (5th Cir. 1978), the Ds were a group of six persons who, among them, committed fraud on investors, arson, passing of counterfeit auto titles, theft, drug sales, and murder. Only one D was connected with all the offenses, and several Ds had no idea of the activities of the others (e.g., that two were committing murder). Nonetheless, all but one were convicted of conspiracy, since each had committed or agreed to commit two crimes falling within the definition of "racketeering," and all activities were part of what the court found to be a criminal "enterprise." (The remaining D, although he committed two or more crimes, was held not to have agreed to participate in a "pattern" of racketeering in connection with the enterprise, since only one crime was part of the enterprise.)

E. **Party who comes late or leaves early:** In handling any problem involving multiple parties, it is important to give special attention to the fact that a conspirator has entered the conspiracy *after it has begun*, or left it *before it is finished*.

   1. **Party who leaves early:** A person who *leaves a conspiracy before it's finished* is liable for the *later activities* of those who remain only if those activities are fairly *within the confines of the conspiracy as he understands them* while he was still present.

   2. **Party who joins late:** Conversely, a person who belatedly enters a conspiracy whose other members have *already committed substantive acts* will be a conspirator as to those acts only if he not only is told about them but *accepts them as part of the general scheme* in which he is participating. For instance, a "fence" who buys from two jewelry thieves may be a conspirator to receive stolen property, but he will *not* normally be a conspirator to commit the original theft crime (unless, perhaps, he were told all about the theft when the goods were fenced to him, and he somehow acknowledged that he was furthering the overall course of conduct).

VI. DURATION OF THE CONSPIRACY

A. **Significance of issue:** It will frequently be of critical importance to determine the *ending point* of a conspiracy. For instance, the longer the conspiracy is found to have gone on, the more likely it is that additional persons will be found to have joined it (or at least portions of it, under the modern "unilateral" view). Also, since the *Statute of Limitations* does not normally start to run until a crime is complete, the longer the conspiracy is found to have gone on, the better chance the prosecution has of satisfying the Statute. Similarly, declarations of conspirators may be admissible against each other, despite the hearsay rule, if those declarations were made while the conspiracy was still in progress.

   1. **Relation to other questions:** The question of a conspiracy's duration is thus closely related to some of the issues discussed above, including the distinction between single and

multiple conspiracies, and the problems of multiple parties with different functions and intents. Here, however, we are concerned solely with the question of finding the ending point of the conspiracy; this involves primarily the problem of distinguishing the conspiracy from a subsequent *"cover-up."*

B. Abandonment: One way that a conspiracy can come to an end, of course, is if it is *abandoned* by the participants.

1. **Abandonment by all:** If *all the parties* abandon the plan, this will be enough to start the Statute of Limitations running. Since it may be difficult to tell at what point abandonment occurred, the court will generally presume that the Statute of Limitations has run if there has been *no overt act* performed by any conspirator within the applicable limitations period. This rule gives the conspirators the benefit of the doubt, by treating them as having abandoned the plan immediately after forming it, if they take no overt acts. Thus if a conspiracy crime has a five-year Statute of Limitations, and the indictment is handed down on June 1, 1979, the prosecution must show that some overt act was taken by at least one of the conspirators after June 1, 1974.

   a. **Abandonment no defense to conspiracy charge:** While abandonment will start the Statute of Limitations running, it will *not serve as defense to the conspiracy charge itself*. The common-law view is that the conspiracy is complete once the agreement is made; therefore, abandonment is logically irrelevant. (The Model Penal Code allows a defense of "renunciation of criminal purpose," which is discussed in the context of withdrawal by a single person, *infra*, this page; it is unclear whether this provision, M.P.C. § 5.03(6), can apply where all the conspirators mutually decide to abandon the plan.)

2. **Withdrawal by individual conspirator:** It frequently happens that an *individual conspirator drops out* of the plan, and the others go on to complete it (or get caught). The issue of whether the drop-out has sufficiently withdrawn is answered differently depending on the purpose for which withdrawal is sought to be shown.

   a. **Procedural issues:** If the reason the defendant tries to show that he withdrew is to establish either: (1) the running of the Statute of Limitations; (2) the non-admissibility of declarations by other conspirators after he left; or (3) his non-liability for the substantive crimes committed by the others after his departure, the rule is fairly liberal; the defendant must merely show that he made an *"affirmative act* bringing home the fact of his withdrawal to his confederates." L, p. 603. It is not necessary that the defendant thwart the success of the conspiracy.

      i. **Notice to each:** It is generally required that the notice be given to *each* of the other conspirators, although in the case of a far-flung conspiracy, this requirement may not be strictly construed.

      ii. **Notification of police:** Alternatively, notification of the *police* will suffice for this purpose.

   b. **Defense to conspiracy charge:** But if the defendant tries to show withdrawal as a *substantive defense* against the conspiracy charge itself, he will have a much tougher row to hoe. The common-law rule is that *no act of withdrawal*, even thwarting the conspiracy by turning the others in to the police, will be a defense; this stems from the principle that the crime is complete once the agreement has been made. See L, p. 604.

  i. More liberal Model Penal Code view: But the Model Penal Code allows a limited defense of *"renunciation of criminal purpose."* Under Code § 5.03(6), "it is an affirmative defense that the actor, after conspiring to commit a crime, thwarted the success of the conspiracy, under circumstances manifesting a complete and voluntary renunciation of his criminal purpose." Under this section, not only must the defendant show that his renunciation was *"voluntary"* (as opposed to having been motivated by a fear of immediate detection), but he must also show that the *conspiracy was thwarted*. In general, to do this it will be necessary to *inform the police*. Furthermore, as the Code commentary makes clear, even a notification to the police which would ordinarily be sufficient to thwart the conspiracy but which, due to police inefficiency, fails to have that result, will not meet the requirements of the defense. See Comment 6 to M.P.C. § 5.03(6).

3. Crime completed: If, rather than abandoning the plan, the conspirators carry through with it to the point of committing substantive offenses, it will be more difficult to determine when the conspiracy has ended, for purposes of Statute of Limitations, admissibility of co-conspirators' declarations, etc. The difficulty arises principally from the fact that virtually every crime in history has been followed by attempts to *avoid discovery*. If the conspirators attempt to conceal their traces, are they to be regarded as continuing the conspiracy during this cover-up?

  a. Acts of concealment not sufficient: It is well accepted that *acts of concealment* are *not*, by themselves, sufficient to continue the conspiracy.

  Example: D1 is charged with conspiring with D2, a woman, to transport X, another woman, from New York to Florida for purposes of prostitution (a violation of the Mann Act). The prosecution introduces into evidence a statement made by D2 more than a month after the alleged violation; the statement is part of an attempt by D2 to prevent D1 from being implicated in the crime. The prosecution argues that the statement is therefore part of the original conspiracy, which included a subsidiary conspiracy to avoid detection, and that the statement therefore is admissible.

  Held, attempts at concealment are not to be treated as part of the original conspiracy. Accepting the prosecution's argument would require major inroads to the rule against hearsay, and would be applicable to all conspiracies. (A concurring opinion by Justice Jackson stressed the many respects in which a conspiracy trial is often unfair to the individual defendants. These unfair results include wide-ranging venue, proof of conspiracy based solely upon hearsay declarations by co-conspirators, the risk that the jury will convict a defendant solely by reason of his association with the others, and the likelihood that co-defendants can be "prodded into accusing or contradicting each other," in which case "they convict each other.") *Krulewitch v. U.S.*, 336 U.S. 440 (1949).

  b. Original intent concealed: However, it is theoretically possible for the prosecution to prove that when the crime itself was planned, there was also an *explicit plan* to continue acting in concert to avoid detection following the crime's consummation. If so, the detection-avoiding steps *would* be deemed part of the conspiracy.

    c.   **Concealment as fulfillment of original crime:**   But acts of concealment may be shown to be part of the original conspiracy on a different theory entirely. The prosecution may be able to demonstrate that such acts were not merely attempts to avoid detection, but attempts to ***consummate the crime itself***. The most obvious example is kidnappers who go into hiding while waiting for the ransom to be paid; they are acting to avoid detection, but they are also acting to fulfill an element of the kidnapping scheme itself, i.e., collection of payment.

VII. PLURALITY

    A.   **Significance of plurality requirement:**   Since conspiracy is defined in terms of an "agreement," it necessarily involves two or more persons. This requirement of more than one person is sometimes called the *"plurality"* requirement. There are a number of situations where it may not be certain whether this requirement has been satisfied. The most important issues are: (1) whether there can be a conspiracy when no more people are involved than are *logically necessary* to commit the substantive offense that is the object of the conspiracy (the so-called *"Wharton's Rule"* problem); (2) whether a conspiracy can exist where the only conspirators are a *man* and *wife*, or a *corporation* and its *officer or agent*; and (3) whether a person can be found guilty of conspiracy if *none* of the other conspirators is *convicted* (either because they are acquitted or for other reasons).

    B.   **Wharton's Rule:**   *Wharton's Rule*, named after the commentator who articulated it, provides that where a substantive offense is defined so as to necessarily require more than one person, a prosecution for the substantive offense must be brought, rather than a conspiracy prosecution. Examples include ***adultery, incest, bigamy***, ***bribery*** and ***gambling***. Thus if a married man and a woman have intercourse, they cannot be charged with conspiracy to commit adultery; prosecution must be for adultery itself.

        1.   **Degree of acceptance:** Some courts — but probably only a minority — apply Wharton's Rule as a *substantive rule* of law. Other courts hold that the "Rule" is not a substantive limitation on the law of conspiracy, but merely a rebuttable *presumption* about what the legislature intended. (This is true of federal courts, as the result of *Iannelli v. U.S.*, discussed below.) Still other courts don't follow Wharton's Rule at all.

        2.   **Rationale:**   The rationale for Wharton's Rule is that where a crime has been defined so as to require a plurality of participants, the legislature was presumably aware of the danger stemming from group criminality, and has presumably factored these dangers into its punishment scheme for that crime. The prosecution should not be allowed to thwart this scheme by charging a general conspiracy (particularly since, in some jurisdictions, conspiracy has a punishment scheme all its own, often unrelated to the object crime; see *infra*, p. 195).

        3.   **More persons than necessary:**   One well-established exception to Wharton's Rule is that there is no bar to a conspiracy conviction when there were ***more participants*** than were logically necessary to complete the crime. For instance, if A persuades and assists his friend B, a married man, to have intercourse with C, ***all three*** can be convicted of conspiracy to commit adultery. This is because there were more persons involved than merely the two necessary direct parties to the adultery. See L, p. 609.

4. **Only one participant punishable:**   Another exception is that if a substantive crime is defined so as to require two or more participants, but ***only one*** of them is ***punishable*** under the substantive statute, ***all*** may be convicted of conspiracy. For instance, if the sale of liquor is prohibited, but penalties are prescribed only for the seller, both seller and buyer may be convicted of conspiracy to violate the prohibition law. L, p. 610-11. (But there may be "policy reasons" for not permitting a conspiracy conviction in this situation; see the discussion of *Gebardi v. U.S., infra*, p. 193.)

5. **Merely a presumption:**   The U.S. Supreme Court has indicated that in the case of many federal crimes, Wharton's Rule should be treated not an inflexible principle but merely as a ***presumption*** that will not apply if the legislative history behind the substantive crime fails to indicate a legislative intent to bar convictions of conspiracy to violate the substantive law. See *Iannelli v. U.S.*, 420 U.S. 770 (1975).

   a. **Facts of Iannelli:**   In *Iannelli*, the Ds were charged with conspiring to violate a provision of the Organized Crime Control Act of 1970 ("OCCA"), which makes it a substantive federal offense for five or more persons to conduct, manage, finance, own, etc., a gambling business prohibited by state law. The Ds argued that since the substantive offense required participation of at least five persons, Wharton's Rule prohibited a charge of conspiring to commit that offense.

   b. **Holding:** But the Supreme Court disagreed, holding that the fact that the substantive offense required five or more participants merely created a rebuttable presumption that Congress did not intend to allow conviction of conspiracy to commit the OCCA. The Court also found that this presumption had not been rebutted (so the conspiracy prosecution was allowed to go forward.) The Court gave two reasons:

      i. **Large-scale social implications:**   First of all, the Court asserted that in the case of the classic Wharton's Rule offenses, such as adultery and dueling, ***only the participants*** are typically ***affected*** by commission of the substantive offense. Here, by contrast, operation of a gambling business will inevitably draw into it ***additional persons*** (gamblers), and is more likely to be part of a generalized pattern of criminal conduct. (So the Court seemed to hold that any time attempts to commit a particular federal crime are likely to involve additional persons beyond those logically required for completion of the crime, Wharton's Rule will not apply.)

      ii. **Congressional intent:**   Furthermore, according to Court, the legislative history of the Organized Crime Control Act showed no ***intent*** on the part of Congress to merge conspiracy charges into the substantive crime. On the contrary, the majority stated, the requirement of five or more participants "reflects no more than a concern to avoid federal prosecution of small-scale gambling activities which pose a limited threat to federal interests and normally can be combatted effectively by local law enforcement efforts." Therefore, the Ds could be convicted of *both* conspiracy and violation of the substantive provision of the Act.

6. Model Penal Code rejects Rule: Wharton's Rule is almost completely ***rejected*** by the Model Penal Code. The draftsmen note that the Rule "completely overlook[s] the functions of conspiracy as an inchoate crime. That an offense inevitably requires concert is no reason to immunize criminal preparation to commit it." (See Comment 4 to M.P.C. § 5.04.) For instance, although it might be unfair and contrary to legislative intent to subject two participants in a non-fatal duel to both a dueling conviction and one for conspiracy to duel, there is nothing illogical about convicting two persons who plan to have a duel and are stopped from going through with it, of conspiracy to duel.

    a. No conviction for conspiracy and substantive offense: Thus the Code provides simply that one may not be convicted of both a substantive crime and a conspiracy to commit it. M.P.C. § 1.07(1)(b).

C. Statutory purpose not to punish one party: A related problem, but distinct from Wharton's Rule, arises where a crime necessarily requires two or more persons, but the legislature has ***imposed punishment only on one***. Although this situation is not covered by Wharton's Rule (see *supra*, p. 191), the court may conclude that, since the legislature has not authorized a party's punishment on the substantive crime, he should not be punished for conspiracy either.

    1. *Gebardi* case: The best-known such case is *Gebardi v. U.S.*, 287 U. S. 112 (1932). The Ds, a man and a woman both married but not to each other, were charged with conspiracy to violate the Mann Act, in that they jointly arranged for the man to transport the woman across state lines, for purposes of having sexual intercourse with each other. The court held first that the Mann Act should not be construed so as to permit punishment of a woman who simply acquiesces in her transportation by others. The legislative intent not to punish her would be thwarted if she could be convicted of conspiracy. Similarly, the court stated, it would not make sense to punish a woman under the age of consent as a co-conspirator with a man to commit statutory rape on herself.

        a. Man's conviction reversed: Since the woman in *Gebardi* could not be convicted of conspiracy, and since there was no evidence that there were any other parties than she and the man, the man's conviction was also reversed (apparently on the theory that there cannot be one conspirator). However, it is not clear that, under the modern approach, the man's conviction would necessarily be vitiated by the reversal of the woman's conviction. See *infra*.

    2. Model Penal Code view: The Model Penal Code accepts part but not all of the *Gebardi* rationale. Under M.P.C. § 5.04(2), one may not be convicted of conspiracy to commit a crime if one could not be convicted of the substantive crime itself, or of being an accomplice to that crime. Thus in the *Gebardi* situation, since the Mann Act is construed so as to prevent conviction of the woman of a Mann Act violation itself, or of aiding and abetting such a violation, she could not be guilty of conspiracy either.

        a. Man could be convicted under Code: But the Code would produce a different result from that in *Gebardi* as to the man, because of the Code's "unilateral" approach. That is, the fact that the woman must be acquitted of conspiracy does not mean that man's conviction also must be reversed; the man is guilty of "agreeing" with the woman, regardless of her immunity. This aspect of the Code is discussed further *infra*, in the treatment of inconsistent disposition.

D. Spouses and corporations: Two common situations in which it may be argued that there are not two distinct conspirators are: (1) where the only alleged conspirators are a married couple; and (2) where the only alleged conspirators are a corporation and its stockholder, officer, or other agent.

1. **Spouses:** The traditional common-law rule was that a *husband* and his *wife* could *not* by themselves make up a conspiracy. This rule was the product of the common-law theory that a man and his wife were one person in the eyes of the law. (But if a third person was part of the conspiracy, they could all be convicted.) L, pp. 607-08.

   a. **Modern view:** But virtually all modern courts have *rejected* this common-law rule, and a conspiracy composed solely of husband and wife is punishable. L, p. 608.

2. **Corporations:** It is necessary that at least two members of the conspiracy be *human beings*. Thus although a corporation can be punished as a conspirator, there can be no conspiracy when only one *corporation* and one human being (e.g., an *officer* or stockholder of the corporation) are implicated. L, p. 609.

E. Inconsistent disposition: Suppose that the evidence shows that, if there was a conspiracy, it involved only two persons, A and B. If A is not convicted (either because of acquittal, lack of prosecution, immunity, failure of the police to find him, etc.), does the plurality requirement mean that B's conviction may not stand? The answer depends mostly on whether the two alleged co-conspirators are tried in the same, or different, proceedings.

1. **Same trial:** Where A and B are tried in the *same proceeding*, and A is acquitted, it is universally agreed that *B must also be acquitted*. This result is due principally to the "community sense of a just outcome." L, p. 605.

   a. **May not be any other defendants:** Of course, this rule assumes that A and B are the only persons alleged to be part of the conspiracy. If A, B and C are charged, the fact that A is acquitted does not require the acquittal of B and C, even if the prosecution's evidence suggests that A was the ringleader. But conversely, if A and B are both acquitted, C must be acquitted also; the premise is that there must be more than one guilty party.

2. **Different trials:** But now suppose that A and B are tried in *different trials*. (This happens frequently, because courts often order that the two trials be *"severed"* from each other in order to prevent unfairness to one party or the other. For instance, a particular confession may be admissible against one of the co-conspirators but not the other.) In this "different trials" situation, most courts today hold that A's acquittal does *not* require B's release.

   a. **Rationale:** The fact that different evidence may have been presented in the two trials, and the fact that the two juries have a different composition, are enough to eliminate the rationale present in the "single trial" situation, that inconsistent results offend the community's sense of justice. See, e.g., *Marquiz v. Colorado*, 726 P.2d 1105 (Col. 1986), following this modern majority view and thus upholding D's conspiracy conviction despite the previous acquittal of his two alleged co-conspirators in separate trials.

3. **One conspirator not brought to justice:** If one of the two alleged conspirators is not *brought to justice* at all, this will *not* prevent conviction of the other. However, the prosecution must of course show that both participated in the agreement. L, p. 606-07.

4. **Model Penal Code rejects consistency requirement:** The Model Penal Code, as a result of its "unilateral" approach, would never release a conspirator solely because of an inconsistent verdict in a different trial. Thus if A and B are the only two alleged conspirators, and A is acquitted in one trial, B may nonetheless be convicted in another trial under the Code. See Comment 2(b) to M.P.C. § 5.03. But the Code leaves open the question of whether one conspirator may be acquitted and the other convicted if both are tried in the same proceeding.

VIII. PUNISHMENT

A. **Typical penalty schemes:** There are a number of statutory schemes for punishing conspiracies. In some states, conspiracy is a misdemeanor, regardless of its objective. In other states, conspiracy is a felony whose maximum sentence remains the same, regardless of the seriousness of the object crime; this can produce the result that the sentence for conspiracy is more severe than that for the completed crime could have been.

    1. **Model Penal Code:** The Model Penal Code does not permit the sentence for conspiracy to be greater than the maximum sentence allowed for the object crime. Generally speaking, the Code authorizes penalties equal to those that could be imposed for the most serious object crime intended (except that a conspiracy to commit a first-degree felony is a second-degree felony). M.P.C. § 5.05(1).

B. **Cumulative sentencing:** Suppose that members of a conspiracy intend to commit only one substantive offense, and they complete this offense. May they be convicted of both conspiracy to commit that crime and the crime itself?

    1. **Cumulative sentencing usually allowed:** Most states allow a *cumulative sentence* (i. e., conviction for both conspiracy and the underlying crime). The rationale generally given for this is that a conspiracy presents additional dangers inherent in group activity, and should therefore be punishable separately from the underlying offense. See L, p. 613.

    2. **Model Penal Code limits cumulative sentencing:** The Model Penal Code rejects the assertion that a conspiracy that is limited solely to committing crime X can be more dangerous than the actual commission of crime X. Therefore, provided that all object crimes of the conspiracy are carried out, the court is not permitted under the Code to convict for both the conspiracy and the underlying crime. M.P.C. § 1.07(1)(b).

        a. **Some objectives not realized:** If, however, the conspiracy has a number of objectives, and only one or some of these are carried out, there can be a conviction of both the conspiracy and the carried-out crimes. See Comment 2(a) to M.P.C. § 5.03. Thus if it is shown that the defendants conspired to run a gambling and loansharking operation, and only the gambling offenses are proved to have been carried out, separate sentences for conspiracy and gambling may be imposed.

43. Che, an internationally-famous left-wing guerilla from South America, migrates to the U.S. He decides to try to overthrow the government of Miami Beach, Florida. To that end, he approaches Sam Surplus, a dealer in excess Army supplies. He tells Sam, "I'll be planning a little insurrection over at City Hall sometime soon, and I'll need some supplies." Sam is himself a pretty right-wing kind of a guy, but he figures that Che's bucks are as green as anyone else's. Therefore, Sam sells Che, at his standard prices, some military uniforms, knapsacks, and surplus Uzis. (All items are ones that appropriately-licensed government-surplus dealers are legally permitted to sell in the ordinary course of business.) Che uses the supplies to outfit his army, and he successfully — though very temporarily — ousts the elected government of Miami Beach. A federal statute makes it a crime to overthrow a municipal government. Is Sam guilty of conspiracy to overthrow the government?

44. Sitting Bull wants to get revenge on Custer by burning down Custer's barn. Therefore, Sitting Bull tells Crazy Horse that the barn is on Bull's property, and asks Crazy Horse to help him raze it to "clear the land."

(A) For this part only, assume that Crazy Horse believes Bull's bull, and agrees to help Bull light a fire to burn down the property. Before they can light the fire, both are arrested and charged with conspiracy to commit arson. Assume that the crime of arson is defined as intentionally burning the property of another without the owner's consent. Is Crazy Horse guilty of conspiracy to commit arson?

(B) Assume the same facts, except this time, Sitting Bull tells Crazy Horse that he wants to use a particular substance, dextromethorpan, or DXM, as the igniter in the fire. As Crazy Horse knows, it is illegal to possess DXM without a license. Crazy Horse nonetheless agrees to purchase some DXM from a crooked dealer. After he buys the DXM, but before he can light the fire with Bull, they are both arrested and charged with conspiracy to commit arson (defined as in part (A)). Is Crazy Horse guilty of conspiracy to commit arson?

45. Penguin intends to rob the Gotham City Bank. He asks Joker to help him out. Joker agrees to go through with the plan — although secretly Joker intends to inform the police of Penguin's plan. No one else is involved in the planning. Shortly before the scheduled robbery, Joker informs the police of the plan, and Penguin (but not Joker) is charged with conspiracy to commit bank robbery. May Penguin properly be convicted, under the modern/M.P.C. approach?

46. Boris Badenov, Snidely Whiplash, and Natasha Fatale conspire to kill Dudley Doright. They draw elaborate diagrams of the proposed murder, and plan the act to the last detail. To insure that all the parties remain silent, they execute a blood oath not to reveal their plans. In the end, their plans are never acted upon because Doright gets a job on a daytime soap opera and moves to another state. Are Boris, Snidely and Natasha guilty of conspiracy to commit murder ...

(A) under the common-law approach?

(B) under the Model Penal Code?

47. The Flying Albatrosses are a team of six circus aerialists. Five of the members hate the sixth, Alva. The five therefore decide that one of them should loosen the fastener on Alva's trapeze so that it will break when Alva grabs it. Accordingly, Ariel Albatross, the most mechanically-minded of the five, is given this task, and loosens the fastener. No other member of the team takes any physical action to help the plan.

When Alva does the routine, due to his recent weight loss the trapeze does not break, and the routine goes flawlessly. The police learn of the plot, and arrest the five immediately afterwards, before they can try again. Are the four members of the Albatrosses other than Ariel guilty of conspiracy to commit murder? (Assume this all takes place in a jurisdiction that requires an overt act in furtherance of the conspiracy.)

48. Tarzan is planning to rob the Jungle and Vine Bank, and make off with a load of bananas. Jane offers to act as a lookout and driver of the getaway car. Jane knows that Tarzan will be armed, and that he's determined not to get caught no matter what (because he's terrified of being returned to the jungle.) When they get to the bank, Jane waits outside with the motor running. Tarzan goes in and meets Sheena, who (unbeknownst to Jane) has previously agreed to help him out. During the robbery, a bank guard, trying to stop the robbery and arrest the suspects, tackles Tarzan. Sheena, who knows how Tarzan feels about getting caught, takes Tarzan's gun and shoots the guard to death, so they can all escape. Alas, all three are apprehended outside the bank. Is *Jane* guilty of murder in the guard's death?

49. Blacque Jacques Shellacque, a criminal sort, makes $1 million in counterfeit money, and by pre-arrangement sells it all to Boodles at a steep discount. Boodles sells $50,000 of that money to Ken Gelt, who sells it all to Minnie Moolah. (Boodles sells the other $950,000 to a variety of buyers.) Minnie does not know anything about any of the activities further upstream; she only knows that Gelt is a source of counterfeit currency. Minnie passes her $50,000 off as real money to stores and banks. A statute makes it a Class A felony to distribute, or conspire to distribute, in excess of $100,000 in counterfeit currency. Distribution or conspiracy to distribute less than $100,000 is a Class B felony. What is the highest felony of which Minnie can be convicted?

50. Winken, Blinken and Nod agree to work together to kill the Calico Cat. A few days later, about a week before the killing is to take place, Winken gets cold feet — he quits the conspiracy, telling the others he wants nothing further to do with the plan and asking them to abandon it. Blinken and Nod carry out the murder of Calico Cat anyway. Is Winken guilty of:

    (A) conspiracy to commit murder?

    (B) murder?

51. Bob is married to Carol. Alice is married to Ted. Bob and Alice have been attracted to each other for several years, but have not done anything about it. Finally, one day, Bob telephones Alice and asks her to meet him at the Ames Acres Motel, where they will conduct an assignation. Alice agrees. Unbeknownst to them, Carol is listening on an extension. She arranges to have the police meet her at the Motel at the appointed time. The police arrest Bob and Alice in their room, while they are in a state of partial undress but have not yet committed adultery. In the state of which Ames is a part, adultery is a substantive crime. The prosecutor charges Bob and Alice with conspiracy to commit adultery.

    (A) If you are defending Bob or Alice, (i) what defense should you assert? and (ii) will it be successful?

    (B) Same basic fact pattern as Part (A). Now, however, assume that the way Bob and Alice come to be together in the motel room is that Bob's friend Peter says to both Bob and Alice, "You know, you'd make a great couple, you should really try to get something going together." In a jurisdiction which would recognize the defense you asserted in your answer to Part (A), may Peter, Bob and Alice all be charged with and convicted of conspiracy to commit adultery?

    (C) Suppose that the jurisdiction follows the Model Penal Code approach to relevant issues. Assume that the facts of Part (A) (not Part (B)) apply. Will the defense you asserted in response to Part (A) succeed?

52. Abbot and Costello are charged with conspiracy to defraud retirees in a scheme to sell retirement homes

in the Florida Everglades. Abbot is acquitted at trial, but Costello is found guilty.

(A) Assume for this part that Abbot and Costello are tried in a single, joint trial. On Costello's appeal on the grounds that the inconsistent verdicts should entitle him to acquittal, will the appellate court find for Costello?

(B) Assume for this part that Abbot and Costello are tried in separate trials. In Costello's appeal on the grounds of the inconsistent verdicts, will the appellate court find for Costello under: (i) the prevailing approach; and (ii) the Model Penal Code approach?

―――――――――――

Answers

43. **Probably not.** To be guilty of conspiracy, the defendant must be shown to have *intended* to further a criminal objective — it's generally not enough that the defendant merely *knew* that his acts would or might enable others to pursue criminal ends. This rule applies to suppliers: the fact that the supplier knows or strongly suspects that the merchandise may be used for particular illegal purposes is generally not sufficient to make the supplier guilty of conspiracy. There are certain other factors that might change this result as to a particular supplier (e.g., that the supplier has agreed to be paid out of proceeds of the upcoming crime, or is charging much higher prices than are commonly charged in the absence of a criminal purpose, or is selling contraband), but none of these special factors applies here. Therefore, especially when one considers that Sam doesn't support left-wing politics, it's unlikely that a court would find Sam to have had the requisite intent to help commit the overthrow.

44. **(A) No.** A party cannot be guilty of conspiracy to commit crime X unless he has the mental state required for crime X. Conspiracy to commit arson therefore requires the defendant to have the intent to burn the property of another without the other's consent. Here, Crazy Horse believed that the property belonged to Bull and was being burned with Bull's consent. Therefore, Crazy did not have an intent to burn the property without the owner's consent. (Note, by the way, that it wouldn't even matter if Crazy's belief about who owned the property was unreasonable — as long as the trier of fact believed that Crazy honestly, though stupidly, thought the property belonged to Bull, Crazy didn't have the requisite mental state for the completed crime and therefore can't be guilty of conspiracy.)

(B) No. The analysis is the same as for part (A): since Crazy's belief that Bull owns the farm prevents Crazy from having the mental state required for arson, he can't be guilty of conspiracy to commit arson. The fact that Crazy has agreed to commit some other crime (illegal possession of DXM) in preparation for their joint effort is irrelevant — Crazy may be convicted of illegal DXM possession, and even conspiracy to illegally possess DXM, but he can't be convicted of conspiracy to commit arson.

45. **Yes.** Under the traditional view, the definition of conspiracy required that there actually be an agreement between two or more people; under that approach, Penguin couldn't be convicted, because there was no one else who was in actual agreement with Penguin. But the modern and M.P.C. approach applies a **"unilateral"** standard: an individual is guilty of conspiracy if he makes an agreement with another person, even if the other person is merely feigning agreement. So under the modern/M.P.C. approach, it's enough that Penguin thought he had (and attempted to have) an agreement with someone else, and the fact that the someone else was secretly not agreeing at all doesn't make any difference.

46. **(A) Yes.** At common law, a conspiracy is complete once the agreement is made — no further act is required. (It's true that about half the states have *statutes* requiring, in some instances, that some overt act in furtherance of the conspiracy must occur. But the question asks you about the common-law approach.)

(B) Yes. The M.P.C. does contain an overt-act requirement, but it applies only where the object crime is a relatively unserious one. If the object crime is a first- or second-degree felony (and murder certainly falls within that group), no overt act is required under the M.P.C. See Comment 5 to M.P.C. § 5.03(5).

47. **Yes.** In those states that require an overt act, an overt act committed by one member, in furtherance of the conspiracy that all have joined, will be attributable to all. So Ariel's act of loosening the trapeze (which is obviously an act in furtherance of the conspiracy) serves as the overt act for all, not just for Ariel.

48. **Yes.** Virtually all courts would agree with this result, but they might differ in how to get there. Some courts follow the approach of the Supreme Court in the *Pinkerton* case: under that approach, a member of a conspiracy is liable for *any substantive crimes* committed by his colleagues, as long as those crimes are committed in furtherance of the conspiracy's aims. Since Sheena was attempting to further one of the conspiracy's goals (escaping from the bank after the robbery) when she fired the fatal shot, under *Pinkerton* Jane as a co-conspirator will be guilty of the substantive crime of murder, even though she didn't have any interaction with Sheena or even know of her existence. (As long as all acts are properly viewed as being part of a single conspiracy, as they clearly would be here, the fact that one particular conspirator didn't know of or interact with another particular one won't make any difference.)

   Many other courts (and the Model Penal Code) reject the *Pinkerton* view that mere membership in a conspiracy, without more, makes each conspirator automatically liable for any substantive crime committed by any member in furtherance of the conspiracy's objectives. Instead, these courts say that liability for the substantive crimes must depend on the law of *accomplice liability* (aiding and abetting): if, and only if, a particular conspirator can be said to have aided and abetted — i.e., encouraged or facilitated — the substantive crime carried out by another can the former be convicted of that substantive crime. However, even under that rule Jane would almost certainly be on the hook. She has helped bring about the entire conspiracy (it probably wouldn't have happened without a lookout/getaway-driver) and she has at least tacitly encouraged Tarzan's carrying of a gun to the scene and his willingness to use it. A court would therefore almost certainly say that Jane "aided and abetted" Sheena's act, even though she didn't know Sheena and had no direct interaction with her. Once the court decided that Jane aided and abetted the shooting, then ordinary principles of accomplice liability (discussed in the next chapter) make her liable for the substantive crimes carried out by her principal(s) in furtherance of the aided crime.

49. **Class B, probably.** The question is really whether Minnie will be deemed to have participated in the original $1 million conspiracy between Shellacque and Boodles. Here, this is an unlikely outcome: since Minnie never knew any of the details of the upstream transactions (indeed, never even knew that any upstream transactions occurred), she's unlikely to be found to be part of the overall conspiracy in which Shellacque and Gelt participated. Therefore, although Shellacque and Gelt might be found to have conspired with Minnie (since she furthered their plan of disseminating the counterfeits until they entered the stream of ordinary business), she won't be found to have conspired with them. (Under the modern/M.P.C. approach, upstream members can be part of a conspiracy extending far downstream even if the downstream members are not deemed part of that same conspiracy back to the top. In other words, there can be a "unilateral" approach to determining who the members of a given conspiracy are.)

50. **(A) Yes.** The traditional rule is that once a conspiratorial agreement occurred, no subsequent act of withdrawal or repudiation by a conspirator could prevent that conspirator from being guilty of conspiracy. The modern / M.P.C. approach recognizes a limited defense of "renunciation of criminal purpose," but even that defense requires that the renouncing conspirator voluntarily **thwart** the conspiracy — mere withdrawal is not enough. So since Winken did not prevent the conspiracy's aims from being fulfilled, he'll be guilty even under this more liberal modern view.

(B) No. Most courts hold that if a conspirator withdraws, the withdrawal alone is enough to prevent the withdrawer from being guilty of any substantive crimes committed by the others in furtherance of the conspiracy. That's true even if the withdrawer doesn't try to thwart the conspiracy — however, the withdrawer must bring home to the remaining members that he is in fact withdrawing. So here, once Winken let the other two know he was no longer part of the team, any substantive crime they later committed may not be attributed to him.

51. **(A) (i) Wharton's Rule; (ii) yes, probably.** Wharton's Rule provides that where a substantive offense is defined so as to necessarily require more than one person, a prosecution for the substantive offense must be brought, rather than a conspiracy prosecution. The Rule is commonly applied to adultery, and thus provides that where a man and woman would be guilty of adultery if they had intercourse, they may not be prosecuted for conspiracy to commit adultery (whether they have sex or merely prepare to have it). Many states would apply Wharton's Rule as a substantive rule on these facts; therefore, regardless of whether the legislature intended to allow a prosecution for conspiracy-to-commit-adultery, in these states the prosecution would not be allowed. In other states, on these facts Wharton's Rule would be treated as a rebuttable *presumption* as to legislative intent; in that situation, the prosecution could try to rebut the presumption by showing (perhaps by legislative history) that the legislature in fact intended to allow conspiracy-to-commit-adultery prosecutions. However, it's unlikely that the prosecution could make that rebuttal showing in an adultery case, because the legislature is unlikely to have even thought about the issue. So all in all, in a state accepting any form of Wharton's Rule the prosecution would probably not be allowed to proceed.

(B) Yes. One well-established exception to Wharton's Rule is that there is no bar to a conspiracy conviction when there are *more participants* than are logically necessary to complete the crime. Here, we have three participants, not merely the two who were logically necessary to commit the crime. Therefore, all three may be convicted even in a jurisdiction that recognizes Wharton's Rule.

(C) No. The Model Penal Code basically rejects Wharton's Rule. See Comment 3 to §5.04(2). The M.P.C. does bar "cumulative" punishment, so that if Bob and Alice had consummated their liaison, neither could have been punished for ***both*** adultery and conspiracy to commit adultery. But the M.P.C. does not prevent a conspiracy conviction merely on the grounds that both parties would be necessary to the substantive crime, had that crime been committed.

52. **(A) Yes.** Where two conspirators are tried together in a single trial, and they are the only ones accused of conspiring, all courts agree that if one is acquitted the other must be. (Note, however, that if the conspiracy involves at least three parties and one is acquitted, the others can still be convicted, even if this occurs in the same trial as the acquittal.)

(B) (i) Probably not; and (ii) No. Where the conspirators are tried in separate trials, the community's sense of injustice at inconsistent verdicts is not nearly as great as where the inconsistency occurs in a single trial. Therefore, most courts will not overturn the guilty verdict. M.P.C. § 5.03 agrees that inconsistent verdicts in separate trials do not necessitate overturning the guilty verdict.

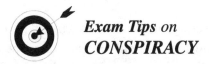

Exam Tips on
CONSPIRACY

This topic is heavily tested. Some key aspects to keep in mind:

Agreement and Intent

☛ **Agreement required:** Remember that the co-conspirators must somehow *agree* to pursue a joint objective.

   ☞ **Agreement without active participation:** But a party may make the necessary agreement without doing so explicitly, and without formally committing to do any specific thing. It's usually enough if the party somehow (by word, by silence, by deed, or whatever) *encourages* the project to move forward. *"Aiding and abetting,"* for instance, is usually enough.

    Example: Z operates a store across the street from, and competitive to, Y's store. Because of Z's unfair business practices, Y worries that Z may force him out of business. Y tells X in a half-jesting manner that if X were a real friend he would "take care" of Z. As a result of Y's remark, X plans for another party to break into Z's store and destroy Z's merchandise. When X tells Y of his plan, Y says, "Sounds great, but don't ask me to do anything to help." X replies, "All you have to do is sit back and let it happen." Because Y made it clear to X that he and X shared a common goal, his actions indicate an agreement and he is guilty of conspiracy to vandalize the store.

   ☞ **Surrounding circumstances:** Words of agreement are not needed — actions and even silence may be sufficient in the circumstances to indicate agreement. Look for defendants who conduct themselves in such a manner as to manifest jointness of action.

    Example: X and Y are suspected of having committed a series of recent robberies. P, an undercover police agent, invites X and Y to her home for drinks and mentions to them that she is impressed with the perpetrators of the recent robberies in the neighborhood. X then suggests that a neighborhood drugstore would be an easy target for a robbery. Y says nothing. P decides to pretend to join in the robbery, in order to obtain evidence of X's and Y's past crimes. All three immediately drive to the store. X is about to enter the store to rob it (with Y waiting in the car) when P arrests both X and Y. Y can be found to have agreed on the robbery plan with X — although Y never verbally agreed to participate in the robbery, his silence plus his driving to the site and waiting is enough to show that he agreed with X to pursue the robbery plan. Therefore Y (as well as X) can be found guilty of conspiracy to rob.

☛ **Only one person holds intent ("unilateral" conspiracy):** If *only one party* has the requisite intent to pursue the criminal objective, then you must address in your essay the issue of whether that party alone may be prosecuted for conspiracy. Remember that: (1) Under the traditional view, unless there were at least two parties holding the requisite intent, there could be *no* prosecution for conspiracy; but (2) Most modern courts (and the MPC) *allow* prosecution for such a "unilateral" conspiracy.

☞ **Feigned agreement:** Many fact patterns will present a party who ***pretends to agree*** to commission of the crime.

> ☞ *Example (undercover agent):* U, an undercover agent, pretends to agree with D, a professional thief, that the two will rob a drugstore. D really intends to cooperate with U in the crime. They drive together to the crime scene, at which point D is arrested before either enter the store. Under the modern view, D is guilty of conspiracy — he had the requisite mental state (agreement to commit a crime with a third person's help), and the fact that U's apparent agreement was fake doesn't change this result.

☛ **D furnishes assistance without agreement:** Don't be fooled by a D who shares the objective of the conspirator(s), but secretly helps without anybody knowing. Although D may be guilty of aiding and abetting, he probably can't be prosecuted for conspiracy.

> *Example:* X and Y, summer campers, decide to kill V, a camp counselor who has punished them. To accomplish their plan, they agree to steal V's asthma medicine. Z, another camper, overhears their conversation and decides to help them without letting them know. He goes to V's room, searches for the medicine, and puts it on V's night table so that X and Y will find it. Several minutes later, X and Y find the medicine on the night table and throw it away. Because he is unable to find the medicine later, V dies. Z would not be liable for conspiracy, because he never made an actual agreement with any other conspirator. (But Z *could* be found guilty of murder as an accomplice.)

> ☞ **Stake in venture:** On the other hand, the requisite agreement probably *will* exist if D1 furnishes preliminary help (goods or services) to D2 with an intent to help D2 commit the crime, and D2 knows that D1 intends to help. Here, the supplying shows the requisite agreement. The issue is whether D1 can be said to have a ***"stake in the venture,"*** i.e., whether D1 has an active desire for the venture to succeed and is trying to bring about that success.

> *Example:* X asks Y to join him in robbing a bank. When Y refuses, X says that he will rob the bank himself if Y will provide a hiding place for him to use after the robbery. Y agrees, if X will pay him $200 from the robbery proceeds. Since Y has a stake in the criminal enterprise, his advance agreement to furnish services may constitute a conspiracy. (The same would be true if Y agreed, in return for similar profit-sharing, just to drive X to the crime scene, or just to act as lookout, or just to drive the getaway car).

Overt act

☛ **States split:** Remember that states are split about whether the conspiracy can be complete even though no conspirator has committed an overt act in furtherance of the conspiracy. So on any fact pattern where there doesn't seem to be an overt act, mention that states may or may not recognize a conspiracy as already existing.

> ☞ **Act of one attributable to all:** Also, remember that even in states requiring an overt act, the overt act of *any* individual conspirator will be deemed an act by *all* conspira-

tors.

Vicarious liability for substantive crimes by other conspirators

☞ In almost any fact pattern involving a conspiracy, you'll have to deal with whether each conspirator is guilty of the substantive crimes carried out by other conspirators. This is especially likely where D1 doesn't expect that D2 will carry out some particular crime as part of the conspiracy, but D2 does so anyway, in order to help the conspiracy succeed.

☞ Remember that in this situation, courts are *split* between two positions, with the second being the modern, and probably majority, view:

❑ **View 1 (traditional):** Under this traditional *"Pinkerton"* view, the *mere fact* that D is part of a conspiracy *automatically* makes him *liable for any substantive crime committed by other conspirators in furtherance of the conspiracy*, at least if the crime was a foreseeable outcome of the conspiracy.

❑ **View 2 (modern):** Under the modern / MPC view, D1 is only liable for substantive crimes by a co-conspirator (call him D2) if D1 meets the standards for *aiding-and-abetting* that crime (i.e., D1 was an "accomplice" to that substantive crime). Usually, if a substantive crime was in furtherance of the conspiracy, D1 will be found to have aided-and-abetted (encouraged or helped) the substantive crime, but this won't always be true.

☞ **Physically absent:** Especially be on the lookout for situations where one of the co-conspirators is *not physically present* when his fellow co-conspirator perpetrates the crime — this is the situation most likely to present the automatic-liability-for-substantive-crimes problem. So look for co-conspirators who *get cold feet*, and also those that are absent for other reasons, such as they're in prison or they're asleep.

☞ *Example:* D1 and D2 agree to commit a burglary by entering V's house to steal her diamonds. They break in, but D1 rapidly gets discouraged when they can't find the diamonds, and leaves. Shortly thereafter, D2 finds the diamonds, and is putting them in his pocket when he is confronted by V. D2, in an attempt to escape with the diamonds, pushes V down stairs, seriously injuring her. (Assume that D2's conduct constitutes battery.) In a "traditional" state, D1 will be liable for the battery committed by D2, since the battery was in furtherance of the objectives of the conspiracy (getting the diamonds), and the traditional rule is that a conspirator is automatically guilty of any substantive crime foreseeably committed by another conspirator in furtherance of the conspiracy's aims. But in a modern / MPC state, D1 will not be liable for battery unless he's found to have "aided and abetted" the battery, which he probably didn't.

Abandonment

☞ When a party *withdraws* his participation before the substantive crime is completed, keep in mind these rules:

☞ **Liability for substantive crimes:** To avoid guilt for the *substantive crimes* committed by the co-conspirators (in a state where being part of the conspiracy is automatically enough to make one guilty of the crimes committed in furtherance of it) it's *not* *necessary* that the withdrawing D try to ***thwart*** the success of the conspiracy. All D has to do is to ***give notice*** of withdrawal (prior to the substantive crime) to each of the co-conspirators, or, alternatively, notify the police that the conspiracy is going on.

☞ **Liability for conspiracy itself:** But the withdrawal does ***not*** avoid guilt for the ***conspiracy itself,*** according to the traditional view (since as soon as the agreement is made, the crime of conspiracy is complete).

    ☞ **MPC gives renunciation defense:** But the MPC *does* recognize a defense of ***renunciation*** in this case, if the conspiracy was ***thwarted*** *and* the renunciation was ***voluntary.***

Wharton's rule

☛ **Wharton's rule summarized:** Keep Wharton's Rule in mind at all times: When a substantive offense is defined so as to require two or persons, the Rule says that there can't be conspiracy to commit that crime unless at least one extra person (i.e., one more than the logically required minimum for the substantive crime) is involved. Watch for this especially on fact patterns involving ***bribery.*** (But remember that many jurisdictions, and the MPC, ***reject*** the Rule, or treat it as merely a rebuttable presumption).

Example: A statute provides: "Any person who shall give or accept a fee not authorized by law as consideration for the act of any public employee is guilty of bribery," a felony. Contractor needs a building permit that normally takes 30 days to issue. Clerk, a clerk in the buildings department, offers to create a false entry in the department's records indicating that the required permit was already issued, if Contractor will pay Clerk $500. They agree to meet the next morning to consummate the transaction. When Contractor arrives with the money, he finds that Clerk has been fired. In a jurisdiction following Wharton's Rule (and treating it as a substantive rule rather than just a presumption about what the legislature intended), neither Contractor nor Clerk can be convicted of conspiracy to bribe, because bribery requires two parties and here, only the minimum two parties were involved.

Conspiracy vs. the Substantive Crime

☛ Distinguish a prosecution for conspiracy from a prosecution for the substantive crime.

☞ **Success not needed:** Don't be fooled by a fact pattern where the conspirators ***never actually accomplish*** what they conspired to do — this ***doesn't matter***, because a conspiracy is committed ***as soon as the agreement is made*** (except in jurisdictions requiring an overt act).

☞ **No merger:** Remember that a defendant can be convicted of *both* conspiracy *and* the substantive crime the conspirators agreed to commit — these ***don't merge*** together. Even the crime of *attempt* does not merge with conspiracy. So make sure to analyze each possible charge separately.

CHAPTER 7

ACCOMPLICE LIABILITY AND SOLICITATION

Introductory note: This chapter examines two ways in which one person can become criminally liable for exhorting another to commit a criminal act. If one encourages or aids another to perform a criminal act, and the latter does so, the former will be liable for the latter's substantive crime; he is said to be, in modern terms, an *"accomplice."* If, on the other hand, one encourages another to do a criminal act, and the latter declines, the former is guilty of the crime of *"solicitation."*

I. PARTIES TO CRIME

A. Various parties: The common law developed a fairly complex scheme for labeling parties according to their relationship to a criminal act. The labels were "principal in the first degree," "principal in the second degree," "accessory before the fact" and "accessory after the fact." Although the first three of these categories are no longer of great significance, it is worthwhile to understand how they have been used, so that one may comprehend older cases.

1. "Principal in first degree": The person who personally performed the *actus reus* of the completed substantive crime was called, in the common-law scheme, a *"principal in the first degree."* Thus if A and B plan to shoot C to death, and A is the one who actually pulls the trigger, A is the principal in the first degree. Every completed substantive crime must have at least one first-degree principal. It is possible for a crime to have more than one, if two or more people each commit an act forming a part of the *actus reus* (e.g., A shoots C in the leg for the purpose of immobilizing him, so that B can then shoot to kill).

2. Principal in second degree: A *principal in the second degree* is one who is present at the crime's commission, and aids and abets its commission, but does not personally perform any acts that constitute the *actus reus*. Thus if A and B decide to murder C, and B is present when A does the shooting, B is a second-degree principal.

a. Constructive presence: Although the second-degree principal must be "present" at the commission of the crime, this requirement may be satisfied by what is sometimes called *"constructive"* presence. For instance, if B, acting as *look-out*, stays outside the building within which A is murdering C, B is probably "constructively present" at the crime, and is therefore a second-degree principal. See L, p. 616.

3. Accessory before the fact: An *accessory before the fact*, like a principal in the second degree, aids and abets the crime rather than committing the *actus reus* himself. He differs from the second-degree principal, however, in that he is *not present* when the crime is carried out. The accessory before the fact may either be the "brains" who organizes the whole operation, or merely one who furnishes slight assistance. L, pp. 616-17.

4. **Accessory after the fact:** An *accessory after the fact* is one who does not participate in the crime itself, but who furnishes post-crime assistance to the perpetrator, in order to prevent him from being arrested. See the fuller discussion *infra*, p. 221.

B. **Procedural effects of classification:** The common law attached great significance to the category within which a particular defendant fell. The classification was of greatest significance in the following respects: (1) an accessory could not be tried before his principal, and could not be acquitted if the principal was convicted; and (2) if the indictment charged the defendant with being an accessory, he could not be convicted of being a principal (and vice versa). See L, pp. 618.

   1. **Categories merged or abolished:** Virtually all states have *abolished* the distinction between a second-degree principal and an accessory before the fact. Thus if one has aided and abetted the commission of a crime, one's punishment is not dependent on presence or absence at the crime scene. The person who assists the crime, but does not commit the *actus reus*, is generally referred to today as an *"accomplice,"* and the person committing the *actus reus* is called the *"principal."* The two are said to have a relationship of *"complicity."*

   2. **Some consequences remain:** There remain some respects in which one who has not committed the *actus reus* is treated differently from one who has. For instance, it is still generally true that an accomplice may not be convicted unless it is proved that his principal is guilty of the substantive crime in question; see *infra*, p. 216. Similarly, an indictment charging the defendant with being an accomplice and acting only prior to the crime may not be sufficient to support a conviction if evidence at trial shows that the defendant in fact carried out the *actus reus*. By and large, however, the only distinction that has to be made is between responsibility for one's own acts and responsibility for the acts of others. It is with this latter sort of responsibility that this chapter is concerned.

II. ACCOMPLICES — THE ACT REQUIREMENT

A. **Aiding and abetting:** The fundamental principle of accomplice liability is that one who *aids, abets, encourages* or *assists* another to perform a crime, will himself be *liable for that crime.*

   1. **Words may be enough:** *Words*, by themselves, may be enough to constitute the requisite link between accomplice and principal. The test is whether the words constituted encouragement and approval of the crime, and thereby assisted it.

   2. **Mere presence not sufficient:** *Mere presence* at the scene of the crime is *not*, by itself, enough to render one an accomplice. It must also be shown that the defendant was at the crime scene for the *purpose of approving and encouraging* commission of the offense. Thus in *Hicks v. U.S.*, 150 U.S. 442 (1893), the Supreme Court held that D could not be convicted of murder merely on the grounds that he was present when his friend shot the deceased; however, his presence, plus a showing that he had previously agreed with the friend that the latter should commit the killing, would have been enough.

      a. **Presence plus flight not sufficient:** Nor is it sufficient that the defendant was not only present at the scene of the crime, but *fled* afterward.

b. Presence as evidence: Although the defendant's presence at the crime scene will not by itself be enough to make him an accomplice, that presence can constitute *evidence* that the defendant intended to give aid, encouragement, etc. Thus in *State v. Parker*, 164 N.W.2d 633 (Minn. 1969), D was one of three hitchhikers picked up by X; D remained in the car without speaking or acting while the other two robbed and beat X. The court held that "if the proof shows that a person is present at the commission of a crime without disapproving or opposing it, it is competent for the jury to consider this conduct in connection with other circumstances and thereby reach the conclusion that he assented to the commission of the crime, lent to it his approval, and was thereby aiding and abetting its commission."

   i. Presence as "look-out": Thus if other evidence suggested that the defendant's presence at the crime was for the purpose of serving as *"look-out,"* this would certainly be enough to allow him to be convicted as an accomplice.

3. Failure to intervene: Normally, the mere fact that the defendant *failed to intervene* to prevent the crime will *not* make him an accomplice, even if the intervention could have been accomplished easily. Nor will the fact that he failed even to speak out against the crime usually be sufficient. (Failure to intervene or speak out is, however, conduct which may be *evidence* of other assistance given by the defendant, such as encouragement before the crime.)

   a. Duty to intervene: There are some situations, however, in which the defendant has an *affirmative legal duty to intervene*. If he fails to do so, this will be enough to make him an accomplice. For instance, if a father were to physically abuse his child, and the child's mother failed to intervene or speak out, she would probably be held to be an accomplice to the father's crime of battery, on the grounds that she had a legal duty to protect her child.

   i. Duties rarely found: However, recall that there are relatively few situations in which a duty to take affirmative action will be imposed (*supra*, pp. 6-8). Thus a driver has been held not to have a duty to try to protect a hitchhiker whom he picks up, even when the hitchhiker is robbed at knife point by the driver's friend and co-passenger. *Pace v. State*, 224 N.E.2d 312 (Ind. 1967).

B. Aid not crucial: It will sometimes be the case that the defendant gives assistance in furtherance of a crime, but that the assistance turns out *not to have been necessary*. In this situation, is the defendant saved from being an accessory?

1. Not a defense: The general answer seems to be "no." That is, as long as the defendant intended to aid the crime, and made its commission easier or more probable in any way, he is an accomplice. The classic illustration of this principle is the case set forth in the following example.

Example: X has seduced the sister-in-law of D (a judge). Her brothers, A and B, pursue X to the nearby town of Stevenson, in order to kill him. One of X's relatives sends X a telegram warning him of the danger. D, learning of this, sends his own telegram to the Stevenson telegraph operator (whom he knows) telling him not to deliver the warning telegram. The warning telegram is not delivered, A and B catch up with X, and kill him. D is charged with being an accomplice in the killing.

Held, it is irrelevant that A and B might have caught up with X and killed him even if the warning telegram had been delivered. "It is quite sufficient if [D's act] facilitated a result that would have transpired without it. It is quite enough if the aid merely renders it easier for the principal actor to accomplish the end intended by him and the aider and abettor, though in all human probability the end would have been attained without it." *State ex rel. Attorney General v. Tally*, 15 So. 722 (Ala. 1894).

2. **Attempted aid:** Suppose that the defendant's acts are not only not necessary to the resulting crime, but *do not influence it at all*. In this situation, which might be termed that of *"attempted assistance"*, most courts would probably *not* treat the defendant as an accomplice to the completed crime. This situation could be compared with that in which the defendant secretly intends to give assistance to another's criminal plans if it turns out to be necessary, but it does not so turn out. See L, p. 624.

    a. **Model Penal Code view:** But the Model Penal Code would make the defendant an accomplice in this "attempted assistance" situation. M.P.C. § 2.06(3)(a)(ii) makes a person liable as an accomplice if, with the purpose of "promoting or facilitating the commission of the offense," he "…attempts to aid such other person in planning or committing it." Thus if, in the *Tally* case, *supra*, the telegraph operator had delivered the warning message anyway, but A and B had nonetheless been able to kill X, D would have been liable as an accomplice to murder under the Code.

3. **Attempts to aid where no crime occurs:** If the assistance attempted to be given by the defendant is unsuccessful, not in the sense that it fails to assist a crime which occurs anyway, but rather, in the sense that the crime sought to be furthered *never takes place*, it is not clear whether the defendant is criminally liable, and if so, for what.

    a. **Crime attempted by principal:** If the principal *attempts* the crime, but fails, it seems reasonable to hold the defendant guilty of *aiding and abetting the attempt*. He would thus be an accomplice to attempt, and would be punishable the same way as if he had made the attempt himself.

    b. **Crime not attempted by principal:** If, on the other hand, the principal does not even attempt the crime, it is not possible to hold the defendant guilty of any crime on accomplice theory, since accomplice liability must be founded upon a crime by the person sought to be aided. (See *infra*, p. 216, regarding the requirement that the principal be guilty.) In many jurisdictions, the defendant would, however, be guilty of the crime of "solicitation" (see *infra*, p. 222).

        i. **Attempt liability:** Additionally, under the Model Penal Code, the defendant might be liable for *attempting* to commit the crime. Thus Comment 7 to M.P.C. § 5.01(3) states that if the judge in *Tally* had sent his telegram, but X was nonetheless able to escape before A and B could try to kill him, the judge would be guilty of attempted murder.

C. **Conspiracy as meeting the act requirement:** It is occasionally held that if the defendant is found to have been in a *conspiracy* with another, he is automatically liable for any crimes committed by that other in furtherance of the conspiracy. See, e.g., the discussion of *Pinkerton v. U.S.*, *supra*, p. 184.

1. **Insufficient under modern view:** However, the modern view seems to be that the act of joining a conspiracy is *not, by itself, enough* to make one an accomplice to all crimes carried out by any conspirator in furtherance of the conspiracy; see *supra*, p. 185. But such membership will, of course, frequently have extremely great evidentiary value in showing that the defendant granted the relevant assistance, encouragement, etc. to the commission of the substantive crimes by other conspirators.

III. ACCOMPLICES — MENTAL STATE

A. **General confusion:** There is great confusion about what *mental state* is required for one to be an accomplice to the crimes of another. In most situations, what is required is that the defendant *intentionally* aid or encourage another's criminal act, and that the defendant also have the mental state necessary for the crime actually committed by the other. In some situations, however, it may be sufficient that the defendant acts with knowledge that the person being assisted will or may commit a criminal offense, but without a purpose that that person do so.

B. **Intentional aid:** The defendant's conduct in rendering assistance or encouragement must generally be intentional in two respects: (1) first, the defendant must intend to commit the acts which in fact give aid or encouragement; and (2) secondly, by committing those acts, the defendant must intend to *help bring about* the other party's criminal act.

1. **Must have purpose to further crime:** Thus it is not enough that the defendant intends acts which have the effect of inducing another person to commit a crime, if it was not the defendant's purpose to help bring that crime about. For instance, in *Hicks v. U.S.*, 150 U.S. 442 (1893), D was charged with being an accomplice to murder, on the grounds that he spoke words to his friend X that had the effect of encouraging X to shoot Y to death. The Supreme Court reversed D's conviction, on the grounds that the trial judge's charge to the jury did not make it clear that it was not enough that D intended to speak the words that he spoke, and that it also had to be proved that D's words were "used by the accused with the intention of encouraging and abetting [X]."

2. **Knowledge not usually enough:** Thus under the most common view, even if the defendant *knows* that the other party intends to commit a crime, and the defendant's conduct is shown to have assisted or encouraged that criminal conduct, the defendant will not be liable unless he *intended* to help bring that crime about. For instance, in *State v. Grebe*, 461 S.W.2d 265 (Mo. 1970), D was charged with inducing her thirteen-year-old son, Kenneth, to kill X. Her conviction as an accomplice was reversed on the grounds that, although she was found by the jury to have in fact encouraged or assisted her son's act of killing, and to have known that he planned to do it, she was not found to have intended to encourage him or assist him. (See the fuller discussion of knowledge without intent *infra*, p. 210).

3. *Mens rea* **of underlying crime:** One way courts have expressed this principle is by holding that the defendant must, in addition to intending to engage in acts which have the effect of assisting or encouraging criminal conduct, have the *mens rea for the crime committed* by the other person.

a. **Ulterior motives:** Thus if the defendant's purpose in rendering aid or encouragement is not to bring about the criminal result, but to accomplish *some other objective*, the defendant might not be liable as an accomplice. This may be true, for instance, where the defendant's purpose is *to trap* the person being "assisted."

Example: D, after spending an evening drinking with X, discovers that his watch is missing. He accuses X of stealing it, but X denies it. The two then agree to pull off a burglary together. D boosts X through a transom; while X is inside, D telephones the police. He returns to receive bottles of whiskey that X hands him through the transom. The police arrest both D and X, and D explains that he never planned to steal the whiskey, but merely wanted to get even with X for stealing his watch.

Held, D is not an accomplice to burglary, because he did not have the mental state required for burglary (i.e., *inter alia*, the intent to permanently take the store's property). *Wilson v. People*, 87 P.2d 5 (Col. 1939).

Note: But it should be recognized that it was not D's desire to trap X, *per se*, that prevented him from being an accomplice. Rather, it was the coincidental fact that this desire *prevented D from having the mental state required for burglary* (in this case, the intent to permanently deprive the store of its goods) that exculpated him. A mere intent to trap the other will not always be sufficient to do this. For instance, suppose that D's scheme to trap X was to encourage X to murder Y. If D then turned in X after the murder, D would not be able to defend on the grounds that he bore no particular ill will against Y; he would still have had the requisite *mens rea* for murder (intent to take another's life).

C. **Knowledge, but not intent, as to criminal result:** Suppose that the defendant *knows* that his conduct will encourage or assist another person in committing a crime, but the defendant does not particularly *intend or desire* to bring about that criminal result. Is this enough to make the defendant liable as an accomplice to the crime?

1. **Not usually sufficient:** Most courts hold that the defendant is *not* an accomplice in this situation. The best-known case so holding is *U.S. v. Peoni*, 100 F.2d 401 (2d Cir. 1938), in which Learned Hand wrote that in order for the defendant to aid and abet another's crime, it is necessary "that he in some sort associate himself with the venture, that he participate in it as in something that he wishes to bring about, that he seek by his action to make it succeed. All the words used, even the most colorless 'abet', carry an implication of purposive attitude towards it." The definitions of accomplice liability "have nothing whatever to do with the probability that the forbidden result would follow upon the accessory's conduct...."

2. **Model Penal Code in agreement:** The Model Penal Code agrees, with *Peoni*, that *mere knowledge* by the defendant that the person he is aiding intends to commit a crime, is *insufficient* to make the defendant liable as an accomplice. M.P.C. § 2.06(3)(a) allows accomplice liability only where the defendant has acted "with the *purpose* of promoting or facilitating the commission of the offense...." (But a preliminary draft of the Code, ultimately rejected by the American Law Institute, would have allowed accomplice liability based on the defendant's "knowledge that such other person was committing or had the

purpose of committing the crime," provided that the defendant "substantially facilitated" the crime's commission. M.P.C. § 2.04(3)(b) (Tent. Dr. No. 1).

3. **Recommendation of source for drugs:** The sufficiency of "mere knowledge" arises frequently in cases where the defendant *recommends a source for illegal drugs*, and is then charged with being an accomplice to the resulting illegal sale. Courts have almost never been willing to make the defendant an accomplice on such facts.

4. **Knowledge may be sufficient for serious crime:** As we've just discussed, mere knowledge (without intent) that a crime will result is not usually enough to make one an accomplice. However, where the defendant knows that the person he is assisting intends to commit a *serious* crime, courts are somewhat more likely to hold the defendant to be an accomplice than where only a minor crime is involved. As one court stated, "one who sells a gun to another knowing that he is buying it to commit a murder, would hardly escape conviction as an accessory to the murder by showing that he received full price for the gun." *Backun v. U.S.,* 112 F.2d 635 (4th Cir. 1940). See also *People v. Lauria, supra*, p. 181, which stated that where a supplier furnishes equipment with knowledge that a serious crime will be committed with it, this knowledge may by itself be enough to impute to the supplier an intent to produce the criminal result.

5. **Criminal facilitation:** Some states have dealt with the defendant who supplies goods knowing that they are to be used for a criminal purpose, but without any particular intent that they be so used, by making him liable for a separate, non-accessory crime. Thus in New York, a person who, "believing it probable that he is rendering aid to a person who intends to commit a...felony,...engages in conduct which provides such person with means or opportunity for the commission thereof and which in fact aids such person to commit such...felony," is guilty of second-degree *"criminal facilitation."* N.Y. Penal Law § 115.05.

D. **Assistance with crime of recklessness or negligence:** As noted, the generally-accepted *mens rea* requirement for accomplice liability is that the defendant have the same mental state as is needed for the crime committed by the principal. If that crime is not one that requires intent, but merely *recklessness or negligence*, can the defendant be liable as an accomplice upon a mere showing that he was reckless or negligent (as the case may be) concerning the risk that the principal would commit the crime?

1. **Lending car to drunk driver:** The issue arises most frequently where the defendant *lends his car to one that he knows to be drunk*. If the drunken driver then kills, or wounds, a pedestrian or other driver, is the car owner liable as an accomplice to manslaughter or battery? A number of courts have indeed *found accomplice liability* in this situation. Such a result can be defended on the grounds that it does not violate the general rule that an accomplice must have at least the same mental state as would be needed to convict him of the crime if he were the principal.

2. **Liability sometimes rejected:** But other courts have held that only an *intent* on the part of the defendant to produce the crime, not merely recklessness or negligence as to the risk of it, will suffice for accomplice liability. See, e.g., *People v. Marshall*, 106 N.W.2d 842 (Mich. 1961), a case in which the drunk driver caused a death; the court refused to find the owner liable for manslaughter as an accomplice, on the grounds that the death "was not

counselled by him, accomplished by another acting jointly with him, nor did it occur in the attempted achievement of some common enterprise." (But the defendant was guilty of the statutory misdemeanor of lending one's car to a drunk driver.)

    a. Liability possible without accomplice theory: But it is important to realize that a defendant like the one in *Marshall* may, depending on the state's statutory scheme, be criminally liable *without respect to accomplice theory*. For instance, in many states there is a statutory form of manslaughter for which one becomes liable by committing an "unlawful act" which is the legal cause of another's death. (*Infra*, p. 259.) In such a state, the defendant in *Marshall*, by committing the misdemeanor of lending his car to a drunk, could then be liable *as a principal* for involuntary manslaughter (assuming that the drunk's conduct was held not to break the causal chain between the defendant's act and the death). (Apparently, the state of Michigan at the time *Marshall* was tried did not recognize the crime of unlawful act-manslaughter.)

        i. Negligence-manslaughter: Alternatively, if a state defines the crime of "criminal negligence-manslaughter" (*infra*, p. 257), the defendant who lent his car keys to a drunk could be liable as a principal for manslaughter upon a showing that his conduct constituted *criminal negligence* (again assuming that the negligence was found to be the proximate cause of the death). See L, p. 631-32.

E. Strict liability: Suppose the defendant's conduct has the effect of encouraging or aiding another to commit a *strict-liability offense*. If the defendant not only had no intent to bring about the offense, but neither knew nor should have known that the offense would occur, should the defendant be liable as an accomplice? Such liability would not violate the rule that the accomplice's mental state must be that which would be necessary for commission of the crime as a principal, since, by hypothesis, a strict-liability offense requires no mental state.

    1. Liability rejected: Nonetheless, most courts have *refused* to impose such accomplice liability.

    2. Vicarious liability: However, the legislature is always free to establish, by statute, that one person is *vicariously liable* for the acts of another, at least where the offense is of a "public welfare" type (i.e., one that does not carry with it great social opprobrium or severe punishment; see *supra*, p. 25). In this situation, the person made vicariously liable is not really an "accomplice to crime." Rather, he is made accountable under a regulatory scheme.

    Example: Suppose a state makes the owner of any vehicle liable for any parking violation committed by one who borrows the car from the owner. The owner is not really being held liable "as an accomplice" — instead, the state is simply imposing vicarious liability on car owners for parking violations by drivers, regardless of whether the owner was at fault.

IV. ACCOMPLICES — ADDITIONAL CRIMES BY PRINCIPAL

A. Results that are "natural and probable" but not intended: Suppose that the defendant has assisted or encouraged his principal to commit a particular offense (call it the *"target"* crime), but that the principal commits not only this offense, but *others as well* (call them *"non-target"* crimes). To what extent is the defendant liable, as an accomplice, for these additional non-target crimes which he did not intend to assist or encourage?

1. **Majority rule:** Courts vary on how they handle this problem. But the majority approach seems to be as follows: If the non-target offenses are the *"natural and probable"* (even though unintended) consequences of the conduct that the defendant *did* intend to assist, the defendant is ***liable as an accessory*** for these crimes as well. The case in the following example represents this majority approach.

    Example: D1 agrees to help two other Ds burglarize a tavern. D1 waits in a car outside the tavern while the other two Ds, at this time unarmed, go inside to commit the burglary. While they are inside, they are surprised by the owner; one of them picks up a gun from the bar and shoots the owner, wounding him. D1 is convicted of being an accomplice not only to the burglary, but to attempted murder.

    Held, D1's conviction affirmed. The statute makes one accountable for another's conduct "during the commission of an offense," if one aided or abetted that offense. Since D1 aided and abetted the offense of burglary, and since the attempted murder occurred during the course of, and in furtherance of, the burglary offense, he is liable as an accomplice for that attempted murder. *People v. Kessler,* 315 N.E.2d 29 (Ill. 1974).

    Note: A dissent in *Kessler* stressed that D1's companions were not armed when they went inside the tavern, and that there was no evidence that D1 intended to encourage any shootings by them. Furthermore, according to the dissent, the legislative history showed that the statute was meant only to cover conduct which the alleged accomplice intends to bring about.

2. **Trial court's duty to identify "target" crime:** In order for a defendant to be convicted of a non-target crime based on the "natural and probable consequences" doctrine, at least one state, California, now requires the trial court to ***identify and describe to the jury*** the target crimes that the defendant might have assisted or encouraged. Without such an instruction, the California Supreme Court has said, the jury has no way to decide whether the resulting crime was the "natural and probable consequence" of the target crime. *People v. Prettyman,* 926 P.2d 1013 (Cal. 1996).

    Example: H and W are husband and wife. W temporarily gives her wallet to V, who then refuses to give it back. W asks H to beat V up in order to teach V a lesson. (Exactly what W says, and what kind of a beating she intends, are later disputed at trial). H beats V repeatedly in the head with a lead pipe, and V dies. H is charged with murder, and W is charged with murder on an accomplice theory.

    Held (on appeal), once the trial judge instructed the jury that W would be liable for any "natural and probable consequences" stemming from a target crime that she urged H to commit, the judge should have identified for the jury exactly what target crimes W may have committed. Only with this information could the jury figure out whether the fatal beating was a natural and probable consequence of the target crime. For instance, if W asked H to commit an ordinary assault on V, but had no idea (or desire) that H would use a lead pipe, the jury could *not* properly find that the murder of V was a natural and probable consequence of the assault encouraged by W. On the other hand, if W asked H to use a lead pipe in the assault, then the murder *could* properly be found to be the natural and probable result of the assault. (However, the error was harmless.) *People v. Prettyman, supra.*

3. **Model Penal Code rejects extended liability:** The Model Penal Code rejects the principle allowing an accomplice to be held liable for "natural and probable" crimes beyond those which he intended to aid or encourage. As the Code draftsmen state, "Probabilities have an important evidential bearing on these issues [of intent to aid or encourage]; to make them independently sufficient is to predicate the liability on negligence when, for good reason, more is normally required before liability is found." Comment 6(b) to M.P.C. § 2.06(3).

4. **Felony-murder and misdemeanor-manslaughter:** Many of the cases which apparently involve application of the "natural and probable consequences" rule are really founded on the separate doctrines of *felony-murder* and *misdemeanor-manslaughter*. The felony-murder rule, discussed *infra*, p. 237, provides that if, in the course of certain dangerous felonies, the felon kills another, even *accidentally*, he is liable for murder. Since in this situation the *mens rea* for the murder charge is not intent-to-kill but intent-to-commit-a-felony, it is not unjust to impose murder liability not only on the person who actually fires the accidental shot, but upon those who are assisting him in the felony. Thus accomplice liability in this situation does not run afoul of the theoretical principle that one should not be liable as an accomplice unless one has the *mens rea* required for the crime.

    a. **Principal commits murder intentionally:** But if A aids or abets B to commit one of the enumerated dangerous felonies (e.g., robbery), and B *intentionally* kills the robbery victim, it is not so clear that A should be liable as an accomplice to murder, based on the felony-murder theory. B is obviously liable for ordinary intent-to-kill murder; A is liable as an accomplice if the murder can be said to be *"in furtherance of"* the robbery (whether or not A specifically intended or contemplated that the robbery might require use of lethal force by himself or B). If the murder is not directly in furtherance of the robbery, but committed during its course, the courts are split: the court in the following example took a hard line.

        Example: D and Whiteside agree to rob a cab driver, X. While D puts a choke-hold on X's head, Whiteside shoots X (apparently intentionally) through the head, killing him. D is charged with murder, on the theory that he was an accomplice to Whiteside, and that regardless of Whiteside's actual intent, Whiteside is guilty of felony-murder since he killed during the perpetration of robbery. D defends on the ground that he never intended for Whiteside to shoot X, and that he deplored the shooting.

        Held, D's conviction of murder affirmed. D clearly participated in the robbery, and the killing occurred "in perpetrating" the robbery, thus making the killing felony-murder. Therefore, even though "it may be true that the ultimate tragedy of the cab driver's senseless murder was far from [D's] mind," his being an accomplice to the robbery makes him liable for the felony-murder committed by Whiteside. *U.S. v. Carter*, 445 F.2d 669 (D. C. Cir. 1971).

        Note: A dissent argued that to convict D of felony-murder, the jury should have been required to find that the shooting by Whiteside occurred not only "during the course of" the robbery, but in "furtherance of a common design or purpose" on the part of D and Whiteside. For this, according to the dissent, it should have been necessary to show that D and Whiteside at least had a conditional plan to use lethal force if that was the only way the robbery could be completed. Otherwise, the possibility remains that the killing was the "independent act of [Whiteside], committed to the dismay of [D]."

b. Harshness of doctrine: The *Carter* case shows one aspect of the harshness of the felony-murder doctrine, since under the majority's view, one who agrees to participate in a robbery in which he anticipates that no lethal force will be used may become vicariously liable not just for an accidental death, but for an independent act of rage or will on the part of a co-felon. Accordingly, at least one state, New York, has enacted a limited statutory defense, applicable if the defendant (1) was unarmed, and (2) reasonably believed that his colleagues were unarmed and that they were not planning to cause serious injury. N.Y. Penal Law § 125.25(3).

c. Model Penal Code might give different results: The result in *Carter* might have been different under the Model Penal Code. The Code, as noted, rejects the rule making an accomplice liable for all "natural and probable consequences." A person has accomplice liability if he participates in the conduct causing a particular criminal result, and is "personally culpable with respect to the result to the extent demanded by the definition of the crime." M.P.C. § 2.06, Comment 7. In the case of felony-murder, the accomplice will only be liable if he acts "recklessly under circumstances manifesting extreme indifference to the value of human life." (M.P.C. § 210.2(1)(b).) However, the Code "presumes" such reckless indifference if the defendant is an accomplice in, *inter alia*, robbery. *Id.*

    i. Application to *Carter*: Thus in a jurisdiction following the Model Penal Code approach, the prosecutor in *Carter* would have been the beneficiary of a presumption that D had acted with the requisite recklessness and extreme indifference to human life. However, D could then have attempted to rebut this presumption by showing that he was not reckless and was not extremely indifferent to the value of human life (e.g., by showing that he did not know Whiteside had a gun, or that he told Whiteside not to harm the cabdriver). Thus the result in *Carter* might have been, but would not necessarily have been, different under the Model Penal Code.

d. Misdemeanor-manslaughter: The ***misdemeanor-manslaughter rule*** is similarly a reasonable grounds for imposing liability on an accomplice for an unintended consequence. For instance, suppose A assists B in performing an unlawful abortion (a misdemeanor) on C, and C dies as a result; if the jurisdiction makes B guilty of manslaughter solely because he participated in a misdemeanor that caused a death, it is not unfair to hold A liable for manslaughter as an accomplice. A's mental state (intent to assist a misdemeanor) is no less culpable than B's, and is no less than is required for B's conviction of manslaughter as a principal.

LEXIS®-*NEXIS*® *Searches on* **ADDITIONAL CRIMES BY PRINCIPAL**

Sub-Topic	Suggested Searches
"Natural and probable" additional crimes	`(accomplice or (aid! w/3 abet!)) w/40 ((natural w/3 probable) w/10 (result or crime))`

Accomplice liability in felony-murder and misdemeanor-manslaughter cases	`(accomplice or (aid! w/3 abet!)) w/40 ((felony w/3 murder) or (misdemeanor w/3 manslaughter))`

V. GUILT OF THE PRINCIPAL

A. Principal must generally be guilty: Since the theory behind accomplice liability is that one is made accountable for the crimes of another, it is logical to require the prosecution to prove that the person being aided or encouraged (the principal) is *in fact guilty* of the crime to which the defendant is being charged with being an accomplice. As is discussed below, there are now a few situations in which a court might hold the accomplice liable for a crime as to which the principal did not have the requisite mental state; nonetheless, as a general rule the principal's guilt must be shown.

Example: D and a companion named Bose burglarize a house. Shortly thereafter, when only Bose is in the getaway car, the police stop the car. Bose starts to shoot at the police, in an attempt to escape. The police return fire, and Bose is killed. D is charged with murder, on the theory that he was an accomplice of Bose, and that Bose's death occurred as part of the burglary that they performed together.

Held, D's conviction reversed. Accomplice liability can exist only where the principal could be liable for the crime in question. Here, although Bose may have had one kind of *mens rea* sufficient for murder (reckless indifference to human life, shown by his initiation of the gun-battle), he could not have been convicted of murder because murder is the taking of the life of *another*. Since Bose obviously couldn't be guilty of murdering himself, D cannot be liable as an accomplice. (Nor can D be liable under the felony-murder doctrine, because in California that doctrine does not apply where one of the felons, rather than an innocent person, is killed; see *infra*, p. 241). *People v. Antick*, 539 P.2d 243 (Cal. 1975).

1. **Principal's conviction not necessary:**   But it is not necessary that the principal be *convicted*. For instance, if A is charged with assisting B to commit a robbery, and B is never arrested or brought to trial, A can nonetheless be convicted of being an accomplice to the robbery. The prosecution will have to show, in its case against A, that B committed the robbery, but there does not have to be an independent verdict against B.

2. **Inconsistent verdicts in same trial:**   Suppose, however, that the principal and accomplice are tried in the same trial, and the principal is acquitted. May the accomplice be convicted? The generally-accepted rule is that the accomplice must *also be acquitted*. But in a few situations, if the principal is the beneficiary of some special defense not applicable to the accomplice, the accomplice may, in some courts, be convicted. See, e.g., *U.S. v. Bryan*, *infra*, p. 217.

3. **Collateral estoppel to aid accomplice:**   Although it is not necessary that the principal be convicted prior to the trial of the accomplice, what happens where the principal is *acquitted* prior to the accomplice's trial? May the accomplice use this fact to automatically foreclose his own liability, or must he relitigate the issue of the principal's guilt?

   a. *Taylor* **allows estoppel:**   At least one court, the California Supreme Court, has permitted the accomplice to use the doctrine of *collateral estoppel* to prevent his prosecution. In *People v. Taylor*, 527 P.2d 622 (Cal. 1974), D drove a getaway car as part of a robbery scheme in which A and B committed the actual robbery. B was killed as part of a gun-battle initiated by the robbery victim. A was acquitted of murdering B, apparently because the prosecution failed to show that he had the requisite malice aforethought. (The felony-murder doctrine was ruled inapplicable.) D then argued that A's acquittal should be binding on the prosecution vis a vis D's own liability, and the California Supreme Court agreed.

    i. **Rationale:** The court based its decision principally on the theory that the public's belief in the integrity of the judicial system requires a certain degree of consistency between verdicts. "Few things undermine the layman's faith in the integrity of our legal institutions more than the specter of a system which results in a person being punished for the acts of another, when the actor himself under identical charges had been previously exonerated from responsibility for those very acts."

B. Principal without required mental state: It is generally held that the accomplice cannot be convicted unless the principal is shown to have had the *required mental state* for the crime in question.

    1. **Illustration:** This is illustrated by *State v. Hayes*, 16 S.W. 514 (Mo. 1891). D and Hill agreed to burglarize a general store. D opened the window, and helped Hill climb through into the building. Hill passed out merchandise to D, and the police arrived shortly thereafter. It developed that Hill was in fact a relative of the storeowners, that he never had any intention of committing a burglary, and that he had feigned acquiescence merely to trap D. The court held that since Hill, as principal, did not have the mental state for burglary, D could not be convicted of being an accomplice. (Nor could D be convicted as a principal, since he himself did not enter the store.)

        a. **Criticism:** Observe that if Hill had helped D through the store, instead of vice versa, D would have been liable as a principal notwithstanding Hill's complete lack of criminal intent. It seems unfair to convict or acquit D based solely upon the fortuity of which role in the plan he occupied, since his culpability is roughly the same in either case. See K&S, pp. 701-02.

    2. **Abandonment of *mens rea* requirement:** A few courts have apparently simply abandoned the requirement that the principal have the required mental state, at least where he performs the *actus reus* and the accomplice does have the *mens rea* for the crime.

        a. **Innocent dupe:** Thus in *U.S. v Bryan*, 438 F.2d 88 (3d Cir. 1973), Echols was charged with having stolen cases of scotch from a pier, and Bryan with having aided and abetted him. Echols was a truck driver who picked up the whiskey by presenting false documents; Bryan supplied the documents. The trial judge concluded that there was at least a reasonable doubt as to whether Echols was anything more than an *innocent dupe* (who did not realize that the papers were false). The judge therefore acquitted Echols, but convicted Bryan.

            i. **Rationale:** The Court of Appeals affirmed, holding that although accomplice liability does require at least proof that the physical aspects of the crime (here, the removal of the whiskey) were committed by the "principal," it is not required that the principal be found to have had the necessary *mental state*. Since Echols definitely removed the whiskey, this was sufficient to make Bryan guilty of aiding and abetting, since he was found to have the requisite intent to steal. (The court also held that the conviction could alternatively be affirmed on the theory that Bryan was in fact the principal; the court asserted that the indictment charging Bryan with being merely an aider and abettor was sufficient to give him fair notice of the prosecution's case so as to permit his conviction as principal.)

3. **Complete defense:** A similar result may occur if the "principal" has a ***complete defense***, which the accomplice does not share. For example, assume that the "principal" is able to show that he was ***entrapped*** into committing the offense in question by government agents, but his companion was not entrapped, and participated completely of his own volition. Under these facts, the companion could be convicted of aiding and abetting, notwithstanding the principal's acquittal.

4. **Model Penal Code's attempt theory:** The Model Penal Code has a different way of sometimes making the accomplice guilty when his "principal' is not. M.P.C. § 5.01(3) provides that "a person who engages in conduct designed to aid another to commit a crime which would establish his complicity under Section 2.06 [accomplice liability section] if the crime were committed by such other person, is guilty of an ***attempt*** to commit the crime, although the crime is not committed or attempted by such other person." Thus D would be liable, on the facts of *Hayes*, for ***attempted burglary***.

5. **Use of innocent agent:** Keep in mind that in some "guilty accomplice but innocent principal" cases, it may be possible to charge the "accomplice" with being ***himself a principal***. For instance, M.P.C. § 2.06(2)(a) makes one liable for the acts of another when "acting with the kind of culpability that is sufficient for the commission of the offense, he causes an ***innocent or irresponsible*** person to engage in such conduct." Thus in *U.S. v. Bryan*, *supra*, p. 217, the prosecution could have proceeded on the theory that Echols (the truck driver) was an innocent party who believed the documents were valid, and that Bryan was the principal. This would simply be another application of the well-accepted rule that one may commit the *actus reus* of a crime through the conduct of an innocent person (e.g., a child).

    a. **Rape case:** Such a theory is illustrated by *Regina v. Cogan*, 2 All E.R. 1059 (Eng. 1975), in which D forced his wife, against her will, to have intercourse with his friend Cogan, after duping Cogan into believing that his wife had consented. Cogan was acquitted of the rape, because of his genuine though unreasonable belief as to consent (see *D.P.P. v. Morgan*, *supra*, p. 28). Nonetheless, D's conviction of rape was ***affirmed***, on the grounds that there was certainly a rape (in the sense of unconsented-to sexual intercourse), and that D was simply using Cogan "as a means to procure a criminal purpose." The court stressed that D could have been convicted as a principal (and then went on to hold that he could also be convicted on an "aider and abettor" theory, because "convictions should not be upset because of mere technicalities of pleading an indictment.")

VI. WITHDRAWAL BY THE ACCOMPLICE

A. **Withdrawal as defense:** Just as one charged with conspiracy may sometimes raise the defense that he withdrew (*supra*, p. 189), so one who has given aid or encouragement prior to a crime may, if he changes his mind, be able to ***withdraw*** and thus avoid accomplice liability.

1. **Effect of aid must be undone:** It is not enough that the defendant has a subjective change of heart, and gives no further assistance prior to the crime. He must, at the very least, make it ***clear to the other party*** that he is repudiating his past aid or encouragement.

   Example: X and D witness an altercation between a police officer and two civilians. X, whom D knows to have a gun, suggests that D go with him to a nearby rooftop to "shoot the police." D goes up to the rooftop, and then decides to leave. After he does so, X shoots the police officer to death. D is charged with being an accomplice to first-degree murder.

   Held, D's conviction affirmed. First, D's act of leaving the rooftop was not enough to prevent accomplice liability from arising, since "presence at the scene of a crime is not an essential element to the crime of aiding and abetting." Secondly, D's leaving was not an effective withdrawal, because there is no evidence that D "communicated to [X] that he was leaving or that he disapproved of the contemplated act, or that he otherwise sought to actively withdraw the support to the proposed event which his presence on the roof supplied." *State v. Thomas*, 356 A.2d 433 (N.J. Super. 1976).

2. **Verbal withdrawal sometimes sufficient:** If the defendant's aid has been only ***verbal*** (e.g., encouragement or strategic suggestions), he may be able to withdraw merely by stating to the other party that he now withdraws from the project and disapproves of it. But if his assistance has been more tangible, he may have to take affirmative action to undo his effects. For instance, if he has ***supplied arms***, the court may very well hold that he has not withdrawn unless he has ***gotten the arms back***. See Comment 9(c) to M.P.C. § 2.06(6)(c).

3. **Warning to authorities:** Alternatively, the defendant can almost always make an effective withdrawal by ***warning the authorities*** prior to commission of the crime. Thus M.P.C. § 2.06(6)(c)(ii) grants the defense of withdrawal where the accomplice gives "timely warning to the law enforcement authorities or otherwise makes proper effort to prevent the commission of the offense."

4. **Not required that crime be thwarted:** Regardless of the means used to withdraw, it is generally not required that the crime actually be thwarted. Thus if the defendant in *Thomas, supra*, had told his companion "I don't want any part of this shooting," and had then left the roof, he probably would have had the defense of withdrawal even if the companion went ahead with the murder.

5. **Withdrawal motivated by fear of detection:** A few states impose additional requirements, such as the requirement that the withdrawal be "voluntary," rather than motivated by a particular threat of apprehension. Thus N.Y. Penal Law § 40.10(1) grants the withdrawal defense only to one who manifests a "voluntary and complete renunciation of his criminal purpose," and makes a "substantial effort to prevent the commission [of the crime]."

VII. VICTIMS AND OTHER EXCEPTIONS TO ACCOMPLICE LIABILITY

A. **Defendant who could not be liable as principal:** Many crimes are defined in such a way that they can only be committed by members of a ***certain class***. For instance, statutory rape is defined so that it can only be committed by a male. Does it follow from this that a defendant charged with accomplice liability for such a crime may defend on the ground that he could not be liable as a principal, since he is not part of the class which can commit the crime? The answer is that there is clearly *no general defense* based on these lines. Thus if it were shown that D, a woman, assisted her brother in having intercourse with a girl below the age of consent, D could be liable as an accomplice to statutory rape, even though she could obviously not be guilty of that crime as principal.

B. Exceptions for certain classes: Nonetheless, there are certain classes of persons as to whom a court will conclude that no accomplice liability should be imposed.

1. **Victims:** The most obvious such class is composed of *victims* of the crime in question. Even though the victim may, in a significant sense, have helped bring about the crime, the court will conclude that it would be illogical and unfair to impose accessorial liability.

   a. **Statutory rape:** Thus it is universally held that a *female below the age of consent* will not be liable as an accessory to statutory rape of herself, even though she may have given extensive assistance or encouragement to the male. As a court stated in so holding in *Queen v. Tyrell*, 1 Q.B. 710 (Eng. 1894), the statutory rape provision was passed "for the purpose of protecting women and girls against themselves," and it would be illogical for the persons meant to be protected to be punished.

   b. **Kidnap victims and persons extorted from:** Similarly, a businessman who meets the demands of an extortionist or blackmailer, or a parent who pays a ransom to a kidnapper of his child, will not be liable as an accessory. See Comment 9(a) to M.P.C. § 2.06(6).

2. **Crime logically requiring second person:** A second class of persons who will generally not be liable as accomplices exists where a crime is defined so as to logically require participation by a second person, as to whom *no direct punishment has been authorized* by the legislature. For instance, an abortion cannot be performed without a pregnant woman, nor an act of prostitution without a customer, nor an illegal drug sale without a purchaser. If the legislature has not specifically authorized punishment for the pregnant woman, the prostitute's customer or the purchaser, these persons will generally not be punished as accomplices to the principal crime.

   a. **Rationale:** Such non-liability is usually justified on the grounds that the legislature must have known that these persons would inevitably be part of the crime, and if it chose not to impose punishment, courts should not do so by the indirect means of accomplice theory. See M.P.C. § 2.06(6)(b), making the defendant not liable as an accomplice if "the offense is so defined that his conduct is inevitably incident to its commission."

   b. **Legislature's right to impose specific punishment:** But as a corollary, the legislature is of course free to authorize particular punishment of the person whose participation is inevitable. For instance, New York's so-called "John law" makes it a misdemeanor to "patronize a prostitute." N.Y. Penal Law § 230.02.

VIII. POST-CRIME ASSISTANCE

A. Accessory after the fact: One who knowingly gives assistance to a felon, for the purpose of helping him *avoid apprehension* following his crime, is an *accessory after the fact*. Under present law, the accessory after the fact is not liable for the felony itself as an accomplice would be. Rather, he has committed a distinct violation, based upon the obstruction of justice, and his punishment will not depend upon the penalty attached to the felony committed. See L, pp. 645-46.

B. Elements of the offense: For one to be guilty as an accessory after the fact, the following elements must be shown:

1. **Commission of a felony:** A completed felony must have been committed. It is not enough that the defendant *mistakenly believed* that the person he was assisting had committed a felony. (But it is not necessary that the person aided have been formally charged with the felony, or even that the felony have been discovered.) See L, p. 643.

2. **Knowledge of felony:** The defendant must be shown to have *known*, not merely suspected, that the felony was committed. Also, he must be shown to have had an understanding of the *essential elements* of the crime.

   Example: Suppose D finds a gun, and knows that the gun was illegally in the possession of X, a person known to D to be a felon. (D knows that for a felon to possess a gun is itself a felony.) However, D does not know that X has recently used the gun in a murder. D helps X destroy the gun. D could not be charged as an accessory after the fact to murder, because he did not know the essential elements of the underlying crime, i.e., that the gun had been used in a murder. (However, he *could* be charged as an accessory after the fact to the gun-control violation, since he knew the essential elements of that violation.)

3. **Knowledge of the felon's identity:** The assistance must be given to the *felon personally*. (But it is probably not necessary that the defendant have known the *name* of the felon; one who sees a robber escaping and who helps him do so is probably an accessory even if he never learns the robber's name.)

4. **Failure to inform not sufficient:** The accessory must be shown to have taken *affirmative acts* to hinder the felon's arrest. It is not enough that the defendant *refuses to give information to the authorities*. Thus in *U.S. v. Magness*, 456 F.2d 976 (9th Cir. 1972), D's conviction as an accessory was reversed even though it was shown that he lied by telling authorities that he had not seen the felon for twenty years (when he had in fact seen him several times within that week). (However, the result in *Magness* may be due to the fact that the federal accessory statute in question requires a positive act of concealment. In some states, the act of giving false information with the intent of diverting suspicion may be enough for accessorial liability. But a mere failure to report the felon to the police will not be enough in any jurisdiction.)

C. Misprision of felony: At common law, one who simply failed to report a known felon was guilty of *misprision of felony*. However, as a statutory offense the crime is virtually non-existent in the U.S. See, e.g., *Holland v. State*, 302 So.2d 806 (Fla. App. 1974), refusing to recognize the offense. (D, City Manager of the city of Pinellas Park, Florida, discovered marijuana growing in his assistant's back yard, and reported him to the police, but decided not to press charges; D was indicted for misprision!)

D. Compounding crime: A number of states make **compounding crime** an offense. The offense typically consists of an agreement not to prosecute what one knows to be a crime, in return for **payment of consideration** by the criminal. See L, pp. 648-50 and fn. 82 thereto.

IX. SOLICITATION

A. Solicitation defined: The common-law crime of **solicitation** occurs when one **requests or encourages another** to perform a criminal act, regardless of whether the latter agrees. If he does agree, both parties will generally be guilty of conspiracy; if he goes on to commit the crime, both will be liable for the substantive offense (one as accomplice and the other as principal). Therefore, the practical utility of punishing the offense of solicitation is in those cases where the person who is requested to commit the crime **refuses.**

Example: D1 owes X $30,000 for diamonds he has bought from him and not paid for. X tells D1 that if he is not paid soon, he will have to go bankrupt. D1 instead introduces X to D2, and D1 and D2 propose that X pursue a scheme whereby he increases his credit rating, buys a lot of diamonds, sells them to raise quick money, and goes bankrupt before paying for them. Then, according to the proposal, D1, D2 and X will split the proceeds. X complains to the police, and D1 and D2 are charged with solicitation of larceny.

Held, the Ds' conviction affirmed. It is clear that the Ds intended X to engage in conduct constituting grand larceny, and that they requested him to do so. Also, the solicitation statute is constitutional even though it does not contain a requirement of corroboration. *People v. Lubow*, 272 N.E.2d 331 (N.Y. 1971).

B. No overt act required: Unlike conspiracy, the crime of solicitation is never construed so as to require an *overt act*. As soon as the defendant makes his request or proposal, the crime is complete.

C. No corroboration required: It is not generally necessary for the solicitee's testimony to be *corroborated*. This had led some people to feel that making solicitation a crime raises a great risk of convicting the innocent, and also a risk of blackmail. Suppose, for instance, that X, a married woman, tells the police that D, a man, has proposed that she commit adultery with him. If X's testimony is not required to be corroborated, there is a substantial risk either that: (1) X has misinterpreted ambiguous words spoken by D (e.g., "Why don't we go out and have a good time") or (2) X is lying to get even with D for something else (e.g., jilting her). Alternatively, it would be easy for X to blackmail D by merely threatening to make such a complaint.

1. Some statutes require corroboration: For this reason, some solicitation statutes require either corroborative testimony from someone other than the solicitee, or some other indication that the offense really occurred. See L, p. 528-29.

D. Mental state: As is the case with accomplice liability (see *supra*, p. 209), it is generally required that the defendant have *intended* to induce the solicitee to perform the crime, not merely that he spoke words which he knew might bring about the crime.

1. **Must have requisite mental state:** Furthermore, the defendant must be shown to have had the *mental state required for the completed crime*. For instance, if A requests that B commit a breaking and entering of a dwelling, A is not guilty of solicitation of burglary unless he is shown to have had the desire not only that B break and enter, but also that he commit a felony within.

E. **Solicitation of accomplice:** Normally the solicitor intends that the solicitee perform the crime as principal. But it is theoretically sufficient for the crime of solicitation if the solicitor intends that the solicitee be an *accomplice* to a third person. Thus if A says to B "find a paid assassin to kill my wife," A will be guilty of solicitation even though under the proposed plan B would be an accomplice to the murder, rather than a principal. See L, p. 530.

F. **Communication not received:** Suppose the defendant attempts to communicate his criminal proposal, but is *unsuccessful* in doing so (e.g., the proposal is contained in a letter which is lost in the mail). It is not clear whether the defendant may be held liable for the completed crime of solicitation. Some jurisdictions will probably allow only a conviction of "attempted solicitation" in this situation.

1. **Model Penal Code:** The Model Penal Code, however, expressly makes it irrelevant that the defendant "fails to communicate with the person he solicits," if his conduct was designed to make such a communication. M.P.C. § 5.02(2). The defendant is thus guilty of the completed crime of solicitation under the Code even if the solicitee never learns of the proposal.

G. **Defenses:** Defenses similar to those raised in cases of attempt, conspiracy, and accomplice liability are often raised in solicitation cases.

1. **Renunciation:** It is not clear whether a *voluntary renunciation* by the solicitor is sufficient to purge him of liability. The Model Penal Code, in § 5.02(3), allows the defense of renunciation provided that the defendant prevents the commission of the object crime, under circumstances showing that the renunciation is "complete and voluntary."

2. **Crime requiring two parties:** Some crimes are defined so as to require the participation of two persons. As we saw, it will frequently be a defense in a prosecution for conspiracy or accomplice liability that the legislature chose *not to impose punishment* on one of the necessary parties. A similar defense should be allowed in a solicitation prosecution. For instance, suppose that D solicits a prostitute to have intercourse with him, but she refuses. Assuming that the legislature has not expressly authorized punishment for either soliciting a prostitute or having intercourse with one, D will normally not be held liable for solicitation (any more than he would be liable for being an accomplice to prostitution if he consummated his proposal). See L, p. 533.

3. **Impossibility:** There is no general defense of "impossibility" to a charge of solicitation. That is, it is irrelevant that, unbeknownst to the defendant, the facts are such that the solicitee could not commit the crime.

H. **Solicitation as an attempted crime:** In a state which does not have a comprehensive solicitation statute, the prosecution may argue that the defendant's act of solicitation constituted a criminal *attempt*. Virtually all courts agree that if nothing more than "bare" solicitation (i.e., the proposal itself) occurs, the defendant has not attempted to commit the object crime.

1. **Must go beyond mere preparation:**   Some courts have held that for attempt liability, either the defendant or the solicitee must take acts that amount to more than "mere preparation," so that if the solicitor were acting alone, he would have met the requirements for an attempt. Recall, for instance, *State v. Davis, supra,* p. 153, in which D not only encouraged X to kill D's mistress's husband, but paid X $600 to carry out the plans; the court held that nothing had been done beyond mere preparation, and that D was thus not guilty of attempted murder.

LEXIS®-NEXIS® Searches on **SOLICITATION**

Sub-Topic	Suggested Searches
Solicitation generally	`(crime or criminal) and atleast3(solicit!) and (criminal solicitation)`
Defenses	
Renunciation	`(crime or criminal) and (solicit! w/20 (renuncia! or withdraw! or abandon!))`
Impossibility	`(crime or criminal) and (solicit! w/20 (defense w/10 impossib!))`

Quiz Yourself on

ACCOMPLICE LIABILITY AND SOLICATION (ENTIRE CHAPTER)

53. Dan Hicks sees that the famous outlaw, Ned Kelly, is about to enter the Provincial Bank. Since Ned is wearing a mask and carrying a gun, Dan deduces that Ned plans to rob the bank.

    (A) For this part only, assume the following: Without saying anything to Ned, Dan stands watch outside the bank, ready to warn Ned if the police appear. As it turns out, Dan's help is not necessary, and Ned makes a clean getaway without ever realizing that Dan was standing watch. Ned is later apprehended on robbery charges. The police learn that Dan stood watch. May Dan be convicted of the substantive crime of bank robbery?

    (B) For this part, assume the same facts, except for the following: As Ned was about to enter the bank, Dan called out, "I'll give you a heads-up if any cops come by." Ned said, "That'd be great," and went in to the bank to commit the robbery. As it turned out, however, Ned made a clean getaway without needing Dan's services. When Ned is later apprehended on robbery charges, will Dan be liable for bank robbery?

54. Czar Nicholas wins tickets to a "Tchaikovsky and the Destroyers" concert from a local radio station. Lenin and Trotsky want the tickets, and decide to steal them from Nicholas. Trotsky is not armed, and thinks that Lenin is unarmed. The two hide behind some bushes and jump Nicholas when he walks by. While Trotsky holds Nicholas down, Lenin, instead of grabbing the tickets, whips out his Swiss Army knife and slits Nicholas' throat. Lenin then runs off and leaves the tickets behind. Is Trotsky liable as an accomplice in Nicholas' death?

55. Captain Hook, a pharmacist, fills Peter Pan's prescription for fairy dust, a mild hallucinogen, knowing that Peter intends to sell the dust illegally to Wendy. Peter then sells the dust illegally to Wendy.

    (A) Assume that Captain Hook charges Peter his regular price, and that all other terms and conditions of the sale are the same as Hook would impose if he did not know that any illegal use was planned. Is Hook an accomplice to Peter's illegal sale to Wendy?

(B) Now, assume that the facts are the same, except that Hood charges Peter three times the amount that he would ordinarily charge for filling such a prescription. He does so because he fears that he might be arrested in connection with Peter's plot if things go wrong, and it's simply not worth it to Hood to run that kind of risk for his ordinary prescription-filling rate. Is Hook an accomplice to Peter's illegal sale to Wendy?

56. Wellington gives Robespierre some dynamite and encourages him to blow up Josephine's house in order to kill her. Robespierre blows up the house. The explosion kills not only Josephine, but several passersby as well, including Napoleon Bonaparte. Clearly Wellington is an accessory to Josephine's killing. Is he also an accessory to *Bonaparte's* death?

57. King Arthur is charged with murder in the first degree for killing Childric. Merlin is charged as an accomplice for supplying Arthur with the murder weapon, the singing sword, Excalibur, and for urging Arthur to use the sword on Childric.

   (A) Assume that Arthur and Merlin are tried in the same trial. Arthur is acquitted by a jury, whose members conclude that the slaying was justified. May Merlin be convicted?

   (B) Same facts as above, except that King Arthur is acquitted because he was entrapped into committing the crime. No government agents were involved in Merlin's part of the crime. Can Merlin be convicted as an accomplice under these facts?

58. A state statute makes it a crime to sell narcotics. Neither that statute, nor any other state statute, makes it a crime to buy narcotics. Sherlock Holmes asks Moriarty to sell him some cocaine. Moriarty does so, and is charged with selling narcotics. Holmes is charged as an accomplice to the sale. Can Holmes be convicted?

59. Juliet, age sixteen, seduces Romeo, age twenty-two. A statute makes it statutory rape for a person to have sex with another who is under the age of seventeen, if the defendant is more than four years older that the underage person. Romeo is charged with statutory rape under this statute. Juliet is charged as an accomplice. Can Juliet be convicted?

60. Butch and Sundance rob a bank. They tell Etta Place about the robbery. Etta does not report it to the police. Is Etta an accessory after the fact?

61. Dostoevsky and Raskolnikov have the same landlady, whom Dostoevsky hates. Dostoevsky urges Raskolnikov to murder the landlady by waiting until she is asleep, and then sticking her nose and mouth shut with Crazy Glue so that she'll suffocate. Raskolnikov thinks that Dostoevsky is a dangerous criminal who must be stopped before he causes someone's murder. Therefore, he says, "No way — you're nuts," and tells the police about Dostoevsky's request. The police arrest Dostoevsky, but need something to charge him with. Because Raskolnikov never even pretended to agree to do what Dostoevsky urged, the police can't charge Dostoevsky with conspiracy.

   (A) What common-law crime offers the prosecution's best charge against Dostoevsky?

   (B) Can the prosecution get a conviction on the offense you listed in part (A)?

———————————

Answers

53. **(A) Probably not.** The only way Dan could be guilty of robbery is on an accomplice theory. One who aids and abets another (the principal) in the commission of a substantive crime becomes an accessory, and

as such is equally guilty of the crime. However, where a person merely stands ready to give assistance that turns out to be unneeded, and his participation does not in any way encourage or facilitate the crime, the potential assistance will generally not be considered aiding and abetting.

(B) Yes. A person will be considered an accomplice (and therefore substantively liable for the crimes that he aids and abets) if he in any significant way encourages or facilitates the crime. That's true even if the crime would probably have been successfully completed without the aid. Here, the fact that Dan encouraged Ned by letting Ned know he was there for Ned would almost certainly be found to be encouragement and facilitation. (For instance, Ned might have changed his mind about going through with the robbery had he not known that Dan was serving as lookout).

54. **No.** For a person to be liable as an accomplice to a crime (call it the "target crime") committed by a principal, the accomplice must have the mental state required for the target crime. So for Trotsky to be liable for the intentional murder of Nicholas, Trotsky would have needed a mental state that suffices for murder. Since Trotsky had no intent to kill or seriously injure, he did not have any of the required mental states for murder.

It's conceivable that Trotsky could be guilty on an alternate theory. An accomplice is guilty of additional crimes (i.e., "nontarget" crimes that the accomplice did not expressly aid and abet) committed by his principal if those are a "natural and probable consequence" of the commission of the target crime. However, there are two reasons why this theory probably wouldn't apply here: (1) it's not clear that Lenin committed the nontarget crime of murder *in addition to* robbery, because probably Lenin didn't commit robbery at all (and the theory probably applies only to crimes that are "added-on" to the target crime, not ones substituted for that target crime); (2) more important, it seems very unlikely that a cold-blooded murder would be found to be a "natural and probable consequence" of a robbery like this one, given that the accomplice didn't think the principal was armed and had no reason to think that the principal might commit such a killing, and further given that the killing doesn't even seem to have been in furtherance of the original robbery motive.

55. **(A) No.** A person will only be liable as an accomplice if he ***intends to assist*** the principal in carrying out the target crime. Mere knowledge that the principal will engage in the crime, even when coupled with some degree of assistance, won't by itself be enough. Therefore, one who as part of an ordinary-course transaction supplies an item to another that he knows will be used by the other in a particular crime won't thereby become guilty as an accomplice to that crime.

(B) Yes, probably. Mere knowledge of a buyer's criminal purpose won't, as explained in part (A), by itself be enough to convert a supplier into an accomplice of the buyer. But if the supplier in some sense takes a "stake" in the buyer's criminal enterprise, this will be enough to cross the supplier over into accomplice territory. The fact that the supplier charges a much higher price on account of the buyer's criminal purpose is likely to be interpreted by a court as his having taken such a stake in the venture.

56. **Yes.** Where an accomplice aids and abets a principal in the commission of one particular crime (call it the "target crime"), the accomplice will also be guilty of any additional crime that is a "natural and probable consequence" of the commission of the target crime. Here, the other deaths were a natural and probable consequence of the intended explosion. Therefore, since Wellington aided and encouraged Robespierre to blow up the house, all the ensuing deaths will likely be deemed within the scope of Wellington's liability as an accomplice.

57. **(A) No.** The general rule is that if the principal is acquitted, the accomplice must be acquitted as well. This rule certainly applies where, as here, the two are tried in the same trial — the accomplice cannot be

guilty unless the principal committed the target crime, and the verdict here shows conclusively that the principal was not guilty.

(B) Yes, probably. Although the general rule is that the accomplice must be acquitted if the principal is acquitted, there is an exception where the principal has a complete defense to the crime that the accomplice does not share. That is the case here, so Merlin is out of luck.

58. No. Where an offense is defined so as to logically require two participants, but the statute specifies a punishment for only one of those participants, the other may not be convicted of being an accomplice. See, e.g., M.P.C. § 2.06(6)(b), making D not liable as an accomplice if "the offense is so defined that his conduct is inevitably incident to [the offense's] commission." That's the case here: a "sale" of narcotics can't take place without a buyer, and the state has chosen not to impose specific punishment on buyers; therefore, buyers can't be made accomplices to sales.

59. No. Where a statute is intended to protect a certain class, a member of the protected class is immune from prosecution as an accomplice. In the case of statutory rape, the underaged person is universally considered to be a victim who is in need of protection. Therefore, Juliet cannot be convicted. Note that the same rule would apply to one who pays ransom to a kidnapper, or pays blackmail money to an extortionist.

60. No. The crime of accessory-after-the-fact is committed where a person knowingly gives assistance to a felon, for the purpose of helping the felon avoid apprehension following the crime. The accessory must be shown to have taken affirmative acts to hinder the felon's arrest — it's not enough that the defendant merely fails (or even refuses when asked) to give information to the authorities. So Etta's off the hook. (But if Etta took affirmative steps to help the boys — if, for instance, she gave a phony alibi or gave false info about where the boys had gone when they left town — then she *would* be guilty of being an accessory after the fact.)

61. (A) Solicitation. This crime occurs when one requests or encourages another to perform a criminal act, with the mental state required for that criminal act. The crime is complete at the moment of the request or encouragement.

(B) Yes. The fact that Raskolnikov never agreed with Dostoevsky's proposal (thus making a conspiracy charge not feasible) is no bar to a solicitation charge. Indeed, the scenario of the immediately-unsuccessful request — as well as the scenario of the request which the requestee appears to accept but secretly disagrees with — are the situations in which solicitation is most often charged.

Exam Tips on
ACCOMPLICE LIABILITY AND SOLICITATION

<u>Accomplice Liability, Generally</u>

☛ **Summary:** Remember that D is liable as an accomplice if he intentionally acts or encourages another (call her X) to commit a "target" crime. Accomplice liability means that D will be liable for the target (substantive) crime committed by X. So D must satisfy two requirements — act and mental state — before he'll have accomplice liability:

❑ **Act:** D must commit an *act* that *aids or encourages* X to commit the "target" crime;

and

☐ **Mental state:** He must have the ***mental state*** required for the target crime. Typically, this means that D must ***intend*** to assist X in committing the target crime.

☛ **Act requirement:** The most testable area is whether the act element has been fulfilled. Therefore, look for:

☞ **Silent observer:** Just ***knowing*** that a crime is being committed and ***silently observing*** is ***not*** considered to be aiding and abetting. (But if X *knows* that D stands ready to assist if needed, and this fact encourages X, then D *does* meet the act requirement.)

    ☞ **Trap:** Don't be fooled by a fact pattern that indicates merely that D was present and had criminal intent. Mere presence and intent are not sufficient.

    Example: Y and Z agree to set fire to their neighbor's home because they suspect that drugs are being trafficked there. They start pouring gasoline around the house. A crowd of onlookers begins to gather. X, an onlooker, hopes that Y and Z will burn the house down (and decides to help them if they can't get the fire burning by themselves), but says and does nothing. Y and Z aren't aware that this is how X feels. Z lights a match and the house is burned. X cannot be prosecuted as an accessory, because although he had the requisite intent (desire to have the house be burned) he did not commit the requisite act (aiding or encouraging Y and Z).

☞ **Verbal encouragement:** Generally, ***verbal encouragement satisfies*** the act requirement.

    Example: Suppose that on the facts of the above example, as Y and Z are trying to get the fire started, X shouts to them, "Burn that baby down." At least if Y and Z hear and are encouraged to continue, X has committed the required act, and can be held liable for arson as an accomplice.

☞ **Actions:** Other kinds of actions that are likely to suffice:

    ☐ By pre-arrangement, D operates a ***getaway car*** for X after X commits the substantive crime;

    ☐ D agrees in advance to ***provide a safe harbor*** for X after he commits the crime, and then does so. (Actually, the advance agreement *alone*, if it encourages X to go ahead and commit the crime, will suffice, even if D then changes his mind after the crime is over.)

    ☞ **Trap:** Be on the lookout for a party who does not have a stake in the commission of the crime and becomes involved ***only after the basic crime has been committed.*** This is likely ***not*** to be enough for accomplice liability, just for the lesser crime of ***"accessory after the fact."***

    Example: X, Y, and Z drive to a liquor store to purchase liquor. X stays in the car while Y and Z enter the store. Just before entering, Y and Z realize they have no money. Subsequently they commit a robbery in the store. They run from the store with Z waving a bottle of whiskey and Y holding a gun. As they jump into the car, Y says to X, "Step on it before the cops get here." X drives off. X probably does not have accomplice liability for the robbery (and is therefore not guilty of robbery), because he did not encourage or assist the commission of the crime, which was complete as soon as Y and Z left the store with the money. X has at most accessory-after-the-fact liability.

☛ **Other crimes:** Courts disagree about whether D is substantively liable for additional crimes that are *"natural and probable"* consequences of the target crime, but that D did not intend to bring about.

> *Example:* D agrees to drive X to a store so X can rob it with X's gun. They say nothing about whether X will use the gun. In the store, the owner, V, resists giving the cash, and X shoots him, injuring him. Even assuming that it was a "natural and probable" consequence of the robbery that X would use the gun if the owner resisted, not all states would hold D guilty of being an accomplice to battery. If the shooting was *not* a natural and probable consequence of the robbery, no court would hold D guilty of being an accomplice to battery.

☞ **Distinction:** But don't confuse the natural-and-probable doctrine with the specialized doctrines of felony-murder and misdemeanor-manslaughter — although these doctrines have an effect that's similar to natural-and-probable, they apply *only* in homicide cases.)

Solicitation

☛ **Generally:** Watch for a party *requesting or encouraging another to perform a criminal act*, where the *other party refuses*. This is likely to be the crime of solicitation, defined as:

> the requesting or encouraging of another to commit a crime, done with an intent to persuade the other to do the completed crime.

(It can still be solicitation if the other party *agrees*, but then it's also conspiracy, which is the more serious crime. So only worry about solicitation if the other party refuses, or there's some other obstacle to its being conspiracy.)

☞ **Surrounding circumstances:** Analyze the surrounding circumstances in order to determine whether the requisite intent (intent to induce the other to commit the underlying crime) can be proven. So evidence that the speaker was *joking*, or intended *some other result* than completion of the target crime, will tend to show that the required intent was not present.

> *Example:* Z has opened a competing store across the street from X's store and, because of unfair business practices, will likely force X out of business. X, in a half-jesting manner, tells Y that if Y were a real friend he would "take care" of Z. As a result, Y breaks into Z's store and destroys Z's merchandise. Given that X's statement was made in a half-jesting and casual manner (and that X had no reason to believe that Y was likely to engage in criminal behavior), it is unlikely that a court would find that X intended to encourage or persuade Y to commit any crime, in which case X can't be guilty of solicitation.

CHAPTER 8

HOMICIDE, AND OTHER CRIMES AGAINST THE PERSON

Introductory Note: This chapter examines crimes that may be committed against the person, with a main focus on the various types of homicides. Assault, battery, mayhem, rape, and kidnapping are also discussed. Within the category "homicide," the main one is of course *murder*, with the two other most important ones being *voluntary manslaughter* and *involuntary manslaughter*. Within the category "murder," keep in mind that there are *multiple mental states*, any one of which may suffice (e.g., intent to kill; intent to seriously injure; reckless indifference to the value of life; and intent to commit a dangerous felony).

I. HOMICIDE — INTRODUCTION

A. **Different grades of homicide:** Any unlawful taking of the life of another falls within the generic class "homicide." The two principal kinds of homicide are *murder* and *manslaughter*.

   1. **Degrees of murder:** In many jurisdictions, murder is in turn divided into first-degree and second-degree murder. Generally, first-degree murder is limited to murders committed with "premeditation and deliberation," and to killings committed during the course of certain felonies. See *infra*, p. 246.

   2. **Two kinds of manslaughter:** Similarly, manslaughter is in nearly all jurisdictions divided into *voluntary* manslaughter (in most cases, a killing occurring in the "heat of passion") and *involuntary* manslaughter (an unintentional killing committed recklessly, grossly negligently, or during commission of an unlawful act.)

   3. **Other statutory forms of homicide:** Additional forms of homicide exist by statute in some states. Many states have created the crime of *vehicular homicide* (i.e., an unintentional death caused by the driver of a motor vehicle); this crime is generally defined so as to require a lesser degree of culpability than involuntary manslaughter. Similarly, the Model Penal Code creates the crime of "negligent homicide." See *infra*, p. 259.

II. MURDER

A. **Taking of life:** Murder, like other forms of homicide, exists only where a life has been taken. Therefore, it is sometimes important to know: (1) whether a particular life has begun; and (2) whether a particular life has ended prior to the defendant's act.

1. **When life begins:** Everyone would agree that a baby that has been born is a human being, whose killing can give rise to a murder prosecution. But it is not clear whether a life exists *prior to the moment of birth*.

   a. **Birth process begun:** If the *birth process* has *begun*, but not yet finished, most courts would probably regard the baby as being alive for purposes of a homicide prosecution.

   b. **Fetus:** But where the birth process has *not even begun*, the courts are reluctant to consider the *fetus* a human being for homicide purposes. Thus in the well-known case of *Keeler v. Superior Court*, 470 P.2d 617 (Cal. 1970), D learned that his estranged wife was pregnant by another man, accosted her, said "I'm going to stomp it out of you," and shoved his knee into her abdomen. The baby was delivered stillborn, with a severely fractured skull. Medical evidence indicated that at the time of D's attack, the fetus was more than 28 weeks old, and that it was "viable" (i.e., that if it had been born prematurely at that point, it would have had a 75% to 96% chance of survival).

      i. **Holding:** The California Supreme Court held that despite the fetus' viability, it was *not a "human being"* as that term was used in the state homicide statute. The court stated that when the legislature passed that statute (in 1850), it did not intend to encompass the crime of feticide within the ambit of homicide. To bring the death of a fetus, even a viable one, within the homicide statute would also, in the court's view, violate due process, in that there would not have been "fair warning of the act which is made punishable as a crime."

      Note: Most states have agreed with California, that the killing of a fetus (even a viable one) should not be considered to fall within the state's general murder statute. But at least two states have reached the opposite result, concluding that the general murder statute covers the killing of a viable fetus. See *Commonwealth v. Cass*, 467 N.E.2d 1324 (Mass. 1984), and *State v. Horne*, 319 S.E.2d 703 (S.C. 1984).

   c. **Changed by statute:** Of course, the state legislature is always free to amend the murder statute to explicitly cover the killing of a viable fetus. Alternatively, the state is free to enact a new crime called "murder of a fetus," and even to punish this crime as seriously as the state punishes the killing of a born-alive person (though it is unclear whether the state may enact the death penalty for this crime of feticide). At least seventeen states have enacted statutes essentially making it a form of murder to kill an unborn. One of these states is California; after *Keeler*, *supra*, the California legislature amended its murder statute to include the killing of a fetus (but to exclude, as most such statutes do, an abortion performed with the mother's consent).

      i. **Not limited to viable fetus:** Of the 17 states just mentioned, 13 create liability only if the fetus was "viable" at the moment it was killed. However, there are apparently no serious constitutional problems with a state's decision to punish as murder even the killing of a *non-viable* fetus.

   d. **Fetus born alive:** If the infant is *born alive*, the defendant can be guilty of common-law murder even though his acts may have taken place *before the birth*. Thus if, in the

Keeler case, the attack by D had taken place when it did, but the baby lived for a few moments outside the womb before dying, D could have been convicted of murder.

2. **When life ends:** One can obviously not murder a person who is already dead. Therefore, it is important to be able to pinpoint the moment at which *death occurs*. The problem is particularly likely to occur where a physician *performs an organ transplant* from a donor which he believes to be a corpse. If a vital organ is taken, and the patient was not dead at the time of the transplant, the physician could be prosecuted for murder.

   a. **Brain death vs. heart death:** The problem is a difficult one because there are conflicting opinions about what physical signs should be sufficient to indicate death. Patients in comas, for instance, frequently continue to have a *heart beat* (at least while on a respirator) and breathing activity, even though they no longer produce *brain waves*. Is this *"brain death"* sufficient? If it is not, the utility of organ transplants may be drastically diminished, since transplants have a significantly greater success rate when they occur prior to or immediately after the cessation of breathing and heart activity.

B. **Elements of murder:** The prosecution in a murder case must show the following four elements:

   ❑ *actus reus* (conduct by the defendant);

   ❑ *corpus delicti* (proof of a death);

   ❑ *mens rea* (a culpable mental state);

   ❑ *proximate cause* (a causal link between the defendant's act and the death).

Let's review each of these in turn.

1. *Actus reus*: There must be conduct by the defendant (i.e., an *"actus reus"*), either an affirmative act or an omission where there was a duty to act.

   a. **Participating in events leading up to assisted suicide not sufficient:** One situation in which the issue of *actus reus* comes up is *assisted suicide.* Most modern courts have held that providing another with *the means for that person to kill herself* does *not* constitute a sufficient *actus reus* to sustain a murder charge.

   Example: D (the famed "Dr. Death," Dr. Jack Kevorkian) provides the Vs, two terminally ill women, with a poison-delivery machine they can use to kill themselves. (D is acting at the women's request.) Although D provides the mechanisms, helps hook the Vs up to them, and explains what the Vs need to do to make the machines work, the actual act of introducing the deadly poison into each woman's body is under the exclusive control of the woman herself.

   Held, D is not guilty of murder. "[W]here a defendant merely is involved in the events leading up to the death, such as providing the means, the proper charge is assisting in a suicide," not murder. *People v. Kevorkian*, 527 N.W.2d 714 (Mich. 1994).

2. *Corpus delicti*: A *death* must, of course, be shown to have occurred. But the *corpus delicti* (i.e., the "body of the crime") of murder does not absolutely require that a *corpse be*

found. Like any aspect of any crime, existence of death may be proved by circumstantial evidence

Example: D is known to be on bad terms with V, his grandmother, who has cut him out of her will. V's ranchhouse burns down one day, and neither V's corpse nor any bone fragments are found in the rubble. D is convicted of her murder.

Held, conviction affirmed. The fact of V's death was adequately established by numerous items of circumstantial evidence, including the facts that: none of V's friends or associates ever heard from her again, the strained relationship between D and V, and D's actual knowledge of the fire several hours before anyone informed him of it. *State v. Pyle*, 532 P.2d 1309 (Kan. 1975).

3. *Mens rea*: There must be an accompanying ***mental state***. This mental state is often called ***"malice aforethought."***

   a. **"Malice aforethought" is term of art:** However, for the defendant to have "malice aforethought," it is not necessary either that he have "malice" towards his victim, in the usual sense of that word, or that he have thought about the killing before committing it. Instead, the phrase is a term of art, and can be satisfied by a number of quite distinct mental states. These states, discussed in sequence below, include (depending on the jurisdiction): (1) intent to kill; (2) intent to commit grievous bodily injury; (3) reckless indifference to the value of human life; and (4) intent to commit any of certain non-homicide felonies.

4. **Proximate cause:** There must also be a ***causal relationship*** between the defendant's act and the victim's death. The defendant's conduct must be both the "cause in fact" of the death and also its "proximate" cause. The existence of the necessary causal relationship is determined in substantially the same way in murder cases as in other sorts of criminal cases; see the chapter on Causation, *supra*, p. 44.

   a. **Year-and-a-day rule:** One special rule of proximate cause that applies only in murder cases is the requirement, still imposed in many jurisdictions, that the victim die within ***a year and a day*** of the defendant's conduct. This rule dates back to a time when the quality of medical care was so poor and the usual life expectancy so short, that if the victim lived more than a year and a day from the attack, it could not be said with reasonable certainty that intervening causes (e.g., some unrelated disease) were not more to blame for the death than the defendant. Although the rule is often condemned as being obsolete, it continues on the books of most states. See L, p. 660.

C. **Intent-to-kill murder:** The most common state of mind that will suffice for murder is the ***intent to kill***. The requisite intent exists, of course, when one has the ***desire*** to bring about the death of another.

   1. **Substantial certainty of death:** But the requisite intent also probably exists where one does not actively desire to bring about another's death, but knows that death is ***substantially certain*** to occur.

   Example: D, who is in financial straits, owns a famous painting. He has a fake version of the painting made up, and he sends it as cargo on a commercial plane. In order to collect on his insurance, he puts a bomb aboard the plane and detonates it, killing all passengers.

Even if D can show that he did not desire to kill any of the passengers, he will be guilty of their murder; he knew that, if his plan was successful, they were all substantially certain to die.

2. **Ill will not needed:** It follows from the above example that the requisite intent to kill may exist even where D *does not bear any ill will* towards his victim. For another illustration, consider the case of *mercy killing*, set out in the next example.

    Example: D's beloved wife, V, is dying of incurable and very painful bone cancer. V begs D to kill her. Soon thereafter, as V is sleeping, D smothers her with a pillow. This is murder. The fact that D acted from humanitarian motives will not make any difference. (But if D had merely given V the means to kill herself, most states would say that D had committed only the lesser crime of assisted suicide, not murder. See *People v. Kevorkian, supra*, p. 232.)

3. **Intent proved by circumstantial evidence:**   Intent to kill, like any other element of a crime, may be proved by *circumstantial evidence*. Such evidence is particularly useful in proving intent, since it is only seldom that there will be direct evidence (e.g., a statement by D that "I intended to kill him") on this issue.

    a. **"Deadly weapon" doctrine:**   One kind of circumstantial evidence of intent to kill is embodied in the *"deadly weapon"* doctrine. By this doctrine, if a death occurs as a result of a deadly weapon used by the defendant, the jury is *permitted to infer* that the defendant intended to bring about the death. The jury is *not required* to make this inference, and the defendant is of course free to rebut it (e.g., by testifying that he intended to shoot over the victim's head in order to frighten him). But the point is that use of a deadly weapon may, even in the absence of other evidence, be sufficient to allow the jury to find the requisite intent to kill. See L, pp. 661-63.

        i. **What is "deadly weapon":**   A "deadly weapon" for this purpose is presumably the same kind of weapon that would constitute "deadly force" for purposes of the rules on self-defense (*supra*, p. 109). That is, force which is *likely to cause* death or serious bodily harm is deadly. On the other hand, an instrument that usually does not cause such death or serious harm (e.g., one's fists) will not generally suffice.

4. **Voluntary manslaughter:**   Not all cases involving a death brought about by an intent to kill will be murder. For instance, most cases of *voluntary manslaughter* (generally, a killing occurring in a "heat of passion"; see *infra*, p. 250) will be ones in which the defendant intended to kill. Similarly, most cases of *self-defense* are intentional killings. Thus in a prosecution for intent-to-kill murder, the mental state is an intent to kill not accompanied by other redeeming or mitigating mental or external factors.

5. **Degrees of intent-to-kill murder:**   In most states intent-to-kill murder is divided into two categories, first-degree and second-degree. The former usually consists of murders committed with deliberation and premeditation. Degrees of murder are discussed further *infra*, p. 246.

D. **Intent to do serious bodily injury:**   In most states, the *mens rea* requirement for murder is satisfied if the defendant intended not to kill, but to do *serious bodily injury* to the victim. The typical application of this principle is a case in which the defendant savagely beats the victim, with his intent limited to doing so, and the victim dies from his injuries. The sufficiency of this intent has been approved, on the grounds that "[s]uch conduct may appear at least as dangerous to life as that required for depraved-heart murder" (discussed *infra*, p. 235). L, p. 665.

1. **Knowledge that injury is highly likely:** Just as one may be deemed to have the intent to kill by virtue of one's knowledge that death is substantially certain to ensue (see *supra*, p. 233), so one may be deemed to have had the intent to commit serious bodily injury if one knew that such injury was ***highly likely*** to occur. Thus in *Hyam v. Director of Public Prosecutions*, [1975] A.C. 55 (Eng. 1974), D was a jealous woman who wished to break up a relationship between her lover and another woman, Mrs. Booth. She poured gasoline through the letter-slot of Mrs. Booth's front door, and then inserted a lighted newspaper. Mrs. Booth escaped, but two of her children were killed in the blaze. D testified that her motive was merely to "frighten" Mrs. Booth.

    a. **Holding in *Hyam*:** The House of Lords held that so long as D knew that serious harm to the inhabitants of the house was highly likely, she should be held to have intended that harm. (The court also held that the harm was not required to be "life threatening," but merely "serious.")

2. **Standard is generally subjective:** Suppose the defendant, perhaps because he is stupid, does not realize that serious bodily harm is highly likely to ensue. Can he be liable for murder if a ***reasonable person*** would have realized the extent of the danger? Most jurisdictions would probably answer "no," that it must be shown that the defendant himself realized the high likelihood of serious harm.

3. **What constitutes "serious bodily injury":** An intent to injure is not necessarily an intent to commit serious bodily harm. Some courts hold that only conduct which is likely to be "***life threatening***" will suffice. But, as noted, the court in *Hyam v. Director of Public Prosecutions*, *supra*, held that danger to life is not necessary. Under this view, presumably an intent by the defendant to deprive his victim of an eye or a limb would suffice, even if there was little danger that death would ensue (and it occurs through unintended freak circumstances).

4. **Model Penal Code rejects:** The Model Penal Code does not recognize an intent to do serious bodily harm as sufficing for murder. The Code draftsmen suggest that the standards of "recklessness" and "extreme indifference to the value of human life" are adequate to handle such cases. See Comment 5 to M.P.C. § 210.2. Thus under the Code, one commits murder if one acts "recklessly under circumstances manifesting extreme indifference to the value of human life," and manslaughter if one acts recklessly, but without such "extreme indifference." See M.P.C. § 210.2(1)(b) and 210.3(1)(a).

E. **Reckless indifference to value of human life ("depraved heart"):** If the defendant knows that death is "substantially certain" to result from his conduct, most jurisdictions, as noted, will treat him as having "intended" that result. But suppose the defendant realizes merely that there is a "very high" risk of death, i.e., a risk short of substantial certainty. Nearly all courts are nonetheless willing to hold the defendant liable for murder in this situation. As the idea is put in some statutes, the defendant, by his reckless conduct, has manifested a ***"depraved heart."*** Or, as the Model Penal Code puts it, the defendant is guilty of murder if he has acted "*recklessly* under circumstances manifesting *extreme indifference to the value of human life*." M.P.C. § 201.2(1)(b).

1. **Illustrations:** Illustrations of the necessary recklessness and depravity include the following:

   a. D, under arrest, is riding in the back seat of a police vehicle. He stands up, lunges across the front seat, grabs the steering wheel, and makes the car swerve across the center of the highway. The car smashes into an oncoming vehicle and the driver of D's vehicle is killed. D is guilty of murder, even though he did not desire to bring about the driver's death, since his conduct manifested a "depraved mind, regardless of human life." *Gibson v. State*, 476 P.2d 362 (Ok. Crim. App. 1970).

   b. D, a 17-year-old boy, plays a game of "Russian Roulette" with V, age 13. D places one bullet in a five-chamber pistol, spins the chamber, and pulls the trigger three times while the gun is pointed at V. It goes off the third time, killing V. D is guilty of murder, based upon his "wicked disposition," even though he may not have intended to kill V. *Commonwealth v. Malone*, 47 A.2d 445 (Pa. 1946).

   c. D shoots into a passing passenger train, without an intent to kill any particular person, and his bullet happens to strike and kill V. D is guilty of "depraved heart" murder. See L, p. 668.

   d. D, in order to guard the marijuana plants he is growing, buys a pit bull, which he knows to have been bred and trained to be a fighting dog. D keeps the dog chained but not fenced. V, a 2 1/2-year-old neighbor, wanders into the marijuana patch, and is attacked and killed by the dog. There is evidence that D knew that the dog was dangerous, knew that V lived next door, and knew that anyone who wandered into the marijuana plants could be attacked by the dog. A jury could properly find that D committed murder of the "wanton disregard for life" variety. *Berry v. Superior Court*, 256 Cal.Reptr. 344 (Cal.Ct.App. 1989).

   e. D, in order to frighten V, her rival for the affections of X, pours gasoline through the mail slot of V's house, and sets fire to it, killing V's children. See *Hyam v. Director of Public Prosecutions*, [1975] A.C. 55 (Eng. 1974) (upholding a murder conviction on the related theory of intent to do serious bodily harm; discussed *supra*, p. 235).

2. **Awareness of risk:** Courts are not in agreement as to whether the requisite "reckless indifference to the value of human life" or "depravity" exists where the defendant is *not aware of the risk* involved in his conduct.

   a. **Objective standard:** Some courts have indicated that so long as a "*reasonable man*" would have recognized the extreme danger inherent in the conduct, the defendant is guilty of murder even though, because of his stupidity, he was not aware of the risk.

   b. **Subjective standard:** But other courts would impose liability only where there is an *actual realization* of the danger. Thus the Model Penal Code, by defining "recklessly" to cover only situations where the defendant "consciously disregards a substantial and unjustifiable risk," would require actual awareness of the risk. M.P.C. § 2.02(2)(c).

   c. **Intoxication:** If the defendant fails to appreciate the risk of his conduct because he is *intoxicated*, even courts that would ordinarily impose a subjective standard would probably ***allow a conviction***. "The person who unconsciously creates a risk because he is voluntarily drunk is perhaps morally worse than one who does so because he is sober but mentally deficient." L, p. 670. Thus M.P.C. § 2.08(2) provides that where a defendant's unawareness of a risk is due to his voluntary intoxication, the unawareness is irrelevant. See *supra*, p. 84, for a further discussion of the relevance of intoxication to *mens rea.*

LEXIS®-NEXIS® Searches on **MURDER**

Sub-Topic	Suggested Searches
Murder generally, elements of	`(elements or defin!) w/5 murder`
Intent to do serious bodily injury as sufficing	`murder w/30 (inten! w/20 serious bodily w/5 (harm or injury))`
Reckless indifferent / depraved heart murder	`murder w/10 ((extreme indifference) or (depraved heart))`

III. FELONY-MURDER

A. Felony-murder generally: The various states of mind discussed so far are frequently difficult to prove, since they can usually be shown only by circumstantial evidence. Partly for this reason, courts and legislatures have long recognized various forms of a doctrine called the ***felony-murder rule***, by which the ***intent to commit a felony*** (a felony unrelated to homicide) is sufficient to meet the *mens rea* requirement for murder. In its broadest form, the felony-murder rule provides that ***if the defendant, while he is in the process of committing a felony, kills another (even accidentally), the killing is murder.***

B. Dangerous vs. non-dangerous felonies: Every state today has numerous statutory felonies which were unknown to the common law. Many of these statutory felonies pose virtually no unusual threat of death or bodily harm to anyone. It would therefore be unfair and illogical to hold that one who commits an accidental killing during the commission of such a felony is automatically guilty of murder.

    1. Illustration: For instance, suppose that it is a felony knowingly to file a false income tax return. If the defendant prepares such a return, and while driving to the post office to file it accidentally (and non-negligently) runs over a pedestrian and kills him, there is no good reason to make the defendant automatically liable for murder. The fact that he was engaged in committing a felony when the accident occurred did not make the accident any more likely to happen than if he had been using his car for lawful purposes.

    2. Now limited to dangerous felonies: Therefore, nearly all courts and legislatures now restrict application of the felony-murder doctrine to ***certain felonies***. There are three related schemes for identifying those felonies to which the doctrine should apply: (1) those felonies which are ***inherently dangerous*** to life or health; (2) those felonies which were felonies at ***common law*** (i.e., rape, sodomy, robbery, burglary, arson, mayhem and larceny); and (3) those felonies which are "***malum in se***" rather than "***malum prohibitum***." See L, pp. 672-73.

a. **"Inherently dangerous" is preferred test:**   Most courts have used the *"inherently dangerous"* test. This has the advantage of making the felony-murder doctrine available for such crimes as kidnapping, which would not be included within the common-law-crimes test. Courts have been sharply in dispute, however, about how this "inherently dangerous" test should be applied: should the "inherent dangerousness" of the felony be judged in the *abstract* (i.e., whether, say, larceny is in general a dangerous crime), or should the felony be evaluated in each case based on the facts of that case (so that if the particular larceny in question were committed in a patently dangerous manner, felony-murder could be applied even though most other larcenies might not pose such danger)?

   i. **Judged in abstract:**   The courts that have tested the felony in the *abstract* have apparently done so principally out of their dislike of the felony-murder rule, and their reluctance to expand its application.

      Example: D, a chiropractor, treats V, an 8-year-old girl with fast-growing cancer of the eye. D dissuades V's parents from having the eye removed, saying that he can cure her without surgery by "building up her resistance." The treatment, for which the parents pay $700, lasts six months, but V dies at that time. D is charged with murder, and convicted on a felony-murder theory.

      Held, D's conviction reversed. The only independent felony committed by D was grand larceny. Since the felony-murder doctrine applies only to "inherently dangerous" felonies, the status of grand larceny must be determined. This must be measured by looking to "the elements of the felony in the abstract, not the particular 'facts' of the case." Thus the mere fact that, in this case, D's conduct may have posed a danger to life, will not suffice for application of the felony-murder rule. Otherwise, any time a defendant endangered life in the course of any felony at all, he would automatically be guilty of murder, and the felony-murder rule would be widened "beyond calculation." Since grand larceny is not normally dangerous to life, the felony-murder rule does not apply here. (However, on these facts D might be found to have had a depraved indifference to V's life, and could therefore be guilty of "depraved heart" murder.) *People v. Phillips*, 414 P.2d 353 (Cal. 1966).

   ii. **Examine particular facts:**   Other courts, as noted, are willing to take the *facts of the particular case* into account in determining the dangerousness of the felony. If what is in the abstract not necessarily a dangerous felony is performed in an obviously dangerous manner, these courts would apply the felony-murder rule. These courts would presumably disagree with the result in *Phillips*, *supra*.

C. **Causal relationship:**   There must be a *causal relationship* between the felony and the killing. That is, it is not enough that the death merely occurs at the same time the felony is being committed. In some way or other, the felony must give rise to the killing. Furthermore, something more than a mere "but for" relationship between felony and killing must exist.

1. **Illustration:**   For instance, suppose that D abducts V, brings her back to his house, and is in the process of raping her when lightning strikes the house, and V is killed in the ensuing blaze. It is unlikely that the felony-murder rule would be applied, although V would not have died except for the kidnapping and rape (she would not have been in D's house). A

court would almost certainly conclude that the manner of death was so bizarre and unexpected that it is unfair to make D criminally responsible for it.

2. **"Natural and probable" consequences:** Thus the rules of *proximate cause*, discussed *supra*, p. 46, apply in felony-murder cases just as they do in other situations. Where the victim's death is precipitated by an *intervening act*, this means that the defendant will be liable if the intervention was either: (1) a coincidence (i.e., not a response to the defendant's act) and was foreseeable; or (2) the intervention was a response to the defendant's act (i.e., the intervention was "dependent") and it was not "abnormal" (even though it may have been "unforeseeable"). The overall notion of proximate cause in this context is often summed up by the loose statement that the defendant is only liable where the death is the "*natural and probable consequence*" of his conduct.

3. **Arson cases:** Proximate cause questions frequently arise where the defendant's underlying felony is *arson*. If a person is inside the building at the time the fire is started, and dies, the requisite causal relationship between the arson and the death is almost certain to be found; see, e.g., *Regina v. Serne*, 16 Cox Crim. Cas. 311 (Eng. 1887).

   a. **Firefighters:** Similarly, if a *firefighter is killed* while attempting to fight the blaze, the arsonist will generally be guilty of felony-murder.

   b. **Unlikely event:** But if a *passer-by* decided to run into the building to *loot it*, it is likely that the arsonist would not be liable under the felony-murder rule for such a person's death. Such an act is probably sufficiently "abnormal" that a court would find it unfair to hold the defendant liable for murder. One way this might be expressed is by holding that a looter is not within the "class" of persons endangered by fires (a class which perhaps includes occupants, immediate neighbors and persons who fight the blaze).

4. **Robberies and gunfights:** Proximate cause questions also frequently arise in the case of *robberies*.

   a. **Robber shoots victim:** If the robber *shoots his hold-up victim*, even accidentally, this will obviously be a sufficient causal link for application of the felony-murder doctrine. Similarly, if the robber merely intends to *temporarily disable* his victim (e.g., he hits him on the head to stun him), and death accidentally results, the felony-murder rule will apply. Even in the absence of any physical impact at all, the rule might apply; see, e.g., *People v. Stamp, supra*, p. 52, in which V suffered a fatal heart attack as a result of a robbery of his store, and the robbers' felony-murder convictions were upheld.

   b. **Robber kills bystander:** Similarly, if a robber accidentally *kills a bystander*, the felony-murder rule will apply. This might occur, for instance, if the robbers were attempting a high-speed escape and negligently (or perhaps even non-negligently) ran over a pedestrian.

   c. **Hold-up victim or police officer kills bystander:** It may happen that the *robbery victim*, or a *police officer*, either in an attempt to protect himself, or to kill the robber, accidentally *kills a bystander*. Here, it is not so clear whether the robber will be liable for felony-murder.

i. **California rejects liability:**   California, with its hostility to the felony-murder doctrine, noted earlier, would apparently not allow felony-murder in this situation (or in any situation where the fatal shot comes from the gun of a ***person other than the robber***). See *People v. Washington*, 402 P.2d 130 (Cal. 1965) (dictum).

ii. **Robber initiates gun battle:**   In other states, the result might depend on whether the robber *fired the first shot*. If he did so, then it would not seem unfair to hold him liable for a bystander's death from a subsequent shot fired by the robbery victim, or by police; one who starts a gun battle should certainly anticipate the likelihood that others will fire back, and that they may hit the wrong target.

d. **One felon kills another:**   One robber may accidentally ***kill another***. In this situation, the former has sometimes been held liable for felony-murder. But other courts have felt that the purpose of the felony-murder rule is to protect ***innocent persons***, and that it should not be extended to cover the death of a co-felon. Thus in *State v. Williams*, discussed further *infra*, p. 241, the court held that the felony-murder statute was applicable "only when an innocent person is killed" as a result of the felony.

e. **Victim or police officer kills one robber:**   Where one robber is killed by the robbery victim or by police officers attempting to make an arrest, the weakest case for holding the other robbers liable for felony-murder is presented. First, the defendant has not directly "caused" the death in the same way as he would have if his own gun had, say, misfired. Secondly, to the extent that the felony-murder principle is designed to protect only innocent persons, it would not be applicable in this situation.

i. ***Redline* case:**   The Supreme Court of Pennsylvania, in the well-known case of *Commonwealth v. Redline*, 137 A.2d 472 (Pa. 1958), refused to allow felony-murder in this situation. D and X were co-robbers, and X was killed by a police officer trying to apprehend the pair. The court attempted to distinguish this situation from that in which an innocent bystander is killed by a police officer or robbery victim: in the latter situation, the killing is merely "excusable" on the part of the person who shoots. Where a felon is killed, on the other hand, the killing is "justifiable" by the shooter, and therefore "obviously could not be availed of, on any rational legal theory, to support a charge of murder."

ii. **Criticism of distinction:**   However, the *Redline* court cannot be correct in its contention that a "justifiable" killing by one person can never be the occasion for a murder prosecution of another. Kadish, Schulhofer and Paulsen, p. 539, pose the following counter-example: Two felons are holed up in a house and fighting a gun battle with surrounding police. One tells the other to run out the back door where the coast is clear. He does this because he wants the other felon dead and knows the police have the back door covered. The other felon runs out, and is shot dead by the police. In this situation, it seems both fair and logical to hold the first felon liable for murder, at least of the ordinary intent-to-kill variety, if not felony-murder.

iii. **Alternate explanation:**   The real explanation of the *Redline* decision is probably simply that, as noted, the felony-murder doctrine is intended for the protection of *innocent persons*, and should not be extended to cover co-felons. See L , p. 679.

f. Co-felon accidentally kills self: Suppose that one co-felon accidentally *kills himself* during commission of the felony. May the other felon be convicted of felony-murder? In many situations (e.g., a terrorist bombing), the accidental death of a co-felon is not extraordinary or unforeseeable, any more than the death of an innocent bystander is. Thus a good case can be made for holding the surviving co-felons liable.

   i. Not applicable to co-felon: But, as noted, several states have held the felony-murder doctrine inapplicable where the death is that of one of the *participants in the felony*. Thus in *State v. Williams*, 254 S. 548 (App. Fla. 1971), one arson-conspirator was held not liable for the death of his colleague, even though the death occurred while they were trying to set the fire. The court stated that the felony-murder doctrine is "primarily" designed to protect the *innocent public.*"

g. "Depraved heart" theory as alternative: Keep in mind that even where the felony-murder rule is held not to apply, the robber may be liable for a shooting by the victim or police based on a finding that the robber showed a "depraved heart," "reckless indifference to the value of human life," etc. This might be the case, for instance, if a robber *initiated or provoked a gun-battle*, even though he did not fire what turned out to be the fatal shot.

   i. *Taylor* case: Thus in *Taylor v. Superior Court*, 477 P.2d 131 (Cal. 1970), D1 and V robbed a liquor store owned by X and Y (a husband and wife) while D2 waited in a getaway car. D pointed a gun at X, and made numerous threats to "blow his head off" if he didn't follow orders. Y used a hidden gun to kill V, and D2 (with D1) was charged with V's murder. The California Supreme Court first held that neither D could be liable on a felony-murder theory, since in California felony-murder applies only where the killing is in fact committed by one of the felons, not by a crime victim or the police. (See *People v. Washington, supra*, p. 240.) However, the court then held that D1's conduct, not only the pointing of the gun but also the threats of execution, might be found to constitute "conscious disregard for life." Since these acts provoked the gun-battle, D1 could be liable for murder, even though he did not fire the first shot, or any shot. Consequently, D2 could be liable as an accomplice to murder. (But see *supra*, p. 216, for a later decision in this case that had the result of setting D2 free.)

   ii. Dissent: A dissent in *Taylor* objected that it was illogical to distinguish between a robber who "merely" points a gun at his victim (in which case there would not necessarily be "conscious disregard for life" or provocation of a gun-battle) and a robber who points a gun, and makes an explicit threat to use it. To hold the latter liable for murder but not the former, the dissent said, is not a sensible punishment scheme.

D. Accomplice liability of co-felons: As many of the above cases show, robberies and other dangerous felonies are often committed by two or more felons working together. If one of these commits an accidental killing of, say, a robbery victim, he himself will of course be guilty of felony-murder. But will the *other co-felons* also be guilty of felony-murder?

1. **Accomplice theory:** The answer is "yes," all the co-felons will be liable for an accidental killing committed by one of them if it was committed *in furtherance of the felony*, at least if the killing can fairly be viewed as a "natural and probable" result of the felony. This result is dictated not by the felony-murder doctrine itself, but by the rules on *accomplice liability*, discussed *supra*, p. 212.

   a. **Intentional killing:** If the killing by one co-felon is *intentional* rather than accidental, the other co-felons will probably still be liable under accomplice principles as long as the killing was committed *"in furtherance" of the felony*. This will normally be true even though the other co-felons can show that they did not desire or foresee the killing.

      Example 1: Recall *U.S. v. Carter, supra*, p. 214. D was held liable for his colleague's murder of a cab driver they had both robbed, despite D's lack of desire that the driver be killed.

      Example 2: D1 and D2, brothers, help their father Gary escape from prison, where he is serving time on a murder conviction. D1 and D2 supply weapons and a getaway car to Gary, knowing of his willingness to use lethal force to escape. They help him lock up the guards, and flee with him into the desert. All three then flag down a car carrying a family of four; while D1 and D2 are getting water some distance away, Gary murders all four.

      Held, D1 and D2 may be convicted of felony-murder. (In fact, they may be sentenced to *death*, without violating the Eighth Amendment's ban on "cruel and unusual" punishment. See *infra*, p. 248.) *Tison v. Arizona*, 107 S.Ct. 1676 (1987). (However, the result in *Tison* seems to have stemmed in part from the fact that D1 and D2 *knew* of their father's willingness to kill to escape. Thus D1 and D2 may *themselves* have been "recklessly indifferent to the value of human life," so that they could perhaps have been convicted of murder even without use of the felony-murder doctrine.)

   b. **Not in "furtherance" of felony:** But if the other co-felons can show that the killing was *not* committed for the purpose of furthering the felony, they may be able to escape accomplice liability. For instance, if the actual killer killed a robbery victim solely because of a prior grudge against him, the other robbers would presumably not be liable for murder.

E. **"In the commission of" a felony:** The felony-murder doctrine applies only to killings which occur *"in the commission of"* a felony. Therefore, it is important to have a way of determining the beginning and ending-point of a felony.

   1. **Mere coincidence not enough:** First, keep in mind that this is not merely a question of whether the killing occurs at the same time and in the same place as the felony. There must be a *causal relationship* between felony and killing. See *supra*, p. 238.

   2. **Escape as part of felony:** If the killing occurs while the felons are attempting to *escape*, it will probably be held to have occurred "in the commission of" the felony, at least if it occurred reasonably close, both in *time and place*, to the felony itself.

a. **"Immediate flight":** Thus the New York felony-murder statute explicitly applies to a killing committed while the felon is in *"immediate flight"* from the scene of the crime.

b. **Possession of "booty":** Where the defendant is attempting to escape with *"booty"* (e.g., proceeds of a robbery, or the ransom from a kidnapping), the court is likely to take a more extended view of what constitutes the felony itself. The theory behind this is that the robber's or kidnapper's object is not fulfilled until he gets the booty to a safe place, and anything before that is still part of the crime sequence.

3. **Killing followed by a felony:** It may sometimes happen that the killing occurs *before* the accompanying felony. If the defendant has planned to commit the felony all along, and the killing happens to occur before the felony can be carried out, this will probably be felony-murder. For instance, if D intends to rape V, and in order to quiet her puts his hand over her mouth, thereby suffocating her, he will not escape liability for felony-murder even if he can show that she died before he committed intercourse.

a. **Intent follows killing:** But if the killing occurs before the defendant even *forms the intent* to commit the felony, this will probably not be felony-murder. For instance, suppose D injures V in a street fight, and seeing V lying in the street helpless (and in fact dead), decides to rob him. LaFave and Scott suggest that the killing should not be considered as occurring "in the commission of" the robbery in this situation. L, pp. 686-87.

F. **Felony is includible in homicide:** It will frequently be the case that the carrying out of a homicide will also constitute the completion of *lesser included offenses*. Assuming that one of these offenses is a felony, the prosecution may argue that the case is converted to felony-murder. However, to prevent the felony-murder rule from making virtually any attack culminating in death into automatic murder, courts have generally required that, for application of the felony-murder doctrine, the felony must be *independent* of the killing.

1. **Manslaughter:** This requirement is most clearly demonstrated where the defendant kills his victim in a "heat of passion," on facts which would justify only a conviction of *voluntary manslaughter* (*infra*, p. 250). Yet manslaughter is obviously a dangerous felony, so the felony-murder rule could theoretically be applied. But this would mean that voluntary manslaughter ceases to exist as a distinct crime; all such manslaughters would "automatically ride up an escalator to become felony-murders." L, p. 687. For this reason, manslaughter may not serve as the underlying felony for felony-murder (at least, where the manslaughter victim and the theoretical felony-murder victim are the same person. If separate victims are involved, the courts are split.)

2. **Batteries and assaults:** Similarly, if the defendant intends to commit an *aggravated battery or assault* upon V, and V's death results, it could be argued that D has committed a dangerous felony and ought to be liable for felony-murder. But here, too, courts have generally declined to find felony-murder. One reason is that the defendant would be stripped of his right to show facts negating "malice aforethought." For instance, if the intended battery was motivated by *extreme provocation*, of the sort that would support a voluntary manslaughter verdict, the defendant would lose his ability to show this mitigating factor.

a. **Discharge of firearm at dwelling:** Some states make it a felony to *discharge a firearm* in or at a *dwelling*. At least one of those states, California, has decided that this felony is *not* like assault or battery, and *can* be the basis for a felony-murder conviction if the discharge accidentally kills someone. *People v. Hansen*, 885 P.2d 1022 (Cal. 1994)

> **Example:** D has a dispute with X, who D knows resides in a particular house. D drives up to the house, and fires 5 rifle shots at the house. One of the bullets strikes V, X's daughter, who (unbeknownst to D) is sitting inside. V dies. *Held*, D can be convicted of felony-murder, based on the dangerous felony of discharging a firearm at an occupied dwelling. *People v. Hansen, supra.*

3. **Burglary with intent to assault:** Suppose the defendant commits a breaking and entering with an intent to commit an assault or battery when he gets inside. Since breaking and entering plus felonious intent give rise to the crime of *burglary*, is the defendant liable for felony-murder if his assault culminates in death? The courts are split.

   a. **California rejects felony-murder:** The courts of California hold that this situation is in principle the same as that in which there is simply an intent to commit an aggravated assault, and that the coincidental presence of breaking-and-entering (thus creating burglary) should not change the result. Thus in *People v. Wilson*, 462 P.2d 22 (Cal. 1969), D's felony-murder conviction was reversed, where he had committed a burglary for the purpose of committing assault with a deadly weapon inside the premises, and the assault turned out to be fatal.

   b. **New York allows liability:** But New York *allows felony-murder* in this situation. In *People v. Miller*, 297 N.E.2d 85 (N.Y. 1973), the court observed that the existence of burglary, insofar as it necessarily involves the entry into a *dwelling*, indicates a greater danger of death than will normally be present in an on-the-street assault. The victim is more likely to resist when attacked in his home, and he is more likely to be aided by relatives.

4. **Armed robbery:** Where the death occurs as part of *armed robbery*, even the courts of California are willing to permit application of the felony-murder doctrine. In *People v. Burton*, 491 P.2d 793 (Cal. 1971), the court rejected the defendant's argument that every armed robbery necessarily involves an assault with a deadly weapon, and that such assault cannot be used as the basis for felony-murder. The court noted that although armed robbery may include an assault, it also contains an "independent felonious purpose, namely…to acquire money or property belonging to another."

G. **Future of the felony-murder rule:** Although all but about three states currently have some form of felony-murder on their books (L, p. 690), many states have limited the doctrine's use in recent years, through such means as the "inherently dangerous" requirement (*supra*, p. 238) and the "includible offense" rule just discussed. These limitations probably reflect an unhappiness with the rule itself, which has often been criticized as illogical.

   1. **Illogicality of rule:** These criticisms stem from the belief that *accidental* killings probably do not happen appreciably more frequently in the course of dangerous felonies than in other circumstances. See, e.g., statistics cited in Comment 6 to M.P.C. § 210.2. Obviously *intentional* killings occur with some frequency during the course of other felonies, but

such killings could presumably be punished as intent-to-kill, or even "reckless indifference to life," murders.

    a. Illustration: Justice Holmes pointed out the illogicality of punishing such accidental killings as murders by supposing the case of a person who, wishing to steal some chickens, shoots at them and thereby kills a man in the henhouse whose presence could not have been foreseen. Holmes stressed that the fact that the shooting is felonious does not increase the likelihood that people will be killed. "If the object of the [felony-murder] rule is to prevent such accidents, it should make accidental killing with firearms murder, not accidental killing in the effort to steal; while if its object is to prevent stealing, it would do better to hang one thief in every thousand by lot." (Quoted in L, p. 690.

2. Model Penal Code rejects rule: The Model Penal Code, on similar reasoning, does not adopt the felony-murder rule *per se*.

    a. Presumption: However, M.P.C. § 210.2(1)(b) establishes a ***rebuttable presumption*** of "recklessness…manifesting extreme indifference to the value of human life" where the defendant "is engaged or is an accomplice in the commission of, or an attempt to commit, or flight after committing or attempting to commit robbery, rape or deviant sexual intercourse by force or threat of force, arson, burglary, kidnapping or felonious escape." Thus if an unintentional killing occurs during one of these crimes, the prosecution is presumably entitled to go to the jury on the issue of "indifference-to-the-value-of-human-life" murder.

        i. May be rebutted: But the defendant is free to show that he was not recklessly indifferent to the value of human life, and that he should therefore not be guilty of murder. The Code provision should thus be contrasted with the usual felony-murder provision, by which the defendant is guilty of murder even if he can show that not only was the killing unintentional, but he was not even reckless with respect to the risk of death.

3. Abolition by decision: One state, Michigan, has entirely ***abolished*** felony-murder, by decision rather than statutory change. *People v. Aaron*, 299 N.W.2d 304 (Mich. 1980). The relevant statute, an old one, provided that "murder which is perpetrated by…willful, deliberate, and premeditated killing, or which is committed in the perpetration, or attempt to perpetrate arson [and other enumerated felonies] is murder in the first degree."

    a. Court's reasoning: The Michigan court interpreted this statute as merely grading murder into degrees, not as defining murder. Therefore, the definition of murder was, the court found, left to common law. The court then conceded that at common law, a killing that took place during a violent felony would be murder. However, the court believed that it was free to abolish this incarnation of the felony-murder rule since it was common-law rather than statutory.

        i. How accomplished: The court accomplished this result by changing the common-law definition of malice (the mental element for murder) so that participation in a violent felony no longer automatically constituted malice. Participation in one of the named felonies might, *on particular facts*, show one of the three remaining types of malice (especially the "wanton and willful disregard of the likelihood [of causing] death or great bodily harm"), but it did not *automatically* mean that such malice existed. Rather, the presence of malice, as the court now defined it, must be "left to the jury to infer from all the evidence."

b. Significance: The *Aaron* court thus adopted something close to the Model Penal Code approach, in that participation in the underlying felony may, but need not, show the requisite recklessness. What is extraordinary about the *Aaron* decision is that it managed to abolish felony murder without statutory change. In any event, this approach would not be possible in the vast majority of states, since most states do not have common-law murder, but instead have a detailed statutory formulation that defines as felony-murder any *death* (not just any "murder," as in the Michigan statute) that occurs during the commission of a designated felony. See K&S, p. 517.

LEXIS®-NEXIS® Searches on **FELONY MURDER**

Sub-Topic	Suggested Searches
Dangerous felony, requirement of	`(felony murder) w/30 ((inherently dangerous) w/ 5 felon!)`
Accomplice liability for additional crimes	`(felony murder) w/30 (accomplice or co-felon) w/30 (natural w/2 probable)`

IV. DEGREES OF MURDER

A. Degrees of murder: In many states, murder is divided into *two or more degrees*. Since the authorized punishment typically varies substantially from degree to degree in a particular state, the classification is of great practical importance. In many (perhaps most) murder cases, there is little or no doubt that the defendant committed a killing, and the only issue is the degree of murder (or manslaughter).

B. Death Penalty: At least 35 states presently authorize the *death penalty* for some kinds of murder. Although a capital punishment statute was held by the U.S. Supreme Court to impose unconstitutional "cruel and unusual" punishment in *Furman v. Georgia*, 408 U.S. 238 (1972), most or all of the present death penalty statutes pass muster under current Supreme Court holdings.

1. *Gregg v. Georgia:* The Supreme Court's principal ruling on the constitutionality of present-day death penalty statutes is ***Gregg v. Georgia***, 428 U.S. 153 (1976). In *Gregg*, the Court held that the death penalty is not necessarily "cruel and unusual," at least where it is imposed for murder. The Court relied on post-*Furman* evidence that both the American people and state legislatures find capital punishment to be acceptable.

a. Statute upheld: The Court, in *Gregg*, upheld the Georgia death penalty statute, which provides that a death sentence may be imposed only if one of ten statutory ***aggravating circumstances*** is found by the jury to exist beyond a reasonable doubt. This requirement, plus the statute's bifurcated scheme (in which the jury is called upon to recommend death or life as part of a separate proceeding following rendition of its verdict), and the provision for automatic appeal of all death sentences to the state

Supreme Court, were in the eyes of the Court sufficient guards against "arbitrariness and caprice."

2. **Mandatory sentences not constitutional:** Many states, like Georgia, have attempted to reduce arbitrariness and discrimination by requiring one of a series of statutory aggravating factors to be present before the death sentence may be imposed. Other states have tried to meet constitutional requirements by making a death sentence *mandatory* for certain crimes (e.g., killing of a police officer, or killing by one already under life sentence). Such mandatory schemes have generally been held to be *unconstitutional* by the Supreme Court, on the grounds that they do not solve the problem of unbridled jury discretion (since the jury may make an unguided decision about whether to convict or acquit, and the decision is a potentially discriminatory one based on whether the jury desires imposition of death). See *Woodson v. North Carolina*, 428 U.S. 280 (1976), and *Roberts v. Louisiana*, 428 U.S. 325 (1976).

3. **Racial prejudice:** If a defendant could prove that the judge's or jury's decision to sentence him to death was motivated by *racial* considerations, presumably the Supreme Court would find that use of the death penalty in that situation violated either the defendant's equal protection or Eighth Amendment rights, or both. (For instance, testimony by a juror that several members of the jury voted to recommend the death sentence for D, a black man, because they hated blacks, would probably be enough to lead the Court to nullify the death sentence.) But the Court has made it clear that any proof of impermissible racial bias must be directed to the *facts of the particular case*, and not be proved by large-scale *statistical studies*.

   a. *McCleskey* **case:** Thus in the celebrated case of *McCleskey v. Kemp*, 481 U.S. 279 (1987), D, a black man accused of murdering a white man, was convicted of murder by a Georgia jury, which then recommended the death penalty. D presented statistical evidence that the combination of defendant's race and victim's race heavily influences whether a jury recommends the death penalty in a Georgia trial: the death penalty is assessed in 22% of the cases involving black defendants and white victims, compared with 8% for white defendants/white victims, 1% for black defendants/black victims and 3% for white defendants/black victims. The Supreme Court did not dispute these statistical findings, but held (by a 5-4 vote) that they *made no constitutional difference*: the fact that there was "some risk" that racial prejudice would influence the jury's decision in a particular criminal case was unfortunate, but the study "does not demonstrate a *constitutionally significant risk* of racial bias affecting the Georgia capital-sentencing process," so D's Eighth Amendment claim failed.

4. **Non-intentional killings:** Apart from the procedures that must be followed before a defendant may be sentenced to death for murder, the Eighth Amendment seems to put *some kinds of killings off-limits* for the death penalty. The Supreme Court has held that the Eighth Amendment prohibits the use of the death penalty on a defendant *"who does not himself kill, attempt to kill, or intend that a killing take place or that lethal force may be employed."* *Enmund v. Florida*, 458 U.S. 782 (1982).

   a. **Getaway driver:** Thus in *Enmund*, the state was not permitted to use the death penalty on D, who had waited in a getaway car while two accomplices went into a farmhouse and murdered the elderly couple who lived there. Since D had not committed the killing or desired it (and was guilty of murder only by a combination of the felony-murder doctrine and the rules on accomplice liability), it would be cruel and unusual punishment for D to be treated the same as if he had caused the harm intentionally.

    b. Knowledge that principal may kill: But where an accomplice *knows* that the principal may kill in furtherance of the joint plan, then apparently the Eighth Amendment does *not* prevent the death penalty from being imposed on the accomplice. See *Tison v. Arizona*, (*supra*, p. 242), in which the Ds, who were brothers, helped their father, Gary, escape from prison by supplying him with a gun and a getaway car; the Ds knew that Gary was willing to kill to carry out his escape. Even though the Ds were some distance away when Gary killed four victims, the Ds could be sentenced to death, the Supreme Court held: they had the requisite mental state for murder under state law, i.e., extreme indifference to the value of human life, so it did not violate the Eighth Amendment for them to be executed even though they did not directly carry out the killing.

    c. Summary: So as the result of *Enmund* and *Tison* taken together, an accomplice to murder can be executed if he himself had the requisite mental state for murder, but not if he was merely an accomplice to some other crime (e.g., robbery) and did not desire that deadly force be used or that killing take place.

  5. Non-murder cases: Incidentally, it seems probable that the Court will not allow the death penalty for crimes *other than murder*. See *Coker v. Georgia*, 433 U.S. 584 (1977), holding that capital punishment may not constitutionally be imposed on one who commits *rape*.

C. First-degree murder: A distinct class of murder, generally called *first-degree murder*, exists in most states. (This class sometimes includes murders for which death may be imposed, but such murders are often treated as a separate "capital murder" class.) The most common statutory requirement for first-degree murder is that the killing have been *"premeditated and deliberate."* Like other mental states, premeditation and deliberation are frequently proved by circumstantial evidence.

Example: D and V are prison inmates. After D's cell is searched by guards, D becomes convinced that someone has informed on him, and tells guards that he is determined to find the "snitch." Within an hour after the search, D attacks V, stabbing him 21 times. The attack begins in the prison mop room, and after V momentarily escapes, D resumes the stabbings in a corridor. V dies from the wounds, and D is charged with first-degree (willful, deliberate and premeditated) murder.

    Held, D's conviction affirmed. The jury was justified in concluding that the killing was deliberate and premeditated. This was indicated by the period of time between the search and the beginning of the stabbings (at least five minutes), D's reference to a "snitch," and the period between the first set and second set of stabbings. *U.S. v. Brown*, 518 F.2d 821 (7th Cir. 1975).

  1. Time required for premeditation: Courts are not in agreement on how long the defendant must have thought about the killing before executing it, for it to have been "premeditated."

a. **Traditional view:** The traditional view is that no substantial amount of time need elapse between formation of the intent to kill and execution of the killing. As one famous old case put it, premeditation exists "if sufficient time be afforded to enable the mind fully to frame the design to kill…. The law fixes upon no length of time as necessary to form the intention to kill…." *Commonwealth v. Drum*, 58 Pa. 9 (1868).

Example: D enters V's house and stabs her repeatedly with one of her kitchen knives. When the knife breaks, he goes to the kitchen, retrieves a second knife, and continues his attack. V finally dies. *Held,* D acted with premeditation. "Even if the initial knifing was spontaneous, defendant had time to reflect upon his actions when the knife broke. That he went searching for another knife is indicative of a reasoned decision to kill." *People v. Perez*, 831 P.2d 1159 (Cal. 1992).

b. **Modern view:** But the traditional position has frequently been criticized, on the grounds that it emasculates the distinction between first- and second-degree murder, since any time there is an intent to kill (usually necessary for second-degree murder) the requisite premeditation is automatically found to exist. Most modern courts, therefore, require a ***reasonable period of time*** during which deliberation exists.

2. **Elements which must be shown:** One well-known case has listed three elements tending to show the requisite deliberation: (1) ***"planning"*** activity, occurring prior to the killing; (2) evidence of ***"motive"***; and (3) a ***manner*** of killing "so particular and exacting that the defendant must have intentionally killed according to a 'preconceived design.' " *People v. Anderson*, 447 P.2d 942 (Cal. 1968). The *Anderson* court stated that a first-degree conviction normally would require either (1) "extremely strong" evidence of planning, or else (2) some evidence of motive (tending to show deliberation rather than sudden decision to kill) plus some evidence of either planning or carefully thought-out manner of killing.

3. **Intoxication as negating deliberation:** The defendant's ability to deliberate may be found to have been negated by ***intoxication.***

4. **Criticism of distinction:** Beyond the difficulty of distinguishing situations of "deliberation" from those in which there is merely a well-formed intent to kill without deliberation, the theory of the distinction has frequently been criticized. Many impulsive murders are characterized by greater depravity than some murders that are carefully thought out.

a. **Model Penal Code view:** As the draftsmen of the Model Penal Code point out, "The very fact of long internal struggle may be evidence that the actor's homicidal impulse was deeply aberrational, far more the product of extraordinary circumstances than a true reflection of the actor's normal character, as, for example, in the case of mercy killings, suicide pacts, many infanticides and cases where a provocation gains in its explosive power as the actor broods about his injury…. We think it no less clear that some purely impulsive murders may present no extenuating circumstance." Comment 4(b) to M.P.C. § 210.6. Accordingly, the Code does not divide murder into first- and second-degree. (It does provide for a separate class of murders as to which the death-penalty may be imposed, but even this does not depend upon whether the crime was premeditated.)

5. Lying in wait, torture and poison:　Apart from murders committed with premeditation and deliberation, many statutes make it first-degree murder to kill by ***"lying in wait,"*** ***"torture,"*** *poisoning*, or other special means. At least as to "lying in wait" and "poison," the rationale behind making these automatically first-degree murders is that such methods furnish evidence of premeditation.

6. Felony-murder:　Although most first-degree murders are of the intent-to-kill variety, statutes in some states also make some or all ***felony-murders*** (typically, those involving rape, robbery, arson and burglary) first-degree. See the general discussion of felony-murder *supra,* p. 237.

D. Second-degree murder:　Murders that are not first-degree are second-degree. These will typically include the following classes:

1. No premeditation:　Cases in which there is ***no premeditation.***

2. Intent to seriously injure:　Cases in which there may have been premeditation, but the defendant's intent was not to kill, but to do ***serious bodily injury*** (a *mens rea* sufficient for murder, as discussed *supra,* p. 234).

3. Indifference to human life:　Cases in which the defendant does not intend to kill, but is ***recklessly indifferent to the value of human life*** (discussed *supra,* p. 235).

4. Felony-murders:　Killings committed during the course of felonies other than those specified in the first-degree murder statute (i.e., typically felonies other than rape, robbery, arson and burglary).

V.　MANSLAUGHTER — VOLUNTARY

A. Manslaughter generally:　The term "manslaughter" covers a number of distinct kinds of homicide, whose common feature is that they are deemed not sufficiently heinous to be treated as murder, but still too blameworthy to go completely unpunished. Manslaughters fall into two principal categories: (1) ***voluntary manslaughter***, in which there is generally an intent to kill; and (2) ***involuntary manslaughter***, in which the death is accidental.

B. Voluntary manslaughter based on "heat of passion":　The most common kind of voluntary manslaughter is that in which the defendant kills while in a ***"heat of passion,"*** i.e., an extremely angry or disturbed state.

1. Intent:　Normally, one who commits voluntary manslaughter intends to bring about the death of the other person. But, theoretically at least, a voluntary manslaughter conviction could be based upon an intent to do ***serious bodily harm***, or a reckless indifference to the value of human life, assuming that such a state of mind was accompanied by the requisite "heat of passion." See L, pp. 703-04.

C. Requirements for voluntary manslaughter:　Assuming that the facts establish what would otherwise be murder, the defendant will be entitled to a conviction on the lesser charge of voluntary manslaughter only if he meets all four of the following requirements: (1) he acts in response to a provocation that would be sufficient to cause a reasonable person to lose his self-control; (2) he in fact acts in a "heat of passion"; (3) the lapse of time between the provocation and the killing is not great enough that a reasonable person would have "cooled off" (i.e., regained his self-control); and (4) he had not in fact "cooled off" by the time he kills.

1. **Consequences of not meeting one hurdle:** If the defendant fails to clear hurdles (1) or (3) above (i.e., he is actually provoked, and has not cooled off, but a reasonable person would have either not lost his self-control or would have cooled off), he will normally be liable only for *second-degree* murder, since he will probably be found to have lacked the necessary premeditation. If, on the other hand, the defendant trips up on hurdles (2) or (4) (i.e., he is not in fact driven into a heat of passion, or has already cooled off), he is likely to be convicted of *first-degree* murder, since his act of killing is in "cold blood." See L, pp. 715-16.

D. **Reasonable provocation:** The defendant's act must be in response to a *provocation* sufficiently strong that a "reasonable person" would have been *caused to lose her self-control*. The rule is sometimes stated that the provocation must be such that it would cause a reasonable person to kill, but this is clearly not required; there are presumably very few circumstances under which a truly "reasonable person" will be driven to kill, and it is clear that courts will accept all kinds of provocation as adequate for voluntary manslaughter that would not drive a reasonable person to kill. All the defendant has to establish is that a provocation would have been enough to make a reasonable person *lose her temper*.

1. **Characteristics of the reasonable person:** There has been much dispute about exactly what characteristics peculiar to the defendant should be imputed to the "reasonable person" in determining how the latter would react to the provocation in question.

a. **Physical characteristics:** Courts have sometimes been willing to endow the "reasonable person" with certain of the defendant's *physical characteristics*. For instance, in one case D was a *one-legged man*, who killed V when the latter knocked away one of his crutches. The court held that in determining whether a reasonable person would have been sufficiently provoked, the jury could assume that the reasonable person was one-legged, and that to such a person, a blow to a crutch is highly inflammatory. *R. v. Raney*, 29 Crim. App. 14 (Eng. 1942).

i. **Disagreement:** But other courts have been *unwilling* to ascribe the defendant's physical characteristics, including physical shortcomings, to the reasonable person. For instance, one English case held that a defendant's *impotence* is not to be imputed to the reasonable man. In *Bedder v. Director of Public Prosecutions*, [1954] 2 All E.R. 801 (Eng. 1954), D, who knew he was impotent, tried and failed to have intercourse with a prostitute. She jeered at him, and he responded by stabbing her to death. The court held that the reasonable man should not be given the characteristic of impotence: "it would be plainly illogical not to recognize an unusually excitable or pugnacious temperament in the accused as a matter to be taken into account but yet to recognize for that purpose some unusual physical characteristic, be it impotence or another."

b. **Emotional characteristics:** Courts are almost always *unwilling* to recognize the peculiar *emotional* characteristics of the defendant in determining how a reasonable person would act. Thus it is universally agreed that the fact that the defendant is *unusually pugnacious or bad-tempered* is not to be taken into account. If it were otherwise, the "reasonable person" test would be virtually eviscerated, since the test is of importance only to weed out those cases where the defendant is enraged by something that would not enrage an ordinary person.

    c. **Model Penal Code allows some subjectivity:** The Model Penal Code establishes a test that is somewhat *more subjective* than that applied by most courts. Under M.P.C. § 210.3(1)(b), the crime is manslaughter if it is "committed under the influence of *extreme mental or emotional disturbance* for which there is *reasonable explanation or excuse*. The reasonableness of such explanation or excuse shall be determined from the viewpoint of a person in the actor's situation under the circumstances as he believed them to be."

        i. **Some subjectivity allowed:** The Code commentary indicates that the term "situation" may be interpreted to include at least some mental or emotional characteristics. "[i]f the actor had just suffered a traumatic injury…or were distraught with grief, if he were experiencing an unanticipated reaction to a therapeutic drug, it would be deemed atrocious to appraise his crime for purposes of sentence without reference to any of these matters."

    d. **Intoxication:** If the defendant is particularly excitable because he is *voluntarily intoxicated*, his intoxication will never be imputed to the reasonable person. That is, he will be judged by the standard of a reasonable sober person; only if the latter would have been provoked may the defendant receive a manslaughter verdict.

2. **Particular categories:** In addition to limiting the special characteristics that may be imputed to the reasonable man, courts have also limited the use of voluntary manslaughter by allowing only *certain categories* of provocation to suffice, and excluding others as a matter of law.

    a. **Battery:** For historical reasons, a more-than-trivial *battery* committed on the defendant is almost always considered to be sufficient provocation. L, p. 706. However, if the defendant brought on the battery by his own initial aggressive conduct, he will not be entitled to a manslaughter verdict.

        i. **Assault:** If the other party *attempts* to commit a battery on the defendant, but fails (thereby committing a *criminal assault*), some but not all courts recognize it as sufficient provocation, at least if the threatened battery was a serious one (e.g., use of a firearm). See L, pp. 706-07.

    b. **Mutual combat:** If the defendant and his victim get into a *mutual combat*, in which neither one can be said to be the aggressor, most courts will reduce the defendant's liability to manslaughter. L, p. 706.

    c. **Adultery:** Perhaps the classic voluntary manslaughter situation is that in which the husband surprises his wife in the act of *adultery* with her paramour, and kills either the wife or the lover. This will virtually always be sufficient provocation.

        i. **Non-married couple:** But most courts have limited this rule to *married couples*. The discovery of one's fiancee, not to mention one's steady girlfriend, in the act of infidelity, is generally not sufficient. L, p. 708.

ii. **Second-hand discovery:** Where the defendant discovers the adultery ***second-hand*** (e.g., by being told about it rather than seeing it), the modern tendency is to find the provocation reasonable, despite the lack of "ocular" evidence. See the discussion of the "words alone" rule, *infra*.

iii. **Reasonable mistake:** Also, if the defendant's second-hand evidence would lead a reasonable person to believe that there has been adultery, but the evidence is in fact ***misleading***, most present-day courts would probably nonetheless allow a manslaughter finding. See, e.g., *Maher v. People*, 10 Mich. 212 (1862).

d. **Words alone:** The traditional rule has been that ***words alone*** can never constitute the requisite provocation. Where the words are simply abusive, insulting or harassing, this rule probably remains in force.

i. **Words carrying information:** But if the words ***convey information*** (i.e., "I am having an affair" or "I want a divorce"), courts generally hold that the information may, if it is sufficiently inflammatory, constitute reasonable provocation. Also, words that both convey distressing information and are taunting or insulting may be sufficient, even where the information by itself would not be sufficient.

Example: D, a 46-year-old cook, marries V, a 20-year-old Israeli woman. V returns from a trip to Israel and announces that she has fallen in love with another man, Yako, has had sex with him, and plans to divorce D and return to Yako. She alternately demands and refuses sex with D and intermittently screams at him. Then she leaves. D waits for 20 hours for her to come home; when she does, she starts screaming at him. D then strangles her with a telephone cord.

Held, V's conduct was sufficient to constitute the necessary provocation for manslaughter. Verbal provocation may be sufficient. Here, V's conduct "could arouse a passion of jealousy, pain and sexual rage in an ordinary man of average disposition so as to cause him to act rashly from this passion." (Nor does D lose his right to manslaughter by virtue of the 20-hour "cooling off" period prior to the killing, since D's rage was rekindled when V began screaming at him right before the killing.) *People v. Berry*, 556 P.2d 777 (Cal. 1976).

(1) **Different view:** However, at least in the case of women victims who taunt or insult their mates, a finding of reasonable provocation is probably less likely today than it was when *People v. Berry* was decided in 1976. For instance, it's hard to see how the case in the following Example is different from *Berry*, except for the fact that society's tolerance for abuse by men against women diminished sharply from 1976 to 1991.

Example: D and V meet and marry after knowing each other only three months. Two months into the marriage, in the midst of an argument, V follows D into the bedroom, climbs on his back and pulls his hair, and taunts him verbally. She calls him names, tells him she never wanted to marry him, tells him she wants a divorce, etc. She asks him several times, "What are you going to do?" D gets up and goes to the kitchen. He grabs a large kitchen knife, hides it behind a pillow and returns to the bedroom. V continues her verbal assault and asks again, "What are you going to do?" D then lunges at V and stabs her to death. At trial, D seeks to have his murder conviction mitigated to manslaughter, arguing that his actions were provoked by V.

Held, D was not entitled to a manslaughter conviction. "Words can constitute adequate provocation [only] if they are accompanied by conduct indicating a present intention and ability to cause the defendant bodily harm." Since the victim here was 5'1" and weighed 115 pounds, and the defendant was 6'2" and weighed over 200 pounds, D could not reasonably have feared for his bodily safety. *Girouard v. State*, 583 A.2d 718 (Md. 1991).

3. **No fixed categories:** Traditionally, as noted, courts found a provocation to be sufficient only if it fell within certain well-defined categories, usually limited to some or all of those discussed above. Recently, however, courts have often rejected the need for such categories, and have left to the jury the decision whether, on all the facts, the provocation was such that a reasonable man would have lost his self-control. Thus in *Berry, supra*, the court stated that "no specific type of provocation [is] required...."

4. **Effect of mistake:** If the defendant reasonably but *mistakenly* reaches a conclusion which, if accurate, would constitute sufficient provocation, courts will generally allow manslaughter. For instance, if the defendant reasonably but erroneously believes that his wife has committed adultery, his killing of her will probably be reduced to manslaughter (at least in a jurisdiction where indirect knowledge of adultery would suffice).

E. **Actual provocation:** The provocation must not only be sufficient to cause a reasonable man to lose his self-control, but also sufficient to have *in fact* enraged the defendant. Thus if the defendant is an unusually cool-headed person, who is not enraged by a particular provocation, he will not be able to claim manslaughter even though a reasonable man might have lost his self-control in the circumstances.

F. **Reasonable "cooling off period":** The lapse of time between the provocation and the killing must not be so long that a reasonable man would have *"cooled off"* (i.e., recovered his self-control).

1. **Minority view:** A few jurisdictions, however, do not impose this requirement, and require only that the defendant *in fact* not have cooled off prior to the killing. (Actual non-cooling-off is a separate requirement in all jurisdictions, as discussed *infra*).

2. **Rekindling:** Even if there is a substantial cooling-off period between the initial provocation and the killing, if a *new provocation* occurs which would rekindle the passion of a reasonable man, the cooling-off rule is not violated. This is true even if the new provocation would not by itself be sufficient to inflame a reasonable man. Thus in *People v. Berry, supra*, D waited for V's return (possibly with an intent to kill her) for twenty hours. This would normally have been a period within which a reasonable man would have cooled off. But the California Supreme Court held that V's screaming rekindled D's rage (and implied that the screaming would have been sufficient to re-inflame a reasonable man); therefore, D was entitled to a manslaughter verdict.

G. **Actual cooling off:** The defendant must not have *in fact* "cooled off," or regained his composure, at the time he commits the killing. Thus if he is less passionate than the ordinary man, and after he calms down, deliberately kills, he will not be entitled to manslaughter even though an ordinary man might still have been without self-control at the time of the killing.

H. Killing of one other than provoker: It may happen that the requisite provocation exists, but that the defendant kills *someone other than the provoker*. Depending on the reasons for the error, the defendant may or may not be entitled to a manslaughter verdict.

1. **Bad aim:** If D is trying to hit X (the actual provoker), and through *faulty aim* hits V, a bystander, D will probably be entitled to manslaughter. This will certainly be true if D is no more than negligent in hitting V rather than X. If D is reckless as to the risk of injuring innocent parties, most courts would still probably allow a manslaughter verdict. See L, pp. 716.

2. **Mistake as to who provoked:** If D *erroneously believes* that V, rather than X, is his provoker, and kills V, D will also probably be entitled to manslaughter. This will certainly be the case if his mistake is no worse than merely negligent; where the mistake is reckless, the courts would probably split.

3. **Victim known not to be provoker:** If D is aware that X, not V, is the actual provoker, but he is so enraged that he strikes out and kills V anyway, most courts will not allow manslaughter. See, e.g., *State v. Tilson*, 503 S.W.2d 921 (Tenn. 1974), refusing to allow manslaughter where the person killed was a bystander and a friend of the provokers.

4. **Model Penal Code:** The Model Penal Code does not place an explicit limitation on the identity of the person killed. Thus even in the *Tilson* situation just discussed, the defendant might obtain a manslaughter verdict if he could persuade the court or jury that his disturbance was so extreme that even killing the wrong person should not be treated as murder. See M.P.C. § 210.3(1)(b).

I. Other kinds of voluntary manslaughter: In addition to manslaughter based upon a "heat of passion" killing, there are a number of other situations in which voluntary manslaughter may be found. In general, these are situations in which what would otherwise be a *complete defense or justification* does not exist due to the defendant's unreasonable mistake or some other reason.

1. **"Imperfect" self-defense:** For instance, a defendant who killed in order to defend himself may fail to have a complete excuse of *self-defense* (*supra*, p. 107) because: (1) he is unreasonably mistaken about the existence of danger; (2) he is unreasonably mistaken about the need for deadly force; or (3) he is the aggressor, and therefore forfeits the right of self-defense. In any of these three situations, *some but not most* states permit the defendant's liability to be reduced from murder to manslaughter. See L, pp. 718-19.

2. **"Imperfect" defense of others:** If the defendant uses deadly force in *defense of another*, and does not meet all the requirements for exculpation (*supra*, pp. 121-122), some courts will similarly allow him the lesser charge of manslaughter. For instance, in a jurisdiction where one's right to defend another is no greater than that person's right to defend himself (the "*alter ego*" rule), the defendant might be entitled to a manslaughter verdict if he used deadly force in defense of a person who turned out to have been the aggressor.

3. **"Imperfect" crime-prevention:** Similarly, a defendant might be convicted of manslaughter where he uses deadly force to *prevent a felony*, where the felony is not a danger-

ous one and the jurisdiction does not allow deadly force to be used to prevent it (e.g., D shoots an unarmed burglar). See L, p. 719.

4. **"Imperfect" coercion or necessity:** Suppose the defendant is subjected to *coercion* or *necessity*, but these defenses are not fully merited. There, too, manslaughter might be the outcome. For instance, in a jurisdiction refusing to allow the defense of duress to an intentional killing (*supra*, p. 100), a reduction to manslaughter might be allowed.

5. **Other killings:** There are a few other situations where manslaughter might be found.

     a. **Mercy killings:** A defendant who commits a *mercy killing* (i.e., a killing to terminate the life of one suffering from a painful and incurable disease) might be convicted of manslaughter. L, pp. 720-21.

     b. **Intoxication:** Occasionally, it is even held that the defendant's *voluntary intoxication* is sufficient to negate "malice aforethought," and thus reduce murder to manslaughter. For instance, in *People v. Conley*, 411 P.2d 911 (Cal. 1966), D, after becoming drunk, shot and killed X (a woman with whom he had become romantically involved) and X's husband Y. The California Supreme Court held that it was error not to give the jury a manslaughter instruction, on the grounds that D's intoxication or mental illness may have made him "unable to comprehend his duty to govern his actions in accord with the duty imposed by law." If D had such an inability, the existence of "malice aforethought" would be negated, and a manslaughter verdict would be appropriate, said the Court. This is true even though D may have had the ability to *premeditate* the killings.

         i. **Intoxication not normally enough:** But most states *never* permit intoxication to reduce murder to manslaughter. (However, intoxication may be enough to negate premeditation and deliberation, thereby reducing first-degree murder to second-degree; see *supra*, p. 249).

LEXIS®-NEXIS® Searches on **VOLUNTARY MANSLAUGHTER**

Sub-Topic	Suggested Searches
Reasonable provocation	`(voluntary manslaughter) w/30 (reasonable provocation) and atleast2(manslaughter)`
Particular categories of provocation	
Adultery	`(voluntary manslaughter) w/50 (adultery w/20 (provok! or provoc!))`
Words alone	`(voluntary manslaughter) w/50 ((word or insult) w/20 (provok! or provoc!))`
Reasonable "cooling off" period	`(voluntary manslaughter) and ("cool off" or "cooling off" or "cooled off")`
Imperfect self-defense as giving rise to	`(voluntary manslaughter) and (imperfect self defense)`

VI. MANSLAUGHTER — INVOLUNTARY

A. Involuntary manslaughter based on criminal negligence: One whose behavior is grossly negligent may be liable for *involuntary manslaughter* if his conduct results in the accidental death of another person. When manslaughter liability for negligence is at issue, two principal questions are raised; (1) how far from the standard of reasonable care must the defendant deviate?; and (2) must the defendant actually be *aware* of the risk of death or harm?

1. **Criminal negligence required:** The vast majority of jurisdictions hold that *something more than ordinary tort negligence* must be shown before the defendant can be liable for involuntary manslaughter. Usually "gross" negligence is required, although it is not clear what this means. It is probably necessary to show that there was a very substantial danger not just of bodily harm, but of *serious* bodily harm or death.

   a. **Model Penal Code formulation:** The Model Penal Code requires that the defendant act *"recklessly."* M.P.C. § 210.3(1)(b). The Code defines "recklessly" so as to require a "gross deviation from the standard of conduct that a law-abiding person would observe in the actor's situation." M.P.C. § 2.02(2)(c). (The Code also requires that the defendant be aware of the risk; see *infra*, p. 258).

2. **All circumstances considered:** The existence of the requisite negligence is to be determined in light of *all the "circumstances,"* at least those external to the defendant. The *social utility* of any objective the defendant is trying to fulfill is weighed. For instance, suppose that D kills V, a pedestrian, by driving at 50 miles per hour in a 30-mile-per-hour residential zone. D's conduct may be held to be criminally negligent if D was simply out for a pleasure spin, whereas it might not be criminally negligent if D was rushing his critically ill wife to the hospital.

3. **Defendant's own characteristics:** Suppose the defendant has *physical or mental defects* which influence his conduct. There is some dispute about when such defects should be taken into account in measuring negligence.

   a. **Physical defects:** Most *physical* characteristics are taken into account in determining whether the defendant's conduct was negligent. The issue thus becomes what a reasonable man would have done had he had that physical shortcoming. Sometimes this will work to the defendant's benefit, as where he fails to realize that his house is burning down because he has a defective sense of smell, and a third person is killed.

      i. **Works to defendant's disadvantage:** But probably more often the situation will be one in which a reasonable man, *knowing of his physical defect*, would *not* have engaged in the activity in question. For instance, if the defendant knows that he is subject to epileptic attacks, it may constitute criminal negligence for him to drive, at least without proper medication. If the defendant has an attack while driving, and a fatal accident occurs, the defendant's illness is unlikely to shield him from manslaughter liability. See L, p. 723 and fn. 22 thereto.

   b. **Mental characteristics:** The courts are even less willing to allow the defendant to benefit from any *mental or emotional shortcomings*. For instance, if the defendant while driving sees a child in the road, and because of extreme timidity or inability to concentrate, he fails to hit the brakes in time, his conduct would probably be measured against that of a reasonable man of average calmness and reactions.

    i.   Effect of ignorance of risk: However, as will be noted below, if the physical or mental shortcoming prevents the defendant from being ***aware*** of the risk, in some jurisdictions this may be enough to absolve him of manslaughter liability.

4. "Inherently dangerous" objects: Where the defendant uses an object that is ***"inherently dangerous,"*** the courts are somewhat more willing to hold him guilty of manslaughter even though his negligence is merely "ordinary" rather than "gross" or "criminal." This is especially true where the accident involves a *firearm.*

    a. Application to automobile: A few cases have applied this "inherent danger" rationale to ***automobile*** deaths. For instance, in *State v. Barnett*, 63 S.E.2d 57 (S.C. 1951), the court held that an automobile, like a firearm, is an object "of such character that its negligent use under the surrounding circumstances is necessarily dangerous to human life or limb." Therefore, the court held, only "simple negligence" is necessary for a manslaughter conviction in the case of a car accident.

5. Defendant's awareness of risk: The courts are in sharp disagreement as to whether the defendant may be liable for manslaughter if he was ***unaware*** of the risk posed by his conduct.

    a. Awareness not required: The court's determination is likely to turn in part on the precise wording of the statute. Thus, where one of the few statutes requiring only ordinary negligence was involved, it was held that a defendant could be liable for manslaughter even though he was unaware of the danger to life. *State v. Williams*, 484 P.2d 1167 (Wash. App. 1971).

    b. Awareness required: Where "gross negligence" or "recklessness" is required, it seems probable that most courts would require an actual awareness of danger on the defendant's part.

    c. Model Penal Code agrees: The Model Penal Code, which bases manslaughter only upon a finding of "recklessness," similarly requires actual awareness. This is because, under M.P.C. § 2.02(2)(c), a person acts recklessly only when he "consciously disregards" a substantial and unjustifiable risk.

6. Proximate cause: There must, of course, be a ***causal link*** between the defendant's act of negligence and the ensuing death. The defendant's conduct must not only be the "cause in fact" of the death but also a "proximate" cause, i.e., one whose relationship to the death is not ***bizarre or extraordinary***. (More complete discussions of proximate cause in negligence crimes occur on p. 50, p. 53 and p. 60 *supra*.)

    a. Member of endangered class: The victim must be a ***member of the class*** that was endangered by the defendant's conduct. Thus if D drives at a grossly excessive speed through local streets, and bangs into a car which (unsuspected by anyone) contains explosives, D will not be liable for the death of V, killed when the blast sends broken glass into V's fourth-story office. In this situation, D's conduct posed a foreseeable danger only to persons on or near the street, and V was not a member of this class.

b. **Manner of harm:** Similarly, the defendant will be liable only if the death occurs in a somewhat foreseeable, or at least not "abnormal," fashion. For instance if, on the facts of the above example, X, a nurse standing on the sidewalk, fatally dropped Y, an infant, when she heard the blast, D would almost certainly escape manslaughter liability on the grounds that the overall manner in which Y met his death was bizarre and unforeseeable.

7. **Contributory negligence of victim:** The fact that the victim may have been *contributorily negligent* is not a defense to manslaughter (or to most other crimes; see *supra*, p. 132). However, the victim's contributory negligence may have a bearing on whether the defendant was sufficiently negligent or reckless to have committed manslaughter. For instance, if cars driven by D and V collide, and V is killed, evidence that V drove negligently by, say, crossing into D's path may be relevant to D's degree of care in not avoiding the accident.

8. **Vehicular homicide:** The majority of involuntary manslaughter cases involve death by *automobile*. Because it is often hard to get a manslaughter conviction in such cases (particularly where the statute requires a showing of "recklessness") and because it is often thought to be unfair to convict a motorist of the heinous felony of manslaughter, a number of states have defined the lesser crime of *vehicular homicide.*

   a. **Intoxication statutes:** Conversely, some states have special statutes which make it a crime to cause death by *driving while intoxicated*. These statutes frequently impose a greater punishment than for involuntary manslaughter.

   b. **Criminally negligent homicide:** The Model Penal Code contains no such special auto statute. However, in a belief that negligence leading to death should be punished even where "recklessness" (required for manslaughter under the Code) does not exist, the Code defines the crime of *"negligent homicide."* One acts "negligently," under the Code, when he "should be aware of a substantial and unjustifiable risk," and his failure to perceive that risk, under all the circumstances, involves a "gross deviation from the standard of care that a reasonable person would observe...." M.P.C. § 2.02(2)(d). Thus actual awareness of the risk is not required for negligent homicide.

B. **Unlawful-act manslaughter ("misdemeanor-manslaughter"):** Just as the felony-murder rule permits a murder conviction when a death occurs during the course of certain felonies, so the so-called *"misdemeanor-manslaughter"* rule permits a conviction for involuntary manslaughter when a death occurs accidentally during the commission of a misdemeanor or other *unlawful act*. The unlawful act is treated as a substitute for criminal negligence. While a few states have abolished the full concept of misdemeanor-manslaughter, the substantial majority retain it, although many place significant limitations on its use.

1. **What constitutes "unlawful act":** Any misdemeanor may serve as the basis for application of the misdemeanor-manslaughter doctrine (provided that the requisite causal relation, discussed *infra*, is shown). Additionally, some jurisdictions permit a showing that the defendant violated a *local ordinance* or *administrative regulation*. See L, p. 728. Also, if a particular felony does not suffice for the felony-murder rule (e.g., because it is not "inherently dangerous to life," such as grand larceny), it may be used.

a. **Battery:** One unlawful act that frequently serves as the basis for misdemeanor-manslaughter liability is ***battery.***

Example: D gets into an argument with V, and gives him a light tap on the chin with his fist. Unbeknownst to D, V is a hemophiliac and bleeds to death. Since D has committed the misdemeanor of simple battery, and a death has resulted, he will be liable for manslaughter.

b. **Assault:** Similarly, if D commits a ***criminal assault*** on V, and V dies accidentally, the misdemeanor-manslaughter rule will apply. Thus suppose that D takes a swing at V, and misses (thus committing the attempted-battery variety of assault; see *infra*, p. 267). V, in escaping from the blow, falls down, hits his head on the curb, and dies. D is liable for manslaughter.

c. **Traffic violations:** Another frequent source of misdemeanor-manslaughter liability is the violation of ***traffic laws***. For instance, if a motorist is exceeding the speed limit at the time he kills a pedestrian, he may be liable for manslaughter even without proof that he was criminally negligent. See, e.g., *State v. Hupf*, 101 A.2d 355 (Del. 1953), in which D violated a number of traffic laws, including failing to stop at a stop sign, failing to yield the right of way, and speeding. He was held liable for manslaughter when a fatal collision resulted; the court held that violation of the traffic laws made it unnecessary for the state to prove "conscious or reckless disregard of the lives or safety of others" (which would otherwise have been required for manslaughter.)

2. **Proximate cause:** There must be a causal relation between the violation and the death. In the case of a violation that is "*malum in se*," the requisite causal relationship is often found so long as the conduct is the "cause in fact" of the death, even though it was not "natural and probable" or even "foreseeable" that the death would occur. That is, the usual requirement of "proximate cause" is frequently suspended.

a. *Malum prohibitum:* If, however, the defendant's offense is "*malum prohibitum*" (i.e., not dangerous in itself, but simply in violation of a public-welfare regulation), most jurisdictions require that the conduct bear a closer causal relation to the death. The requirement of proximate cause is usually imposed in one of three ways:

i. **"Natural" or "foreseeable" result:** Some courts hold that the death must be the "*natural*" or "*foreseeable*" consequence of the unlawful conduct.

Example: Suppose that D *fails to renew his driver's license*, and then runs over a pedestrian. A court following the "natural or foreseeable consequence" view is likely to hold that death of a pedestrian is not a "natural" or "probable" consequence of failure to renew one's license, and that there is therefore no manslaughter in the absence of actual criminal negligence. (But a different result might be reached where the defendant never got a license in the first place; the court might reason that unlicensed drivers are more likely to cause death or injury than licensed ones.)

ii. **Unlawful excess:** Other courts require that the "***unlawful excess***," i.e., the respect in which the defendant's conduct goes beyond the lawful, be the cause in fact of the death. For instance, if D drives 50 miles per hour in a 40-mile-per-hour zone, and kills a pedestrian, he will be liable for misdemeanor-manslaughter only if the accident would not have occurred at 40 miles per hour. Observe that this rule will often be more lenient than the "natural or foreseeable consequence" rule discussed above; the latter is likely to be applied on a more general and abstract basis (e.g., "speeding always creates a risk of death or injury").

    iii. Violation irrelevant: Still other courts simply do not apply the misdemeanor-manslaughter rule at all to conduct that is *malum prohibitum*; actual criminal negligence must be shown, just as if there were no violation.

  3. Criticism of doctrine: The misdemeanor-manslaughter rule has been subject to great criticism in recent years, on the grounds that it imposes the extreme sanction of manslaughter on conduct which frequently does not even constitute ordinary, let alone criminal, negligence. Furthermore, there is little reason to believe that death is more likely to result from many unlawful acts than from other, lawful, conduct. For instance, it seems neither fair nor very effective to attempt to deter street fights by punishing with a manslaughter conviction the one defendant in every, say, 10,000 who is unlucky enough to have an opponent with a thin skull or blood disease.

    a. Model Penal Code abolishes: Accordingly, the Model Penal Code *rejects* the misdemeanor-manslaughter rule in its entirety. See Comments 3 and 8 to M.P.C. § 210.3. However, even under the Code the fact that an act is unlawful may have an evidentiary bearing on whether it is reckless (the Code *mens rea* for manslaughter).

LEXIS®-NEXIS® Searches on **INVOLUNTARY MANSLAUGHTER**

Sub-Topic	Suggested Searches
Involuntary manslaughter, generally	`atleast2(involuntary manslaughter) and ((involuntary manslaughter) w/30 (definit! or elements))`
Misdemeanor-manslaughter rule	`misdemeanor-manslaughter rule`

Quiz Yourself on
HOMICIDE (ALL FORMS)

62. Kingsman, holding a lead pipe, walks up to Humpty Dumpty, who is sitting on top of a wall.

(A) Assume for this part only the following additional facts: Kingsman swings his pipe with relatively little force against the side of Humpty's head. His intent is to frighten Humpty into paying his back taxes to the King; Kingsman believes (reasonably) that the pipe will cause only a slight bruise and a little pain, but that it will signify that Kingsman is prepared to get as rough as he has to on later occasions to get Humpty to pay. What Kingsman doesn't realize is that Humpty has an eggshell skull. The tap fractures Humpty's skull, and Humpty dies as a result. Is Kingsman guilty of murdering Humpty?

(B) Assume for this part only that the event happens as described in part (A) with the following differences: Kingsman intends to hit Humpty hard enough that Humpty's skull will be fractured, and he'll be in the hospital for at least a week. He does not intend to kill Humpty, because that would defeat the whole purpose (getting the taxes paid back). Kingsman in fact swings with a force, and in a location, that in most instances would indeed have fractured a person's (or egg's) skull without killing him. In this case, tragically, Humpty's eggshell skull causes the fracture to be so bad that Humpty dies of brain edema. Is Kingsman guilty of murdering Humpty?

63. Brutus stabs Julius Caesar, with intent to kill him, on March 15, 44 B.C. Caesar lingers until April 1, 43 B.C., when he dies as a result of Brutus' attack. Under the common law, is Brutus guilty of murder?

64. Two thrillseekers, Macbeth and Banquo, set out separately one evening to have a rowdy good time. Macbeth heads off for the countryside. He takes out his gun as he drives along, and fires it into an old abandoned hunting cabin for target practice. Unbeknownst to him, a tramp, Polonius, is sleeping inside; Macbeth's shot kills him. At the same time, Banquo drives through Dunsinane, a heavily-populated residential suburb. He fires his gun into the open window of a dark apartment. His shot kills a person sleeping inside the apartment. Neither Macbeth nor Banquo intended to kill anyone. Macbeth believed the cabin was unoccupied. Banquo believed that the room into which he fired was unoccupied, but believed that there were probably people present elsewhere in the building. Is either of them guilty of murder, and if so, on what theory?

65. Señor Delgato agrees to help Speedy Gonzales rob the Limburger Cheese Factory one night. Delgato lends Speedy his gun, although he doesn't believe Speedy will have to use it; he doesn't want anyone killed just for a stinking piece of cheese. Delgato stands as lookout while Speedy breaks into the factory. Speedy is unexpectedly accosted by the night watchman, who tries to tackle him. To avoid capture, Speedy shoots at the watchman, intending to hit him in the leg to disable (but not kill or seriously wound) him. Unfortunately, Speedy's shot is slightly off, and the watchman bleeds to death from his wound. Is *Delgato* guilty of murder, and if so, on what theory?

66. Nero sets a fire to Sabina's house one night, believing (reasonably, based on the facts known to him) that Sabina and her family are away on vacation. In fact, Sabina and her family have returned a day early from vacation, and are asleep inside. The house is soon engulfed in flames. Firemen rush to the scene. One of them, Claudius, is killed while trying unsuccessfully to save Sabina. Another fireman, Maecenas, survives the fire, but is killed when a low-lying tree branch knocks him off the fire truck on the way back to the station. For whose death(s) will Nero be liable under the felony-murder rule: Sabina's, Claudius', and/or Maecenas'?

67. Water-Pistol Kelly is robbing the Smalltown Bank. While he is holding the bank manager at gunpoint in the vault, a customer, Kitty Litter, suffers a heart attack and dies in the lobby.

   (A) For this part only, assume that at the time Kitty had her heart attack, no one in the lobby, including Kitty, knew that a robbery was underway. Is Kelly guilty of murdering Kitty?

   (B) For this part only, assume that just before Kitty had her heart attack, she heard from a teller that someone was holding the bank manager at gunpoint in the vault. Kitty had a nervous disposition, and was frightened (even though others in the lobby were not) that the stickup artist or his confederates might soon threaten her. Her heart attack was brought on by these fears. Is Kelly guilty of murdering Kitty?

68. Derevenko slashes Czarevich Alexis in the arm with a dagger, intending only to cut him. In fact, Alexis is a hemophiliac and, as a result of the cut, Alexis bleeds to death. In the jurisdiction, Derevenko's attack with a dagger would constitute aggravated battery, a felony. Is Derevenko guilty of felony murder?

69. Aunt Pittypat runs up to Rhett Butler and tells him, "Your wife Scarlett is having an affair with Ashley!" (Assume that a reasonable person in Brett's position would believe, as Rhett does, that Aunt Pittypat is

referring to Ashley Wilkes.) In a blind rage, Rhett runs the few blocks over to Ashley Wilkes' house, where he finds Scarlett and Ashley sitting in the living room, sipping tea. Rhett shoots and kills Ashley. In fact, Scarlett has been having an affair with a different Ashley — Ashley Farkus, who lives on the other side of town. What is the most serious crime for which Rhett can be convicted?

70. James Bond's wife, Tracy, is gunned down by Fast Eddie Triggerhand as she sits in the front seat of her car next to James. James is heartbroken, but coolly takes her to the morgue. He spends the next few hours looking calmly for clues as to Triggerhand's whereabouts, tracking him down, and finally killing him with his trusty Walther PPK. What is the most serious crime for which James can be convicted?

71. Deerslay is an avid, and properly-licensed, deer hunter. During deer season one day, he decides to hunt in a region called Acadia, which was once completely uninhabited, but which (as Deerslay knows) is now immediately adjacent to a sizable development of homes. Deerslay is standing at a point he knows to be about 300 yards away from the closest houses, when he sees a moving flash of brown and white in the direction where the houses lie. He thinks this is a deer. He immediately points his rifle and shoots. Unbeknownst to Deerslay, the flash of brown is in fact Dierdre standing in her back yard at the edge of the woods, wearing a brown fox-fur coat trimmed in white mink. The shot strikes Dierdre in the chest, and she dies immediately.

(A) For this part, assume that Deerslay's actions (hunting so close to the houses, shooting in the direction of the houses, and not verifying that what he saw was a deer) constitute gross negligence, but that his actions do not manifest a depraved indifference to the value of human life. What is the most serious crime of which Deerslay is guilty?

(B) Same basic fact pattern as part (A). Now, however, assume that Deerslay is new to the region, and does not know that there are housing developments nearby, in the direction at which he is pointing his gun. Assume further, however, that an ordinarily careful person would have asked questions of hunters who lived in the area, and would probably have discovered that houses were nearby. May Deerslay on these facts be convicted of the same crime which you listed as your answer to the prior question?

72. Jerry insults Tom's mother. To retaliate, Tom punches Jerry in the nose. Tom intends only to injure Jerry slightly — the most he hopes or intends will happen is that Jerry's nose will get bloody. Unbeknownst to Tom, Jerry is a hemophiliac. Consequently, Jerry bleeds to death. What is the most serious crime of which Tom can be convicted, and on what theory, in a jurisdiction following the most common approach to relevant matters?

73. Lady Godiva's horse is being re-shoed, so she is forced to drive into town in her car. She let her driver's license lapse several years ago. It is a misdemeanor in the jurisdiction to drive with a lapsed license. On the way into town, she hits a child who runs out into the street, chasing a ball. The child is killed, although Lady Godiva could not have been any more careful a driver. The jurisdiction follows the most common approach to issues of manslaughter. Can Lady Godiva properly be convicted of manslaughter?

Answers

62. (A) No. Murder in most jurisdictions requires one of the four following mental states: (1) intent to kill; (2) intent to commit grievous bodily injury; (3) reckless or wanton indifference to the value of human life; or (4) intent to commit any of certain dangerous non-homicide felonies (i.e., felony-murder). Here, none of these mental states is present. In particular, (2) is not satisfied, because although Kingsman used a weapon that could be a deadly weapon, he did not use it with intent to commit grievous (i.e., serious) bodily injury — a small bruise, a little pain, and fear, do not add up to serious bodily injury, and that's all that Kingsman intended. So the fact that much worse resulted is irrelevant as far as murder goes — there's no general "you take your victim as you find him" rule in murder, as there is in tort law. (This is, instead, a classic case of manslaughter, perhaps misdemeanor-manslaughter.)

(B) Yes. On these facts, Kingsman has clearly intended to inflict grievous bodily injury. Even if the strictest definition of grievous bodily injury is used (intent to inflict life-threatening injuries), the injuries intended here qualify, since fractured skulls are often fatal. Therefore, Kingsman can be convicted of murder despite the absence of an intent to kill. Alternatively, the brutality and dangerousness of the attack probably qualify for reckless-indifference-to-value-of-life murder.

63. **No.** Under the common-law "year and a day" rule (still in force in many states), a death that occurs more than a year and a day following the defendant's act won't be murder, because the time delay creates a doubt about whether the defendant's act was the proximate cause of the death.

64. **Banquo is guilty of "reckless indifference" murder, but Macbeth is not guilty of any sort of murder.** One of the mental states that will suffice for murder is a *"reckless indifference to the value of human life,"* sometimes called a "depraved heart." Banquo's act of firing into a building that he knew was usually occupied would almost certainly qualify as reckless indifference to the value of human life, even though he thought the particular room was empty — because bullets go through walls, the conduct manifests indifference to the very high risk of death or serious injury. On the other hand, Macbeth had no reason to think his conduct was particularly likely to kill or badly injure someone, so his mental state doesn't meet the "reckless indifference" (or any other) mental state that suffices for murder.

65. **Yes, probably, on a theory of felony-murder coupled with accomplice liability.** First, *Speedy* is guilty of felony murder, because the killing took place during the course of a dangerous felony (robbery). Then, under the rules of accomplice liability Delgato is also guilty of robbery, because by serving as lookout and furnishing a weapon, he encouraged or assisted Speedy's commission of the robbery. The interesting question, of course, is whether Delgato is also guilty of the killing of the watchman. The killing of the watchman was an additional crime beyond the target crime (robbery) that Delgato intended to assist. The rule is that the accomplice will be guilty of additional crimes by the principal if and only if the additional crimes were a "natural and probable result" of the target felony, and were committed in furtherance of that target felony. A court would probably conclude that where an accomplice facilitates what he knows is an armed robbery by the principal, the principal's use of the gun to escape apprehension during the robbery is a natural and probable result of (and is committed in furtherance of) the robbery. In that event, Delgato would be guilty of murder.

66. **Sabina's and Claudius', but not Maecenas'.** When a person commits any of a group of particular dangerous felonies, he will be guilty under the felony-murder rule for any deaths, even accidental ones, that are the natural and probable consequences of the defendant's actions. Arson is universally considered part of this group of dangerous felonies. Therefore, Nero's guilty of any deaths that are the natural and probable consequences of his act of arson. Sabina's death clearly falls in this category: when one sets fire to a dwelling, the risk that the dwelling is unexpectedly occupied is great enough that this occupancy will not be deemed to be a superseding event. Claudius' death also falls into this category: when one commits arson, it is quite predictable that firefighters will respond, and relatively "natural and probable" that a firefighter may die fighting the blaze. On the other hand, death of a firefighter by getting hit by a branch while returning from the fire fight is not very natural and probable: this is not one of the kinds of events that makes fighting fires especially hazardous. So Maecenas' death probably won't be deemed to be a natural-and-probable consequence of the arson, and Nero won't be guilty of his murder.

67. **(A) No, because the requisite causal link is missing.** Even in a felony-murder case, the prosecution must show that the commission of the underlying dangerous felony in some sense was the proximate cause of the death — it's not enough for the death to occur at the same time and place as the dangerous felony is occurring. Here, Kitty's death had nothing to do with the felony

    (B) Yes. Since the heart attack was caused by fear over the felony (the robbery), it's highly likely that a court would say that the felony "caused" the death. That is, although the heart attack was due in some measure to Kitty's unusual fearfulness, the chain of events was not so bizarre or unforeseeable that Kitty's nervous disposition will be viewed as a superseding cause. This case falls within the general rule in felony-murder cases that crime victims' reactions to the crime, unless they are truly bizarre, will be non-superseding.

68. **No, because aggravated battery is not sufficiently "independent" from homicide to be covered by the felony-murder rule.** If crimes consisting solely of intent-to-physically-injure could be the predicate to felony-murder, any battery or assault that unexpectedly ended in death would be "bootstrapped" to murder. For this reason, courts universally say that battery and assault cannot be predicate crimes for felony-murder (at least if the battery and/or assault is directed solely at the person who in fact dies.) So here, Derevenko has committed only battery (he didn't intend to kill or even seriously injure Alexis), and this crime can't be the predicate crime for felony murder.

69. **Voluntary manslaughter.** What would otherwise be murder will be reduced to voluntary manslaughter if: (1) the defendant acts in response to a provocation that would be sufficient to cause a reasonable person to lose self-control; and (2) the defendant in fact acts with such a loss of control ("heat of passion"). Here, these requirements are satisfied. The fact that Rhett made a mistake of identity will not strip him of the defense, as long as his mistake was in some sense reasonable (and perhaps even if the mistake was careless but genuine, as long as it was not reckless). Some older cases say that "words alone" cannot constitute sufficient provocation, but modern courts recognize that words may be enough if they carry factual information (rather than, say, insults); so Aunt Pittypat's words would probably be held to be enough to cause the kind of lost self-control that voluntary manslaughter is designed to deal with.

70. **He'll be liable for murder, not voluntary manslaughter.** That's because one of the requirements for voluntary manslaughter is that the defendant must have in fact been still under the heat of passion at the time of killing. If it's the case either that a reasonable person would have "cooled off" by the time of the killing, or that the defendant himself had actually cooled off (even if a reasonable person wouldn't have), then the defendant can't qualify for v.m. Here, since the facts indicate that James behaved in a quite rational, cool-headed manner, he can't be said to have acted in the heat of passion.

71. **(A) Involuntary manslaughter.** One form of manslaughter is "involuntary manslaughter," which is defined in most states as being the *reckless or the grossly negligent causing of another's death*. It is not necessary for involuntary manslaughter that the defendant have desired to kill, or even that he desired to injure, the victim. It is enough that he behaved in a way that recklessly or grossly negligently disregarded the risk of serious bodily injury or death. Since Deerslay knew that there were houses nearby, in the direction at which he was aiming, it would be quite plausible for a jury to find him guilty of involuntary manslaughter.

    (B) No, probably. If the jurisdiction requires "gross negligence" or "recklessness" for involuntary manslaughter, as most jurisdictions do, Deerslay's conduct here probably did not rise to that level. Most courts hold that gross negligence or recklessness is only established where the defendant was *actually aware* of the danger, regardless of whether he *should* have been aware of it. Similarly, the Model Penal Code would acquit Deerslay of manslaughter here. The M.P.C. requires "recklessness" for manslaughter, and under §2.02(2)(c), a person acts recklessly only when he "consciously disregards" a substantial and unjustifiable risk.

72. **Involuntary manslaughter, under the misdemeanor-manslaughter rule.** That rule permits a conviction for involuntary manslaughter when a death occurs accidentally during (and is proximately caused by) the commission of a misdemeanor or other unlawful act. The rule is not in force in all jurisdictions (and isn't recognized by the M.P.C.), but it's part of the law of most states. For Tom to punch Jerry was a battery, which is a misdemeanor. (Jerry's insult does not furnish Tom with a defense — words of insult are never sufficient provocation to entitle the listener to commit a harmful or offensive touching.) Once that happened, any death that was proximately caused by that battery falls within the misdemeanor-manslaughter rule. The fact that Jerry was a hemophiliac won't furnish Tom with a defense — this event (like *any* unusual frailty of the victim) won't be considered so extraordinary that it should be viewed as superseding.

73. **No.** The only way L.G. could possibly be convicted of manslaughter is if the doctrine of misdemeanor manslaughter applied. We will assume that it does. However, for the doctrine to apply, the commission of the misdemeanor must be the proximate cause of the death. This means at the very least that the death must be attributable to the type of risk that caused the state to make the offense an offense in the first place. It is very unlikely that a court would hold that the state has made driving with an expired (as opposed to, say, a suspended) license a misdemeanor because such driving is especially risky — license renewals are generally required for fiscal and general recordkeeping purposes, not accident-prevention ones. Therefore, the lack of a license wouldn't be considered the proximate cause of the accident.

VII. ASSAULT, BATTERY AND MAYHEM

A. **Battery:** The crime of *battery* exists, in brief, when the defendant causes either: (1) *bodily injury*; or (2) *offensive touching*. Generally the crime is committed intentionally, but in most states it may also be committed recklessly or with criminal negligence.

1. **Injury or offensive touching:** Any kind of physical injury, even a bruise from a blow, will meet the physical harm requirement. Additionally, in most states an *offensive touching* will suffice. An unconsented-to kiss or fondling, for example, may constitute a battery. See L, pp. 737-38.

2. **Mental state:** The *mens rea* for battery will usually be *intent* to do the injury or offensive touching. However, in most states an injury or offensive touching committed *recklessly*, or with criminal negligence, will also suffice. (As is the case with manslaughter, more than "simple" negligence is required; see *supra*, p. 257).

3. **Unlawful act:** Occasionally, the *mens rea* for battery will be found where the injury or touching resulted from an *unlawful act* by the defendant. For instance, if the defendant possessed an unregistered firearm, and it went off and injured another person, the defendant might be liable for battery even without a showing that he was negligent.

4. **Degrees of battery:** Simple battery is generally a misdemeanor. However, most states have one or more additional, aggravated, forms of battery. These are usually felonies.

a. **Serious injury:**   Some statutes refer to the seriousness of the harm caused. Thus under Model Penal Code § 211.1(2)(a), it is an "aggravated assault" (the term "assault" being used loosely) purposely to cause "serious bodily injury" to another.

b. **Use of weapon:**   Similarly, battery may reach an aggravated degree if a ***deadly weapon*** is used, even if serious bodily harm does not result. Thus Model Penal Code § 211.1(2)(b) makes it a felony to cause "bodily injury to another with a deadly weapon." For instance, if D shoots at V with a pistol, he will be liable for some kind of aggravated battery even if V has only a superficial skin wound.

c. **Intent to kill:**   Similarly, a battery committed "with intent to kill," "with intent to rape," or other felonious intent will often be aggravated battery. See L, pp. 741-42.

5. **Defenses:**   Most of the general defenses discussed previously may be used in battery cases. For instance, it may sometimes be a defense that the victim ***consented***, as where two men engage in a friendly scuffle.

B. **Assault:**   The crime of ***assault*** exists where either: (1) one ***attempts to commit a battery***, and fails; or (2) one places another in ***fear of imminent injury***.

1. **Attempted battery assault:**   One who ***unsuccessfully attempts*** to commit a battery is guilty of assault.

   a. **Must be intentional:**   Since the offense is attempt-like, it must be committed ***intentionally***. One who recklessly or negligently nearly causes bodily damage to another (e.g., a drunken motorist who narrowly misses a pedestrian) has not committed assault. L, p. 745.

   b. **Present ability:**   Some states impose the additional requirement that the defendant have the ***present ability*** to cause injury. In such a state, if D pointed his gun at V and pulled the trigger, but the gun turned out to be unloaded, D would not be guilty of assault (at least of the attempted-battery type). L, p. 745.

   c. **Would-be victim need not be aware:**   For assault of the attempted-battery type, it is not necessary that the potential victim be ***aware*** of the danger before it occurs. See, e.g., *U.S. v. Bell*, 505 F.2d 539 (7th Cir. 1974), upholding the conviction for assault with intent to rape of D, where D attempted to rape a female geriatric patient who because of a mental disease could not comprehend what was occurring.

2. **Intentional-frightening assault:**   Some states have recognized an additional form of assault, that in which the defendant intentionally ***frightens his victim*** into fearing ***immediate bodily harm***.

   a. **Intent:**   This form of assault similarly can only be committed ***intentionally***. That is, the defendant must intend to cause fear of injury.

   b. **Conduct:**   ***Words alone*** will almost never suffice for this kind of assault. Thus even if D states to V "I'm going to blow your head off," it will not be an assault unless the words are accompanied by some overt gesture (e.g., the pointing of a gun).

3. **Conditional assault:**   Either attempted-battery assault or intent-to-frighten assault may be committed where the danger or threat is ***conditional*** upon meeting the assailant's demands. For instance, if D tells V, a bystander at a bank robbery, "One false step and I'll

fill you full of lead," this is both attempted-battery assault and intent-to-frighten assault, even though V can avoid all danger by failing to exercise his lawful right to move.

    4. Aggravated assault: Simple assault, like simple battery is a misdemeanor. However, most states have recognized various kinds of felonious *aggravated assault*. The most common form relates to the additional felonious intent of the assailant. Thus it is frequently a felony to commit an assault "with intent to kill" or "with intent to rape." Similarly, one who frightens another by use of a deadly weapon is probably liable for "assault with a deadly weapon."

C. Mayhem: The common law did not recognize aggravated forms of assault and battery. In order to punish as a felony violent attacks that did not culminate in death, the crime of *mayhem* evolved. The crime is committed whenever the defendant intentionally *maims* or permanently *disables* his victim. That is, mayhem is a battery causing *great bodily harm.*

    1. Injury must be permanent: The injury must not only be serious, but *permanent*. For this reason, it is usually not mayhem to break the victim's jaw, or even cut his throat with a knife (providing that no serious permanent damage is done). L, p. 750.

    2. Nature of intent: In most states, mayhem is a crime requiring intent; thus one who negligently or recklessly endangers another, with resulting serious injury, is not guilty of the crime. However, it is not clear precisely what intent is required. Certainly an intent to cause a serious and permanent injury (whether or not that precise injury occurs) will suffice.

        a. Intent to harm but not seriously: Some but not all statutes would permit a mayhem conviction where the defendant intends to harm the victim, but does not intend that the injury be *serious*. Thus if D intends merely to strike a few blows to V's face, but because D is wearing a ring V's eye is taken out, D will in some jurisdictions be liable for mayhem.

    3. Model Penal Code abolishes category: The Model Penal Code, unlike virtually all states, does not recognize a separate crime of mayhem. Such conduct is handled as aggravated assault, under M.P.C. § 211.1(2)(a).

VIII. RAPE

A. Definition of rape: Rape is generally defined as *unlawful sexual intercourse with a female without her consent.*

    1. Intercourse: It is not necessary that the defendant achieve an emission. All that is required is that there be a sexual *penetration*, however slight. However, it is usually required that the penetration be of the vagina rather than the anus (although in the latter case the offense of "deviate sexual intercourse" may exist; see *infra*, p. 271).

        a. Model Penal Code recognizes anal penetration: But the Model Penal Code recognizes anal penetration as sufficing for rape. See M.P.C. § 213.1(1) (last paragraph).

2. **The spousal exemption:** Common-law rape requires that the victim be one *other than the defendant's wife*. The common-law's complete spousal exemption has, however, been weakened by statutory reform.

    a. **Forcible rape even while living together:** A substantial minority of states (about 17) now permit prosecution for *forcible rape* even if husband and wife are living together. In other words, in these states, the spousal exemption is virtually eliminated. K&S, p. 398.

    b. **Separated or living apart:** An additional substantial minority (about 22 states) eliminate the spousal exemption based on the parties' current living arrangements or marital status. Some of these eliminate the exemption where the parties are *not living together*. Others eliminate it only if the parties are separated by court order or one has filed for divorce or separation. See generally 99 Harv. L. Rev. 1255, 1258-60.

3. **Without consent:** The intercourse must occur without the woman's *consent*. The precise meaning of this requirement varies from state to state. Except in a few special circumstances discussed below (e.g., unconsciousness or under-age), the requisite lack of consent will be found only if the woman used words or acts that would make it clear to a reasonable person in the man's position that the woman was not consenting. In other words, a woman who remains silent but subjectively fails to consent will normally not be found to have met the "lack of consent" requirement.

    a. **Victim drunk or drugged:** Some courts find the requisite lack of consent where the victim is *drunk, drugged* or *unconscious*, regardless of whether this state was induced by the defendant. Other jurisdictions, however, find liability only where the defendant caused the insensibility; see, e.g., M.P.C. § 213.1(1)(b).

    b. **Fraud:** If consent is obtained by *fraud*, it will usually nonetheless be regarded as valid for rape purposes. For instance, if D is a doctor who induces V to have intercourse with him by telling her that sex forms part of a treatment, he is not guilty of rape in most jurisdictions. The fraud is said to be merely "in the inducement." P&B, p. 215. Similarly, if D takes V through a sham marriage ceremony, so that she thinks that they are man and wife, this will usually not be held to be rape. B&P, p. 724-37.

        i. **Fraud in the essence:** But if the fraud is such that the victim does not even realize that she is having intercourse at all, this is "fraud in the essence," and may suffice for rape. For instance, if D is a doctor who has sex with V (a not-very-intelligent woman) by telling her that he is treating her with a surgical instrument, D is guilty of rape. B&P, p. 724-37.

    c. **Mistake as to consent:** If the defendant makes a *reasonable mistake* as to whether the victim has consented, he does not have the *mens rea* for rape.

        i. **Reckless or negligent mistake:** If, however, the mistake is a negligent or reckless one, many courts will hold that it furnishes no defense to a rape charge. But see *D.P.P. v. Morgan, supra*, p. 28, following the minority view that an unreasonable, but honest, belief that there has been consent will bar a rape conviction.

4. **Force:** The vast majority of rape statutes apply only where the intercourse is committed by *"force"* or "forcible compulsion." K&S, p. 381. In other words, it is not enough that the

woman fails to consent; she must also be "forced" to have the intercourse. (Where the intercourse is with a minor, or while the woman is mentally incompetent or unconscious, force is not an element of the crime; but for garden-variety rape, force is required.)

a. **Definition of force:** Nevertheless, at least one court has found that the statutory requirement of physical force can be satisfied by the ***act of penetration itself***, provided the court finds that the penetration was involuntary or unwanted. In *New Jersey in the Interest of M.T.S.*, 609 A.2d 1266 (N.J. 1992), the court held that in cases of "acquaintance rape" where there is no evidence of force beyond the penetration itself, the "role of the factfinder is to decide … whether the defendant's belief that the alleged victim had freely given affirmative permission was reasonable."

b. **Threat of force:** The defendant's ***threat*** to commit ***imminent serious bodily harm*** on the woman will be a substitute for the use of actual physical force, in virtually all states. Some states also recognize a threat to do other kinds of acts not involving serious bodily harm; for instance, Model Penal Code § 213.1(a) provides that a threat of "extreme pain or kidnapping" may suffice, and that the threatened harm need not be directed to the victim.

   i. **Implied threats or threats of non-imminent harm:** On the other hand, ***implied threats***, or threats to commit harm on some ***future occasion***, or ***duress*** stemming from the victim's circumstances — none of these will typically suffice, because they are not threats to use force on the particular occasion.

   Example: D has beaten V throughout their six-month relationship. While D and V are taking a walk, V tries to break the relationship off. D tells V he is going to "fix" her face to show her he is "not playing," and then says that at least he has the "right" to have intercourse with V one last time. V goes inside with D to a motel room, and V submits to sex. *Held*, even though V didn't truly consent, there was no rape because there was no force — D's threats to V, even though shortly before the act, were "unrelated to the act of sexual intercourse" and thus didn't count. *State v. Alston*, 312 S.E.2d 470 (N.C. 1984).

c. **Resistance:** Traditionally, rape did not exist unless the woman ***physically resisted***, and in some states she was required to resist "to the utmost." In some states, resistance was specifically required by the statute; in others (probably a majority) resistance was required by the courts as a means of ensuring that force really was used. In any event, the requirement of resistance is gradually being weakened.

   i. **Reasonable resistance:** No state requires resistance "to the utmost" anymore. Typically, the woman must now make merely ***"reasonable"*** resistance, as measured by the circumstances. For instance, in the face of a gun or knife wielded by a stranger, it will presumably be "reasonable" not to resist at all.

   ii. **Requirement eliminated:** Some states (e.g., New York) have eliminated the resistance requirement entirely, and merely rely upon the statutory requirement of "force" or "forcible compulsion."

   iii. **"Unreasonable" failure to resist:** Most states continue to insist that the woman's fear and her consequent failure to physically resist have been "reasonable" under the circumstances — if the woman becomes *"unreasonably" scared*, and submits without resistance, this is not rape in most states, *even if the defendant knew of and capitalized on the fear.*

   d. Requirement of force eliminated: A few states have *eliminated* the requirement of force entirely, and make non-consensual intercourse some sort of crime (though typically not the highest degree of rape) even in the absence of force or threat. See, e.g., Wisconsin Criminal Code § 940.225(3), making it the least-serious form of sexual assault to have "sexual intercourse with a person without the consent of that person" (with "consent" defined to refer to "words or actions by a person who is competent to give informed consent indicating a freely given agreement to have sexual intercourse…."). Delaware and Washington have similar statutes. See K&S, pp. 390-91.

5. **Corroboration:**   Some (but not most) states refuse to allow a rape conviction on the *uncorroborated testimony* of the victim. Of those states imposing some sort of corroboration requirement, some require only corroboration of any part of the victim's testimony, while others require corroboration of such aspects as force, penetration and identity. See, e.g., *U.S. v. Wiley*, 492 F.2d 547 (D.C. Cir. 1973), a case involving a 12-year-old victim, holding that there must be corroboration of the fact of intercourse, not merely of the perpetrator's identity and his association with the victim. Often, medical evidence (i.e., an examination of the woman) is the only way of corroborating the fact of intercourse.

6. **Homosexual rape:**   Because common-law rape is defined so as to require both penetration and a female victim, it was generally held that there could be no *homosexual rape* at common law. However, a substantial majority of states have now amended their rape statutes to be *gender-neutral*. In these states, one man's forcible intercourse with another is rape.

   a. Gender-neutral by judicial decree: At least one state has received a gender-neutral definition of rape by *case law* rather than legislation. See *People v. Liberta*, 474 N.E.2d 567 (N.Y. 1984), holding that it is a violation of equal protection for the state's rape statute to allow only males to be convicted of forcible rape, and therefore removing from the statute the exemption for female defendants.

B. Statutory rape: All jurisdictions establish an *age of consent*, below which the law regards a female's consent as impossible. One who has intercourse with a female below this age is punished for what is usually called *"statutory rape."* Most jurisdictions hold that even a *reasonable belief* by the defendant that the girl was over the age of consent is not a defense, making this in essence a strict liability crime. This can sometimes lead to harsh results, as exemplified by the example that follows.

   Example: D is a 20 year-old retarded man. His I.Q. is only 52, and he has the social skills of an 11 or 12 year-old. He is introduced to Erica, a 13 year-old girl, by a friend. One night D goes to Erica's house with the intention of using the phone. She summons him into her bedroom. They talk and then have sex. Erica becomes pregnant and has D's child. D is tried for statutory rape. Under Maryland's statute, the crime consists of having vaginal intercourse with someone who is under 14 years of age if the person performing the act is at least four years older than the victim. At trial, D proffers evidence to show that Erica and her friends had previously told Raymond she was 16 years old, and that he had acted with that belief.

Held, under Maryland's statute, the crime of statutory rape is a strict liability offense. The state need not prove any *mens rea*, and the defense cannot offer evidence regarding a mistake of age. *Garnett v. State*, 632 A.2d 797 (Md. 1993).

1. **Model Penal Code allows reasonable mistake defense:** But the Model Penal Code allows the "reasonable mistake as to age" defense, at least where the offense is garden-variety statutory rape (i.e., intercourse with a girl under the age of 16). See M.P.C. §§ 213.3(1)(a) and 213.6(1).

IX. KIDNAPPING

A. **Definition of kidnapping:** Kidnapping is generally defined as the unlawful *confinement* of another, accompanied by either a *moving* of the victim ("asportation") or a secreting of him.

   1. **Asportation:** Assuming that the crime does not involve secret imprisonment, it is necessary that the victim be *moved* ("asportation").

      a. **Large distance not required:** The asportation need not be over a large distance. For instance, if D accosts V on the street, and makes her walk a few feet to his car, where he detains her, the requisite transporting will probably be found.

      b. **Must not be incidental to other offense:** However, the transporting must not be merely *incidental to some other offense*. For instance, if D, in order to rob V, forces him to stand up and put his hands against the wall so that his pockets may be emptied, the asportation requirement is not met; there is no independent purpose to the confinement and movement, since robbery is the only real objective. (But if V were then bound and gagged and left in a strange place to facilitate D's escape, this would probably be kidnapping.)

Quiz Yourself on
NON-HOMICIDE CRIMES AGAINST THE PERSON

74. Mother Goose sends one of her children to Br'er Rabbit with a gift of a bottle marked "medicine." Rabbit drinks the contents, and becomes violently ill. The bottle actually contains a mild poison deliberately mislabeled by Mother. (Mother wanted to make Rabbit slightly sick.) What is the most serious crime that Mother is guilty of?

75. Stolitz Naya is driving a streetcar. He is travelling far faster than his bosses have instructed him to travel, and is under the influence of narcotics. Also, he's not watching whether anyone's on the tracks. Anna Karenina, a pedestrian, is reading a magazine as she crosses the street at a crosswalk. Anna doesn't see the streetcar coming, and it hits her, seriously injuring her.

    (A) Has Stolitz committed a criminal assault?

    (B) Has Stolitz committed a criminal battery?

76. Ferdinand, who is very angry at his wife Isabella for funding an extravagant voyage by Columbus, threat-

ens her by pointing a rifle at her and threatening to "blow her in half." Isabella believes that Ferdinand will probably, but not certainly, pull the trigger. Isabella does not know it but the rifle is not loaded. Ferdinand does nothing further. What is the most serious crime of which Ferdinand is guilty?

77. Don Juan wants to have sex with Camille. Camille refuses because they are not married.

(A) For this part only, assume that Don Juan gets a friend of his to pose as a minister and fake a wedding ceremony. Thinking she's now an "honest woman," Camille consents to sex with Don Juan. Is Don Juan guilty of rape?

(B) For this party only, assume instead that Camille refuses to have sex unless she is at least engaged. Don Juan promises to marry Camille next year, and she consents to have sex with him. In fact, he has no intention of marrying her – next year or ever. Is Don Juan guilty of rape under these facts?

78. Clark Kent meets Lois Lane at a singles bar. By the time they meet, it is obvious to Clark that Lois has had quite a few drinks and is seriously drunk. Clark does not buy Lois any additional drinks. Instead, he asks her if she wants to come to his apartment, and she nods, somewhat dreamily. When they get to his apartment, Clark undresses her and begins to make love to her. Lois giggles and makes slurred remarks, which Clark reasonably believes indicate that she is conscious and that she is not objecting. The next day, Lois, now sober, relives the whole episode, and makes a complaint to the prosecutor that she has been raped. Assume that Lois demonstrates to the satisfaction of the court that she would not have consented to sex had she not been drunk, and that Clark knew or should have known that the appearance of consent was due to Lois' drunkenness. May Clark properly be convicted of rape, in a jurisdiction following the Model Penal Code approach?

Answers

74. Criminal battery. The crime of battery exists when the defendant causes a harmful or offensive touching of another. The defendant's mental state may be intentional (intent to make the contact), reckless, or criminally negligent. The touching may be direct or, as here, indirect (contact between the harmful "medicine" and Rabbit's body). Thus the fact that Mother did not touch Br'er with her own body is irrelevant. And since Mother intended to bring about the harmful contact, she meets the mental-state requirement.

75. (A) No. An assault occurs only when the defendant either: (1) intends to bring about a harmful or offensive contact with another, and fails; or (2) intends to create in another a fear of an imminent harmful or offensive contact. Here, (1) is not satisfied because it's clear that Stolitz didn't intend to bring about a contact with Anna (he was just reckless in not noticing the risk). And (2) is not satisfied because Stolitz didn't intend to frighten Anna.

(B) Yes. Where a person brings about a harmful or offensive contact with another, he'll be guilty of battery if he acted intentionally or, in almost every state, recklessly. Stolitz' actions — the speeding combined with inattention and driving under the influence — certainly amount to recklessness. Therefore, he meets the mental state for battery. The fact that the contact was in a sense indirect (i.e., the fact that it was the streetcar, rather Stolitz' own body, that made harmful contact with Anna's body) is irrelevant.

76. Assault. One of the ways in which a person can commit the crime of assault is by intentionally putting another in fear of an imminent harmful or offensive contact. That's what happened here: the trier of fact could infer that Ferdinand desired to put Isabella in fear that he would soon pull the trigger and shoot her. The fact that the rifle was unloaded is irrelevant to the sufficiency of Ferdinand's mental state: as long as Isabella didn't *know* that it was unloaded (and as long as Ferdinand was relying on this lack of knowledge), Ferdinand had the requisite mental state, an intent to cause fear of contact. Also, the defendant's present *ability* to actually cause the threatened contact is not one of the elements of assault, so here too the lack of a bullet irrelevant.

77. **(A) No.** Rape is generally defined as unlawful intercourse with one other than one's wife, without consent. Intercourse based on a man's fraudulently persuading his victim that they are married is generally not deemed to be without consent. Fraud can only negate consent in a rape situation if the fraud prevents the victim from knowing the true nature of the act involved ("fraud in the essence") — the existence of a marriage is viewed as instead involving merely "fraud in the inducement."

(B) No. Fraud in falsely promising to marry someone in the future will not negate consent. As with Part A above, fraud can only negate consent in a rape situation if the fraud prevents the victim from knowing the true nature of the act involved.

78. **No.** The question here, of course, is whether there was consent. Clark clearly has not used force or threats. Under the Model Penal Code, Clark would be liable for rape if he had surreptitiously drugged Lois or administered liquor to her without her knowledge. Similarly, if Lois had been completely unconscious, Clark would be liable for rape, since M.P.C. §213.1(1)(c) makes it rape to have sexual intercourse where the female is "unconscious." But nothing in the Model Penal Code makes it rape to have sex with a woman who has become drunk on her own volition, but who remains conscious — the fact that the woman's drunkenness induces her to behave in a way that she might not if she were sober is treated by the M.P.C. as irrelevant. (But some courts would convict Clark here, on the theory that there can be no valid consent where the woman is drunk, even where this state was not induced by the defendant.)

Exam Tips on
HOMICIDE & OTHER CRIMES AGAINST PERSON

Homicides Generally

Homicides occur regularly on exams. So it's well worth your time mastering the details covered in this chapter.

Intent in Homicide Cases

☛ **Intent, generally:** The issue of whether the defendant had the *requisite intent* for a particular form of homicide is commonly tested. Look for a defendant who is *unconscious* or *intoxicated*.

☞ **Intoxication:** In intoxication scenarios, analyze the situation carefully to determine whether D was sufficiently drunk to *prevent him from forming the requisite intent.* For instance, in a murder case drunkenness might have prevented D from forming an intent to kill or an intent to seriously injure (the two most common mental states for murder).

☞ **Motive vs. intent:** Also, don't confuse *motive* with intent. A defendant needs some sort of qualifying intent, but need not be shown to have any "motive," i.e., any "reason" to kill. So for instance D need not show ill will towards a victim.

☛ **Intent in murder cases:** Remember that there are several different mental states that can suffice for murder. Here's an overview:

☞ **Intent-to-kill murder:** First, of course, there's intent-to-kill murder. Here are some of the twists on this version:

☞ **Acting with the desire to kill:** If D *desires* to kill, that's enough, even though it was *very improbable* that D's conduct actually would result in the death.

Example: D knows that his neighbor, N, has a weak heart and has suffered several heart attacks. D is angry at N and wants to kills him. He decides to scare him into having another heart attack. When N leaves his house, D runs to him shouting, "Look out! Look out! The sky is falling." Although D thinks this probably will not kill N, he hopes it will. When N sees D running towards him shouting he gets frightened and dies of a heart attack. D has an appropriate mental state for murder (desire to kill), and he's in fact guilty of murder, notwithstanding the unlikelihood of his plan's working.

☞ **Substantial certainty of death:** Where D knows that death is *substantially certain* to occur, then the requisite intent will be found, even if D *does not actively desire* the death.

Example: D puts a bomb in a plane owned by X Airlines. He desires that the bomb go off, but only so the plane will explode in the air and hurt X's reputation. However, D knows that people will almost certainly be on board, and will be killed. If the plane explodes in the sky and the passengers die, D will have the mental state required for intent-to-kill murder, because he knew the deaths were substantially certain to occur if his plan succeeded, and the fact that D didn't actively desire the deaths is irrelevant.

☞ **Intent-to-cause-serious-bodily-harm murder:** Next, remember that an intent to *cause serious bodily harm* will suffice, even if D does *not* desire to kill.

☞ **Serious injury highly likely:** In fact, if D knows that serious bodily injury is substantially certain to occur from his act, then this is tantamount to an intent to cause serious harm, and will suffice.

Example: D wants to get revenge on her coworker, V, by exposing her to a poisonous pesticide gas D uses for her work. D does not desire to kill V, but does desire to make her sick enough that she'll have temporary blindness, and have to be hospitalized for several days. (D sees from the manual for the poison gas that such results are common if humans ingest very much of the gas.) D releases the poison in V's car. V unexpectedly dies of the exposure to the poison. Because D desired to cause what a court would consider to be serious bodily harm, D can be prosecuted for murder.

☞ **Inference of intent:** Furthermore, a jury can infer a desire to cause serious bodily harm from the fact that D uses a weapon in a way that will generally inflict such harm.

Example: D is a good marksman. D shoots a rifle at V's legs, in an attempt to coerce V into paying a debt. Unexpectedly, V dies of shock. Since firing a rifle at someone's legs will often cause serious bodily injury, a jury can infer that D desired to cause serious (not just minor) injury. Therefore, D has the intent required for intent-to-inflict-serious-injury murder.

☞ **Reckless-indifference-to-the-value-of-human-life murder:** Profs. love to test this one, because it makes for nice fact patterns. This form exists where D disregards a *high risk* that his act will cause death (or serious bodily harm) to others. The classic illustration is firing a rifle into a building known to be occupied.

   ☞ **Illustrations:** Generally, you should discuss reckless-indifference in these kinds of situations:

      ❑ D *drives a car at extremely high speeds*;

      ❑ D *fires a shot in a public place* with lots of people around;

      ❑ D *gets drunk* while knowing that he often behaves very violently if drunk;

      ❑ D *wants to scare* (but not kill or injure) someone badly, and uses what he knows is a very dangerous method to do so, which then goes awry. (*Example:* D tries to fire a gun near V's head to scare him, but miscalculates and hits V.)

   ☞ **Consciousness of risk:** Remember that courts *disagree* about whether reckless-indifference murder can exist if D is reckless, but is *unaware* that the risk of death or serious injury is very high. So if the facts indicate that D has behaved in a very reckless and dangerous way without being aware of the danger, discuss whether the lack of unaware of the danger would prevent reckless-disregard from existing. (*Example:* D gets so drunk that he doesn't realize that what he's about to do is extremely dangerous — most courts would probably find reckless-disregard here.)

   ☞ **Distinguish from negligence:** Remember that the unthinking creation of an "unreasonable" (but not extremely high) risk is merely negligent behavior, and does not rise to the level of reckless indifference. Reckless-indifference requires a disregard of a *very high* probability of *death or serious harm*.

Felony-murder

Profs love to test felony-murder, because it can involve so many sub-issues. So any time anyone is committing a felony during the course of which someone dies, you've got to think felony-murder (we'll call it f.m. here).

☛ **Definition:** Look for a fact pattern where *during or as a consequence* of D's perpetration of an *inherently-dangerous felony* (other than the homicide itself), D *causes a death*, even accidentally.

☛ **Situations:** Here are the most common felonies that can give rise to f.m.:

     ❑ *Robbery* (most common of all). (*Example:* D robs V's store while pointing a gun at V. V has a fatal heart attack, or D's gun goes off by accident and kills V. In both scenarios, D has committed f.m.)

❏ ***Burglary***. (*Example:* D is breaking into V's house, thinking it's empty. V surprises D, they struggle, V falls and hits her head, then dies from the wound. Even if D wasn't trying to injure V, just escape, D is guilty of f.m.)

❏ ***Arson.*** (*Example:* D sets fire to X's house. V, a firefighter, dies fighting the blaze. D is guilty of f.m. in V's death.)

☛ **D's guilt of underlying crime:** Make sure that D would probably be found guilty of the underlying felony — if not, the death can't be f.m.

☛ **Death of co-felon:** Often the death will be that of a ***co-felon*** (either killed by a victim or by a police officer, or killed by himself in an accident). Here, note that courts are split about whether f.m. can apply where one of the participants in the felony is killed.

☛ **Causal relationship, and intervening acts:** *Causation* is the most testable issue in this area. If the death is brought about by an ***intervening act*** (and is not the direct consequence of D's own act), D will be guilty only if his participation in the felony was the ***"proximate cause"*** of the death. Generally, this means that you must find that the death was the ***"natural and probable consequence"*** of the felony — if the intervening act was too abnormal or bizarre, D will get off the hook.

☞ *Examples of foreseeable consequences & thus causal connection:*

❏ The normal reactions of ***victims, bystanders, and police*** make violence a foreseeable result of any ***robbery***. Therefore, if a death results from these reactions, it's at least arguable that the death was a natural and probable consequence of the robbery. (*Example:* D robs S's store at gun point. If S tries to stop the robbery by shooting at D, and hits-and-kills a bystander V accidentally, that's probably f.m. Ditto if a police officer responding to S's call for help accidentally hits V or S. Not so clear if D's accomplice is accidentally killed — some states say the killing of a co-felon during the felony can't be f.m.)

❏ It is reasonably foreseeable that the occupants of a ***burglarized*** dwelling might return before an intruder has left and confront the burglar. Therefore, a killing that flows naturally from such a confrontation is probably a natural-and-probable result of the burglary, triggering f.m. (*Example:* While D is burglarizing O's house, O pulls a gun and, while trying to stop D, accidentally shoots O's wife V. D's arguably guilty of f.m. for V's death.)

Example of no causal connection: X, Y and Z commit a robbery in a casino. As they are leaving, on the steps of a gambling casino, D approaches them, believing them to be the operators of the casino. D shouts, "Death to gamblers," shoots at them, and kills Y. D was unaware of the robbery. His motive for shooting was to close down the casino because he had lost all his savings there and his life had been ruined. There is no causal relationship between perpetration of the felony and Y's death — the death resulted from a truly independent, intervening event. Therefore, even in a state allowing one felon to be guilty of f.m. for the death of a co-felon, X and Z won't be guilty of f.m.

☛ **"During commission of" the felony:** Make sure the death occurs ***during the perpetration*** *of the felony.*

> *Example:* V, a store owner, returns from vacation to find out that her store was held up the previous day. V becomes so upset that she suffers a cerebral hemorrhage and dies. F.M. doesn't apply to her death, because the death wasn't "during the perpetration" of the felony.

☞ **Immediate flight:** But the "during the perpetration" element is *satisfied* if the death occurs while the defendant is *attempting to escape,* as long as the attempt occurs reasonably close, in time and place, to the felony. (*Example:* D accidentally runs over V while driving the getaway car from the scene of a bank robbery.)

☛ **Lack of desire to hurt is no defense:** Beware a common trap: the fact pattern indicates that D did not want to harm (or at least physically injure) anyone. This doesn't matter — it's still f.m. if the death proximately results from the felony.

> *Example:* D holds up V's store with a toy pistol. V has a heart attack and dies. The fact that D never intended to cause physical injury or any harm other than economic is irrelevant — it's still f.m.

☛ **Accomplice liability:** Be on the lookout for *accomplice liability* in f.m. scenarios. If D2 is guilty of f.m., and D1 is D2's accomplice in the underlying felony, then D1 is guilty of f.m. as well, as long as the killing was the *"natural and probable result"* of the felony.

> *Example:* R tells D that he wants to rob a candy store, and asks D if D wants to join in. D says no, but agrees that he will drive R to the store, and drive the getaway car thereafter. (D does not expect any violence to occur.) D's gun goes off during the robbery, killing V. R is clearly an accomplice to the bank robbery, so he's guilty of the substantive crime of robbery. Then, D (not just R) is guilty of f.m. as well, because he's committed a dangerous felony (robbery, under accomplice rules) which has "caused" a death during its perpetration. The fact that it wasn't D's gun that went off is irrelevant, because a mistaken or accidental shooting is certainly a "natural" result of an armed robbery.

Voluntary manslaughter ("v.m.")

☛ **Provocation:** The most frequently tested issue in this area is whether there was *reasonable provocation* for D's actions. Remember that this is an *objective* test, measured by the characteristics of a person of ordinary temperament.

> *Examples that <u>are</u> probably reasonable provocation (in all cases, V is the dead victim):*

> ❏ V physically attacks, rapes, or murders D's friend or relative.

> ❏ V is D's wife or girlfriend, and has consensual sex with X, which D has just learned of.

> ❏ X is D's wife or girlfriend, and X has consensual sex with V, which D has just learned of.

> *Examples that are probably <u>not</u> reasonable provocation:*

> ❏ V verbally insults D.

❏ V steals some relatively inexpensive items from D.

☞ **Cooling off period:** Also, look for a lapse of time within which a reasonable person would have *cooled off.* If there was such a lapse, then D can't use v.m.

　　☞ **Time frame in fact pattern:** Often the fact pattern will give you a time frame, and help you answer the question, Was there adequate time to cool off?

　　Example 1: Where the facts says that D avenged his wife's rape "the morning after learning about it," there is a question whether enough time went by that a reasonable person would have cooled off.

　　Example 2: Where the facts say that D is too stunned to act "for a moment," the momentary pause would certainly not be sufficient to constitute a cooling-off period, if D had suffered a severe shock.

　　☞ **Retrieval of weapon:** Also, look for a situation where D *goes elsewhere to retrieve a weapon,* then kills the provoker. This is probably your prof's signal that she wants you to at least consider the issue of whether D had time to cool off.

☛ **Imperfect self-defense:** Remember that in some states, liability may be reduced from murder to manslaughter, if the defendant was ***unreasonably mistaken*** in believing that his actions were justified by the need for, say, self-defense. This is the "imperfect self-defense" form of v.m. (*Example:* D unreasonably, but genuinely, believes that V is about to attack him, so he shoots V first.)

Involuntary manslaughter ("i.m.")

☛ **Definition in fact pattern:** If the fact pattern tells you the jurisdiction's definition of i.m., read it carefully to see just how extreme D's negligence must be to trigger i.m.

　　☞ **Gross negligence (or "recklessness") usually required:** If the fact pattern does not contain a statute, remember that typically, D must behave with "gross negligence" or "recklessness." Typically, this means that D must disregard a substantial danger of serious bodily harm or death — garden-variety negligence is not enough.

　　Example: D, the operator of an automobile service station, advises a customer, V, that removing an air pollution device (a state law requires that all cars be equipped with such a device) would increase her car's fuel efficiency. At V's direction, D works carefully to remove the device, but accidentally loosens a connection in the exhaust system. This causes exhaust gases to leak into the car, poisoning and killing V. Probably D would not be convicted of i.m., because there's no indication that he knew (or should have known) that there was a substantial risk of death or serious injury from what he was doing.

☛ **Alternative to reckless-indifference murder:** Generally, if you argue in your answer that the defendant could be prosecuted for reckless-indifference murder, you should argue in the alternative (in case D's behavior does not rise to that level) that his reckless behavior would make him guilty of i.m.

　　Example: V contacts D, his landlord, for the sixth time in two days to report that the heating system in his apartment building is malfunctioning. D does nothing. The furnace explodes and causes a fire, and V is killed while trying to rescue his baby. You should first discuss the possibility that L is guilty of reckless-indifference murder, on the theory that he disregarded a very high risk that the malfunction might cause a fire or explosion. But then, you should say that at the least, D is probably guilty of i.m., since his disregard of the risk was reckless.

Reckless drivers: Drivers who *exceed the speed limit* by a lot, or otherwise drive recklessly (e.g., wrong-way down a 1-way street), should always suggest i.m. to you if a death results. Ditto for people who drive while intoxicated.

☛ **Attempted i.m. not possible:** When D is reckless but V doesn't die, don't be tempted to charge D with *attempted* i.m. Attempt crimes require an intent to bring about a result — i.m., since it's based on recklessness rather than intent, can't be "attempted."

☛ **Misdemeanor-manslaughter rule:** If the defendant is guilty of a *misdemeanor* the commission of which is causally linked to a death, consider the *"misdemeanor manslaughter" rule*: this rule permits a conviction for i.m. if a death occurs accidentally during the commission of a misdemeanor or other unlawful act. (Remember that not all states recognize it; and the MPC doesn't).

☞ **Assault or battery as misdemeanor:** The classic fact patterns for misdemeanor-manslaughter are assaults and batteries.

Example 1 (assault): D tries to frighten V by pointing a gun at him and pretending to fire. D is just playing a joke, but V has a fatal heart attack. Since this was assault, the misdemeanor-manslaughter rule will be triggered if the jurisdiction recognizes it.

Example 2 (battery): V insults D. D hits V with his fist, just intending to injure him slightly (not enough to constitute even "serious bodily harm.") V falls, hits his head on the edge of the sidewalk, and dies of brain trauma from the fall. Since D committed battery, this qualifies for misdemeanor-manslaughter.

☞ **Malum prohibitum:** If the offense is *"malum prohibitum"* — i.e., not dangerous in itself, but just a violation of a regulatory-type rule — in most states this *can't* be used for misdemeanor-manslaughter unless there is a close relationship between the violation and the death (which there usually won't be).

Example: D's license is suspended for non-payment (not for prior accidents). While driving without a license, but otherwise driving properly, he accidentally hits and kills V. This won't be misdemeanor manslaughter, because there was no close causal relationship between D's failure to pay a license fee and his causing V's death.

Battery

☛ **Definition:** Remember that a battery is an intentional, reckless, or criminally negligent application of force that results in either *bodily injury* or an *offensive touching*.

Examples:

[1] D strikes V with a heavy ashtray;

[2] D pushes V

[3] D sticks a pipe against V's back so it feels like a gun

☞ Remember that there must be a physical contact between D (or some instrumental that he controls) and V's body. Some physical effect that V suffers in response to events — but that occurs without any physical contact between D and V — won't suffice.

> *Example:* D shoots X, V's wife, in front of V. V has a stroke when he sees this. D has not committed battery on V, because there was no physical contact between D (or an instrumentality controlled or launched by D) and V's body.

Assault

☛ There are two situations in which you should discuss assault:

☞ **Attempted battery:** Assault can occur where D is unsuccessful in his *attempt to commit a battery.* Remember that: (1) the act must be done with *intent* to commit a harmful or offensive touching (recklessness or negligence aren't enough); and (2) the would-be-victim *need not be aware* of the danger.

> *Example:* The President of the United States is driving in a car with bullet-proof glass. Intending to shoot the President, D shoots three times at the car with a rifle, striking the glass, but not penetrating it. Because of the noise of the crowd, the President is unaware of the shots. A police officer who witnesses the shots being fired arrests D. Because D perpetrated an attempted battery, he is guilty of assault.

☞ **Intentional frightening:** Alternatively, assault occurs if D intentionally *frightens the victim* into fearing immediate bodily harm.

> *Examples:*
>
> ❑ Chasing and shooting at somebody with a hunting rifle;
>
> ❑ Sticking a pipe against somebody's back and saying, "Don't move or I'll shoot."

☞ **Doesn't see attacker:** Analyze the situation carefully where the victim *does not see his attacker* — it's not "intentional-frightening" assault unless there's a moment where V fears an imminent harmful or offensive contact.

> *Example:* D shoots at V, attempting to frighten him. Because of crowd noise, V doesn't learn of the attempt until several seconds later, by which time police have already tackled D. This isn't intentional-frightening assault, because there was no moment when V actually feared an imminent contact.

Rape / Sexual Assault

☛ Rape is not tested too often. When it is, two issues are most likely:

☞ **Statutory rape:** This is a strict liability crime, The defendant needs just to have the intent to have intercourse. *Important:* D's knowledge of V's age is not an element of the crime, so he's guilty even if he (reasonably) thinks V is an adult.

☞ **Intoxication of defendant:** Because rape / sexual assault is a so-called "general intent" crime, D's *voluntary intoxication* is *not* a defense as long as D *intended to have intercourse.* So, for instance, if D's drunkenness prevented him from realizing that V wasn't consenting, D's out of luck. However, if D is so intoxicated that he does not even know that he is engaging in intercourse, then he cannot be guilty of rape (even statutory rape).

Kidnapping

☛ This crime is not heavily tested. Basically look for:

☞ **Intent to confine:** D must intend to confine another.

Example: D steals a car and is unaware that a sleeping child is in the back seat. D does not possess the intent to commit kidnapping, since he has not intended to confine or transport anyone.

☞ **Asportation:** V must either be hidden or moved (*"asportation"*). Many jurisdictions hold that there is no asportation if the movement of the victim was incidental to and a necessary part of the commission of some other substantive crime.

☞ *Example:* During the course of a bank robbery, R points a gun at and orders the bank tellers and manager to go from the bank lobby to the back room while R's partner attempts to open the safe. There has probably been no asportation, in which case there has been no kidnapping.

CHAPTER 9

THEFT CRIMES

Introductory note: The principal focus of this chapter is on the three basic theft crimes: (1) *larceny* (including "larceny by trick"); (2) *embezzlement*; and (3) obtaining property by *false pretenses*. Other property crimes briefly discussed are: (4) receiving stolen property; (5) burglary; (6) robbery; and (7) extortion (blackmail).

I. HISTORICAL OVERVIEW

A. Larceny was judge-made crime: Much of this chapter is devoted to the distinctions between the three major theft crimes, larceny, embezzlement and false pretenses. There could easily have developed one consolidated crime of "theft," but historically things did not work out that way. First, the crime of "larceny" was developed by English judges (rather than Parliament). This crime punished the unconsented-to taking of another's property *from his possession.*

1. **Need to expand "possession":** The requirement that for a taking to be larcenous, the property must be taken without consent from the owner's possession, was a severe limitation. To expand the crime to meet the requirements of trade, judges made several far-fetched manipulations of "possession."

   a. **Employees:** For instance, suppose an employer voluntarily gave his employee or servant goods or money to use on the former's behalf. Under the original, common-sense idea of possession, the employee could not be guilty of larceny if he subsequently appropriated the property for his own purposes — his original possession was consented-to. Therefore, the judges decided that, at least where the employee was a minor one (e.g. a clerk), the employer never voluntarily gave him possession, but merely "custody"; possession remained in the owner until the wrongful appropriation (which was thus larceny).

   b. **Breaking bulk:** Similarly, if a carrier was given bales or other wrapped goods, and he appropriated them to his own use, this would normally not be larceny, since he obtained possession lawfully. But if he "*broke bulk*" by breaking open the bales and taking the contents, the judges instituted the fiction that at the moment of breaking open the bales and taking the contents, the possession flew back to the owner; the taking of the contents thus constituted an unlawful re-taking of possession by the carrier, and it was therefore larceny.

2. **Statutes on embezzlement and false pretenses:** Other stretching of the concept of possession occurred through the years, as will be discussed below. Finally, however, Parliament created an *embezzlement* statute (1799), to deal with employees who received property not directly from the employer, but from a third person for the employer. Similarly, the statutory crime of false pretenses was created (1757) to deal with one who acquires not only possession, but title, without the owner's consent.

    a. No overlap with larceny: Since these statutes were attempts to "plug the holes" in the definition of larceny, they were construed so as to have *no overlap* with larceny. That is, if the defendant's acts fit within the definition of larceny, they could not constitute embezzlement or false pretenses, and vice versa.

    b. Same problem exists today: American jurisdictions adopted the same tripartite scheme, with distinct statutory definitions of larceny, embezzlement and false pretenses. Such a scheme offers the defendant great opportunity to escape conviction on a "technicality."

        i. How to escape conviction: The reason for this is that, even though in some jurisdictions the prosecutor may charge, say, both embezzlement and larceny on the same facts (if he is not sure which category the facts fall into), the *jury may only convict on one*. Suppose that the jury convicts on larceny rather than embezzlement. Then, on appeal, the defendant may argue that the facts presented at the trial constitute embezzlement, rather than larceny; if the appellate court agrees, the conviction is reversed. In some cases the double jeopardy rule may be construed to prevent retrial on embezzlement charges. In any event, the defendant has at least obtained a new trial. See L, p. 849, fn. 2 and 3.

3. Need for understanding distinctions: Some American states have now consolidated the three main theft crimes into one basic crime, "theft." See *infra*, p. 305. However, most states have retained the distinction, and some of the states which have consolidated still require the prosecutor to fit the defendant's conduct into one of the three pigeon-holes. Therefore, the student's principal job in this area is to master: (1) the dividing line between larceny and embezzlement (i.e., was possession originally obtained unlawfully [larceny] or lawfully [embezzlement]?); and (2) the line between larceny and false pretenses (what was obtained unlawfully, mere possession [larceny] or title [false pretenses]?)

II. LARCENY

A. Definition: Common-law larceny is defined so as to include the following six elements:

  1. The *trespassory*

  2. *taking* and

  3. *carrying away* of

  4. *personal property*

  5. of *another*

  6. with *intent to steal*.

    See L, p. 795.

B. Trespassory taking: As noted, larceny is a crime against possession. It requires the wrongful taking of property from another's possession, so that if the defendant is *already in rightful possession* of the property at the time he appropriates it to his own use, he cannot be guilty of larceny.

Example 1: The Ds contract to sell their farm to X. According to X, the deal covers certain items of personal property (e.g. some unattached bathroom accessories) as well as the real estate. X moves in after the closing and discovers that the personal property is missing. The Ds are charged with larceny of these items.

Held, the Ds cannot be convicted of larceny, because at the time of the alleged misappropriation, the Ds were in lawful possession of the items. The terms of the sale were that the Ds could maintain possession until X moved in; since the alleged taking and carrying away occurred before this, there can be no larceny liability. (The Ds might be guilty of fraudulent conversion, or "larceny by bailee," but they were not charged with either of these crimes.) *Commonwealth v. Tluchak*, 70 A.2d 657 (Pa. 1950).

Example 2: D rents a horse from a stable, saying he plans to take a trip and return that same evening. Instead, he sells the horse that same day and cannot be located because he has given a false address to the stable-keeper.

Held, whether D has committed larceny depends on his intent at the time he made the rental arrangements. If at the time of those arrangements he intended to sell the horse, his initial possession was wrongful, and he has committed larceny. But if at the time he made the rental arrangement he really planned to take the trip, and changed his mind later, he has not committed larceny, because he was in rightful possession up until the sale. Here, the issue of what D's intent was at the time he made the arrangements was properly left to the jury, which found that he had a fraudulent intent at that time; therefore, D is guilty of larceny. *King v. Pear*, 168 Eng. Rep. 208 (1779).

1. **Trapped by owner:** One situation in which the requisite trespass may be found lacking is that in which the ***owner learns in advance*** that a thief is planning to take his property, and therefore lies in wait for the theft, perhaps even facilitating it (e.g., by leaving the door unlocked). It is often held that there is ***no trespass*** when the thief takes the goods away, although the rationale for such decisions is not uniform.

   Example: D arranges with Dolan, an employee at the Plankinton Packing Co., for Dolan to put three barrels of the company's meat on the loading platform. The plan is for D to load the barrels on his wagon and drive away like any customer. D informs his boss of the plan, and is instructed to feign cooperation. The barrels are put out on the platform, D drives away with them, and is arrested. He is charged with larceny.

   Held, D's conviction reversed. There can be no larceny without a trespass. Here, the owner of the barrels in effect consented to their being taken. Furthermore, there was a "delivery" of the barrels to D for practical purposes. Therefore, even though D may be as morally culpable as one who took the barrels from the same platform without the owner's knowledge or consent, an essential element of larceny is missing and there can be no conviction. *Topolewski v. State*, 109 N.W. 1037 (Wisc. 1906).

   a. **Criticism:** It is hard to see why the owner's "consent" should bar liability in *Topolewski*. There is no consent, in the sense of a shared objective, as there would be if a woman consented to sexual intercourse (thereby negating the existence of rape). Nor is this a case of entrapment (see *supra*, p. 133), since (1) the police were not involved; and (2) D was clearly the initiator of the plan. Fletcher (pp. 86-88) suggests that the decision's rationale stems from the historical notion that larceny is a "forcible or stealthful act of thieving," and that takings that have the external appearance of routine commercial transactions are not included. (However, as Fletcher notes at p. 88, this would not explain why a clever thief, such as a burglar who dresses up as a moving-man and steals in broad daylight, can be convicted of larceny).

2. **Taking by employee:**   As noted, a *minor employee* is generally held to have only *custody*, so that the employer retains possession. Thus if the employee (e.g. a bank clerk) appropriates the property, he has committed the necessary trespass, and is guilty of larceny at common law.

    a. **High employee:**   If the employee is one who has a *high position* and is given broad authority, he will be deemed to have possession, not just custody, of property that he holds for the employer's benefit. Therefore, if he subsequently appropriates the property for his own purposes, he is not guilty of larceny, since he has not committed a wrongful taking from the owner's possession. He thus falls under the typical embezzlement statute (which applies only where the defendant's original possession is lawful; see *infra*, p. 297).

    b. **Property received from third person:**   The rule that a minor employee has custody only does not apply where the property is received by the employee for the employer's benefit from a *third person*. In this situation, even the minor employee has possession, not custody, and if he later appropriates it, he is not guilty of larceny.

        i.   **Possession transferred to owner:**   But there is an exception to this exception: If the employee receives the property, and transfers it to the employer's possession, he is guilty of larceny if he re-takes it subsequently. Thus in *Nolan v. State*, 131 A.2d 851 (Md. 1957), D worked for a finance company. He collected cash receipts throughout the day, and put them in the office's cash drawer. At the close of business, he would appropriate some of the cash from the drawer. The court held that this was larceny, not embezzlement, since the money went into the cash drawer (thus entering the finance company's possession) and was re-taken later. (A concurrence criticized the formalistic reasoning of the majority, pointing out that the cash drawer was under the defendant's control.)

        ii. **Brief return to employer's possession:**   The case may turn on *how long* the property is returned to the employer's possession before being re-taken. Thus in *Commonwealth v. Ryan*, 30 N.E. 364 (Mass. 1892) the defendant was a cashier who received money from a detective posing as a customer, dropped it in the cash drawer, and *almost immediately thereafter* took it out again. The court (per Judge Holmes) held that this was larceny, not embezzlement, because the defendant intended, at the time he received the money, to appropriate it, and put it into the drawer "for his own convenience."

3. **Transaction in owner's presence:**   If the owner of property delivers it to the defendant as part of a transaction which the owner *intends to be completed in his presence*, the defendant receives only custody, and the owner retains *"constructive possession."* Therefore, if the defendant appropriates the money, the requisite trespass exists, and the crime is larceny.

    Example: D drives into X's gas station. He asks for his tank to be filled up, and drives off without paying.

Held, D is guilty of larceny, not embezzlement or false pretenses. X, when he put the gas in the tank, did not intend to part with title (ownership) of the gas unless he was paid for it. Although he did intend to part with possession, this intent was vitiated by D's fraud, and X retained "constructive possession." Therefore, when D drove off he was taking the property without consent from X's possession. *Hufstetler v. State*, 63 So.2d 730 (Ala. Ct. App. 1953).

Note: The larceny in *Hufstetler* is frequently called *"larceny by trick,"* since actual possession was obtained by deceit. "Larceny by trick," which is discussed further, *infra*, p. 288, is not a distinct crime, but is simply one means by which larceny can be committed (just as it can be committed by a forcible taking not accompanied by deceit).

4. **Bailee who breaks bulk:** As we saw (*supra*, p. 283), a carrier or other **bailee** who **breaks bulk** is guilty of larceny. This rule derives from ***Carrier's case***, Y.B. 13 Edw. IV, f. 9, pl.5 (Eng. 1473), in which a carrier broke open bales consigned to him, and sold the contents. Although the carrier may have had rightful possession of the packaged goods to start with, "constructive possession" returned to the owner when the bales were broken into, and the misappropriation constituted a larcenous taking of possession.

   a. **Extension of doctrine:** The "breaking bulk" doctrine has been extended to cover the situation where the carrier or other bailee (e.g., a warehouseman) is given a quantity of un-packaged goods, and appropriates some (but not all) of them. See L, p. 799. Some American states continue to apply the "breaking bulk" doctrine, so that there is larceny if bulk is broken, and embezzlement if it is not. In other states, a separate offense called "larceny by bailee" exists, covering all taking by bailees regardless of whether bulk is broken; e.g., *Burns v. State, infra*, p. 298, construing such a statute.

5. **Finders of lost or mislaid property:** One who finds *lost or mislaid property* commits the requisite trespass if he *intends to keep it* at the time he finds it. If he lacks such an intent at the time of finding (e.g., he intends to try to return it to the owner), his possession is rightful and there is no trespass. Then, if he later changes his mind and does keep it, he is *not guilty of larceny*, since he is already in lawful possession. (This result may also be viewed as an application of the rule that there must be concurrence of intent to steal with taking of possession; see *infra*, p. 293.) Such a finder may, however, be guilty of embezzlement in some states; see *infra*, p. 298.

   a. **Means of returning to owner necessary:** Furthermore, even one who does not intend to return the property at the time he finds it will not be guilty of larceny unless either: (1) he knows who the owner is (e.g., a wallet with the owner's name and address in it) or (2) he has reason to believe that he *may be able to find out* who and where the owner is (e.g., a pet wearing a partially identifying tag or collar). See L, p. 800. Under the common-law view, if such knowledge or reasonable belief is lacking at the time of finding, the finder will not become guilty of larceny even if, subsequently, he discovers the owner's identity.

   b. **Property delivered by mistake:** The same rules apply where the owner of property *delivers it by mistake* to the defendant. That is, the defendant is not guilty of larceny unless, *at the time he receives the property*, he: (1) realizes the mistake; and (2) intends to keep the property.

Example: D brings a check for $97.92 to the bank, and asks Teller to credit $80.00 to an account, and to give him the rest in cash. Teller, being inexperienced, misreads the date (12 06 59) as the amount payable. She therefore deducts the $80.00 deposit, and gives D $1,126.59. D takes the money and leaves; he is charged with and convicted of larceny.

Held, conviction reversed. The trial judge was wrong to instruct the jury that they could convict if they believed that D's original receipt of the money was innocent (i.e., he failed to realize the error) and that he subsequently realized the error and decided to keep the money. A larceny conviction may be based only upon a finding that D realized the error at the time he received the money, and immediately decided to keep it. *U.S. v. Rogers*, 289 F.2d 433 (4th Cir. 1961).

    c. **Model Penal Code changes rule:** The Model Penal Code substantially changes the trespass rules in cases of lost, mislaid, or misdelivered property. Under M.P.C. § 223.5, the recipient's intent at the time he obtains the property is *irrelevant*. Instead, he becomes liable for theft "if, with purpose to deprive the owner thereof, he fails to take *reasonable measures to restore the property* to a person entitled to have it." Thus D's conviction in *Rogers* would have been affirmed under the Code, since D, whatever his intent at the time he received the property, failed to return it to the bank.

  6. **Larceny by trick:** For a taking of property to be larcenous, the original possession by the defendant must be wrongful. As we saw in *Hufstetler, supra*, p. 286, possession will be wrongful if it is obtained by *fraud or deceit*. The larceny in this situation is said to be "*by trick*"; larceny by trick is simply one way in which larceny may be committed, not a separate crime.

    a. **Distinguished from false pretenses:** One who obtains *title*, as opposed to mere possession, from another is not guilty of common-law larceny. Where possession is obtained by fraud or deceit, it will often be hard to tell whether title has passed as well. If it has, the crime is that of false pretenses, discussed *infra*, p. 299. The means of distinguishing between larceny by trick and false pretenses are treated in the discussion of the latter.

    b. **Need for conversion:** Where the larceny is by trick, one additional requirement exists that is not necessary for other forms of larceny: The property must be *converted* by the defendant (i.e. destroyed, sold, or otherwise deprived of much of its utility to its owner). Contrast the following two situations:

       i. **Burglar:** First, consider a burglar who is caught right outside the scene of the crime carrying away a stereo. He is guilty of larceny (as well as burglary) because he has taken the property and "carried it away" (see *infra*, 289), even though he has not yet had a chance to "convert" it (i.e., deprive its owner of a substantial part of its value).

       ii. **Larceny by trick:** Now consider a person who obtains possession of the same stereo by falsely telling its owner that he will return it tomorrow, when he intends not to return it at all. The possession here is trespassory (since it is obtained "by trick"), but if the recipient is caught the next day, with the stereo unharmed, he will not be guilty of larceny by trick, since there has been no conversion. This is true even though there may have been an ***intent*** to convert (e.g., an intent to resell the unit). If, on the other hand, six months were to pass, without a return of the unit, then the taker would be guilty of larceny by trick, since a substantial portion of the stereo's value to the owner would have been lost. See L, pp. 799-800.

C. Carrying away ("asportation"): The defendant, to commit larceny, must not only commit a trespassory taking (discussed *supra*), but must also ***carry the property away***. The technical term for this requirement is ***"asportation."***

1. Slight distance sufficient: However, as long as every portion of the property is moved, even a ***slight distance*** will suffice. And, in fact, if the defendant merely brings the property under his "dominion and control" without physical movement, in many courts today that's enough.

Example: D enters V's car, turns on the lights and starts the engine. At that point he is arrested. At common law, this would probably not be enough movement to satisfy the asportation requirement. But many courts today would hold that since D brought the car under his dominion and control, he did enough to satisfy the requirement. If D drove the car a few feet, *all* courts would agree that this was enough to meet the asportation requirement.

2. Innocent purchaser transports property: Suppose the defendant falsely pretends to own certain property, and sells it to X, who carries it off. Is this carrying off by an ***innocent third person*** sufficient to meet the asportation requirement? Most courts follow the reasonable view that the innocent purchaser is the defendant's ***agent*** for purposes of the trespassory taking and asportation requirements, and that the defendant is therefore guilty of larceny. See L, p. 804.

D. Personal property of another: Common-law larceny exists only where the property that is taken is ***tangible personal property***.

1. Tangible personal property: Thus one could not commit common-law larceny of ***real estate***. Nor could one steal ***intangible*** personal property, such as stocks, bonds, checks or promissory notes. See L, pp. 805-06.

2. Modern expansion: All states have expanded larceny to cover more than just tangible personal property. ***Intangible items***, such as stocks and bonds, are always covered. Some items that would formerly have been considered real property (e.g. minerals in the ground), are also usually covered. ***Gas and electricity*** are brought within some statutes, as are ***services***. Thus one who makes a telephone call or stays in a hotel room without making payment may be guilty of larceny.

a. Trade secrets: Some courts have held that the taking of ***trade secrets*** can constitute larceny.

b. Model Penal Code "theft of services": The Model Penal Code contains a separate provision, § 223.7, establishing the crime of ***"theft of services."*** The statute explicitly refers to professional services, hotel accommodations, restaurant meals, and admission to exhibitions. A refusal to pay after the rendering of the service (such as in a hotel or restaurant) gives rise to a "presumption that the service was obtained by deception as to intention to pay."

    c. **Theft of the right to "honest government":** Even in jurisdictions recognizing intangible items, including services, as being the kind of property that can be stolen, the services in question may be found by the court to be *too intangible* to be covered by the theft statute. For instance, in *McNally v. U.S.*, 107 S.Ct. 2875 (1987), the two Ds (one of whom was a public official at the time in question) were charged with violating the federal *mail fraud* statute by entering into a self-dealing patronage scheme under which the citizens of Kentucky were defrauded of the "intangible right" to have the state's affairs conducted honestly. (The government charged that D1 sent the state's insurance business to D2's insurance agency, in return for a kickback of some of the commissions.)

        i. **Result:** The Supreme Court held that Congress, when it passed the federal mail fraud statute, intended only to protect "property rights," and that the right asserted here — the intangible right of the citizenry to good government — was not a "property" right, so that the Ds could not be prosecuted. (But Congress responded to *McNally* by amending the statute to cover a scheme "to deprive another of the intangible right of honest services." See 18 U.S.C. § 1346.)

E. Property of another: The property taken must, to constitute larceny, be property *belonging to another*. Where the defendant and another person are *co-owners*, the common-law view is that there can be no larceny. Thus a partner who steals property of the partnership would not be guilty of larceny. However, a few states have changed this rule by statute. See L, p. 809.

    1. **Embezzlement or false pretenses:** Some states which do not allow a co-owner to be guilty of larceny may nonetheless allow a conviction of embezzlement or false pretenses if the other aspects of these crimes are met. See *infra*, p. 296 and p. 303.

    2. **Recapture of chattel:** If the defendant is attempting to *retake* a *specific chattel* that belongs to him, the defendant will not be guilty of larceny, because he is not taking property "of another". In most states, this is also true if the defendant is genuinely *mistaken* (even if unreasonably) in thinking that the thing he is taking belongs to himself rather than the other person. But this rule does not apply where the defendant is taking *cash* or other property in satisfaction of a *debt* — in this situation, the "claim of right" defense may be available (see *infra*, p. 292) but that is conceptually different.

    Example: D's bicycle is stolen. Two days later, he sees, chained to a lamp post, what appears to be the same bike. D genuinely believes that this is his own, stolen, bike. He cuts the chain and removes the bike. If the bike was in fact his own, clearly D is not guilty of larceny, because he has not taken property "of another." If D genuinely believes that the bike was his — even if this belief is unreasonable — most courts will similarly hold that he has not committed larceny. (Of course, the fact that the bike was not in fact the one previously stolen from D may make it hard, as an evidentiary matter, for D to convince the court that he genuinely held the belief that the bike was his own.)

    But now, suppose that D is owed $100 by V, and that D sees V's bicycle parked on the street. If D takes the bike in payment, he probably cannot defend on the grounds that the bike is not "property of another." On the other hand, most states would allow him to raise the "claim of right" defense, discussed *infra*, p. 292. (If D took the bike forcibly from V's person, in an attempt to get satisfaction of the debt, even the "claim of right" defense probably won't work, since that defense usually does not apply in cases of violent crime such as robbery. See *infra*, p. 292.)

F. Intent to steal: Larceny is a crime that can only be committed ***intentionally***, not negligently or recklessly. The Latin phrase often used to describe the intent is "***animus furandi***" (literally "intent to steal").

1. **Intent to permanently deprive owner:**   As a general rule, the defendant must be shown to have an intent to ***permanently deprive*** the owner of his property. An intent to take property temporarily is not sufficient.

   Example: D, a 17-year-old boy, enters the house of X (another boy), and takes his bicycle. He testifies that he took it to get even with X for something X had done, and that he intended to bring it back, but got caught before he could do so.

   Held, D's conviction of burglary (based on intent to commit larceny) reversed. One must have an intent to deprive the owner of his property permanently, not temporarily. *People v. Brown*, 38 P. 518 (Cal. 1894).

   a. **Must have actual ability to return:**   However, an intent to return the property will not negate liability if one's intent is to use it in a way that makes it likely that the owner will not get it back. For instance, if one intends to take a car, drive it hundreds of miles, and ***abandon it***, the requisite intent to steal will be found, even though there is no intent to keep it permanently; the reason is that the intended use makes it likely that the owner will not recover the car. See L, p. 813.

   b. **Substantial deprivation:**   Similarly, if one intends to use the property for such a long time, or in such a way, that the owner is deprived of a ***significant portion of its economic value***, the requisite intent to steal exists. Thus a Comment 6 to Model Penal Code § 223.2 poses the case of a D who takes a lawnmower belonging to V, with an intent to keep it all summer and fall. According to the Code, this constitutes larceny, because D is intending to deprive his neighbor of a "substantial part of the useful life of the mower."

   c. **Issue is intent, not result:**   But the issue, both as to abandonment and as to use for a substantial period, is the defendant's ***intent***, not what actually happens. For instance, if D intends to borrow V's car for a brief round-trip and return it, D does not meet the intent-to-steal requirement even if he gets into an accident after one block that destroys the car.

2. **Intent to return equivalent property:**   As noted, an intent to return the very property taken negates an intent-to-steal. But where the defendant intends to return ***equivalent*** property, not the very property taken, it is not clear whether intent-to-steal is present.

   a. **Offered for sale:**   If the property is being ***offered for sale***, and the defendant intends to pay for it shortly thereafter, he is almost certainly not guilty of larceny. Thus if a newspaper stand is momentarily untended, and D takes a newspaper without paying for it (because of a lack of change), and intends to pay for it the following day, he will not be a thief. See M.P.C., § 223.1(3)(c), explicitly granting a defense where one takes property "exposed for sale," intending to pay and "reasonably believ[ing] that the owner, if present, would have consented."

b. Property not for sale: Where the property is not being offered for sale, the defendant might be found to have the requisite intent-to-steal despite his intent to pay or return equivalent property. This is particularly likely to be the case if the property is unique, something for which there is no exact monetary value (e.g., an original painting). See L, p. 814.

c. Embezzlement: The requisite intent for larceny should be distinguished from that for embezzlement; intent to return the equivalent property is virtually never a defense to an embezzlement charge. See *infra*, p. 299.

3. **Claim of right:** If the defendant takes another's property with intent to *collect a debt* which the other owes him, or to *satisfy a claim* against the other, this will generally negate intent-to-steal.

   a. Money taken against liquidated claim: The taking in such circumstances is quite likely to be non-criminal if the defendant takes *money* in satisfaction of a liquidated debt or claim (i.e., one with a fixed monetary value). This will generally be true even if the defendant is *mistaken* (even unreasonably mistaken) about whether the debt is owed or the claim valid, so long as his belief is an honest one.

   > **Example:** D works for V. V fires D, and refuses to pay him for three weeks of vacation pay, which D genuinely believes is owed to him. Assume that under applicable legal principles, and as any reasonably knowledgeable employee would understand, D was not entitled to any vacation pay, because D had taken all the vacation to which he was entitled up to the moment he was fired. D nonetheless reaches into V's cash register and removes three weeks' pay. D is not guilty of larceny, because he took pursuant to an honest, though unreasonable and mistaken, belief that he had a legally-enforceable claim against V for the money.

   b. Unliquidated claim or property taken: If, on the other hand, either the defendant's claim is unliquidated (e.g., a claim for damages from a car accident), or he takes the victim's property rather than money, it is less clear that his claim of right will negate intent-to-steal. But if what he takes is clearly less than what he is owed (or honestly believes is owed him), the defense of claim of right will nonetheless probably be recognized. See L, p. 815.

   c. Usually not a defense to robbery: Most states hold that the "claim of right" defense is *not available* where D is charged with a crime of *violence*, including *robbery*.

   > **Example:** D is charged with robbery, for having taken $25 by force from V. At trial, D testifies that V had previously owed him $25 and agreed to pay him back $15 of this. D, by his account, saw that V had enough money to pay back the whole $25, but that V refused to pay back more than $15. D then forcibly took the entire $25 owed to him from V's stack of cash. D asserts the defense of claim of right, in that he merely took back what was owed to him.
   >
   > *Held*, for the prosecution. The New York legislature did not intend the "claim of right" defense to be available in crimes involving force, including robbery. This is "consistent with what appears to be the emerging trend of decisions from other jurisdictions." *People v. Reid*, 508 N.E.2d 661 (N.Y. 1987).

Note: The court in *Reid* suggested that the result might be different if D had been trying to take back a *specific chattel* which he owned, and which V had taken from him. In that event, D would not be guilty of robbery, because he was not taking property "from an owner thereof." But here, D was merely taking *fungible cash* to satisfy a claimed debt, so the cash was clearly "property of another." That being the case, the only issue was whether the legislature had intended to authorize the "claim of right" defense, and, as noted, the court found that the legislature had not so intended.

4. **Concurrence of taking and intent; mistake:** As with any other crime, larceny requires a *concurrence* between the *actus reus* (the taking) and the *mens rea* (the intent-to-steal). Thus if the defendant commits the taking under innocent circumstances, he does not commit larceny even if he subsequently decides to keep the property. This is true, for instance, if D *mistakenly believes that the property is his ow*n (and, indeed, it's true even if the mistake is an *unreasonable* one).

   Example: D, an absent-minded professor, picks up his colleague's black umbrella thinking that it is his own. Subsequently he realizes the error, but decides to keep the umbrella anyway. D is not guilty of larceny, because at the time of taking he did not have an intent to steal, and at the time he had the intent to steal, he no longer met the *actus reus* requirement for larceny.

   a. **Bank overpayment:** Thus in *U.S. v. Rogers, supra*, p. 288 (the bank overpayment case), the court held that the defendant would not be guilty of larceny if he received the overpayment without realizing the error, and only later formed an intent to keep it.

   b. **Model Penal Code:** But, as noted, Model Penal Code § 223.5 imposes a different rule, making a person guilty of theft if he "fails to take reasonable measures to restore the property to a person entitled to have it," regardless of whether there was an intent to steal at the time he came into possession of lost, mislaid or misdelivered property.

       i. **Container rule:** Suppose the lost or misdelivered property is in an envelope or *container* (e.g., money inside an envelope). A few states hold that the defendant does not take possession of the enclosed property until he discovers it, and can thus be guilty of larceny if at the time of discovery he decides to keep it. Thus if D in *Rogers, supra*, had received the overpayment in an envelope, and realized the mistake only when he arrived home and looked at the contents, he would be guilty of larceny in these minority states if he at that time decided not to return the money. See L, pp. 817.

   c. **Continuing trespass:** Some states apply the doctrine of "*continuing trespass*," in order to make the defendant's trespassory taking coincide with his guilty intent. The doctrine applies where the defendant's original taking, while not done with intent to steal, is nonetheless *somewhat culpable*; his trespass is said to continue up until the time he decides to keep the property. For instance, if D decides to borrow V's car for a short time and return it (a culpable taking even though one not made with intent to steal), he will be liable for larceny under the "continuing trespass" doctrine if he subsequently decides not to return the car. (But if he took the car honestly, believing that it was his own, his original taking would not be trespassory, and the doctrine would not apply at all. Thus he would not be guilty of larceny even if he subsequently decided to keep the car). See L, pp. 817-18.

G. Degrees of larceny: Almost all states divide larceny into at least two degrees, *petit* and *grand*. Grand larceny usually consists of cases where the property stolen has a market value of more than a certain amount (e.g., $500). Theft of an automobile and theft from the *person* of another (e.g., pickpocketing) are often treated as grand larceny regardless of amount.

  1. Aggregation: Where the defendant has stolen several items, which together meet the amount for grand larceny, but no item meets it separately, the status of the offense depends on the circumstances. If the items were stolen *at one time* from one victim, the aggregate value will usually be considered. Also, property taken at the same time from several people will usually be aggregated, on the grounds that all the takings are part of a single scheme. See L, p. 808.

LEXIS®-NEXIS® Searches on **LARCENY**

Sub-Topic	Suggested Searches
Definition of larceny	`larceny w/10 (definit! or defined or elements)`
Trespassory taking	`larceny w/10 (trespas! w/3 tak!)`
Asportation requirement	`larceny w/30 ((carry! w/2 away) or (asportation))`
Intent to steal	`larceny w/30 (inten! w/10 (steal or permanently deprive))`
Larceny by trick	`atleast2(larceny by trick)`

III. EMBEZZLEMENT

A. Definition: Embezzlement varies somewhat from state to state, but in general it is composed of the following elements:

  1. A *fraudulent*

  2. *conversion* of

  3. the *property*

  4. of *another*

  5. by one who is *already in lawful possession* of it.

  See L, p. 818.

B. Need for embezzlement crime: As we saw, larceny occurs only where the defendant wrongfully obtains possession. If he obtains possession lawfully (e.g., with the owner's consent), and later misappropriates it, he has not committed larceny. To deal with this situation, the crime of embezzlement exists.

1. **No overlap:** Embezzlement statutes are generally construed so as ***not to overlap*** with larceny. That is, a given fact pattern must be either larceny or embezzlement, and cannot be both. L, pp. 818-19.

C. **Conversion:** For most larceny, it is only necessary that the defendant take and carry away the property. But for embezzlement, he must ***convert it*** (i.e., deprive the owner of a significant part of its usefulness). Thus if he merely uses it for a short time, or moves it slightly, he is not guilty of embezzlement (regardless of whether he intended to convert it).

Example: D's boss lends him the company car to do a company errand, and D decides to abscond with it or sell it. If he is stopped before he has traveled very far, he will not technically be guilty of embezzlement, since he has not yet converted the car.

D. **Property of another:** To be the subject of embezzlement, property must fall within certain classes, and must also belong to someone other than the embezzler.

1. **Kind of property which may be embezzled:** Larceny statutes often provide that any property which may be the ***subject of larceny*** may also be embezzled. Thus tangible personal property (covered by common-law larceny), plus any other classes of property (e.g., stocks and bonds) covered by the larceny statute will be covered by the embezzlement statute as well.

   a. **Extension beyond larceny:** Furthermore, some embezzlement statutes are even ***broader*** with respect to property covered than the corresponding larceny statute. For instance, although one generally cannot commit larceny of real estate (for one thing, it cannot be "carried away"), one can easily embezzle it (e.g., by using a power of attorney received from the owner to deed the property to oneself or to mortgage it for one's own purposes). L, p. 820.

2. **Property "of another":** One can only embezzle property belonging to ***another***, rather than to oneself.

   a. **Owner to pay from own funds:** Thus if defendant has an obligation to ***make payment from his own funds,*** he ***cannot embezzle*** even if he fraudulently fails to make the payment. Two famous cases involving this principle are set forth in the following examples.

   Example 1: D, a coal mine operator, has his employees sign orders directing him to deduct from their wages the amount that each owes to a grocery store. D deducts the amount, but then fails to pay the store owner.

   Held, D is not guilty of "fraudulent conversion" (a kind of embezzlement). D did not misappropriate his employee's money, but rather, failed to make payment from his own funds. It is true that he owed money to the employees as unpaid wages, but this gives rise only to civil liability, not criminal. *Commonwealth v. Mitchneck*, 198 A. 463 (Pa. 1938).

   Example 2: D runs both a loan company and a collection agency. His loan company receives a promissory note for $200 from X. He gives her only $7 in cash, and agrees to use the rest of the loan proceeds to pay off certain of X's creditors. D then goes to two of the creditors, to whom she owes $57, and convinces them to retain his collection agency to collect the sum (without telling them of his relationship to X). He pays them $38 and keeps the remaining $19 as his own collection fee.

Held, D's conviction of larceny reversed. D may have been a debtor of X for $193, but he was not a custodian of her money. Even had he failed to make any payments at all, he would have had only civil liability. Furthermore, X did not lose anything by D's conduct, since she would not have gotten the $19 anyway. (And while the creditors might have lost, the indictment did not charge D with stealing from them.) *State v. Polzin*, 85 P.2d 1057 (Wash. 1939).

    i. Model Penal Code critical: The Model Penal Code draftsmen are highly critical of the logic behind *Mitchneck* and *Polzin*. As the draftsmen point out, Mitchneck could have been convicted of theft if he had paid his employees their full wages at one window and received the grocery money back again at a different window. Similarly, Polzin could have been convicted if he had handed $200 over to X, and she had immediately handed him back $197 with which to pay the creditors. As the draftsmen state, "the physical manipulation of greenbacks has no conceivable criminologic significance." (Tent. Dr. No. 1 at 114.)

    ii. Code changes rule: Therefore, the Code establishes the new crime of "theft by failure to make required disposition of funds received." (M.P.C. § 223.8.) The provision applies wherever the person with the obligation to pay agrees to *reserve funds* for the obligation. Thus Mitchneck and Polzin would be liable under the provision, but one who buys goods on credit and does not pay for them would not be (since he has not agreed to reserve particular funds). See Comment 1 to § 223.8.

  b. Co-owners of property: One who is *co-owner* of property together with another cannot, according to the usual rule, embezzle the joint property, because it is his "own." This is true, for instance, of *joint tenants* in real estate, or *partners* in a business. Occasionally, however, the embezzlement statute explicitly applies to co-owned property

  c. Agent for collection: A person may undertake to *collect money* for another, and to remit it (usually minus a commission). When such a person collects and then fails to remit, the courts are split as to whether this is embezzlement. See, e.g., *State v. Riggins*, 132 N.E.2d 519 (Ill. 1956), in which D ran a collection agency, one of whose clients was X. D's arrangement with X was that he could collect from her debtors and commingle all funds received in one bank account; furthermore, he was not required to pay anything to X on a particular account until it was paid in full. He made collections over a period of time (including full collection from some accounts), and did not remit. The court held that D could be guilty of embezzlement, because he was not a co-owner of the funds, but merely an "agent." (A dissent criticized the finding that D was an "agent," arguing that the embezzlement statute's use of the term "agent" was intended to be narrow, and did not apply to an independent businessman who works for hundreds of clients.)

  d. Purchaser who gives security interest: One who buys *goods on credit* frequently gives the seller a "security interest," sometimes called a "chattel mortgage." This gives the seller the right to ***repossess*** the equipment if the price is not paid. If the purchaser misappropriates the property (e.g., by selling it in violation of the agreement with the seller), this will usually ***not*** be treated as embezzlement; the property is held to be that of the purchaser, even though the seller has an interest in it.

Example: D, a car dealer, finances the purchase and sale of used cars through Finance Company, which keeps formal "title" to the cars until they are paid for. D sells the cars in the course of his business, but is unable to repay the money.

Held, D is not guilty of "fraudulent conversion" (a type of embezzlement). Despite the fact that Finance Company held nominal title to the cars, the real substance of the transaction was that D owned them, and was simply a debtor of Finance Company. *Commonwealth v. Stahl*, 127 A.2d 786 (Pa. 1966).

    i. Model Penal Code follows this view: The Model Penal Code follows the approach of *Stahl*. M.P.C. § 223.0(7) provides that "property in possession of the actor shall not be deemed property of another who has only a security interest therein, even if legal title is in the creditor pursuant to a conditional sales contract or other security agreement."

E. By one in lawful possession: As noted, the principal distinction between larceny and embezzlement is that the latter is committed by one who is ***already in lawful possession*** of the property before he appropriates it to his own use.

Example: D drives a truck for a company that purchases scrap meat and bones from butcher shops. The arrangement with one customer, Hill Field, is that, in order to pay Hill Field for the scraps in cash, the company issues a check for their value, payable to D, who cashes it and pays Hill Field. All other customers simply receive credit slips showing the poundage of the scrap picked up, and later receive a check from the scrap company. One day, D submits a slip showing that he has picked up $84.25 of scrap from Hill Field; he turns in that much scrap, and receives a check. It develops that the scraps did not in fact come from Hill Field, but rather, were obtained by D from other customers, and not reflected in shorted weight slips given to those customers. D keeps the $84.25 check for himself.

Held, D's embezzlement conviction reversed. The scraps that D turned in to get the $84.25 were unlawfully obtained by him (by issuing the shorted weight slips). Therefore, D cannot have embezzled either the scraps or the $84.25, since "one could not embezzle that which he had already stolen." (D could be guilty of larceny, but this is not what the indictment charges.) *State v. Taylor*, 378 P.2d 352 (Ut. 1963).

    1. Limited to certain classes of persons: Embezzlement statutes in most states list ***certain classes of persons*** who may be guilty of embezzlement (e.g., employees, bailees, attorneys, guardians, etc.) A person who does not fall within one of the listed classes cannot be an embezzler, even though he may have misappropriated property the possession of which he had previously obtained lawfully. Some states have attempted to fill such loopholes by drafting broad embezzlement statutes applying to anyone to whom property is "entrusted," or some similar formulation. See L, p. 823.

    2. Employees: Virtually all embezzlement statutes apply to ***employees*** who misappropriate property with which they have been entrusted. However, since common-law embezzlement exists only where the employee is originally in lawful possession (not merely custody), some misappropriation by employees will be larceny.

    a. **Minor employee:** Thus as noted (*supra*, p. 286), a **minor employee** (e.g., a bank clerk) may be held to have received only **custody** of the item, with "constructive possession" remaining in the employer. When the employee takes it for his own purposes, he is therefore committing larceny (by unlawfully obtaining possession).

        i. **Possession from third person:** But if the property is obtained by the employee directly from a **third person,** not from the employer, this will usually constitute possession rather than custody. See, e.g., *Commonwealth v. Ryan, supra*, p. 286, holding a bank clerk liable for embezzlement rather than larceny where he received cash from a third person, briefly deposited it in the employer's cash drawer, and withdrew it for his own use.

    b. **Broad statutes:** A number of states, however, now have broad embezzlement statutes that make it embezzlement rather than larceny for an employee to take property in his possession or "under his care." Under such a statute, even a minor employee who at common law would have had only "custody" is guilty of embezzlement when he misappropriates. See L, pp. 824-25.

3. **Finders:** One who finds **lost or mislaid property**, or to whom property is **mistakenly delivered**, cannot be guilty of larceny if he gains possession without intent to steal. (*Supra*, pp. 287-288.) However, many embezzlement statutes may not be drawn so as to make such a person an embezzler either. Thus he may go free. See L, p. 825.

    a. **Bailee statutes may cover:** However, some states have special *"larceny by bailee"* statutes, and others have embezzlement statutes explicitly covering finders and other bailees. In either event, the finder is likely to be liable. See, e.g., *Burns v. State*, 128 N.W. 987 (Wisc. 1911), wherein D, a constable, finds a roll of money thrown away by an insane man. D fails to return the money, and is convicted of "larceny by bailee." Conviction affirmed, on the grounds that there has been a "bailment," even though there was not a formal contractual arrangement between the insane man, as bailor, and D, as bailee.

F. **Fraudulent taking:** The embezzler must not only intend to take the property, but his taking must be *"fraudulent."* The principal issue with respect to the defendant's mental state is whether a **claim of right** or an **intent to repay** negates a fraudulent state of mind.

1. **Claim of right:** If the defendant honestly believes he has a **right** to take the property, this will often negate the existence of fraud. For instance, if he mistakenly believes that the property is **his**, or that he is authorized to use it in a certain way, this will be a defense (perhaps even if the mistake is unreasonable; see L, p. 826).

2. **Collection of debt:** Similarly, if the defendant takes the property in order to **collect a debt** owed him by the owner, there will probably be no fraud. For instance, in *Regina v. Feely*, [1973] 2 W.L.R. 201 (Eng. 1972) D was branch manager of a bookmaking firm, and "borrowed" 30 from the cash drawer. He defended on the grounds that his employers owed him 70, and that the 30 should be treated as partial payment of this debt. *Held*, it should have been left to the jury to consider whether the taking was "dishonest" (the term used in the statute). It cannot be said as a matter of law that one who takes in this situation has the necessary fraudulent intent.

3. **Intent to repay:** It is very commonly raised as a defense to embezzlement that the defendant *intended to return the property taken.*

    a. **Intent to return the very property:** If the defendant intends to return the *very property taken*, and has a substantial ability to do so at the time of taking, this may be a defense. One who uses his employer's car, intending to return it, for instance, would probably escape conviction. See L, pp. 826-27.

    b. **Intent to return equivalent property:** But much more commonly, the property taken is *money*, and the intent is not to return the same dollars, but an *equivalent sum*. Perhaps because it is precisely along these lines that most embezzlements occur, it is uniformly accepted that such an intent to return the equivalent is *no defense.*

        i. **Ability to repay irrelevant:** Generally, of course, the embezzler does not have a realistic possibility of paying back the money. But *even if he does,* this will not help him. See, e.g., *People v. Talbot*, 28 P.2d 1057 (Cal. 1934), affirming D's embezzlement conviction where he used corporate funds of the Richfield Oil Co., of which he was President, to speculate in the 1929 stock market. The fact that he intended to repay the money, and at the time of the taking had a net worth of several million dollars, an amount far greater than that taken, was held irrelevant. (By the time the prosecution was instituted, D had gone bankrupt in the Crash.)

LEXIS®-NEXIS® Searches on **EMBEZZLEMENT**

Sub-Topic	Suggested Searches
Embezzlement, generally	`atleast2(embezzlement) and (embezzle! w/30 (definit! or elements))`
Lawful possession, requirement of	`embezzle! w/30 (lawful! w/3 possess!)`
Employee, embezzlement by	`atleast2(embezzlement) and (embezzle! w/10 employe!)`

IV. FALSE PRETENSES

A. Definition: The crime of obtaining property by false pretenses, usually referred to as simply *"false pretenses,"* generally consists of the following elements:

1. A *false representation* of a

2. *Material present or past fact*

3. Which *causes* the person to whom it is made

4. To *pass title to*

5. His *property* to the misrepresenter who

6. *Knows* that his representation is false, and *intends to* defraud.

See L, p. 828.

B. **Need for crime:** Larceny, as noted, exists where the defendant obtains possession unlawfully, but does not obtain title. If a person uses fraud or deceit to obtain not only possession but also ownership (title), he must be prosecuted for the crime of false pretenses, which exists in all jurisdictions.

    1. **No overlap:** Like the crime of embezzlement, false pretenses was first enacted as a Parliamentary statute in order to supplement larceny. Therefore, the courts have always construed false pretenses statutes in such a way that there is no overlap with larceny; either one is guilty of larceny or of false pretenses, but not of both.

    2. **Difficulty of distinguishing from larceny to trick:** Since one kind of larceny (larceny "by trick") is accomplished with the use of fraud or deceit to obtain possession, it will sometimes be difficult to tell whether an appropriation is larceny or false pretenses (i.e., whether title or merely possession has passed). This issue is discussed further *infra*, p. 302.

C. **False representation of present or past fact:** There must be a *false representation* of a *material present or past fact.*

    1. **Non-disclosure and concealment:** Normally the misrepresentation will be an explicit one, made by use of words. But courts have recognized other kinds of misrepresentations.

        a. **Reinforcing false impression:** For instance, it may be a misrepresentation to *reinforce a false impression* held by another. Model Penal Code § 223.3(a) includes such conduct within the crime of "theft by deception." The Code Commentary gives the following example: D buys a glass ring from Woolworth's. V, who mistakenly fancies himself to be a diamond expert, sees the ring, and says to V "That is a nice diamond ring you're wearing. How much will you sell it for?" D responds saying "$500" (which he knows to be much more than the value of the ring). D would be liable for "theft by deception" under the Code, since he has reinforced what he knows to be V's false impression. (Comment 3(a) to § 223.3.)

        b. **Concealment:** Similarly, active non-verbal conduct may suffice. For instance, if D sold V a car with a broken engine block, and painted the engine block in such a way as to *conceal* the defect, he might be liable for false pretenses.

        c. **Fiduciary relationship:** Also, if the defendant is in a *fiduciary relationship* with the other party (e.g., attorney and client), he may have an affirmative duty to speak the truth, and if he remains silent with knowledge that the other person is mistaken, he may be liable. See M.P.C. § 223.3(c).

        d. **Silence normally not enough:** But there is no general duty on the part of a party to a bargaining situation to speak the truth rather than remaining silent. That is, one may generally *remain silent* even though one knows that the other party is under a false impression (provided that one did not cause that false impression in the first place). See L, p. 830.

2. False promises not sufficient: The representation, according to most courts, must relate to a *past or present fact*. The majority rule is that *false promises*, even when made with an intent not to keep them, are not sufficient.

  a. Rationale: The rationale for this majority view is that a contrary rule might lead to *imprisonment of debtors*, who borrow with an honest intent to repay, but later get into financial difficulties. The theory is that it will often be nearly impossible to tell whether D borrowed with intent to repay, or with a dishonest intent not to.

  b. Minority view: But there has been a tendency in some courts to allow false statements as to future facts, including false promises, to suffice.

  Example: D obtains the life savings of two elderly women, by promising to give them mortgages on certain properties. The money is never repaid, and the mortgages are never tendered.

  Held, D can be convicted (of the consolidated crime of "theft," one form of which is false pretenses) if it is shown that he did not intend to perform the promises at the time he made them. It is true that there is a risk of prosecuting one who is "guilty of nothing more than a failure or inability to pay his debts," but this danger can be guarded against by requiring something more than the mere non-performance to prove the fraudulent intent. *People v. Ashley*, 267 P.2d 271 (Cal. 1954).

  Note: A concurrence argued that there is no effective way to guard against this danger, since juries will often reason that the defendant "should" have known he couldn't keep the promise, and that therefore that he did in fact not intend to keep it.

  c. Distinguished from larceny by trick: Although a false promise will not, as noted, usually suffice for false pretenses, for no logical reason such a promise *will suffice for larceny by trick*. For instance, if one rents a car by promising to return it in two days, and then keeps the car permanently, this will suffice for larceny by trick. See L, pp. 831-32.

D. Reliance: There must, of course, be a causal relation between the false representation and the passing of title. This requirement is usually expressed by stating that the victim must *"rely"* upon the representation. Thus if the victim does *not believe* the representation, the crime does not exist. See L, p. 833.

1. Representation must be "material":   Also, the false representation must be a *"material"* one. That is, it must be one which would play an important role in a reasonable man's decision whether to enter into the transaction. The courts have not been very liberal to defendants in determining what is material.

Example: D purchases two television sets on credit from V by stating that he is the free-and-clear owner of a Packard car worth over $4,000, and giving V a chattel mortgage on the car. D fails to disclose that there is a prior mortgage on the car, for $3,000. The car is then in a collision, sustaining $1,000 worth of damage, and is repossessed by the first mortgagee. D is prosecuted for obtaining the television sets by false pretenses. He defends on the grounds that the sets were only worth a total of $272, and that even with the first mortgage he had an equity in the car of $1,000 (five times the value of the sets); therefore, he argues, the misrepresentation was not material.

Held, conviction affirmed. There was evidence that V would not have sold the sets had it known the true facts. Therefore, D's misrepresentation was material. (A dissent argued that, insofar as D gave security that was worth, by any standards, more than three times the value of the property being purchased, he should not be found to have materially defrauded V.) *Nelson v. U.S.*, 227 F.2d (D.C. Cir. 1955).

E. Passing of title: To decide whether a case involves larceny (usually by trick) or false pretenses, it is necessary to determine whether the victim has passed title (ownership) to the property, or merely possession. ***Only if the title has passed*** will the crime be false pretenses. In general, the question will be what the victim ***intends*** to do.

1. **The victim has only possession:** For the victim to pass title, he himself must of course have something more than mere possession. One who finds lost property, for instance, or who purchases stolen goods from a fence, does not have title; if he is swindled, therefore, this is larceny rather than false pretenses. See L, pp. 835-36.

2. **Sale as opposed to loan or lease:** Where the victim parts with property (as opposed to money), there is a transfer of title if a ***sale*** occurs. If, on the other hand, the property is merely ***lent*** or ***leased***, only possession has been transferred, so the offense is larceny by trick.

3. **Purchase of goods on conditional sale:** Suppose the defendant ***buys goods*** under a conditional sale contract, by which the seller retains a ***security interest*** in the property until it is completely paid for. In this situation the buyer probably gets a significant enough ownership interest to qualify for false pretenses, if he has lied in the negotiations (e.g., by ***misrepresenting his ability to pay***). See L, p. 836.

4. **Handing over of money:** If the victim ***hands over money***, it is probably the case that he does not expect to get the money back (but rather expects to get something else of value in return). If so, the crime is false pretenses. For instance, if D sells V a glass ring claiming that it is a diamond, and V pays an exorbitant price, D has obtained ownership of the money, not merely possession, and is guilty of false pretenses.

   a. **For specified purpose:** But occasionally, a person gives money to another with the understanding that the latter will apply it towards a ***particular purpose***. In this situation, it is usually held that possession, not title, is all that passes. The crime is therefore larceny.

      Example: V, an immigrant, asks D, a lawyer, to assist him in straightening out a disorderly conduct arrest (which he fears will prevent him from getting U.S. citizenship). D tells V that it will be necessary to bribe the arresting policeman, and V gives D $2,000 for this purpose (in addition to a $200 legal fee). D never pays the money to the policeman, and is charged with larceny.

      Held, D is guilty of larceny by trick, not embezzlement. V did not intend that title to the money would pass from him until it was actually paid over to the policeman. Therefore, D obtained only possession. *Graham v. U.S.*, 187 F.2d 87 (D.C. Cir. 1950).

   b. **Loan of money:** If, on the other hand, the victim makes a ***loan*** of money without explicit restrictions on how the recipient is to spend it, this will be false pretenses rather than larceny. Thus if D borrows money from Bank by misrepresenting his assets, he receives title to the money, not merely possession. See L, p. 838. See, e.g., *Nelson v. U.S.*, discussed *supra*, p. 301 (D borrows by lying about whether his automobile is already mortgaged; held liable for false pretenses).

F. Property of another: The defendant must have received property, and it must be property belonging to "another."

1. **Property that qualifies:** Originally the crime of false pretenses was limited to property that could be the subject of larceny, i.e., tangible personal property. But modern statutes have generally extended the crime to cover at least documents representing rights (e.g., stocks, bonds, insurance policies, etc.).

    a. **Some limitations remain:** But some intangibles, even though they have value, are beyond the scope of most statutes. For instance, in *State v. Miller*, 233 P.2d 786 (Ore. 1951), D falsely told V that he owned a tractor free of liens, thus inducing V to guarantee D's indebtedness to a third person; in return, V received a mortgage on the tractor (which was in fact being bought under a conditional sales contract). The court held that a loan guarantee was not "property" within the meaning of the false pretenses statute. The court relied on the fact that such a guarantee could not be "possessed" nor the title to it transferred.

    b. **Extended to cover anything of value:** Some statutes, however, are broad enough to cover anything that has value. Thus Model Penal Code § 223.0(6) defines property, for theft purposes, to include *"anything of value."*

2. **Joint ownership:** Since the property received by the defendant must belong to "another," most courts still hold that property D *co-owns* with V does not qualify.

    a. **Modern view finds liability:** But modern courts are increasingly likely to hold that where D takes property belonging to himself and a co-owner, at least part of what was taken *is* property of "another" (the other's co-ownership interest), and can thus give rise to false pretenses.

G. Defendant's mental state: False pretenses, like embezzlement and larceny, is essentially a crime requiring intent. However, since one of the elements of the crime is that the representation be false, too strict a construction of the intent requirement might allow scoundrels to escape. Therefore, the intent requirement is met if either (1) the defendant *knows* that the representation is untrue; (2) he *believes*, but does not know, that the representation is untrue; or (3) he *knows that he does not know* whether the representation is true or false. See L, pp. 839-40.

1. **Practical significance:** Thus if the prosecutor can show that the representation was false, he can gain a conviction merely by showing that the defendant had no way of knowing whether it was true or false. This will often be much easier to demonstrate than it would be to show actual knowledge by the defendant of the falsity.

2. **Reasonable belief in truth of representation:** But if the defendant believes the representation to be true, he will not be liable for false pretenses *even if his belief was completely unreasonable*. That is, as to the falsity of the statements, the crime is not one that can be committed by gross negligence. (Of course, the fact that such a belief would be extremely unreasonable will be evidence that the defendant did not really hold it.)

3. **Intent to defraud:** Even if the defendant knows or believes that the statement is false, he cannot be convicted if his intent was not "*fraudulent*." The principal significance of this additional requirement is that a *claim of right* (e.g., collection of a debt) may be a defense to false pretenses just as to embezzlement (*supra*, p. 298) or larceny.

   a. **Attempt to collect debt:** Suppose, for instance, that D sells V a bicycle, and V does not promptly pay the purchase price. D makes reasonable attempts to collect, but is unsuccessful. V then complains that the bike is defective, and D tells him that if he will bring it in, D will obtain a new replacement bike for him. V gives back the bike, and D refuses to give the new one. On these facts, it seems probable that D would not be guilty of false pretenses, since although he made a false promise (which in some states may suffice; see *supra*, p. 301), he had no intent to defraud — he was trying to collect a legitimate debt. See L, p. 841, fn. 84.

H. **Defenses:** Two defenses are particularly likely to be raised in false pretenses cases:

   1. **Gullibility of victim:** The defendant may claim that the representation, although false, was not one which would have deceived an ordinarily intelligent man, and that the *victim's gullibility* should therefore furnish a defense. This defense is *extremely unlikely to succeed*, since one purpose of the criminal law is to protect those who cannot take care of themselves. See L, pp. 841-42.

   2. **No pecuniary loss:** The defendant may argue that despite the representation's falsity, the victim has suffered no actual *pecuniary loss*. For instance, suppose D sells V what he claims to be a fabulous set of stainless-steel kitchen knives, for the unbelievably low price of $2.95. The knives are really a weak alloy which rusts easily, but they are nonetheless worth $2.95. The fact that there has been no actual pecuniary loss will probably *not be a valid defense*. See L, pp. 842-43.

I. **Crimes related to false pretenses:** A number of statutory crimes are related to false pretenses, in that they typically involve the obtaining of title to property by fraud or deceit. A full discussion of these crimes is beyond the scope of this outline; however, they may be summarized as follows:

   1. **Bad checks:** If a person obtains property by writing a *bad check* (either one for which there are insufficient funds at the bank, or one for which there is no valid account) it may be possible to convict him of false pretenses. But this approach will not always work; for one thing, the court may hold that title to the property does not pass until the check is cashed, so that if it never clears, there can be no false pretenses. See L, p. 852.

      a. **Bad check statutes:** Therefore, many states have enacted special bad check statutes, which make it a crime to write a check with knowledge that there are insufficient funds to cover it. Most such statutes provide that if the check is returned for insufficient funds, and the issuer fails to make good on it within a short statutory period of time (usually ten days), knowledge of the insufficiency, and an intent to defraud, may be presumed. See L, pp. 852-54.

   2. **Mail fraud:** The federal *mail fraud* statute makes it a federal crime to use the mails as part of a scheme to defraud a victim of his property. One significant aspect of the crime is that *the scheme does not have to be successful* for liability to exist.

3. **Forgery:** The crime of *forgery* exists where a document is falsified (usually a check or other negotiable instrument). The falsification must relate to the *genuineness* of the instrument itself (e.g., a signature purporting to be that of someone other than the actual signer). It is not necessary that the forged document actually be used to obtain property from another; thus one who acquires stolen checks and signs the account holder's name to them will be liable even if the checks never leave the forger's possession. See L, pp. 844-45.

4. **Confidence games:** Some states have a separate *"confidence game"* statute. Such statutes are generally quite vague, and cover many devices that would ordinarily be considered either larceny by trick or false pretenses (such as the "bunco scheme" almost attempted in *People v. Orndorff, supra*, p. 152). See L, p. 843.

LEXIS®-NEXIS® Searches on **FALSE PRETENSES**

Sub-Topic	Suggested Searches
False pretenses, generally	`(crime or criminal) and atleast2(false pretenses) and ((false pretense!) w/10 (defin! or elements))`
Reliance, requirement of	`(crime or criminal) and ((false pretense!) w/20 (reliance or rely))`

V. CONSOLIDATION OF THEFT CRIMES

A. Need for consolidation: As has been noted throughout this chapter, it will often be extremely important to determine on which side of the dividing line between larceny and embezzlement, or between larceny and false pretenses, a particular case lies. The jury must take its choice of one or the other, and if it picks the wrong one, its verdict will be overruled on appeal. Furthermore, the dividing line can be extremely blurry.

1. **Consolidation by some states:** Therefore, a number of states (still a minority) have joined larceny, embezzlement and false pretenses into *one unified crime*, usually called "theft." California and New York are among the states which have adopted this approach.

   a. **Advantage for prosecution:** It is still necessary that the prosecution establish facts which would fall within one of the three traditional theft classes, larceny, embezzlement or false pretenses. But the advantage for the prosecution is that the indictment need not specify which theory will be proceeded on, and the jury does not have to make an election; it simply returns a verdict of guilty of theft. Then, on appeal, so long as the facts are found to support guilt of one of the traditional offenses, the conviction will be affirmed.

2. **Model Penal Code consolidation:** The Model Penal Code goes even further in the direction of consolidation. The Code establishes a number of theft crimes which, among them, cover not only larceny, embezzlement and false pretenses, but also receiving stolen property and blackmail or extortion.

    a. New classifications: What were formerly larceny and embezzlement are now consolidated as "theft by unlawful taking or disposition" (§ 223.2). What were formerly false pretenses and that form of larceny called "larceny by trick" are now "theft by deception" (§ 223.3). Blackmail and extortion are now "theft by extortion" (§ 223.4). Receiving stolen property is treated by itself (§ 223.6). Finally, there are sections for "theft of property lost, mislaid, or delivered by mistake" (§ 223.5) (which previously could have been either larceny or embezzlement, depending on the facts); "theft of services" (§ 223.7); and "theft by failure to make required disposition of funds received" (§ 223.8) (which might formerly have been no crime at all, as in *Commonwealth v. Mitchneck* and *State v. Polzin*, both *supra*, p. 295).

VI. RECEIVING STOLEN PROPERTY

A. Need for punishing receipt: A thief, like a wholesaler, does not find it practical to deal with ultimate consumers. He therefore uses a middleman, known as a "fence," who typically buys the goods at an extremely small fraction of their market value, and resells them to end-users who may or may not be aware that the goods are stolen property. Statutes punishing *receipt of stolen property* are directed primarily at such fences (though they can be used as well against end-users who purchase with knowledge that the property is stolen).

B. Elements of offense: A detailed analysis of typical receipt of stolen property statutes is beyond the scope of this outline. Briefly, such statutes are violated if it is shown that the defendant has: (1) received (2) stolen property, (3) knowing that it has been stolen, and (4) done with intent to deprive the owner. See L, p. 855.

    1. Stolen property: Most statutes, even though they may refer to "stolen" property (which would normally imply larceny), have been construed to apply to property taken by *embezzlement* or *false pretenses* as well. L, p. 857.

    2. Trap laid by police: Suppose the police, or the owner of property, catch a thief who has stolen it, before he has sold to his fence. They may be able to persuade the thief to cooperate (in order to reduce his punishment) in trapping the fence, by passing the property on to the latter. In this situation the fence is not guilty of receiving stolen property, since the property has lost its character as stolen. (He may be guilty of *attempted* receipt of stolen goods, though even here he might escape with the defense of "impossibility," as in *People v. Jaffe, supra*, p. 159).

    3. Knowledge that it is stolen: The principal issue in most prosecutions for receiving stolen property is whether the defendant *knew* that the property had been stolen. It is usually not enough that the defendant merely *suspected* (or still less that he should have suspected) that the property was stolen. L, pp. 858-59.

    Example: The Ds, editor and owner of the Los Angeles Free Press, publish a list of names, home addresses and home telephone numbers of undercover narcotics agents working for the state of California. They obtain the list from X, who got it while working in the mailroom of the L.A. office of the Attorney General. The Ds refuse X's request for payment for the list, and refuse to return it to him. The Ds are convicted of receiving stolen property.

Held, the Ds' conviction reversed. The list was in fact stolen by X, since at the time he gave it to the Ds he was no longer working for the Attorney General's office, and could not conveniently return it. But the Ds were not shown to have been put on notice that the document was stolen. It is true that they were on notice that there would be great official displeasure if the list was published, but this is not equivalent to knowledge that the document was stolen. Nor were the Ds aware that X no longer worked for the Attorney General, and that he had therefore more than simply "borrowed" the list. *People v. Kunkin*, 507 P.2d 1392 (Cal. 1973).

    a. Strong belief is sufficient: However, it is not required that the defendant know, with 100% certainty, that the goods are stolen. It is sufficient, in virtually all jurisdictions, that he *believes them to be stolen.*

        i. Knowledge requirement circumscribed: Some states have weakened the requirement of knowledge even more. A few, for instance, punish one who merely has "reason to know" the stolen status of the goods. L, p. 859.

    b. Model Penal Code applies presumption: Other statutes require knowledge, but establish a *presumption* of knowledge in certain circumstances. Model Penal Code § 223.6(2), for instance, institutes a presumption that a *dealer* (defined as one who is "in the business of buying or selling goods") possesses the required knowledge or belief if he: (a) is found in possession of property stolen from two or more persons on separate occasions; (b) has received stolen goods in another transaction within one year prior to the transaction charged; or (c) is a dealer in the kind of property received, and buys for a consideration which he knows is far below its reasonable value. (This presumption can, of course, be rebutted by the dealer.)

VII. BURGLARY

    A. Common-law burglary: The common-law crime of burglary was defined to be the *breaking and entering of the dwelling of another at night with intent to commit a felony*. Nearly all states punish as burglary conduct which fails to meet one or more of these requirements; however, the requirements are sometimes maintained for higher degrees of the crime.

    B. Breaking: The common law required that there be a *"breaking."* The principal significance of this was that an opening must be created by the burglar. If the owner simply left his door or window *open*, the requisite breaking did not exist. (However, no force or violence was needed; the mere opening of a closed but *unlocked* door sufficed.)

    1. Consentual entry: Nor did breaking exist when the defendant was *invited* into the house (assuming that he did not stray into a portion of the house where he had not been invited).

    2. Most states abandon breaking requirement: Most American jurisdictions no longer require breaking for burglary. Instead, there is typically a requirement that D's presence on the property be "unlawful." L, p. 885.

    C. Entry: There must also be, under the common-law view, an *entry* following the breaking. However, it is sufficient that *any part* of the defendant's anatomy entered the structure, even for a moment (e.g., D reaches his hand through a window to unlock it). See L, p. 886.

1. **Requirement maintained:**   Nearly all American states continue to impose the requirement of an entry.

D. **Dwelling of another:**   The common law required that the structure entered be the ***dwelling of another.***

   1. **Dwelling:**   Thus the structure was normally required to be a ***house.*** A place of business did not suffice (unless the proprietor or one of his employees usually slept there). However, it was not required that the house be occupied ***at the particular moment of entry.*** L, pp. 887-88.

   2. **Statutory modification:**   All states now have at least one form of statutory burglary that does not require that the structure be a dwelling. However, many states require a dwelling for higher degrees of burglary; see, e.g., Model Penal Code § 221.1(2).

E. **Nighttime:**   At common law, the breaking and entering had to occur ***at night***; this requirement reflected the belief that the greatest danger to honest homeowners occurred after dark. If the sun had set, however, it was no defense that the dwelling was artificially illuminated. See L, p. 890.

   1. **No longer a requirement:**   No state now requires, for all degrees of burglary, that entry be at night. However, about half the states impose this as a requirement for higher degrees of burglary. L, p. 890.

F. **Intent to commit a felony:**   At the time of entry, the common-law burglar must have ***intended to commit a felony*** once he got inside. Today, an intent to commit a felony is not required; however, all states require that the defendant have an intent to commit ***some crime*** within the structure. In some states, the statute provides that the intent must be to commit either a felony or a theft crime (though the latter may be a misdemeanor, e.g., petty larceny). L, pp. 890-91.

LEXIS®-NEXIS® Searches on **BURGLARY**

Sub-Topic	Suggested Searches
Burglary, generally	`atleast2(burglary) and (burglary w/30 (defini! or defined or element))`
Breaking, requirement of	`atleast2(burglary) and burglary w/30 break!`
Dwelling of another, requirement of	`atleast2(burglary) and (burglary w/30 (dwelling w/10 another))`
Intent to commit a felony within	`atleast2(burglary) and (burglary w/30 (inten! w/30 felony))`

VIII. ROBBERY

A. **Definition of robbery:**   Robbery is generally defined as larceny committed with two additional elements: (1) the property is taken from the ***person*** or ***presence*** of the owner; and (2) the taking is accomplished by using ***force*** or putting the owner in ***fear.***

B. From the person or presence of owner: The property must be taken from the *presence* or *person* of its owner. There will normally not be much question about whether the property is taken from the victim's "person." The taking from the victim's *"presence"* is a bit trickier. The test for "presence" is whether the victim, if he had not been intimidated or forcibly restrained, could have prevented the taking. Thus if D enters V's house and confines him to one room, and then takes property from the opposite end of the house, this will be robbery. L, p. 869.

C. Use of violence or intimidation: The taking must be by use of *violence* or *intimidation*.

   1. Violence: Violence will exist if the thief engages in a struggle with the victim before taking the property, ties the victim up, hits him on the head, or otherwise uses substantial physical force to accomplish the taking. But *pickpocketing* is not robbery (assuming no struggle by the victim).

      a. Purse-snatching: If the thief simply *snatches* property from the owner's grasp (e.g., a purse), before the owner has a chance to resist, it is almost always held that the requisite violence is *not present*. L, p. 870. (However, if the owner is able to put up a struggle, the requisite force will be found to exist even if the thief uses only his hands.)

   2. Intimidation: Alternatively, a *threat of harm* may suffice in lieu of violence. For instance, if D pulls a gun on V, and says, "Your money or your life," this is robbery even though no actual force is used.

      a. Apprehension, not fear: All that is required is that the victim be placed in *apprehension* of harm (in the sense that he expects harm to occur); it is not required that he be *afraid*. Also, the requisite apprehension probably exists even though the victim believes that he could prevent the harm by using force of his own. For instance, if D says to V, "Give me your money or I'll kick you in the face," robbery exists if V complies, even though V knows that he could shoot D with a revolver secreted in his pocket and thereby prevent the attack.

      b. "Reasonable man" standard not applied: It is irrelevant that a "reasonable man" would not have been apprehensive of bodily harm. Thus if the victim is unusually timid, robbery can exist even though most people would not have been afraid in the situation. L, p. 875.

   3. Taking must concur with violence or intimidation: The violence or intimidation must occur either *before* or *simultaneously* with the taking. Thus if D snatches V's purse before V can resist (so that the requisite violence does not exist), the taking will not become a robbery merely because D subsequently has to use violence or threats to prevent V from recapturing the property. L, pp. 875-76.

D. Aggravated robbery: Most jurisdictions recognize several degrees of robbery. One aggravated form is "armed robbery," which exists where the defendant uses a deadly weapon. (Such "armed robbery" statutes are usually held to apply although the gun is unloaded; occasionally even a *toy pistol* has been held to suffice. This view is criticized in L, pp. 878-79.)

IX. BLACKMAIL AND EXTORTION

A. Nature of offense: The crime of robbery exists only where property is taken by use of violence or a threat of immediate harm. If the defendant obtains property by a threat of *future harm*, he is guilty of *extortion* (or, as the crime is called in some states, *"blackmail"*).

B. Nature of threat: The threat can be to cause physical harm to the property owner or, in some cases, the latter's family or relatives. A threat to cause economic injury may sometimes be sufficient, as where a corrupt union leader threatens to call a strike unless the employer pays him off. See L, p. 881.

    1. Threat to accuse victim of crime: Perhaps the most common kind of threat that will suffice is a threat to *accuse the victim of a crime*. Also, threats to expose some non-criminal secret of the victim that would subject him to disgrace are usually covered by extortion statutes. L, pp. 881-82.

C. Attempt to recover property: The fact that the victim is guilty of the crime or disgrace in question is, of course, no defense to a charge of extortion or blackmail. However, suppose the victim has taken property *from the defendant*, and the defendant threatens him with exposure or prosecution merely in order to recover the property. The courts are split on whether this constitutes extortion.

    1. Yes: Some courts have held that such conduct is extortion, despite the claim of right. See, e.g., *People v. Fichtner*, 118 N.Y.S.2d 392 (App. Div. 1952), in which the Ds, managers of a supermarket, threatened X, a suspected shoplifter, with arrest and publicity unless he signed a confession that he had taken $50 worth of goods from the store over a four-month period, and repaid the $50. The Ds did not take the money for their own use, but rung it up on the store register. The court held that this was extortion, even though X may in fact have stolen the $50 worth of goods (which he denied).

        a. Rationale: The court theorized that one of the purposes of the extortion statute was to prevent "the concealment and compounding of a felony to the injury of the State," and that the existence of a just debt was irrelevant to this statutory purpose.

    2. No: Other courts have held that this is not extortion, at least if the amount obtained by the defendant is no more than the amount actually taken from him by the victim. See, e.g., *State v. Burns*, 297 P. 212 (Wash. 1931), holding that if V had really embezzled from D, and D's threat of prosecution was an attempt to recover no more than the amount stolen, this would negate corrupt intent on D's part.

        a. Model Penal Code: See also M.P.C. § 223.4, making it a defense to extortion, in some circumstances, that the defendant "honestly claimed [the property] as restitution or indemnification for harm done in the circumstances to which [the] accusation, exposure, lawsuit or other official action relates, or as compensation for property or lawful services."

Quiz Yourself on
THEFT CRIMES *(ENTIRE CHAPTER)*

    NOTE: For all questions in this chapter, assume unless otherwise noted that the common-law definitions of all theft crimes are in effect.

79. Bunter, the manservant of Lord Peter Wimsey, is given certain grooming aids — barber's tools and the like — belonging to Wimsey that Bunter is to use in performing the services of his job. After several years of faithful service, Bunter decides to leave Wimsey's employ and announces that he will be leaving on July 1, following the June 30 expiration of his correct contract. On July 1, having formed an attachment to the tools of his trade, Bunter decides to take the grooming aids with him when he leaves, which he does later that day. What theft crime, if any, is Bunter guilty of?

80. Racer X covets Speed Racer's car, the Mach V, which is unattended in Speed's driveway.

(A) For this part only assume that, succumbing to impulse, Racer X hops in and rolls the car several feet out of the driveway, intending to keep the car until he can sell it. As he is about to start driving down the street, X's conscience overcomes him, and he returns the car to the driveway. Speed Racer, who witnesses the incident from his window, becomes furious, and decides to file a criminal complaint. Is Racer X guilty of common-law larceny?

(B) For this part only, assume the following: Racer X never intends to keep the car or sell it. Instead, he intends just to take it for a little spin, to see how it accelerates. He hops in, drives around the block, and returns the car exactly where he found it. Is Racer X guilty of larceny?

81. Pandora leaves her magic box in the cloakroom of a restaurant. Hope leaves her magic box next to Pandora's. After having a few too many cocktails at dinner, Hope returns first and picks up Pandora's box by mistake, even though Pandora's box is somewhat bigger than hers, and a slightly different color. (Assume that Hope's mistake was honest but that a reasonably sober person wouldn't have made the error.) Hope takes Pandora's box home and never looks at it again. Is Hope guilty of larceny?

82. Genie loses her black wine bottle at the beach. She puts up signs all over the place offering a reward for its return. Anthony Nelson subsequently finds the bottle.

(A) Assume for this part only that: Anthony, believing the bottle he's found is the one he's seen signs about, picks up the bottle, intending to return it to Genie. However, it sits in his car for a while, and he subsequently decides to keep it. Is he guilty of larceny?

(B) Assume for this part only that: Genie never put up the signs, and there are no indications of ownership on the bottle. Nelson finds the bottle and intends to keep it. A couple of days later, during a return visit to the beach, he overhears Genie telling another beachcomber about her lost bottle. He says nothing, and gets in his car and drives home. Is Nelson guilty of larceny?

83. T. Pott, presidential advisor to President Warren Harding, has been given a government-owned shredder for his office use. He takes it home one night (to use it to shred cheese for pizza), and never brings it back. Three months later he's fired. What theft crime, if any, has Pott committed?

84. Wanda Oceanview is a real estate agent. Charles Foster Kane authorizes her to sell his home, Zanadoo, for $100,000. Wanda sells it for $102,000. She pockets the extra $2,000, honestly believing she's entitled to the extra money as a commission. In fact, however, as a matter of local law governing real estate brokers, Wanda is not entitled to any commission, because she doesn't have a written agreement providing for any commission. An ordinarily prudent real estate broker would know this. As soon as these facts of law are explained to Wanda by Kane's lawyer (two weeks after she deposits the money), Wanda reluctantly refunds the money. Is Wanda guilty of embezzlement?

85. Tokyo Rose is the manager of an army base PX during World War II. Silk stockings, which the PX sells for $5 a pair, are in short supply. Rose takes three pair of stockings from the PX, and sells them to civilians for $20 a pair. At the moment she takes the stockings, she intends to put the $5 per pair PX price back in the register as soon as she can sell the stockings and get the cash for them. The next morning, Rose does exactly that, so the PX ends up with the same $5 a pair as if they had been sold in the regular course of business. Is Rose guilty of embezzlement?

86. Guido tells Jules that he is going to dredge land from the continental shelf off Florida and build an offshore casino. He asks Jules to invest, and, with visions of golden poker ships dancing in his head, Jules does so.

(A) For this part only, assume that Guido in fact has no intention of actually building the casino — he plans to invest Jules' funds at the racetrack instead. Under the majority view, is Guido guilty of false pretenses?

(B) Same facts as part (A), except that Guido says he's already received the necessary permits to build the casino. In fact, he has not, and has no intention of building the casino. Under the majority view, is he guilty of false pretenses?

87. Old Mother Hubbard applies for welfare benefits. Her caseworker asks her if she is receiving funds from any other source. Hubbard says no. Although she receives unemployment benefits, Hubbard believes the question referred to other earnings, not benefits. (Assume that Hubbard's belief about what the caseworker means is honest but unreasonable.) Based on her response to the question, Hubbard receives the welfare benefits. Is Hubbard guilty of false pretenses?

88. Jessie James, a professional criminal, knows that J.P. Morgan, a rich banker, will be away from home for several days. Therefore, at 1:00 a.m. on a Tuesday, Jessie goes to J.P.'s house, jimmies a lock on J.P.'s rear door, and enters the house. At the time of his entry, Jessie's intent is to steal whatever cash and jewelry he can find. However, Jessie inadvertently sets off J.P.'s alarm. Jessie is arrested by police before he has a chance to place any of J.P.'s possessions into the sack that he has brought with him. What is the most serious common-law crime of which Jessie may be convicted?

89. Bonnie & Clyde, a crack theft team, decide to try to steal from the First National Bank. They break into the Bank at 10 PM one night, when they suspect no one is there. Their purpose is to steal as much gold bullion as they can from the vault (to which they have previously learned the combination by bribing a bank employee). They break in, and are in fact able to take $100,000 worth of bullion before an alarm rings and frightens them off. Have Bonnie & Clyde committed common-law burglary?

90. Prince Charming breaks into his friend Cinderella's home at midnight one evening, intending only to leave a note demonstrating to Cinderella how simple it would be to burglarize her home. While inside, he sees a valuable painting that he falls in love with and decides to make off with it. Is Prince Charming guilty of burglary?

Answers

79. **Larceny.** The point of this question, of course, is for you to figure out whether this is larceny or embezzlement. Where at the time of the trespassory taking the defendant is in lawful possession (not just "custody") of the items, the taking is embezzlement; if the defendant is just in custody at that moment, the taking is larceny. Here, had Bunter absconded with the tools during his actual employment, the crime might have been embezzlement, on the theory that Wimsey had given possession (not just custody) of them to Bunter; the case could have gone either way on the issue of possession vs. custody. But by July 1,

given that the employment contract had ended, Bunter could not have had more than temporary custody of the tools, not true possession, since he no longer had any job-related reason to have them. At that point, the taking was a taking from Bunter's possession, so the crime was larceny.

80. **(A) Yes.** Larceny is defined at common law as the trespassory taking and carrying away of the personal property of another, with intent to steal. The two interesting issues here are: (1) was there a "carrying away"?; and (2) was there an intent to steal at the appropriate time? (1) is satisfied, because even a very small movement of the goods meets the carrying-away ("asportation") requirement, so rolling the car into the street sufficed. As to (2), the intent to steal must occur at the time of the carrying-away, and need not occur at any other time. Since the facts make it clear that at the moment the car was driven into the street, X intended to keep it and permanently deprive Speed Racer of it, this requirement was satisfied, and the crime was complete. The fact that X changed his mind (and returned the goods) shortly thereafter is irrelevant.

(B) No. Larceny requires the taking and carrying away of another's personal property with the "intent to steal." An intent to steal is generally deemed present only if the defendant has an intent to **permanently deprive** the owner of the property. Since Racer X did not intend to deprive Speed of the use of the car permanently, he hasn't met this requirement. (That's why most jurisdictions have special "joyriding" statutes to deal with this kind of situation.)

81. **No, because her mistake was honest.** Larceny requires an intent to take the property of another. If a person takes property believing that it is his own, the requisite intent to take another's property is not present. That's true even if the mistake is an unreasonable one. So larceny is in effect a "specific intent" crime — the requisite intent includes a belief about title, and even voluntary intoxication can negate that intent.

82. **(A) No.** A finder of lost property is only liable for larceny if, at the moment he finds the property, (1) he has reason to believe he can find the owner's identity *and* (2) he intends at that moment to steal the item. Here, (2) is not satisfied, because at the time Nelson found the bottle, he intended to return it. Since his intent to steal and finding the bottle do not coincide, he is not liable for larceny. The fact that Nelson later formed an "intent to steal" is irrelevant, at least under the common law. (But Model Penal Code § 223.5 *does* make it larceny for a defendant to "fail to take reasonable measures to restore [lost or mislaid] property to a person entitled to have it," regardless of whether there was an intent to steal at the time the defendant came into possession. So Nelson *would* be guilty of larceny under the M.P.C.)

(B) No. For larceny to exist, there must be an intent, existing at the time the defendant comes into possession of the property, to deprive the rightful owner of permanent possession. Where property is lost or mislaid, and at the time it comes into the defendant's possession there's no clue to its ownership, the defendant cannot have the requisite intent to "deprive the owner" of it. Therefore, Nelson won't be guilty of common-law larceny, even though he later discovered the owner's identity. (At that later point, he has the requisite intent, but it doesn't coincide with the moment of "taking," so it doesn't count.) (Again, under M.P.C. § 223.5 the result would be different, since by not speaking up Nelson would be "fail[ing] to take reasonable measures to restore [the] property to a person entitled to have it.")

83. **Embezzlement.** Embezzlement is the fraudulent conversion of the property of another by one who is already in lawful possession of it. That's the case here. The main issue is whether Pott was already in lawful possession of the shredder when he converted it to his own use. Since he was a relatively high-level official, and was given physical use of the shredder for as long as he held the government post, a court would almost certainly hold that Pott had possession, not just temporary custody, of the shredder. That makes his conversion embezzlement, rather than larceny (which could have occurred only if he had cus-

tody rather than possession at the time of the conversion.)

84. No. Embezzlement requires the "fraudulent" conversion of another's property by one in lawful possession of that property. The issue here is whether Wanda's conversion was "fraudulent." If a person honestly believes that she has a right to take the property — as where she is taking it in satisfaction of what she believes to be a valid debt — the conversion will not be deemed to be fraudulent. And that's true no matter how unreasonable the defendant's belief in her claim of right is. So the fact that Wanda "should have known better" is irrelevant. (Of course, the more unreasonable the defendant's belief, the more likely the trier of fact is to conclude that the belief was not in fact genuinely held. But if the trier *does* believe the belief was genuine, then its unreasonableness is irrelevant.)

85. Yes. When a person takes property and intends to replace equivalent property later, that's not a defense to embezzlement. Embezzlement requires only a fraudulent conversion of property by one with lawful possession of the property. Since these elements are satisfied here, Rose will be liable. (Note that this most frequently happens when an employee takes money from his employer to pay off personal debts, intending to replace it later. The "intent to replace" is no defense.)

86. (A) Amazingly enough, no. False pretenses requires a "factual" misrepresentation. Furthermore, the fact being misrepresented must be a past or present one — a promise that something will or won't happen in the future does not suffice as a factual misrepresentation, under the oft-criticized majority view. And that's so even if the promisor has absolutely no intention of keeping the promise. (But a minority of courts find liability where the speaker never intends to keep the promise.)

(B) Yes. Here, Guido has knowingly made a false representation about a present or past fact: that he has received the necessary permits. Therefore, the transaction meets all the requirements for the crime of false pretenses: (1) a false representation of a (2) material present or past fact (3) which causes the person to whom it is made to (4) pass title to his property to the misrepresenter, who (5) knows that his representation is false, and intends to defraud.

87. No, because she had an honest belief that her statement was true. False pretenses requires a *knowing* misrepresentation intended to convince the victim to pass title to property. Here, the intent to defraud is missing. Even an unreasonable belief in the truth of one's statement will negate intent, as long as it's an honest belief.

88. Burglary. The common-law crime of burglary is defined to be the breaking and entering of the dwelling of another at night with intent to commit a felony therein. The "trick" here is that Jessie is guilty of burglary *even though he in fact did not carry out the crime he had intended* (larceny). That is, once Jessie broke into and entered J.P.'s premises at night with an intent to commit larceny, he had already completed the crime of burglary.

89. No. The definition of common-law burglary requires the breaking and entering of a *dwelling* of another at night. The bank is not a dwelling, it's a place of business. (But many modern statutes have expanded the definition to cover the breaking/entering of any structure, dwelling or not.)

90. No. Burglary requires breaking and entering the dwelling house of another at night with the intention to commit a felony therein. At the moment Charming broke and entered, he had no intent to commit an act that was a felony therein (since leaving a warning note, even if it's a malicious prank, is not a felony). It's true that Charming later formed an intent to commit a felony (steal the painting), but to count, the felonious intent must exist at the moment of entry. Therefore, Charming is not guilty of burglary (but will, however, be guilty of larceny for taking the painting).

 *Exam Tips* on
THEFT CRIMES

Larceny and *burglary* are the theft crimes most frequently tested.

Larceny

☞ If you think you have larceny in your facts, confirm that all the required elements of common-law larceny have been met: The (1) trespassory (2) taking and carrying away of (3) personal property of (4) another (5) with the intent to steal.

☞ **Trespassory taking:** Look for a defendant who is *already in rightful possession* of the property at the time he decides to appropriate it for his own purposes — if so, he is *not* guilty of larceny because the "trespassory" taking element is missing.

> *Example:* D is walking in the street at night and finds a watch (with the owner's name engraved on it) lying on the ground near a pawnshop. He decides to take it home and to try to locate the owner. However, once he gets home, he decides to keep it. Since D was already in lawful possession of the watch at the moment he decided to keep it, he will not be guilty of common-law larceny.

☞ **Carrying away:** Determine whether the defendant assumed *dominion and control* over the object. Generally, but not always, this means that there must be a physical *movement* of the object.

> ☞ **Slight distance sufficient:** But if D causes even a *slight movement* of the object (after forming the intent to misappropriate), this will suffice for the dominion-and-control element.
>
> > *Example:* D is having dinner in a restaurant with V. V leaves the table to go to the restroom and D notices V's expensive watch on the table. She decides to steal it and puts it into her pocket. D begins to feel guilty, so when V returns to the table, D hands her the watch and says, "Here, you dropped this, and I put it into my pocket for safekeeping." Since D moved the watch from the table to her pocket with the intention of keeping it, she carried it away. She was actually guilty of larceny at that moment. (The fact that D changed her mind shortly thereafter and tried to "undo" the crime doesn't change this result.)

☞ **Intangible property:** Be on the lookout for property that is intangible. Remember that at common law, only tangible property could be the subject of larceny. But if your fact pattern has intangible property (e.g., a check, or services), say that under modern statutes, larceny has usually been expanded to cover intangibles.

> *Example:* D, a student, breaks into the offices of X, her professor, and photographs the original text of the exam that X will be giving the next day. (D never physically moves the original.) Although the original text is intangible property in a sense, a modern larceny statute would probably still cover it, making this larceny.

☛ **Property of "another":** Be on the lookout for property that appears to be property of one other than D, but really belongs to D. When this happens, D can't be guilty of larceny for taking the property, because it's not property of *"another."*

☞ *Example:* D pawns his watch to X, a pawnbroker. The pawn agreement says that D may reclaim the watch by paying $100 at any time during the next month. Two weeks later, D breaks in to X's store and takes the watch. D has at least a good argument that he hasn't committed common-law larceny, because he hasn't taken property of "another" (he himself still has title to the watch, subject to X's right to possess it as security for repayment).

☞ **Collecting a debt:** As a twist on "property of another," watch for a situation in which *V owes D money* or an item, and D takes a different item (or money) with an equal or lesser value, as a form of *self-help.* Here, V probably *won't be guilty* of larceny — his honest claim of "right" will negate the intent to take property "of another". And that's probably true even if D is *wrong* (though honest) in his belief that V owes him the debt.

Example: V has borrowed $50 from D, and has also borrowed D's watch (worth $50). V has repeatedly refused either to give back the watch or repay the $50 debt. While D is visiting V, he finds V's wallet on a table. D takes $100 from the wallet, intending this to constitute repayment for both the $50 and the watch. D is not guilty of c/l larceny, because he took under a claim of right. (Probably the same result would apply if D honestly but mistakenly believed that V had never repaid the $50 loan.)

☛ **Intent to permanently deprive:** This issue frequently arises on exams. The two rules to keep in mind are: (1) The only intent that matters is the intent *at the time of the taking* (not at some point after); and (2) There must be an intent to *permanently* deprive the owner of the property (or at least of a significant portion of the property's economic value).

☞ **Intent to borrow item:** Often, the defendant has a viable argument that he merely wanted to *borrow* the item. If so, there's no c/l larceny, because there's no intent-to-permanently-deprive.

Example: D breaks into her the office of V, her professor, to photocopy his notes. While in the office, she notices a gold-plated pen on V's desk and takes it with the intent of returning it in a week or two, hoping in the meantime that V will be so distressed about losing his pen that he will not notice that his notes have been disturbed. The next day, the pen is stolen from D's briefcase. D is not guilty of c/l larceny, because at the time she took the pen she did not intend to permanently deprive V of it (and the fact that the pen was later stolen by someone else, so as to prevent her from returning it, is irrelevant).

☞ **Actual ability to return:** But in intent-to-borrow situations, keep in mind that D will lack the requisite intent only if, viewed as of the time of D's taking, there is a substantial likelihood that D will in fact be able to return the property to V in pretty much its original form. If the facts show that the property probably won't be returned to V (or will likely be returned in damaged form), then D will be found to have the requisite intent-to-steal despite the intent to "return" it.

Example: Outside and during the night, D robs V of his billfold in order to retrieve a memorandum from it. After removing only the memorandum from the billfold, D throws V's billfold into the gutter, where he "expects" V to find it. In your answer, you should analyze the probability of the billfold being found and returned to V. If a jury finds that D should have realized that leaving the billfold there made it unlikely that D would get it back, then D probably has the requisite intent-to-steal the billfold even though D may have hoped or expected that D would get it back.

☞ **Property returned:** Conversely, don't be fooled by a fact pattern which indicates that the item was ***actually returned***. That fact is inconsequential if D's decision to return it was formed subsequent to the taking. (*Example:* In the fact pattern above where D puts V's watch in her pocket at the restaurant and then changes her mind and returns it, this is still larceny.)

☞ **Contingent borrowing:** Lastly, be on the lookout for what could be termed a "contingent intent" to return "borrowed" property. For an intent-to-return to negate intent, D's intent must clearly be to return the item and not be contingent on any circumstances.

Example: D, V's employee, "borrows" money from V's cash register, intending to gamble with it and to return it if she wins. She does in fact win, and returns the full amount. Regardless, D had the requisite intent to steal, because her intent-to-return was subject to a contingency.

☛ **Larceny by trick:** It can still be c/l larceny when D obtains possession of the property by fraud or deceit, instead of by force. But in this situation, make sure V was induced only to transfer temporary possession (not ownership or title) — if title is transferred, it's false pretenses, not larceny-by-trick.

Example: V rents a car to D, who pays with what turns out to be a worthless check. D keeps the car (as he intended all along). This is c/l larceny (of the larceny-by-trick variety), because D has fraudulently induced V to part with mere possession, not title. But if V had *sold* (transferred title) to the car to V in return for the worthless check, this would be false pretenses rather than c/l larceny, since in that situation title (rather than mere possession) would have been procured by D's deceit.

☛ **Where V doesn't have lawful possession:** Don't be tricked by a fact pattern which indicates that the *victim* of the theft *does not have lawful possession of the property*. As long as V's claim to the property is better than D's, that's enough for larceny. So, for instance, the fact that V himself previously stole the property, or possessed it illegally, is irrelevant. (*Example:* D may commit a larceny by stealing V's illegal-to-possess marijuana plant.)

Robbery

☛ **Definition:** Remember that robbery is defined as larceny with two additional elements: (1) the property is *taken from the person or presence* of the owner, and (2) the taking is accomplished by *force or putting the owner in fear*. Remember to note in your answer that the crime of larceny merges into that of robbery.

☛ **Intent:** Since robbery is built on larceny, D must have the specific intent to permanently deprive another of the other's personal property. Refer to the discussion regarding larceny above. So watch for situations where D believes that the property actually belongs to him, or where his intent at the time of the taking is not to permanently deprive — there can't be robbery in these situations, since there's no underlying larceny.

☛ **Force:** This element is occasionally tested. Generally, it's obvious when a taking is accomplished by using force or a threat of force, but there can be close questions, where your job is to notice that there's an issue about whether force-or-threat-of-force is present.

> *Example:* V is shot while driving his car. The car rolls into a tree and comes to a stop. D, a bystander, opens the driver's door with the intention of helping V. However, when he sees that V has been shot, he decides there's nothing he can do. D notices that V is wearing an expensive watch and begins to remove it. V opens one eye and faintly motions D away. D takes the watch and says, "You won't need this where you're going." V dies moments later. Given the circumstances, V's faint protestations were adequate to demonstrate he was not relinquishing the watch freely. Therefore, D probably would be deemed to have obtained the watch by force or threat of force.

Embezzlement

☛ **Definition:** In many fact patterns, embezzlement should be argued as an alternative to larceny. Remember the definition of c/l embezzlement: A fraudulent conversion of the property of another, by one who is ***already in lawful possession*** of that property.

☛ **Employees:** Think of embezzlement anytime an employee misappropriates the employer's money. Remember that c/l embezzlement exists only where the employee is originally in lawful *possession* of the employer's property (not merely *custody*). This means that if an employee has custody of the employer's property, but not true "possession," the misappropriation would be larceny, not embezzlement. Point this out whenever the employee is a minor, clerical-type person.

> *Example:* D is a cashier at the V supermarket. D periodically pocket $5 or $10 from the cash register. D's minor-employee status indicates that she probably has only temporary custody of the cash in the drawer, and that "constructive possession" remains with V. If so, D's conduct is probably larceny, not embezzlement. (But if D was V's controller, entrusted with investing the company's cash, his misappropriation would probably be embezzlement, since his seniority indicates he was given "possession," not just temporary custody, of the funds.)

☛ **Bailees:** Also think of embezzlement where the property is in the lawful possession of a ***bailee*** (repair-person, pawnbroker, etc.), who then appropriates it.

> *Example:* V's watch is broken, so he gives it to D, a jeweller, to be repaired. D takes it, fixes it, and then (because he's deeply in debt to bookies) puts it for sale in his store. X buys it. D has committed embezzlement, since he was in lawful possession of the watch at the time he sold it.

☛ **Possession must be lawful:** Remember that the defendant's possession must be ***lawful***, not produced by fraud or other crime.

> *Example:* D offers for "sale" various cars that he doesn't in fact own. He collects a

$100 cash down payment from V, then vanishes without producing the car. D cannot be guilty of embezzling money because his possession of the $100 is the result of fraud and was never lawful. (In other words, his crime is larceny, not embezzlement.)

☞ **Intent to repay:** Remember that if what's embezzled is money, D's *intent to repay* the money is never a defense to embezzlement charges. And that's true even if the repayment actually occurs.

False pretenses

☞ The crime of obtaining property by false pretenses is not heavily tested.

    ☞ **Definition:** This crime is committed when, with the intent to cause V to transfer title to personal property, D makes a fraudulent misrepresentation which causes V to make the transfer.

    ☞ **Title passes:** Distinguish false pretenses from larceny by trick. In false pretenses, title passes. In larceny by trick, only possession passes.

    ☞ **Purchase with bad check:** Think false-pretenses if D purchases V's property with what D knows is a *bad check.*

    ☞ **Swindle:** Also, think false pretenses if D *swindles* V, by charging V money for something that doesn't have the qualities D says it has.

        Example: D sells V a potion that D says will cure impotence. D knows it's actually a completely inert substances. This is obtaining money by false pretenses.

Burglary

☞ When a question requires you to analyze whether a defendant can be convicted of burglary, first attempt to ascertain the particular jurisdiction's required elements of the crime. If the fact pattern does not mention them, discuss the common-law requirements: (1) the *breaking & entering* of (2) the *dwelling* of *another* (3) in the *night*; (4) with *intent to commit a felony* therein. Some things to keep in mind about this definition:

    ☞ **Breaking:** Remember that *no force* is required.

        ☞ **Unlocked door:** So for instance, a defendant who *opens a closed door or window* (even an unlocked one) has fulfilled the "breaking" requirement, if this is done without the owner's authorization.

        ☞ **Use of key:** But if D uses a *key* to gain *authorized* entry, this is not "breaking." (*Example:* V gives D her key so she can water her plants while V is on vacation. D then enters and steals. This is not "breaking," and therefore not burglary.)

        ☞ **Closed area:** Watch for a fact pattern that describes an initial entry that clearly does not involve a "breaking," but the defendant subsequently breaks into a *large enclosed structure* located within the larger structure. In some states, breaking and entering such a closed area within which a person is capable of standing is sufficient.

        Example: X, Y, and Z enter a casino shortly before closing and hide in the bathroom until it closes. After closing, they hold the employees at gun point. A heavy safe, large enough to walk into, is blown open by X; Y and Z enter it and grab sacks of money from it. Although their initial entry into the casino did not constitute a breaking, blowing open the safe probably does, in which case X has committed burglary (and Y and Z are his accomplices to that burglary).

☞ **Entry:** Remember that an *entry* must follow the breaking. But it doesn't take much to satisfy this element — even putting a hand or foot into the previously-enclosed space will suffice.

> *Example:* X kicks in the door to someone's room and fires a shot at somebody inside. The bullet certainly entered the room and X's foot probably did when he kicked in the door. So either probably qualifies as an entry, making the whole transaction a burglary.

☞ **Dwelling of another:** Although the c/l definition requires that the entry be into the "dwelling" of another, you may want to note in your answer that some jurisdictions have *broadened* the definition. So it may be sufficient that the structure is *attached* to a dwelling, such as a garage, or a pawnshop that has living quarters upstairs. Additionally, note that many jurisdictions have extended the definition to *any* structure, even one with no connection to a residence (e.g., an office; a warehouse; or a store.)

☞ **Nighttime:** Pay attention to the *time of day.* If there's no mention of this in the fact pattern, write that you're assuming that the burglary occurred at night or that the jurisdiction has abandoned the nighttime requirement for all degrees of burglary.

☞ **Intent to commit crime inside structure:** Under the common law, the defendant must have intended to commit a *felony* inside the structure. But where appropriate, note in your answer that in some states today, all that's required is the intent to commit some crime, whether felony or non-felony theft crime. Two key points:

> ☞ **Not just theft:** Don't mistakenly assumes that burglary requires an intent to commit a *theft* crime within. Intent to commit *any* felony will do, even at common law.
>
> *Example:* D breaks into a house with the intent to shoot and kill V, the house's owner. At the moment D breaks and enters at night, he's committed burglary, because he had an intent to commit a felony (murder) inside.

> ☞ **Intent at time of entering:** Make sure that D intended, at the time of the breaking and entering, to later commit a felony. Don't be tricked by a defendant's *subsequent* decision to take something or to commit some other crime within the structure.

> ☞ **Recovering own property:** Even though D has the intent to take something at the time of entering the structure, if he *believes (even incorrectly) that it belongs to him*, there is *no intent* to commit a crime.
>
> *Example:* Although D knows that V is out of town, he goes to V's apartment to retrieve his own camera so that he can take pictures at his sister's wedding. V's apartment door is locked, but D shakes the doorknob and the door opens. D searches for the camera, but can't find it. On his way out he takes a silver candy dish from a shelf to give as a wedding present. Although V committed a breaking

and entering and a larceny, the fact that he entered only with the intent to recover his own camera prevented him from having the requisite intent to be convicted of burglary. (And the later decision to take the candy dish doesn't count, because it wasn't an act that D intended at the moment of the breaking-and-entering.)

Receiving stolen property

☛ Two key issues:

☞ **Stolen property:** Remember that for D to be guilty of receiving stolen property, the property must *in fact be stolen,* under the jurisdiction's theft statute. So you'll have to carefully analyze the property in terms of larceny, embezzlement, etc.

Example: X is walking in the street and finds a watch lying on the ground. He decides to take it home and to try to locate the owner. However, once he gets home, he decides to keep it. He then becomes nervous and gives the watch to his friend D saying, "Here, you can have this watch, but be careful, it's hot." D keeps the watch. Since X was not guilty of c/l larceny (he did not have the intent to permanently deprive the owner of possession at the time of the taking), the watch was not the subject of larceny. Therefore, D was not guilty of receiving stolen property.

☞ **Decoy:** Look for a fact pattern where the police are attempting to trap a thief or receiver of stolen goods. The decoy property used in such a scheme has probably been recovered by the police and has therefore *lost its character as stolen.* Therefore, D can't be guilty of receiving stolen property.

☞ **Knowledge that it's stolen:** Make sure D *knew* the property was stolen *at the moment he acquired possession* of it.

Example: D's friend T gives him a new television as a birthday gift. The next day D asks T for the warranty document. T informs D that there isn't any because the television was stolen. D keeps the television. D is not guilty of receiving stolen property, because he did not know it was stolen when he received it.

ESSAY EXAM
QUESTIONS AND ANSWERS

The following questions were asked on various Criminal Law examinations given at Harvard Law School. The questions are reproduced as they actually appeared, with only slight modifications. The sample answers are not "official" and represent merely one approach to handling the questions. Page references are to the main text of the outline.

QUESTION 1: Sapo and Crapaud agreed to commit a holdup at the First County Bank, in which Badger worked as a teller. They obtained her cooperation in the plan. The three of them agreed that Sapo and Crapaud would enter the bank and carry out the "holdup" at Badger's window. She would give them the money, apparently under the threat of the holdup. Later the three of them would meet and divide up the money. It was agreed that the plan would be carried out on January 12.

On January 9, Badger became frightened. After thinking about it, she called the apartment where Sapo and Crapaud lived together. Someone who was cleaning the apartment answered and said that neither Sapo nor Crapaud was at home. Badger asked the person to leave a message for them saying, "Can't go through with it. Sorry. Badger." The person on the telephone misunderstood (!) and left a note saying that someone had called and left the message, "Aunt Flo threw a fit. Sorry. Alger." When Sapo and Crapaud came home, they saw the message, concluded that someone was playing some sort of silly joke, and thought no more about it.

On January 12, as planned, Sapo and Crapaud went on foot to the bank and entered, brandishing guns. Sapo ordered everyone to stand still. Crapaud went to Badger's window and, pointing a gun at her, demanded money. As he did so, he winked at her. Startled that the "holdup" was taking place despite her message and frightened that her part in the plan would be discovered, Badger passed over the money. Crapaud grabbed it and he and Sapo ran out of the bank. Badger fainted.

As they ran onto the street, Sapo bumped into Wale (who knew nothing about the holdup) and knocked him to the sidewalk. Sapo and Crapaud kept running. Furious at Sapo's rudeness, Wale pulled out a gun and fired. The shot hit Sapo in the heart and killed him instantly.

Crapaud kept running and turned a corner. He bumped into Gark who had heard the shots (but knew nothing about the holdup). "What's the matter, friend?" Gark shouted.

"Oh, help me, they're after me," Crapaud shouted. He kept running.

"They are, are they? I'm with you, friend," Gark said.

As people from the bank came running around the corner after Crapaud, Gark tackled the first of them, who was named Dasher. As he did so, he said to Dasher, "Leave that poor man alone, friend."

The people behind Dasher tripped over the bodies of him and Gark and there was great confusion. In the melee, Dasher shouted at Gark, "You idiot, that was a bank robber."

"And I'm the king of diamonds. Relax, friend," Gark said, and pushed Dasher down again. Dasher fought back. Haley, one of the bank people who was behind Dasher concluded that Gark was one of the holdup men and that Dasher was trying to capture him. He grabbed Gark around the neck from behind, and tried to pull him off Dasher. Thinking that he had fallen among a gang of dangerous thugs or lunatics and thoroughly frightened, Gark grabbed a brick lying on the pavement and reached around and hit Haley in the head with it. Haley fell to the ground and lost consciousness.

The police arrived and restored order. Haley was put in an ambulance to be taken to the hospital. Speeding through an intersection with the siren sounding, the ambulance was struck by an automobile driven by Leek, who had heard the siren but paid no attention to it because he was preoccupied by an argument he had had with his boss earlier that day. By the time another ambulance arrived at the scene of the accident, Haley had died from head injuries.

In the meantime, Crapaud had boarded a bus and escaped. He arrived home and found that he had $5,742 of bank money. He spent $42 on a floral wreath, which he sent anonymously to Sapo's funeral, and put the remainder in his desk.

So far as you can tell from these facts, what crimes were committed by Sapo, Crapaud, Badger, Wale, Gark, Dasher, Haley, and Leek? Explain your conclusions, where that is necessary.

QUESTION 2: Your boss has asked you to write a memorandum outlining the legal issues in the following case:

A 22-year-old heiress of a wealthy family was kidnapped by a small band of revolutionaries, who held her captive in a closet for several weeks, and repeatedly threatened to kill her unless she sent taped messages to her family. After 10 days of such threats and abuse coupled with deprivation of food and sleep, the heiress [hereafter H] heard a commotion and several shots in the room adjoining her closet. Fearing that she would be killed, she opened the closet door and observed the following scene: a member of the revolutionary group [hereafter M] was lying in a pool of blood; another member of the group [hereafter A] was standing over him with a smoking pistol. Seeing that H had emerged from the closet, A pointed the pistol at H and said, "Now you'll have to die, because you can pin the murder on me. I won't kill you now, since you're still valuable to us. But you'll never leave here alive; we can't afford to let you go now; we will kill you eventually — maybe next week, maybe next month, maybe next year. There's only one way out for you. M is dying, but he's not dead yet. If you kill him, I will be able to trust you. What'll it be? Do you kill him or do I kill you? M has only 5 or 10 minutes to live, so you have two minutes to make up your mind." Fearing that she would be killed, H said she would kill M. She was then given a pistol and told it had one bullet in it. Still covered by A's pistol, she was told to shoot M — through the head, which she did.

Over the next several weeks H became convinced that she was guilty of first degree murder and she began to identify more and more with the group. Soon she was allowed out of the closet. A month after the shooting of M, the police received an anonymous telephone tip that H was being held in the house where she was, in fact, being held. The police — without a warrant — surrounded the house and burst through the front and back doors with their guns drawn. H was sitting at a table with A when the raid took place; nobody else was in the house at the time. As the police came through the door, A handed H one of the two sub-machine guns that were under the table, shouting, "It's the pigs; they're going to kill us; we have to protect ourselves!" H and A began shooting and one policeman was killed before A and H were subdued and taken prisoner. The bullet that killed the policeman came either from A's gun or from H's gun but it cannot be determined from which, since the guns were mixed up in the excitement. After A and H were arrested, handcuffed, and removed from the building, the police — without a search warrant — conducted a search of the entire house, claiming that they were looking for other members of the group. In the process of searching for other members, they opened closets, drawers and cabinets, and seized numerous papers, including a diary kept by A from the beginning of the kidnapping and a diary kept by H beginning the day after the shooting of M. A's diary reveals that on the morning of the shooting of M, A discovered that M was an undercover agent for the F.B.I. Deciding that M had to be killed, A contrived to have H kill him. A knocked M unconscious and spilled animal blood around his body and then fired two shots into the air. H then killed M as A had planned (as previously described). A's diary also revealed that he had put LSD into H's drinking water the day before the killing of M. H's diary revealed that she did not know that M was an informant, and that she believed that M was alive but dying at the time she shot him. It also reveals that she did not think that A would kill her immediately if she refused to shoot M, but she did think there was a good chance she would be killed at some future time. The diary also reveals that H hated M because M had constantly threatened to rape and kill her in the early days of her kidnapping and that H felt pleasure when she shot M. There is a statute, enacted just before the kidnapping of H, which provides for a mandatory sentence of death for the first degree murder of a law enforcement official.

You are an assistant either to the prosecuting attorney or the defense attorney for H (pick either one). Your boss has asked you to write a memorandum outlining the issues in the case, including the crimes that the defendants (both H and A) can reasonably be charged with and the defenses they can reasonably raise. If any facts are unclear or if facts that you deem critical are not stated, indicate what they are and how they would affect your analysis.

QUESTION 3: Foyle and Pierce went to Smitty's Novelty Shop to buy masks that they intended to use in a holdup of the Lightheart Liquor Store, which was a few hundred yards away from Smitty's, in the same block of stores. While he was waiting on them, Smitty overheard Foyle say Pierce, "We can hit Lightheart at night, when there are no customers. They'll have the whole day's receipts then too." Smitty concluded that the two women planned to hold up the liquor store. He sold them masks. He said nothing about the holdup. He decided that he would watch to see when the holdup took place and that if he had an opportunity to help Foyle and Pierce he would do so, in hope of sharing in the loot.

Three nights later, Foyle and Pierce, wearing masks, entered the Lightheart Liquor Store. They displayed revolvers and ordered Bear and Wolf, two clerks, to go around to the back of the counter with their hands up. Foyle opened the cash register, which was empty. Wolf said, "There's no money there. The store is closed today because we are taking inventory." Pierce ordered the clerks not to leave the store, and both women ran out. When they got outside, they found that their "getaway" car (which was a stolen car) was blocked by another car illegally double-parked beside it, in which Driver was sitting. Pierce shouted at him, "Move that car."

"Take it easy, lady, you got a roast in the oven?" Driver responded. Angered, Pierce shot him.

"You fool," Foyle shouted to Pierce. "There was't supposed to be any shooting." They both started to run down the street.

Smitty had heard the shot and guessed what was happening. As Foyle and Pierce ran by his shop, he opened the door and said, "In here." The women ran into his shop. He led them through the back of the shop to an exit onto an alley. They ran out. Smitty shouted after them, "Don't forget me now."

As they came out of the alleyway, Lindsey, who was carelessy not looking where he was going, crashed into Foyle and knocked her down. "Oh, I'm terribly sorry, madam," Lindsey said, and bent down to help her up. Foyle punched Lindsey in the face. He fell down.

"That's dumb," said Pierce. They ran up the street.

A policeman who had seen Foyle punch Lindsey (but knew nothing about the preceding events) ran after them. When they failed to stop in response to his shouted command, he fired his pistol twice, both times aiming high with the intention of firing over their heads. He failed to reckon sufficiently on the steep upward incline of the street. One shot hit Foyle in the leg. The other shot hit the tire of a car.

The car was being driven by Sport, whose license had expired ten days previously, as he knew, and had not been renewed. The tire burst. The car careened and hit Morton, who was crossing the street against the traffic light, which constituted jaywalking, a minor traffic offense for which the maximum fine was $5.00. Morton was crushed under the car and died instantly.

Driver died in the hospital the next day, from the bullet wound. Lindsey recovered from his fall and went home, which was several blocks away. He was in a disturbed state. After he told his wife about the incident, he lay down on a couch. Two hours later, his wife discovered that he was breathing badly, and called an ambulance. He died that night. The attending physician said that he had suffered a heart attack.

In the Lightheart Liquor Store, Wolf took the opportunity afforded by the excitement to remove a bottle of brandy from the shelf and place it in his coat pocket. He took the brandy home without paying for it and drank it that night to calm his nerves. What crimes were committed, and by whom?

ANSWER TO QUESTION 1:

Conspiracy by Sapo, Crapaud and Badger: Sapo, Crapaud and Badger have all agreed to commit the crime of larceny (and perhaps the crime of robbery). Therefore, they are guilty of *conspiracy* to commit those crimes.

Badger might argue that she has not agreed to do anything unlawful; she has simply agreed to hand over money to gunmen, which is probably in accord with the policies of the Bank anyway. However, she has clearly agreed to be party to a crooked scheme, and will receive money if all goes well; this should suffice for conspiracy liability.

Badger may also argue that she *withdrew* from the conspiracy. However, the common law does not recognize a defense of withdrawal from a conspiracy at all (p. 189). Some states, and the Model Penal Code, might recognize withdrawal as a defense, but even these require that the conspiracy be thwarted. It is not sufficient that Badger took action which could reasonably be expected to thwart the robbery, if this did not happen. (p. 190).

Robbery by Sapo, Crapaud and Badger: Sapo and Crapaud (and perhaps Badger) are guilty of robbery, which is defined as theft from the person or presence of another, by force or intimidation (p. 308). Since Badger was originally part of the plan, it is not clear whether force or intimidation should be deemed to have been used against her. Also, the facts indicate that she passed over the money not out of fear of violence, but fear that her part in the plan would be discovered. In any event, if it can be shown that anyone else in the bank was placed in fear, robbery would exist, since the property would have been taken from the "presence" of these others.

Badger may also be liable for robbery, as an *accomplice*. She certainly gave aid and encouragement at the beginning, which would be enough for accomplice liability. But she may be able to raise the defense of *withdrawal*. Less is required for withdrawal by an accomplice than by a conspirator (p. 218). However, even an accomplice must bring home his withdrawal to the other conspirators, which Badger has not done. A court might, however, hold that her attempt to do so sufficed. Alternatively, Badger could argue that she cannot be an accomplice to the robbery of herself; this argument might be rebutted by showing that other persons present were placed in fear of the gun.

Larceny and embezzlement by Sapo, Crapaud and Badger: Sapo and Crapaud have committed either larceny or embezzlement. If Badger is regarded as still having been part of the plan when she handed over the money, the crime is probably embezzlement by all three, since modern embezzlement statutes cover an employee who appropriates property already in her lawful possession. (Sapo and Crapaud would be viewed as accomplices to Badger's embezzlement in this situation.)

If, on the other hand, Badger is not regarded as part of the theft, the crime by Sapo and Crapaud is larceny, since they took the property unlawfully from the possession of Badger and the bank.

Battery by Sapo: Sapo may be guilty of battery. He did not intend to collide with Wale, but it may suffice that he was *criminally negligent* in doing so (p. 266). Alternatively, Sapo, since he was in the process of committing an "unlawful act" (the robbery), might be guilty on that ground alone, by analogy to the misdemeanor-manslaughter rule (p. 259). If Sapo were guilty of battery on either of these theories, Crapaud might be liable as an accomplice.

Murder or manslaughter by Wale: Wale is almost certainly liable for some kind of homicide in the death of Sapo. He might argue that he acted in self-defense or in order to apprehend the felon, but both of these defenses require that the actor have been aware of the necessity for them (p. 114). The factors indicate that Wale did not know anything about the holdup at the time he did the shooting.

Wale may be able to get the charge reduced to *voluntary manslaughter*; a more-than-trivial battery is generally considered to be sufficient provocation (p. 252). However, it is not clear that there was a battery, and even if there was, the court might hold that only a battery which Wale could reasonably have regarded as intentional should suffice. Nor, of course, will Wale be entitled to have his own highly excitable temperament taken into account in determining whether the provocation was sufficient (p. 251).

Felony-murder of Sapo by Crapaud: Arguably, Crapaud may be liable for the felony-murder of Sapo, since Sapo's death occurred "in the commission of" the robbery. However, many courts now refuse to apply the felony-murder doctrine where the person killed is a co-felon, on the theory that the doctrine only covers the death of innocent persons (pp. 240-241). Also, some courts have refused to apply the doctrine to a shooting by a bystander (p. 239). A felony-murder conviction is even less likely here, since the shooting by Wale was not even in resistance to the robbery, or done in an attempt to apprehend Sapo.

Battery by Gark against Dasher: Gark is probably guilty of battery against Dasher. Gark had the necessary intent, since he intended to make the bodily contact, even though he may have been mistaken as to other facts.

Gark could raise the defense that he was defending another (Crapaud). His success depends in part on whether the jurisdiction is one which follows the "alter ego" rule (p. 122); if it does, Gark has no defense, since Crapaud would not have been privileged to use force against his pursuers. If the "alter ego" rule is not in effect, and Gark can show that his mistake as to who was the aggressor was reasonable, his defense will probably be valid, at least as to the first tackle. But it is unlikely that his second pushing-down of Dasher is justifiable, since here, a reasonable man would probably have believed Dasher's statement about Crapaud's being a bank robber, and would therefore have known that force against Dasher was not lawful.

Battery by Haley against Gark: Haley has committed a battery against Gark, unless he can establish the defense that he reasonably believed Gark to be one of the robbers, and was trying to prevent his escape. Escape prevention is a grounds for use of reasonable force (p. 129), provided that the belief in the need for it is either correct or reasonably mistaken.

Battery by Gark against Haley: Gark is guilty of a battery (and perhaps manslaughter) against Haley, unless he can establish ***self-defense***. It is usually held that one may use force to defend against only if the latter is ***unlawful*** (pp. 107-108). Since Haley's use of force against Gark may have been lawful (if Haley reasonably believed Gark to be one of the bank robbers), this requirement for self-defense would not be met. However, a court would probably allow self-defense if Gark showed that his mistake as to the lawfulness of Haley's motives was in turn a reasonable one. But since Gark was already on notice that this was a bank robbery, he might be unable to make this showing.

Even if Gark is able to show a reasonable mistake, it may nonetheless be held that he used a greater degree of force than necessary in the circumstances. The use of the brick to hit Haley in the head might even be considered ***deadly force*** (force intended or likely to cause serious bodily injury), so that in some states Gark would have had a duty to retreat if he could have safely done so (p. 112).

Involuntary manslaughter of Haley by Leek: Leek may be guilty of involuntary manslaughter of Haley. This will depend on whether Leek was reckless or criminally negligent (depending on the jurisdiction). It seems doubtful that mere inattention to a siren would constitute anything more than ordinary civil negligence. But if Leek is held to be reckless or grossly negligent, he can try to raise the defense that he was not the proximate cause of death, since the death occurred from head injuries inflicted by Gark. However, it is surely a foreseeable consequence of failing to pay heed to an ambulance siren that a collision may result and that the patient may die because he cannot receive treatment for his pre-existing injuries. This would seem to be an extension of the rule that one takes one's victim as one finds him (p. 52).

Alternatively, if Leek's failure to pull over at the sound of the siren constituted a violation of traffic laws, this might trigger application of the ***misdemeanor-manslaughter*** rule. In that event, Leek's proximate cause argument would have even less chance of success, since proximate cause is often virtually suspended in misdemeanor-manslaughter cases based upon ***malum in se*** violations (p. 260).

Murder or manslaughter by Gark: Gark may be liable for the murder of Haley, since murder may be based upon an intent to do serious bodily injury, or a "reckless indifference to the value of human life." Gark can, of course, raise self-defense, but this will not necessarily succeed (as discussed above in the context of the battery of Haley). Gark may also claim that his blow was not a proximate cause of Haley's death, because of the intervening traffic accident. However, assuming that the head injuries which proved fatal to Haley were from the blow (rather than the collision), the proximate cause defense is unlikely to work, since the case will probably come within the rule that a third party's failure to act will never be a superseding cause. (p. 57). That is, the ambulance driver's failure to get Haley to the hospital cannot absolve Gark of liability. (However, Leek's act of affirmative negligence might be sufficiently abnormal and unforeseeable so as to be held to have broken the chain of causation).

If Gark's proximate cause defense fails, but he is not shown to have had the requisite intent for murder, he will probably be liable for involuntary manslaughter. This might be founded on the fact that he committed a battery, triggering the misdemeanor-manslaughter rule. It is not clear whether the death occurred "in the commission of" the battery. But since the blow itself is what finally killed Haley, the requisite link between the battery and the death probably exists.

Felony-murder by Crapaud: It is possible that Crapaud is liable for the felony-murder of Haley. However, this is unlikely, since: (1) the killing was not from the hand of Crapaud or his co-robbers; and (2) the chain of events leading from the robbery to Haley's death is quite bizarre and unforeseeable.

ANSWER TO QUESTION 2:

CRIMES BY A

Murder of M as accomplice or principal: A is probably guilty of the murder of M, either as accomplice or as principal. A has obviously aided and abetted H's shooting of M, so he is potentially liable as an accomplice (p. 206). However, it is usually required that, for accomplice liability, the principal be guilty (p. 216). As is discussed below, H may have a defense to murder (perhaps duress); if so, A may escape accomplice liability. However, a modern tendency has been to allow an accomplice to be held guilty even though certain defenses are available to the "principal" (p. 218).

Alternatively, A may be guilty of murder as a *principal*. A court might take the view that H was merely an innocent agent, whose conduct was controlled by A. See, e.g., *R.v. Cogan* (p. 218). If A is found to have been a principal to murder, it might well be held to be first-degree, since A was aware that M was a law enforcement official.

Alternatively, A may be liable for *felony-murder*. That is, the killing of M might be viewed as having been in furtherance of the kidnapping scheme. But it seems to me that A can successfully argue that the killing of M was unrelated to the kidnapping, and was not a "natural and probable" result of it (p. 212).

Conspiracy to murder M: A may be guilty of conspiring to murder M. However, it seems probable that there has been no "agreement" between A and H, but rather, duress used against H. If H's duress defense is found not to be valid, perhaps the necessary agreement would exist.

Battery of M: A is clearly guilty of committing a battery on M, since he knocked M unconscious.

Battery of H: A, by placing LSD in H's drink, may be guilty of committing a battery against her. Battery is the intentional causing of bodily injury, and administering of a hallucinogenic drug would probably qualify. It is not necessary that the injury be caused directly (e.g., by a blow).

Murder of policeman: A is probably guilty of murdering the policeman, either as an accomplice or as a principal. Obviously, if the prosecution can show that the fatal bullet came from A's gun, he is liable as principal. But even if this cannot be shown, A clearly aided H in the shooting (by giving her the gun). This would be enough to make A an accomplice to murder. Under modern procedural rules, it is probably not necessary that the prosecution specify in the indictment whether A is charged with being an accomplice or a principal, so long as enough facts are stated to allow A to defend himself.

Conspiracy to murder the policeman: A may also be guilty of conspiring to murder the policeman, since there was probably a tacit agreement (even though very hurriedly reached) between A and H to shoot at the policeman. See *U.S. v. James* (p. 176).

CRIMES BY H

Murder of M: H is probably guilty of the murder of M. She had the necessary intent to kill, despite the fact that she believed that M was already dying; it is probably enough that one intends to hasten the already inevitable death of another. (Certainly H's shot would have been the "cause in fact" of M's death even if he had actually been dying prior to the shot; p. 45).

H may be able raise the defense of *duress*. However, the court might very well hold that the duress defense is not available where the charge is murder as a principal, which the threatened shooting of H by A was not. However, the Model Penal Code would not impose such a requirement, provided that a person of "reasonable firmness" would have been "unable to resist" the threat; in view of H's deprivation of food and sleep, and the previous abuse directed to her, the Model Penal Code's test might be met.

Assuming that H can overcome these hurdles to a duress defense, the defense is probably not lost by the fact that H hated M, and took pleasure in killing him. These factors would, of course, have some evidentiary bearing on whether H really acted out of duress, but as long as duress was the principal motivation, the other facts would probably be disregarded.

It is conceivable that H may be able to raise the defense of *involuntary intoxication*, based on A's having given her LSD (p. 89). However, H would probably have to show that the drug contributed materially to her shooting of M; that this was the case is not indicated by the facts as given.

If the duress and intoxication defenses fail, the murder will probably be *first-degree*. Assuming that one of the purposes of the statute imposing severe penalites on killings of law enforcement personnel is to protect such personnel, the killer's lack of knowledge that an officer was involved would probably be irrelevant. The problem is similar to that posed in *U.S. v. Feola* (p. 180), where the Supreme Court held that one could be guilty of conspiracy to assault a federal enforcement official without knowledge that the victim was an official.

H may be able to get the charge reduced from murder to **voluntary manslaughter**. She might argue that M's mistreatment of her brought her to a rage, of the sort that would have provoked a "reasonable man." However, since M's misconduct occurred early on in the kidnapping, a "cooling off" period may have passed (p. 254). Alternatively, a manslaughter verdict might be justified by a theory of "imperfect" duress, since H was obviously acting under a fair amount of coercion (p. 256).

Conspiracy to murder M: H may also be guilty of conspiring to murder M. Again, however, it is not clear that she has made the necessary "agreement." Also, she can raise the same defenses against the conspiracy charge as against the murder charge.

Murder of policeman: If it cannot be determined whose gun the bullet that killed the policeman came from, H can probably escape liability for murder. H can assert that the bullet came from A's gun. On that hypothesis, H would probably not be an accomplice to the killing, since there is not much evidence that she aided or abetted A's conduct. (However, the prosecution might succeed in arguing that merely by virtue of H's participating in the shoot-out with A, she gave him encouragement, thus making her an accomplice.)

Felony-murder of policeman: Since the killing of the policeman took place in the course of an assault on a group of police, the felony-murder rule might apply. The assault, since it was made with a deadly weapon, was probably the felony of aggravated assault. However, H can argue that the assault here was included in the killing, and that the requirement of an independent felony is therefore not met (p. 243). But the prosecution can counter that several police were being assaulted, and that a felonious assault against the ones other than the dead officer can support a felony-murder conviction.

Conspiracy to murder policeman: Finally, there is a small chance that H might be liable for conspiring to murder the policeman, again on the grounds that she participated in the shoot-out and thereby acted in concert with A.

ANSWER TO QUESTION 3:

Conspiracy to rob by Foyle and Pierce: Foyle and Pierce are clearly guilty of **conspiracy to rob** the liquor store. They have obviously reached an agreement to commit the robbery, and have met any overt act requirement.

Conspiracy to rob by Smitty: It is not so clear whether Smitty has joined this conspiracy. A person who sells non-contraband items with knowledge that they will be used for criminal purposes will not usually be held to have joined a conspiracy, if he does not actively desire a criminal result. (p. 180). However, Smitty's additional intent to assist if he can do so may be enough to give him the required mental state. As there has been no agreement by Smitty on the one hand and Foyle and Pierce on the other that Smitty will help them, Smitty might escape conspiracy liability (p. 176).

Attempted robbery by Foyle and Pierce: Foyle and Pierce have committed **attempted robbery**, regardless of what test is used to determine the sufficiency of their acts. They might try to raise the defense of "factual impossibility," but this defense is extremely unlikely to succeed — the situation is not very different from that of a pickpocket who finds that his victim is not carrying a wallet; the pickpocket would certainly be guilty of attempted larceny (pp. 157-158).

Attempted robbery by Smitty: Smitty might be liable for attempted robbery as an **accomplice**. Such accomplice liability for an unsuccessful attempt seems allowable in principle (p. 208). However, Smitty has not directly aided or encouraged the attempt (as distinguished from the escape) except by selling goods. It is questionable whether his sale of goods, coupled with his knowledge that the attempt would take place, and intent to render assistance in the future, if needed, add up to accomplice liability. Certainly the sale of the goods with knowledge is not by itself sufficient (p. 210).

Robbery by Foyle and Pierce: Foyle and Pierce are not guilty of robbery, because that crime requires an underlying taking of property, and nothing was taken from the liquor store.

Murder of Driver by Pierce and Foyle: Pierce seems clearly guilty of murdering Driver. She might try to get this reduced to *voluntary manslaughter* on the theory that Driver provoked her, and she acted in a heat of passion. However, words of harrassment or abuse are almost never accepted as the sort of provocation that will cause a "reasonable person" to lose his temper. (p. 253).

Foyle may be liable for the *felony-murder* of Driver. Pierce committed the killing while attempting to commit a dangerous felony (robbery), and the killing could be viewed as "in the commission of" the robbery. Foyle might then be an accomplice to Pierce's felony-murder. However, since Pierce killed out of anger, and not directly in furtherance of a felony, Foyle might be able to show that the killing was not the "natural or probable" result of the robbery. But this case seems a lot like *U.S. v. Carter* (p. 214), where the accomplice was found guilty of felony-murder, despite his disapproval of the killing.

It is conceivable that Smitty might also be found guilty of the felony-murder of Driver. However, it is not even clear that he was an accomplice to the robbery, so the connection between him and the death of Driver is probably too attenuated for liability.

Accessory after the fact by Smitty: Smitty is probably an accessory after the fact to attempted robbery. Although he did not know the precise details of the robbery attempt, or that it had failed, he probably still had the requisite knowledge of the essential elements of the crime. (p. 221). He might also conceivably be guilty of attempted compounding of crime, since he was hoping to receive money from the robbers for his help (p. 222).

Murder or manslaughter of Lindsey by Pierce and Foyle: Foyle might conceivably be guilty of murdering Lindsey, based upon an intent to do *serious bodily injury*. However, it would probably be found that Foyle intended to commit merely a minor battery, rather than serious bodily harm.

Alternatively, Foyle may be guilty of *felony-murder* in Lindsey's death. The episode took place while the two were attempting to escape, and this might be viewed as having been part of the "commission" of the attempted robbery. However, the requisite causal relationship between the punch and the heart attack may be lacking. If Lindsey would have had a fatal heart attack exactly when he did, even without the punch in the face, the punch is not a "cause in fact" of death. If, however, the heart attack occurred earlier than it would have (even if it would have happened eventually) the punch is probably both a cause in fact and a proximate cause of the death. This is an application of a "pre-existing weakness" rule (p. 52).

Foyle may, alternatively, be liable for *misdemeanor-manslaughter* in the death of Lindsey. She has committed a battery, which will suffice for misdemeanor-manslaughter liability (pp. 259-260). Again, however, the necessary causal relationship between the blow and Lindsey's death may be lacking; this is likely to be determined in essentially the same way as causation in the felony-murder context (discussed in the preceding paragraph).

Whatever homicide Foyle is found liable for in Lindsey's death, Pierce may have the same liability on an *accomplice* basis. However, she can argue that neither the collision between Lindsey and Foyle, nor Foyle's punch, was the "natural and probable" consequence of a robbery attempt, and that accomplice liability should therefore not apply (p. 213). This issue is similar to the question of whether Foyle is liable as an accomplice to Pierce's killing of Driver.

Battery and manslaughter liability of Policeman: If Policeman is found to have been grossly negligent or reckless in the way he shot towards Foyle and Pierce, he may be liable for battery of Foyle. This is because intent is not necessary where gross negligence or recklessness exist (p. 266). He may be able to raise the defense of *attempted arrest*.

However, as far as Policeman knew, Foyle was merely a misdemeanant; *deadly force* may not be used against misdemeanants (p. 127). The court would probably find that firing a gun constitutes use of deadly force, even if the intent is to shoot over the target's head. (The Model Penal Code would make the shooting deadly force if the gun was fired "in the direction" of another person, which Policeman seems to have done (p. 111).)

Policeman might also claim that Foyle and Pierce were in reality *felons,* and that he was therefore permitted to use deadly force against them. However, it does not seem likely that the fact that they were, unbeknownst to Policeman, felons, will shield Policeman; for instance, self-defense may not be claimed where one was not aware of the danger until later (p. 114).

Policeman may also be guilty of *manslaughter* in the death of Morton. He may have *misdemeanor-manslaughter* liability, if his using his gun against persons believed to be mere misdemeanants constitutes a misdemeanor (perhaps assault or, in the case of the shot which hit Foyle, battery). Alternatively, he may be guilty of ordinary involuntary manslaughter, if his failure to take the steepness of the hill into account constitutes recklessness or gross negligence (whichever the jurisdiction requires) (p. 257). Some jurisdictions may require an actual awareness of the risk on Policeman's part, in which case he will probably not be liable. (p. 258). Policeman might also try to show that his shot was not the proximate cause of Morton's death, since it was somewhat unlikely that the shot would puncture the tire, and lead to a traffic accident. However, this chain of events is not completely "bizarre" or "abnormal", and the necessary causal relationship may well be found. (pp. 51, 54-54).

Finally, Policeman may rely on the same "attempted arrest" defense as he will use on the battery charge. However, even assuming that the other requirements for the defense are met (which, as noted, is questionable), the defense only exists if his act presented no unreasonable danger to persons other than the fleeing criminals. (See p. 119 as to the same issue in the context of self-defense).

Misdemeanor-manslaughter by Sport: Sport might conceivably be liable for misdemeanor-manslaughter in the death of Morton. Sport's failure to renew his license is probably a misdemeanor. However, it is *"malum prohibitum"* rather than *"malum in se."* No matter which of the three tests for proximate cause is used (pp. 260-261), it is hard to see how Sport's failure to renew his license has any direct causal relationship to the accident (except for the fact that had he not been driving at all the accident would not have occurred). Therefore, Sport will probably escape liability.

Larceny or embezzlement by Wolf: Wolf has probably committed either larceny or embezzlement. He was probably not entrusted with "possession" of liquor sitting out on the shelves, so his taking is probably larceny (i.e., an unlawful taking from the liquor store's possession). (p. 286). However, he will not be guilty of larceny if, at the time he took the liquor, he intended to pay for it subsequently. This is true regardless of whether he ultimately changed his mind and decided not to pay (p. 291). If he did not intend to pay at the time he took the liquor, he might try to claim the defense of necessity or duress, since he used the liquor to calm his nerves. However, these defenses are available only where there was no third, non-criminal alternative (p. 104). Since Wolf was free to pay for the liquor, these two defenses seem not to apply.

MULTIPLE CHOICE QUESTIONS

Here are 26 multiple-choice questions, in a Multistate Bar Exam style. These questions are taken from *"The Finz Multistate Method"*, a compendium of 1100 questions in the Multistate subjects (*Contracts*, *Torts*, *Property*, *Evidence*, *Criminal Law* and *Constitutional Law*) written by Professor Steven Finz of National University School of Law, San Diego, CA, and published by us. This book is available at your bookstore or directly from Emanuel Publishing Corp.

1. On Darr's birthday, his friend Mead gave him a new television as a gift. The following day, when Darr opened the box and began using the television, he noticed that there was no warranty document with it. Darr phoned Mead and asked Mead for the missing warranty document. Mead said, "I can't give it to you because the television was stolen." Darr kept the television and continued using it.

   Darr was guilty of

   (A) receiving stolen property only.

   (B) larceny only.

   (C) receiving stolen property and larceny.

   (D) no crime.

Questions 2-3 are based on the following fact situation.

   Tom, John and Sam were teenaged boys staying at a summer camp. One evening Vanney, a camp counselor, ordered Tom and John to go to bed immediately after dinner. Outside the dining hall, Tom and John decided to get even with Vanney. Having seen Vanney take medicine for an asthma condition, they agreed to kill Vanney by finding his medicine and throwing it away. Tom and John did not know whether Vanney would die without the medicine, but they both hoped that he would.

   Sam, who disliked Vanney, overheard the conversation between Tom and John and hoped that their plan would succeed. He decided to help them without saying anything about it. Going into Vanney's room, Sam searched through Van-

ney's possessions until he found the medicine. Then he put it on a night table so that Tom and John would be sure to find it.

   As Tom and John were walking towards Vanney's room, John decided not to go through with the plan. Because he was afraid that Tom would make fun of him for chickening out, he said nothing to Tom about his change of mind. Instead, saying that he needed to use the bathroom, he ran away. Tom went into Vanney's room by himself, found the medicine where Sam had left it on the night table, and threw the medicine away. Later that night, Vanney had an asthma attack and died because he was unable to find his medicine.

   A statute in the jurisdiction provides that persons the age of Tom, John and Sam are adults for purposes of criminal liability.

2. If Sam is charged with conspiracy, a court will probably find him

   (A) guilty, because he knowingly aided and abetted in the commission of a crime.

   (B) guilty, because he committed an overt act in furtherance of an agreement to throw away Vanney's medicine.

   (C) not guilty, because he did not agree to commit any crime.

   (D) not guilty, because John effectively withdrew from any conspiracy which existed.

3. If John is charged with the murder of Vanney, a court will probably find him

(A) guilty, because he and Tom agree to throw away Vanney's medicine in the hope that doing so would cause Vanney's death.

(B) guilty, because he aided and abetted in causing Vanney's death.

(C) not guilty, because he did not physically participate in throwing away Vanney's medicine.

(D) not guilty, because he withdrew from the conspiracy before any overt act was committed.

4. Larraby worked as a lifeguard from 5 P.M. to 8 P.M. every night at a public swimming pool operated by the City of Muni. At 8 P.M., Larraby told her boss she was going and left, although the pool had become quite crowded with adults and young children. At 9 P.M., Susan, a nine-year-old child, fell into the pool, striking her head against its edge. Watcher, one of the adults swimming in the pool, saw Susan fall and realized that the child would drown if someone did not rescue her. Watcher had seen Larraby leave and knew that there was no lifeguard present, but made no effort to rescue Susan although Watcher was a strong swimmer and could easily have done so with no risk to herself. Susan drowned. If Watcher is charged with criminal homicide in the death of Susan, the court should find her

(A) guilty, because she could have saved Susan without any risk to herself.

(B) guilty, if she knew that she was the only person present who was aware of Susans's plight and who was able to rescue her.

(C) not guilty, unless she was related to Susan.

(D) not guilty, because she had no duty to aid Susan.

5. Diller purchased an ounce of cocaine and divided it into fifty packets of about one-half gram each. She was selling them outside the local high school when Gunn, a cocaine user, noticed her and saw the opportunity to get some free drugs. Gunn stepped up beside her. With his hand in the pocket of his jacket, he thrust his finger forward inside the pocket and jabbed her in the ribs with it. Snarling, he said, "I've got a gun. Give me the dope or I'll blow you away." Diller reached into her purse, drew a small pistol which she kept there, and shot Gunn, killing him.

If Diller is charged with the murder of Gunn, she should be found

(A) guilty, because it was unreasonable for her to use deadly force to protect illegal contraband.

(B) guilty, if Gunn was unarmed.

(C) guilty, because Diller was committing a crime and therefore had no privilege of self-defense.

(D) not guilty, if it was reasonable for her to believe that her life was in danger.

6. Anthony was a resident patient at the state mental hospital, where he had been receiving treatment for a mental illness diagnosed as chronic paranoid schizophrenia. As a result of his illness, he believed that the governor of his state was part of a nationwide plot to turn all voting citizens into drug addicts. He felt that the only way to foil the plot was to kill the governor, but realized that the law prohibited such an act. He knew that if he was caught making any attempt on the governor's life he would be punished, but concluded that it would be better to be convicted and punished for a crime than to be turned into a drug addict.

Knowing that the governor visited the hospital every few months, and that when he did he usually ate in the hospital dining room, Anthony volunteered for a job in the hospital kitchen. On the governor's next visit, Anthony placed poison in food he knew would be served to the governor, intending to cause the governor's death. The governor ate the food and died as a result. If Anthony is charged with murder in a jurisdiction which has adopted only the M'Naghten test of insanity, Anthony should be found

(A) guilty, since he knew the nature of his act, and that it was prohibited by law.

(B) guilty, unless Anthony can establish that his mental illness made him unable to resist the impulse to kill the governor.

(C) not guilty, since Anthony's conduct was the result of mental illness.

(D) not guilty, if his delusion was the result of mental disease, and if his conduct was reasonable within the context of that delusion.

7. Ventana was a professional basketball player scheduled to play in an important basketball game on Sunday. On Friday, after wagering heavily on the game, Duggan attacked Ventana with a baseball bat. Duggan's intent was to inflict injuries severe enough to require hospitalization and thus keep Ventana from playing as planned. As a result of the beating, Ventana was taken to a hospital, where he was treated by Dr. Medich. The following day, Dr. Medich injected Ventana with a medicine to relieve his pain. Because of an allergic reaction to the drug, Ventana died within minutes.

If Duggan is charged with the murder of Ventana, he should be found

(A) not guilty, because Ventana's allergic reaction to the drug was an intervening cause of death.

(B) not guilty, if Ventana's death was proximately caused by Dr. Medich's negligence.

(C) guilty, only if Ventana's death was proximately caused by Duggan's attack.

(D) guilty, unless Dr. Medich's conduct is found to be reckless or grossly negligent.

8. Darrel knew that his neighbor Volmer had a weak heart and that Volmer had suffered several heart attacks in the past. Because he was angry at Volmer, Darrel decided to try to frighten him into another heart attack. He watched Volmer's house and when he saw Volmer leaving through the front door, he ran towards him shouting, "Look out. Look out. The sky is falling," Although Darrel was not sure that this would kill Volmer, he hoped it would. When Volmer saw Darrel running toward him, shouting, he became frightened, had a heart attack and died on the spot.

The jurisdiction has statutes which define first degree murder as "the deliberate and premeditated killing of a human being," and second degree murder as "any unlawful killing of a human being with malice aforethought, except for a killing which constitutes first degree murder." In addition, its statutes adopt common law definitions of voluntary and involuntary manslaughter.

Which of the following is the most serious crime of which Darrel can properly be convicted?

(A) First degree murder.

(B) Second degree murder.

(C) Voluntary manslaughter.

(D) Involuntary manslaughter.

Questions 9-10 are based on the following fact situation.

Angry because her co-worker Ventura had insulted her, Delman decided to get revenge. Because she worked for an exterminator, Delman had access to cans of a poison gas called Terminate which was often used to kill termites and other insects. She did not want to kill Ventura, so she carefully read the use manual supplied by the manufacturer. The manual said that Terminate was not fatal to human beings, but that exposure to it could cause serious ailments including blindness and permanent respiratory irritation. When she was sure that no one would see her, Delman brought a can of Terminate to the parking lot and released the poison gas into Ventura's car. At lunchtime, Ventura and his friend Alex sat together in Ventura's car. As a result of their exposure to the Terminate in the car, Alex died and Ventura became so ill that he was hospitalized for over a month.

9. If Delman is charged with the murder of Alex, she should be found

(A) guilty, because Alex's death resulted from an act which Delman performed with the intent to cause great bodily harm to a human being.

(B) guilty, because the use of poison gas is an inherently dangerous activity.

(C) not guilty, because she did not know that Alex would be exposed to the poison gas.

(D) not guilty, because she did not intend to cause the death of any person.

10. If Delman is charged with the attempted murder of Ventura, she should be found

(A) guilty, because Ventura suffered a serious illness as the result of a criminal act which she performed with intent to cause him great bodily harm.

(B) guilty, because her intent to cause great bodily harm resulted in the death of Alex.

(C) not guilty, because she did not intend to cause the death of any person.

(D) not guilty, because the crime of attempted murder merges with the crime of murder.

Questions 11-12 are based on the following fact situation.

Conn had just been released from prison after serving a three year term for aggravated assault. In need of money, he called his old friend Delbert and asked whether Delbert would be interested in joining Conn in the robbery of Perry's Pawnshop. Delbert agreed, but only after making Conn promise that there would be no violence. Upon Delbert's insistence, they carried realistic-looking toy guns and when they entered Perry's Pawnshop, they drew their toy guns and ordered Perry to give them all the money in his cash register and all the gems in his safe. Perry took a gun from the safe and shot Conn, killing him. Perry then aimed the pistol at Delbert, who fled from the store. As Perry ran out into the street with his pistol in his hand, Delbert jumped into the car which he and Conn had left parked at the curb. Speeding away from the scene, Delbert acciden-

tally struck Nora, a pedestrian, who died of her injuries. By statute, the jurisdiction has adopted the felony-murder rule.

11. If Delbert is charged with the murder of Conn, Delbert's most effective argument in defense is that

(A) Conn was not a victim of the felony which resulted in his death.

(B) Perry was justified in shooting Conn.

(C) the use of toy guns made it unforeseeable that the robbery would result in the death of any person.

(D) Delbert lacked malice aforethought.

12. If Delbert is charged with the murder of Nora, the court should find him

(A) guilty, because Nora's death resulted from Delbert's attempt to commit a robbery.

(B) guilty, only if he drove the car in a criminally negligent manner.

(C) not guilty, if he was in reasonable fear for his own life when attempting to flee in the automobile.

(D) not guilty, because Nora's death did not occur during the commission of a felony.

13. After looking at a car which Samson had advertised for sale, Berrigan agreed to purchase it for three thousand dollars. Berrigan gave Samson one hundred dollars cash, promising to bring the balance and to pick up the car the following day. In fact Samson was a thief who had no intention of selling the car, and had been collecting cash down payments from buyers all over the state. As soon as Berrigan left, Samson ran off with the hundred dollars. One week later, Samson was arrested and charged with embezzlement and larceny by trick. He can properly be convicted of

(A) embezzlement only.

(B) larceny by trick only.

(C) embezzlement and larceny by trick.

(D) neither embezzlement nor larceny by trick.

14. Dafton came home from work to find that his wife and two of his children had been slashed and cut and were lying dead in a pool of blood. His third child was also cut and bleeding severely. As Dafton approached, the child said, "Valens hurt Mommy." Dafton said, "I'll kill that son of a bitch." Then he loaded his shotgun and went next door to the home of the Valens. He knocked on the door, and when Valens opened the door Dafton shot and killed him. State statutes codify the common law definitions of voluntary and involuntary manslaughter, and define first degree murder as "the deliberate and premeditated killing of a human being," and second degree murder as "the killing of a human being with malice aforethought."

If Dafton is charged with voluntary manslaughter, the court should find him

(A) guilty, if he intended the death of Valens because he believed that Valens had killed his wife and children.

(B) guilty, because the killing of Valens was deliberate and premeditated.

(C) not guilty, because the killing of Valens was deliberate and premeditated.

(D) not guilty, if Valens was the killer of Dafton's wife and children.

15. Mildred and Bonnie were college students who needed money. One night, Mildred suggested that they hold up a local convenience store. When Bonnie told her that she was afraid to get involved in a robbery, Mildred offered to go into the store alone if Bonnie would wait outside in the car with the engine running so that they could make a getaway after the robbery. Bonnie agreed on condition that they split the take. The following day, they went together to a sporting goods store where Mildred purchased a shotgun. That night, Bonnie drove Mildred to the convenience store and waited in the parking lot with the engine running. Mildred went into the store with the shotgun hidden in a paper bag. Once inside, she pointed it at the store clerk and made him give her the contents of the cash register. Then she ran out to the car. When Bonnie saw Mildred running toward the car, she became frightened and drove away without waiting for Mildred.

Bonnie is guilty of

(A) conspiracy only.

(B) robbery only.

(C) conspiracy and robbery.

(D) either conspiracy or robbery, but not both.

16. A statute prohibited the sale of liquor between the hours of midnight and 8 A.M. When a customer came into Donohue's liquor store and asked to buy a bottle of liquor, Donohue looked at the clock and saw that it said five minutes past eleven, so he sold the liquor to the customer. Donohue believed that the clock was correct and did not realize that the previous day the state had changed from standard time to daylight savings time. In fact, the correct time was five minutes past midnight.

If Donohue is charged with attempting to violate the statute, he should be found .Q6

(A) guilty, because he sold liquor between midnight and 8 A.M.

(B) guilty, if he should have known the actual time.

(C) not guilty, unless the statute did not require specific intent.

(D) not guilty, because he believed that the time was five minutes past eleven.

Questions 17-18 are based on the following fact situation.

Dailey and Reavis had been in the same cell together while serving time in prison. Soon after their release, Reavis asked Dailey to join with him in robbing a bank. Dailey refused, stating that he did not want to go back to prison. Reavis then said that he would rob the bank himself if Dailey would provide him with a place to hide afterwards. Dailey agreed that Reavis could hide in Dailey's apartment following the robbery in return for one fourth of the proceeds of the robbery. The following day, Reavis robbed the bank. While he was attempting to leave the bank, a security guard began shooting at him, and Reavis fired back, killing a bystander. One week later, Reavis was arrested at Dailey's apartment where he had been hiding, and was charged with robbery and felony murder.

17. Assume for the purpose of this question only that Dailey was subsequently charged with felony murder on the ground that he was an accomplice to the robbery committed by Reavis which resulted in the death of a bystander. The court should find Dailey

   (A) not guilty, because he was an accessory after the fact.

   (B) not guilty, if he did not know that Reavis was going to use deadly force to accomplish the robbery.

   (C) guilty, only if it was foreseeable that someone would be shot during the course of the robbery.

   (D) guilty, because an accomplice is responsible for all crimes committed in furtherance of the crime to which he is an accomplice.

18. Assume for the purpose of this question only that Dailey was charged with conspiracy to commit robbery. The court should find Dailey

   (A) not guilty, because he did not agree to participate in the actual perpetration of the robbery.

   (B) not guilty, because Dailey's agreement to permit Reavis to stay at his apartment following the robbery was not per se unlawful.

   (C) guilty, because he was an accessory to the robbery.

   (D) guilty, because he agreed to furnish Reavis with a place to hide in return for a portion of the proceeds of the robbery.

Questions 19-20 are based on the following fact situation.

Okner was the owner of a department store. One day, Okner asked Shafer, who was employed in the store's shoe department, to temporarily replace a sporting goods salesman who did not show up for work. Yule, who was 15 years of age, subsequently entered the sporting goods department and asked Shafer to sell her ammunition for a pistol. Shafer placed a box of ammunition on the counter and said, "That'll be nine dollars, please." Realizing that she did not have any money with her, Yule left the store without the ammunition, saying that she would return for it later. A statute in the jurisdiction provides as follows: "Any person who sells ammunition for a firearm to a person below the age of 16 years shall be guilty of a felony. The employer of any person who violates this section during the course of such employment shall be guilty of a misdemeanor punishable by a fine not to exceed $250. It shall not be a defense to a violation of this section that the defendant had no knowledge of the age of the person to whom the sale was made."

19. Assume for the purpose of this question only that Yule did not return to the store. If Shafer is charged with attempting to violate the above statute, which of the following would be Shafer's most effective argument in defense against that charge?

   (A) Shafer did not know of the statute or its provisions.

   (B) Shafer did not know that Yule was below the age of 16 years.

   (C) Okner should be prosecuted under the statute, since she was Shafer's employer.

   (D) Shafer is customarily employed in the shoe department, and should not be held to the same standard as a person in the business of selling firearms and ammunition.

20. Assume for the purpose of this question that

Yule subsequently returned to the store with money and that Shafer sold her the ammunition. If Okner is prosecuted under the statute, Okner should be found

(A) guilty, because her employee sold ammunition to a person under the age of 16 years.

(B) guilty, only if it was unreasonable for Okner to assign Shafer to the sporting goods department without properly instructing him regarding the statute.

(C) not guilty, unless Okner was present when Shafer made the sale to Yule.

(D) not guilty, because holding one person vicariously liable for the crime of another violates the constitutional right to due process of law.

Questions 21-22 are based on the following fact situation.

Alice and Bonnie were roommates until they began arguing bitterly. During one argument, Alice moved out of the apartment which they shared. As she left, she said, "I'm going to get even with you for all the grief you've caused me." The following day, Bonnie's friend Frieda told Bonnie that Alice had purchased a gun. Frieda also said that Alice told her that she was going to shoot Bonnie the next time she saw her. As a result, Bonnie began carrying a loaded pistol. Several days later, realizing that she still had the key to Bonnie's apartment, Alice went back to return it. Bonnie was leaving her apartment when she saw Alice walking toward her. As Alice reached into her pocket for the apartment key, Bonnie drew her pistol and shot Alice, aiming to hit her in the chest. The bullet grazed Alice's shoulder, inflicting a minor injury. Alice immediately drew her own pistol and shot Bonnie with it, striking her in the thigh, and inflicting a serious injury.

21. If Bonnie is charged with attempted murder, which of the following would be her most effective argument in defense?

(A) Alice's injury was not serious enough to result in death.

(B) Bonnie did not succeed in striking Alice in the chest as she intended.

(C) It was reasonable for Bonnie to believe that Alice was reaching into her pocket for a gun.

(D) The force which Bonnie used was not deadly.

22. Assume that Alice is charged with attempted murder. If Alice asserts the privilege of self-defense, she will most probably be found

(A) guilty, if it was reasonable for Bonnie to believe that Alice was reaching into her pocket for a gun.

(B) guilty, because Alice's injury was not serious enough to result in death.

(C) guilty, because the fact that Alice was carrying a pistol is evidence of premeditation.

(D) not guilty.

23. Dennison was having dinner in a restaurant with his employer Vale, when Vale left the table to go the restroom. As Vale walked away, Dennison noticed that Vale's wristwatch had fallen off Vale's wrist onto the table. Since it looked like a rather valuable watch, Dennison decided to steal it. Picking up the watch, he put it into his pocket. A few moments later, he began to feel guilty about stealing from his employer, so when Vale returned to the table, Dennison handed him the watch and said, "Here, you dropped this, and I put it into my pocket for safekeeping."

Which is the most serious crime of which Dennison can be properly convicted?

(A) Larceny.

(B) Attempted larceny.

(C) Embezzlement.

(D) No crime.

Questions 24-25 are based on the following fact situation.

Vena was addicted to heroin, and frequently committed acts of prostitution to obtain the money she needed to buy drugs. One night she was out looking for customers for prostitution when she was approached by Dorian who asked what her price was. When she told him that she would have intercourse with him for $20, he said that he would get the money from a friend and see her later. When Vena went home several hours later, Dorian was waiting inside her apartment. He said that he wanted to have sex with her, but when Vena repeated her demand for $20, he said that he had no money. She told him to get out or she would call the police. Dorian took a knife from his pocket, saying that if she did not have intercourse with him he would kill her. Silently, Vena took off her clothes and had intercourse with him.

Immediately afterwards, Dorian fell asleep. Vena tied his hands and feet to the four corners of the bed, and woke him. She said, "Now you are going to be punished for what you have done. I should kill you, but I won't because I want to make sure that you suffer for the rest of your life." Using his own knife, she began to cut and jab him with it, planning to torture but not to kill him. She stabbed and blinded him in both eyes, then cut off his sex organs. She also severed the tip of his nose and made a series of cuts across his face and chest.

24. If Dorian is charged with rape, the court should find him

   (A) guilty, because he overcame Vena's refusal to have intercourse with him by threatening to kill her with his knife.

   (B) not guilty, because Vena's demand for twenty dollars made her resistance conditional and therefore less than total.

   (C) not guilty, because Vena offered no resistance and Dorian did not use physical force.

   (D) not guilty, because of the injuries inflicted by Vena.

25. Assume for the purpose of this question only that

Dorian dies as a result of the injuries inflicted by Vena. Assume further that she is charged with first degree murder in a jurisdiction which defines that crime as "the unlawful killing of a human being committed intentionally, with deliberation and premeditation." The court should find Vena

   (A) not guilty, because Vena did not intend to cause Dorian's death.

   (B) not guilty, because Vena was acting in self-defense.

   (C) guilty, because Dorian's death resulted from Vena's commission of a dangerous felony.

   (D) guilty, because Dorian's death resulted from torture.

26. Dingle had suspected for some time that his wife Wilma was unfaithful to him. One night when she came home later than usual, Dingle confronted her, demanding to know where she had been. Tearfully, Wilma confessed that she had been out with a male friend, and that she had sexual intercourse with him. Dingle flew into a rage, striking Wilma repeatedly about the face and head with his clenched fist. The following day, Wilma died as a result of the injuries which Dingle had inflicted. Dingle was subsequently charged with murder. At Dingle's trial, his attorney asserted that under the circumstances Dingle should not be convicted of any crime more serious than voluntary manslaughter.

Which of the following would be the prosecuting attorney's most effective argument in response to that assertion?

   (A) Dingle's conduct indicated an intent to kill Wilma.

   (B) Dingle's conduct indicated an intent to inflict great bodily harm on Wilma.

   (C) Dingle did not catch Wilma "in flagrante delicto."

   (D) In Dingle's position, a person of ordinary temperament would not have become angry enough to lose normal self-control.

ANSWERS TO
MULTIPLE CHOICE QUESTIONS

1. **D**   The crime of receiving stolen property consists of acquiring stolen property with the knowledge that it was stolen and the intent to permanently deprive the owner thereof. Since Darr did not know that the television was stolen when he acquired possession of it, he cannot be guilty of receiving stolen property. **A** and **C** are, therefore, incorrect.

    The crime of larceny consists of the trespassory taking and carrying off of personal property known to be another's with the intent to permanently deprive the owner thereof. Since Darr did not know that the television was the property of another when he took it (i.e., received it from Mead), he cannot be guilty of larceny. **B** and **C** are, therefore, incorrect.

2. **C**   A criminal conspiracy is an agreement to commit a crime and is complete when two or more persons make such an agreement. Although Sam privately decided to assist Tom and John in the commission of a crime, he did not agree with them that he would do so. He is, therefore, not guilty of conspiracy, and **C** is correct.

    One who knowingly aids and abets in the commission of a crime is guilty of that crime as an accessory. For this reason, Sam might be guilty of murder. **A** is incorrect, however, because Sam is charged not with murder but with conspiracy. Some jurisdictions hold that to convict for conspiracy it is necessary to prove an overt act in addition to an agreement to commit a crime. Even in these jurisdictions, however, Sam would not be guilty of conspiracy because he did not agree to commit a crime. **B** is, therefore, incorrect. Co-conspirators are guilty of the crime of conspiracy when their agreement is made and are not rendered innocent by the withdrawal of one or more of them from the conspiracy. **D** is incorrect for this reason, and because Sam was never part of the conspiracy in the first place.

3. **A**   Murder is the unjustified killing of a human being with malice aforethought. Malice aforethought includes the intent to kill, which means the desire or knowledge that the defendant's act will bring about the death of another person. Since Tom threw away Vanney's medicine with the desire that doing so would bring about the death of Vanney and since Vanney died as a result, Vanney was murdered. A criminal conspiracy is an agreement to commit a crime. Since Tom and John agreed to kill Vanney, they were involved in a criminal conspiracy. Co-conspirators are vicariously liable for any crimes committed in furtherance of the conspiracy. Since the murder of Vanney was committed by Tom in furtherance of his agreement with John, John is vicariously liable for it. **A** is, therefore, correct.

    Since John did no physical act which enabled Tom to bring about Vanney's death, he did not aid or abet him in bringing it about. **B** is, therefore, incorrect. **C** is incorrect because the principle of vicarious liability as explained above makes it unnecessary for John to physically participate in the commission of the crime with which he is charged. One who effectively withdraws from a conspiracy before its goal is accomplished may avoid vicarious guilt for the substantive crime, although not for the crime of conspiracy. In order for a withdrawal to be effective, however, the withdrawing conspirator must at least do something which places his co-conspirator on notice of his withdrawal. Since John did not do so, he has not effectively withdrawn from the conspiracy, and **D** is incorrect.

4. **D** In the absence of special circumstances, no person is under a legal duty to render aid to another. Since a failure to act can lead to criminal responsibility only in the face of a duty to act, Watcher's failure to rescue Susan was not a crime.

This is true even though she could have saved Susan without risk to herself, even though she knew that there was no one else who could rescue the child, and even if she was related to Susan. **A**, **B** and **C** are, therefore, incorrect.

5. **D** Self defense is a privilege to use reasonable force to protect oneself against aggression. In determining whether force was reasonable, courts usually balance the danger likely to result from its use against the benefit of using it. If the benefit which would be apparent to the reasonable person in the defendant's situation outweighs the danger which would be apparent to the reasonable person in defendant's situation, the force which the defendant used was reasonable. Since it is generally understood that the reasonable person would consider the benefit of saving her own life to be of greater weight than the danger of killing an assailant, it is usually held that lethal force (i.e., force likely to kill or do serious bodily harm) is reasonable if used by a person who reasonably believes that she is being attacked with lethal force. Thus, if it was reasonable for Diller to believe that her life was in danger, it was probably reasonable for her to use lethal force to protect it.

A is incorrect because Diller was attempting to protect herself rather than the cocaine. Even if Gunn was actually unarmed, Diller's reasonable belief that he had a pistol might have privileged her use of lethal force in self defense. **B** is, therefore, incorrect. A person who is committing a crime has no right to defend herself against a lawful arrest. Since Gunn was not attempting to arrest Diller, however, the fact that she was committing a crime at the time of his attack is irrelevant. **C** is, therefore, incorrect.

6. **A** Under the M'Naghten test, a person may be found not guilty by reason of insanity only if mental illness prevented him from knowing the nature and quality of his act or from knowing that the act was legally wrong. Since Anthony knew what he was doing (i.e., that he was poisoning the Governor) and knew that it was against the law, he was not insane.

B refers to the irresistible impulse supplement, and is incorrect because the facts indicate that the jurisdiction has adopted only the M'Naghten test. **C** is incorrect because it refers to the Durham rule, which is no longer applied in any jurisdiction. In some jurisdictions, a defendant is insane under the M'Naghten rule if mental disease caused him/her to suffer from a delusion within the context of which the defendant's act would be lawful. **D** is incorrect, however, because even within the context of Anthony's delusion, Anthony knew that killing the governor was an unlawful act.

7. **C** Murder involves malice aforethought coupled with an act which proximately results in the unlawful killing of a human being. Since malice aforethought includes the intent to inflict great bodily harm, and since it was Duggan's intention to severely injure Ventana, the only issue to be resolved in determining Duggan's guilt is whether Duggan's act was a proximate cause of Ventana's death. If it was, then Duggan is guilty of murder.

Intervening proximate causes of Ventana's death would not prevent Duggan's act from also being a proximate cause, unless those intervening causes could be characterized as unforeseeable or independent. Although Ventana's allergic reaction to the drug was an intervening cause of harm, there is no indication that such an allergic reaction was unforeseeable. Since the drug was given to relieve pain which resulted from the beating, neither its administration nor the patient's allergic reaction to it can be termed independent. **A** is, therefore, incorrect. **B** is incorrect because Ventana's death may have had several proximate causes. The fact that Dr. Medich's conduct was one of them does not mean that Duggan's conduct was not also one of them. Since Ventana's death would not have occurred without Dr. Medich's conduct, Dr. Medich's conduct was a *factual* cause of death. Since Dr. Medich's conduct occurred after Duggan's, Dr. Medich's conduct was an *intervening* cause of that death. But an intervening cause does not break the chain of proximate causation, unless that intervention was unforeseeable. Sometimes gross negligence or recklessness by an intervenor is held to be unforeseeable. This is not an inflexible rule, however. Under some circumstances, even reckless conduct or gross negligence has been held foreseeable. For this reason, a finding that Dr. Medich's conduct was reckless or grossly negligent — without an additional finding that it was unforeseeable — would not be sufficient to result in the conclusion that Duggan's conduct was not one of the proximate causes of Ventana's death. **D** is, therefore, incorrect.

8. **A**   A killing is intentional if the defendant desired or knew to a substantial degree of certainty that it would result from his act. A killing is deliberate and premeditated if the defendant was capable of reflecting upon it with a cool mind and did in fact do so. Since Darrel hoped for (i.e., desired) Volmer's death, the killing was intentional. Since he reflected on it in advance with a cool mind, it was deliberate and premeditated.

Since first degree murder is the most serious crime listed, **B**, **C** and **D** are incorrect. Voluntary manslaughter is an intentional killing resulting from extreme emotional disturbance or in the mistaken belief that it is justified. **C** is also incorrect because there is no indication that Darrel was emotionally disturbed or mistakenly believed that his act was justified. Involuntary manslaughter is an unintended killing which results from criminal negligence. **D** is also incorrect because Darrel intended the death of Volmer.

9. **A**   Murder is the unjustified killing of a human being with malice aforethought. Malice aforethought includes the intent to cause great bodily harm to a human being. A defendant "intends" a particular consequence if she desires or knows to a substantial degree of certainty that it will occur. Since Delman desired and/or knew that exposure to Terminate was likely to result in great bodily harm to Ventura, she intended to cause great bodily harm to a human being. Since Alex died, Delman may be found guilty of his murder. **A** is, therefore, correct.

B is incorrect because engaging in an inherently dangerous activity is not equivalent to malice aforethought. **C** is incorrect because Delman's intent to cause great bodily harm to any human being is sufficient to make her guilty of murder in causing the death of Alex. Although the intent to kill is a form of malice aforethought, **D** is incorrect because the intent to cause great bodily harm is also a form of malice aforethought.

10. **C**   A person is guilty of a criminal attempt when, with the specific intent to bring about a prohibited result, she comes substantially close to doing so. Thus, all attempts are "specific intent" crimes. This means that although murder does not require a specific intent to cause the death of a person, attempted murder does. Since Delman did not intend to cause the death of a human being, she lacks the intent required to make her guilty of

attempted murder.

A is, therefore, incorrect. The death of Alex does not satisfy the specific intent requirement unless Delman intended to bring it about. For this reason, **B** is also incorrect. Although the attempt to murder a person may merge with the actual murder of the person, **D** is incorrect because Ventura did not die, and so could not have been murdered.

11. **B**   Many jurisdictions hold that the defendant will not be guilty of the murder of a co-felon under the felony murder rule if the co-felon's death resulted from a justifiable attempt by the crime-victim to prevent the crime. Although this is not the law in all jurisdictions, it is the only argument listed which would provide Delbert with any defense at all.

          A is incorrect because the felony murder rule is applied to deaths which occur during the commission of a felony, even though the person killed is not the intended crime-victim. **C** is incorrect because the normal reactions of victims, bystanders, and police, make violence a foreseeable result of any robbery. **D** is incorrect because jurisdictions which apply the felony murder rule regard the intent to commit a felony as a form of malice aforethought.

12. **A**   The felony murder rule provides that the intent to commit a felony is malice aforethought, and that a death which results from the perpetration of a felony is, therefore, murder. For this purpose, the perpetration of a felony continues during the defendant's attempt to escape to a place of seeming safety. Nora's death thus occurred during the perpetration of a robbery, and Delbert could be convicted of murder even if he was driving carefully at the time it occurred.

          B, **C**, and **D** are, therefore, incorrect.

13. **D**   Embezzlement is the conversion of personal property known to be another's with the intent to defraud, by a person in lawful possession of the property. Since Samson's possession was the result of fraud and therefore not lawful, he is not guilty of embezzlement. **A** and **C** are, therefore, incorrect. Larceny by trick is committed when the defendant fraudulently induces the victim to deliver *temporary possession* of personal property to the defendant. If the victim transfers title to the property involved, the crime of larceny by trick has not been committed. Since Berrigan's intention was to make Samson the owner of the money, he transferred title to the money, and **B** and **C** are incorrect. The crime actually committed by Samson was false pretenses, since Samson knowingly made a false representation to Berrigan to induce Berrigan to part with title to the money.

14. **A**   Voluntary manslaughter is committed when the defendant, with the intent to cause death or great bodily harm, causes the death of a human being under circumstances such that the defendant is acting in the "heat of passion." The belief that Valens brutally murdered his family probably is sufficient to furnish the heat of passion which reduces the crime from murder to manslaughter.

          B is incorrect for two reasons: first, deliberation and premeditation require a mind which is capable of thinking coolly and rationally, and under the circumstances Dafton's probably wasn't and, second, deliberation and premeditation are not elements of voluntary manslaughter. Since voluntary manslaughter is a lesser offense included in first degree murder, Dafton could be convicted of voluntary manslaughter even if he were guilty of first degree murder. **C** is incorrect because it suggests that guilt of first degree murder would prevent a conviction for voluntary manslaughter. Convicting and sentencing for crime are functions of the court, not of the family of the crime's victim. **D** is incorrect because it suggests a law of vendetta (i.e., that if Valens was the killer Dafton could punish him without incurring criminal responsibility).

15. **C**   One who intentionally aids or facilitates the commission of a crime is guilty of the crime as an accessory. Robbery is larceny committed by force or threat of force. Although Bonnie did not point a gun and demand money, she aided and abetted Mildred by operating the getaway car. She is thus guilty as an accessory. Conspiracy is an agreement to commit a crime made by two or more people who have specific intent. Bonnie and Mildred committed the crime of conspiracy when they agreed on the commission of the robbery.

   A , **B** and **D** are incorrect because the crime of conspiracy is separate from and does not merge into the substantive crime which the conspirators agreed to commit.

16. **D**   A person is guilty of a criminal attempt when, with the specific intent to bring about a result which is criminally prohibited, he comes substantially close to accomplishing that result. Since Donohue believed that the time was five minutes past eleven, and since it would have been lawful to sell liquor at that time, he did not have the specific intent to bring about a result which was criminally prohibited. For this reason, he could not be guilty of attempting to violate the statute.

   A and **B** are, therefore, incorrect. Attempt always requires specific intent, even where the substantive crime does not. Thus, even if the statute did not require specific intent, Donohue could not be guilty of *attempting* to violate it without specifically intending to sell liquor after midnight. **C** is, therefore, incorrect.

17. **C**   One who intentionally aids, abets, or facilitates the commission of a crime is criminally responsible for the crime as an accomplice. In addition, an accomplice is criminally responsible for all the foreseeable consequences of the crime which he facilitated. Since the use of Dailey's apartment to escape detection was part of Reavis' plan in preparing for the robbery, Dailey's agreement to permit Reavis to use it facilitated the robbery, making Dailey an accomplice to it. As such, Dailey may be guilty of felony murder in the death which resulted from the robbery, but only if it was foreseeable that such a death would occur.

   One who becomes an accessory after a crime has been committed (i.e., accessory after the fact) by knowingly harboring the person who committed it is not criminally responsible for prior acts committed by the person harbored. A person who facilitates the commission of a crime by agreeing in advance that he will harbor the perpetrator after the crime is committed is guilty as an accomplice (i.e., accessory before the fact), however. As such he is criminally responsible for all foreseeable consequences of the crime to which he was an accomplice. **A** is, therefore, incorrect. Since an accomplice is criminally responsible for those consequences which were foreseeable, the fact that Dailey did not actually know that Reavis would use a gun does not protect him from liability if Reavis' use of a gun was foreseeable. **B** is, therefore, incorrect. A conspirator is criminally responsible for all crimes committed by co-conspirators in furtherance of the subject of the conspiracy. **D** is incorrect, however, because an accessory is criminally responsible only for consequences which were foreseeable.

18. **D**   A conspiracy is an agreement by two or more persons to commit a crime. Ordinarily, one who agrees to furnish services to another which the other will use in committing a crime is not guilty of conspiracy merely because he knows the purpose to which the services will be put. Where, however, the supplier has a stake in the criminal enterprise, his agreement to furnish services may constitute a conspiracy to commit the crime. Since Dailey knew that Reavis would be using his apartment as a hideout following the robbery, and since Reavis' promise to compensate Dailey by paying him a percentage of the loot gave Dailey a stake in the criminal enterprise, Dailey may be guilty of conspiracy.

A is, therefore, incorrect. **B** is incorrect for two reasons: first, Dailey's agreement probably was per se unlawful, since he knew that Reavis would be hiding in his apartment to escape detection (i.e., that he would be harboring a felon); and, second, Dailey had a personal stake in Reavis' crime. The crime of conspiracy to commit robbery is complete when the defendant agrees with another to commit the robbery, and is a separate crime from the robbery itself. Thus, the fact that a defendant is guilty of robbery is not relevant to the issue of whether he conspired (i.e., agreed) to commit it. For this reason, **C** is incorrect.

19. **B**   A person is guilty of a criminal attempt when, with the specific intent to bring about a criminally prohibited result, he comes substantially close to bringing about that result. Thus, while certain crimes may be committed without intending the prohibited consequences, criminal attempt always requires the specific intent to bring about the prohibited result. Although Shafer could be convicted of violating the statute if he actually sold ammunition to Yule who was under the age of 16, he could not be convicted of attempting to violate the statute unless he knew that Yule was under the age of 16 and intended to sell her the ammunition.

For obvious practical reasons, there is usually an irrebuttable presumption that all persons know the law. Ignorance of the law, therefore, would not provide Shafer with a defense. **A** is, therefore, incorrect. The fact that Okner is vicariously liable under the statute would not furnish Shafer with a defense, since the statute imposes liability on both employee and employer. **C** is incorrect for this reason, and because the statute imposes vicarious liability on the employer only if the employee actually makes a sale, which Shafer did not do. **D** is incorrect because the statute does not make knowledge or experience an element of guilt.

20. **A**   Some cases have held that the imposition of a prison term on the basis of vicarious liability for a strict-liability crime committed by a defendant's employee is a violation of due process. It is generally understood, however, that the imposition of a fine on this basis is constitutionally valid. Since this statute makes an employer vicariously liable for the payment of a fine if an employee sells ammunition to a minor, and since Okner's employee sold ammunition to a minor, Okner may be convicted.

B and **C** are incorrect because of the specific language of the given statute: **B** because the statute imposes strict liability, and does not make negligence or unreasonable behavior a basis of guilt; and **C** because the statute does not make the employer's presence an element of guilt. **D** is incorrect because it is overinclusive: there are many situations in which the criminal law may validly impose vicarious liability for the crime of another (e.g., co-conspirators are vicariously liable for each other's crimes committed in furtherance of the conspiracy).

21. **C**   A person is privileged to use reasonable force to protect herself from what she reasonably believes to be a threat of imminent bodily harm. Potentially lethal force is reasonable when used in response to what the defendant reasonably perceives to be a threat of potentially lethal force. Thus, if Bonnie reasonably believed that Alice was reaching for a gun, her use of a gun in response may have been reasonable, and therefore privileged. While it is not certain that a court would come to this conclusion, the argument in **C** is the only one listed which could possibly provide Bonnie with an effective defense.

A person is guilty of a criminal attempt when, with the intent to bring about a criminally prohibited result, she comes substantially close to achieving it. **A** is incorrect because the fact that a death did not actually occur will not prevent a conviction for attempting to cause one. If Bonnie had the intent to kill Alice when she aimed her pistol at Alice's chest, she would be guilty of attempted murder if she came subsequently close to causing Alice's death. this might be so even if she did not strike Alice in the chest, or even if she did not strike Alice at all. for this reason, **B** is incorrect. **D** is incorrect because deadly force is force which is likely to result in death or great bodily harm. The use of a pistol thus constitutes deadly force even though the harm which it actually causes happens to be slight.

22. **D**   A person is privileged to use reasonable force to protect herself from what she reasonably believes to be a threat of imminent bodily harm. Since Bonnie fired a pistol at Alice, and was (or appeared to be) capable of firing it again, it was reasonable for Alice to believe herself threatened with imminent bodily harm, and was probably reasonable for her to respond with deadly force.

If Bonnie's belief that Alice was about to shoot her was a reasonable one, Bonnie's use of force may have been privileged. **A** is incorrect, however, because, although an aggressor has no right of self-defense against a reasonable response to her initial aggression, Alice committed no act of aggression until after Bonnie fired at her. Self-defense may privilege the use of deadly force in response to what is reasonably perceived as deadly force. Even though the force used by Bonnie had not yet caused death or serious injury, it was capable of doing so, and can, therefore, be regarded as deadly force. **B** is, therefore, incorrect. **C** is incorrect because even a premeditated killing may be privileged by self-defense.

23. **A**   Larceny is defined as a trespassory taking and carrying off of personal property known to be another's with the intent to permanently deprive the owner thereof. A trespassory taking is an acquisition of possession contrary to the rights of the owner and without the owner's consent. Since Dennison acquired possession without Vale's permission, he committed a trespassory taking. A carrying off occurs when the defendant moves the property, even slightly, with the intention of exercising dominion over it. Since Dennison moved the watch from the table to his pocket with the intention of keeping it, he carried it off. Since he knew that the watch belonged to Vale and intended to keep it for himself, he had knowledge that the property was another's and intended to deprive the owner of it. He, therefore, committed a larceny, making **A** correct.

A person is guilty of a criminal attempt when with the specific intent to bring about a criminally prohibited result, he comes substantially close to bringing it about. Although Dennison is probably guilty of attempted larceny, **B** is incorrect because larceny is a more serious crime. Embezzlement is defined as a criminal conversion of personal property by one in lawful custody of that property. Employees who steal property from their employers while in custody of it because of the employment relationship may be guilty of embezzlement. **C** is incorrect, however, because Dennison did not come into possession of the watch as a result of his employment relationship with Vale. **D** is incorrect because Dennison is guilty of larceny for the reasons stated above.

24. **A**   Rape is committed when the defendant intentionally has sexual intercourse with a female not his wife without consent. Although it is necessary that the victim be unwilling, it is not necessary for her to put up a fight if it would be futile for her to do so or if she reasonably believes that resisting will cause her to sustain serious injury. Since Vena's refusal was overcome by a threat which would have led a reasonable person in her place to fear for her life, the intercourse was without her consent.

If her resistance had been overcome by payment, the intercourse would not have been against her will. But the fact that she was willing to accept payment does not mean that she consented to intercourse with one who did not offer payment, or even with one who did. **B** is, therefore, incorrect. **C** is incorrect because Vena's resistance was overcome by Dorian's threat of physical force. Since Vena inflicted the injuries after the intercourse occurred, her conduct in inflicting them could not possibly relate to whether she consented to the intercourse. **D** is, therefore, incorrect.

25. **A**   Since the statute requires intent, and since Vena did not intend Dorian's death, she is not guilty of first degree murder under the statute.

B is incorrect because once Dorian was asleep (and certainly once he was tied to the bed), Vena was no longer in danger and therefore not privileged to use force in self-defense. Although some first degree murder statutes include deaths resulting from the commission of dangerous felonies, this particular statute does not. **C** is, therefore, incorrect. Many first degree murder statutes include death resulting from torture, but this one does not. **D** is, therefore, incorrect.

26. **D**   Voluntary manslaughter is the killing of a human being with the intent to kill or inflict great bodily harm, under circumstances of extreme emotional distress (or mistaken justification). Frequently, the rage which accompanies a discovery of infidelity by a spouse has been held to be sufficient emotional distress to reduce an intentional homicide from murder to voluntary manslaughter. Most jurisdictions apply an objective standard, however, in judging a defendant's emotional distress. Thus, if a person of ordinary temperament would not have lost self-control, Dingle's emotional distress would not have been sufficient to result in a reduction of his crime from murder to manslaughter.

A and **B** are incorrect because although a killing with the intent to kill or inflict great bodily harm *may* be murder, extreme emotional distress may reduce it to voluntary manslaughter even though the defendant intended to kill or inflict great bodily harm. Although anger which results from the defendant's catching his spouse in *flagrante delicto* (i.e., in the act) may justify reducing a murder charge to one of manslaughter, **C** is incorrect because there is no requirement that defendant's emotional distress result from this particular circumstance.

TABLE OF
MODEL PENAL CODE REFERENCES

TABLE OF CASES

SUBJECT MATTER INDEX

Products for 2000-01 Academic Year

emanuel ®

Emanuel Law Outlines

Steve Emanuel's Outlines have been the most popular in the country for years. Twenty years of graduates swear by them. In the 1999–00 school year, law students bought an average of 3.0 Emanuels each – that's 130,000 Emanuels.

Civil Procedure ◆	$19.95
Constitutional Law	23.95
Contracts ◆	19.95
Corporations	19.95
Criminal Law ◆	17.95
Criminal Procedure	17.95
Evidence	19.95
Property ◆	19.95
Secured Transactions	15.95
Torts (General Ed.) ◆	19.95
Torts (Casebook Ed.)	19.95

Keyed to '94 Ed. Prosser, Wade & Schwartz

Also, Steve Emanuel's First Year Q&A's (see below)	$19.95

First Year Set

All outlines marked ◆ *plus* Steve Emanuel's First Year Q & A's *plus* Strategies & Tactics for First Year Law. Everything you need to make it through your first year.

Complete Set	*$105.50*

Siegel's Essay & Multiple–Choice Q & A's

Each book contains 20–25 essay questions with model answers, plus 90–120 Multistate-style multiple-choice Q & A's.

Civil Procedure ◆	$15.95
Constitutional Law	15.95
Contracts ◆	15.95
Corporations	15.95
Criminal Law ◆	15.95
Criminal Procedure	15.95
Evidence	15.95
Professional Responsibility	15.95
Real Property ◆	15.95
Torts ◆	15.95
Wills & Trusts	15.95

Siegel's First Year Set

All titles marked ◆ included in the this set.

Complete Set	*$64.95*

CrunchTime Series (New)

Designed to get you through the final days before exams. Each title contains: a Capsule Summary; Exam Tips; Flowcharts; Short-Answer Q&A's; and Essay Q&A's. All in a small, easy-to-carry format with less than 300 pages. And they come with a *30-day money-back guarantee* (see www.emanuel.com for details).

Civil Procedure*	$15.95
Constitutional Law*	15.95
Contracts*	15.95
Corporations**	15.95
Criminal Law*	15.95
Criminal Procedure**	15.95
Evidence**	15.95
Property**	15.95
Torts*	15.95

* Available Sept. 2000
**Available by late '00 or early '01

Emanuel Law Tapes - Constitutional Law

Includes mnemonics, skits, a special night-before-the-exam review tape, and a printed supplement.

11 Cassette Set, '98-99 Ed.	*$37.95*

Steve Finz's Multistate Method

967 MBE (Multistate Bar Exam) – style multiple choice questions and answers for all six Multistate subjects, each with detailed answers – *Plus* a complete 200 question practice exam modeled on the MBE – perfect for law school and **bar exam** review.

	$35.95

Steve Emanuel's First Year Q&A's

1,144 Objective–style short-answers question with detailed answers, in first year subjects. A single volume covers Contracts, Torts, Civil Procedure, Property, Criminal Law & Criminal Procedure.

	$19.95

Law In A Flash

Flashcards or Software

Civil Procedure 1 ♦	$19.95
Civil Procedure 2 ♦	19.95
Constitutional Law ▲	19.95
Contracts ♦▲	19.95
Corporations	19.95
Criminal Law ♦▲	19.95
Criminal Procedure ▲	19.95
Evidence ▲	19.95
Federal Income Taxation	19.95
Future Interests ▲	19.95
Professional Responsibility (950 cards)	37.95
Real Property ♦▲	19.95
Sales (UCC Art.2) ▲	19.95
Torts ♦▲	19.95
Wills & Trusts	19.95

Law In A Flash Sets

First Year Law Set	115.00

(includes all sets marked ♦ *plus* the book
Strategies & Tactics for First Year Law.)

Multistate Bar Review Set	195.00

(includes all sets marked ▲ *plus* the book
Strategies & Tactics for MBE)

Professional Responsibility Set	57.95

(includes the *Professional Responsibility* flashcards
plus the book Strategies & Tactics for the MPRE Exam.)

Professor Series

All titles in this series are written by leading law professors. Each follows the Emanuel style and format. Each has big, easy-to-read type, extensive citations and notes, and clear, crisp writing. Most have capsule summaries and sample exam Q & A's.

Agency & Partnership	$17.95
Bankruptcy	17.95
Environmental Law	17.95
Family Law	17.95
Federal Income Taxation	17.95
Intellectual Property	19.95
International Law	17.95
Labor Law	17.95
Neg. Instruments & Payment Systems	17.95
Professional Responsibility	18.95
Property	18.95
Torts	17.95
Wills & Trusts	17.95

Lazar Emanuel's Latin for Lawyers

This book defines every word and phrase derived from the Latin in common use by lawyers. Each listing gives the Latin derivation and meaning. Many of these will help you to understand how the law developed from its earliest days.

$15.95

Strategies & Tactics Series

Strategies & Tactics for the MBE

Packed with the most valuable advice you can find on how to successfully attack the MBE. Each MBE subject is covered, including Criminal Procedure (part of Criminal Law), Future Interests (part of Real Property), and Sales (part of Contracts). The book contains 350 actual past MBE questions broken down by subject, plus a full-length 200-question practice MBE. Each question has an answer which describes in detail not only why the correct answer is correct, but why each of the wrong answer choices is wrong.

Covers all the new MBE specifications on and after July, 1997.

$35.95

Strategies & Tactics for the First Year Law Student

A complete guide to your first year of law school, from the first day of class to studying for exams. Packed with the inside information that will help you survive what most consider the worst year of law school and come out on top.

$13.95

Strategies & Tactics for the MPRE

Packed with exam tactics that help lead you to the right answers and expert advice on spotting and avoiding the traps set by the Bar Examiners. Contains actual questions from past MPRE's with detailed answers.

$21.95

 **emanuel** ®

We'd like to know . . . .
Emanuel on *Criminal Law* (4th Edition)

We value your opinions on our study aids. After all, we design them for *your* use, and if you think we could do something better, we want to know about it. Please take a moment to fill out this survey and feedback form and return it to us.

We'll enter you in our monthly drawing, in which 5 people will win the study aid of their choice! If you don't want to identify yourself, that's OK, but you'll be ineligible for the drawing.

Name: _____ Address: _____

City: _____ State: _____ Zip: _____ E-mail: _____

Law school attended: _____ Graduation year: _____

Please rate this product on a scale of 1 to 5:

General readability (style, format, etc.)......................................*Poor* ① ② ③ ④ ⑤ *Excellent*

Length of outline (number of pages)...*Too short* ① ② ③ ④ ⑤ *Too long*

Capsule Summary: Length..*Too short* ① ② ③ ④ ⑤ *Too long*

　　　　　　　　　Usefulness.......................................*Not useful* ① ② ③ ④ ⑤ *Useful*

Casebook Correlation Chart ....*Not useful* ① ② ③ ④ ⑤ *Useful*

Quiz Yourself sections...*Not useful* ① ② ③ ④ ⑤ *Useful*

Exam Tips sections ....*Not useful* ① ② ③ ④ ⑤ *Useful*

Essay exam Q&A's (at end of book)...........................*Not useful* ① ② ③ ④ ⑤ *Useful*

Outline's coverage of material presented in class ....*Incomplete* ① ② ③ ④ ⑤ *Complete*

OVERALL RATING...*Poor* ① ② ③ ④ ⑤ *Excellent*

Suggestions for improvement: _____

_____

_____

☛ **What other study aids did you use in this course?** _____

_____

☛ **If you liked any features of these other study aids, describe them:** _____

_____

_____

☛ **What casebook(s) did you use in this course?** _____

☛ **For other subjects, what study aids other than Emanuel do you use, and what features do you like about them?** _____

_____

☛ **Please list the items you would like us to add to our product line:**

　Outline subjects: _____

　Flashcard subjects: _____

　Other products (e.g., software, multimedia, etc.): _____

☛ **If you win our drawing, what one study aid would you like?** _____

Send to: *Emanuel Law* **Survey** 　OR 　Fax to: *(914) 834-5186*
　　　　1328 Boston Post Road
　　　　Larchmont, NY 10538

Cut here

Please complete & return the Survey Form on the other side